EVERY VOTE EQUAL:
A State-Based Plan for Electing the President by National Popular Vote

John R. Koza
Barry Fadem
Mark Grueskin
Michael S. Mandell
Robert Richie
Joseph F. Zimmerman

FOREWORDS BY

John B. Anderson
Birch Bayh
John Buchanan
Tom Campbell

NATIONAL POPULAR VOTE PRESS
First Edition — Eighth Printing

Yale University Press is gratefully acknowledged for permission to use figure 2.13 from *The People's President: The Electoral College in American History and Direct-Vote Alternative* by Neal R. Peirce and as the copyright owner of that figure.

First edition — First Printing (February 6, 2006)
First edition — Second Printing (February 17, 2006)
First edition — Third Printing (March 6, 2006)
First edition — Fourth Printing (March 13, 2006)
First edition — Fifth Printing (April 5, 2006)
First edition — Sixth Printing (May 8, 2006)
First edition — Seventh Printing (July 6, 2006)
First edition — Eighth Printing (December 20, 2006)

ISBN-13 978-0-9790107-0-5

National Popular Vote Press
Box K
Los Altos, California 94023
Phone: 650-472-1587
Email: info@NationalPopularVote.com
www.every-vote-equal.com
www.NationalPopularVote.com

CHAPTER-LEVEL TABLE OF CONTENTS

DETAILED TABLE OF CONTENTS

BIOGRAPHIES

 **JOHN B. ANDERSON** served in Congress as a Republican Representative from Illinois from 1961 to 1981. He was Chairman of the House Republican Conference for 10 years. In 1980, he ran for President as an Independent and won 6.6% of the national vote. He currently a professor of law at Nova Southeastern University and is the President of the Board of Directors of The Center for Voting and Democracy (Fair Vote) in Washington, D.C.

 **BIRCH BAYH** was a member of the Indiana House of Representatives from 1955 to 1963, its Speaker from 1961 to 1962, and a United States Senator from Indiana from 1963 to 1980. He is currently partner in the law firm of Venable LLP in Washington, D.C. Senator Bayh authored two amendments to the U.S. Constitution— the 25th Amendment on presidential and vice-presidential succession, and the 26th Amendment lowering the voting age to 18. He also sponsored and led the efforts to adopt a federal constitutional amendment on direct nationwide election of the president in the 1960s and 1970s.

 **JOHN BUCHANAN** is an ordained Baptist minister who has served churches in Virginia, Tennessee, Alabama and Washington, D.C. A life-long Republican, he was Alabama Republican State Finance Director and Jefferson County Chairman prior to his service for sixteen years as the first Republican to represent Birmingham in the Congress in the city's history. A legislative consultant and public interest advocate, he has served as Chairman of the Council for the Advancement of Citizenship and as National Vice-Chairman of the Republican Mainstream Committee. Presently, he is Chairman of the Board of Managers of the Nexus Group.

TOM CAMPBELL earned his bachelor's and master's degrees in economics simultaneously at the University of Chicago, a law degree from Harvard, and a Ph.D. in economics from the University of Chicago. He served as law clerk to U.S. Supreme Court Justice Byron White, a White House Fellow in the Office of the Chief of Staff, and Executive Assistant to the U.S. Deputy Attorney General. He was a law professor at Stanford University Law School for 19 years, beginning in 1983. He was elected as a California state senator once and elected five times to represent the Silicon Valley area of California in the United States House of Representatives. Campbell served as Director of the California Department of Finance under Governor Arnold Schwarzenegger. He is currently the Bank of America Dean and Professor at the Haas School of Business at the University of California Berkeley. His book, *Separation of Powers in Practice*, published by Stanford University Press in 2004, examines the constitutionally defined roles and powers of the judicial, legislative, and executive branches of government, in the context of some of America's most contentious policy issues.

BARRY F. FADEM is a partner in the law firm of Fadem & Associates in Lafayette, California. He specializes in all aspects of campaign and election law, and provides expert consultation in the area of initiatives and referendums.

MARK GRUESKIN is a shareholder at Isaacson Rosenbaum P.C. in Denver and chairs the firm's Public Law and Policy practice.

JOHN R. KOZA, originator of the plan described in this book, received his Ph.D. in computer science from the University of Michigan in 1972. He published a board game involving electoral college strategy in 1966. From 1973 through 1987, he was co-founder, chairman, and CEO of Scientific Games Inc. where he co-invented the rub-off instant lottery ticket used by state lotteries. In the 1980s, he and attorney Barry Fadem (see above) were active in promoting adoption of lotteries by various states through the citizen-initiative process and legislative action. He has taught a course on genetic algorithms and genetic programming at Stanford University since 1988. He is currently a consulting professor in the Biomedical Informatics Program in the Department of Medicine and in the Department of Electrical Engineering at Stanford University.

MICHAEL S. MANDELL has been an associate with the law firm of Perkins Coie Brown & Bain in Phoenix and is currently the general counsel to the Arizona State Senate. He received his J.D. with honors from Arizona State University, where he was an editor of the *Arizona State Law Journal.*

ROBERT RICHIE has been the executive director of FairVote—The Center for Voting and Democracy (www.fairvote.org), a non-profit organization dedicated to advancing fair elections, since its founding in 1992. His political writings have appeared in many newspapers and in eight books, including the feature essay in Whose Votes Count. He has been a guest on C-SPAN, NBC News, National Public Radio, CNN, FOX, and MSNBC. Richie has addressed numerous events, including the annual conventions of the National Association of Counties, and National Conference of State Legislatures and has drafted several pieces of federal and state legislation.

 **JOSEPH F. ZIMMERMAN** is Professor of Political Science at the State University of New York at Albany. He has authored of *Interstate Cooperation: Compacts and Administrative Agreements (2002)*, *Interstate Relations: The Neglected Dimension of Federalism (1996)*, *Contemporary American Federalism: The Growth of National Power (1992)*, *The Initiative: Citizen Law-Making (1997)*, *The Referendum: The People Decide Public Policy (1997)*, and *The Recall: Tribunal of the People (1997)*.

ACKNOWLEDGMENTS

The authors are especially grateful to Paul F. Eckstein of Perkins Coie Brown & Bain in Phoenix for his invaluable advice in the early stages of formulation of their proposal.

Chris Pearson of the Center for Voting and Democracy (Fair Vote) in Washington, DC, made numerous valuable contributions to this book including researching items for this book.

The authors appreciate legal comments from
- Catherine Carroll,
- Edward DuMont,
- Kevin O. Faley,
- Tom Goldstein,
- Martin S. Lederman,
- Spencer Overton,
- Jamin Raskin,
- Leonard Shambon,
- Sonja Starr,
- Laurence H. Tribe, and
- Eugene Volokh.

In addition, the authors gratefully acknowledge the following people who were helpful in preparation of this book:
- David Andre,
- Christie Carter at the Vermont State Archives,
- Susan Cumberpatch,
- Neil Erikson at the Nebraska Secretary of State's office,
- Deb Fadem,
- Kate Gottfredson,
- Terri Hudoba,
- Adam Johnson,
- David Johnstone,
- Lee W. Jones,
- Natalie Marie Koss,
- Alex Michael,

- Bob Michaud, *Reference Librarian, Maine State Law and Legislative Reference Library,*
- John Mountjoy, *Director, National Center for Interstate Compacts The Council of State Governments,*
- William Mydlowec,
- Elisabeth Higgins Null,
- Timothy Sahd of the Cook Political Report in Washington, DC,
- Ernie Sowada and Amy Bunk of the Office of the Federal Register at the National Archives and Records Administration,
- Matthew J. Streeter,
- Barbara Wardenburg of the League of Women Voters of Mountain View, California, and
- Natalie Young-Lee.

Cheryl Fuller of Proteus Graphics in Mountain View, California, did the typesetting and preparation of this book.

FOREWORD
By John B. Anderson

I believe the occupant of the nation's highest office should be determined by a nationwide popular vote by legally registered voters.

The current system of allocating electoral votes on a statewide winner-take-all basis divides us on regional lines, undercuts accountability, dampens voter participation, and can trump the national popular vote. The system is not based on majority rule, and it fails to provide political equality.

The anti-democratic nature of the Electoral College is deeply grounded in our history. The Framers distrusted democracy and saw the Electoral College as a deliberative body that would pick the best candidate. However, the lofty view of the Founding Fathers was based on a wildly mistaken understanding of the way our political system would evolve.

Many believe that the Electoral College was included in the Constitution to satisfy the last-ditch efforts of the "states' righters" of 1787 to preserve as much of the Articles of Confederation as possible. This group was intent on denying direct popular election of the President and preserving the power of the states. Just as they had succeeded in establishing a provision allowing state legislatures to elect the members of the U.S. Senate, they wanted the primary power to elect a President to be lodged in the states—not in a mass electorate of individual voters.

The initial impact was to give slave states additional weight. The infamous constitutional provision counting slaves as three-fifths of a person for the purpose of apportioning Representatives in Congress (and apportioning electoral votes) was designed to favor Southern states. Slaves could not vote, but they could give their owners extra power in both congressional and presidential elections. It is no accident that slave-owning Virginians served as President for thirty-two of the nation's first thirty-six years.

The rule for apportioning electoral votes according to the number of each state's members of Congress is anti-democratic because it makes electoral power in the presidential race dependent on the population of a state, rather than on its number of voters. For this reason, there is no national incentive to spur turnout in a state and expand the franchise.

Majority rule and political equality are fundamental tenets of democracy. The power of one's vote should be equal, no matter where one lives. Candidates for our most important national office should have incentives to speak to everyone. In the past century we have amended the Constitution to elect Senators directly, to guarantee women's right to vote, and to lower the voting age to 18. We have passed the Voting Rights Act to provide access to the ballot regardless of race or ethnicity. The Electoral College has escaped the move to greater democracy only because of institutional inertia and misguided, parochial considerations.

A large majority of Americans have consistently supported direct election of the President for many years and it is time to listen to them. This book describes the "Agreement Among the States to Elect the President by National Popular Vote," an innovative approach that is a politically practical way to achieve the goal of nationwide popular election of the President. It has my enthusiastic support.

FOREWORD
By Birch Bayh

On January 10, 1977, I introduced S.J. Res.1, a proposed Amendment to the Constitution to abolish the Electoral College and provide for direct election of the President and Vice President of the United States. As Chairman of the Senate Subcommittee on Constitutional Amendments, I held five days of hearings on this and related proposals that year, receiving testimony from 38 witnesses and hundreds of pages of additional statements and academic studies. This series of hearings was not the first time the Subcommittee on Constitutional Amendments undertook a review of the workings and implications of the Electoral College. In fact, my Subcommittee held its first hearing on the process of electing the President on February 28, 1966, and had amassed a record on the need for electoral reform of nearly 2,600 pages prior to the 1977 hearings.

At the end of this process, I was even more firmly convinced that the Electoral College had outlived whatever positive role it once played as a choice of convenience and compromise. Long overdue, the President and Vice President should be chosen by the same method every other elective office in this country is filled—by citizen voters of the United States in a system which counts each vote equally. In 1979 we came close to getting S.J.Res.1 through the Senate but in the end we could not get enough votes to end the filibuster blocking the Resolution. Our effort, like many before it, was relegated to the Congressional history books.

Unfortunately, Congress has continued to block this basic reform that has long-standing, overwhelming public support. Gallup polls have shown strong public support for nationwide popular election of the President for over five decades.[1] Numerous other polls have confirmed a high level of public support for this reform. Polls consistently show 60–80% of Americans believe they should be able to cast votes in the direct election of the President. That is why I unequivocally support this new strategy to provide for the direct election of the President and Vice

---

[1] Gallup News Service. 2000. Americans have historically favored changing the way presidents are elected: Historical polling data show majority favored abolishing electoral college system more than 50 years ago. November 10, 2000.

President. This new approach is consistent with the Constitution but does not rely on the arduous process of a Constitutional Amendment.

Today more than ever, the Electoral College system is a disservice to the voters. With the number of battleground states steadily shrinking, we see candidates and their campaigns focused on fewer and fewer states. While running for the nation's highest office, candidates in 2004 completely ignored three-quarters of the states, including California, Texas, and New York, our three most populous states. Why should our national leaders be elected by only reaching out to 1/4 of our states? It seems inherently illogical, and it is.

Opponents of the direct election often point to the wisdom of the Founding Fathers in drafting the Constitution. No question, the Founders had incredible wisdom and foresight, but they were dealing with a much different society and the Electoral College was designed for the realities of the 18th Century. The landmass of the country was huge; travel and communication were arduous and primitive; and education was limited at best. Lack of information about possible Presidential candidates among the general public was a very real consideration. Also, there were issues involving slavery. At the time, 90% of the slave population lived in the South. Since the slaves could not vote, without the weighted vote of the Electoral College, the South faced electoral domination from Northern states. While not the first choice of any Founder, the Electoral College system solved these tricky considerations with a compromise which allowed them to complete the monumental task of creating our country's Constitution.

However, it soon became apparent that the Electoral College process devised by the Founders was flawed. In 1804 the initial Electoral College system was changed through the adoption of the 12th Amendment. Additional weaknesses became apparent. In the 1800s, there were three instances when the popular vote winner lost the Presidency. In 1824, John Quincy Adams was a minority vote winner over Andrew Jackson, as were Rutherford B. Hayes over Samuel J. Tilden (1876), and Benjamin Harrison over Grover Cleveland (1888). This anomaly is not that rare in the Electoral College system. In fact, a small shift of votes in one or two states would have thrown the election to the second-place vote winner five additional times in the last 60 years.

For example, in 1976, Jimmy Carter won a nationwide popular vote victory of 1.7 million votes. However, a change of only 25,579 votes in the states of Ohio and Mississippi would have reelected President Gerald Ford in the Electoral College. With a switch of 18,488 votes in the states of Ohio and Hawaii, the Electoral College normally would have produced a Ford victory. However, because a renegade elector from Washington state cast his vote for non-candidate Ronald Reagan, the final electoral vote count would have been Carter – 268, Ford – 269, and Reagan – 1. Under this scenario, with no candidate receiving the necessary 270 electoral votes, the President would have been chosen by the House of Representatives.

In recent history, we all remember the 2000 election, which awarded the Presidency to the candidate who came in second in the popular vote. In the last election, President Bush defeated Senator Kerry by more than 3 million votes nationwide. However, it is easy to overlook that a change of less than 60,000 votes would have put Ohio in the Kerry column under the Electoral College system and would have elected him President.

In the final analysis, the most compelling reason for directly electing our president and vice president is one of principle. In the United States every vote must count equally. One person, one vote is more than a clever phrase, it's the cornerstone of justice and equality. We can and must see that our electoral system awards victory to the candidates chosen by the most voters. In this day and age of computers, television, rapidly available news, and a nationwide public school system, we don't need nameless electors to cast our votes for president. The voters should cast them directly, themselves. Direct election is the only system that counts every vote equally and where the voters cast their ballots directly for the candidates of their choice. It has the additional virtue of operating in the way most Americans think the electoral process operates—and is expected to operate.

It is heartening to see the Every Vote Equal strategy described in this book which will correct the flawed system we maintain for electing our top two leaders. Our federation of states must band together to solve this long-standing, vexatious problem. Since Congress has repeatedly refused to act, it's refreshing to know states have the ability under the Constitution to step up and create the sensible solution Americans have long been supporting. I hope you will join me in supporting this important effort.

The election of President of the United States should not be a contest between red states and blue states. The President should be chosen by a majority of our citizens, wherever they may live. Direct popular election would substitute clarity for confusion, decisiveness for danger, and popular choice for political chance.

FOREWORD
By John B. Buchanan

The founder of my party, Abraham Lincoln, described the American political system as "Government of the people, by the people, for the people." Yet in the first presidential election of the twenty-first century, once again the presidential candidate who won the popular vote lost the election, and the will of the people who cared enough to be present and voting was frustrated rather than fulfilled. In the next election the then incumbent President won the popular vote, but a change in the electoral vote of a single state could have cost him the election.

Denying the American people the right to determine by their votes who the President and Vice-President shall be is a flaw in our system, and one that needs fixing. It is time for "the world's greatest democracy" to in fact become one at the highest level of elective office as is already the case at all other levels.

As a member of Congress I voted in support of the direct election of the president and nearly saw the system change during my tenure. At the time it was a controversial idea, but not overburdened by the partisan bickering so much as regional concerns. Many of my colleagues in Southern states, for example, believed the Electoral College system, as it stood, benefited their state.

Today, any discussions, although there have been too few, seem to give rise to partisan concerns. Yet this is not, nor should it be, either a regional or a partisan matter. We should rather be guided by patriotism and principle to do what is right for our country and for the American people as a whole. When we look at the method by which we elect the president, we should have a system that is fair, guarantees votes are counted equally, puts residents of each state on equal footing, and promotes vote-seeking across the nation.

Today, the Electoral College system means that campaigns are focused on dangerously few states. In 2004, over two-thirds of the country was completely neglected during the one nationwide political contest. Candidates spend more and more money to reach fewer and fewer voters. In the close states, which do get attention, under the winner take all system of allotting electoral votes practiced by most states, all who end up on the losing end of even a 50.1% to 49.9% statewide vote are denied the right for their votes to count toward the election of the candidate of their choice at the national level in a national election. Hence, too many people in too many places have no meaningful role in the election process.

In 1969, I was one of 337 members of the U.S. House of Representatives who passed an amendment for direct election of the president. We had overwhelming support and outside help from the US Chamber of Commerce, the American Bar Association, and others who agreed this was a needed change to our system. Unfortunately the effort went down in the Senate. Yet from that time to the present, a large majority of the American people has continued to support the direct election of the president.

Since 1969, Congress has not taken meaningful action to address this issue. While doing away with the Electoral College would be my preference, that requires a Constitutional amendment. Yet the states themselves have the power to achieve the result of the popular election of the President and Vice-President without such an amendment. The time has come for them to act.

The strength of our country and its democracy lies in the public. The people have supported the direct election of the president for over fifty years. In this book, Dr. Koza suggests a way for states to come together and make it happen. If every vote counts equally, if every voter has an equal say in the election of the president and can cast a meaningful vote, then we can better address issues of confidence in our political system, and in fact and fully become a true democracy.

I strongly support and applaud any good-faith effort to make the direct election of the president a reality and commend to you the intriguing approach offered in the "Agreement Among the States to Elect the President by National Popular Vote" described in this book.

I want your vote and my vote to count in the most important elections of all. It can happen. It should happen. If enough of us care enough, it will be done.

FOREWORD
By Tom Campbell

California has 35,893,799 residents. Wyoming has 506,520 residents. California casts 55 electoral votes for President. Wyoming casts 3. The result: A Wyoming voter is worth 4 times a California voter in selecting America's President. If a Third World country, coming into democratic principles out of tyranny, announced a scheme with some citizens worth 4 times as much as others in their governance, it would be told to try again. Indeed, America would tell it to try again!

No Californian should accept the present way we elect Presidents. No American should accept it.

The ingenious approach put forward in this book provides, for the first time, a solution that is achievable. It does not rely on unrealistic assumptions. It can be implemented, if the very people who are relatively disenfranchised in our country will only be awakened to how to do it.

1 | Introduction

In elections for President and Vice President of the United States, every vote should be equal. Every person's vote should be equally important, regardless of the state in which the vote is cast. The presidential and vice-presidential candidate who receive the most popular votes throughout the United States should win those offices. The current system for electing the President and Vice President does not satisfy these principles. This book presents a politically practical way by which action at the state level can bring presidential elections into conformity with these principles.

This chapter

- describes what the U.S. Constitution says—and does not say—about presidential elections (section 1.1),
- highlights three significant shortcomings of the current system for electing the President and Vice President of the United States and identifies the common cause of all three problems (section 1.2),
- identifies nationwide popular election as a remedy for the shortcomings of the current system (section 1.3),
- notes the fortuitous convergence of factors favoring reform at the present time (section 1.4),
- provides a roadmap to the remainder of this book (section 1.5), and
- identifies additional sources of information (section 1.6).

1.1 WHAT THE U.S. CONSTITUTION SAYS—AND DOES NOT SAY—ABOUT PRESIDENTIAL ELECTIONS

The method of selecting the President and Vice President of the United States is not set forth in detail in the U.S. Constitution. In fact, the Founding Fathers never reached agreement on a complete system for selecting the President. Aside from scheduling and administrative provi-

1

sions,[1] the U.S. Constitution specifies only four aspects of presidential elections:

- **Indirect Election:** The Constitution specifies that the President and Vice President are to be chosen every four years by a small group of people who are individually referred to as presidential "electors." The electors are often collectively referred to as the "Electoral College," although this term does not appear in the Constitution.

- **Allocation of Electoral Votes to the States:** The Constitution specifies that each state is entitled to one presidential elector for each of its U.S. Representatives and Senators. Today, there are a total of 538 electoral votes.[2]

- **Majority of Electoral College Required for Election:** The Constitution specifies that a presidential or vice-presidential candidate must win a majority of the electoral votes in order to be elected to office (that is, 270 of the 538 electoral votes). In the absence of such a majority, the U.S. House of Representatives chooses the President, and the U.S. Senate chooses the Vice President.[3]

---

[1] The Constitution contains provisions concerning setting the date for appointing presidential electors, setting the date for the meeting of presidential electors, recording the electoral votes, and counting the electoral votes by Congress. For the reader's convenience, appendix A contains the provisions of the U.S. Constitution relating to presidential elections.

[2] The total of 538 electoral votes corresponds to the 435 U.S. Representatives from the 50 states *plus* the 100 U.S. Senators from the 50 states *plus* the three electoral votes that the District of Columbia received under the 23rd Amendment to the Constitution (ratified in 1961). Every 10 years, the 435 U.S. Representatives are reapportioned among the states in accordance with the latest federal census, thereby automatically reapportioning the electoral votes among the states. The number of U.S. Representatives is set by federal statute.

[3] More precisely, a majority of the presidential electors "appointed" are required for election. There have been several occasions when a state has failed to appoint its presidential electors. For example, New York failed to appoint its electors for the nation's first presidential election in 1789, and 11 southern states failed to appoint their electors for the 1864 election during the Civil War. In the event that no candidate receives an absolute majority of the number of presidential electors who are "appointed" for a particular presidential election, the Constitution provides that the House of Representatives chooses the President (with each state casting one vote regardless of the size of its congressional delegation) and that the Senate chooses the Vice President (with each Senator casting one vote).

- **The Way That the Presidential Electors Cast Their Votes:** Under the original Constitution, each presidential elector cast two votes. The leading candidate became President, and the second-place candidate became Vice President. Under the 12th Amendment to the Constitution (ratified in 1804), each presidential elector casts a separate vote for President and Vice President.

As can be seen from the above, the U.S. Constitution is silent about many of the most politically important features of presidential elections, most notably including:

(1) **Who Votes for the Presidential Electors?** Do the nation's voters, for example, have any direct voice in choosing the presidential electors?

(2) **How Are Votes Counted for Presidential Electors?** Regardless of who may be entitled to vote for the presidential electors, are the votes to be counted on a statewide basis? By congressional district? In regional multi-member districts? In specially created presidential elector districts? In a proportional way? In some other way?

The Constitution does not answer these (and other politically important) questions about the conduct of presidential elections. Instead, the Founding Fathers created a system with considerable built-in flexibility. The Constitution leaves these questions to be decided by the individual states. It provides:

"Each State shall **appoint,** in such **Manner as the Legislature thereof may direct,** a Number of Electors, equal to the whole Number of Senators and Representatives to which the State may be entitled in the Congress...."[4] [Emphasis added]

The above delegation of power to the states concerning presidential elections is unusually unconstrained. It contrasts significantly with the limitations contained in the Constitution on state power over congressional elections.

---

[4] U.S. Constitution. Article II, section 1, clause 2.

"The Times, Places and Manner of holding Elections for Senators and Representatives, shall be prescribed in each State by the Legislature thereof; **but the Congress may at any time by Law make or alter such Regulations**...."[5] [Emphasis added]

Accordingly, the U.S. Supreme Court has characterized state power concerning the manner of appointing presidential electors as "supreme," "plenary,"[6,7] and exclusive. As the Court wrote in 1892:

"In short, the appointment and mode of appointment of electors belong **exclusively** to the states under the constitution of the United States."[8]

In a 1919 case involving a state statute entitled "An act granting to women the right to vote for presidential electors," the Maine Supreme Judicial Court wrote:

"[E]ach state is thereby clothed with the **absolute power to appoint electors in such manner as it may see fit, without any interference or control on the part of the federal government,** except, of course, in case of attempted discrimination as to race, color, or previous condition of servitude...."[9] [Emphasis added]

Over the years, the states have used the Constitution's built-in flexibility concerning presidential elections in a remarkable variety of ways. Many of the most familiar features of present-day presidential elections

---

[5] U.S. Constitution. Article II, section 4, clause 1.

[6] In the 1892 case of *McPherson v. Blacker*, the U.S. Supreme Court wrote, "[F]rom the formation of the government until now the practical construction of the clause has conceded **plenary** power to the state legislatures in the matter of the appointment of electors" (146 U.S. 1 at 36) [Emphasis added].

[7] In the 2000 case of *Bush v. Gore*, the U.S. Supreme Court wrote, "The individual citizen has no federal constitutional right to vote for electors for the President of the United States unless and until the state legislature chooses a statewide election as the means to implement its power to appoint members of the Electoral College. U.S. Const., Art. II, §1. This is the source for the statement in *McPherson v. Blacker*, 146 U.S. 1, 35 (1892), that the State legislature's power to select the manner for appointing electors is **plenary**; it may, if it so chooses, select the electors itself, which indeed was the manner used by State legislatures in several States for many years after the Framing of our Constitution. *Id.*, at 28–33." (531 U.S. 98. 2000) [Emphasis added].

[8] *McPherson v. Blacker*. 146 U.S. 1 at 29. 1892.

[9] *In re Opinion of the Justices*. 107 A. 705. 1919.

were not in widespread use immediately after ratification of the Constitution.

(1) **Who Votes for the Presidential Electors?** In the nation's first presidential election in 1789, only four states gave the voters a direct voice in electing the presidential electors. In most states, there was no election at all, and the legislature simply "appointed" the presidential electors. By 1836, the voters elected the presidential electors in all states except South Carolina. No state legislature has appointed presidential electors since Colorado did so in 1876.[10]

(2) **How Are Votes Counted for Presidential Electors?** In 1789, only three states awarded their electoral votes using the system that is now in almost universal use throughout the United States—that is, the statewide "winner-take-all" rule. Under this rule, a majority (or, nowadays, a plurality) of each state's voters controls the election of 100% of the state's presidential electors. In 1789, Virginia permitted the voters to elect presidential electors in specially created presidential elector districts, thereby creating the possibility that minority sentiment within the state would control some of the state's electoral votes. At various times in other states, voters elected presidential electors from congressional districts or from multi-member regional districts. Various indirect methods have been used occasionally, including a miniature state-level electoral college in Tennessee to choose the state's members of the national Electoral College.[11] Today, the voters in Maine and Nebraska elect presidential electors by congressional district.

In short, there was no consensus among the Founding Fathers in favor of two of the most politically salient features of present-day

---

[10] Section 2.2 covers the history of methods of selecting presidential electors.

[11] As detailed in section 2.2.2, in 1796, in Tennessee, specific citizens from various groups of counties were named in the state law establishing this system. The specifically named individuals then chose the presidential electors for their part of the state. In 1828, the New York legislature created an indirect system in which the presidential electors who were elected by the voters from each of the state's congressional districts selected the state's two senatorial presidential electors (section 2.2.4).

presidential elections—namely voting by the people and the statewide winner-take-all rule. These features are not mandated by the U.S. Constitution. These features were not implemented by amending the U.S. Constitution. Instead, these now-familiar features came into existence because the states used the flexibility that the Founders built into the Constitution to make these features part of our political landscape. These features are strictly a matter of state law.

The piecemeal adoption by the states of the winner-take-all rule is particularly instructive. As the U.S. Supreme Court noted in 1892, many of the Founding Fathers considered the district system (such as that used by Virginia in the nation's first presidential election) to be "the most equitable."[12] However, as early as the nation's first competitive presidential election (1796), it had become clear to political observers that the district system diminished a state's political influence because it fragmented the state's electoral votes. As historian Noble Cunningham wrote:

> "The presidential election of 1796 had been extremely close, and in examining the results of that contest Republican Party managers had been struck by the fact that **Adams' 3-vote margin of victory in the electoral college could be attributed to 1 vote from Pennsylvania, 1 from Virginia, and 1 from North Carolina.** In each of these states, the Republicans had won an impressive victory, amassing in the three states a total of 45 electoral votes. The loss of 3 votes in these strongly Jeffersonian states was due to the district method of electing presidential electors. **In looking for ways to improve their chances for victory in the next presidential election, Republican managers thus turned their attention to state election laws.**"[13] [Emphasis added]

On January 12, 1800, Thomas Jefferson (the losing Republican[14] candidate from the 1796 election) wrote James Monroe (then a member of the legislature in Jefferson's home state of Virginia):

[12] *McPherson v. Blacker:* 146 U.S. 1 at 29. 1892.

[13] Cunningham, Noble E., Jr. In Schlesinger, Arthur M., Jr. and Israel, Fred L. (editors). 2002. *History of American Presidential Elections 1878–2001.* Philadelphia, PA: Chelsea House Publishers. Pages 104–105. See section 2.2.3 for additional details on the 1796 election.

[14] Jeffersonians were originally called Anti-Federalists, later Republicans or Democratic-Republicans, and eventually Democrats.

"On the subject of an election by a general ticket [the statewide winner-take-all rule], or by districts, most persons here seem to have made up their minds. All agree that an **election by districts would be best, if it could be general; but while 10 states chuse either by their legislatures or by a general ticket, it is folly & worse than folly** for the other 6. not to do it."[15] [Emphasis added; spelling and punctuation as per original]

Thus, although the statewide winner-take-all system may not have been "best," Virginia changed from its original district system to the winner-take-all system, thereby ensuring Jefferson 100% of his home state's electoral votes in the 1800 elections.

Over a period of years, more and more states gravitated to the statewide winner-take-all rule to avoid the "folly" of fragmenting their electoral votes. By 1836, all but one state had adopted the statewide winner-take-all rule.[16] Except for Florida in 1868, Colorado in 1876, and Michigan in 1892, all states used the statewide winner-take-all rule between 1860 and 1972.

More recently, Maine (since 1972) and Nebraska (since 1992) have awarded one electoral vote to the candidate who carries each congressional district in the state and two electoral votes to the presidential candidate carrying the state.[17] The present-day state laws in Maine and Nebraska are reminders of the flexibility that the Founders built into the U.S. Constitution. They are reminders that the manner of conducting presidential elections is strictly a matter of state law. Most importantly,

---

[15] The January 12, 1800 letter is discussed in greater detail and quoted in its entirety in section 2.2.3. Ford, Paul Leicester. 1905. *The Works of Thomas Jefferson.* New York: G. P. Putnam's Sons. 9:90.

[16] The South Carolina legislature elected the state's presidential electors until 1860, so South Carolina's electoral votes were also cast as a solid bloc. See chapter 2 for a detailed history of the proliferation of the statewide winner-take-all rule.

[17] In all 13 presidential elections in which the district system has been used by Maine and Nebraska, the presidential candidate carrying the state has carried all of the state's congressional districts. The reason why the congressional district system has not produced a division of the electoral votes in Maine and Nebraska is that Maine has only two congressional districts and Nebraska has only three. The presidential candidate carrying a state with only a few districts is apt to carry each of the state's individual districts. Thus, in terms of the practical political outcome, the statewide "winner take all" rule is universal throughout the United States despite the Maine and Nebraska laws.

they are reminders that the now-prevailing statewide winner-take-all rule may be changed, at any time, by the states—merely by passage of a state law.

1.2 SHORTCOMINGS OF THE CURRENT SYSTEM

The current system for electing the President and Vice President of the United States has three major shortcomings:

- **Voters Are Effectively Disenfranchised in Two Thirds of the States in Presidential Elections.** Under the now-prevailing statewide winner-take-all rule, presidential candidates do not campaign in states in which they are far ahead because they do not receive any additional electoral votes by winning such states by a larger margin. Similarly, candidates ignore states where they are far behind because they have nothing to gain by losing those states by a smaller margin. Instead, presidential candidates concentrate their public appearances, organizational efforts, advertising, polling, and policy attention on states where the outcome of the popular vote is not a foregone conclusion. In practical political terms, a vote matters in presidential politics only if it is cast in a closely divided battleground state. To put it another way, the question of whether a voter matters in presidential politics depends on whether *other* voters in the voter's own state happen to be closely divided. In the five most recent presidential elections (1988–2004), about two thirds of the states have been non-competitive, including six of the nation's 10 most populous states (California, Texas, New York, Illinois, New Jersey, and North Carolina), 12 of the 13 least populous states,[18] and the vast majority of medium-sized states.
- **The Current System Does Not Reliably Reflect the Nationwide Popular Vote.** The statewide winner-take-all

---

[18] There are 13 states with just one or two U.S. House members (and hence three or four electoral votes). Of the 13 smallest states, only New Hampshire has been competitive in recent presidential elections (having gone Republican in 1988, 1992, and 2000 and having gone Democratic in 1996 and 2004). The small states tend to be non-competitive in presidential elections because they are apt to be one-party states.

rule makes it possible for a candidate to win the Presidency without winning the most popular votes nationwide. This has occurred in one of every 14 presidential elections (as detailed in section 1.2.2). In the past six decades, there have been six presidential elections in which a shift of a relatively small number of votes in one or two states would have elected (and, of course, in 2000, did elect) a presidential candidate who lost the popular vote nationwide.

* **Not Every Vote Is Equal.** The statewide winner-take-all rule creates variations of 1000-to-1 and more in the weight of a vote (as illustrated in section 1.2.3).

1.2.1 Voters in Two Thirds of the States Are Effectively Disenfranchised

Most people who follow political news are aware of the fact that presidential campaigns are concentrated on a tiny handful of battle-ground states; however, few are aware of the extreme degree of this concentration.

Although there is no single definition of a "battleground" state, these states can be readily identified by examining where presidential campaigns pay close attention to public opinion, where they spend their advertising money, and where they campaign.

In terms of polling, presidential candidates pay hardly any attention to the concerns of voters in states that are not closely divided in presidential elections. As Charlie Cook reported in 2004:

> "Senior Bush campaign strategist Matthew Dowd pointed out yesterday that the Bush campaign hadn't taken a national poll in almost two years; instead, it has been polling 18 battle-ground states."[19]

Kerry similarly pursued an 18-state strategy in 2004.

Battleground states can be readily identified by "following the money." Fully 99% of the $237,423,744 reported advertising expenditures in the last month of the 2004 presidential campaign was spent in only 17

---

[19] Cook, Charlie. 2004. Convention dispatches—As the nation goes, so do swing states. Charlie Cook's Political Report. August 31, 2004.

Table 1.1 THE 17 STATES RECEIVING 99% OF THE ADVERTISING MONEY

PER CAPITA AD SPENDING	STATE	AD SPENDING
$4.45	New Mexico	$8,096,270
$4.30	Nevada	$8,596,795
$4.16	Ohio	$47,258,386
$4.02	Florida	$64,280,557
$3.73	New Hampshire	$4,608,200
$3.22	Iowa	$9,412,462
$3.00	Pennsylvania	$36,813,492
$2.70	Wisconsin	$14,468,062
$2.18	Minnesota	$10,734,683
$1.70	Maine	$2,171,101
$1.63	Colorado	$7,015,486
$1.36	Michigan	$13,518,566
$1.22	West Virginia	$2,213,110
$0.67	Oregon	$2,280,367
$0.42	Missouri	$2,361,944
$0.32	Hawaii	$388,095
$0.20	Washington	$1,198,882
	Total	**$235,416,458**

states. Table 1.1 lists the 17 states in order of per capita spending.[20] The nine states where per capita spending exceeded $2.00 correspond to the top-tier battleground states and account for seven eighths (87%) of the $237,423,744. Five states (Florida, Iowa, Ohio, Pennsylvania, and Wisconsin) account for three quarters (72%) of the money.

A mere 1% of the money was spent in the remaining 34 of the 51 jurisdictions entitled to vote in presidential elections. The 1% was split among 11 jurisdictions, while nothing at all was spent in 23 states.

Advertising expenditures were similarly concentrated during the earlier part of the presidential campaign period.[21]

Candidate travel is another way to identify battleground states. The major-party presidential or vice-presidential candidates appeared at 307

---

[20] The period covered was October 2 to November 4, 2004. See FairVote. 2005. *Who Picks the President?* Takoma Park, MD: The Center for Voting and Democracy. www.fairvote.org/whopicks. See also http://www.cnn.com/ELECTION/2004/special/president/campaign.ads/.

[21] An article by Chuck Todd in the *New York Times* (November 3, 2004) reported that five states accounted for 66% of the TV ad spending over the entire campaign period ($380 million of the $575 million spent).

Table 1.2 THE 16 STATES RECEIVING 92% OF THE VISITS BY THE PRESIDENTIAL AND VICE-PRESIDENTIAL CANDIDATES

STATE	CAMPAIGN EVENTS
Florida	61
Ohio	48
Iowa	37
Wisconsin	31
Pennsylvania	23
Michigan	19
Minnesota	14
Colorado	10
Nevada	7
New Hampshire	6
New Mexico	6
Oregon	5
Missouri	5
Arizona	4
New Jersey	4
California	2
Total	**282**

campaign events in the last month of the 2004 campaign. These 307 events were concentrated in 27 states.[22] If one excludes from consideration the six states receiving only one visit,[23] the home states of the four candidates,[24] and the District of Columbia (where all four candidates had day jobs),[25] 92% of the 307 campaign events were concentrated in just 16 states (as shown in table 1.2). Two thirds (200 of the 307) of the events were concentrated in Florida, Ohio, Iowa, Wisconsin, and Pennsylvania (the same five states that accounted for three quarters of the money).

As can be seen from table 1.2, 35 (over two thirds) of the 51 jurisdictions entitled to vote in presidential elections cumulatively received

[22] For simplicity, we often refer to the District of Columbia as a "state" in this book. The 23rd Amendment provides that the District of Columbia's three electoral votes "shall be considered, for the purposes of the election of President and Vice President, to be electors appointed by a state."

[23] Hawaii, Kansas, Maine, Maryland, West Virginia, and New York.

[24] There were four events in Texas (Bush's home state) and Massachusetts (Kerry), three in Wyoming (Cheney), and two in North Carolina (Edwards).

[25] There were six events in the District of Columbia.

Table 1.3 NINETEEN CLOSE STATES IN THE 2000 PRESIDENTIAL ELECTION

STATE	ELECTORAL VOTES	DEMOCRATIC PERCENTAGE
Louisiana	9	46.06%
Arizona	8	46.72%
West Virginia	5	46.76%
Arkansas	6	47.20%
Tennessee	11	48.04%
Nevada	4	48.14%
Ohio	21	48.18%
Missouri	11	48.29%
New Hampshire	4	49.33%
Florida	25	50.00%
New Mexico	5	50.03%
Wisconsin	11	50.12%
Iowa	7	50.16%
Oregon	7	50.24%
Minnesota	10	51.29%
Pennsylvania	23	52.15%
Michigan	18	52.63%
Maine	4	52.75%
Washington	11	52.94%
Total	**200**	

only 8% of the campaign visits. Almost half of the states received no visits at all.

In short, polling, advertising, and campaigning are not merely skewed toward about a dozen and a half states in presidential campaigns, but the remaining two thirds of the states are, for all practical purposes, *excluded* from the campaign. They are mere spectators in the election process.

Not surprisingly, this concentration of polling, advertising, and travel corresponds closely to the states where the presidential election was close. Table 1.3 shows the 19 states in which the two-party vote for President was between 46% and 54% in the 2000 presidential election, starting with the least Democratic state.[26]

---

[26] Not all of the states in the tables are full-fledged battleground states. The 2004 Kerry campaign made efforts to pick up three states that Bush had carried in 2000 (Missouri, Colorado, and Nevada), and the 2004 Bush campaign made similar efforts to reverse the 2000 results in Delaware, Washington, New Jersey, and Oregon. Nonetheless, as the 2004 campaign progressed, it became apparent that none of these states would actually change hands. By the end of the campaign, there were few actual battleground states.

Table 1.4 SIXTEEN CLOSE STATES IN THE 2004 PRESIDENTIAL ELECTION

STATE	ELECTORAL VOTES[27]	DEMOCRATIC PERCENTAGE
Missouri	11	46.33%
Colorado	9	47.35%
Florida	27	47.47%
Nevada	5	48.67%
Ohio	20	48.75%
New Mexico	5	49.42%
Iowa	7	49.54%
Wisconsin	10	50.20%
New Hampshire	4	50.68%
Pennsylvania	21	51.13%
Michigan	17	51.73%
Minnesota	10	51.76%
Oregon	7	51.97%
New Jersey	15	53.13%
Washington	11	53.60%
Delaware	3	53.82%
Total	**182**	

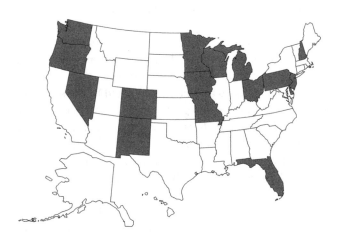

Figure 1.1 Sixteen close states in the 2004 presidential election

---

[27] Some states in tables 1.3 and 1.4 have a different number of electoral votes because of the reallocation of electoral votes resulting from the 2000 federal census.

Table 1.4 and figure 1.1 show the 16 states in which the two-party vote for President was between 46% and 54% in the 2004 presidential election, starting with the least Democratic state.

The 16 states in table 1.4 and figure 1.1 together represent 182 electoral votes—34% of the total (538).

Because each state receives one electoral vote for each of its U.S. Representatives, the Founding Fathers expected that the Constitution's formula for allocating electoral votes would give the most populous states the greatest amount of influence in presidential elections. Glances at tables 1.1 through 1.4 and figure 1.1 show that the Founders did not achieve this objective. Large states are not necessarily important in presidential elections. Six of the nation's 10 most populous states (California, Texas, New York, Illinois, New Jersey, and North Carolina) are non-competitive in presidential elections. Non-competitive states—regardless of their size or number of electoral votes—simply do not matter in presidential elections.

The Founders' intended allocation of political influence in favor of the most populous states was not achieved because of the cumulative effect of the nearly universal adoption by the states of the winner-take-all rule. Political power resides in the scattered collection of states of various sizes where the popular vote happens to be closely divided—that is, the battleground states. In short, the Founders' attempt to allocate political influence was trumped by the decisions—taken separately by the individual states—to adopt the winner-take-all rule.

The less populous states are similarly affected by the statewide winner-take-all rule. As part of the political compromise that led to the Constitution, the Founding Fathers intended to confer a certain amount of extra influence on the less populous states by giving every state a bonus of two electoral votes corresponding to its two U.S. Senators.[28] Again, tables 1.1 through 1.4 and figure 1.1 show that the Founding Fathers did not achieve their objective. Because small states are apt to be one-party states, 12 of the 13 (92%) least populous states are non-competitive in presidential elections. Non-competitive states—with or without a bonus of two extra electoral votes—simply do not matter in

---

[28] In present-day terms, about 81% of the current pool of 538 electoral votes are allocated according to population. The 13 smallest states collectively possess about 4% of the nation's population and have 8% of the electoral votes (44 of 538).

presidential politics. The Founders' intended allocation of political influence was not achieved because the political effect of the mathematical bonus provided by the Constitution was trumped by the nearly universal adoption by the states of the winner-take-all rule.

The effective disenfranchisement of voters in two thirds of the states has additional negative effects.

First, the absence of a meaningful presidential campaign in two thirds of the states diminishes voter turnout in those states. A 2005 Brookings Institution report entitled *Thinking About Political Polarization* pointed out:

> "The electoral college can depress voter participation in much of the nation. Overall, the percentage of voters who participated in last fall's election was almost 5 percent higher than the turnout in 2000. Yet, most of the increase was limited to the battleground states. Because the electoral college has effectively narrowed elections like the last one to a quadrennial contest for the votes of a relatively small number of states, people elsewhere are likely to feel that their votes don't matter."[29,30]

Second, diminished voter turnout in presidential races in non-competitive states weakens the candidates of the state's minority party for state and local offices, thereby making the state even less competitive in the future. In turn, political divisiveness may be increased because a lack of competition may increase the influence of each party's fringe elements.

The number of battleground states has been declining for many decades, and this decline appears to be continuing, as detailed in *The Shrinking Battleground* by the Center for Voting and Democracy.[31]

[29] Nivola, Pietro S. 2005. *Thinking About Political Polarization.* Washington, DC: The Brookings Institution. Policy Brief 139. January 2005.

[30] Voter turnout is adversely affected in non-competitive states because voters of both parties in non-competitive states realize that their votes do not matter in presidential elections. As reported by the Committee for the Study of the American Electorate, "Turnout in battleground states increased by 6.3 percentage points, while turnout in the other states (and the District of Columbia) increased by only 3.8 percentage points." Committee for the Study of the American Electorate (2004). "President Bush, Mobilization Drives Propel Turnout to Post-1968 High." November 4, 2004.

[31] FairVote. 2005. *The Shrinking Battleground: The 2008 Presidential Election and Beyond.* Takoma Park, MD: The Center for Voting and Democracy. www.fairvote.org/shrinking.

Table 1.5 PRESIDENTIAL ELECTIONS IN WHICH THE CANDIDATE WITH MOST
POPULAR VOTES DID NOT WIN THE PRESIDENCY

YEAR	CANDIDATE WITH THE MOST POPULAR VOTES NATIONWIDE	CANDIDATE WITH THE MOST ELECTORAL VOTES	POPULAR VOTES FOR THE CANDIDATE WITH THE MOST POPULAR VOTES	POPULAR VOTES FOR THE CANDIDATE WHO PLACED SECOND IN THE POPULAR VOTE	POPULAR VOTE DIFFERENCE
1824	Andrew Jackson	John Q. Adams	151,271	113,122	38,149
1876	Samuel J. Tilden	Rutherford B. Hayes	4,288,191	4,033,497	254,694
1888	Grover Cleveland	Benjamin Harrison	5,539,118	5,449,825	89,293
2000	Al Gore	George W. Bush	50,992,335	50,455,156	537,179

1.2.2 The Current System Does Not Accurately Reflect the Nationwide Popular Vote

Of the 55 presidential elections between 1789 and 2004, there have been four elections—approximately once every five decades—in which the candidate with the most popular votes nationwide did not win the Presidency (table 1.5).[32]

In the past six decades, there have been six presidential elections in which a shift of a relatively small number of votes in one or two states would have elected a presidential candidate who lost the popular vote nationwide. In 1976, for example, Jimmy Carter led Gerald Ford by 1,682,970 votes nationwide; however, a shift of 3,687 votes in Hawaii and 5,559 votes in Ohio would have elected Ford. As shown in table 1.6, there has been an average of one problematic election each decade.[33]

In 2004, President George W. Bush was ahead by about 3,500,000 popular votes nationwide on election night; however, the outcome of the election remained in doubt until Wednesday morning because it was not clear which candidate was going to win Ohio's 20 electoral votes. In the end, Bush received 118,785 more popular votes than Kerry in Ohio,[34] thus winning all of the state's 20 electoral votes and ensuring his reelection.

---

[32] Congressional Quarterly. 2002. *Presidential Elections 1789–2002*. Washington, DC: CQ Press.

[33] Congressional Quarterly. 2002. *Presidential Elections 1789–2002*. Washington, DC: CQ Press.

[34] Ohio Certificate of Ascertainment, December 6, 2004.

Table 1.6 **SIX PROBLEMATIC PRESIDENTIAL ELECTIONS IN THE PAST SIX DECADES**

YEAR	POPULAR VOTE WINNER	ELECTORAL VOTE WINNER	NATIONWIDE POPULAR VOTE LEAD	ELECTORAL VOTES RECEIVED BY NATIONWIDE POPULAR VOTE WINNER	ELECTORAL VOTES RECEIVED BY ELECTORAL VOTE WINNER	POPULAR VOTE SWITCH THAT WOULD HAVE CHANGED THE OUTCOME
2004	Bush	Bush	3,319,608	286	286	59,393 in Ohio
2000	Gore	Bush	537,179	267	271	269 in Florida
1976	Carter	Carter	1,682,970	297	297	5,559 in Ohio and 3,687 in Hawaii
1968	Nixon	Nixon	510,645	301	301	10,245 in Missouri and 67,481 in Illinois
1960	Kennedy	Kennedy	114,673	303	303	4,430 in Illinois and 4,782 in South Carolina
1948	Truman	Truman	2,135,570	303	303	3,554 in Ohio and 42,835 in New Jersey

However, if 59,393 Bush voters in Ohio had switched in 2004, Kerry would have ended up with 272 electoral votes (two more than the 270 required to be elected to the Presidency). The 59,393 Bush voters in Ohio were decisive, whereas Bush's 3,500,000-vote nationwide lead was irrelevant.[35] The illusion of closeness in 2004 resulted from the statewide winner-take-all system used in Ohio—not because the election was genuinely close on the basis of the nationwide popular vote.

Given the relative closeness of the five most recent presidential elections and the current closely divided political environment, additional problems with the electoral system should be considered probable.

[35] Ohio was not the only key state in the Electoral College in 2004. A switch of 6,743 votes in Iowa (with 7 electoral votes), 4,295 in New Mexico (with 5 electoral votes), and 10,784 in Nevada (with 5 electoral votes) would have given George W. Bush and John Kerry each 269 electoral votes. If this switch of 21,822 popular votes had occurred, the presidential election would have been thrown into the House of Representatives (with each state casting one vote and states with an equal division casting no vote), and the vice-presidential election would have thrown into the Senate (with each Senator having one vote).

Interestingly, the 1991 book *Wrong Winner: The Coming Debacle in the Electoral College* by David Abbott and James P. Levine[36] predicted that emerging political and demographic trends would lead to an increasing number of elections in which the candidate with the most popular votes nationwide would not win a majority in the Electoral College.

1.2.3 Not Every Vote Is Equal

There are numerous examples of large disparities in the value of votes under the statewide winner-take-all system. For example, Gore won five electoral votes by carrying New Mexico by 365 popular votes in the 2000 presidential election, whereas Bush won five electoral votes by carrying Utah by 312,043 popular votes—an 855-to-1 disparity in the importance of a vote.

In 2000, George W. Bush received 2,912,790 popular votes in Florida, whereas Al Gore received 2,912,353—a difference of 537 popular votes. Meanwhile, Gore had a nationwide lead of 537,179 popular votes. Gore's shortfall of 537 votes in Florida was less than 1/1000th of Gore's nation-wide lead of 537,179 votes. However, under the winner-take-all rule in effect in Florida, Bush's 537-vote lead in Florida entitled him to all of Florida's 25 electoral votes, thereby giving him the Presidency.[37]

The large differences in the value of a vote in various states in presidential elections has the additional negative side effect of increasing the likelihood of contested presidential elections and recounts. Because the statewide winner-take-all system divides the nation's 122,000,000 popular votes into 51 separate pools, it regularly manufactures artificial crises even when the nationwide popular vote is not particularly close. There are fewer opportunities for razor-thin outcomes when there is one single large pool of votes than when there are 51 separate smaller pools.

The 2000 presidential election is remembered as having been close because George W. Bush's popular vote in Florida was a mere 537 more than Gore's statewide total. There was, however, nothing particularly close about the 2000 election on the basis of the nationwide popular vote. Al Gore's nationwide lead of 537,179 popular votes was larger than, for

---

[36] Abbott, David W. and Levine, James P. 1991. *Wrong Winner: The Coming Debacle in the Electoral College.* Westport, CT: Praeger.

[37] George W. Bush received 271 electoral votes when the Electoral College met in December 2000—one more than the minimum required for election.

example, Nixon's lead of 510,314 in 1968 and Kennedy's lead of 118,574 in 1960.[38] The closeness of the 2000 presidential election was an artificial crisis manufactured by Florida's use of the statewide winner-take-all system.

In the controversial 1876 presidential election, Democrat Samuel J. Tilden received 4,288,191 popular votes—254,694 more than the 4,033,497 popular votes received by Rutherford B. Hayes. Tilden's lead of 3.05% was substantial. It was, for example, greater than George W. Bush's popular vote lead of 2.8% in 2004. The 1876 election is remembered as having been close because Hayes's one-vote lead in the Electoral College resulted from his winning several states by extremely narrow margins:

- 889 votes in South Carolina,
- 922 votes in Florida,
- 1,050 votes in Oregon,
- 1,075 votes in Nevada, and
- 2,798 votes in California.[39]

The closeness of the 1876 election was an artificial crisis created by the statewide winner-take-all system—it was not due to anything particularly close about the nationwide popular vote for President.

The six problematic presidential elections in the past six decades (table 1.6) are reminders that the operation of the winner-take-all system in 51 separate jurisdictions makes razor-thin margins more likely and electoral fraud more rewarding. As Senator Birch Bayh said in a Senate speech in 1979:

> "[O]ne of the things we can do to limit fraud is to limit the benefits to be gained by fraud.
>
> "Under a direct popular vote system, one fraudulent vote wins one vote in the return. In the electoral college system, one fraudulent vote could mean 45 electoral votes, 28 electoral votes."[40]

---

[38] Congressional Quarterly. 2002. *Presidential Elections 1789–2002*. Washington, DC: CQ Press. Pages 146 and 148.

[39] Congressional Quarterly. 2002. *Presidential Elections 1789–2002*. Washington, DC: CQ Press. Page 125.

[40] *Congressional Record.* March 14, 1979. Page 5000.

1.3 NATIONWIDE POPULAR ELECTION AS A REMEDY FOR THE SHORTCOMINGS OF THE CURRENT SYSTEM

Nationwide popular election of the President is the only system that

* makes all states competitive,
* guarantees that the candidate with the most popular votes nationwide wins the Presidency, and
* makes every vote equal.

The authors of this book believe that George W. Bush's lead of 3.5 million popular votes in 2004 should alone have guaranteed him the Presidency in 2004—regardless of who ended up carrying Ohio. Similarly, Al Gore's lead of 537,179 alone should have been sufficient to elect him as President in 2000—regardless of whether one candidate or the other carried Florida by 537 votes.

1.4 FORTUITOUS CONVERGENCE OF FACTORS FAVORING REFORM AT THE PRESENT TIME

There is, at the present time, a fortuitous convergence of factors favoring reform of the current system.

First, the public has come to realize that voters are effectively disenfranchised in presidential elections in about two thirds of the states. Because of the closeness of the last five presidential elections, the media has spotlighted the operation of the winner-take-all rule and the notion of reliably "red" states, reliably "blue" states, and battleground states. In addition, the six problematic presidential elections in the past six decades (table 1.6) have further focused public attention on the mechanics of the Electoral College.

Second, neither major political party gains a partisan advantage from the small states. The small states have been equally divided between the major political parties in the five most recent presidential elections (1988 through 2004).

* Six of the 13 smallest states (Alaska, Idaho, Montana, North Dakota, South Dakota, and Wyoming) have almost always given their combined 19 electoral votes to the Republican presidential candidate.[41]

---

[41] Among the six Republican-leaning small states, the one exception was that Clinton carried Montana in 1992.

- Six other small jurisdictions (Delaware, the District of Columbia, Hawaii, Maine, Rhode Island, and Vermont) have almost always given their combined 21 electoral votes to the Democratic presidential candidate.[42]
- One small state (New Hampshire) is a battleground state that has gone Republican three times and Democratic twice.

As it happens, the small states are disadvantaged by the statewide winner-take-all rule to a considerably greater degree than the larger ones. Overall, two thirds of the states have been politically non-competitive in the last five presidential elections, whereas 92% (12 of the 13) of the smallest states have been non-competitive.

The 13 smallest states have a combined population of 11,448,957.[43] Coincidentally, Ohio has almost the same population (11,353,140) as the 13 smallest states combined. Excluding the one competitive small state (New Hampshire) from consideration, the Constitution gives 40 electoral votes to the 12 non-competitive small states (16 electoral votes warranted by population and 24 bonus electoral votes). The Constitution gives Ohio only 20 electoral votes—half as many as the 12 non-competitive small states. If it were true that the two-vote bonus enhanced the influence of small states, the 12 small states should exert considerably more influence than Ohio in presidential elections. This is not, of course, the case. The battleground state of Ohio (with its "mere" 20 electoral votes) is very important in presidential elections, whereas the 12 non-competitive small states (with their seemingly hefty cache of 40 electoral votes) are irrelevant.[44] Table 1.2 (on 2004 campaign events) dramatically shows the irrelevance of the 12 non-competitive small states in presidential elections—there was not one visit by any major-party presidential or vice-presidential candidate to those states. Almost none of the $237,423,744 in table 1.1 was spent in the 12 non-competitive small states.

---

[42] Among the six Democratic-leaning small states, the three exceptions were that, in 1988, George H. W. Bush carried Delaware, Maine, and Vermont.

[43] Unless otherwise stated, population figures in this book refer to the 2000 federal census.

[44] The 12 non-competitive small states have 16 electoral votes warranted by population plus 24 bonus electoral votes, for a total of 40.

The nearly universal use by *other* states of the winner-take-all rule has trumped the voices of the 11 million people in the 12 non-competitive small states and has also trumped the potential benefit of the two-vote bonus that each state receives in the Electoral College.

In short, the two-vote bonus established by the Constitution to enhance the influence of the small states exists today in *form;* however, the nearly unanimous use by the states of the winner-take-all rule robs these bonus electoral votes of any political *substance.* If, hypothetically, the Constitution had given each state a bonus of *four* electoral votes (instead of just two), the 12 non-competitive small states would then collectively have 64 electoral votes (16 warranted by population plus 48 bonus electoral votes). Even then, these states still would not have any meaningful influence in presidential elections. A competitive state, such as Ohio with only 20 electoral votes, would remain far more important in terms of practical politics than the 12 non-competitive small states. Political power in a system based on the statewide winner-take-all rule comes from being a closely divided battleground state—not from mathematical bonuses.

The argument that the Electoral College confers an enormous amount of influence on the most populous states is another superficially plausible and arithmetically correct argument that simply does not reflect political reality. A large state (such as California, Texas, or New York) receives electoral votes approximately in direct proportion to its population. The Constitution allocates 81% of the electoral votes according to population.[45] If size mattered, the nation's three most populous states (California, Texas, and New York) would be at center stage in presidential elections. But this is not the case. The political reality is that these three largest states suffer from the same spectator status as the 12 non-competitive small states—none has mattered in presidential elections for decades. If, hypothetically, California, Texas, and New York were to suddenly each acquire 10 extra electoral votes, they still would not matter in presidential elections. Presidential candidates would continue to take the

---

[45] Out of the 538 electoral votes, the 435 corresponding to the 435 U.S. Representatives are allocated according to population.

non-competitive states for granted and to concentrate on the closely divided battleground states.

Civics books often recite the argument that a vote in a small state is worth more than a vote in a large state because of the bonus of two electoral votes that each state receives in the Electoral College. The argument is that a Wyoming vote is worth 3.74 times that of a California vote because one electoral vote corresponds to 164,594 people in Wyoming, compared to 615,848 people in California.[46] This argument is arithemetically and legally correct, but it does not reflect political reality. A vote in a small state such as Wyoming and a vote in a large state such as California simply do not matter because everyone knows, well in advance of the voting in November, which candidate will win the electoral votes from those states. From the perspective of presidential candidates operating under the winner-take-all system, a vote in Wyoming is equal to a vote in California in presidential elections—*both are equally worthless.*

Third, there has been long-standing support for nationwide popular election among the public and from members of Congress in both political parties from small, medium, and large states in all parts of the country. As shown in appendix S of this book, there has been at least one Senator or Representative in each of the 50 states who has either sponsored a bill for nationwide popular election or voted for nationwide popular election of the President in a roll call vote in Congress.

1.5 ROADMAP OF THIS BOOK

Chapter 2 of this book describes the current system of electing the President, including the federal constitutional and statutory provisions that govern presidential elections (section 2.1). Section 2.2 reviews the history of the various methods that the states have used over the years to elect their presidential electors, and section 2.3 discusses present-day methods.

---

[46] Wyoming has a population of 493,782 (according to the 2000 federal census) and has three electoral votes (one warranted by population plus its two-vote bonus). California (with a population of 33,871,648) has 55 electoral votes (53 warranted by population plus its two-vote bonus). Thus, one electoral vote corresponds to 164,594 people in Wyoming, compared to 615,848 people in California.

The chapter also discusses the certification of the popular vote for President by the states (section 2.4), the meeting of the Electoral College in mid-December (section 2.5), the certification of the votes cast by the presidential electors (section 2.6), and the counting of the electoral votes in Congress (section 2.7). The chapter also covers write-in voting for President (section 2.8), voting for individual presidential electors (section 2.9), fusion voting in presidential races (section 2.10), unpledged presidential electors (section 2.11), and faithless presidential electors (section 2.12).

Chapter 2 identifies five salient features of present-day presidential elections that did not exist or that were not prominent at the time of ratification of the U.S. Constitution, namely

- popular voting for presidential electors,
- the non-deliberative nature of the Electoral College,
- the statewide winner-take-all rule,
- nomination of presidential candidates by political parties, and
- the short presidential ballot.

As chapter 2 demonstrates, these present-day features of the system evolved over a period of many decades as a result of the piecemeal passage of laws by individual states and the emergence of political parties. As summarized in section 2.13, none of these features is contained in the U.S. Constitution or any federal law. None reflects a consensus of the Founding Fathers. None came into being because of the adoption of any federal constitutional amendment. Instead, these features came into existence because the states used the built-in flexibility of the Constitution to make them part of our present-day political landscape.

Chapter 3 examines the three most prominent approaches to presidential election reform that have been proposed in the form of a federal constitutional amendment, including

- fractional proportional allocation of electoral votes (section 3.1),
- district allocation of electoral votes (section 3.2), and
- nationwide popular election (section 3.3).

Each of these three proposed approaches is examined in light of three criteria:

- whether the proposed approach accurately reflects the nationwide popular vote;
- whether the proposed approach makes every state competitive; and
- whether every vote is equal.

Chapter 4 examines the two most prominent approaches to presidential election reform that can be enacted at the state level (i.e., without a federal constitutional amendment and without action by Congress), namely

- the whole-number proportional approach (section 4.1), and
- the congressional-district approach (section 4.2).

Again, each proposed approach is examined in light of the above three criteria.

Chapter 5 provides background on interstate compacts—the contractual arrangement authorized in the Constitution by which states can act in concert to address an issue that cannot be readily solved by unilateral action. The chapter begins with the constitutional basis for interstate compacts starting with the Articles of Confederation (section 5.1), the legal standing of compacts (section 5.2), and the history of compacts (section 5.3). The chapter then covers the wide variety of subjects addressed by compacts (section 5.4), the variety of parties that may participate in compacts (section 5.5), the procedures for drafting, negotiating, and formulating compacts (section 5.6), the methods by which a state may adopt an interstate compact (section 5.7), and the contingent nature of compacts (section 5.8). Section 5.9 discusses congressional involvement in interstate compacts and the process of congressional consent; section 5.10 discusses the effect of congressional consent; section 5.11 gives examples of compacts that are contingent on the enactment of federal legislation; and section 5.12 gives examples of compacts that do not require congressional consent. Section 5.13 discusses enforcement of compacts; section 5.14 discusses amendments to compacts; section 5.15 discusses the duration of compacts and the process of terminating and withdrawing from compacts; section 5.16 discusses administration of compacts; and section 5.17 discusses the style of drafting compacts. Section 5.18 compares treaties and compacts; section 5.19 compares uniform state laws and compacts; and section 5.20 compares federal multi-state commissions and compacts. The future of interstate compacts is discussed in section 5.21.

Chapter 6 presents the authors' proposal to reform the presidential election process—an interstate compact entitled the "Agreement Among the States to Elect the President by National Popular Vote." The compact is a proposed state law. The compact would not become immediately effective when any one or two states enact it. Instead, the compact would come into effect only after it is enacted by states collectively possessing a majority of the electoral votes (i.e., 270 of the 538 electoral votes).

The proposed compact would not change any state's internal procedures for conducting or counting its presidential vote. After the people cast their ballots in early November of presidential election years, the popular vote counts from all 50 states and the District of Columbia would be added together to obtain a national grand total for each presidential slate. At the present time, the Electoral College reflects the voters' state-by-state choices for President or, in the cases of Maine and Nebraska, the voters' district-wide choices. The compact would change the Electoral College from an institution that reflects the voters' state-by-state choices or district-wide choices into a body that reflects the voters' nationwide choice. Specifically, the proposed compact specifies that each member state will award all of its electoral votes to the presidential candidate who received the largest total number of popular votes in all 50 states and the District of Columbia. Because the compact would become effective only when it encompasses states collectively possessing a majority of the electoral votes, the presidential candidate receiving the most popular votes in all 50 states and the District of Columbia would be guaranteed enough electoral votes in the Electoral College to be elected.

Note that membership in the proposed compact is not required for the popular votes of a state to count. Every state's popular vote is included on an equal footing in the nationwide total regardless of whether the state is a member of the compact. Note also that the political complexion of the states belonging to the compact does not affect the outcome produced by the compact. The presidential candidate receiving the most popular votes in all 50 states and the District of Columbia is ensured enough electoral votes (that is, at least 270 of the 538) to be elected to the Presidency regardless of what states happen to belong to the compact.

Chapter 7 outlines a possible timeline for securing adoption of the proposed interstate compact.

Chapter 8 addresses several legal questions concerning the proposed interstate compact, namely

- Is the subject matter of the proposed compact appropriate for an interstate compact (section 8.1)?
- May the citizen-initiative process be used to enact interstate compacts in general (section 8.2)?
- May the citizen-initiative process be used to enact a state law concerning the manner of choosing presidential electors (section 8.3)?
- Does the proposed compact encroach on the power of non-member states (section 8.4)?
- Does the proposed compact impermissibly delegate a state's sovereign power (section 8.5)?
- Is the six-month blackout period for withdrawals from the proposed compact enforceable (section 8.6)?

Chapter 9 addresses various administrative aspects of the proposed interstate compact.

- Does the proposed compact impose any significant additional financial cost or administrative burdens on a state's election officials (section 9.1)?
- How would recounts be handled (section 9.2)?

Chapter 10 is the epilogue.

1.6 SOURCES OF ADDITIONAL INFORMATION

There is a large literature analyzing the arguments for and against the current electoral system and possible alternatives. This book limits its discussion of the various possible approaches to three criteria that seem particularly pertinent to the electoral system at the present time—namely whether a particular approach makes every state competitive in presidential elections; whether the approach accurately reflects the nationwide popular vote; and whether the approach makes every vote equal.

Additional information is available from a variety of sources. The congressional hearings held in 1967,[47] 1969,[48,49,50] 1975,[51] 1977,[52] 1979,[53] 1993,[54] and 1999[55] contain numerous detailed discussions of the current system and its alternatives from various experts, members of the public, organizations, and members of Congress. Books on these same subjects include:

[47] U.S. Senate Committee on the Judiciary. 1967. *Election of the President: Hearings on S.J. Res. 4, 7, 11, 12, 28, 58, 62, 138 and 139, 89th Congress; and S.J. Res. 2, 3, 6, 7, 12, 15, 21, 25, 55, 84, and 86.* 89th Congress, 2nd Session and 90th Congress, 1st Session. February 28–August 23, 1967. Washington, DC: U.S. Government Printing Office.

[48] U.S. House of Representatives Committee on the Judiciary. 1969. *Electoral College Reform: Hearings on H.J. Res. 179, H.J. Res. 181, and Similar Proposals to Amend the Constitution Relating to Electoral College Reform.* 91st Congress, 1st Session. February 5, 6, 19, 20, 26, and 27; March 5, 6, 12, and 13, 1969. Washington, DC: U.S. Government Printing Office.

[49] U.S. Senate Committee on the Judiciary. 1969. *Electing the President: Hearings on S.J. Res. 1, S.J. Res. 2, S.J. Res. 4, S.J. Res. 12, S.J. Res. 18, S.J. Res. 20, S.J. Res 25, S.J. Res. 30, S.J. Res 31, S.J. Res 33, S.J. Res 71, and S.J. Res 72 to Amend the Constitution Relating to Electoral College Reform.* 91st Congress, 1st Session. January 23–24, March 10, 11, 12, 13, 20, 21, April 30, May 1–2, 1969. Washington, DC: U.S. Government Printing Office.

[50] U.S. Senate Committee on the Judiciary. 1969. *Direct Popular Election of the President: Report, with Additional Minority, Individual, and Separate Views on H.J. Res. 681, Proposing an Amendment to the Constitution of the United States Relating to the Election of the President and Vice President.* 91st Congress, 1st Session. Washington, DC: U.S. Government Printing Office.

[51] U.S. Senate Committee on the Judiciary. 1975. *Direct Popular Election of the President: Report (to Accompany S.J. Res. 1).* 94th Congress, 1st Session. Washington, DC: U.S. Government Printing Office.

[52] U.S. Senate Committee on the Judiciary. 1977. *The Electoral College and Direct Election: Hearings on the Electoral College and Direct Election of the President and Vice President (S.J. Res. 1, 8, and 18): Supplement.* 95th Congress, 1st Session. July 20, 22, and 28, and August 2, 1977. Washington, DC: U.S. Government Printing Office.

[53] U.S. Senate Committee on the Judiciary. 1979. *Direct Popular Election of the President and Vice President of the United States: Hearings on S.J. Res. 28, Joint Resolution Proposing an Amendment to the Constitution to Provide for the Direct Popular Election of the President and Vice President of the United States.* 96th Congress, 1st Session. March 27 and 30, April 3 and 9, 1979. Washington, DC: U.S. Government Printing Office.

[54] U.S. Senate Committee on the Judiciary. 1993. *The Electoral College and Direct Election of the President: Hearing on S.J. Res. 297, S.J. Res. 302, and S.J. Res 312, Measures Proposing Amendments to the Constitution Relating to the Direct Election of the President and Vice President of the United States.* 102nd Congress, 2nd Session. July 22, 1992. Washington, DC: U.S. Government Printing Office.

[55] U.S. House Committee on the Judiciary. 1999. *Proposals for Electoral College Reform: Hearing on H.J. Res. 28 and H.J. Res. 43.* 105th Congress, 1st Session. September 4, 1997. Washington, DC: U.S. Government Printing Office.

- *Wrong Winner: The Coming Debacle in the Electoral College* by David Abbott and James P. Levine (1991),[56]
- *Choice of the People? Debating the Electoral College* by Judith A. Best (1996),[57]
- *The Case Against Direct Election of the President: A Defense of the Electoral College* by Judith Vairo Best (1975),[58]
- *Why the Electoral College Is Bad for America* by George C. Edwards III (2004),[59]
- *The Importance of the Electoral College* by George Grant (2004),[60]
- *Securing Democracy: Why We Have an Electoral College*, a collection of articles edited by Gary L. Gregg II (2001),[61]
- *The Electoral College* by Suzanne LeVert (2004),[62]
- *The Politics of Electoral College Reform* by Lawrence D. Longley and Alan G. Braun (1972),[63]
- *The People's President: The Electoral College in American History and Direct-Vote Alternative* by Neal R. Peirce (1968),[64]
- *Enlightened Democracy: The Case for the Electoral College* by Tara Ross (2004),[65]

---

[56] Abbott, David W. and Levine, James P. 1991. *Wrong Winner: The Coming Debacle in the Electoral College*. Westport, CT: Praeger.

[57] Best, Judith A. 1996. *Choice of the People? Debating the Electoral College*. Lanham, MD: Rowman & Littlefield.

[58] Best, Judith Vairo. 1975. *The Case Against Direct Election of the President: A Defense of the Electoral College*. Ithaca, NY: Cornell University Press.

[59] Edwards, George C. III. 2004. *Why the Electoral College Is Bad for America*. New Haven, CT: Yale University Press.

[60] Grant, George. 2004. *The Importance of the Electoral College*. San Antonio, TX: Vision Forum Ministries.

[61] Gregg, Gary L. II (editor). 2001. *Securing Democracy: Why We Have an Electoral College*. Wilmington, DE: ISI Books.

[62] LeVert, Suzanne. 2004. *The Electoral College*. New York, NY: Franklin Watts.

[63] Longley, Lawrence D. and Braun, Alan G. 1972. *The Politics of Electoral College Reform*. New Haven, CT: Yale University Press.

[64] Peirce, Neal R. 1968. *The People's President: The Electoral College in American History and Direct-Vote Alternative*. New York, NY: Simon and Schuster.

[65] Ross, Tara. 2004. *Enlightened Democracy: The Case for the Electoral College*. Los Angeles, CA: World Ahead Publishing Company.

- *Choosing a President,* a collection of articles edited by Paul D. Schumaker and Burdett A. Loomis (2002),[66]
- *History of American Presidential Elections 1878–2001* an 11-volume collection of articles edited by Arthur M. Schlesinger, Jr. and Fred L. Israel (2002),[67]
- *A History of the Presidency from 1788 to 1897*[68] and *A History of the Presidency from 1897 to 1916* by Edward Stanwood (1924),[69] and
- *The Electoral College* by Lucius Wilmerding (1958).[70]

Among books that have come out since the 2000 presidential election, the 2004 book *Enlightened Democracy: The Case for the Electoral College*[71] contains some of the clearest arguments supporting the existing system. On the other side of the argument, the 2004 book *Why the Electoral College Is Bad for America*[72] is noteworthy because it closely examines and analyzes many of the most commonly invoked arguments in favor of the existing system—such as protection of federalism and protection of state interests.

The Center for Voting and Democracy (FairVote) published two insightful reports on presidential elections in 2005:

- *The Shrinking Battleground: The 2008 Presidential Election and Beyond*[73] and
- *Who Picks the President?*[74]

---

[66] Schumaker, Paul D. and Loomis, Burdett A. (editors). 2002. *Choosing a President.* New York, NY: Chatham House Publishers.

[67] Schlesinger, Arthur M., Jr. and Israel, Fred L. (editors). 2002. *History of American Presidential Elections 1878–2001.* Philadelphia, PA: Chelsea House Publishers. 11 volumes.

[68] Stanwood, Edward. 1924. *A History of the Presidency from 1788 to 1897.* Boston, MA: Houghton Mifflin Company.

[69] Stanwood, Edward. 1916. *A History of the Presidency from 1897 to 1916.* Boston, MA: Houghton Mifflin Company.

[70] Wilmerding, Lucius, Jr. 1958. *The Electoral College.* Boston, MA: Beacon Press.

[71] Ross, Tara. 2004. *Enlightened Democracy: The Case for the Electoral College.* Los Angeles, CA: World Ahead Publishing Company.

[72] Edwards, George C. III. 2004. *Why the Electoral College Is Bad for America.* New Haven, CT: Yale University Press.

[73] FairVote. 2005. *The Shrinking Battleground: The 2008 Presidential Election and Beyond.* Takoma Park, MD: The Center for Voting and Democracy. www.fairvote.org/shrinking.

[74] FairVote. 2005. *Who Picks the President?* Takoma Park, MD: The Center for Voting and Democracy. www.fairvote.org/whopicks.

This book's bibliography contains numerous additional references to books about particular problematic elections (e.g., 1800, 1876, and 2000) as well as the history and operation of the present system over the years.

2 | How the Electoral College Works

The current system for electing the President and Vice President of the United States is governed by a combination of federal and state statutory and constitutional provisions. This chapter discusses the:

- federal constitutional and federal statutory provisions governing presidential elections (section 2.1),
- history of various methods for choosing presidential electors (section 2.2),
- current state laws governing the election of presidential electors (section 2.3),
- certification of the popular vote by the states (section 2.4),
- meeting of the Electoral College (section 2.5),
- certification of the votes cast by a state's presidential electors (section 2.6),
- counting of the electoral votes in Congress (section 2.7),
- write-in votes for president (section 2.8),
- state laws permitting a voter to cast separate votes for individual candidates for presidential elector (section 2.9),
- fusion voting (section 2.10),
- unpledged electors (section 2.11),
- faithless presidential electors (section 2.12), and
- five major changes that have been implemented without a federal constitutional amendment (section 2.13).

2.1 FEDERAL CONSTITUTIONAL AND STATUTORY PROVISIONS

The President and Vice President of the United States are not elected directly by the voters. Instead, the President and Vice President are elected by a group of 538 people who are known individually as "presidential electors" and collectively as the "Electoral College." Each political party nominates its own candidates (typically long-standing party activists) for the position of presidential elector.

Presidential electors are chosen separately by each state and the District of Columbia on the Tuesday after the first Monday in November in presidential election years. The 538 presidential electors cast their votes for President and Vice President in mid-December in separate meetings held in the 50 state capitals and the District of Columbia.

The U.S. Constitution provides:

> "The executive Power shall be vested in a President of the United States of America. He shall hold his Office during the Term of four Years, and, together with the Vice President, chosen for the same Term, be elected, as follows:

> "Each State shall appoint, in such Manner as the Legislature thereof may direct, a Number of Electors, equal to the whole Number of Senators and Representatives to which the State may be entitled in the Congress...."[1]

For the reader's convenience, appendix A contains the provisions of the U.S. Constitution relating to presidential elections, and appendix B contains the relevant provisions of federal law.

The number of seats in the House of Representatives is set by federal statute. There are currently 435 U.S. Representatives. There are, in addition, two Senators from each state. Consequently, the 50 states together have 535 electoral votes. The District of Columbia acquired three electoral votes as a result of the ratification of the 23rd Amendment to the U.S. Constitution in 1961. Thus, in total, there are currently 538 electoral votes. If all 538 electors are appointed, 270 electoral votes (i.e., a majority of 538) are required to elect the President and the Vice President.

After each decennial federal census, the 435 seats in the United States House of Representatives are reapportioned among the 50 states. The 2000 federal census determined the distribution of electoral votes among the states for the 2004 and 2008 presidential elections. The 2010 census will determine the distribution of electoral votes for the 2012, 2016, and 2020 presidential elections.

Table 2.1 shows the distribution of electoral votes among the 51 jurisdictions that appoint presidential electors. Because each state has two Senators and at least one Representative, no state has fewer than three

---

[1] U.S. Constitution. Article II, section 1, clauses 1 and 2.

electoral votes. The average number of electoral votes is about 11. The states with the most electoral votes are California (55), Texas (34), and New York (31). There are 13 states with three or four electoral votes.

Table 2.1 DISTRIBUTION OF ELECTORAL VOTES AMONG THE 50 STATES AND THE DISTRICT OF COLUMBIA

JURISDICTION	REPRESENTATIVES	SENATORS	ELECTORAL VOTES
Alabama	7	2	9
Alaska	1	2	3
Arizona	8	2	10
Arkansas	4	2	6
California	53	2	55
Colorado	7	2	9
Connecticut	5	2	7
Delaware	1	2	3
District of Columbia	0	0	3
Florida	25	2	27
Georgia	13	2	15
Hawaii	2	2	4
Idaho	2	2	4
Illinois	19	2	21
Indiana	9	2	11
Iowa	5	2	7
Kansas	4	2	6
Kentucky	6	2	8
Louisiana	7	2	9
Maine	2	2	4
Maryland	8	2	10
Massachusetts	10	2	12
Michigan	15	2	17
Minnesota	8	2	10
Mississippi	4	2	6
Missouri	9	2	11
Montana	1	2	3
Nebraska	3	2	5
Nevada	3	2	5
New Hampshire	2	2	4
New Jersey	13	2	15
New Mexico	3	2	5
New York	29	2	31
North Carolina	13	2	15
North Dakota	1	2	3
Ohio	18	2	20

Table 2.1 DISTRIBUTION OF ELECTORAL VOTES AMONG THE 50 STATES AND THE DISTRICT OF COLUMBIA (cont.)

JURISDICTION	REPRESENTATIVES	SENATORS	ELECTORAL VOTES
Oklahoma	5	2	7
Oregon	5	2	7
Pennsylvania	19	2	21
Rhode Island	2	2	4
South Carolina	6	2	8
South Dakota	1	2	3
Tennessee	9	2	11
Texas	32	2	34
Utah	3	2	5
Vermont	1	2	3
Virginia	11	2	13
Washington	9	2	11
West Virginia	3	2	5
Wisconsin	8	2	10
Wyoming	1	2	3
Total	**435**	**100**	**538**

The Electoral College meeting in mid-December is governed by the 12th Amendment to the U.S. Constitution:

"The Electors shall meet in their respective states, and vote by ballot for President and Vice-President, one of whom, at least, shall not be an inhabitant of the same state with themselves; they shall name in their ballots the person voted for as President, and in distinct ballots the person voted for as Vice-President, and they shall make distinct lists of all persons voted for as President, and of all persons voted for as Vice-President, and of the number of votes for each, which lists they shall sign and certify, and transmit sealed to the seat of the government of the United States, directed to the President of the Senate."

The Constitution further provides:

"The Congress may determine the Time of chusing the Electors, and the Day on which they shall give their Votes; which Day shall be the same throughout the United States." [Spelling as per original]

Federal election law establishes the date for the choosing of presidential electors. In 2004, the date was Tuesday, November 2.

"The electors of President and Vice President shall be appointed, in each State, on the Tuesday next after the first Monday in November, in every fourth year succeeding every election of a President and Vice President."[2]

The date for the meeting of the Electoral College is established by federal election law. In 2004, the designated day for the meeting of the Electoral College was Monday, December 13.

"The electors of President and Vice President of each State shall meet and give their votes on the first Monday after the second Wednesday in December next following their appointment at such place in each State as the legislature of such State shall direct."[3]

This statute was enacted in 1934 after the 20th Amendment (ratified in 1933) changed the date for the presidential inauguration from March 4 to January 20.

The people have the right, under the Constitution, to vote for United States Representatives. The 17th Amendment (ratified in 1913) gave the people the right to vote for United States Senators (who were elected by state legislatures under the original Constitution). The people, however, have no federal constitutional right to vote for President or Vice President or for presidential electors. Instead, the Constitution provides:

"Each State shall appoint, in such Manner as the Legislature thereof may direct, a Number of Electors, equal to the whole Number of Senators and Representatives to which the State may be entitled in the Congress...."[4]

As the U.S. Supreme Court observed in the 1892 case of *McPherson v. Blacker:*

"The constitution does not provide that the appointment of electors shall be by popular vote, nor that the electors shall be voted for upon a general ticket, nor that the majority of those who exercise the elective franchise can alone choose the electors."[5]

---

[2] United States Code. Title 3, chapter 1, section 1.

[3] United States Code. Title 3, chapter 1, section 7.

[4] U.S. Constitution. Article II, section 1, clause 2.

[5] *McPherson v. Blacker.* 146 U.S. 1 at 27. 1892.

The full text of the Court's decision in *McPherson v. Blacker* can be found in appendix O.

In 2000, the U.S. Supreme Court in *Bush v. Gore* reiterated the principle that the people have no federal constitutional right to vote for President.

> "The individual citizen has no federal constitutional right to vote for electors for the President of the United States unless and until the state legislature chooses a statewide election as the means to implement its power to appoint members of the Electoral College."[6]

There is only one state where the right of the people to vote for presidential electors is guaranteed by a state constitution. The Colorado Constitution provides:

> "The general assembly shall provide that after the year eighteen hundred and seventy-six the electors of the electoral college shall be chosen by direct vote of the people."[7]

2.2 HISTORY OF METHODS OF SELECTING PRESIDENTIAL ELECTORS

In 1787, the Constitutional Convention considered a variety of methods for electing the President and Vice President, including election by

- state governors,
- Congress,
- state legislatures,
- nationwide popular vote, and
- electors.

The delegates debated the method of electing the President on 22 separate days and held 30 votes on the topic.[8,9] As described in George Edwards's recent book:

> "The delegates were obviously perplexed about how to select the president, and their confusion is reflected in their voting. On July 17, for example, the delegates voted for selection of

---

[6] *Bush v. Gore.* 531 U.S. 98. 2000.

[7] Section 20 of the article of the Colorado Constitution governing the transition from territorial status to statehood.

[8] Peirce, Neal R. 1968. *The People's President: The Electoral College in American History and Direct-Vote Alternative.* New York, NY: Simon and Schuster. Pages 28–57.

[9] Longley, Lawrence D. and Braun, Alan G. 1972. *The Politics of Electoral College Reform.* New Haven, CT: Yale University Press. Pages 22–41.

the president by the national legislature. Two days later they voted for selection by electors chosen by state legislatures. Five days after that, they again voted for selection by the nation legislative, a position they rejected the next day and then adopted again the day after that. Then, just when it appeared that the delegates had reached a consensus, they again turned the question over to a committee. This committee changed the convention's course once more and recommended selection of the president by electors...."[10]

The Constitutional Convention never agreed on a method for choosing the presidential electors. The matter was simply turned over to the states.

The U.S. Constitution gave the states considerably more discretion in choosing the manner of appointing their presidential electors than it did in choosing the manner of electing their U.S. Representatives and Senators. The states' power to chose the manner of conducting congressional elections is subject to congressional oversight. Article I, section 4, clause 1 of the U.S. Constitution provides:

"The Times, Places and Manner of holding Elections for Senators and Representatives, shall be prescribed in each State by the Legislature thereof; **but the Congress may at any time by Law make or alter such Regulations,** except as to the Places of chusing Senators." [Emphasis added]

In contrast, article II, section 1, clause 2 of the U.S. Constitution gives Congress no comparable oversight power concerning a state's choice of the manner of appointing its presidential electors.

"Each State shall appoint, in such Manner as the Legislature thereof may direct, a Number of Electors, equal to the whole Number of Senators and Representatives to which the State may be entitled in the Congress...."

As the U.S. Supreme Court wrote in *McPherson v. Blacker:*

"In short, the appointment and mode of appointment of electors belong **exclusively** to the states under the constitution of the United States."[11] [Emphasis added]

---

[10] Edwards, George C., III. 2004. *Why the Electoral College Is Bad for America.* New Haven, CT: Yale University Press. Pages 79–80.

That is, the states have plenary power in choosing the manner of appointing their presidential electors. Of course, the state's power in this area is limited by various general constitutional limitations, such as the equal protection clause of the 14th Amendment, the 15th Amendment (outlawing the denial of vote based on race, color, or previous condition of servitude), the 20th Amendment (women's suffrage), the 24th Amendment (outlawing poll taxes), and the 26th Amendment (18-year-old vote).

2.2.1 THE FIRST AND SECOND PRESIDENTIAL ELECTIONS

The states employed three distinct methods for choosing presidential electors in the nation's first presidential election (1789), including

- appointment of all the state's presidential electors by the legislature,
- popular election by district, and
- statewide popular election.

In five of the 10 states that participated in the first presidential election, the legislatures simply designated themselves as the appointing authority for all of the state's electors. Thus, the voters had no direct involvement in choosing presidential electors in Connecticut, Delaware, Georgia, New Jersey, and South Carolina.

Massachusetts used a more complicated system; however, a majority of the legislature[12] effectively retained the power to choose all of the state's 10 presidential electors. In each of the state's eight congressional districts, the voters cast ballots in a popular election for their choice for the district's presidential elector. However, the actual selection of the presidential elector for each district was then made by the state legislature from among the two elector candidates receiving the most popular votes in each district. The state legislature also chose the state's two senatorial electors.

Appointment of presidential electors by a state legislature did not seem as odd in 1789 as it would today. In 1789, the states legislatures had the power to elect United States Senators[13] and, in most states, the state's Governor.

---

[11] *McPherson v. Blacker.* 146 U.S. 1 at 35. 1892.

[12] Sitting in a joint convention of both houses.

[13] Under the original constitution, United States Senators were elected by state legislatures. The ratification of the 17th Amendment in 1913 permitted the voters to elect Senators.

In four of the 10 states that participated in the first presidential election, the voters chose all of the presidential electors.

In Virginia (which, at the time, had 10 congressional districts and hence 12 electoral votes), the state was divided into 12 presidential elector districts. Each voter cast a vote for an elector in his district.

In New Hampshire, Maryland, and Pennsylvania, presidential electors were elected in a statewide popular vote. This method (sometimes called the "general ticket" system) resembled the modern-day system in that a majority of the state's voters controlled all of the state's electoral votes. It differed from the present-day system in that the names of the presidential and vice-presidential candidates did not appear on the ballot. Instead, each voter cast votes for individual candidates for presidential elector. For example, in a state with five electoral votes (such as New Hampshire), a voter could (and ordinarily would) cast a vote for five individual candidates for presidential elector. In Maryland, all the state's voters voted for three electors from the Eastern Shore and five from the Western Shore.

In summary, nine of the 10 states chose presidential electors in a way that permitted a majority to control all of the state's presidential electors. In six states, a legislative majority controlled all of the state's electors. In three states, a popular majority controlled all of the state's electors. Only Virginia used a system that, under normal circumstances, was likely to produce a division of the state's electoral votes.

The Supreme Court noted the "disadvantage" of such "division of their strength" in 1892 in *McPherson v. Blacker*:

> "The district system was largely considered the most equitable, and Madison wrote that it was that system which was contemplated by the framers of the constitution, although it was soon seen that its adoption by some states might place them at a disadvantage by a division of their strength, and that a uniform rule was preferable."[14]

Three of the original 13 states did not participate in the nation's first presidential election. Rhode Island and North Carolina did not ratify the Constitution in time to participate. In New York, the legislature could not agree on a method for choosing presidential electors, so New York

---

[14] *McPherson v. Blacker.* 146 U.S. 1 at 29. 1892.

did not cast any votes in the first presidential election. The missing votes mattered little because George Washington received a vote from all of the 69 presidential electors who voted in the Electoral College in 1789.[15]

In 1792, the Massachusetts legislature loosened its grip on the choice of presidential electors and permitted the voters to elect all of the state's presidential electors directly. The state was divided into four regional multi-member districts for the purpose of electing the state's 16 electors.[16] Under the 1792 plan in Massachusetts, the legislature would become involved in the choice of presidential electors only in the event that a presidential elector candidate failed to receive a majority of the popular votes cast in a district.

In 1792, George Washington again received a vote from all of the presidential electors who voted.

2.2.2 THE FIRST COMPETITIVE PRESIDENTIAL ELECTION

In the early years of the republic, Thomas Jefferson led the opposition to the policies of the ruling Federalist Party.

George Washington's decision not to run for a third term in 1796 opened the way for a contested presidential election between the country's two emerging political parties.

In the summer of 1796, the Federalist members of Congress caucused and nominated John Adams of Massachusetts as their candidate for President and nominated Thomas Pinckney for Vice President. Meanwhile, the opposition caucus in Congress (originally called the Anti-Federalists, later the Republicans or the Democratic-Republicans, and eventually the Democrats) voted to support the candidacies of Thomas Jefferson of Virginia for President and Aaron Burr for Vice President.[17,18,19]

In preparation for the 1796 presidential election, the legislature of the newly admitted state of Tennessee created a state-level electoral

---

[15] In addition, two presidential electors from Maryland and two from Virginia failed to vote in the Electoral College in 1789.

[16] As a consequence of the 1790 federal census, Massachusetts became entitled to choose 16 presidential electors in the 1792 presidential election (as compared to 10 in the 1789 election).

[17] Peirce, Neal R. 1968. *The People's President: The Electoral College in American History and Direct-Vote Alternative.* New York, NY: Simon and Schuster. Page 63.

[18] Grant, George. 2004. *The Importance of the Electoral College.* San Antonio, TX: Vision Forum Ministries. Pages 23–26.

[19] The congressional caucus was replaced by the national nominating convention during the 1820s.

college to choose the state's members of the national Electoral College. The legislative act asserted that its aim was that the presidential electors

"be elected with as little trouble to the citizens as possible."[20]

To this end, the legislature specifically named, in the statute, certain prominent local persons from Washington, Sullivan, Green, and Hawkins counties to select one presidential elector from their part of the state. Then, it named another group of individuals from Knox, Jefferson, Sevier, and Blount counties to select their area's presidential elector. Finally, it named yet another group from Davidson, Sumner, and Tennessee counties to select a presidential elector from their district.

For the 1796 election, Massachusetts switched from multi-member elector districts to a system in which the voters elected the presidential electors by congressional district (with the legislature being involved only in the event that a presidential elector candidate failed to receive a majority of the popular votes cast in his district). Under the 1796 plan, the state legislature appointed the state's two senatorial electors.

Maryland used a district system in 1796.

The Founding Fathers anticipated that the Electoral College would act as a deliberative body wherein the presidential electors would exercise independent and detached judgment as to the best persons to serve as President and Vice President. Hamilton wrote in *Federalist 64*:

"As the select assemblies for choosing the President … will in general be composed of the most enlightened and respectable citizens, there is reason to presume that their attention and their votes will be directed to those men only who have become the most distinguished by their abilities and virtues."

The Founding Fathers' lofty expectations that the Electoral College would be a deliberative body were dashed by the political realities of the nation's first competitive presidential election.[21] In 1796, both political parties nominated candidates for President and Vice President on a centralized basis (the party's caucus in Congress). Both parties campaigned throughout the country for their nominees. It was only logical that the presidential

---

[20] Laws Tenn. 1794, 1803, p. 209; Acts 2d Sess. 1st Gen. Assem. Tenn. c. 4.

[21] White, Theodore H. 1969. *The Making of the President 1968*. New York, NY: Atheneum Publishers. Page 471.

electors associated with each political party would be expected to cast their votes in the Electoral College for the party's nominees.

As the Supreme Court observed in *McPherson v. Blacker*:

> "Doubtless it was supposed that the electors would exercise a reasonable independence and fair judgment in the selection of the chief executive, but experience soon demonstrated that, **whether chosen by the legislatures or by popular suffrage on general ticket or in districts, they were so chosen simply to register the will of the appointing power** in respect of a particular candidate. In relation, then, to the independence of the electors, the original expectation may be said to have been frustrated."[22] [Emphasis added]

Table 2.2 shows the distribution, by state, of the 71 electoral votes received by John Adams and the 68 electoral votes received by Thomas Jefferson in the nation's first contested presidential election in 1796.[23,24]

In 1796, presidential electors were effectively chosen by state legislatures in nine of the 16 states.[25] Despite the distinguished qualifications of both Adams and Jefferson, there was no hint of independent judgment by any of the presidential electors chosen by the legislatures. As table 2.2 demonstrates, all 66 presidential electors from these nine states voted in unison for Jefferson or Adams in accordance with "the will of the appointing power"—that is, the will of the legislative majority.

In the one state (New Hampshire) in which the voters elected the state's presidential electors in a statewide popular election in 1796, all of the state's presidential electors voted for Adams. That is, the voters were "the appointing power," and they chose electors who faithfully did their bidding.

---

[22] *McPherson v. Blacker.* 146 U.S. 1 at 36. 1892.

[23] Congressional Quarterly. 2002. *Presidential Elections 1789-2002.* Washington, DC: CQ Press. Page 176.

[24] The table simplifies the results of the 1796 election by presenting only the number of electoral votes received by Adams and Jefferson. Thirteen different people received electoral votes in the 1796 election. Under the original Constitution, each presidential elector cast two votes. The candidate with the most electoral votes (provided that it was a majority of the electors appointed) became President. The second-ranking candidate (if he received a majority of the electors appointed) became Vice President.

[25] This count treats Tennessee as a state in which the legislature, in effect, chose the state's presidential electors. When Tennessee's three presidential electors cast their votes in the Electoral College in 1796, they unanimously supported Thomas Jefferson— the candidate who was popular with a majority of the Tennessee legislature.

All of the presidential electors in Massachusetts voted for their home state candidate, Adams. All four presidential electors in Kentucky voted for Jefferson.

In three of the 16 states (Virginia, North Carolina, and Maryland), the electoral votes were fragmented because the presidential electors were elected from districts. One elector from Virginia, one from North

Table 2.2 ELECTORAL VOTES FOR ADAMS AND JEFFERSON IN THE NATION'S FIRST CONTESTED PRESIDENTIAL ELECTION (1796)

STATE	ELECTORAL VOTES	ADAMS	JEFFERSON	METHOD OF ELECTING PRESIDENTIAL ELECTORS
Connecticut	9	9		Legislature
Delaware	3	3		Legislature
Georgia	4		4	Legislature
Kentucky	4		4	Popular voting in elector districts
Maryland	11	7	4	Popular voting in districts
Massachusetts	16	16		Popular voting in congressional districts (with the legislature choosing the two senatorial electors)
New Hampshire	6	6		Popular voting statewide
New Jersey	7	7		Legislature
New York	12	12		Legislature
North Carolina	12	1	11	Popular voting in elector districts
Pennsylvania	15	1	14	Popular voting statewide
Rhode Island	4	4		Legislature
South Carolina	8		8	Legislature
Tennessee	3		3	Presidential electors chosen by county electors chosen by the state legislature
Vermont	4	4		Legislature
Virginia	21	1	20	Popular voting in 21 elector districts
Total	**139**	**71**	**68**	

Carolina, and four electors from Maryland voted differently from the majority of their state's electors. These presidential electors were not demonstrating independence or detached judgment—they were merely voting in accordance with "the will of the appointing power" at the level of the district that elected them.

Although Pennsylvania employed the general ticket system in 1796, its electoral votes were divided because voters were required to cast separate votes for the 15 positions of presidential elector. As Stanwood reported in *A History of the Presidency from 1788 to 1897*:

> "In Pennsylvania, the vote was extremely close. There were … two tickets, each bearing fifteen names. The highest number polled by any candidate for elector was 12,306; the lowest of the thirty had 12,071. Thus 235 votes only represented the greatest difference; and two of the Federalist electors were chosen."[26]

Fourteen of Pennsylvania's presidential electors (13 Anti-Federalists and one Federalist) duly voted for their party's designated nominee for President. One of the two Federalist electors from Pennsylvania in 1796 did not, however, vote as expected.

Samuel Miles cast his vote in the Electoral College for Thomas Jefferson—instead of John Adams.[27] A Federalist supporter complained in the December 15, 1796, issue of *United States Gazette*:

> 'What, do I chufe Samuel Miles to determine for me whether John Adams or Thomas Jefferfon is the fittest man to be President of the United States? No, I chufe him to **act,** not to **think.**'" [Emphasis as per original; spelling as per original].[28]

The expectation that presidential electors should "act" and not "think" has remained strong ever since political parties began nominating their presidential candidates on a centralized basis. Of the 21,915 electoral votes cast for President in the 55 presidential elections between 1789 and 2004, only 11 were cast in an unexpected way. Moreover, among

---

[26] Stanwood, Edward. 1924. *A History of the Presidency from 1788 to 1897*. Boston, MA: Houghton Mifflin Company. Page 48.

[27] Peirce, Neal R. 1968. *The People's President: The Electoral College in American History and Direct-Vote Alternative*. New York, NY: Simon and Schuster. Page 64.

[28] This piece was signed "CANDOUR."

these 11 cases in 217 years, the vote of Samuel Miles for Thomas Jefferson in 1796 remains the only instance when the elector might have thought, at the time he cast his unexpected vote, that his vote might affect the national outcome.[29]

In summary, the Electoral College never operated as the deliberative body envisioned by the nation's Founding Fathers. In the nation's first two presidential elections, the Electoral College was a rubberstamp of the national consensus in favor of George Washington. By the time of the nation's first contested presidential election (1796), the Electoral College had become a rubberstamp that simply affirmed "the will of the appointing power" of each separate jurisdiction. Thus, in practice, the Electoral College had the form, but never the substance, of a deliberative body.

2.2.3 THE SECOND COMPETITIVE PRESIDENTIAL ELECTION

Thomas Jefferson lost the Presidency in the nation's first competitive election (1796) by a mere three electoral votes (table 2.2). As Cunningham wrote in *History of American Presidential Elections 1878–2001*:

> "The presidential election of 1796 had been extremely close, and in examining the results of that contest Republican Party managers had been struck by the fact that Adams' 3-vote margin of victory in the electoral college could be attributed to 1 vote from Pennsylvania, 1 from Virginia, and 1 from North Carolina. In each of these states, the Republicans had won an impressive victory, amassing in the three states a total of 45 electoral votes. The loss of 3 votes in these strongly Jeffersonian states was due to the district method of electing presidential electors. **In looking for ways to improve their chances for victory in the next presidential election, Republican managers thus turned their attention to state election laws.** No uniform system of selection of presidential electors prevailed. In some states electors were chosen by the state legislature; in others they were elected on a general ticket throughout the state; in still others they were elected in districts. This meant that the party that controlled the state legislature was in a position to enact the system of

---

[29] As discussed in greater detail in section 2.12, all but one of the other instances of faithless electors are considered grand-standing votes. One electoral vote (in 2004) was cast by accident.

selection that promised the greatest partisan advantage. Thus, in January 1800 the Republican-controlled legislature of Virginia passed an act providing for the election of presidential electors on a general ticket instead of districts as in previous elections. By changing the election law, Republicans in Virginia, confident of carrying a majority of the popular vote throughout the state but fearful of losing one or two districts to the Federalists, ensured the entire electoral vote of the Union's largest state for the Republican candidate."[30] [Emphasis added]

Vice-President Thomas Jefferson (soon to be a candidate for President in the 1800 election) summed up the reasons for Virginia's switch from the district system to the statewide winner-take-all system in a January 12, 1800, letter to James Monroe:

"On the subject of an election by a general ticket, or by districts, most persons here seem to have made up their minds. All agree that an election by districts would be best, if it could be general; but while 10 states chuse either by their legislatures or by a general ticket, **it is folly & worse than folly** for the other 6. not to do it. In these 10. states the minority is entirely unrepresented; & their majorities not only have the weight of their whole state in their scale, but have the benefit of so much of our minorities as can succeed at a district election. This is, in fact, ensuring to our minorities the appointment of the government. To state it in another form; it is merely a question whether we will divide the U S into 16. or 137. districts. The latter being more chequered, & representing the people in smaller sections, would be more likely to be an exact representation of their diversified sentiments. But a representation of a part by great, & a part by small sections, would give a result very different from what would be the

[30] Cunningham, Noble E., Jr. In Schlesinger, Arthur M., Jr. and Israel, Fred L. (editors). 2002. *History of American Presidential Elections 1878-2001*. Philadelphia, PA: Chelsea House Publishers. Pages 104–105. The quotation from Cunningham contains a small error. Pennsylvania did not use a district system in 1796. The split vote in Pennsylvania resulted from the closeness of the statewide popular vote, as explained in section 2.2.2.

sentiment of the whole people of the U S, were they assembled together."[31] [Emphasis added; spelling and punctuation as per original]

Thus, in 1800, Virginia ended its "folly" and adopted the statewide winner-take-all system to replace the district system used in the state in the first three presidential elections. As a result of this change in Virginia's election law, Jefferson received all of Virginia's electoral votes in the 1800 election.[32]

Meanwhile, Virginia's "folly" of dividing its electoral votes did not go unnoticed by the Federalist Party in Massachusetts. In the 1796 election, Adams had succeeded in winning all his home state's electoral votes under the congressional-district approach. The Jeffersonians, however, were making such significant inroads into Massachusetts that the Federalist-controlled legislature feared that the Jeffersonians might win as many as two districts in Massachusetts in the upcoming 1800 election.[33]

---

[31] Ford, Paul Leicester. 1905. *The Works of Thomas Jefferson*. New York: G. P. Putnam's Sons. 9:90.

[32] The remainder of Thomas Jefferson's January 12, 1800, letter to James Monroe is interesting in that it discusses the political calculations in the decisions by the New York and New Jersey legislatures not to permit the voters to participate in choosing the state's president electors. The letter continues, "I have today had a conversation with 113 [Aaron Burr] who has taken a flying trip here from N Y. He says, they have really now a majority in the H of R, but for want of some skilful person to rally round, they are disjointed, & will lose every question. In the Senate there is a majority of 8. or 9. against us. But in the new election which is to come on in April, three or 4. in the Senate will be changed in our favor; & in the H of R the county elections will still be better than the last; but still all will depend on the city election, which is of 12. members. At present there would be no doubt of our carrying our ticket there; nor does there seem to be time for any events arising to change that disposition. There is therefore the best prospect possible of a great & decided majority on a joint vote of the two houses. They are so confident of this, that the republican party there will not consent to elect either by districts or a general ticket. They chuse to do it by their legislature. I am told the republicans of N J are equally confident, & equally anxious against an election either by districts or a general ticket. The contest in this State will end in a separation of the present legislature without passing any election law, (& their former one is expired), and in depending on the new one, which will be elected Oct 14. in which the republican majority will be more decided in the Representatives, & instead of a majority of 5. against us in the Senate, will be of 1. for us. They will, from the necessity of the case, chuse the electors themselves. Perhaps it will be thought I ought in delicacy to be silent on this subject. But you, who know me, know that my private gratifications would be most indulged by that issue, which should leave me most at home. If anything supersedes this propensity, it is merely the desire to see this government brought back to it's republican principles. Consider this as written to mr. Madison as much as yourself; & communicate it, if you think it will do any good, to those possessing our joint confidence, or any others where it may be useful & safe. Health & affectionate salutations."

Thus, the Massachusetts legislature eliminated the district system and, just to be safe, eliminated the voters and decided to choose all of the state's presidential electors themselves for the 1800 presidential election.[34]

Similarly, the Federalist-controlled New Hampshire legislature feared losing the statewide vote to the Jeffersonians under the state's existing statewide winner-take-all popular election system and decided to choose all of the state's presidential electors themselves.

Cunningham describes election law politics in New York and Pennsylvania in 1800 as follows:

> "In New York, Republicans introduced a measure to move from legislative choice to election by districts, but the proposal was defeated by the Federalists, an outcome that ultimately worked to the advantage of the Republicans when they won control of the legislature in the state elections of 1800. In Pennsylvania, a Republican House of Representatives and a Federalist Senate produced a deadlock over the system to be used to select electors, and the vote of that state was eventually cast by the legislature in a compromise division of the 15 electoral votes, eight Republican and seven Federalist electors being named." [35,36]

2.2.4 THE EMERGENCE OF THE CURRENT SYSTEM

The method of choosing presidential electors varied from state to state and from election to election over the next several decades.

Chief Justice Melville Fuller of the U.S. Supreme Court recounted the history of methods used to appoint presidential electors between 1804 and 1828 in his opinion in *McPherson v. Blacker*:

---

[33] Cunningham, Noble E., Jr. In Schlesinger, Arthur M., Jr. and Israel, Fred L. (editors). 2002. *History of American Presidential Elections 1878–2001*. Philadelphia, PA: Chelsea House Publishers. Page 105.

[34] Congressional Quarterly. 2002. *Presidential Elections 1789–2002*. Washington, DC: CQ Press.

[35] Cunningham, Noble E., Jr. In Schlesinger, Arthur M., Jr. and Israel, Fred L. (editors). 2002. *History of American Presidential Elections 1878–2001*. Philadelphia, PA: Chelsea House Publishers. Page 105.

[36] It is interesting to note that, by the time of the nation's second competitive presidential election (1800), both of the states (Pennsylvania and New Hampshire) in which presidential electors were elected in a statewide popular vote in 1796 had switched to a system of legislative election of the state's presidential electors. That is, no state used a statewide popular vote system in the 1800 presidential election.

"[W]hile most of the states adopted the general ticket system, the district method obtained in Kentucky until 1824; in Tennessee and Maryland until 1832; in Indiana in 1824 and 1828; in Illinois in 1820 and 1824; and in Maine in 1820, 1824, and 1828. Massachusetts used the general ticket system in 1804, … chose electors by joint ballot of the legislature in 1808 and in 1816, … used the district system again in 1812 and 1820, … and returned to the general ticket system in 1824 … In New York, the electors were elected in 1828 by districts, the district electors choosing the electors at large…. The appointment of electors by the legislature, instead of by popular vote, was made use of by North Carolina, Vermont, and New Jersey in 1812."[37]

By 1824, presidential electors were chosen by popular vote (either by districts or statewide) in 18 of the 24 states. State legislatures chose presidential electors in Delaware, Georgia, Louisiana, New York, South Carolina, and Vermont.

By 1832, the people, rather than the state legislatures, chose presidential electors in 22 of the 23 states, with South Carolina being the only exception.[38]

By 1832, Maryland was the only state where presidential electors were elected by district. Maryland changed to a statewide system in 1836. In 1836, presidential electors were elected on a statewide basis in all of the states (that is, either by the people or, in the case of South Carolina, by the legislature).

As previously noted, the Founding Fathers did not advocate the use by the states of a statewide winner-take-all system to allocate their electoral votes. Nonetheless, once the states acquired the exclusive power to choose the manner of appointing their presidential electors, it was probably inevitable that they would realize the disadvantage of dividing their electoral votes and that they would consequently gravitate to the unit rule. Thus, the Constitution's grant of the power to the states to choose the manner of allocating their electoral votes resulted in the emergence throughout the country of a system that the Founding Fathers never envisioned. This fundamental change in the system for electing the President did not come about from a federal constitutional amendment but,

---

[37] *McPherson v. Blacker.* 146 U.S. 1 at 32. 1892.

instead, from the use by the states of a power that Article II of the U.S. Constitution specifically granted to them. As Stanwood noted in *A History of the Presidency from 1788 to 1897,*

> "the [statewide] method of choosing electors had now become uniform throughout the country, **without the interposition of an amendment to the Constitution.**"[38] [Emphasis added]

The South Carolina legislature last chose presidential electors in 1860. Since the Civil War, there have been only two instances when presidential electors have been chosen by a state legislature. In 1868, the Florida legislature did so because reconstruction was not complete in Florida in time for the presidential election. In 1876, Colorado did so because it was admitted as a new state in the midst of the presidential election.

By 1876, the principle that the people should elect presidential electors was so well established that the Colorado Constitution specifically addressed the exceptional nature of the appointment of the state's presidential electors by the legislature in 1876:

> "**Presidential electors, 1876.** The general assembly shall, at their first session, immediately after the organization of the two houses and after the canvass of the votes for officers of the executive department, and before proceeding to other business, provide by act or joint resolution for the appointment by said general assembly of electors in the electoral college, and such joint resolution or the bill for such enactment may be passed without being printed or referred to any committee, or read on more than one day in either house, and shall take effect immediately after the concurrence of the two houses therein, and the approval of the governor thereto shall not be necessary."[39]

[38] Stanwood, Edward. 1924. *A History of the Presidency from 1788 to 1897.* Boston, MA: Houghton Mifflin Company. Page 165. See also Busch, Andrew E. 2001. The development and democratization of the electoral college. In Gregg, Gary L. II (editor). 2001. *Securing Democracy: Why We Have an Electoral College.* Wilmington, DE: ISI Books. Pages 27–42.

[39] Section 19 of the article of the Colorado Constitution governing the transition from territorial status to statehood.

The next section of the Colorado Constitution then mandated a segue from legislative appointment to popular election of presidential electors by providing that after 1876:

"[T]he electors of the electoral college shall be chosen by direct vote of the people."[40]

The inclusion of the above section in the Colorado Constitution was a congressional condition for Colorado's admission to the Union.

2.2.5 DEVELOPMENTS SINCE 1876

Since 1876, the norm has been that a state's voters directly elect presidential electors in a statewide popular election under the winner-take-all system (with only the three exceptions described below).

The first exception arose as a consequence of the controversial 1888 presidential election. In that election, President Grover Cleveland received 5,539,118 popular votes in his re-election campaign, whereas Republican challenger Benjamin Harrison received only 5,449,825 popular votes.[41] Despite Cleveland's margin of 89,293 popular votes, Harrison won an overwhelming majority of the electoral votes (233 to Cleveland's 168) and was elected President. In the 1890 mid-term elections, the Democrats won political control of the then-usually-Republican state of Michigan. Under the Democrats, Michigan switched from the statewide winner-take-all system (then prevailing in all the states) to an arrangement in which one presidential elector was elected from each of Michigan's 12 congressional districts; one additional presidential elector was elected from a specially created eastern district (consisting of the 1st, 2nd, 6th, 7th, 8th, and 10th congressional districts); and the state's final presidential elector was elected from a western district (consisting of the state's other six congressional districts). The Republicans contested the constitutionality of the change to the district system before the U.S. Supreme Court in the 1892 case of *McPherson v. Blacker* mentioned earlier in this chapter. In that case, the Court upheld Michigan's right to choose the method of allocating its electoral votes. As a result, in the 1892 presidential election, Democrat Grover Cleveland received

---

[40] Section 20 of the article of the Colorado Constitution governing the transition from territorial status to statehood.

[41] Congressional Quarterly. 2002. *Presidential Elections 1789–2002*. Washington, DC: CQ Press. Page 128.

five electoral votes from Michigan, and Republican Benjamin Harrison received the other nine. When the Republicans regained political control in Michigan, they promptly restored the statewide winner-take-all system.

The second exception arose in 1969 when Maine adopted a system in which the state's two senatorial presidential electors are awarded to the presidential slate winning the statewide vote and one additional presidential elector is awarded to the presidential slate carrying each of the state's two congressional districts.

The third exception arose in 1992 when Nebraska adopted Maine's system of district and statewide electors. Nebraska law provides:

> "Receipt by the presidential electors of a party or a group of petitioners of the highest number of votes statewide shall constitute election of the two at-large presidential electors of that party or group of petitioners. Receipt by the presidential electors of a party or a group of petitioners of the highest number of votes in a congressional district shall constitute election of the congressional district presidential elector of that party or group of petitioners."[42]

In practice, the approach currently used in Maine and Nebraska has never resulted in a political division of either state's presidential electors. The reason is that, in states with only a few congressional districts (two in Maine and three in Nebraska), the presidential candidate carrying the state is very likely to carry all of the state's congressional districts.

2.2.6 THE SHORT PRESIDENTIAL BALLOT

Until the middle of the 20th century, voters generally cast separate votes for individual candidates for presidential elector. In other words, in a state with 20 electoral votes, the voter was entitled to cast 20 separate votes. Inevitably, some voters would accidentally invalidate their ballot by voting for more than 20 candidates—something that was especially easy to do on the paper ballots that were in general use at the time. Other voters would accidentally vote for fewer than 20 electors (thereby diminishing the value of their franchise). Still other voters would mistakenly vote for just one presidential elector (thereby drastically diminishing

---

[42] Nebraska election law. Section 32-1038.

their franchise). A small number of voters intentionally split their ticket and voted for presidential electors from opposing parties (perhaps because they liked or disliked individual candidates for presidential elector). One result of these "bed sheet" ballots was that a state's electoral vote would occasionally become split between two political parties. For example, in 1916, Woodrow Wilson received one of West Virginia's electoral votes, with Charles Evans Hughes receiving seven. In 1912, Wilson received two of California's electoral votes, with Theodore Roosevelt receiving 11. The statewide winner came up short by one electoral vote in California in 1880, in Ohio and Oregon in 1892, in California and in Kentucky in 1896, and in Maryland in 1904.[43] The Federalists elected two presidential electors in Pennsylvania in 1796 (one of whom was the faithless elector Samuel Miles).

The *short ballot* was developed to simplify voting. It enables a voter to cast a single vote for a presidential slate composed of the name of a candidate for President and the name of a candidate for Vice President. By 1940, 15 states had adopted the short ballot. The number increased to 26 states by 1948 and to 36 by 1966.[44]

The presidential ballot in Ohio in 1948 was particularly confusing. Ohio employed the short ballot for established political parties. The newly formed Progressive Party (supporting Henry Wallace for President) failed to qualify as a regular party in Ohio in time for the 1948 presidential elections. Consequently, the individual names of its 25 candidates for presidential elector appeared on the ballot. In the confusion caused by this hybrid system, an estimated 100,000 ballots were invalidated because voters mistakenly voted for some individual presidential electors while also voting for either Democrat Harry Truman or Republican Thomas Dewey. Truman carried Ohio by 7,107 votes.

Vermont used a combination of the short presidential ballot and the traditional long ballot until 1980. Figure 2.1 shows a 1964 sample presidential ballot in Vermont. As can be seen, the voter had the option of casting a straight-party vote for all three of a party's presidential electors; voting for one, two, or three individual candidates for presidential elector on

---

[43] Congressional Quarterly. 2002. *Presidential Elections 1789–2002*. Washington, DC: CQ Press. Pages 158–159.

[44] Peirce, Neal R. 1968. *The People's President: The Electoral College in American History and Direct-Vote Alternative*. New York, NY: Simon and Schuster. Page 120.

PRESIDENTIAL ELECTORS

OFFICIAL BALLOT

Town of

WINDSOR

for the

General Election November 3, 1964

Electors of President and Vice-President of the United States

To vote a straight party ticket, make a cross (X) in the square at the head of the party column of your choice.
If you desire to vote for a person whose name is not on the ballot, fill in the name of the candidate of your choice in the blank space provided therefor.

If you do not wish to vote for every person in a party column, make a cross (X) opposite the name of each candidate of your Choice; or you may make a cross (X) in the square at the head of the party column of your choice which shall count as a vote for every name in that column, except for any name through which you may draw a line, and except for any name representing a candidate for an office to fill which you have otherwise voted in the manner heretofore prescribed.

REPUBLICAN PARTY	DEMOCRATIC PARTY
For President	For President
BARRY M. GOLDWATER of Arizona	LYNDON B. JOHNSON of Texas
For Vice-President	For Vice-President
WILLIAM E. MILLER of New York	HUBERT H. HUMPHREY of Minnesota
☐	☐

For Electors of President and Vice-President of the United States	Vote for THREE	For Electors of President and Vice-President of the United States	Vote for THREE
MABEL STAFFORD, Republican, South Wallingford		MARGARET M. FARMER, Democratic, Burlington	
LEE EMERSON, Republican, Barton		PETER J. HINCKS, Democratic, Middlebury	
OLIN GAY, Republican, Springfield		HAROLD RAYNOLDS, Democratic, Springfield	

Figure 2.1 1964 presidential ballot in Vermont

the ballot; or voting for one, two, or three write-in candidates for presidential electors.

Since 1980, all states have employed the short presidential ballot. Nonetheless, it is still possible today, in some states, to cast write-in votes for individual presidential electors (section 2.8), to cast votes for unpledged presidential electors (section 2.11), and, on an exceptional basis, to cast separate votes for individual candidates for presidential elector (section 2.9).

2.3 CURRENT METHODS OF ELECTING PRESIDENTIAL ELECTORS

As stated previously, the people have no federal constitutional right to vote for President or Vice President of the United States. In Colorado, the people have a state constitutional right to vote for presidential electors. In all the other states, the people have acquired the presidential vote by means of state law.

In this book, we will frequently refer to the laws of Minnesota to illustrate the way in which one state implements the process of electing the President and Vice President. As a convenience for the reader, appendix D contains the provisions of Minnesota election law that are relevant to presidential elections.

Section 208.02 of Minnesota election law gives the people of Minnesota the right to vote for presidential electors.

> "Presidential electors shall be chosen at the state general election held in the year preceding the expiration of the term of the president of the United States."

In Minnesota, the presidential ballot is prepared and printed by county auditors in accordance with state law. Accordingly, when a voter walked into a polling place in Hennepin County, Minnesota on November 2, 2004, he or she received a "short presidential ballot" resembling the sample ballot shown in figure 2.2 containing nine presidential slates, including the Republican slate consisting of George W. Bush for President and Dick Cheney for Vice President and the Democratic slate consisting of John F. Kerry and John Edwards.

As demonstrated by figure 2.2, Minnesota's presidential ballot is silent as to the existence of the Electoral College or the state's 10 electoral votes. The ballot simply reads,

> "U.S. President and Vice President—Vote for one team."

The linkage between a vote cast for a presidential slate on Minnesota's ballot and the state's 10 presidential electors is established by state law.

> "When Presidential electors are to be voted for, a vote cast for the party candidates for president and vice-president **shall**

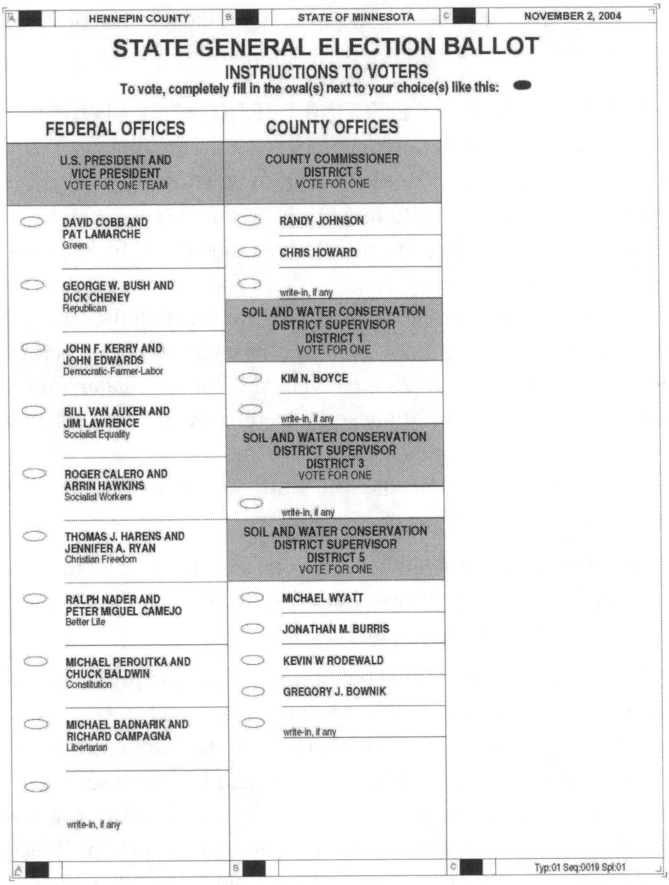

HENNEPIN COUNTY | STATE OF MINNESOTA | NOVEMBER 2, 2004

STATE GENERAL ELECTION BALLOT

INSTRUCTIONS TO VOTERS

To vote, completely fill in the oval(s) next to your choice(s) like this:

FEDERAL OFFICES	COUNTY OFFICES
U.S. PRESIDENT AND VICE PRESIDENT VOTE FOR ONE TEAM	COUNTY COMMISSIONER DISTRICT 5 VOTE FOR ONE
DAVID COBB AND PAT LAMARCHE Green	RANDY JOHNSON
	CHRIS HOWARD
GEORGE W. BUSH AND DICK CHENEY Republican	write-in, if any
	SOIL AND WATER CONSERVATION DISTRICT SUPERVISOR DISTRICT 1 VOTE FOR ONE
JOHN F. KERRY AND JOHN EDWARDS Democratic-Farmer-Labor	KIM N. BOYCE
BILL VAN AUKEN AND JIM LAWRENCE Socialist Equality	write-in, if any
	SOIL AND WATER CONSERVATION DISTRICT SUPERVISOR DISTRICT 3 VOTE FOR ONE
ROGER CALERO AND ARRIN HAWKINS Socialist Workers	write-in, if any
THOMAS J. HARENS AND JENNIFER A. RYAN Christian Freedom	SOIL AND WATER CONSERVATION DISTRICT SUPERVISOR DISTRICT 5 VOTE FOR ONE
RALPH NADER AND PETER MIGUEL CAMEJO Better Life	MICHAEL WYATT
	JONATHAN M. BURRIS
MICHAEL PEROUTKA AND CHUCK BALDWIN Constitution	KEVIN W RODEWALD
	GREGORY J. BOWNIK
MICHAEL BADNARIK AND RICHARD CAMPAGNA Libertarian	write-in, if any
write-in, if any	

Typ:01 Seq:0019 Spl:01

Figure 2.2 2004 presidential ballot in Minnesota

> **be deemed** a vote for that party's electors as filed with the secretary of state."[45] [Emphasis added]

Thus, a voter filling in the oval next to the names of George W. Bush and Dick Cheney on November 2, 2004, was not directly casting a vote for Bush and Cheney but, instead, for a slate of 10 Republican candidates for presidential elector who, if elected on November 2, 2004, were expected to vote for Bush and Cheney when the Electoral College met on December 13, 2004.

---

[45] Minnesota election law. Section 208.04, subdivision 1.

Minnesota law outlines the procedure by which the Minnesota Secretary of State becomes officially informed of the names of the persons running for President and Vice President and the names of the candidates for presidential elector:

> "Presidential electors for the major political parties of this state shall be nominated by delegate conventions called and held under the supervision of the respective state central committees of the parties of this state. On or before primary election day the chair of the major political party shall certify to the secretary of state the names of the persons nominated as Presidential electors and the names of the party candidates for president and vice-president."[46]

Thus, it is the state chair of each major political party in Minnesota who officially informs the Minnesota Secretary of State as to the name of the person nominated for President by the party's national convention, the name of the person nominated for Vice President by the party's national convention, and the names of the 10 persons nominated for the position of presidential elector by the party's state convention.

Twenty-nine states follow Minnesota's approach of nominating elector candidates at state party conventions. In six other states and the District of Columbia, the state party committee (or district committee) nominates the party's presidential electors. Many of the remaining states permit each party in the state to choose its method for itself. In Pennsylvania, each party's presidential nominee directly nominates the elector candidates who will run under his name in the state.[47]

Minnesota law also provides the procedure by which the county auditors become officially notified of the names of the persons running for President and Vice President:

> "The secretary of state shall certify the names of all duly nominated Presidential and Vice-Presidential candidates to the county auditors of the counties of the state."[48]

---

[46] Minnesota election law. Section 208.03.

[47] Berns, Walter (editor). *After the People Vote: A Guide to the Electoral College.* Washington, DC: The AEI Press. Page 11. See section 2.12 for Pennsylvania law.

[48] Minnesota election law. Section 208.04, subdivision 1.

Laws in the other states and the District of Columbia operate in a broadly similar way to accomplish the above objectives.

There are currently three major types of presidential ballots that a voter encounters in presidential elections:

- Presidential ballots in eight states (Arizona, Idaho, Kansas, North Dakota Oklahoma, South Dakota, Tennessee, and Virginia) explicitly mention the names of all of the candidates for presidential elector associated with each presidential slate. For example, the 2004 presidential ballot in North Dakota (figure 2.3) makes it clear that a vote for "Bush-Republican" is, in fact, a vote for the Republican Party's three candidates for presidential elector in 2004-namely Betsy Dalrymple, Evan Lips, and Ben Clayburgh. Curiously, in North Dakota, the name of the candidate for Vice President does not appear on the ballot even though the ballot is headed by the words "President & Vice President of the United States—Vote for no more than one team."
- Presidential ballots in most states mention that the voter is voting for presidential electors but do not explicitly identify the electors. Figure 2.4 shows the 2004 ballot for Michigan. It refers to "Presidential: Electors of President and Vice President of the United States—4 Year Term."
- Oregon's presidential ballot is unusually explicit and informs the voter: "Your vote for the candidates for United States President and Vice President shall be a vote for the electors supporting those candidates."
- Presidential ballots in many states[49] make no reference at all to the existence of the Electoral College or presidential electors.

2.4 CERTIFICATION OF THE PRESIDENTIAL VOTE BY THE STATES

After the popular voting for presidential electors takes place on the Tuesday after the first Monday in November, the votes cast by the people are counted at the precinct level. The vote counts are then aggregated at the local level (e.g., city, town, village, township, or county) and are finally aggregated at the statewide level.

---

[49] Including Minnesota, Alaska, Florida, Georgia, Illinois, Iowa, Maryland, North Carolina, Texas, Washington, and West Virginia.

SAMPLE BALLOT
GENERAL ELECTION BALLOT - NOVEMBER 2, 2004
COUNTY OF BURLEIGH   STATE OF NORTH DAKOTA

INSTRUCTIONS TO VOTER

To vote for the candidate of your choice, you must completely blacken the oval (●) opposite the name of the candidate.

To vote for a person whose name is not printed on the ballot, write or paste that person's name in the blank space provided for that purpose and completely blacken the oval opposite the space provided (●).

PARTY BALLOT

President & Vice President of the United States
Vote for no more than ONE team

Presidential Electors

○ **NADER** Independent — Mathew Reister, Patrick Jund, Mary Jund

○ **BADNARIK** Libertarian — Roland Riemers, James Foster, Keith Hanson

○ **PEROUTKA** Constitution — Charlene Nelson, Leland Wetzel, Herb Mittelstedt

○ **KERRY** Democratic-NPL — Jocelyn Burdick, Heidi Heitkamp, Rolland Redlin

○ **BUSH** Republican — Betsy Dalrymple, Evan Lips, Ben Clayburgh

○ _____

Member of House of Representatives 8TH DISTRICT
Vote for no more than TWO names

○ Dwight Wrangham, Republican
○ Jeff Delzer, Republican
○ Ken Baker, Democratic-NPL
○ Muriel Kisse, Democratic-NPL
○ _____
○ _____

Governor and Lt. Governor
Vote for no more than ONE set of names

○ Joseph A. Satrom & Deb Mathern, Democratic-NPL
○ John Hoeven & Jack Dalrymple, Republican
○ Roland Riemers & Mitchell S. Sanderson, independent nomination
○ _____

Secretary of State
Vote for no more than ONE name

○ Douglas Melby, Democratic-NPL

Attorney General
Vote for no more than ONE name

○ Wayne Stenehjem, Republican
○ Bruce Schoenwald, Democratic-NPL
○ _____

Commissioner of Insurance
Vote for no more than ONE name

○ Terry Barnes, Democratic-NPL
○ Jim Poolman, Republican
○ _____

Commissioner of Agriculture
Vote for no more than ONE name

○ Roger Johnson, Democratic-NPL
○ Doug Goehring, Republican
○ _____

Public Service Commissioner
Vote for no more than ONE name

○ Ron Gumeringer, Democratic-NPL
○ Kevin Cramer, Republican
○ _____

Figure 2.3 2004 presidential ballot in North Dakota

Minnesota law specifies that the state canvassing board shall ascertain the number of votes cast for each presidential slate in the state.

"The state canvassing board at its meeting on the second Tuesday after each state general election shall open and canvass the returns made to the secretary of state for Presidential electors, prepare a statement of the number of votes cast for the persons receiving votes for these offices, and **declare the person or persons receiving the highest number of votes for each office** duly elected. When it appears that more than the number of persons to be elected

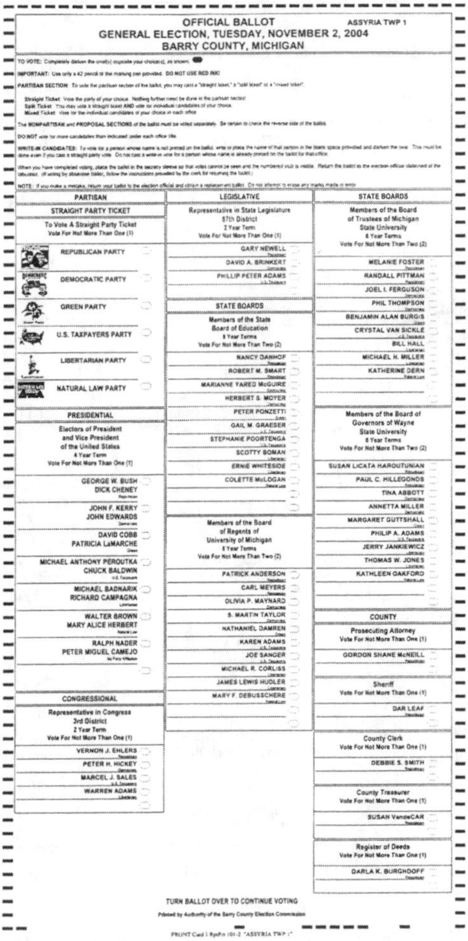

Figure 2.4 2004 presidential ballot in Michigan

as Presidential electors have the highest and an equal number of votes, the secretary of state, in the presence of the board shall decide by lot which of the persons shall be declared elected. The governor shall transmit to each person declared elected a certificate of election, signed by the governor, sealed with the state seal, and countersigned by the secretary of state."[50] [Emphasis added]

---

[50] Minnesota election law. Section 208.05.

Thus, it is the above section of Minnesota election law that establishes the statewide winner-take-all system in Minnesota.

Minnesota law (in common with the laws of many states) calls for the use of a lottery in the event of a tie vote for presidential electors. In some states (including Maine and Michigan), the state legislature would break a tie among presidential electors. For example, Maine law provides:

> "If there is a tie vote for presidential electors, the Governor shall convene the Legislature by proclamation. The Legislature by joint ballot of the members assembled in convention shall determine which are elected."[51]

Although elections are primarily controlled by state law, various federal laws also govern presidential elections. For example, federal law requires each state to create seven "Certificates of Ascertainment" certifying the number of votes cast for each presidential slate. One of these certificates is sent to the Archivist of the United States in Washington, D.C., and six are supplied to the presidential electors for their use during the meeting in mid-December. Title 3, chapter 1, section 6 of the United States Code specifies:

> "It shall be the duty of the executive of each State, as soon as practicable after the conclusion of the appointment of the electors in such State by the final ascertainment, under and in pursuance of the laws of such State providing for such ascertainment, to communicate by registered mail under the seal of the State to the Archivist of the United States a certificate of such ascertainment of the electors appointed, setting forth the names of such electors and the canvass or other ascertainment under the laws of such State of the number of votes given or cast for each person for whose appointment any and all votes have been given or cast; and it shall also thereupon be the duty of the executive of each State to deliver to the electors of such State, on or before the day on which they are required by section 7 of this title to meet, six duplicate-originals of the same certificate under the seal of the State...."

---

[51] Maine 21-A M.R.S, section 732. The State of Maine claims a copyright in its codified statutes. All copyrights and other rights to statutory text are reserved by the State of Maine.

STATE of MINNESOTA

EXECUTIVE DEPARTMENT

TIM PAWLENTY
GOVERNOR

CERTIFICATE OF ASCERTAINMENT
OF APPOINTMENT OF ELECTORS
FOR PRESIDENT AND VICE PRESIDENT
OF THE UNITED STATES
FOR THE STATE OF MINNESOTA

To: John W. Carlin
       Archivist of the United States
       National Archives and Records Administration
       c/o Office of the Federal Register (NF)
       8601 Adelphi Road
       College Park, MD 20740-6001

I, Tim Pawlenty, Governor of the State of Minnesota, do hereby certify the following:

In accordance with Article 2, Section 1 of the Constitution of the United States, the Legislature of the State of Minnesota directed that the electors for President and Vice President of the United States be elected at the General Election conducted on November 2, 2004.

At the General Election held in this State on November 2, 2004, the following persons received the greatest number of votes cast for the office of Electors for President and Vice President of the United States, and are duly elected to fill such office:

Figure 2.5 First page of Minnesota's 2004 Certificate of Ascertainment

Figures 2.5, 2.6, and 2.7 show the first three pages of Minnesota's 2004 Certificate of Ascertainment (with all eight pages being shown in appendix E). Minnesota's Certificate of Ascertainment is signed by the Governor and Secretary of State, bears the state seal, and was issued on November 30, 2004 (four weeks after the voting by the people on November 2).

The second page of Minnesota's Certificate of Ascertainment (figure 2.6) shows that 1,445,014 popular votes were cast for each of the 10 presidential electors associated with the presidential slate consisting of John Kerry for President and John Edwards for Vice President of the

State of Minnesota
Certificate of Ascertainment, 2004, Page 2 of 8

Minnesota Democratic-Farmer-Labor Party
Electors pledged to John F. Kerry for President of the United States
and John Edwards for Vice President of the United States.
These candidates for presidential elector each received 1,445,014
votes:

> Sonja Berg, of St. Cloud
> Vi Grooms-Alban, of Cohasset
> Matthew Little, of Maplewood
> Michael Meuers, of Bemidji
> Tim O'Brien, of Edina
> Lil Ortendahl, of Osakis
> Everett Pettiford, of Minneapolis
> Jean Schiebel, of Brooklyn Center
> Frank Simon, of Chaska
> Chandler Harrison Stevens, of Austin

I further certify that the returns of the votes cast for Presidential Electors at the General Election were canvassed and certified by the State Canvassing Board on the 16th day of November, 2004 in accordance with the laws of the State of Minnesota, and that the number of votes cast for each candidate for Presidential Elector at the General Election is as follows:

Green Party of Minnesota
Electors pledged to David Cobb for President of the United States
and Pat LaMarche for Vice President of the United States.
These candidates for presidential elector each received 4,408 votes:

> Scott Bol
> Kellie Burriss
> Michael Cavlan
> Amber Garlan
> Jenny Heiser
> Molly Nutting
> Douglas Root
> Mark Wahl
> Annie Young
> Dean Zimmermann

Figure 2.6 Second page of Minnesota's 2004 Certificate of Ascertainment showing that the Kerry-Edwards slate received 1,445,014 popular votes and carried the state

Minnesota Democratic-Farmer-Labor Party. All 10 elector candidates received the identical number of votes because Minnesota law specifies that a vote cast for the Kerry-Edwards presidential state "shall be deemed" to be a vote for each of the 10 presidential electors associated with that slate.[52]

---

[52] Minnesota election law. Section 208.04, subdivision 1.

State of Minnesota
Certificate of Ascertainment 2004, Page 3 of 8

Republican Party of Minnesota
Electors pledged to George W. Bush for President of the United States
and Dick Cheney for Vice President of the United States.
Each elector received 1,346,695 votes:

      George Cable
      Jeff Carnes
      Ronald Eibensteiner
      Angie Erhard
      Eileen Fiore
      Walter Klaus
      Michelle Rifenberg
      Julie Rosendahl
      Lyall Schwarzkopf
      Armin Tesch

Socialist Equality Party
Electors pledged to Bill Van Auken for President of the United States
and Jim Lawrence for Vice President of the United States.
These candidates for presidential elector each received 539 votes:

      Nathan Andrew
      Dan W. Blais
      William J. Campbell-Bezat
      Christopher M. Isett
      Cory R. Johnson
      Cynthia B. Moore
      Thomas G. Moore
      Stephen M. Paulson
      Emanuele Saccarelli
      James Strouf

Figure 2.7 Third page of Minnesota's 2004 Certificate of Ascertainment showing that the Bush-Cheney slate received 1,346,695 popular votes

Similarly, the third page of Minnesota's Certificate of Ascertainment (figure 2.6) shows that 1,346,695 popular votes were cast for presidential electors associated with the presidential slate consisting of George W. Bush and Dick Cheney of the Republican Party.[53]

---

[53] Minnesota's 2004 Certificate of Ascertainment goes on to report the votes cast for candidates of the Better Life Party, Libertarian Party, Green Party, Constitution Party, Christian Freedom Party, Socialist Equity Party, and Socialist Workers Party.

The Certificate of Ascertainment reflects Minnesota's use of the winner-take-all system of awarding electoral votes. In particular, the second page (figure 2.6) of the certificate states that the 10 presidential electors associated with the presidential slate consisting of John Kerry for President and John Edwards for Vice President of the Minnesota Democratic-Farmer-Labor Party

> "received the greatest number of votes for the office of Electors of President and Vice President of the United States and are duly elected to fill such office."

In the two states that use the district system (Maine and Nebraska), the Certificate of Ascertainment shows the statewide vote (which decides the state's two senatorial electors) as well as the district vote (which decides the presidential elector for each congressional district). Maine's 2004 Certificate of Ascertainment is shown in appendix F, and Nebraska's 2004 Certificate of Ascertainment is shown in appendix G.

Controversies about the voting for presidential electors generally focus on the issuance of the Certificate of Ascertainment in the contested state. Title 3, chapter 1, section 5 of the United States Code creates a "safe harbor" date six days before the scheduled meeting of the Electoral College for resolving disputes concerning the November voting for presidential electors. Title 3, chapter 1, section 5 of the United States Code states:

> "If any State shall have provided, by laws enacted prior to the day fixed for the appointment of the electors, for its final determination of any controversy or contest concerning the appointment of all or any of the electors of such State, by judicial or other methods or procedures, and such determination shall have been made at least six days before the time fixed for the meeting of the electors, such determination made pursuant to such law so existing on said day, and made at least six days prior to said time of meeting of the electors, shall be conclusive, and shall govern in the counting of the electoral votes as provided in the Constitution, and as hereinafter regulated, so far as the ascertainment of the electors appointed by such State is concerned."

This "safe harbor" date played a central role in the decision of the U.S. Supreme Court in *Bush v. Gore*[54] concerning the disputed counting of the popular votes in Florida in the 2000 presidential election.

Many states finalize their Certificate of Ascertainment in late November. Maine's 2004 Certificate of Ascertainment (shown in appendix F) was issued on November 23, 2004. Almost all states have a law setting a specific deadline for finalizing the canvassing of their statewide elections (sometimes with an earlier deadline for presidential electors). Appendix T lists these deadlines.

Most states regard the federal "safe harbor" date established by Title 3, chapter 1, section 5 of the United States Code as a deadline for finalizing their Certificate of Ascertainment. For example, New York's 2004 Certificate of Ascertainment (shown in appendix H) was issued on December 6, 2004 (i.e., six days before the scheduled December 13 meeting of the Electoral College). States tend to regard the federal "safe harbor" date as a deadline if there is any controversy about the presidential vote count in the state. For example, various issues were raised about the presidential voting in Ohio in 2004, and Ohio finalized its Certificate of Ascertainment on December 6, 2004.

On the other hand, if there is no controversy involving a state's presidential vote, some states fail to finalize their Certificate of Ascertainment until the day that the Electoral College meets. For example, in 2004, 14 states finalized their Certificate of Ascertainment on December 13, 2004. Appendix J shows the date on which each state's Certificate of Ascertainment was finalized.

2.5 MEETING OF THE ELECTORAL COLLEGE

The U.S. Constitution[55] specifies that electors must meet on the same day throughout the United States.

Federal law specifies the particular day for the meeting of the Electoral College (December 13 for the 2004 presidential elections).

> "The electors of President and Vice President of each State shall meet and give their votes on the first Monday after the second Wednesday in December next following their

---

[54] *Bush v. Gore.* 531 U.S. 98. 2000.
[55] U.S. Constitution. Article II, section 1, clause 4.

appointment at such place in each State as the legislature of such State shall direct."[56]

State law, in turn, specifies the place and time of the meeting of the Electoral College. For example, Minnesota law provides:

> "The Presidential electors, before 12:00 [P.]M. on the day before that fixed by congress for the electors to vote for president and vice-president of the United States, shall notify the governor that they are at the state capitol and ready at the proper time to fulfill their duties as electors. The governor shall deliver to the electors present a certificate of the names of all the electors. If any elector named therein fails to appear before 9:00 a.m. on the day, and at the place, fixed for voting for president and vice-president of the United States, the electors present shall, in the presence of the governor, immediately elect by ballot a person to fill the vacancy. If more than the number of persons required have the highest and an equal number of votes, the governor, in the presence of the electors attending, shall decide by lot which of those persons shall be elected."[57]

2.6 CERTIFICATION OF VOTES OF THE PRESIDENTIAL ELECTORS

Federal law requires that the presidential electors sign six separate Certificates of Vote reporting the outcome of their voting for President and Vice President. Of the seven Certificates of Ascertainment created by each state, one is sent to the National Archivist in Washington, D.C., and six are given to the presidential electors for use at their meeting. At the Electoral College meeting, the electors attach one Certificate of Ascertainment to each of the six required "Certificates of Vote."

> "The electors shall make and sign six certificates of all the votes given by them, each of which certificates shall contain two distinct lists, one of the votes for President and the other of the votes for Vice President, and shall annex to each of the certificates one of the lists of the electors which shall have been furnished to them by direction of the executive of the State."[58]

---

[56] United States Code. Title 3, chapter 1, section 7.

[57] Minnesota election law. Section 208.06.

[58] United States Code. Title 3, chapter 1, section 9.

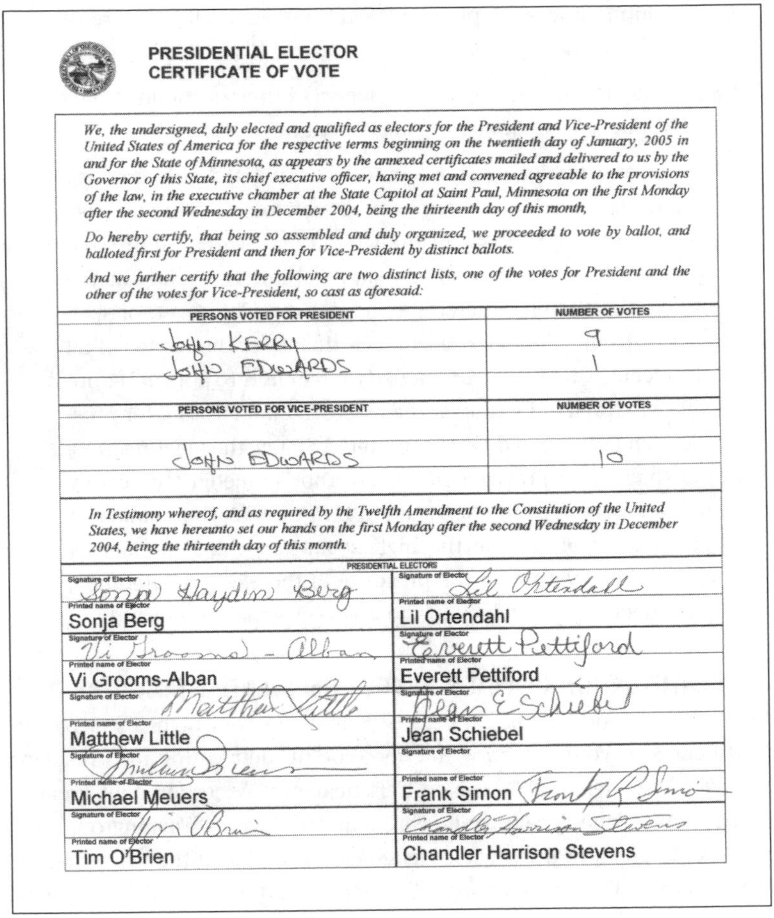

Figure 2.8 Minnesota 2004 Certificate of Vote

In addition, federal law[59] specifies that one of these sets of documents be sent to the President of the Senate in Washington, D.C.; two be sent to the Secretary of State of the United States; two be sent to the Archivist of the United States in Washington, D.C.; and one to the federal district court in the judicial district in which the electors assemble. In the event that no certificates are received from a particular state by the fourth

---

[59] United States Code. Title 3, chapter 1, section 11.

Wednesday in December, federal law[60] establishes procedures for sending a special messenger to the local federal district court in order to obtain the missing certificates.

In Minnesota in 2004, the Kerry-Edwards presidential slate received the most votes in the statewide popular election held on November 2, 2004. Thus, all 10 Democratic-Farmer-Labor Party presidential electors were elected. Figure 2.8 shows Minnesota's 2004 Certificate of Vote.

In Minnesota, the presidential electors vote by secret ballot. In accordance with the 12th Amendment to the Constitution, each presidential elector is to cast one vote for President and a separate vote for Vice President. As can be seen in figure 2.8, all 10 of Minnesota's presidential electors voted for John Edwards for Vice President. However, one of the 10 electors also voted for John Edwards for President. That vote was apparently accidental because, after the count was announced, all 10 electors said that they had intended to vote for John Kerry for President. The result of this error was that John Kerry officially received only 251 electoral votes for President in 2004 (with John Edwards receiving one electoral vote for President and George W. Bush receiving 286). The vote for Edwards for President in 2004 was, apparently, the only electoral vote ever cast by accident.[61]

2.7 COUNTING OF THE ELECTORAL VOTES IN CONGRESS

Federal law specifies that the electoral votes are to be counted on January 6th of the subsequent year.

> "Congress shall be in session on the sixth day of January succeeding every meeting of the electors. The Senate and House of Representatives shall meet in the Hall of the House of Representatives at the hour of 1 o'clock in the afternoon on that day, and the President of the Senate shall be their presiding officer. Two tellers shall be previously appointed on the part of the Senate and two on the part of the House of Representatives, to whom shall be handed, as they are opened by the President of the Senate, all the certificates and

---

[60] United States Code. Title 3, chapter 1, sections 13 and 14.

[61] See section 2.12 for a discussion of the related issue of faithless electors.

papers purporting to be certificates of the electoral votes, which certificates and papers shall be opened, presented, and acted upon in the alphabetical order of the States, beginning with the letter A; and said tellers, having then read the same in the presence and hearing of the two Houses, shall make a list of the votes as they shall appear from the said certificates; and the votes having been ascertained and counted according to the rules in this subchapter provided, the result of the same shall be delivered to the President of the Senate, who shall thereupon announce the state of the vote, which announcement shall be deemed a sufficient declaration of the persons, if any, elected President and Vice President of the United States, and, together with a list of the votes, be entered on the Journals of the two Houses."[62]

The 12th Amendment to the Constitution governs the counting of the electoral votes by Congress. In order to be elected president, a candidate must receive "a majority of the whole number of Electors appointed." Assuming that all 538 electors are appointed, 270 electoral votes are necessary for election. The 12th Amendment states in part:

"[T]he President of the Senate shall, in the presence of the Senate and House of Representatives, open all the certificates and the votes shall then be counted;—The person having the greatest number of votes for President, shall be the President, if such number be a majority of the whole number of Electors appointed...."

In the event that no candidate receives the required majority, the 12th Amendment provides a procedure (appendix A) for a "continent election" in which the House of Representatives chooses the President (with each state having one vote), and the Senate chooses the Vice President (with each Senator having one vote).

The President and Vice President are inaugurated on January 20th in accordance with the terms of the 20th Amendment (ratified in 1933).

---

[62] United States Code. Title 3, chapter 1, section 15.

2.8 WRITE-IN VOTES FOR PRESIDENT

Write-in votes for the offices of President and Vice President are inherently more complex than those for any other office because when the people go to the polls in November, they are voting for candidates to fill the office of presidential elector—not for candidates to fill the office of President and Vice President of the United States.

Minnesota law permits a voter to cast presidential write-in votes in two ways.

- **Advance Filing of Write-Ins:** Under this approach, supporters of a write-in presidential slate may file a slate of presidential electors prior to the election. Such advance filing makes write-in voting more convenient because it enables the voter to write in the name of a presidential slate, without having to write in the names of 10 (in the case of Minnesota) individual candidates for presidential elector.
- **Election-Day Write-Ins:** Under this approach, there is no advance filing, and the voter must write in the names of up to 10 individual presidential electors.

Minnesota law implements the method of advance filing of write-ins as follows:

"(a) A candidate for state or federal office who wants write-in votes for the candidate to be counted must file a written request with the filing office for the office sought no later than the fifth day before the general election. The filing officer shall provide copies of the form to make the request.

"(b) A candidate for president of the United States who files a request under this subdivision must include the name of a candidate for vice-president of the United States. The request must also include the name of at least one candidate for Presidential elector. The total number of names of candidates for Presidential elector on the request may not exceed the total number of electoral votes to be cast by Minnesota in the presidential election."[63]

---

[63] Minnesota election law. Section 204B.09, subdivision 3.

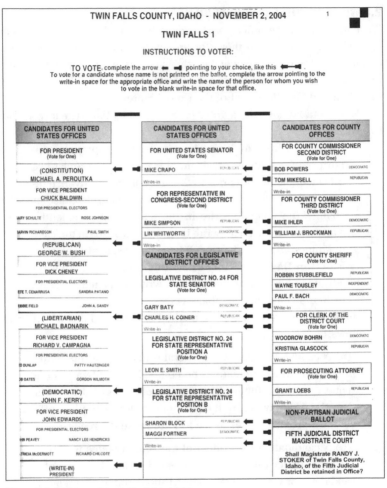

Figure 2.9 2004 presidential ballot in Idaho

Minnesota's 2004 Certificate of Ascertainment (appendix E) shows that 1, 1, 2, 2, and 4 votes were cast for the presidential electors associated with the five officially declared write-in slates in the presidential election in Minnesota in 2004.

Many other states permit advance filing of write-ins.

Election-day write-ins (without advance filing) are permitted in fewer states. This method is allowed in Minnesota as the consequence of a 1968

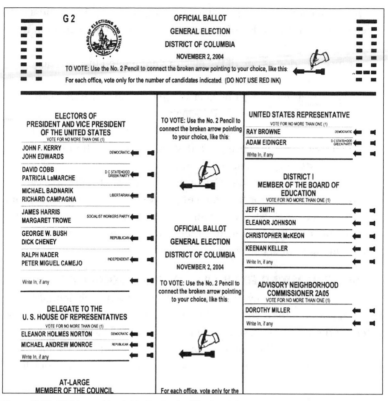

Figure 2.10 2004 presidential ballot in the District of Columbia

opinion of the Minnesota Attorney General.[64] That ruling declared that a presidential write-in vote may be cast in Minnesota by writing between one and 10 names of persons for the position of presidential elector. The Minnesota Attorney General also ruled that a pre-printed sticker containing the names of between 1 and 10 presidential electors may be employed in Minnesota. Given the small amount of space available for a write-in for president on Minnesota's ballot (figure 2.2), a pre-printed sticker is the most practical way to cast such a vote.

A similar small space (figure 2.9) is provided on the ballot for presidential write-ins in Idaho (which has four electoral votes) and the District of Columbia (figure 2.10).

---

[64] Op. Atty. Gen., 28c-5. October 5, 1968.

In Minnesota, it is possible for an individual candidate to receive votes for the office of presidential elector in Minnesota in three ways:

- by appearing as one of the electors nominated by a political party under section section 208.03;
- by appearing on a list of electors filed in advance under subdivision 3 of section 204B.09; and
- by receiving a write-in vote for the position of presidential elector (e.g., on a pre-printed sticker) as permitted by the 1968 Attorney General's opinion.

When the Minnesota State Canvassing Board meets, all votes cast for a particular individual for the office of presidential elector are added up. The 10 elector candidates receiving the most votes are elected to the office of presidential elector. In other words, there can be a fusion of votes from more than one source.

2.9 SEPARATE VOTING FOR INDIVIDUAL PRESIDENTIAL ELECTORS

Notwithstanding the now-universal use of the short presidential ballot, it is still possible for a voter to cast separate votes for individual candidates for the office of presidential elector in some states.

Section 23–15–431 of Mississippi election law entitled "Voting irregular ballot for person whose name does not appear on voting machine" provides:

"Ballots voted for any person whose name does not appear on the machine as a nominated candidate for office, are herein referred to as irregular ballots. In voting for presidential electors, a voter may vote an irregular ticket made up of the names of persons in nomination by different parties, or partially of names of persons so in nomination and partially of persons not in nomination, or wholly of persons not in nomination by any party. Such irregular ballots shall be deposited, written or affixed in or upon the receptacle or device provided on the machine for that purpose. With that exception, no irregular ballot shall be voted for any person for any office whose name appears on the machine as a nominated candidate for that office; any irregular ballot so voted shall not be counted. An irregular ballot must be cast in its appropriate place on the machine, or it shall be void and not counted."[65]

In addition, Mississippi election law concerning "Electronic Voting Systems" provides:

"No electronic voting system, consisting of a marking or voting device in combination with automatic tabulating equipment, shall be acquired or used in accordance with Sections 23-15-461 though 23-15-485 unless it shall ...

"(c) Permit each voter, at presidential elections, by one (1) mark or punch to vote for the candidates of that party for President, Vice-President, and their presidential electors, or to vote individually for the electors of his choice when permitted by law."[66]

Although Mississippi law permits such "irregular" voting, Mississippi's 2004 Certificate of Ascertainment (appendix I) and the state's 2000 Certificate indicate that no such votes were actually cast in the state in either the 2004 or 2000 presidential elections.

2.10 FUSION VOTING IN NEW YORK

Fusion voting is a major aspect of partisan politics in the state of New York. In New York, candidates for political office may appear on the ballot in the general election as nominees of more than one political party. For example, George Pataki has run for Governor as the candidate of both the Republican Party and the Conservative Party. That is, Pataki's name appeared more than once on the same ballot. Under New York election law, the votes that a candidate receives on each ballot line are added together in a process called *fusion*.

One of the political effects of fusion is that it enables a minor party to make a nominee of a major political party aware that he or she would not have won without the minor party's support. In the past, fusion voting played an important role in Minnesota politics prior to the merger that

---

[65] Mississippi election law. Section 23-15-431.

[66] Mississippi election law. Section 23-15-465. Similar statutory provisions are applicable to other voting systems that may be used in Mississippi (e.g., optical mark-reading equipment).

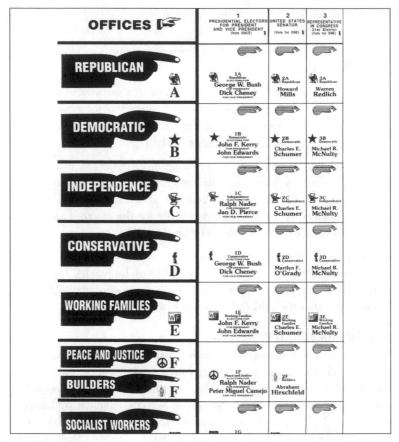

Figure 2.11 2004 New York presidential ballot

resulted in the formation of that state's present-day Democratic-Farmer-Labor Party.

New York is not the only state that currently allows fusion voting. For example, fusion voting is currently permitted under Vermont election law.

Figure 2.11 shows the 2004 New York presidential ballot. As can be seen, the Bush-Cheney presidential slate ran with the support of both the Republican Party and the Conservative Party, and the Kerry-Edwards slate ran with the support of the Democratic Party and Working Families Party.

STATE OF NEW YORK, ss:

Statement of the whole number of votes cast for all the candidates for the office of ELECTOR OF PRESIDENT and VICE-PRESIDENT at a General Election held in said State on the Second day of November, 2004.

The whole number of votes given for the office of ELECTOR OF PRESIDENT and VICE-PRESIDENT was **7,448,266** of which

		REPUBLICAN	CONSERVATIVE	TOTAL
George E. Pataki	received	2,806,993	155,574	2,962,567
Alexander F. Treadwell	received	2,806,993	155,574	2,962,567
Joseph Bruno	received	2,806,993	155,574	2,962,567
Charles Nesbitt	received	2,806,993	155,574	2,962,567
Mary Donohue	received	2,806,993	155,574	2,962,567
Rudolph Giuliani	received	2,806,993	155,574	2,962,567
Charles Gargano	received	2,806,993	155,574	2,962,567
Joseph Mondello	received	2,806,993	155,574	2,962,567
J. Patrick Barrett	received	2,806,993	155,574	2,962,567
John F. Nolan	received	2,806,993	155,574	2,962,567
Robert Davis	received	2,806,993	155,574	2,962,567
Peter J. Savago	received	2,806,993	155,574	2,962,567
Maggie Brooks	received	2,806,993	155,574	2,962,567
Catherine Blaney	received	2,806,993	155,574	2,962,567
Howard Mills	received	2,806,993	155,574	2,962,567
John Cahill	received	2,806,993	155,574	2,962,567
Rita DiMartino	received	2,806,993	155,574	2,962,567
Libby Pataki	received	2,806,993	155,574	2,962,567
Stephen Minarik	received	2,806,993	155,574	2,962,567
Raymond Meier	received	2,806,993	155,574	2,962,567
Thomas M. Reynolds	received	2,806,993	155,574	2,962,567
Adam Stoll	received	2,806,993	155,574	2,962,567
Herman Badillo	received	2,806,993	155,574	2,962,567
Jane Forbes Clark	received	2,806,993	155,574	2,962,567
James Garner	received	2,806,993	155,574	2,962,567
Shawn Marie Levine	received	2,806,993	155,574	2,962,567
Viola J. Hunter	received	2,806,993	155,574	2,962,567
Laura Schreiner	received	2,806,993	155,574	2,962,567
Carmen Gomez Goldberg	received	2,806,993	155,574	2,962,567
Bernadette Castro	received	2,806,993	155,574	2,962,567
Cathy Jimino	received	2,806,993	155,574	2,962,567

Figure 2.12 Third page of New York's 2004 Certificate of Ascertainment

When fusion voting is applied to presidential races, the question arises as to how to handle the presidential electors associated with the candidate. New York law permits two parties to nominate a common slate of presidential electors. For example, the Republican and Conservative parties nominated the same slate of presidential electors for the 2004 presidential election. Similarly, the Democratic and Working Families parties nominated the same slate of presidential electors.

Figure 2.12 shows the third page of New York's 2004 Certificate of Ascertainment indicating that the Bush-Cheney presidential slate received

2,806,993 votes on the Republican Party line and an additional 155,574 votes on the Conservative Party line, for a grand total of 2,962,567 votes.

Similarly, the fourth page of New York's 2004 Certificate of Ascertainment (appendix H) shows that the Kerry-Edwards presidential slate received 4,180,755 votes on the Democratic Party line and an additional 133,525 votes on the Working Families Party line, for a grand total of 4,313,280 votes.

The second page of New York's 2004 Certificate of Ascertainment states that the 31 presidential electors shared by the Democratic Party and the Working Families Party (i.e., the Kerry-Edwards electors)

> "were, by the greatest number of votes given at said election, duly elected elector of President and Vice-President of the United States."

The presidential ballot in New York in 2004 (figure 2.11) shows that the presidential election in New York is indeed conducted on the basis of distinct presidential slates. Ralph Nader appeared on the ballot in New York as the presidential nominee of both the Independence Party and the Peace and Justice Party. Nader, however, ran with Jan D. Pierce for Vice President on the Independence Party line but with Peter Miguel Camejo for Vice President on the Peace and Justice Party line. Thus, there were two different "Nader" presidential slates in New York in 2004, each with a different slate of presidential electors. The Nader-Pierce presidential slate received 84,247 votes on the Independence Party line (shown on the fifth page of the Certificate of Ascertainment in appendix H). The Nader-Camejo presidential slate received 15,626 votes on the Peace and Justice Party line (shown on the sixth page of the Certificate of Ascertainment in appendix H). Because there were two distinct presidential slates and two distinct slates of presidential electors, there was no fusion of votes between the Independence Party and the Peace and Justice Party.

2.11 UNPLEDGED PRESIDENTIAL ELECTORS

Unpledged electors were a prominent feature of presidential voting in many southern states immediately before and after passage of the civil rights legislation of the mid-1960s.

In 1960 (figure 2.13), for example, Alabama's presidential ballot contained 11 separate lines, each with the name of one candidate for the office of presidential elector and a separate lever that the voter could pull.[67] The 11 electors of the Alabama Democratic Party appeared under the party's rooster logo and the slogan "White Supremacy-For the Right." Similarly, there were lists of 11 elector candidates for the Alabama Republican Party and 11 elector candidates for each of several other political parties in Alabama that year. The name of no presidential or vice-presidential candidate appeared anywhere on the 1960 Alabama presidential ballot.

Current Mississippi law provides for unpledged presidential electors:

"(1) When presidential electors are to be chosen, the Secretary of State of Mississippi shall certify to the circuit clerks of the several counties the names of all candidates for President and Vice-President who are nominated by any national convention or other like assembly of any political party or by written petition signed by at least one thousand (1,000) qualified voters of this state.

"(2) The certificate of nomination by a political party convention must be signed by the presiding officer and secretary of the convention and by the chairman of the state executive committee of the political party making the nomination. Any nominating petition, to be valid, must contain the signatures as well as the addresses of the petitioners. Such certificates and petitions must be filed with the State Board of Election Commissioners by filing the same in the office of the Secretary of State not less than sixty (60) days previous to the day of the election.

"(3) Each certificate of nomination and nominating petition must be accompanied by a list of the names and addresses of persons, who shall be qualified voters of this state, equal in number to the number of presidential electors to be chosen. Each person so listed shall execute the following statement which shall be attached to the certificate or petition when the same is filed with the State Board of Election Commissioners:

---

[67] The 1960 Alabama presidential ballot is shown in appendix K of Peirce, Neal R. 1968. *The People's President: The Electoral College in American History and Direct-Vote Alternative.* New York, NY: Simon and Schuster. The 1960 Alabama presidential ballot is reprinted as figure 2.13 in this book with the permission of Yale University Press.

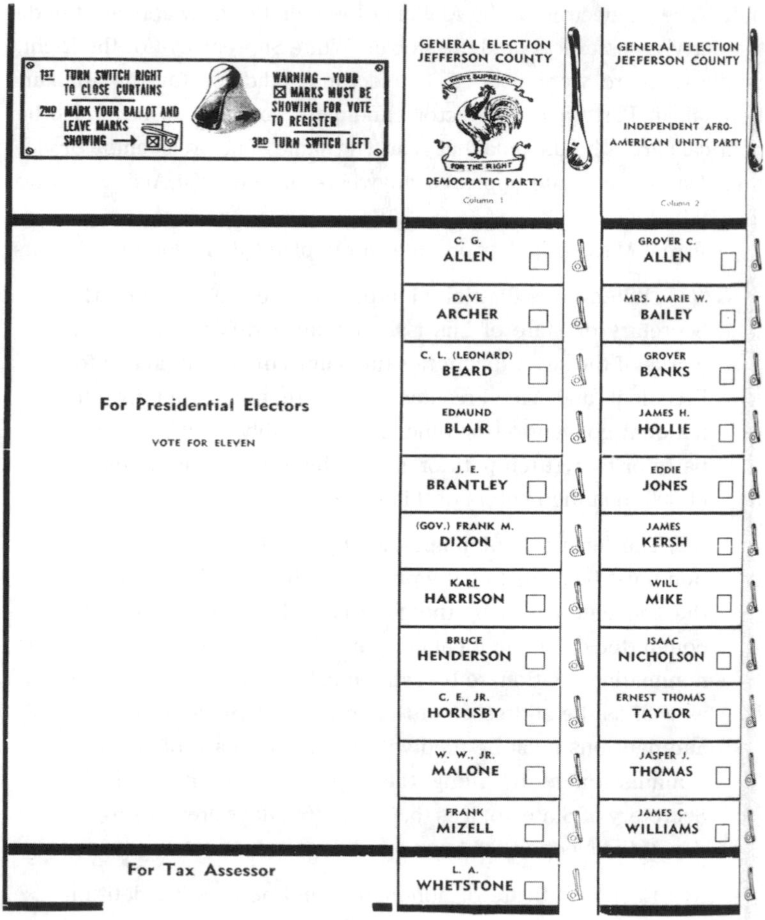

1ST TURN SWITCH RIGHT TO CLOSE CURTAINS
2ND MARK YOUR BALLOT AND LEAVE MARKS SHOWING →
WARNING—YOUR ☒ MARKS MUST BE SHOWING FOR VOTE TO REGISTER
3RD TURN SWITCH LEFT

	GENERAL ELECTION JEFFERSON COUNTY — WHITE SUPREMACY — FOR THE RIGHT — DEMOCRATIC PARTY — Column 1	GENERAL ELECTION JEFFERSON COUNTY — INDEPENDENT AFRO-AMERICAN UNITY PARTY — Column 2
For Presidential Electors — VOTE FOR ELEVEN	C. G. ALLEN	GROVER C. ALLEN
	DAVE ARCHER	MRS. MARIE W. BAILEY
	C. L. (LEONARD) BEARD	GROVER BANKS
	EDMUND BLAIR	JAMES H. HOLLIE
	J. E. BRANTLEY	EDDIE JONES
	(GOV.) FRANK M. DIXON	JAMES KERSH
	KARL HARRISON	WILL MIKE
	BRUCE HENDERSON	ISAAC NICHOLSON
	C. E., JR. HORNSBY	ERNEST THOMAS TAYLOR
	W. W., JR. MALONE	JASPER J. THOMAS
	FRANK MIZELL	JAMES C. WILLIAMS
For Tax Assessor	L. A. WHETSTONE	

Figure 2.13 1960 Alabama presidential ballot

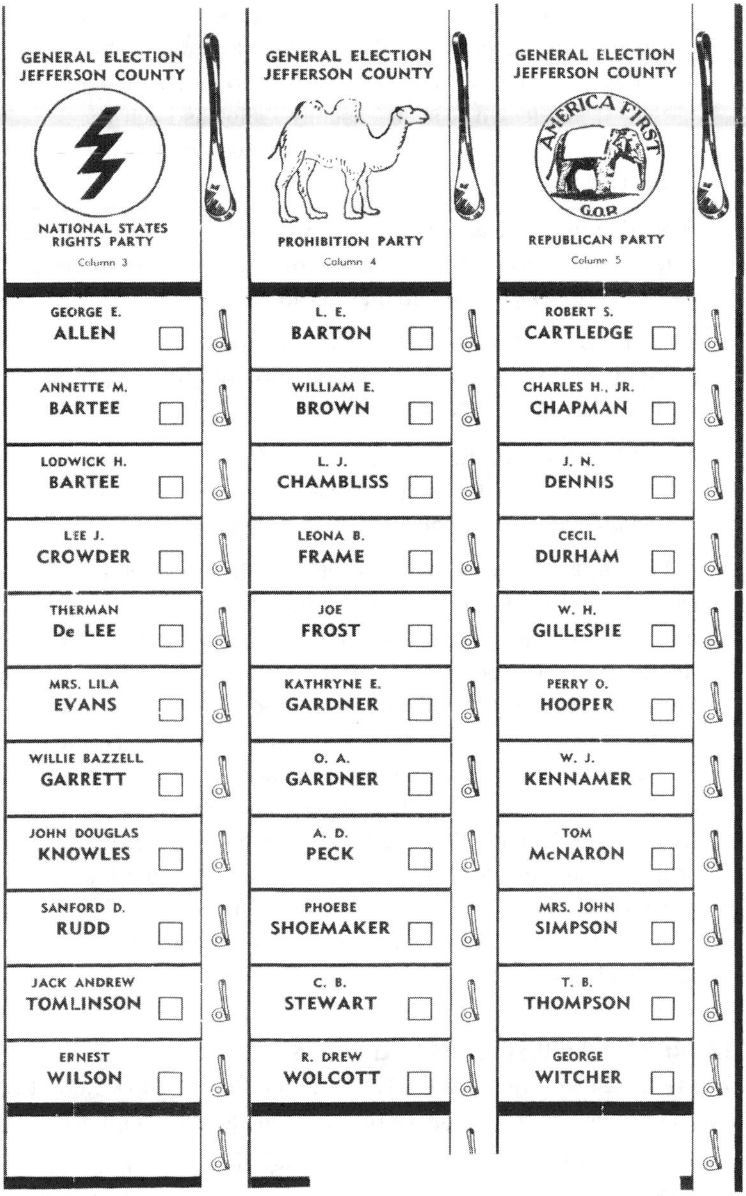

GENERAL ELECTION JEFFERSON COUNTY	GENERAL ELECTION JEFFERSON COUNTY	GENERAL ELECTION JEFFERSON COUNTY
NATIONAL STATES RIGHTS PARTY Column 3	**PROHIBITION PARTY** Column 4	**REPUBLICAN PARTY** Column 5
GEORGE E. **ALLEN** ☐	L. E. **BARTON** ☐	ROBERT S. **CARTLEDGE** ☐
ANNETTE M. **BARTEE** ☐	WILLIAM E. **BROWN** ☐	CHARLES H., JR. **CHAPMAN** ☐
LODWICK H. **BARTEE** ☐	L. J. **CHAMBLISS** ☐	J. N. **DENNIS** ☐
LEE J. **CROWDER** ☐	LEONA B. **FRAME** ☐	CECIL **DURHAM** ☐
THERMAN **De LEE** ☐	JOE **FROST** ☐	W. H. **GILLESPIE** ☐
MRS. LILA **EVANS** ☐	KATHRYNE E. **GARDNER** ☐	PERRY O. **HOOPER** ☐
WILLIE BAZZELL **GARRETT** ☐	O. A. **GARDNER** ☐	W. J. **KENNAMER** ☐
JOHN DOUGLAS **KNOWLES** ☐	A. D. **PECK** ☐	TOM **McNARON** ☐
SANFORD D. **RUDD** ☐	PHOEBE **SHOEMAKER** ☐	MRS. JOHN **SIMPSON** ☐
JACK ANDREW **TOMLINSON** ☐	C. B. **STEWART** ☐	T. B. **THOMPSON** ☐
ERNEST **WILSON** ☐	R. DREW **WOLCOTT** ☐	GEORGE **WITCHER** ☐

Figure 2.13 1960 Alabama presidential ballot (cont.)

'I do hereby consent and do hereby agree to serve as elector for President and Vice-President of the United States, if elected to that position, and do hereby agree that, if so elected, I shall cast my ballot as such for _____ for President and _____ for Vice-President of the United States'

(inserting in said blank spaces the respective names of the persons named as nominees for said respective offices in the certificate to which this statement is attached).

"(4) The State Board of Election Commissioners and any other official charged with the preparation of official ballots shall place on such official ballots the words

'PRESIDENTIAL ELECTORS FOR (here insert the name of the candidate for President, the word 'AND' and the name of the candidate for Vice-President)'

in lieu of placing the names of such presidential electors on such official ballots, and a vote cast therefore shall be counted and shall be in all respects effective as a vote for each of the presidential electors representing such candidates for President and Vice-President of the United States. In the case of unpledged electors, the State Board of Election Commissioners and any other official charged with the preparation of official ballots shall place on such official ballots the words 'UNPLEDGED ELECTOR(S) (here insert the name(s) of individual unpledged elector(s) if placed upon the ballot based upon a petition granted in the manner provided by law stating the individual name(s) of the elector(s) rather than a slate of electors).' "[68]

2.12 FAITHLESS PRESIDENTIAL ELECTORS

In the 1952 case of *Ray v. Blair*, U.S. Supreme Court Justice Robert H. Jackson summarized the history of presidential electors as follows:

"No one faithful to our history can deny that the plan originally contemplated, what is implicit in its text, that electors

---

[68] Mississippi election law. Section 23-15-785.

would be free agents, to exercise an independent and non-partisan judgment as to the men best qualified for the Nation's highest offices....

"This arrangement miscarried. Electors, although often personally eminent, independent, and respectable, officially become voluntary party lackeys and intellectual nonentities to whose memory we might justly paraphrase a tuneful satire:

'They always voted at their party's call

'And never thought of thinking for themselves at all' "[69]

Among the 21,915 electoral votes cast in the 55 presidential elections in the 217 years between 1789 and 2004, there have been 11 cases when a presidential elector has cast a vote for President in an unexpected way.[70,71,72]

- In 1796, Samuel Miles was one of the two Federalist presidential electors chosen in Pennsylvania; however, he voted for Thomas Jefferson (the Democratic-Republican candidate) instead of for Federalist John Adams (section 2.2.2).
- In the uncontested presidential election of 1820, a New Hampshire Democratic-Republican presidential elector who had been expected to vote for James Monroe instead voted for John Quincy Adams, thereby preventing Monroe from duplicating George Washington's 1789 and 1792 unanimous votes in the Electoral College.
- In 1948, a Truman elector (Preston Parks) in Tennessee voted for Strom Thurmond, the Dixiecrat presidential nominee.
- In 1956, a Stevenson elector (W. F. Turner) in Alabama voted for Walter B. Jones, a local judge.
- Nixon lost one electoral vote on each of the three occasions (1960, 1968, and 1972) when he ran for President. In 1960,

---

[69] *Ray v. Blair* 343 U.S. 214 at 232. 1952.

[70] Congressional Quarterly. 2002. *Presidential Elections 1789-2002.* Washington, DC: CQ Press. Page 159.

[71] Peirce, Neal R. 1968. *The People's President: The Electoral College in American History and Direct-Vote Alternative.* New York, NY: Simon and Schuster. Pages 122–127.

[72] Edwards, George C., III. 2004. *Why the Electoral College Is Bad for America.* New Haven, CT: Yale University Press. Pages 21–27.

an Oklahoma Republican elector (Henry D. Irwin) voted for United States Senator Harry F. Byrd (a Democrat). In 1968, a North Carolina Republican elector (Lloyd W. Bailey) voted for Governor George Wallace (that year's nominee of the American Independent Party). In 1972, a Virginia Republican elector (Roger L. MacBride) voted for John Hospers (a Libertarian).

- In 1976, one Ford elector from the state of Washington voted for Ronald Reagan (who had lost the presidential nomination to Ford at the closely contested 1976 Republican nominating convention).
- In 1988, a Democratic elector (Margaret Leach) from West Virginia voted for Lloyd Bentsen for President and Michael Dukakis for Vice President, saying that she thought that the Democratic ticket would have been better in opposite order.
- In 2000, a Democratic presidential elector from the District of Columbia (Barbara Lett-Simmons) did not vote for Al Gore, as a protest against the lack of representation in Congress for the District.
- In 2004, an unknown Democratic presidential elector from Minnesota accidentally voted for John Edwards for both President and Vice President (section 2.6).

These 11 cases can be divided into three categories:

- **Clear Case of a Faithless Elector:** In 1796, Samuel Miles cast his electoral vote in an unexpected way in an election in which the overall electoral vote was very close (71 for Adams and 68 for Jefferson). Given the slow communications of the day, Miles might have had reason to believe, at the time he voted, that his vote might affect the outcome of the election in the Electoral College (section 2.2.2).
- **Grand-Standing Votes:** There have been nine cases (one in 1820 and eight others between 1948 and 2000) of presidential electors who cast an unexpected vote; however, these nine electors knew, at the time they voted, that their vote would not affect the outcome of the election in the Electoral College.
- **Accidental Vote:** In 2004 in Minnesota, there was one accidentally miscast electoral vote for President (section 2.6).

Thus, after 55 presidential elections, the vote of Samuel Miles in 1796 was the only case when an electoral vote was cast in an unexpected way by a presidential elector who might have had reason to think, at the time he cast the vote, that his vote might have affected the outcome.

Table 2.3 shows the number of presidential electors voting in the 55 presidential elections between 1789 and 2004 (a total of 21,915 electoral votes), the number of electoral votes that were cast as expected (a total of 21,904 electoral votes), and the 11 electoral votes that were cast in an unexpected way (that is, one clear faithless elector, nine grand-standing votes, and one accidental vote).[73,74]

Most recently, Richie Robb, one of the candidates nominated by the Republican Party as presidential elector from West Virginia in 2004, threatened, prior to the November 2004 voting, not to vote for George W. Bush in the Electoral College. Ultimately, Robb changed his mind and voted for Bush when the Electoral College met on December 13, 2004.

The laws of a majority of the 51 jurisdictions that appoint presidential electors (including Minnesota) do not mention the way that a presidential elector should vote. Nineteen states have laws that assert that the presidential elector is obligated to vote for the nominee of his or her party, but contain no enforcement provision.[75,76] For example, Maine law provides:

"The presidential electors at large shall cast their ballots for the presidential and vice-presidential candidates who received the largest number of votes in the State. The presidential electors of each congressional district shall cast their ballots for the presidential and vice-presidential candidates who received the largest number of votes in each respective congressional district."[77]

[73] Congressional Quarterly. 2002. *Presidential Elections 1789-2002*. Washington, DC: CQ Press. Page 159.

[74] There were, arguably, three additional faithless electors in the 1796 presidential election. As *Congressional Quarterly* notes, "Some historians and political scientists claim that three Democratic-Republican electors voted for Adams. However, the fluidity of political party lines at that early date, and the well-known personal friendship between Adams and at least one of the electors, makes the claim of their being 'faithless electors' one of continuing controversy." See Congressional Quarterly. 1979. *Presidential Elections Since 1789*. Second Edition. Washington, DC: CQ Press. Page 7.

[75] Berns, Walter (editor). *After the People Vote: A Guide to the Electoral College*. Washington, DC: The AEI Press. Pages 10–13 and 86–88.

[76] Concerning pledges by presidential electors, see *Ray v. Blair*. 343 U.S. 214. 1952.

[77] Maine 21-A M.R.S. section 805.

Table 2.3 FAITHLESS ELECTORS

ELECTION	ELECTORS VOTING	CAST AS EXPECTED	CLEAR FAITHLESS ELECTOR	GRAND-STANDING VOTE	ACCIDENTAL VOTE
1789	69	69			
1792	132	132			
1796	138	138			
1800	138	137	1		
1804	176	176			
1808	175	175			
1812	218	218			
1816	221	221			
1820	232	231		1	
1824	261	261			
1828	261	261			
1832	288	288			
1836	294	294			
1840	294	294			
1844	275	275			
1848	290	290			
1852	296	296			
1856	296	296			
1860	303	303			
1864	234	234			
1868	294	294			
1872	366	366			
1876	369	369			
1880	369	369			
1884	401	401			
1888	401	401			
1892	444	444			
1896	447	447			
1900	447	447			
1904	476	476			
1908	483	483			
1912	531	531			
1916	531	531			
1920	531	531			
1924	531	531			
1928	531	531			
1932	531	531			
1936	531	531			
1940	531	531			

Table 2.3 FAITHLESS ELECTORS (cont.)

ELECTION	ELECTORS VOTING	CAST AS EXPECTED	CLEAR FAITHLESS ELECTOR	GRAND-STANDING VOTE	ACCIDENTAL VOTE
1944	531	531			
1948	531	530		1	
1952	531	531			
1956	531	530		1	
1960	537	536		1	
1964	538	538			
1968	538	537		1	
1972	538	537		1	
1976	538	537		1	
1980	538	538			
1984	538	538			
1988	538	537		1	
1992	538	538			
1996	538	538			
2000	538	537		1	
2004	538	537			1
Total	**21,915**	**21,904**	**1**	**9**	**1**

Pennsylvania election law (section 2878) addresses the potential problem of faithless electors by providing that each party's presidential nominee shall have the power to nominate the entire slate of candidates for the position of presidential elector in Pennsylvania:

> "The nominee of each political party for the office of President of the United States shall, within thirty days after his nomination by the National convention of such party, nominate as many persons to be the candidates of his party for the office of presidential elector as the State is then enti-tled to. If for any reason the nominee of any political party for President of the United States fails or is unable to make the said nominations within the time herein provided, then the nominee for such party for the office of Vice-President of the United States shall, as soon as may be possible after the expi-ration of thirty days, make the nominations. The names of such nominees, with their residences and post office address-es, shall be certified immediately to the Secretary of the Commonwealth by the nominee for the office of President or

Vice-President, as the case may be, making the nominations. Vacancies existing after the date of nomination of presidential electors shall be filled by the nominee for the office of President or Vice-President making the original nomination. Nominations made to fill vacancies shall be certified to the Secretary of the Commonwealth in the manner herein provided for in the case of original nominations."

Five states (New Mexico, North Carolina, Oklahoma, South Carolina, and Washington) have laws imposing penalties of up to $1,000 on faithless electors.

North Carolina's election law specifies that failure to vote as pledged constitutes resignation from the office of the elector, cancels the vote cast by the faithless elector, and provides for another person to be appointed to cast the vote by the remaining electors.[78] North Carolina law (section 163-212) provides:

"Any presidential elector having previously signified his consent to serve as such, who fails to attend and vote for the candidate of the political party which nominated such elector, for President and Vice-President of the United States at the time and place directed in G.S. 163-210 (except in case of sickness or other unavoidable accident) shall forfeit and pay to the State five hundred dollars ($500.00), to be recovered by the Attorney General in the Superior Court of Wake County. In addition to such forfeiture, refusal or failure to vote for the candidates of the political party which nominated such elector shall constitute a resignation from the office of elector, his vote shall not be recorded, and the remaining electors shall forthwith fill such vacancy as hereinbefore provided."

In short, the states have ample power to enact various preventive measures (e.g., Pennsylvania's system of empowering each presidential nominee to directly nominate the elector candidates who run under his name) as well as to provide remedies for faithless electors (e.g., North Carolina's approach).[79]

---

[78] Berns, Walter (editor). *After the People Vote: A Guide to the Electoral College.* Washington, DC: The AEI Press. Pages 12 and 87–88.

[79] Edwards, George C., III. 2004. *Why the Electoral College Is Bad for America.* New Haven, CT: Yale University Press. Pages 25–27.

In summary, faithless electors are a historical curiosity associated with the Electoral College, but they never have had any practical effect on any presidential election.

2.13 FIVE MAJOR CHANGES IN THE PRESIDENTIAL ELECTION SYSTEM THAT HAVE BEEN IMPLEMENTED WITHOUT A FEDERAL CONSTITUTIONAL AMENDMENT

Five of the most salient features of the present-day system of electing the President and Vice President of the United States are:

- popular voting for president,
- the statewide winner-take-all rule,
- nomination of candidates by nationwide political parties,
- the non-deliberative nature of the Electoral College, and
- the short presidential ballot.

Although some people today mistakenly believe that the current system of electing the President and Vice President of the United States was designed by the Founding Fathers, none of the above five features reflected a consensus of the Founding Fathers or is mentioned in the original U.S. Constitution. None of these features was implemented by means of a federal constitutional amendment. None was the creation of federal legislation.

Instead, three of these five features came into being by the piecemeal enactment of state laws over a period of years, and two resulted from actions taken by non-government entities—namely the political parties that emerged at the time of the nation's first competitive presidential election (1796).

- **Popular Vote:** As recounted in section 2.2, there was no consensus among the Founding Fathers as to whether the voters should be directly involved in process of choosing presidential electors. The Constitution left the manner of choosing presidential electors to the states. Popular election was not the norm in the nation's first presidential election (1789). In fact, the voters were allowed to choose presidential electors in only four states. However, state laws changed over years. By 1824, voters were allowed to choose presidential electors in three quarters of the states, and by 1832, voters were able to choose presidential electors in all but one state.[80] Since 1876, all presidential electors have been elected directly by the voters. In short, direct popular voting for presidential electors became the norm by virtue of the piecemeal enactment of state laws— not because the Founders advocated popular voting, not because the original Constitution required it, and not because of any federal constitutional amendment. The states used the built-in flexibility of the Constitution to change the system.

- **Statewide Winner-Take-All Rule:** The Founding Fathers certainly did not advocate that presidential electors be chosen on a statewide winner-take-all basis in a popular election. In fact, this approach was used by only three of the states participating in the nation's first presidential election. "Madison wrote that it was [the district system] which was contemplated by the framers of the constitution,"[81] and some states elected presidential electors by districts in the early years of the Republic. However, those states soon came to realize what Thomas Jefferson called the "folly"[82] of diminishing their influence by fragmenting their electoral votes, and the states gravitated to the winner-take-all rule. Since 1836, the presidential slate receiving the most popular votes statewide has won all of a state's presidential electors—with only occasional and isolated exceptions.[83] The statewide winner-take-all rule emerged over a period of years because of the piecemeal enactment of state laws— not because the Founders advocated the winner-take-all rule, not because the original Constitution required it, and not because of any federal constitutional amendment.

---

[80] The South Carolina legislature chose presidential electors up to 1860. There were two isolated instances of the election of presidential electors by the state legislature since then—Florida in 1868 and Colorado in 1876.

[81] *McPherson v. Blacker:* 146 U.S. 1 at 29. 1892.

[82] Letter from Thomas Jefferson to James Monroe on January 12, 1800. Ford, Paul Leicester. 1905. *The Works of Thomas Jefferson.* New York: G. P. Putnam's Sons. 9:90.

[83] The exceptions include the present-day use of the district system in Maine (since 1969) and Nebraska (since 1992) and the one-time use of a district system by Michigan in 1892.

- **Nomination of Presidential Candidates by Political Parties:** Since the nation's first competitive presidential election (1796), candidates for President and Vice President have been nominated on a nationwide basis by a central body of a political party (e.g., by the congressional caucus of each party starting in 1796 and by the national conventions of each party starting in the 1820s). This feature of the present-day system of electing the President emerged because of the actions taken by non-government entities— namely the political parties. This change did not come about because the Founders wanted it, because the original Constitution required it, or because of any federal constitutional amendment.

- **Non-Deliberative Nature of the Electoral College:** The Founding Fathers intended that the Electoral College would act as a deliberative body in which the presidential electors would exercise independent judgment as to the best persons to serve as President and Vice President. However, once political parties began nominating presidential and vice-presidential candidates on a centralized basis, and once political parties began actively campaigning for their nominees throughout the country (1796), the presidential elector necessarily became a rubberstamp. "[W]hether chosen by the legislatures or by popular suffrage on general ticket or in districts, [the presidential electors] were so chosen simply to register the will of the appointing power."[84] Thus, since 1796, presidential electors have been expected to vote for the candidates nominated by their party—that is, "to act, not to think."[85] Moreover, this expectation has been achieved with remarkable fidelity. Of the 21,915 electoral votes cast for President in the 55 presidential elections in the 217 years between 1789 and 2004, the vote of Samuel Miles for Thomas Jefferson in 1796 was the only instance when a presidential elector might

---

[84] *McPherson v. Blacker.* 146 U.S. 1 at 36. 1892.
[85] *United States Gazette.* December 15, 1796. Item signed "CANDOUR."

have thought, at the time he cast his unexpected vote, that his vote might affect the national outcome.[86] The change in character of the Electoral College—from the deliberative body envisioned by the Founding Fathers—to a rubberstamp came about because of the emergence of political parties. This change did not come into being because the Founders wanted it, because the original Constitution required it, or because of any federal constitutional amendment.

- **Short Presidential Ballot:** Since the later part of the 20th century, voters have not cast separate votes for individual candidates for presidential elector but, instead, have cast a single vote for a presidential slate consisting of a candidate for President and a candidate for Vice President. Moreover, in all but a few states, the names of the individual presidential electors have entirely disappeared from the ballot. The universal adoption of the short presidential ballot has almost entirely erased the presidential elector from the public's consciousness. This feature of modern-day presidential elections emerged over a period of years because of the piecemeal enactment of laws by the individual states—not because the Founders advocated it, not because the original Constitution required it, and not because of any federal constitutional amendment.

In short, the original U.S. Constitution did not specify in detail the manner of electing the President and Vice President. The flexibility built into the original U.S. Constitution permitted the development of a system that is very different from the one that the Founding Fathers originally envisioned. The built-in flexibility of the original U.S. Constitution concerning the manner of choosing presidential electors remains today.

---

[86] As discussed in greater detail in section 2.12, nine of the other instances of faithless electors are considered to have been grand-standing votes, and one electoral vote (in 2004) was cast by accident.

3 | Three Previously Proposed Federal Constitutional Amendments

There have been hundreds of proposals to change the current system of electing the President and Vice President over the years. This chapter examines the three most prominent approaches to presidential election reform that have been proposed as a federal constitutional amendment. The next chapter (chapter 4) will analyze two approaches that can be enacted entirely at the state level (without a federal constitutional amendment and without action by Congress). Later, chapter 6 will discuss this book's suggested approach for reform.

The three most discussed proposals for a federal constitutional amendment are:

- **Fractional Proportional Allocation of Electoral Votes** in which a state's electoral votes are divided proportionally according to the percentage—carried out to three decimal places—of votes received in that state by each presidential slate (section 3.1);

- **District Allocation of Electoral Votes** in which the people elect two presidential electors statewide and one presidential elector for each district (section 3.2); and

- **Direct Nationwide Popular Election** in which all the popular votes are added together on a nationwide basis (section 3.3).[1]

The chapter analyzes how each of these three approaches would operate in terms of the following criteria:

---

[1] Numerous variations on each of the three approaches presented in this chapter have been introduced in Congress over the years. The major differences include the extent to which the proposal empowers Congress to adopt uniform federal laws governing presidential elections, whether the casting of electoral votes is made automatic (i.e., the office of presidential elector is eliminated), the percentage of the vote required to trigger a contingent election, and the procedures for a contingent election (e.g., separate voting by the two houses of Congress, voting in a joint session of Congress, or a nationwide run-off popular election).

- Would it accurately reflect the nationwide popular vote?
- Would it improve upon the current situation in which most areas of the country are non-competitive?
- Would every vote be equal?

Interest in reform tends to follow troublesome presidential elections.

Under the original Constitution, each presidential elector cast two votes. The candidate with the most electoral votes (provided that the candidate had a majority) became President, and the second-place candidate became Vice President (again, provided that the candidate had a majority). The nation's first two presidential elections (1789 and 1792) were unanimous in the sense that George Washington received a vote from each presidential elector who voted.[2]

The problems inherent with doubling voting surfaced as soon as political parties formed and presidential elections became competitive. In 1796, the Federalist members of Congress caucused and nominated John Adams of Massachusetts for President and Thomas Pinckney of South Carolina for Vice President. Meanwhile, the Republicans in Congress nominated Thomas Jefferson of Virginia for President and Aaron Burr of New York for Vice President. The Federalists were strongest in the north, and the Republicans were strongest in the south. Thus, each party had a presidential nominee from the part of the country where the party was strongest and a vice-presidential candidate from the other part of the county. Vice-presidential nominee Pinckney was, however, more highly regarded than Burr. In particular, Pinckney was expected to be able to win electoral votes from his Republican-leaning home state of South Carolina (where the state legislature chose the electors), whereas Burr was not expected to be able to make counter-balancing inroads in the New York legislature's solid support for the Federalist ticket of Adams and Pinckney. The Federalist Party thus faced the dilemma of whether to give its wholehearted support to its own ticket. If Federalist presidential electors were to uniformly cast one vote for Adams and one vote for Pinckney, and if Pinckney then won additional electoral votes in his home state of South Carolina, their own party's nominee for Vice President would end up as President. As Stanwood reports,

---

[2] In 1789, two Maryland electors and two Virginia electors did not vote. In 1796, two Maryland electors and one Vermont elector did not vote. Congressional Quarterly. 2002. *Presidential Elections 1789-2002.* Washington, DC: CQ Press. Pages 174–175.

> "No less than eighteen [Federalist] electors in New England resolved that Pinckney's vote should not exceed Adam's, withheld their votes from the candidate for Vice president, and scattered them upon others.[3]

This "strategic voting" by the Federalists to ensure the Presidency to their own party's nominee for President enabled the Republican presidential nominee (Jefferson) to end up with the second-highest number of electoral votes. Thus, Federalist John Adams was elected President, and his chief critic, Thomas Jefferson, was elected Vice President.[4,5]

In 1800, Thomas Jefferson and Aaron Burr again ran together as candidates of the Anti-Federalist Party. Anti-Federalist presidential electors won a majority in the Electoral College. In 1800, all of the winning party's presidential electors cast one vote for each of their party's nominees. Thus, Jefferson and Burr each received an equal number of votes in the Electoral College, thereby creating a tie. Under the Constitution, such ties are resolved by a "contingent election" in which the House of Representatives elects the President and the Senate elects the Vice President. In the House, each state is entitled to cast one vote for President (with equally divided states being unable to cast a vote). In the Senate, each Senator is entitled to cast one vote for Vice President. After a bitter dispute in Congress, Thomas Jefferson emerged from the House of Representatives as President.[6]

Given the emergence of political parties that centrally nominated presidential and vice-presidential candidates and given that it was necessary for each presidential elector to vote for both of his party's nominees (to prevent a recurrence of the 1796 debacle), it was apparent that tied presidential elections would be the norm for future elections. Congress

---

[3] Stanwood, Edward. 1924. *A History of the Presidency from 1788 to 1897*. Boston, MA: Houghton Mifflin Company. Page 49.

[4] Peirce, Neal R. 1968. *The People's President: The Electoral College in American History and Direct-Vote Alternative*. New York, NY: Simon and Schuster. Pages 63–64.

[5] Stanwood, Edward. 1924. *A History of the Presidency from 1788 to 1897*. Boston: Houghton Mifflin Company. Pages 49-53. There is considerable historical controversy concerning Alexander Hamilton's possible motives and role in the "strategic voting" by Federalist presidential electors in the 1796 election. The main point, for the purposes of this chapter, is that the original Constitution's provision for double voting by presidential electors was unworkable in the context of political parties and competitive presidential elections.

[6] Dunn, Susan. 2004. Jefferson's Second Revolution: *The Elections Crisis of 1800 and the Triumph of Republicanism*. Boston, MA: Houghton Mifflin.

therefore passed the 12th Amendment specifying that each presidential elector would cast a separate vote for President and Vice President. Separate voting enables the winning political party to elect its nominees to both nationwide offices. The states quickly ratified the amendment, and it was in effect in time for the 1804 election.[7]

In 1824, there was a four-way race for President. The presidential election was again thrown into the U.S. House and Senate. This controversial election spotlighted various undemocratic practices, including the continued selection of presidential electors in many states by the state legislature.[8] After the 1824 election, the laws of many states were changed to empower the voters to choose the state's presidential electors directly. Within two presidential elections, the voters directly elected presidential electors in all but one state (South Carolina).

In 1876, Democrat Samuel J. Tilden received 254,694 more popular votes than the 4,033,497 votes received by Rutherford B. Hayes; however, Hayes led by one electoral vote by virtue of carrying a number of states by extremely small margins (e.g., South Carolina by 889 votes, Florida by 922 votes, Oregon by 1,050 votes, Nevada by 1,075 votes, and California by 2,798 votes).[9] Moreover, conflicting returns were submitted from three southern states that still had reconstruction governments (South Carolina, Florida, and Louisiana). A 15-member electoral commission eventually awarded the Presidency to Hayes.[10,11,12] The contested Tilden-Hayes 1876 election led to the passage of federal legislation governing the handling of controversies involving presidential elections.[13]

In the 1888 election, President Grover Cleveland received 5,539,118 popular votes to Benjamin Harrison's 5,449,825. Harrison won in the

---

[7] Kuroda, Tadahisa. 1994. *The Origins of the Twelfth Amendment: The Electoral College in the Early Republic, 1787–1804.* Westport, CT: Greenwood Press.

[8] Schlesinger, Arthur M., Jr. and Hewson, Martha S. 2002. Philadelphia, PA: Chelsea House Publishers. Pages 34–36.

[9] Congressional Quarterly. 2002. *Presidential Elections 1789–2002.* Washington, DC: CQ Press. Page 125.

[10] Morris, Roy B. 2003. *Fraud of the Century: Rutherford B. Hayes, Samuel Tilden, and the Stolen Election of 1876.* Waterville, ME: Thorndike Press.

[11] Robinson, Lloyd. 1996. *The Stolen Election: Hayes versus Tilden—1876.* New York, NY: Tom Doherty Associates Books.

[12] Rehnquist, William H. 2004. *Centennial Crisis: The Disputed Election of 1876.* New York, NY: Alfred A. Knopf.

[13] The federal election laws resulting from the 1876 election evolved into what is now Title 3 of the United States Code (found in appendix B).

Electoral College by a substantial margin—233 to 168 despite Cleveland's 89,293-vote lead in the popular vote. In the 1890 mid-term elections, the Democrats won control in Michigan (then regularly Republican). The Democrats passed a law switching Michigan from the statewide winner-take-all system to a system in which one presidential elector was to be elected from each of the state's congressional districts and in which the state's two senatorial electors were to be elected from two special districts, each comprising half of the state's congressional districts. Republicans contested the constitutionality of Michigan's change from the statewide winner-take-all system to the district system. In the 1892 case of *McPherson v. Blacker* (discussed in chapter 2), the U.S. Supreme Court upheld Michigan's right to change its law concerning the method of choosing its presidential electors.

The 1968 presidential election was held in the midst of continuing controversy over recently passed civil rights laws, urban rioting, and the war in Vietnam. Governor George Wallace of Alabama ran for President against Richard Nixon and Hubert Humphrey.[14] Wallace hoped to win enough electoral votes to prevent either major-party nominee from winning a majority of the electoral votes. His primary goal was not to throw the election into the Congress. Instead, he planned to negotiate with one of the major-party candidates before the meeting of the Electoral College in mid-December to extract policy concessions on civil rights and cabinet positions. To aid in these anticipated post-November negotiations, Wallace obtained affidavits from each of his presidential electors committing them to vote in the Electoral College for Wallace or "for whomsoever he may direct."[15]

Wallace won 45 electoral votes in 1968 by carrying Alabama, Arkansas, Georgia, Louisiana, and Mississippi. Richard Nixon ended up with 43.42% of the popular vote (compared to Hubert Humphrey's 42.72%) as well as a majority of the electoral votes. Although Nixon was elected President by a majority of the Electoral College, a shift of only 10,245 popular votes in Missouri and 67,481 popular votes in Illinois would have left Nixon without a majority of the electoral votes (while still leading Humphrey by more than 300,000 popular votes on a nationwide basis).

---

[14] Longley, Lawrence D. and Braun, Alan G. 1972. *The Politics of Electoral College Reform.* New Haven, CT: Yale University Press. Pages 7–21.

[15] Congressional Quarterly. 1979. *Presidential Elections Since 1789.* Second Edition. Washington, DC: CQ Press. Page 8.

Faithless presidential electors had begun to emerge as an irritant in presidential politics in several southern states during the period immediately before and after passage of the civil rights legislation of the mid-1960s. In the 1968 presidential election, George Wallace received one electoral vote from a faithless Republican presidential elector from North Carolina. This was one of three occasions when Nixon suffered the loss of an electoral vote because of a faithless Republican elector.

Thus, shortly after taking office as President in 1969, Nixon sent a message to Congress saying:

> "I have in the past supported the proportional plan. But I am not wedded to the details of this plan or any other specific plan. I will support any plan that moves toward … the abolition of individual electors … allocation of presidential candidates of the electoral vote of each state and the District of Columbia in a manner that may more closely approximate the popular vote than does the present system … making a 40 percent electoral vote plurality sufficient to choose a President."[16]

President Nixon's message ignited a flurry of activity in the 91st Congress.

- Senator Howard Cannon (D–Nevada) introduced a proposed constitutional amendment for a fractional proportional allocation of each state's electoral votes (section 3.1).
- Senator Karl Mundt (R–South Dakota) introduced a proposed amendment for electing presidential electors by congressional district (section 3.2).
- Representative Emmanuel Celler (D–New York) and Senator Birch Bayh (D–Indiana) introduced amendments for nationwide popular election of the president (section 3.3).

Celler's proposal (House Joint Resolution 681 of the 91st Congress) passed in the House of Representatives by a 338–70 vote in 1969. After the strong bipartisan vote in the House, President Nixon urged the Senate to adopt the House bill. That bill, however, was filibustered and died in the Senate.[17]

---

[16] February 20, 1969.

[17] Congressional Quarterly. 2002. *Presidential Elections 1789-2002*. Washington, DC: CQ Press. Page 169.

Interest in electoral reform was rekindled after the 1976 presidential elections. A shift of 3,687 popular votes in Hawaii and 5,559 popular votes in Ohio would have elected Gerald Ford, even though Jimmy Carter led Ford by 1,682,970 popular votes nationwide.

President Carter, President Ford (the losing presidential candidate in 1976), and Senator Robert Dole (the losing vice-presidential candidate) publicly supported nationwide popular election of the President. In 1979, a majority of the Senate voted in favor a proposed constitutional amendment (Senate Joint Resolution 28) sponsored by Senator Birch Bayh that closely resembled the bill that had passed in the House in 1969. Lacking the required two-thirds support, the bill was defeated.

The 2000 election resulted in the election of a President who had not received the most popular votes nationwide. After the 2000 election, former Presidents Jimmy Carter and Gerald Ford created a bipartisan Commission to make recommendations for improving the nation's electoral system. Many of the reforms proposed by the Carter-Ford Commission became part of the Help America Vote Act (HAVA) of 2002.

If 59,393 Ohio votes had switched in the 2004 presidential election, Kerry would have been elected President despite George W. Bush's lead of about 3,500,000 votes in the nationwide popular vote. After the 2004 election, former President Jimmy Carter and former Secretary of State James Baker formed another bipartisan commission to review the implementation of HAVA in light of the nation's experience in the 2004 election and to make additional recommendations concerning election administration.

Potential problems with the current statewide winner-take-all system appear to be becoming increasingly common.[18] As shown in table 1.3, there have been six presidential elections—1948, 1960, 1968, 1976, 2000, and 2004—in the past six decades in which the shift of a relatively small number of votes in one or two states would have elected a presidential candidate who had not received the most popular votes nationwide.

Meanwhile, the 2004 presidential election made it clear that the number of battleground states is decreasing. Although voter turnout increased in the battleground states in 2004, it decreased in noncompetitive states.[19]

---

[18] Abbott, David W. and Levine, James P. 1991. *Wrong Winner: The Coming Debacle in the Electoral College.* Westport, CT: Praeger.

[19] Committee for the Study of the American Electorate (2004). "President Bush, Mobilization Drives Propel Turnout to Post-1968 High." November 4, 2004.

3.1 FRACTIONAL PROPORTIONAL ALLOCATION OF ELECTORAL VOTES

In the fractional proportional approach, a state's electoral votes are divided proportionally—carried out to three decimal places—according to the percentage of votes received in the state by each presidential slate.

Senator Howard Cannon (D–Nevada) introduced the following proposed federal constitutional amendment (Senate Joint Resolution 33 in the 91st Congress) to implement the fractional proportional approach:

> *"Resolved by the Senate and House of Representatives of the United States of America in Congress assembled (two-thirds of each House concurring therein),*

> That the following article is proposed as an amendment to the Constitution of the United States, which shall be valid to all intents and purposes as part of the Constitution if ratified by the legislatures of three-fourths of the several States:

> 'Article—
> 'SECTION 1. The Executive power shall be vested in a President of the United States of America. He shall hold his office during the term of four years, and, together with the Vice President, chosen for the same term, be elected as provided in this article. No person constitutionally ineligible for the office of President shall be eligible for the office of Vice President.

> 'SECTION 2. The President and Vice President shall be elected by the people of the several States and the District of Columbia. The electors in each State shall have the qualifications requisite for electors of the most numerous branch of the State legislature, except that the legislature of any State may prescribe lesser qualifications with respect to residence therein. The electors of the District of Columbia shall have such qualifications as the Congress may prescribe. The places and manner of holding such election in each State shall be prescribed by the legislature thereof, but the Congress may at any time by law make or alter such regulations.

The place and manner of holding such election in the District of Columbia shall be prescribed by the Congress. The Congress shall determine the time of such election, which shall be the same throughout the United States. Until otherwise determined by the Congress, such election shall be held on the Tuesday next after the first Monday in November of the year preceding the year in which the regular term of the President is to begin.

'**SECTION 3.** Each state shall be entitled to a number of electoral votes equal to the whole number of Senators and Representatives to which each State may be entitled in the Congress. The District of Columbia shall be entitled to a number of electoral votes equal to the whole number of Senators and Representatives in Congress to which such District would be entitled if it were a State, but in no event more than the least populous State.

'**SECTION 4.** Within forty-five days after such election, or at such time as Congress shall direct, the official custodian of the election returns of each State and the District of Columbia shall make distinct lists of all persons for whom votes were cast for President and the number of votes cast for each person, and the total vote cast by the electors of the State of the District for all persons for President, which lists he shall sign and certify and transmit sealed to the seat of Government of the United States, directed to the President of the Senate. On the 6th day of January following the election, unless the Congress by law appoints a different day not earlier than the 4th day of January and not later than the 10th day of January, the President of the Senate shall, in the presence of the Senate and House of Representatives, open all certificates and the votes shall then be counted. Each person for whom votes were cast shall be credited with such proportion of the electoral votes thereof as he received of the total vote cast by the electors therein for President. In making the computation, fractional numbers less than one one-thousandth shall be disregarded. The person having the greatest aggregate number of electoral votes of the States and the District of Columbia for President shall be President, if such number be at least 40 per centum of the whole number of such electoral votes, or if two persons have received an identical number of such electoral votes which is at least 40 per centum of the whole number of electoral votes, then from the persons having the two greatest number of such electoral votes for President, the Senate and the House of Representatives sitting in joint session shall choose immediately, by ballot, the President. A majority of the votes of the combined membership of the Senate and House of Representatives shall be necessary for a choice.

'SECTION 5. The Vice President shall be likewise elected, at the same time, in the same manner, and subject to the same provisions as the President.

'SECTION 6. The Congress may by law provide for the case of the death of any of the persons from whom the Senate and the House of Representatives may choose a President whenever the right of choice shall have devolved upon them, and for the case of death of any of the persons from whom the Senate and the House of Representatives may choose a Vice President whenever the right of choice shall have devolved upon them. The Congress shall have power to enforce this article by appropriate legislation.

'SECTION 7. The following provisions of the Constitution are hereby repealed: paragraphs 1, 2, 3, and 4 of section 1, Article II; the twelfth article of amendment; section 4 of the twentieth article of amendment; and the twenty-third article of amendment.

'**SECTION 8.** This article shall take effect on the 1st day of February following its ratification, except that this article shall be inoperative unless it shall have been ratified as an amendment to the Constitution by the legislatures of three-fourths of the States within seven years from the date of its submission to the States by the Congress.' "

The remainder of this section analyzes how the proposed fractional proportional approach would operate in terms of the following criteria:

- Would it accurately reflect the nationwide popular vote?
- Would it improve upon the current situation in which most areas of the country are non-competitive?
- Would every vote be equal?

Almost any electoral system will work well in a landslide. Thus, we start our analysis of the fractional proportional approach with data from a close recent presidential election—the 2000 election.

Table 3.1 shows how the fractional proportional approach would have operated in the 2000 presidential election. Columns 3, 4, and 5 of this table show, for each state, the number of population votes received by Al Gore, George W. Bush, and Ralph Nader. Column 6 shows, for each state, the number of electoral votes that Gore would have received under the fractional proportional approach (expressed as a fraction with three decimal places of precision, as specified by Senator Cannon's proposal). This number of electoral votes is obtained by dividing Gore's popular vote in the state by the total popular vote received by Gore, Bush, and Nader together, and then multiplying this quotient by the number of electoral votes possessed by the state. Columns 7 and 8 show the same information for Bush and Nader. For each state, the number of electoral votes for the three presidential candidates (columns 6, 7, and 8) adds up to the number of electoral votes possessed by the state (column 2). As can be seen from the bottom line of the table, Al Gore would have received 259.969 electoral votes; George W. Bush would have received 260.323 electoral votes; and Ralph Nader would have received 17.707 electoral votes if the 2000 presidential election had been run under the fractional proportional approach.[20]

---

[20] In this book, all analyses of the results of hypothetically using some alternative electoral system are based on the data available from the actual election using the current electoral system.

Table 3.1 2000 ELECTION UNDER THE FRACTIONAL PROPORTIONAL APPROACH (CONSIDERING THREE PARTIES)

STATE	ELECTORAL VOTES	POPULAR VOTES GORE	POPULAR VOTES BUSH	POPULAR VOTES NADER	ELECTORAL VOTES GORE	ELECTORAL VOTES BUSH	ELECTORAL VOTES NADER
Alabama	9	692,611	941,173	18,323	3.773	5.127	0.100
Alaska	3	79,004	167,398	28,747	0.861	1.825	0.313
Arizona	8	685,341	781,652	45,645	3.625	4.134	0.241
Arkansas	6	422,768	472,940	13,421	2.790	3.121	0.089
California	54	5,861,203	4,567,429	418,707	29.178	22.737	2.084
Colorado	8	738,227	883,748	91,434	3.447	4.126	0.427
Connecticut	8	816,015	561,094	64,452	4.529	3.114	0.358
Delaware	3	180,068	137,288	8,307	1.659	1.265	0.077
DC	3	171,923	18,073	10,576	2.571	0.270	0.158
Florida	25	2,912,253	2,912,790	97,488	12.293	12.295	0.412
Georgia	13	1,116,230	1,419,720	134,322	5.434	6.912	0.654
Hawaii	4	205,286	137,845	21,623	2.251	1.512	0.237
Idaho	4	138,637	336,937	122,922	0.927	2.252	0.822
Illinois	22	2,589,026	2,019,421	103,759	12.087	9.428	0.484
Indiana	12	901,980	1,245,836	185,312	4.639	6.408	0.953
Iowa	7	638,517	634,373	29,374	3.432	3.410	0.158
Kansas	6	399,276	622,332	36,086	2.265	3.530	0.205
Kentucky	8	638,898	872,492	23,192	3.331	4.548	0.121
Louisiana	9	792,344	927,871	20,473	4.097	4.797	0.106
Maine	4	319,951	286,616	37,127	1.988	1.781	0.231
Maryland	10	1,145,782	813,797	53,768	5.691	4.042	0.267
Massachusetts	12	1,616,487	878,502	173,564	7.269	3.950	0.780
Michigan	18	2,170,418	1,953,139	84,165	9.285	8.355	0.360
Minnesota	10	1,168,266	1,109,659	126,696	4.858	4.615	0.527
Mississippi	7	404,614	572,844	8,122	2.874	4.069	0.058
Missouri	11	1,111,138	1,189,924	38,515	5.224	5.595	0.181
Montana	3	137,126	240,178	24,437	1.024	1.794	0.182
Nebraska	5	231,780	433,862	24,540	1.679	3.143	0.178
Nevada	4	279,978	301,575	15,008	1.877	2.022	0.101
New Hampshire	4	266,348	273,559	22,198	1.895	1.947	0.158
New Jersey	15	1,788,850	1,284,173	94,554	8.471	6.081	0.448
New Mexico	5	286,783	286,417	21,251	2.412	2.409	0.179
New York	33	4,107,697	2,403,374	244,030	20.067	11.741	1.192
North Carolina	14	1,257,692	1,631,163	0	6.095	7.905	0.000
North Dakota	3	95,284	174,852	9,486	1.022	1.876	0.102
Ohio	21	2,186,190	2,351,209	117,857	9.862	10.606	0.532
Oklahoma	8	474,276	744,337	0	3.114	4.886	0.000
Oregon	7	720,342	713,577	77,357	3.337	3.305	0.358
Pennsylvania	23	2,485,967	2,281,127	103,392	11.740	10.772	0.488
Rhode Island	4	249,508	130,555	25,052	2.464	1.289	0.247

Table 3.1 2000 ELECTION UNDER THE FRACTIONAL PROPORTIONAL APPROACH (CONSIDERING THREE PARTIES) (cont.)

STATE	ELECTORAL VOTES	POPULAR VOTES			ELECTORAL VOTES		
		GORE	BUSH	NADER	GORE	BUSH	NADER
South Carolina	8	565,561	785,937	20,200	3.298	4.584	0.118
South Dakota	3	118,804	190,700	0	1.152	1.848	0.000
Tennessee	11	981,720	1,061,949	19,781	5.233	5.661	0.105
Texas	32	2,433,746	3,799,639	137,994	12.223	19.084	0.693
Utah	5	203,053	515,096	35,850	1.347	3.416	0.238
Vermont	3	149,022	119,775	20,374	1.546	1.243	0.211
Virginia	13	1,217,290	1,437,490	59,398	5.830	6.885	0.284
Washington	11	1,247,652	1,108,864	103,002	5.580	4.959	0.461
West Virginia	5	295,497	336,475	10,680	2.299	2.618	0.083
Wisconsin	11	1,242,987	1,237,279	94,070	5.311	5.287	0.402
Wyoming	3	60,481	147,947	46,252	0.712	1.743	0.545
Total	**538**	**50,999,897**	**50,456,002**	**2,882,955**	**259.969**	**260.323**	**17.707**

Concerning the accurate reflection of the nationwide popular vote, table 3.1 shows that, if the fractional proportional approach had been in use throughout the country in the 2000 presidential election, it would not have awarded the most electoral votes to the candidate receiving the most popular votes nationwide. Gore would have received 0.354 fewer electoral votes than George W. Bush even though Gore led by 537,179 popular votes nationwide. Because Bush would have received "the greatest aggregate number of electoral votes" and such number would have been "at least 40 per centum of the whole number of such electoral votes," Bush would have been elected under Senate Joint Resolution 33 as proposed by Senator Cannon in 1969.

Under some variants of the proposed fractional proportional approach, no electoral votes are awarded to a presidential slate receiving less than a specified "cut-off" percentage (e.g., 5%) of a state's popular vote (or the national popular vote). Table 3.2 shows how the fractional proportional approach would have operated in the 2000 presidential election if only the two major political parties are considered. Column 2 shows Gore's popular vote percentage for each state. Columns 3 and 4 show, for each state, the electoral votes (rounded off to three decimal places) that Gore and Bush, respectively, would have received under the fractional proportional approach with a cut-off. Columns 5 and 6 show the actual numbers of electoral votes that Gore and Bush, respectively, received in the 2000 presidential election.

Table 3.2 2000 ELECTION UNDER THE FRACTIONAL PROPORTIONAL APPROACH (CONSIDERING THE TWO MAJOR PARTIES)

STATE	GORE POPULAR VOTES	GORE FRACTIONAL ELECTORAL VOTES	BUSH FRACTIONAL ELECTORAL VOTES	GORE ACTUAL ELECTORAL VOTES	BUSH ACTUAL ELECTORAL VOTES
Alabama	42.393058%	3.815	5.185		9
Alaska	32.063051%	0.962	2.038		3
Arizona	46.717401%	3.737	4.263		8
Arkansas	47.199310%	2.832	3.168		6
California	56.202990%	30.350	23.650	54	
Colorado	45.514080%	3.641	4.359		8
Connecticut	59.255658%	4.740	3.260	8	
Delaware	56.740065%	1.702	1.298	3	
DC	90.487694%	2.715	0.285	3	
Florida	49.995391%	12.499	12.501		25
Georgia	44.016246%	5.722	7.278		13
Hawaii	59.827296%	2.393	1.607	4	
Idaho	29.151510%	1.166	2.834		4
Illinois	56.180010%	12.360	9.640	22	
Indiana	41.995217%	5.039	6.961		12
Iowa	50.162779%	3.511	3.489	7	
Kansas	39.083093%	2.345	3.655		6
Kentucky	42.272213%	3.382	4.618		8
Louisiana	46.060754%	4.145	4.855		9
Maine	52.747842%	2.110	1.890	4	
Maryland	58.470825%	5.847	4.153	10	
Massachusetts	64.789344%	7.775	4.225	12	
Michigan	52.634606%	9.474	8.526	18	
Minnesota	51.286412%	5.129	4.871	10	
Mississippi	41.394515%	2.898	4.102		7
Missouri	48.288051%	5.312	5.688		11
Montana	36.343638%	1.090	1.910		3
Nebraska	34.820519%	1.741	3.259		5
Nevada	48.143162%	1.926	2.074		4
New Hampshire	49.332200%	1.973	2.027		4
New Jersey	58.211409%	8.732	6.268	15	
New Mexico	50.031926%	2.502	2.498	5	
New York	63.087885%	20.819	12.181	33	
North Carolina	43.536003%	6.095	7.905		14
North Dakota	35.272603%	1.058	1.942		3
Ohio	48.181568%	10.118	10.882		21
Oklahoma	38.919329%	3.114	4.886		8
Oregon	50.235892%	3.517	3.483	7	

Table 3.2 2000 ELECTION UNDER THE FRACTIONAL PROPORTIONAL APPROACH (CONSIDERING THE TWO MAJOR PARTIES) (cont.)

STATE	GORE POPULAR VOTES	GORE FRACTIONAL ELECTORAL VOTES	BUSH FRACTIONAL ELECTORAL VOTES	GORE ACTUAL ELECTORAL VOTES	BUSH ACTUAL ELECTORAL VOTES
Pennsylvania	52.148479%	11.994	11.006	23	
Rhode Island	65.649116%	2.626	1.374	4	
South Carolina	41.846973%	3.348	4.652		8
South Dakota	38.385287%	1.152	1.848		3
Tennessee	48.037133%	5.284	5.716		11
Texas	39.043730%	12.494	19.506		32
Utah	28.274495%	1.414	3.586		5
Vermont	55.440351%	1.663	1.337	3	
Virginia	45.852764%	5.961	7.039		13
Washington	52.944771%	5.824	5.176	11	
West Virginia	46.757926%	2.338	2.662		5
Wisconsin	50.115068%	5.513	5.487	11	
Wyoming	29.017694%	0.871	2.129		3
	50.268045%	**268.766**	**269.234**	**267**	**271**

Table 3.2 shows that, if the fractional proportional approach had been used in the 2000 presidential election (with a cut-off percentage excluding all but the two major-party candidates), it would not have awarded the most electoral votes to the candidate receiving the most popular votes nationwide. Even though Al Gore led by 537,179 popular votes nationwide, he would have received only 268.766 electoral votes, whereas George W. Bush would have received 269.234 electoral votes. Since 269.234 is more than half of 538, George W. Bush would have been elected President.

Concerning competitiveness, the fractional proportional approach improves upon the current situation in which about three-quarters of states are non-competitive. Winning a few hundred more popular votes in any state will earn a presidential candidate an additional 0.001 electoral votes, thus giving some political importance to every vote, regardless of the state in which it is cast.

On the other hand, not every vote is equal under the fractional proportional approach. In fact, there are three different inequalities inherent in the fractional proportional approach as explained below. These inequalities (3.79-to-1, 1.76-to-1, and 1.27-to-1) are substantial and, in particular, are considerably larger than the small variations that are considered to be constitutionally tolerable nowadays when congressional and other types of districts are drawn within states.[21]

The inequalities under the fractional proportional approach arise from the

- two bonus electoral votes that each state receives regardless of its population,
- inequalities in the apportionment of the membership of the House of Representatives among the several states, and
- differences in voter turnout in various states.

First, a vote cast in a large state has less weight than a vote cast in a small state because of the two bonus in the Electoral College that each state receives regardless of its population. For example, in the 2000 presidential election, Wyoming (with a population of 453,588 in 1990) had three electoral votes, whereas California (with a population of 29,760,021 in 1990) had 54 electoral votes. As shown in table 3.3, in the presidential elections of 1992, 1996, and 2000, one electoral vote corresponded to 151,196 people in Wyoming but to 572,308 in California. The last column of this table shows the ratio of California's population per electoral vote compared to that of Wyoming—a 3.79-to-1 variation.

Table 3.3 DIFFERENCE IN WEIGHT OF A POPULAR VOTE ARISING FROM EACH STATE'S BONUS OF TWO ELECTORAL VOTES

STATE	POPULATION	REPRESENTATIVES	SENATORS	ELETORAL VOTES	POPULATION CORRESPONDING TO ONE ELECTORAL VOTE	RATIO TO LOWEST
California	29,760,021	52	2	54	572,308	3.79
Wyoming	453,588	1	2	3	151,196	1.00

Second, a vote cast in certain states has less weight than a vote cast in certain other states because of inequalities in the apportionment of membership of the House of Representatives among the several states. For example, Wyoming (with a population of 453,588 in 1990) and Montana (with a population of 799,065 in 1990) each had one member in the House of Representatives (and hence three electoral votes). As

---

[21] Of course, if the fractional proportional approach were enacted in the form of a federal constitutional amendment, it could not be successfully challenged in court on the grounds that it countenances inequalities that are greater than those constitutionally allowed for election districts for other offices.

shown in table 3.4, in the presidential elections of 1992, 1996, and 2000, one electoral vote corresponded to 151,196 people in Wyoming but to 266,355 in Montana. The last column of this table shows the ratio of Montana's population per electoral vote compared to the ratio for Wyoming—a 1.76-to-1 variation. There are numerous other pairs of states with similar variations.[22]

Table 3.4 I **DIFFERENCE IN WEIGHT OF A POPULAR VOTE ARISING FROM CONGRESSIONAL APPORTIONMENT**

STATE	POPULATION	POPULATION CORRESPONDING BY ONE ELECTORAL VOTE	RATIO TO LOWEST
Montana	799,065	266,355	1.76
Wyoming	453,588	151,196	1.00

Third, voter turnout within a voter's own state changes the weight of a given voter's vote. For example, a vote cast in a state with a low turnout has a greater weight than a vote cast in a state where more total votes are cast. Column 4 of table 3.5 shows the numbers of popular votes cast in the 2000 presidential election in the four states with five electoral votes (Nebraska, New Mexico, Utah, and West Virginia). As can be seen in column 5 of the table, one electoral vote corresponds to 118,900 popular votes in New Mexico but to 150,800 popular votes in Utah. Column 6 shows the ratio of the number of votes representing one electoral vote in each state compared to that of the lowest in the table (New Mexico). The greatest variation is between Utah and New Mexico—a 1.27-to-1 variation.

Table 3.5 COMPARISON OF WEIGHT OF A POPULAR VOTE CAST IN FOUR STATES WITH THE SAME NUMBER OF ELECTORAL VOTES

STATE	1990 POPULATION	2000 POPULATION	VOTES CAST IN 2000 PRESIDENTIAL ELECTION	POPULAR VOTES CORRESPONDING TO ONE ELECTORAL VOTE	RATIO TO LOWEST
Nebraska	1,578,385	1,711,263	690,182	138,000	1.16
New Mexico	1,515,069	1,819,046	594,451	118,900	1.00
Utah	1,722,850	2,233,169	753,999	150,800	1.27
West Virginia	1,793,477	1,808,344	642,652	128,600	1.08

[22] These include pairs of states with more than three electoral votes and pairs of states with different numbers of electoral votes.

The total number of votes cast in states with the same number of electoral votes varies for at least two reasons.

- First, the actual population of the state at the moment of the election might have increased or decreased since the last census.
- Second, the number of voters turning out for the particular election depends on the degree of civic participation in the state.

As to the first of these factors, a state's allocation of electoral votes depends on its number of Representatives and Senators. The number of Representatives to which a state is entitled changes every 10 years based on the federal census. For example, the 1992, 1996, and 2000 presidential elections were conducted under the apportionment that resulted from the 1990 census. This means that the 2000 presidential election was conducted using an allocation of electoral votes based on 10-year-old population data. Thus, the weight of a citizen's vote in a rapidly growing state is diminished. Column 2 of table 3.5 shows the population of each state according to the 1990 census. Column 3 shows the population of each state according to the 2000 census. The 2000 census was taken in the spring of 2000 but was not applicable to the 2000 presidential election. These numbers closely approximate each state's population in the 2000 presidential election held a few months later. As can be seen, Utah, a fast-growing state, had 510,319 more people in 2000 than it did in 1990, whereas West Virginia barely grew at all during the 10-year period (only 14,867 more people than in 1990). New Mexico also experienced rapid population growth during the 1990s. Because of the time lag in reallocating electoral votes (a full 10 years in the case of the 2000 election), Utah and New Mexico had the same number of electoral votes in the 2000 presidential election as West Virginia.

Concerning the second of the above factors, voter turnout within a state also affects the relative weight of a vote under the fractional proportional approach. A citizen's vote gets less weight if it happens to be cast in a state with a high degree of civic participation. For example, Utah consistently has high voter turnout in its elections.

In summary, if the fractional proportional approach had been in use throughout the country in the 2000 presidential election,

- it would not have more accurately reflected the nationwide popular vote;

- it would have made all states competitive; and
- not every vote would have been equal.

It should be noted that the fractional proportional approach discussed above differs significantly from the whole-number proportional approach (discussed in section 4.1). In the whole-number proportional approach, the office of presidential elector is not abolished and, therefore, the states continue to choose presidential electors. Because human presidential electors each have one indivisible vote, it is not possible to divide the electoral votes precisely (e.g., to three decimal places as specified in Senator Cannon's proposal). Thus, a state's electoral votes must necessarily be rounded off to the nearest whole number in the whole-number proportional approach. The counter-intuitive effects of this rounding-off, in the context of a system in which the average state has only 11 electoral votes, is discussed in detail in section 4.1.

3.2 DISTRICT ALLOCATION OF ELECTORAL VOTES

In the district approach, voters elect two presidential electors statewide and one presidential elector for each district.

Senator Karl Mundt (R–South Dakota) was the leading sponsor of a proposed federal constitutional amendment to implement the district system in 1969. Senate Joint Resolution 12 of the 91st Congress provided (in part):

> *"Resolved by the Senate and House of Representatives of the United States of America in Congress assembled (two-thirds of each House concurring therein),*

That the following article is proposed as an amendment to the Constitution of the United States, which shall be valid to all intents and purposes as part of the Constitution if ratified by the legislatures of three-fourths of the several States within seven years from the date of its submission by the Congress:

> 'Article—
> 'SECTION 1. Each State shall choose a number of electors of President and Vice President equal to the whole number of Senators and Representatives to which the State may be entitled in the Congress; but no Senator or Representative, or person holding an office of trust or profit under the United States shall be chosen elector.

'The electors assigned to each State with its Senators shall be elected by the people thereof. Each of the electors apportioned with its Representatives shall be elected by the people of a single-member electoral district formed by the legislature of the State. Electoral districts within each State shall be of compact and contiguous territory containing substantially equal numbers of inhabitants, and shall not be altered until another census of the United States has been taken. Each candidate for the office of elector of President and Vice President shall file in writing under oath a declaration of the identity of the persons for whom he will vote for President and Vice President, which declaration shall be binding on any successor to his office. In choosing electors the voters in each State have the qualifications requisite for electors of the most numerous branch of the State legislature.

'The electors shall meet in their respective States, fill any vacancies in their number as directed by the State legislature, and vote by signed ballot for President and Vice President, one of whom, at least, shall not be an inhabitant of the State with themselves....

"Any vote cast by an elector contrary to the declaration made by him shall be counted as a vote cast in accordance with his declaration.' "

Senate Joint Resolution 12 of the 91st Congress in 1969 was sponsored by the following Senators:

- Mundt (R–South Dakota),
- Boggs (R–Delaware),
- Byrd (D–West Virginia),
- Cotton (R–New Hampshire),
- Curtis (R–Nebraska),
- Dominick (R–Colorado),
- Fong (R–Hawaii),
- Goldwater (R–Arizona),
- Hansen (R–Wyoming),
- Hruska (R–Nebraska),
- Jordan (R–Idaho),
- Miller (R–Iowa),
- Sparkman (D–Alabama),
- Stennis (D–Mississippi),
- Thurmond (R–South Carolina),
- Tower (R–Texas),
- Williams (R–Delaware), and
- Young (R–North Dakota).

The characteristics of the congressional-district approach are analyzed in detail in section 4.2, where it is demonstrated that

- it would not accurately reflect the nationwide popular vote;
- it would not improve upon the current situation in which most areas of the country are non-competitive but, instead, would simply create a small set of battleground congressional districts (with most districts being non-competitive), and
- not every vote would be equal.

The Mundt proposal was noteworthy in that it retained the office of presidential elector while eliminating the possibility of a faithless presidential elector. First, Mundt's proposed amendment provided that each candidate for presidential elector must take an oath to vote in the Electoral College for particular persons for President and Vice President (and made the original candidate's oath binding on any replacement). Second, Mundt's proposal then stated that regardless of the way the presidential elector actually voted in the Electoral College, his or her vote would "be counted as a vote cast in accordance with his declaration."

3.3 DIRECT NATIONWIDE POPULAR ELECTION

In 1969, the House of Representatives approved, by a 338–70 vote, a federal constitutional amendment sponsored by Representative Emmanuel Celler for direct nationwide popular election. Celler's proposal (House Joint Resolution 681 of the 91st Congress) provided:

> *"Resolved by the Senate and House of Representatives of the*
> *United States of America in Congress assembled (two-thirds*
> *of each House concurring therein),*

That the following article is proposed as an amendment to the Constitution of the United States, which shall be valid to all intents and purposes as part of the Constitution when ratified by the legislatures of three-fourths of the several States within seven years from the date of its submission by the Congress:

> 'Article—
> 'SECTION 1: The people of the several States and the District constituting the seat of government of the United States shall elect the President and Vice President. Each elector shall cast a single vote for two persons who shall have consented to the joining of their names as candidates for the offices of President and Vice President. No candidate shall

consent to the joinder of his name with that of more than one other person.

'**SECTION 2:** The electors of President and Vice President in each State shall have the qualifications requisite for electors of the most numerous branch of the State legislature, except that for electors of President and Vice President, the legislature of any State may prescribe less restrictive residence qualifications and for electors of President and Vice President the Congress may establish uniform residence qualifications.

'**SECTION 3:** The pair of persons having the greatest number of votes for President and Vice President shall be elected, if such number be at least 40 per centum of the whole number of votes cast for such offices. If no pair of persons has such number, a runoff election shall be held in which the choice of President and Vice President shall be made from the two pairs of persons who received the highest number of votes.

'**SECTION 4:** The times, places, and manner of holding such elections and entitlement to inclusion on the ballot shall be prescribed in each State by the legislature thereof; but the Congress may at any time by law make or alter such regulations. The days for such elections shall be determined by Congress and shall be uniform throughout the United States. The Congress shall prescribe by law the time, place, and manner in which the results of such elections shall be ascertained and declared.

'**SECTION 5:** The Congress may by law provide for the case of the death or withdrawal of any candidate for President or Vice President before a President and Vice President have been elected, and for the case of the death of both the President-elect and Vice-President-elect.

'**SECTION 6:** The Congress shall have power to enforce this article by appropriate legislation.

'**SECTION 7:** This article shall take effect one year after the 21st day of January following ratification.' "

When it was first introduced, House Joint Resolution 681 was sponsored by the following Representatives:

- Biester (R–Pennsylvania),
- Cahill (R–New Jersey),
- Celler (D–New York),
- Conyers (D–Michigan),
- Donohue (D–Massachusetts),
- Edwards (D–California),
- Eilberg (D–Pennsylvania),
- Feighan (D–Ohio),
- Fish (R–New York),
- Hungate (D–Missouri),
- Jacobs (D–Indiana),
- Kastenmeier (D–Wisconsin),
- MacGregor (R–Minnesota),
- McClory (R–Illinois),
- McCulloch (R–Ohio),
- Meskill (R–Connecticut),
- Mikva (D–Illinois),
- St. Onge (D–Connecticut),
- Railsback (R–Illinois),
- Rodino (D–New Jersey),
- Rogers (D–Colorado),
- Ryan (D–New York),
- Sandman (R–New Jersey),
- Smith (R–New York), and
- Waldie (D–California).

Congressman George Herbert Walker Bush (R–Texas), like many of his colleagues in Congress, supported all three of the prominent approaches to abolish the present Electoral College system. He spoke in favor of nationwide direct popular election (House Joint Resolution 681) on September 18, 1969, saying:

> "Frankly I think this legislation has a great deal to commend it. It will correct the wrongs of the present mechanism because by calling for direct election of the President and Vice President it will eliminate the formality of the electoral college and by providing for a runoff in case no candidate receives 40 percent of the vote it eliminates the unrealistic ballot casting in the House of Representatives. Yet, in spite of these drastic reforms, the bill is not, when viewed in the light of current practice, one that will be detrimental to our federal system or one that will change the departmentalized and local nature of voting in this country.

> "In electing the President and Vice President, the Constitution establishes the principle that votes are cast by States. This legislation does not tamper with that principle. It only changes the manner in which the States vote. Instead of voting by intermediaries, the States will certify their popular vote count to the Congress. The states will maintain primary

responsibility for the ballot and for the qualifications of voters. In other words, they will still designate the time, place, and manner in which elections will be held. Thus, there is a very good argument to be made that the basic nature of our federal system has not been disturbed.

"On the walls of the Jefferson Memorial are written these words that we might well consider today:

> 'I am not an advocate for frequent changes in laws and constitutions, but laws and constitutions must go hand in hand with the progress of the human mind as that becomes more developed, more enlightened, as new discoveries are made, new truths discovered, and manners and opinions change. With the change of circumstances institutions must advance also to keep pace with the times.'

"The world has changed a great deal since the 12th amendment was approved, and the system it perpetuates is one fraught with a history of fraud, leaves our country open to constitutional crisis, and is clearly unresponsive to the desires of the American people. I do support the proposal before us today because I believe it combines the best features of our current practice with the desirable goal of a simpler, more direct voting system."[23]

Senator Birch Bayh (D–Indiana) introduced Senate Joint Resolution 1 in the 91st Congress in 1969 (with substantially the same provisions as Representative Celler's House Joint Resolution 681). The sponsors of Senate Joint Resolution 1 included the following Senators:

- George D. Aiken (R–Vermont),
- Birch Bayh (D–Indiana),
- Henry Bellmon (R–Oklahoma),
- Alan Bible (D–Nevada),
- Quentin Burdick (D–North Dakota),
- Robert C. Byrd (D–West Virginia),
- Clifford P. Case (R–New Jersey),

---

[23] *Congressional Record.* September 18, 1969. Pages 25,990–25,991.

- Frank Church (D–Idaho),
- Marlow Cook (R–Kentucky),
- Alan Cranston (D–California),
- Thomas F. Eagleton (D–Missouri),
- Charles E. Goodell (R–New York),
- Mike Gravel (D–Alaska),
- Fred R. Harris (D–Oklahoma),
- Mark O. Hatfield (R–Oregon),
- Vance Hartke (D–Indiana),
- Daniel K. Inouye (D–Hawaii),
- Henry M. Jackson (D–Washington),
- Jacob K. Javits (R–New York),
- Warren G. Magnuson (D–Washington),
- Mike Mansfield (D–Montana),
- Charles McC. Mathias, Jr. (R–Maryland),
- George McGovern (D–South Dakota),
- Thomas J. McIntyre (D–New Hampshire),
- Lee Metcalf (D–Montana),
- Walter F. Mondale (D–Minnesota),
- Joseph M. Montoya (D–New Mexico),
- Edmund S. Muskie (D–Maine),
- Gaylord Nelson (D–Wisconsin),
- Robert W. Packwood (R–Oregon),
- John O. Pastore (D–Rhode Island),
- James B. Pearson (R–Kansas),
- Claiborne Pell (D–Rhode Island),
- William Proxmire (D–Wisconsin),
- Jennings Randolph (D–West Virginia),
- Abraham Ribicoff (D–Connecticut),
- Richard S. Schweiker (R–Pennsylvania),
- Joseph D. Tydings (D–Maryland),
- Harrison A. Williams, Jr. (D–New Jersey), and
- Stephen M. Young (D–Ohio).

After the 338–70 vote in the House of Representatives in favor of House Joint Resolution 681 in 1969, the House bill was filibustered and died in the Senate.

Throughout the 1970s, Senator Bayh repeatedly introduced constitutional amendments for nationwide popular election of the President. For example, the sponsors of Senate Joint Resolution 1 in the 95th Congress in 1977 included the following Senators:

- Abourezk (R–South Dakota),
- Anderson (D–Minnesota),
- Baker (R–Tennessee),
- Bartlett (R–Oklahoma),
- Bayh (D–Indiana),
- Bellmon(R–Oklahoma),
- Brooke (R–Massachusetts),
- Chafee (R–Rhode Island),
- Church (D–Idaho),
- Clark (D–Iowa),
- Cranston (D–California),
- Danforth (R–Missouri),
- DeConcini (D–Arizona),
- Dole (R–Kansas),
- Ford (D–Kentucky),
- Garn (R–Utah),
- Glenn (D–Ohio),
- Gravel (D–Alaska),
- Hart (D–Michigan),
- Haskell (D–Colorado),
- Hatfield (R–Oregon),
- Hathaway (D–Maine),
- Huddleston (D–Kentucky),
- Humphrey (D–Minnesota),
- Inouye (D–Hawaii),
- Jackson (D–Washington),
- Javits (R–New York),
- Kennedy (D–Massachusetts),
- Leahy (D–Vermont),
- Magnuson (D–Washington),
- Mathias (R–Maryland),
- Matsunaga (D–Hawaii),
- McIntyre (D–New Hampshire),
- Metzenbaum (D–Ohio),
- Packwood (R–Oregon),
- Randolph (D–West Virginia),
- Ribicoff (D–Connecticut),
- Riegle (D–Michigan),
- Schweiker (R–Pennsylvania),
- Stafford (R–Vermont),
- Stevenson (D–Illinois),
- Williams (D–New Jersey), and
- Zorinsky (D–Nebraska).

The sponsors of Senate Joint Resolution 28[24] in the 96th Congress in 1979 included the following Senators:

- Baker (R–Tennessee),
- Bayh (D–Indiana),
- Bellmon (R–Oklahoma),
- Burdick (D–North Dakota),
- Chafee (R–Rhode Island),
- Cranston (D–California),
- Danforth (R–Missouri),
- DeConcini (D–Arizona),
- Dole (R–Kansas),
- Kennedy (D–Massachusetts),
- Leahy (D–Vermont),
- Levin (D–Michigan),
- Magnuson (D–Washington),
- Mathias (R–Maryland),
- Matsunaga (D–Hawaii),
- Packwood (R–Oregon),
- Pell (D–Rhode Island),
- Proxmire (D–Wisconsin),

---

[24] Senate Joint Resolution 28 of the 96th Congress in 1979 was substantially the same as Celler's House Joint Resolution 681 that the House of Representatives passed in 1969.

- Durenberger (R–Minnesota),
- Ford (D–Kentucky),
- Garn (R–Utah),
- Gravel (D–Alaska),
- Hatfield (R–Oregon),
- Huddleston (D–Kentucky),
- Inouye (D–Hawaii),
- Jackson (D–Washington),
- Javits (R–New York),
- Johnston (D–Louisiana),
- Pryor (D–Arkansas),
- Randolph (D–West Virginia),
- Ribicoff (D–Connecticut),
- Riegle (D–Michigan),
- Stafford (R–Vermont),
- Stevenson (D–Illinois),
- Tsongas (D–Massachusetts),
- Williams (D–New Jersey), and
- Zorinsky (D–Nebraska).

Senator Robert E. Dole of Kansas, the Republican nominee for Vice President in 1976 and later Republican nominee for President in 1996, spoke in the Senate on January 14, 1979 on the subject of nationwide popular election of the President and Vice President, saying:

> "That candidates for these two positions should be selected by direct election is an idea which I have long supported....
>
> "The electoral college system was provided for in the Constitution because, at one time, it seemed the most fair way to select the President and Vice President. Alexander Hamilton apparently expressed the prevailing view when we wrote that a small number of persons selected from the general population would most likely have the ability and intelligence to select the best persons for the job. I have no doubt but that in the 18th century, the electoral college was well suited for our country. However, already by the early 19th century, misgivings were being voiced about the college.
>
> "The skepticism seems to be related to the formation of political party candidates and the difference they made in the selection of the President and Vice President. In the years since then, the electoral college has remained in use. It has served us fairly well—except for three times when it allowed a candidate to gain the Presidency who did not have the most popular votes.
>
> "There have been numerous other elections in which a shift of a few thousand votes would have changed the outcome of the electoral college vote, despite the fact that the would-be

winner came in second place in popular votes. Mr. President, I think we are leaving a little too much to chance, and to hope, that we will not witness yet another unrepresentative election."[25] [Emphasis added]

Senator Dole then specifically addressed the question of the effect of the bonus of two electoral votes that each state receives regardless of its population.

"Many persons have the impression that the electoral college benefits those persons living in small states. I feel that this is somewhat of a misconception. Through my experience with the Republican National Committee and as a Vice Presidential candidate in 1976, it became very clear that the populous states with their large blocks of electoral votes were the crucial states. It was in these states that we focused our efforts.

"Were we to switch to a system of direct election, I think we would see a resulting change in the nature of campaigning. While urban areas will still be important campaigning centers, there will be a new emphasis given to smaller states. **Candidates will soon realize that all votes are important, and votes from small states carry the same import as votes from large states. That to me is one of the major attractions of direct election. Each vote carries equal importance.**

"Direct election would give candidates incentive to campaign in States that are perceived to be single party states. For no longer will minority votes be lost. Their accumulated total will be important, and in some instances perhaps even decisive.

"The objections raised to direct election are varied. When they are analyzed, I think many objections reflect not so much satisfaction with the electoral college, but rather a reluctance to change an established political system. While I could never advocate change simply for the sake of changing, neither should we defer action because we fear change.

---

[25] *Congressional Record.* January 14, 1979. Page 309.

"In this situation, I think the weaknesses in the current system have been demonstrated, and that the prudent move is to provide for direct election of the President and Vice President.

"I hope that the Senate will be able to move ahead on this resolution. As long as we continue with the electoral college system, we will be placing our trust in an institution which usually works according to design, but which sometimes does not. There are remedies available to us and I trust the Senate will act to correct this weakness in our political system."[26] [Emphasis added]

In a 1979 Senate speech, Senator Henry Bellmon (R–Oklahoma) described how his views on the Electoral College had changed while he had served as Governor, Senator, national campaign director for Richard Nixon, and a member of the American Bar Association's commission studying electoral reform.

"While the consideration of the electoral college began–and I am a little embarrassed to admit this–I was convinced, as are many residents of smaller States, that the present system is a considerable advantage to less populous States such as Oklahoma, and that it was to the advantage of the small States for the electoral college concept be preserved.

"I think if any Member of the State has that concept he would be greatly enlightened by the fact that the Members of the Senate from New York are now actively supporting the retention of the electoral college system....

"Mr. President, as the deliberations of the American Bar Association Commission proceeded and as more facts became known, I came to the realization that the present electoral system does not give an advantage to the voters from the less populous States. Rather, it works to the disadvantage of small State voters who are largely ignored in the general election for President.

---

[26] *Congressional Record.* January 14, 1979. Page 309.

"It is true that the smaller States which are allowed an elector for each U.S. Senator and for each Congressman do, on the surface, appear to be favored; but, in fact, the system gives the advantage to the voters in the populous States. The reason is simple as I think our friends from New York understand: A small State voter is, in effect, the means whereby a Presidential candidate may receive a half-dozen or so electoral votes. On the other hand, a vote in a large State is the means to 20 or 30 or 40 or more electoral votes. Therefore, Presidential candidates structure their campaigns to appeal to the States with large blocs of electors. This gives special and disproportionate importance to the special interest groups which may determine the electoral outcome in those few large States.

"Here, Mr. President, let me say parenthetically that during 1967 and part of 1968 I served as the national campaign director for Richard Nixon, and I know very well as we structured that campaign we did not worry about Alaska, about Wyoming, or about Nevada or about New Mexico or about Oklahoma or Kansas. We worried about New York, California, Pennsylvania, Texas, Michigan, Illinois, all of the populous States, where there are these big blocks of electors that we could appeal to, provided we chose our issues properly and provided we presented the candidates in an attractive way.

"The result, Mr. President, is that the executive branch of our National Government has grown and is continuing to become increasingly oriented toward populous States, to the disadvantage of the smaller, less populous areas. An examination of past campaign platforms and campaign schedules of the major party candidates will bear out this position. Therefore, it is obvious that any political party or any candidate for President or Vice President will spend his efforts primarily in the populous States. The parties draft their platforms with the view in mind of attracting the voters of the populous States and generally relegate the needs of the smaller States to secondary positions.

"This whole situation would change if we go for a direct election and, therefore, **make the voters of one State equally important with the voters of any other State.**"[27] [Emphasis added]

Senator Carl Levin (D–Michigan) spoke in the Senate on June 21, 1979, and said:

"Mr. President, the direct election of the President and the Vice President of the United States is an electoral reform which is long overdue. It is long overdue because of its basic fairness, democratic nature, and its inherent simplicity. There is no principle which is more basic to our concept of democracy than equal treatment under the law. And yet when this Nation goes to the polls every 4 years in the only truly national election that we have, that principle is abrogated. The effect of the electoral college system on our Presidential election is often drastically unequally treatment of individual voters and their votes. The discrepancies are real and widespread, and they defy our basic sense of fairness....

"Mr. President, we ask the wrong question when we ask who gains and who loses under the electoral college, and how will this group lose its advantage under direct election? The function of the President is to serve the interests of all persons, all citizens of this country, and, therefore, all citizens should have an equal say as to who the President will be. In the debate over who will gain and who will lose, there is only one real winner in implementing direct election, and that is the American people who will finally be able to participate in a democratic and fair national election where **each vote counts for as much as every other vote.**

"The American people will also win because we have eliminated the threat which the electoral college has always posed—that is the possibility that a candidate who has not won the popular vote will, through the mechanisms of the

---

[27] *Congressional Record.* July 10, 1979. Page 17748.

electoral college, be elevated to the Presidency."²⁸ [Emphasis added]

In a Senate speech on July 10, 1979, Senator Charles McC. Mathias, Jr. (R–Maryland) listed the faults of the existing system, including the "state-by-state winner-take-all" system and the possibility of electing the second-place candidate, saying:

"Direct election is the most effective method to remedy these faults. As the late Senator Hubert Humphrey noted, only direct election insures that

'the votes of the American people wherever cast [are] counted directly and equally in determining who shall be President of the United States.'

"Only by direct election can the fundamental principle of equal treatment under the law for all Americans be incorporated into our Presidential selection process."²⁹ [Emphasis added]

After discussing the ever-present possibility that the presidential candidate receiving the most popular votes nationwide might not win the Presidency, Senator David Durenberger (R-Minnesota) said:

"[T]he most damaging effect of the electoral system has already occurred, in **every** State and in **every** Presidential election. For with its 'winner take all' requirement, the electoral college effectively disenfranchises every man and woman supporting the candidate who fails to carry their State. Under that system, votes for the losing candidate have no significance whatsoever in the overall outcome of the election. And for this reason, candidates who either pull far ahead or fall far behind in a State have the incentive to 'write it off'— simply ignore it—in planning their campaign appearances. In contrast, **the proposed amendment would grant every vote the same degree of significance in determining the final outcome.** Candidates would be forced to consider their margins in every State, and the tendency to ignore a 'safe' or

---

²⁸ *Congressional Record.* June 21, 1979. Page 15095.
²⁹ *Congressional Record.* July 10, 1979. Page 17751.

'lost' State would be sharply diminished. By restoring the significance of every vote, Senate Joint Resolution 28 increases the incentive to vote, which in itself is a significant argument for passage."

"Had the Founding Fathers adopted a direct election system, it is inconceivable that anyone would be rising after 200 years to propose replacing that system with the electoral college."[30] [Emphasis added]

On July 20, 1979, 51 senators voted in favor of Senate Joint Resolution 28 (with one additional senator being announced in favor).

Appendix W contains the March 14, 1979, speech of Senator Birch Bayh on his proposed constitutional amendment.

In subsequent years, numerous other proposed federal constitutional amendments for nationwide popular election of the President have been introduced. For example, Senator J. James Exon of Nebraska introduced a proposed federal constitutional amendment in 1992. The sponsors included the following Senators:

- Exon (D–Nebraska),
- Murkowski (R–Alaska),
- Burdick (D–North Dakota),
- Boren. (D–Oklahoma),
- Adams (D–Washington),
- D'Amato (R–New York),
- Kennedy (D–Massachusetts),
- Coats (R–Indiana),
- Reid (D–Nevada),
- Dixon (D–Illinois),
- Durenberger (R–Minnesota),
- Glenn (D–Ohio),
- Lieberman (D–Connecticut), and
- Hollings (D–South Carolina).

The Exon proposal (Senate Joint Resolution 302) reads as follows:

"Resolved by the Senate and House of Representatives of the United States of America in Congress assembled,

"That the following article is proposed as an amendment to the Constitution of the United States, which shall be valid to all intents and purposes as part of the Constitution when ratified by the legislatures of three-fourths of the several States within seven years from the date of its submission by the Congress:

---

[30] *Congressional Record.* July 10, 1979. Pages 17706–17707.

'Article—

'**SECTION 1.** The people of the several States and the District constituting the seat of government of the United States shall elect the President and Vice President. Each elector shall cast a single vote for two persons who shall have consented to the joining of their names as candidates for the offices of President and Vice President.

'**SECTION 2.** The electors of President and Vice President in each State shall have the qualifications requisite for electors of the most numerous branch of the State legislature, except that for the electors of President and Vice President, any State may prescribe by law less restrictive residence qualifications and for electors of President and Vice President the Congress may by law establish uniform residence qualification.

'**SECTION 3.** The persons joined as candidates for President and Vice President having the greatest number of votes shall be elected President and Vice President, if such number be at least 50 per centum of the whole number of votes cast and such number be derived from a majority of the number of votes cast in each State comprising at least one-third of the several States. If, after any such election, none of the persons joined as candidates for President and Vice President is elected pursuant to the preceding paragraph, a runoff election shall be held within sixty days in which the choice of President and Vice President shall be made from the two pairs of persons joined as candidates for President and Vice President receiving the greatest number of votes in such runoff election shall be elected President and Vice President.

'**SECTION 4.** The times, places, and manner of holding such elections and entitlement to inclusion on the ballot shall be prescribed by law in each State; but the Congress may by law make or alter such regulations.

The days for such elections shall be determined by Congress and shall be uniform throughout the United States. The Congress shall prescribe by law the times, places, and manner in which the results of such elections shall be ascertained and declared. No such election, other than a runoff election, shall be held later than the first Tuesday after the first Monday in November, and the results thereof shall be declared no later than thirty days after the date on which the election occurs.

'**SECTION 5.** The Congress may by law provide for the case of the death, inability, or withdrawal of any candidate for President or Vice President before a President and Vice President have been elected, and for the case of the death of either the President-elect or the Vice President-elect.

'**SECTION 6.** Sections 1 through 4 of this article shall take effect two years after ratification of this article.

'**SECTION 7.** The Congress shall have power to enforce this article by appropriate legislation.' "

In 2005, Representatives Jesse Jackson Jr. (D–Illinois) and Barney Frank (D–Massachusetts) introduced a federal constitutional amendment for nationwide popular election of the President (House Joint Resolution 36). Like the Exon proposal of 1992, this proposal would have required that a candidate receive "a majority of the votes cast" in order to be elected.

In addition, Senator Dianne Feinstein (D–California) introduced Senate Joint Resolution 11 in March 2005 as follows:

"Resolved by the Senate and House of Representatives of the United States of America in Congress assembled (two-thirds of each House concurring therein),

That the following article is proposed as an amendment to the Constitution of the United States, which shall be valid to all intents and purposes as part of the Constitution when ratified by the legislatures of three-fourths of the several States within seven years after the date of its submission to the States for ratification:

'Article—

'**SECTION 1.** The President and Vice President shall be elected by the people of the several States and the district constituting the seat of government of the United States. The persons having the greatest number of votes for President and Vice President shall be elected.

'**SECTION 2.** The voters in each State shall have the qualifications requisite for electors of Representatives in Congress from that State, except that the legislature of any State may prescribe less restrictive qualifications with respect to residence and Congress may establish uniform residence and age qualifications. Congress may establish qualifications for voters in the district constituting the seat of government of the United States.

'**SECTION 3.** Congress may determine the time, place, and manner of holding the election, and the entitlement to inclusion on the ballot. Congress shall prescribe by law the time, place, and manner in which the results of the election shall be ascertained and declared.

'**SECTION 4.** Each voter shall cast a single vote jointly applicable to President and Vice President in any such election. Names of candidates shall not be joined unless both candidates have consented thereto, and no candidate shall consent to being joined with more than one other person.

'**SECTION 5.** Congress may by law provide for the case of the death of any candidate for President or Vice President before the day on which the President-elect or the Vice President-elect has been chosen, and for the case of a tie in any such election.

'**SECTION 6.** This article shall take effect one year after the twenty-first day of January following ratification.' "

The Exon proposal of 1992 provided that a run-off election would be held if no presidential slate were to receive at least 50% of the popular vote. In contrast, the constitutional amendment introduced by Senator

Feinstein in 2005 (Senate Joint Resolution 11) required only a plurality of the popular votes.

> "The persons having the greatest number of votes for President and Vice President shall be elected."

The 2005 Feinstein proposal also differed from the 1992 Exon proposal in that the Feinstein proposal provided that

> "Congress may determine the time, place, and manner of holding the election, and the entitlement to inclusion on the ballot ..."

The Exon proposal provided that

> "The times, places, and manner of holding such elections and entitlement to inclusion on the ballot shall be prescribed by law in each State; but the Congress may by law make or alter such regulations."

Appendix S shows, state by state, members of Congress who have sponsored proposed constitutional amendments for nationwide popular election of the President in recent years or who voted in favor of constitutional amendments in the 1969 roll call in the House of Representatives or the 1979 roll call in the Senate. As shown in appendix S, there has been at least one supporter in Congress from each of the 50 states.

In summary, in terms of the three criteria mentioned at the beginning of this chapter, nationwide popular voting for President would

- accurately reflect the nationwide popular vote,
- make every area of the country competitive, and
- make every vote equal.

4 | Two Previously Proposed Approaches for State-Level Action

Chapter 3 analyzed the three most discussed proposals for federal constitutional amendments for changing the current system of electing the President and Vice President. This chapter examines the two most prominent approaches to presidential election reform that can be unilaterally enacted at the state level (i.e., without a federal constitutional amendment and without action by Congress). Later, chapter 6 will discuss this book's suggested approach for reform.

The office of presidential elector is established by the Constitution (as discussed in section 2.1), and therefore cannot be eliminated without a federal constitutional amendment. However, the manner of choosing the presidential electors is determined on a state-by-state basis by means of state legislation. As the U.S. Supreme Court stated in *McPherson v. Blacker* in 1892:[1]

> "In short, the appointment and mode of appointment of electors belong **exclusively** to the states under the constitution of the United States." (Emphasis added).

Two proposals for changing the current system of electing the President and Vice President that can be enacted at the state level have received attention in recent years. Neither approach involves abolition of the office of presidential elector or of the Electoral College (and hence neither requires a federal constitutional amendment). Both proposals can be enacted at the state level without any involvement of Congress. Both approaches involve dividing a state's electoral votes in a manner that is different from the statewide winner-take-all system that is currently used by all states except Maine and Nebraska. The two approaches are the:

- **Whole-Number Proportional Approach** in which a state's electoral votes are divided proportionally—*rounded*

---

[1] *McPherson v Blacker.* 146 U.S. 1 at 35. 1892.

off to the nearest whole number—according to the percentage of votes received in the state by each presidential slate (section 4.1); and

- **Congressional-District Approach** in which one presidential elector is elected from each congressional district and two presidential electors are elected statewide (section 4.2).

4.1 WHOLE-NUMBER PROPORTIONAL APPROACH

The whole-number proportional approach was considered by Colorado voters in the November 2, 2004, election. The proposition, called Amendment 36, was placed on the ballot by initiative petition. It was defeated by the voters.

The *whole-number* proportional approach is distinctly different from the *fractional* proportional approach (discussed in section 3.1). The two approaches differ in that the whole-number proportional approach divides a state's electoral votes *to the nearest whole number*, whereas the fractional proportional approach carries out the division of a state's electoral votes *to three decimal places*. As will be seen below, the whole-number proportional approach operates in a highly counter-intuitive way because of this seemingly minor difference.

The voting in Colorado in the 2004 presidential election can be used to illustrate the difference between the two approaches. George W. Bush received 1,068,233 popular votes (52.6508712%), and John Kerry received 960,666 popular votes (47.3606128%) in Colorado. The state has nine electoral votes.

Under the fractional proportional approach, Bush would have received 4.739 electoral votes, and Kerry would have received 4.261 electoral votes. The fractional numbers from Colorado—4.739 and 4.261—would be added together with fractional numbers from all the other states (and the District of Columbia) in order to yield a nationwide grand total. It is possible for candidates to receive fractional numbers of electoral votes from each state because the fractional proportional approach would be implemented by a federal constitutional amendment that would abolish the office of presidential elector. Fractions (carried out to three decimal places) would be possible because the human electors (each casting one *indivisible* vote) would be eliminated under the fractional proportional approach.

As discussed in section 3.1, Senator Cannon's proposed federal constitutional amendment implementing the fractional proportional approach would definitely increase the competitiveness of presidential elections. Additional popular votes would matter in every state. A presidential candidate could, for example, earn an additional 0.001 electoral vote by winning an additional hundred or so popular votes in any state. Thus, no state would be written off by any presidential candidate. All states would be battleground states.

In contrast, the whole-number proportional approach (i.e., Colorado's Amendment 36) was proposed as a *state* constitutional amendment—not as a *federal* constitutional amendment. A state may not abolish the office of presidential elector or the Electoral College—it may simply choose the method by which it allocates its own electoral votes within the Electoral College. Any approach adopted unilaterally in Colorado must necessarily award 0, 1, 2, 3, 4, 5, 6, 7, 8, or 9 presidential electors to each presidential slate. Only whole numbers—not fractions— are allowed because Colorado must choose nine human presidential electors, each casting one *indivisible* vote in the Electoral College. Based on the fact that Bush received 52.6508712% of the popular vote in the November 2004 voting in Colorado, he would have received five of Colorado's nine electoral votes, and Kerry would have received four under the whole-number proportional approach. In other words, the whole-number proportional approach would have produced a 5–4 division of Colorado's electoral votes, compared to the 9–0 division produced by the current statewide winner-take-all rule.

The problem with the whole-number proportional approach stems from the fact that there are only 538 electoral votes in the Electoral College (i.e., one for each U.S. Representative and Senator). The average number of electoral votes per state is, therefore, about 11. As it happens, about three-quarters (36) of the states have a below-average number of electoral votes. The important difference between *whole numbers* and *fractions carried out to three decimal places* arises because the number of electoral votes possessed by a typical state is so small. For example, in an average-sized state with 11 electoral votes, one electoral vote corresponds to a 9.09% share of the state's popular vote under the whole-number proportional approach. In Colorado (a slightly below-average sized state), one electoral vote corresponds to an 11.11% share of the popular vote. In states with only three electoral votes, one electoral vote corresponds to a 33.3% share of the popular vote. Except for occasional landslides (e.g., Reagan's 60% in 1984, Nixon's 61% in 1972, and Johnson's 61% in 1964), most elections are decided by only a few percentage points. A system that requires a 33% share, an 11% share, or a 9% share of the popular vote in order to win one electoral vote is fundamentally out of sync with the small-percentage vote shifts that are encountered in non-landslide elections.

As will be shown in the detailed analysis below, if the whole-number proportional approach were adopted nationwide,

* it would not accurately reflect the nationwide popular vote; and
* it would not make every state competitive but, instead, would simply create a small new group of battleground states in presidential elections.

In fact, if the whole-number proportional approach were adopted nationwide,

* it would amount to a "winner-take-one" system in all states except California—that is, the presidential election would revolve around winning a single electoral vote, here and there, from a small group of battleground states; and
* it would retain the political importance of carrying a state only if the state happens to have an odd number of electoral votes, while eliminating that importance if the state happens to have an even number of electoral votes.

Of course, almost any electoral system will yield a reasonable outcome in a landslide election. The test of an electoral system is how it works in a close election. Therefore, our analysis here starts with data from a close recent presidential election (i.e., 2000).

Column 2 of table 4.1 shows the number of electoral votes possessed by each of the 50 states and the District of Columbia in the 2000 presidential election. The table is sorted in order of electoral votes, with the smallest states listed first. Columns 3 and 4 show the respective percentage of the two-party popular vote received by Al Gore and George W. Bush. Columns 5 and 6 show the number of electoral votes received respectively by Al Gore and George W. Bush under the existing statewide winner-take-all system.[2]

---

[2] Maine and Nebraska use the congressional-district approach for allocating their electoral votes. However, since the adoption of this system (1969 for Maine and 1992 for Nebraska), the candidate carrying the state has always also carried all the congressional districts.

Table 4.1 RESULTS OF 2000 PRESIDENTIAL ELECTION

STATE	ELECTORAL VOTES	GORE POPULAR VOTE	BUSH POPULAR VOTE	GORE ELECTORAL VOTES	BUSH ELECTORAL VOTES
Alaska	3	32%	68%		3
Delaware	3	57%	43%	3	
District of Columbia	3	90%	10%	3	
Montana	3	36%	64%		3
North Dakota	3	35%	65%		3
South Dakota	3	38%	62%		3
Vermont	3	55%	45%	3	
Wyoming	3	29%	71%		3
Hawaii	4	60%	40%	4	
Idaho	4	29%	71%		4
Maine	4	53%	47%	4	
Nevada	4	48%	52%		4
New Hampshire	4	49%	51%		4
Rhode Island	4	66%	34%	4	
Nebraska	5	35%	65%		5
New Mexico	5	50%	50%	5	
Utah	5	28%	72%		5
West Virginia	5	47%	53%		5
Arkansas	6	47%	53%		6
Kansas	6	39%	61%		6
Iowa	7	50%	50%	7	
Mississippi	7	41%	59%		7
Oregon	7	50%	50%	7	
Arizona	8	47%	53%		8
Colorado	8	46%	54%		8
Connecticut	8	59%	41%	8	
Kentucky	8	42%	58%		8
Oklahoma	8	39%	61%		8
South Carolina	8	42%	58%		8
Alabama	9	42%	58%		9
Louisiana	9	46%	54%		9
Maryland	10	58%	42%	10	
Minnesota	10	51%	49%	10	
Missouri	11	48%	52%		11
Tennessee	11	48%	52%		11
Washington	11	53%	47%	11	
Wisconsin	11	50%	50%	11	
Indiana	12	42%	58%		12
Massachusetts	12	65%	35%	12	

Table 4.1 RESULTS OF 2000 PRESIDENTIAL ELECTION (cont.)

STATE	ELECTORAL VOTES	GORE POPULAR VOTE	BUSH POPULAR VOTE	GORE ELECTORAL VOTES	BUSH ELECTORAL VOTES
Georgia	13	44%	56%		13
Virginia	13	46%	54%		13
North Carolina	14	44%	56%		14
New Jersey	15	58%	42%	15	
Michigan	18	53%	47%	18	
Ohio	21	48%	52%		21
Illinois	22	56%	44%	22	
Pennsylvania	23	52%	48%	23	
Florida	25	50%	50%		25
Texas	32	39%	61%		32
New York	33	63%	37%	33	
California	54	56%	44%	54	
Total	**538**			**267**	**271**

4.1.1 JURISDICTIONS WITH THREE ELECTORAL VOTES

There were eight jurisdictions with three electoral votes in the 2000 presidential election—Alaska, Delaware, the District of Columbia, Montana, North Dakota, South Dakota, Vermont, and Wyoming (as shown in the top eight rows of table 4.1).

Under the whole-number proportional approach, one electoral vote corresponds to a 33.3% share of the state's popular vote for the states with three electoral votes.

To implement the whole-number proportional approach, the number of popular votes that each presidential slate received statewide is divided by the total number of votes cast statewide in order to obtain that slate's percentage of the statewide popular vote. This percentage is then multiplied by the state's number of electoral votes. The number of electoral votes received by each presidential slate is then rounded off to the nearest whole number.

There are four possibilities in states with three electoral votes:[3]

    • If a presidential slate receives less than 16.66% of the popular

---

[3] If there are more than two presidential slates on the ballot in a state with three electoral votes and no minor-party slate receives at least 16.66% of the popular vote in the state, it may be necessary to repeat the calculation without the minor parties in order to allocate all of the state's electoral votes.

vote (that is, less than one half of the 33.3% share necessary to win one electoral vote), then it gets no electoral votes.

- If a presidential slate receives between 16.67% and 50.00% of the popular vote, then it gets one electoral vote.
- If a presidential slate receives between 50.01% and 83.33% of the popular vote, then it gets two electoral votes.
- Finally, at the high end of the scale, if a presidential slate receives more than 83.33% of the popular vote, then it gets all three of the state's electoral votes.

Table 4.2 summarizes the number of electoral votes (from zero to three) that a presidential slate receives for various ranges of percentages of the popular vote in the states with three electoral votes. Column 3 shows the *breakpoints* (i.e., 16.67%, 50.00%, and 83.33%) in the ranges of percentages of popular votes. These breakpoints are the spots, along the percentage scale, where the number of electoral votes changes. The breakpoints are the critical numbers that would dictate campaign strategy under the whole-number proportional approach.

Table 4.2 TABLE OF BREAKPOINTS FOR STATES WITH THREE ELECTORAL VOTES

PERCENT OF POPULAR VOTE	NUMBER OF ELECTORAL VOTES	BREAKPOINT
0.00% to 16.66%	0	16.67%
16.67% to 50.00%	1	50.00%
50.01% to 83.33%	2	83.33%
83.33% to 100.00%	3	NA

Figure 4.1 graphically presents the breakpoints (16.67%, 50.0%, and 83.33%) for states with three electoral votes. The horizontal line in the figure represents a presidential candidate's percentage share of the popular vote—from 0% to 100%. The vertical tick marks show the breakpoints (16.67%, 50.0%, and 83.33%) for states with three electoral votes. The small numbers (0, 1, 2, or 3) immediately under the horizontal line show the number of electoral votes that a candidate would receive by winning a particular share of the popular vote.

Figure 4.1 Scale showing the number of electoral votes that a candidate would receive under the whole-number proportional approach by winning a particular share of the popular vote in a state with three electoral votes

For example, a candidate receiving 58% of the popular vote would get two electoral votes under the whole-number proportional approach.

Table 4.3 shows the consequences of the whole-number proportional approach in the eight jurisdictions with three electoral votes in the 2000 presidential election.

Table 4.3 2000 ELECTION UNDER THE WHOLE-NUMBER PROPORTIONAL APPROACH IN JURISDICTIONS WITH THREE ELECTORAL VOTES

STATE	GORE VOTE	GORE EV UNDER WTA	BUSH EV UNDER WTA	GORE EV UNDER WNP	BUSH EV UNDER WNP	BREAKPOINT JUST BELOW GORE VOTE	BREAKPOINT JUST ABOVE GORE VOTE	CHANGE NEEDED TO GAIN OR LOSE 1 ELECTORAL VOTE UNDER WNP
AK	32.06%	0	3	1	2	16.67%	50.00%	-15.39%
DE	56.74%	3	0	2	1	50.00%	83.33%	-6.74%
DC	90.49%	3	0	3	0	83.33%	100.00%	-7.16%
MT	36.34%	0	3	1	2	16.67%	50.00%	+13.66%
ND	35.27%	0	3	1	2	16.67%	50.00%	+14.18%
SD	38.39%	0	3	1	2	16.67%	50.00%	+11.61%
VT	55.44%	3	0	2	1	50.00%	83.33%	-5.44%
WY	29.02%	0	3	1	2	16.67%	50.00%	-12.35%
Total		**9**	**15**	**12**	**12**			

Column 2 of table 4.3 shows Al Gore's percentage share of the two-party presidential vote for the 2000 presidential election for the eight jurisdictions with three electoral votes.

Columns 3 and 4 present the respective number of electoral votes (abbreviated "EV" in the table) that Al Gore and George W. Bush received under the existing statewide winner-take-all system (abbreviated "WTA" in the table) in the 2000 presidential election.

Columns 5 and 6 show the respective number of electoral votes that Gore and Bush would have received if the whole-number proportional approach (abbreviated "WNP") had been in effect for the 2000 presidential election.

Column 7 of table 4.3 shows the breakpoint (taken from table 4.2) that is just below the percentage that Gore actually received in the 2000 presidential election.

Column 8 shows the breakpoint that is just above the percentage that Gore actually received in the 2000 presidential election.

Column 9 of table 4.3 shows the percentage change in popular votes that Gore would have needed to change his electoral vote count in the state. That is, column 9 shows the difference between the percentage of the vote that Gore actually received (column 2) and the *nearer* of the two breakpoints in columns 7 and 8. The percentage in column 9 is the most important number in understanding how the whole-number proportional approach would work in practice in a particular state. It shows whether it is likely for a candidate to gain or lose one electoral vote in the state. Unless this percentage is reasonably small, it will prove very difficult for a candidate to gain or lose one electoral vote in that state in a non-landslide election. In other words, unless this percentage is small, candidates will simply write the state off (just as they now write states off under the statewide winner-take-all system).

In column 9 of table 4.3, an entry with a positive sign, such as +11.61% for South Dakota, means that if Gore had received an additional 11.61% share of the popular vote (i.e., 11.61% added to the 38.39% share of the popular vote that he actually received in South Dakota), he would have gained one electoral vote under the whole-number proportional approach. The reason why Gore would have gained one electoral vote is that he would have risen above the breakpoint of 50.00%—the breakpoint between one and two electoral votes in a state with three electoral votes. Gore would have received one fewer electoral vote (i.e., no electoral votes) in South Dakota under the whole-number proportional approach if his share of the popular vote had dropped below 16.67% (the breakpoint between one and zero electoral votes). This would occur by losing a 21.72% share of the popular vote (i.e., 21.72% subtracted from the 38.39%). Column 9 contains an entry of "+11.61%" because the breakpoint at 50.00% is closer to Gore's actual popular vote (38.39%) than the break-point at 16.67%.

Figure 4.2 presents, along a horizontal line, Gore's percentage share (38.39%) of the two-party popular vote in South Dakota in the 2000

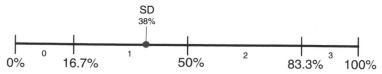

Figure 4.2 2000 presidential vote in South Dakota (with the Democrat receiving 38% of the popular vote)

presidential election. As in figure 4.1, the figure contains tick marks along the horizontal line representing the breakpoints of 16.67%, 50.00%, and 83.33% applicable to states with three electoral votes under the whole-number proportional approach. The small numbers (0, 1, 2, or 3) immediately under the horizontal line show the number of electoral votes that a candidate would receive under the whole-number proportional approach by winning a particular share of the popular vote. The figure shows that Gore's vote share in South Dakota was not close to the 16.67% or 50.00% breakpoints. Because Gore's vote share was so distant from these breakpoints, it is unlikely that a Democratic presidential candidate could gain or lose even a single electoral vote in South Dakota under the whole-number proportional approach in a non-landslide election. In terms of practical politics, figure 4.2 shows that South Dakota would be written off by both the Democrats and Republicans because there would be no realistic possibility that either party could win or lose an electoral vote under the whole-number proportional approach in that state.

An entry with a negative sign in column 9 of table 4.3, such as -7.16% for the District of Columbia, means that if Gore's share of the popular votes had been 7.16% less than he actually received in the District of Columbia (that is, 7.16% subtracted from the 90.49%), he would have lost one electoral vote under the whole-number proportional approach. The reason why Gore would have lost one electoral vote is that he would have fallen below the breakpoint of 83.33%—the boundary between two and three electoral votes in the District of Columbia.

Table 4.3 shows the division of electoral votes for the eight jurisdictions with three electoral votes in the 2000 presidential election. The division was 9–15 under the existing statewide winner-take-all system (columns 4 and 5) and would be 12–12 under the whole-number proportional approach (columns 6 and 7).

Overall, table 4.3 shows that the effect of the whole-number proportional approach for awarding electoral votes in the states with three electoral votes is generally to convert the existing statewide winner-take-all system (yielding either three or zero electoral votes to each presidential slate) into a "statewide winner-take-one" system. Indeed, the discussion below will establish, for states of all sizes, that the whole-number proportional approach is, as a practical matter, a "statewide winner-take-one" system (except that two electoral votes might occasionally be in play in California).

Under the existing statewide winner-take-all system, Gore carried three of the eight jurisdictions with three electoral votes and, therefore, received nine of the 24 available electoral votes (column 3 of table 4.3). George W. Bush carried five of the eight jurisdictions and, therefore, received 15 of the 24 (column 4). Under the whole-number proportional approach, the 24 electoral votes available in these eight jurisdictions would have divided 12–12 (columns 5 and 6).

None of the eight jurisdictions with three electoral votes is politically competitive under the existing statewide winner-take-all system. Accordingly, none received any significant attention from any presidential campaign in 2000. Under the whole-number proportional approach, all eight jurisdictions would remain politically irrelevant. The reason for their non-competitiveness can be seen from the percentages in column 9 of table 4.3, namely -15.39%, -6.74%, -7.16%, +13.66%, +14.18%, +11.61%, -5.44%, and -12.35%. These percentages (averaging 10.8%) are so large that it is unlikely that a presidential slate could gain or lose even a single electoral vote in a non-landslide election in any of these eight jurisdictions under the whole-number proportional approach.

Figure 4.3 summarizes the information in table 4.3. The figure presents, along a horizontal line, Gore's percentage share of the two-party popular vote in the 2000 presidential election for the eight jurisdictions with three electoral votes (obtained from column 2 of table 4.3). As in figure 4.1, the figure contains tick marks along the horizontal line at 16.67%, 50.00%, and 83.33% representing the breakpoints applicable to jurisdictions with three electoral votes under the whole-number proportional approach. The small numbers (0, 1, 2, or 3) immediately under the horizontal line show the number of electoral votes that a candidate would receive under the whole-number proportional approach by winning a particular share of the popular vote. Figure 4.3 shows graphically that Gore's share of the vote is not close to 50.00% in any of the eight jurisdictions. Thus, none of the eight is competitive under the existing statewide winner-take-all system. The figure also shows that Gore's vote

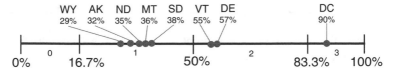

Figure 4.3 2000 presidential vote in jurisdictions with three electoral votes

share is not close to any of the three breakpoints (16.67%, 50.00%, and 83.33%).

4.1.2 STATES WITH FOUR ELECTORAL VOTES

There were six states with four electoral votes in the 2000 presidential election—Hawaii, Idaho, Maine, Nevada, New Hampshire, and Rhode Island.

For the states with four electoral votes, one electoral vote corresponds to a 25.0% share of the state's popular vote under the whole-number proportional approach.

Table 4.4 shows the number of electoral votes that a presidential slate would receive for various ranges of percentages of the popular vote in the states with four electoral votes. Column 3 shows the breakpoints that are applicable to states with four electoral votes.

Table 4.6 is constructed in the same manner as table 4.2. The general rule for constructing this table (and others in the section) is that if x is the number of electoral votes,

- $\frac{1}{2x}$ is the breakpoint between 0 and 1 electoral vote (0.1250 when x is 4);
- $\frac{1}{2x}+\frac{1}{x}$ is the breakpoint between 1 and 2 electoral votes (0.3750 when x is 4);
- $\frac{1}{2x}+\frac{2}{x}$ is the breakpoint between 2 and 3 electoral votes (0.6250 when x is 4); and
- $\frac{1}{2x}+\frac{3}{x}$ is the breakpoint between 3 and 4 electoral votes (0.8750 when x is 4).

Thus, the breakpoints are 12.50%, 37.50%, 62.50%, and 87.50% for states with four electoral votes.

Table 4.4 TABLE OF BREAKPOINTS FOR STATES WITH FOUR ELECTORAL VOTES

PERCENT OF POPULAR VOTE	NUMBER OF ELECTORAL VOTES	BREAKPOINT
0.00% to 12.50%	0	12.50%
12.51% to 37.50%	1	37.50%
37.51 to 62.50%	2	62.50%
62.51% to 87.50%	3	87.50%
87.51% to 100.00%	4	NA

In table 4.4, there is no breakpoint at 50.00% for the states with four electoral votes under the whole-number proportional approach. In fact, this observation is true for every state with an even number of electoral votes under the whole-number proportional approach. Thus, it no longer would matter which presidential slate carries a state with an even number of electoral votes. The winner of the state would get no particular reward for carrying a state. This characteristic contrasts with the situation in the states with an odd number of electoral votes (where carrying the state would still matter). In other words, the whole-number proportional approach operates in a manner that is politically different in states with an even number of electoral votes from the manner it does in states with an odd number of electoral votes.

Table 4.5 is constructed in the same manner of table 4.3 and shows the consequences of the whole-number proportional approach in the six states with four electoral votes in the 2000 presidential election.

Table 4.5 2000 ELECTION UNDER THE WHOLE-NUMBER PROPORTIONAL APPROACH IN STATES WITH FOUR ELECTORAL VOTES

STATE	GORE VOTE	GORE EV UNDER WTA	BUSH EV UNDER WTA	GORE EV UNDER WNP	BUSH EV UNDER WNP	BREAKPOINT JUST BELOW GORE VOTE	BREAKPOINT JUST ABOVE GORE VOTE	CHANGE NEEDED TO GAIN OR LOSE 1 ELECTORAL VOTE UNDER WNP
HI	59.83%	4	0	2	2	37.50%	62.50%	+2.67%
ID	29.15%	0	4	1	3	12.50%	37.50%	+8.35%
ME	52.75%	4	0	2	2	37.50%	62.50%	+9.75%
NV	48.14%	0	4	2	2	37.50%	62.50%	-10.64%
NH	49.33%	0	4	2	2	37.50%	62.50%	-11.83%
RI	65.65%	4	0	3	1	62.50%	87.50%	-3.15%
Total		**12**	**12**	**12**	**12**			

Table 4.5 shows the division of electoral votes for the six states with four electoral votes in the 2000 presidential election. The division was 12–12 under the existing statewide winner-take-all system (columns 4 and 5) and would remain at 12–12 under the whole-number proportional approach (columns 6 and 7).

Despite not affecting the overall 12–12 allocation of electoral votes between the presidential candidates, the whole-number proportional approach has a dramatic effect on the particular states within this group of states in terms of their competitiveness.

Figure 4.4 presents, along a horizontal line, Gore's percentage share of the popular vote in the 2000 presidential election for the six states with four electoral votes (from column 2 of table 4.5). The figure contains tick marks along the horizontal line at 12.50%, 37.50%, 62.50%, and 87.50% representing the breakpoints (from table 4.4) that are applicable to states with four electoral votes under the whole-number proportional approach. The small numbers between zero and four immediately under the horizontal line show the number of electoral votes that a candidate would receive under the whole-number proportional approach by winning a particular share of the popular vote.

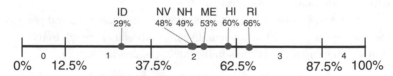

Figure 4.4 2000 presidential vote in states with four electoral votes

New Hampshire (where Gore received 49.33% of the popular vote) and Nevada (where Gore received 48.14%) were competitive under the existing statewide winner-take-all system. However, both New Hampshire and Nevada would become non-competitive under the whole-number proportional approach because there is no breakpoint at 50% for states with an even number of electoral votes. In states with four electoral votes, a candidate gets two electoral votes for receiving anywhere between 37.50% and 62.50% of the popular vote. The Democratic vote shares (49.33% and 48.14%) are almost in the middle of the band between 37.50% and 62.50%. Thus, in anything other than a landslide election, both the Democrats and Republicans would be virtually certain to win two electoral votes each in New Hampshire and Nevada. In New Hampshire, for example, it would take a downswing of 11.83% in the share of the Democratic vote (from 49.33%) for the Democratic candidate to lose one electoral vote. It would take an upswing of 13.19% by the Democrat to gain one electoral vote in New Hampshire. Neither is likely to happen in an ordinary election.

Similarly, Maine (where Gore received 52.75% of the popular vote) becomes distinctly non-competitive under the whole-number proportional approach because a presidential candidate gets two electoral votes for receiving anywhere between 37.50% and 62.50% of the popular vote. The Democratic vote in Maine (52.75%) is far from either 37.50% or 62.50%.

As will be seen in the sections below relating to other states with an even number of electoral votes, the whole-number proportional approach frequently converts current battleground states into non-competitive states.

On the other hand, Hawaii (which is non-competitive under the statewide winner-take-all system) becomes somewhat competitive under the whole-number proportional approach. In Hawaii, a change of +2.67% would result in a gain for the Democrats of one electoral vote.

Thus, the overall effect of the whole-number proportional approach in terms of competitiveness is to make New Hampshire, Nevada, and Maine non-competitive and to make Hawaii borderline competitive.

4.1.3 STATES WITH FIVE ELECTORAL VOTES

There were four states with five electoral votes in the 2000 presidential election—Nebraska, New Mexico, Utah, and West Virginia. For such states, one electoral vote corresponds to a 20% share of the state's popular vote under the whole-number proportional approach.

Table 4.6 shows the number of electoral votes that a presidential slate would receive for various ranges of percentages of the popular vote in the states with five electoral votes.

Table 4.6 TABLE OF BREAKPOINTS FOR STATES WITH FIVE ELECTORAL VOTES

PERCENT OF POPULAR VOTE	NUMBER OF ELECTORAL VOTES	BREAKPOINT
0.00% to 10.00%	0	10.00%
10.01 to 30.00%	1	30.00%
30.01% to 50.00%	2	50.00%
50.01% to 70.00%	3	70.00%
70.01% to 90.00%	4	90.00%
90.01% to 100.00%	5	NA

Table 4.7 shows the consequences of the whole-number proportional approach in the four states with five electoral votes in the 2000 presidential election.

Gore received five electoral votes in 2000 in the four states with five electoral votes but would have received eight under the whole-number proportional approach.

Figure 4.5 presents, along a horizontal line, Gore's percentage share (column 2 of table 4.7) of the popular vote in the 2000 presidential election for the four states with five electoral votes. The figure contains tick

Table 4.7 2000 ELECTION UNDER THE WHOLE-NUMBER PROPORTIONAL
APPROACH IN STATES WITH FIVE ELECTORAL VOTES

STATE	GORE VOTE	GORE EV UNDER WTA	BUSH EV UNDER WTA	GORE EV UNDER WNP	BUSH EV UNDER WNP	BREAKPOINT JUST BELOW GORE VOTE	BREAKPOINT JUST ABOVE GORE VOTE	CHANGE NEEDED TO GAIN OR LOSE 1 ELECTORAL VOTE UNDER WNP
HI	59.83%	4	0	2	2	37.50%	62.50%	+2.67%
NB	34.82%	0	5	2	3	30.00%	50.00%	-4.82%
NM	50.03%	5	0	3	2	50.00%	70.00%	-0.03%
UT	28.27%	0	5	1	4	10.00%	30.00%	+1.73%
WV	46.76%	0	5	2	3	30.00%	50.00%	+3.24%
Total		5	15	8	12			

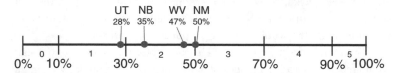

Figure 4.5 2000 presidential vote in states with five electoral votes

marks along the horizontal line at 10%, 30%, 50%, 70%, and 90% representing the breakpoints that are applicable to states with five electoral votes (from table 4.6). The small numbers from zero to five immediately under the horizontal line show the number of electoral votes that a candidate would receive under the whole-number proportional approach by winning a particular share of the popular vote.

As a general rule, states with an odd number of electoral votes always have a breakpoint at 50%. Thus, states that have an odd number of electoral votes and are competitive under the existing statewide winner-take-all system will remain competitive under the whole-number proportional approach. For instance, New Mexico is very competitive under the existing statewide winner-take-all system and would remain so under the whole-number proportional approach.

Utah is an example of a state that is non-competitive under the existing statewide winner-take-all system but that becomes competitive under the whole-number proportional approach. In a state with a lopsided partisan balance, the breakpoint at 30.00% can become politically important under the whole-number proportional approach. Specifically, Gore could have gone from one to two electoral votes by increasing his popular vote by 1.73% from 28.27% to 30.00%. This is an example of the phenomenon of a non-competitive state becoming a battleground state because of a breakpoint other than 50.00%.

4.1.4 STATES WITH SIX ELECTORAL VOTES

Arkansas and Kansas each had six electoral votes in the 2000 presidential election. For these states, one electoral vote corresponds to a 16.67% share of the state's popular vote under the whole-number proportional approach. Table 4.8 shows the number of electoral votes that a presidential slate would receive in states with six electoral votes for various ranges of percentages of the popular vote.

Table 4.8 TABLE OF BREAKPOINTS FOR STATES WITH SIX ELECTORAL VOTES

PERCENT OF POPULAR VOTE	NUMBER OF ELECTORAL VOTES	BREAKPOINT
0.00% to 8.33%	0	8.33%
8.34% to 25.00%	1	25.00%
25.01% to 41.66%	2	41.66%
41.67% to 58.33%	3	58.33%
58.34% to 75.00%	4	75.00%
75.00% to 91.677%	5	91.66%
91.67% to 100.00%	6	NA

Table 4.9 shows the consequences of the whole-number proportional approach in the two states with six electoral votes in the 2000 presidential election.

Table 4.9 2000 ELECTION UNDER THE WHOLE-NUMBER PROPORTIONAL APPROACH IN STATES WITH SIX ELECTORAL VOTES

STATE	GORE VOTE	GORE EV UNDER WTA	BUSH EV UNDER WTA	GORE EV UNDER WNP	BUSH EV UNDER WNP	BREAKPOINT JUST BELOW GORE VOTE	BREAKPOINT JUST ABOVE GORE VOTE	CHANGE NEEDED TO GAIN OR LOSE 1 ELECTORAL VOTE UNDER WNP
AR	47.20%	0	6	3	3	41.66%	58.33%	-5.54%
KS	39.08%	0	6	2	4	25.00%	41.66%	+2.58%
Total		0	12	5	7			

Gore received no electoral votes in 2000 in the two states with six electoral votes, but he would have received five under the whole-number proportional approach.

Figure 4.6 presents, along a horizontal line, Gore's percentage share of the popular vote in the 2000 presidential election for the two states with six electoral votes.

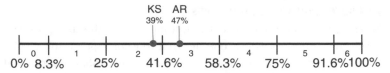

Figure 4.6 2000 presidential vote in states with six electoral votes

Arkansas is borderline competitive under the existing statewide win-ner-take-all system (requiring a change of 2.80% in the popular vote to switch its six electoral votes). The whole-number proportional approach would make Arkansas considerably less competitive because a change of 5.54% in the popular vote would be necessary to affect one electoral vote there. Meanwhile, Kansas (which is non-competitive under the existing statewide winner-take-all system) would become somewhat more com-petitive under the whole-number proportional approach.

4.1.5 STATES WITH SEVEN ELECTORAL VOTES

Iowa, Mississippi, and Oregon each had seven electoral votes in the 2000 presidential election. For states with seven electoral votes, one electoral vote corresponds to a 14.29% share of the state's popular vote under the whole-number proportional approach. Table 4.10 shows the number of electoral votes that a presidential slate would receive in states with seven electoral votes for various ranges of percentages of the popular vote.

Table 4.10 TABLE OF BREAKPOINTS FOR STATES WITH SEVEN ELECTORAL VOTES

PERCENT OF POPULAR VOTE	NUMBER OF ELECTORAL VOTES	BREAKPOINT
0.00% to 7.14%	0	7.14%
7.15% to 21.43%	1	21.43%
21.44% to 35.71%	2	35.71%
35.72% to 50.00 %	3	50.00%
50.01% to 64.28%	4	64.28%
64.29% to 78.57%	5	78.57%
78.58% to 92.86%	6	92.86%
92.87% to 100.00%	7	NA

Table 4.11 shows the consequences of the whole-number proportional approach in the three states with seven electoral votes.

Table 4.11 2000 ELECTION UNDER THE WHOLE-NUMBER PROPORTIONAL APPROACH IN STATES WITH SEVEN ELECTORAL VOTES

STATE	GORE VOTE	GORE EV UNDER WTA	BUSH EV UNDER WTA	GORE EV UNDER WNP	BUSH EV UNDER WNP	BREAKPOINT JUST BELOW GORE VOTE	BREAKPOINT JUST ABOVE GORE VOTE	CHANGE NEEDED TO GAIN OR LOSE 1 ELECTORAL VOTE UNDER WNP
IA	50.16%	7	0	4	3	50.00%	64.28%	-0.16%
MS	41.39%	0	7	3	4	35.71%	50.00%	-5.68%
OR	50.24%	7	0	4	3	50.00%	64.28%	-0.24%
Total		**14**	**7**	**11**	**10**			

Gore received 14 electoral votes in 2000 in the three states with seven electoral votes, but he would have received 11 under the whole-number proportional approach.

Figure 4.7 presents, along a horizontal line, Gore's percentage share of the popular vote in the 2000 presidential election for the two states with seven electoral votes.

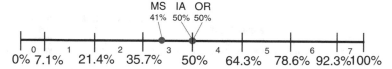

Figure 4.7 2000 presidential vote in states with seven electoral votes

Iowa and Oregon are competitive under the existing statewide winner-take-all system. They would remain so under the whole-number proportional approach because Gore's popular vote in those states was near the breakpoint of 50.00%. Mississippi, however, would have been noncompetitive under both systems.

4.1.6 STATES WITH EIGHT ELECTORAL VOTES

Arizona, Colorado, Connecticut, Kentucky, Oklahoma, and South Carolina each had eight electoral votes in the 2000 presidential election. For those states, one electoral vote corresponds to a 12.5% share of the state's popular vote under the whole-number proportional approach.

Table 4.12 shows the number of electoral votes that a presidential slate would receive in states with eight electoral votes for various ranges of percentages of popular votes.

Table 4.12 TABLE OF BREAKPOINTS FOR STATES WITH EIGHT ELECTORAL VOTES

PERCENT OF POPULAR VOTE	NUMBER OF ELECTORAL VOTES	BREAKPOINT
0.00% to 6.25%	0	6.25%
6.26% to 18.75%	1	18.75%
18.76% to 31.25%	2	31.25%
31.26% to 43.75%	3	43.75%
43.76% to 56.25%	4	56.25%
56.26% to 68,75%	5	68.75%
68.76% to 81.25%	6	81.25%
81.26% to 93.75%	7	93.75%
92.9% to 100.0%	8	NA

Table 4.13 shows the consequences of the whole-number proportional approach in the six states with eight electoral votes in the 2000 presidential election.

Table 4.13 2000 ELECTION UNDER THE WHOLE-NUMBER PROPORTIONAL APPROACH IN STATES WITH EIGHT ELECTORAL VOTES

STATE	GORE VOTE	GORE EV UNDER WTA	BUSH EV UNDER WTA	GORE EV UNDER WNP	BUSH EV UNDER WNP	BREAKPOINT JUST BELOW GORE VOTE	BREAKPOINT JUST ABOVE GORE VOTE	CHANGE NEEDED TO GAIN OR LOSE 1 ELECTORAL VOTE UNDER WNP
AZ	46.72%	0	8	4	4	43.75%	56.25%	-2.97%
CO	45.51%	0	8	4	4	43.75%	56.25%	-1.76%
CT	59.26%	8	0	5	3	56.25%	68.75%	-3.01%
KY	42.27%	0	8	3	5	31.25%	43.75%	+1.48%
OK	38.92%	0	8	3	5	31.25%	43.75%	+4.83%
SC	41.85%	0	8	3	5	31.25%	43.75%	+1.90%
Total		**8**	**40**	**22**	**26**			

Among these six states, Gore carried only Connecticut in 2000. His popular vote was in the 40% range in the other five states of this group. Gore, therefore, received only eight electoral votes out of the 48 available from these six states. He would have received 22 under the whole-number proportional approach.

Figure 4.8 presents, along a horizontal line, Gore's percentage share of the popular vote in the 2000 presidential election for the six states with eight electoral votes.

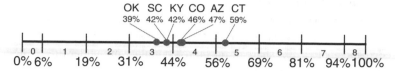

Figure 4.8 2000 presidential vote in states with eight electoral votes

Only Arizona was even border-line competitive under the existing statewide winner-take-all system in the six states with eight electoral votes. Colorado, Kentucky, and South Carolina become competitive under the whole-number proportional approach.

4.1.7 STATES WITH NINE ELECTORAL VOTES

Alabama and Louisiana each had nine electoral votes in the 2000 presidential election. For these states with nine electoral votes, one electoral vote corresponds to an 11.11% share of the state's popular vote under the whole-number proportional approach.

Table 4.14 shows the consequences of the whole-number proportional approach in these states. The relevant breakpoints for this table are at 38.88% (the boundary between three and four electoral votes) and 50.00% (the boundary between four and five electoral votes).

Table 4.14 2000 ELECTION UNDER THE WHOLE-NUMBER PROPORTIONAL APPROACH IN STATES WITH NINE ELECTORAL VOTES

STATE	GORE VOTE	GORE EV UNDER WTA	BUSH EV UNDER WTA	GORE EV UNDER WNP	BUSH EV UNDER WNP	BREAKPOINT JUST BELOW GORE VOTE	BREAKPOINT JUST ABOVE GORE VOTE	CHANGE NEEDED TO GAIN OR LOSE 1 ELECTORAL VOTE UNDER WNP
AL	42.39%	0	9	4	5	38.88%	50.00%	-3.51%
LA	46.06%	0	9	4	5	38.88%	50.00%	+3.94%
Total		**0**	**18**	**8**	**10**			

Figure 4.9 presents, along a horizontal line, Gore's percentage share of the popular vote in the 2000 presidential election for the two states with nine electoral votes.

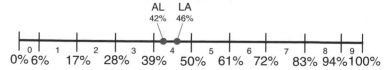

Figure 4.9 2000 presidential vote in states with nine electoral votes

4.1.8 STATES WITH 10 ELECTORAL VOTES

There were two states with 10 electoral votes in the 2000 presidential election—Maryland and Minnesota. For those states, one electoral vote corresponds to a 10% share of the state's popular vote under the whole-number proportional approach.

Table 4.15 shows the consequences of the whole-number proportional approach in these states. The relevant breakpoint for this table is at 55.00% (the boundary between five and six electoral votes).

Table 4.15 2000 ELECTION UNDER THE WHOLE-NUMBER PROPORTIONAL APPROACH IN STATES WITH 10 ELECTORAL VOTES

STATE	GORE VOTE	GORE EV UNDER WTA	BUSH EV UNDER WTA	GORE EV UNDER WNP	BUSH EV UNDER WNP	BREAKPOINT JUST BELOW GORE VOTE	BREAKPOINT JUST ABOVE GORE VOTE	CHANGE NEEDED TO GAIN OR LOSE 1 ELECTORAL VOTE UNDER WNP
MD	58.47%	10	0	6	4	55.00%	65.00%	-3.47%
MN	51.29%	10	0	5	5	45.00%	55.00%	+3.71%
Total		**20**	**0**	**11**	**9**			

Figure 4.10 presents, along a horizontal line, Gore's percentage share of the popular vote in the 2000 presidential election for the two states with 10 electoral votes.

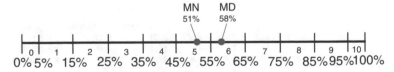

Figure 4.10 2000 presidential vote in states with 10 electoral votes

4.1.9 STATES WITH 11 ELECTORAL VOTES

There were four states with 11 electoral votes in the 2000 presidential election—Missouri, Tennessee, Washington, and Wisconsin. For states with 11 electoral votes, one electoral vote corresponds to a 9.09% share of the state's popular vote under the whole-number proportional approach.

Table 4.16 shows the consequences of the whole-number proportional approach in these states. The relevant breakpoint for this table is at 50.00% (the boundary between five and six electoral votes).

Table 4.16 2000 ELECTION UNDER THE WHOLE-NUMBER PROPORTIONAL APPROACH IN STATES WITH 11 ELECTORAL VOTES

STATE	GORE VOTE	GORE EV UNDER WTA	BUSH EV UNDER WTA	GORE EV UNDER WNP	BUSH EV UNDER WNP	BREAKPOINT JUST BELOW GORE VOTE	BREAKPOINT JUST ABOVE GORE VOTE	CHANGE NEEDED TO GAIN OR LOSE 1 ELECTORAL VOTE UNDER WNP
MO	48.29%	0	11	5	6	40.91%	50.00%	+1.71%
TN	48.04%	0	11	5	6	40.91%	50.00%	+1.96%
WA	52.94%	11	0	6	5	50.00%	59.09%	-2.94%
WI	50.12%	11	0	6	5	50.00%	59.09%	-0.12%
Total		22	22	22	22			

Figure 4.11 presents, along a horizontal line, Gore's percentage share of the popular vote (column 2 of table 4.16) in the 2000 presidential election for the four states with 11 electoral votes.

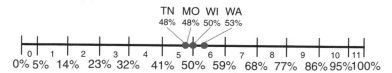

Figure 4.11 2000 presidential vote in states with 11 electoral votes

Because Gore's percentage was reasonably close to 50.00% in all four of the states with 11 electoral votes in the 2000 presidential election (table 4.16), the whole-number proportional approach makes no difference in terms of the degree of competitiveness for these particular states.

4.1.10 STATES WITH 12 ELECTORAL VOTES

Indiana and Massachusetts each had 12 electoral votes in the 2000 presidential election. For these two states, one electoral vote corresponds to an 8.33% share of the state's popular vote under the whole-number proportional approach.

Table 4.17 shows the consequences of the whole-number proportional approach in states with 12 electoral votes. The relevant breakpoints for this table are at 45.83% (the boundary between five and six electoral votes) and 62.50% (the boundary between seven and eight electoral votes).

Table 4.17 2000 ELECTION UNDER THE WHOLE-NUMBER PROPORTIONAL APPROACH IN STATES WITH 12 ELECTORAL VOTES

STATE	GORE VOTE	GORE EV UNDER WTA	BUSH EV UNDER WTA	GORE EV UNDER WNP	BUSH EV UNDER WNP	BREAKPOINT JUST BELOW GORE VOTE	BREAKPOINT JUST ABOVE GORE VOTE	CHANGE NEEDED TO GAIN OR LOSE 1 ELECTORAL VOTE UNDER WNP
IN	42.00%	0	12	6	6	37.50%	45.83%	+3.83%
MA	64.79%	12	0	7	5	62.50%	70.83%	-2.29%
Total		**12**	**12**	**13**	**11**			

Figure 4.12 presents, along a horizontal line, Gore's percentage share of the popular vote in the 2000 presidential election for the two states with 12 electoral votes.

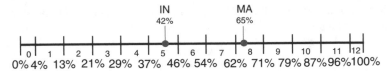

Figure 4.12 2000 presidential vote in states with 12 electoral votes

4.1.11 STATES WITH 13 ELECTORAL VOTES

There were two states with 13 electoral votes in the 2000 presidential election—Georgia and Virginia. For the states with 13 electoral votes, one electoral vote corresponds to a 7.69% share of the state's popular vote under the whole-number proportional approach.

Table 4.18 shows the consequences of the whole-number proportional approach in the states with 13 electoral votes. The relevant breakpoints for this table are at 42.31% (the boundary between five and six electoral votes) and 50.00% (the boundary between six and seven electoral votes).

Table 4.18 2000 ELECTION UNDER THE WHOLE-NUMBER PROPORTIONAL APPROACH IN STATES WITH 13 ELECTORAL VOTES

STATE	GORE VOTE	GORE EV UNDER WTA	BUSH EV UNDER WTA	GORE EV UNDER WNP	BUSH EV UNDER WNP	BREAKPOINT JUST BELOW GORE VOTE	BREAKPOINT JUST ABOVE GORE VOTE	CHANGE NEEDED TO GAIN OR LOSE 1 ELECTORAL VOTE UNDER WNP
GA	44.02%	0	13	6	7	42.31%	50.00%	-1.71%
VA	45.85%	0	13	6	7	42.31%	50.00%	-3.54%
Total		**0**	**26**	**12**	**14**			

Figure 4.13 presents, along a horizontal line, Gore's percentage share of the popular vote for the two states with 13 electoral votes in the 2000 presidential election.

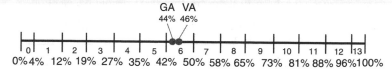

Figure 4.13 2000 presidential vote in states with 13 electoral votes

Under the whole-number proportional approach, Gore would have received 12 of the 26 electoral votes available from these two states (compared to none under the statewide winner-take-all system).

One of Georgia's electoral votes would have been contested under the whole-number proportional approach.

4.1.12 THE 10 STATES WITH 14 OR MORE ELECTORAL VOTES
The remaining 10 states (North Carolina, New Jersey, Michigan, Ohio, Illinois, Pennsylvania, Florida, Texas, New York, and California) each had a different number of electoral votes (between 14 and 54) in the 2000 presidential election.

Table 4.19 shows the percentage share of the popular vote that corresponds to one electoral vote under the whole-number proportional approach for the 10 states with 14 or more electoral votes in the 2000 election.

Table 4.19 SHARE OF THE POPULAR VOTE CORRESPONDING TO ONE ELECTORAL VOTE FOR THE 10 LARGEST STATES

STATE	ELECTORAL VOTE	SHARE OF POPULAR VOTE CORRESPONDING TO 1 ELECTORAL VOTE
North Carolina	14	7.1%
New Jersey	15	6.7%
Michigan	18	5.6%
Ohio	21	4.8%
Illinois	22	4.5%
Pennsylvania	23	4.4%
Florida	25	4.0%
Texas	32	3.1%
New York	33	3.0%
California	54	1.9%
Total	**254**	

The breakpoints for the 10 states with 14 to 54 electoral votes were different because each of these states had a different number of electoral votes. Table 4.20 shows the consequences of the whole-number proportional approach for these 10 states for the 2000 presidential election.

Table 4.20 2000 ELECTION UNDER THE WHOLE-NUMBER PROPORTIONAL APPROACH FOR THE 10 STATES WITH 14 OR MORE ELECTORAL VOTES

STATE	GORE VOTE	GORE EV UNDER WTA	BUSH EV UNDER WTA	GORE EV UNDER WNP	BUSH EV UNDER WNP	BREAKPOINT JUST BELOW GORE VOTE	BREAKPOINT JUST ABOVE GORE VOTE	CHANGE NEEDED TO GAIN OR LOSE 1 ELECTORAL VOTE UNDER WNP
NC	43.54%	0	14	6	8	39.28%	46.42%	+2.88%
NJ	58.21%	15	0	9	6	56.66%	63.33%	-1.55%
MI	52.63%	18	0	10	8	47.22%	52.78%	+0.15%
OH	48.18%	0	21	10	11	45.23%	50.00%	+1.82%
IL	56.18%	22	0	12	10	52.27%	56.82%	+0.18%
PA	52.15%	23	0	12	11	50.00%	54.35%	-2.15%
FL	49.99%	0	25	12	13	46.00%	50.00%	+0.01%
TX	39.04%	0	32	12	20	35.94%	39.06%	+0.02%
NY	63.09%	33	0	20	13	62.12%	65.15%	-0.97%
CA	56.20%	54	0	30	24	54.63%	56.48%	+0.28%
Total		**165**	**92**	**133**	**124**			

Figure 4.14 presents, along a horizontal line, Gore's percentage share of the popular vote in the 2000 presidential election in North Carolina (14 electoral votes). As can be seen, the Democrats were within 2.88% of the breakpoint (46.42%) between getting six and seven electoral votes in North Carolina and therefore could have gained one electoral vote in North Carolina under favorable circumstances. This opportunity is, however, not symmetrical. There would have been little likelihood of the Republicans being able to reduce Gore's share of the electoral vote from six to five.

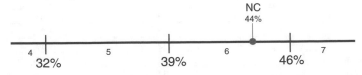

Figure 4.14 2000 presidential vote in North Carolina (14 electoral votes)

Figure 4.15 presents, along a horizontal line, Gore's percentage share of the popular vote in New Jersey (15 electoral votes) in the 2000 presidential election. As can be seen, the Democrats were within 1.55% of the breakpoint between getting nine and eight electoral votes. Thus, the Republicans could have gained one electoral vote in New Jersey under favorable circumstances. This opportunity to affect one electoral vote is not, however, symmetrical. There would have been little likelihood of the Democrats being able to increase their share of the electoral vote from nine to 10.

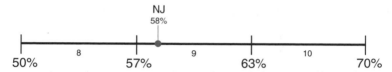

Figure 4.15 2000 presidential vote in New Jersey (15 electoral votes)

Figure 4.16 presents, along a horizontal line, Gore's percentage share of the popular vote in the 2000 presidential election in Michigan (18 electoral votes). The Democrats were within 0.15% of getting 11 (as compared to 10) electoral votes from Michigan. Neither party, however, has any realistic chance of gaining or losing as many as two electoral votes in Michigan in anything other than a landslide election.

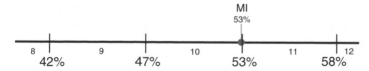

Figure 4.16 2000 presidential vote in Michigan (18 electoral votes)

Figure 4.17 presents, along a horizontal line, Gore's percentage share of the popular vote in the 2000 presidential election in Ohio (which had 21 electoral votes in 2000). The Democrats were within 1.82% of the breakpoint between getting 10 and 11 electoral votes in Ohio and could have gained one electoral vote in the state under favorable circumstances. There would have been little likelihood, however, of the Republican's decreasing the Democrat's share of the electoral vote in Ohio from 10 to nine.

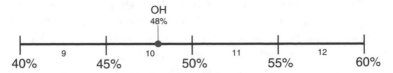

Figure 4.17 2000 presidential vote in Ohio (21 electoral votes)

Figure 4.18 presents, along a horizontal line, Gore's percentage share of the popular vote in the 2000 presidential election in Illinois (which had 22 electoral votes in 2000). The Democrats were within 0.18% of the breakpoint between getting 12 and 13 electoral votes in Illinois.

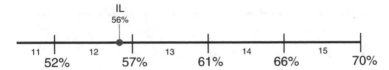

Figure 4.18 2000 presidential vote in Illinois (22 electoral votes)

Figure 4.19 presents, along a horizontal line, Gore's percentage share of the popular vote in the 2000 presidential election in Pennsylvania (23 electoral votes). The Democrats were within 2.15% of the nearest break-point, and the Republicans were within 2.20% of the nearest breakpoint. Thus, one electoral vote is potentially in play for both parties. Because both parties are more than 2% away from gaining or losing one electoral vote, it is entirely conceivable that Pennsylvania might be passed over in favor of states where less effort would be necessary to affect one electoral vote.

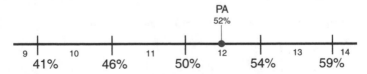

Figure 4.19 2000 presidential vote in Pennsylvania (23 electoral votes)

Figure 4.20 presents, along a horizontal line, Gore's percentage share of the popular vote in the 2000 presidential election in Florida (which had 25 electoral votes in 2000). The Democrats were within +0.01% of the breakpoint between getting 12 and 13 electoral votes in Florida.

Figure 4.20 2000 presidential vote in Florida (25 electoral votes)

Figure 4.21 presents, along a horizontal line, Gore's percentage share of the popular vote in the 2000 presidential election in Texas (32 electoral votes in 2000). The Democrats were within +0.02% of the breakpoint between getting 12 and 13 electoral votes in Texas.

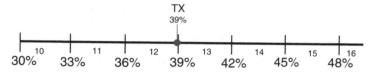

Figure 4.21 2000 presidential vote in Texas (32 electoral votes)

Figure 4.22 presents, along a horizontal line, Gore's percentage share of the popular vote in the 2000 presidential election in New York (which had 33 electoral votes in 2000). The Democrats were within 0.97% of the breakpoint between getting 20 and 19 electoral votes in New York. Thus, the Republicans could possibly have gained one electoral vote in the state under favorable circumstances. The opportunity is not, however, symmetrical. It is less likely that the Democrats would have been able to increase their share of the electoral vote from 20 to 21.

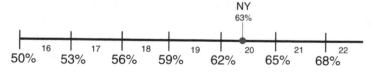

Figure 4.22 2000 presidential vote in New York (33 electoral votes)

Figure 4.23 presents, along a horizontal line, Gore's percentage share of the popular vote in California (which had 54 electoral votes in the 2000 presidential election). The Democrats were within 0.28% of getting 31 (as compared to 30) electoral votes from California. One electoral vote was in play in California for both parties. Moreover, two electoral votes might sometimes be in play in California because one electoral vote corresponds to a mere 1.85% share of the state's popular vote. For example, if the Democrats were to increase their share of the popular vote by 2.13% (0.28% plus 1.85%), they would pick up two electoral votes. That is, the whole-number proportional approach could operate as a "statewide winner-take-two" system for the Democrats in California. Note that this opportunity is not symmetric. A change of 3.43% in the popular vote would have been necessary for the Bush 2004 campaign to pick up two electoral votes in California.

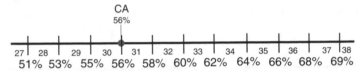

Figure 4.23 2000 presidential vote in California (54 electoral votes)

In summary, table 4.20 shows that all of the 10 most populous states are competitive to some degree under the whole-number proportional approach.

In particular, the six biggest states (North Carolina, New Jersey, Illinois, Texas, New York, and California) that are spectator states under the statewide winner-take-all system become battleground states under the whole-number proportional approach. The "battle" would only be for one electoral vote ("winner-take-one") in five of these six states. In California, the battle would sometimes be for two electoral votes ("winner-take-two").

Michigan, Ohio, Pennsylvania, and Florida are battleground states under the current statewide winner-take-all system. These four states would remain competitive under the whole-number proportional approach. However, the battle would not be for 18, 21, 23, or 25 electoral votes but, instead, for only one electoral vote in each state.

4.1.13 NATIONWIDE ANALYSIS OF THE WHOLE-NUMBER PROPORTIONAL APPROACH

This section addresses two questions. The first is whether the whole-number proportional approach would, if adopted by every state, more accurately reflect the nationwide popular vote than the existing statewide winner-take-all system. The second question is whether the whole-number proportional approach would, if adopted by every state, improve the competitiveness of presidential elections on a nationwide basis.

Table 4.21 combines the information from 12 of the foregoing tables in order to show the overall consequences of the whole-number proportional approach for all 50 states and the District of Columbia for the 2000 presidential election. Table 4.21 is sorted in descending order according to the percentage change (column 9) in popular votes that Gore would have needed to change his electoral vote count by one electoral vote in each jurisdiction.

Table 4.21 shows that, if the whole-number proportional approach had been in use throughout the country in the 2000 presidential election, it would not have awarded the most electoral votes to the candidate receiving the most popular votes nationwide. Instead, the result would have been a tie of 269–269 in the electoral vote, even though Al Gore led by 537,179 popular votes across the nation.[4] That is, the whole-number proportional approach would not have accurately reflected the nation-wide popular vote.

In order to analyze competitiveness, let us try to visualize how each political party might have approached the 2004 presidential election if all states had used the whole-number proportional approach.

The best starting point for planning a strategy in any election is the outcome of the previous election. Thus, under the whole-number proportional approach, the starting point for planning a strategy for the 2004 presidential election would have been the data in table 4.21 (showing both parties tied at 269 electoral votes). The central question for each party's campaign would have been focused on the way to win more than 269 electoral votes. Each party's campaign would have been aware that the whole-number proportional approach is predominantly a "statewide winner-take-one" system. Thus, the challenge to each party would be to

---

[4] If there had been a tie when the electoral votes for the 2000 presidential election were counted on January 6, 2001, the election for President would have been thrown into the House of Representatives (voting on a one-state-one-vote basis). Based on the party alignment of the newly elected House, George W. Bush would have been elected President. However, the newly elected Senate—responsible for electing the new Vice President—was equally divided after the 2000 elections. The U.S. Constitution is not entirely clear as to whether Vice President Gore (whose term of office ran until January 20, 2001) would have been entitled to vote to break the tie in the Senate in order to elect a new Vice President.

Table 4.21 2000 ELECTION UNDER THE WHOLE-NUMBER PROPORTIONAL APPROACH

STATE	GORE VOTE	GORE EV UNDER WTA	BUSH EV UNDER WTA	GORE EV UNDER WNP	BUSH EV UNDER WNP	BREAKPOINT JUST BELOW GORE VOTE	BREAKPOINT JUST ABOVE GORE VOTE	CHANGE NEEDED TO GAIN OR LOSE 1 ELECTORAL VOTE UNDER WNP
ND	35.27%	0	3	1	2	16.67%	50.00%	14.18%
MT	36.34%	0	3	1	2	16.67%	50.00%	13.66%
SD	38.39%	0	3	1	2	16.67%	50.00%	11.61%
ME	52.75%	4	0	2	2	37.50%	62.50%	9.75%
ID	29.15%	0	4	1	3	12.50%	37.50%	8.35%
OK	38.92%	0	8	3	5	31.25%	43.75%	4.83%
LA	46.06%	0	9	4	5	38.88%	50.00%	3.94%
IN	42.00%	0	12	6	6	37.50%	45.83%	3.83%
MN	51.29%	10	0	5	5	45.00%	55.00%	3.71%
WV	46.76%	0	5	2	3	30.00%	50.00%	3.24%
NC	43.54%	0	14	6	8	39.28%	46.42%	2.88%
HI	59.83%	4	0	2	2	37.50%	62.50%	2.67%
KS	39.08%	0	6	2	4	25.00%	41.66%	2.58%
TN	48.04%	0	11	5	6	40.91%	50.00%	1.96%
SC	41.85%	0	8	3	5	31.25%	43.75%	1.90%
OH	48.18%	0	21	10	11	45.23%	50.00%	1.82%
UT	28.27%	0	5	1	4	10.00%	30.00%	1.73%
MO	48.29%	0	11	5	6	40.91%	50.00%	1.71%
KY	42.27%	0	8	3	5	31.25%	43.75%	1.48%
CA	56.20%	54	0	30	24	54.63%	56.48%	0.28%
IL	56.18%	22	0	12	10	52.27%	56.82%	0.18%
MI	52.63%	18	0	10	8	47.22%	52.78%	0.15%
FL	49.99%	0	25	12	13	46.00%	50.00%	0.01%
TX	39.04%	0	32	12	20	35.94%	39.06%	-0.02%
NM	50.03%	5	0	3	2	50.00%	70.00%	-0.03%
WI	50.12%	11	0	6	5	50.00%	59.09%	-0.12%
IA	50.16%	7	0	4	3	50.00%	64.28%	-0.16%
OR	50.24%	7	0	4	3	50.00%	64.28%	-0.24%
NY	63.09%	33	0	20	13	62.12%	65.15%	-0.97%
NJ	58.21%	15	0	9	6	56.66%	63.33%	-1.55%
GA	44.02%	0	13	6	7	42.31%	50.00%	-1.71%
CO	45.51%	0	8	4	4	43.75%	56.25%	-1.76%
PA	52.15%	23	0	12	11	50.00%	54.35%	-2.15%
MA	64.79%	12	0	7	5	62.50%	70.83%	-2.29%
WA	52.94%	11	0	6	5	50.00%	59.09%	-2.94%

Table 4.21 2000 ELECTION UNDER THE WHOLE-NUMBER PROPORTIONAL APPROACH (cont.)

STATE	GORE VOTE	GORE EV UNDER WTA	BUSH EV UNDER WTA	GORE EV UNDER WNP	BUSH EV UNDER WNP	BREAKPOINT JUST BELOW GORE VOTE	BREAKPOINT JUST ABOVE GORE VOTE	CHANGE NEEDED TO GAIN OR LOSE 1 ELECTORAL VOTE UNDER WNP
AZ	46.72%	0	8	4	4	43.75%	56.25%	-2.97%
CT	59.26%	8	0	5	3	56.25%	68.75%	-3.01%
RI	65.65%	4	0	3	1	62.50%	87.50%	-3.15%
MD	58.47%	10	0	6	4	55.00%	65.00%	-3.47%
AL	42.39%	0	9	4	5	38.88%	50.00%	-3.51%
VA	45.85%	0	13	6	7	42.31%	50.00%	-3.54%
NB	34.82%	0	5	2	3	30.00%	50.00%	-4.82%
VT	55.44%	3	0	2	1	50.00%	83.33%	-5.44%
AR	47.20%	0	6	3	3	41.66%	58.33%	-5.54%
MS	41.39%	0	7	3	4	35.71%	50.00%	-5.68%
DE	56.74%	3	0	2	1	50.00%	83.33%	-6.74%
DC	90.49%	3	0	3	0	83.33%	100.00%	-7.16%
NV	48.14%	0	4	2	2	37.50%	62.50%	-10.64%
NH	49.33%	0	4	2	2	37.50%	62.50%	-11.83%
WY	29.02%	0	3	1	2	16.67%	50.00%	-12.35%
AK	32.06%	0	3	1	2	16.67%	50.00%	-15.39%
Total		**267**	**271**	**269**	**269**			

devise a strategy for accumulating additional electoral votes by targeting particular states.

Landslides take care of themselves. Thus, the planning process for a political campaign inevitably concentrates on what might happen if the upcoming election turns out to be close. Planners for the Bush 2004 campaign would have carefully considered what might happen if they were to improve their nationwide popular vote by various reasonably attainable percentages—1%, 2%, or 3%.

We *now* know that the Republicans increased their share of the two-party popular presidential vote by 1.98% (from 49.72% in 2000 to 51.71% in 2004). Hindsight of this sort is not, however, required for us to know that, at the beginning of the 2004 presidential campaign, it was imperative for each campaign to consider small percentage swings such as 1%, 2%, or 3%.

Referring to table 4.21, those involved in planning the Bush 2004 campaign would have immediately identified the nine battleground states where a gain of 2% or less in the popular vote could yield them one additional electoral vote under the whole-number proportional approach. These nine states (shown in table 4.22 and in figure 4.24) would have been the highest-priority "upside" battleground states for Bush in 2004.

Table 4.22 shows that the Bush 2004 campaign could have picked up nine electoral votes in the following way under the whole-number proportional approach:

- **Lowest-Hanging Fruit:** Pick up one electoral vote in Texas by reducing the Democratic share of the vote there by a mere 0.02% (from 39.04% to the breakpoint of 39.02%).

- **Easy Pickings:** Pick up one electoral vote in each of four states by reducing the Democratic share of the vote by 0.03% in New Mexico, 0.16% in Iowa, 0.12% in Wisconsin, and 0.24% in Oregon.

- **1% Neighborhood:** Pick up one electoral vote in New York by reducing the Democratic share of the vote by 0.97% (from 63.09% to the breakpoint of 62.12%).

- **2% Neighborhood:** Pick up one electoral vote by reducing the Democratic share of the vote by 1.55% in New Jersey, 1.71% in Georgia and 1.76% in Colorado.

Similarly, those involved in planning the Kerry 2004 campaign under the whole-number proportional approach would surely have considered the consequences of improving upon Gore's popular vote in 2000 by various attainable small percentages. Referring to table 4.21, planners for the Kerry 2004 campaign surely would have quickly identified the 10 battleground states where a gain of 2% or less could yield them one additional electoral vote. These 10 states (shown in table 4.23 and in figure 4.25) would have been the highest-priority "upside" battleground states for Kerry in 2004.

Table 4.23 shows that the Kerry 2004 campaign could have picked up 10 electoral votes in the following way under the whole-number proportional approach:

- **Lowest-Hanging Fruit:** Pick up one electoral vote in Florida by increasing the Democratic share of the vote in Florida by 0.01% (from 49.99% to the breakpoint of 50.00%).

- **Easy Pickings:** Pick up one electoral vote by increasing the Democratic share of the vote by 0.15% in Michigan, 0.18% in Illinois, and 0.28% in California.

Table 4.22 THE NINE "UPSIDE" BATTLEGROUND STATES FOR BUSH IN 2004 UNDER THE WHOLE-NUMBER PROPORTIONAL APPROACH

STATE	GORE VOTE	GORE EV UNDER WTA	BUSH EV UNDER WTA	GORE EV UNDER WNP	BUSH EV UNDER WNP	BREAKPOINT JUST BELOW GORE VOTE	BREAKPOINT JUST ABOVE GORE VOTE	CHANGE NEEDED TO GAIN OR LOSE 1 ELECTORAL VOTE UNDER WNP
TX	39.04%	0	32	12	20	35.94%	39.06%	-0.02%
NM	50.03%	5	0	3	2	50.00%	70.00%	-0.03%
WI	50.12%	11	0	6	5	50.00%	59.09%	-0.12%
IA	50.16%	7	0	4	3	50.00%	64.28%	-0.16%
OR	50.24%	7	0	4	3	50.00%	64.28%	-0.24%
NY	63.09%	33	0	20	13	62.12%	65.15%	-0.97%
NJ	58.21%	15	0	9	6	56.66%	63.33%	-1.55%
GA	44.02%	0	13	6	7	42.31%	50.00%	-1.71%
CO	45.51%	0	8	4	4	43.75%	56.25%	-1.76%
Total		**78**	**53**	**68**	**63**			

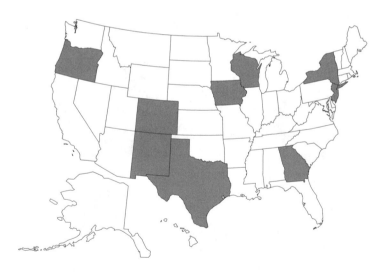

Figure 4.24 The nine "upside" battleground states for Bush in 2004 under the whole-number proportional approach

168 | *Chapter 4*

Table 4.23 THE 10 "UPSIDE" BATTLEGROUND STATES FOR KERRY IN 2004 UNDER THE WHOLE-NUMBER PROPORTIONAL APPROACH

STATE	GORE VOTE	GORE EV UNDER WTA	BUSH EV UNDER WTA	GORE EV UNDER WNP	BUSH EV UNDER WNP	BREAKPOINT JUST BELOW GORE VOTE	BREAKPOINT JUST ABOVE GORE VOTE	CHANGE NEEDED TO GAIN OR LOSE 1 ELECTORAL VOTE UNDER WNP
TN	48.04%	0	11	5	6	40.91%	50.00%	1.96%
SC	41.85%	0	8	3	5	31.25%	43.75%	1.90%
OH	48.18%	0	21	10	11	45.23%	50.00%	1.82%
UT	28.27%	0	5	1	4	10.00%	30.00%	1.73%
MO	48.29%	0	11	5	6	40.91%	50.00%	1.71%
KY	42.27%	0	8	3	5	31.25%	43.75%	1.48%
CA	56.20%	54	0	30	24	54.63%	56.48%	0.28%
IL	56.18%	22	0	12	10	52.27%	56.82%	0.18%
MI	52.63%	18	0	10	8	47.22%	52.78%	0.15%
FL	49.99%	0	25	12	13	46.00%	50.00%	0.01%
Total		**94**	**89**	**91**	**92**			

Figure 4.25 The 10 "upside" battleground states for Kerry in 2004 under the whole-number proportional approach

- **1% Neighborhood:** Pick up one electoral vote in Kentucky by increasing the Democratic share of the vote by 1.48% (from 42.27% to the breakpoint of 43.75%).
- **2% Neighborhood:** Pick up one electoral vote by increasing the Democratic share of the vote by 1.71% in Missouri, 1.73% in Utah, 1.82% in Ohio, 1.90% in South Carolina, and 1.96% in Tennessee.

Of course, the 10 "upside" states for the Kerry 2004 campaign would have been the same states where the Bush 2004 campaign would have had to play defense under the whole-number proportional approach. Conversely, the nine "upside" states for the Bush 2004 campaign are the states where Kerry would have been on the defensive.

Of course, those planning a campaign would have, in practice, added or deleted certain states from the above list of 19 battleground states for numerous reasons, including the following:

First, planners of both campaigns would have considered adding or deleting a state with various unusual local political factors, such as a noticeable shift in partisan alignment since the last election, significant demographic changes since the last election, the localized impact of a controversial existing or planned government policy, the effect of an unusually popular or unpopular state administration, the home states of the candidates, or other political considerations.

Second, those involved in planning the Bush 2004 campaign would have given some consideration to the three states where they could have picked up one electoral vote each by reducing the Democratic share of the popular vote by between 2% and 3% (e.g., 2.29% in Massachusetts, 2.94% in Washington, and 2.97% in Arizona). Similarly, planners for the Kerry 2004 campaign would have given some consideration to the four states where they could have picked up one electoral vote each by increasing the Democratic share of the popular vote by between 2% and 3% (e.g., 2.15% in Pennsylvania, 2.29% in Massachusetts, 2.94% in Washington, and 2.97% in Arizona). Both campaigns would have glanced briefly at states where they might conceivably pick up an electoral vote by increasing their popular vote by 4% or more.

Third, California is the one exception to the statement that, except in landslide elections, the whole-number proportional approach is a "winner-take-one" system. In California, one electoral vote corresponds to a

1.85% share of the state's popular vote. If, for example, the 2004 Kerry campaign could have increased the Democratic share of the vote by 2.13% (0.28% plus 1.85%), it would have picked up two electoral votes in California. It would have required a change of 3.43% in the popular vote for the Bush 2004 campaign to have gained two electoral votes in California. In states other than California, the share of popular vote corresponding to one electoral vote is considerably larger than 1.85%. For example, for the two next largest states (New York and Texas), the shares of the popular vote corresponding to one electoral vote were 3.0% and 3.1%, respectively. For the fourth largest state (Florida), the percentage was 4.0%. As mentioned earlier, 41 of the 51 jurisdictions that are entitled to appoint presidential electors had 13 or fewer electoral votes in 2000. The share of the popular vote corresponding to one electoral vote is 7.69% for states with 13 electoral votes. The share of the popular vote corresponding to one electoral vote is 33.33% for states with three electoral votes.

Notwithstanding the above caveats, the political reality is that campaign strategies in ordinary elections are based on trying to change a reasonably achievable small percentage of the votes—1%, 2%, or 3%. The bottom line is that the number of battleground states under the whole-number proportional approach would approximate the list of 19 states shown in tables 4.22 and 4.23. Something like 32 states would be non-competitive.

Table 4.24 presents the 19 battleground states in 2004 (based on a 2% swing) under the whole-number proportional approach. The states in this table are sorted in order of the absolute value of the percentage change that would have been needed in order to gain or lose one electoral vote under the whole-number proportional approach.

Figure 4.26 summarizes the information in table 4.24. The figure presents, along a horizontal line, Gore's percentage share of the popular vote in the 19 battleground states listed in table 4.24.

Several observations can be made by comparing the 19 battleground states under the whole-number proportional approach listed in table 4.24 with the 19 closest states in the 2000 presidential election (table 1.3) and the 16 closest states in the 2004 presidential election (table 1.4 and figure 1.1).

First, over half of the 19 battleground states under the whole-number proportional approach in table 4.24 are different from the actual battleground states of the 2004 election. The 19 battleground states under the

Table 4.24 THE 19 BATTLEGROUND STATES IN 2004 UNDER THE WHOLE-NUMBER PROPORTIONAL APPROACH

STATE	CHANGE NEEDED TO GAIN OR LOSE 1 ELECTORAL VOTE UNDER THE WHOLE-NUMBER PROPORTIONAL APPROACH
Florida	0.01%
Texas	-0.02%
New Mexico	-0.03%
Wisconsin	-0.12%
Michigan	0.15%
Iowa	-0.16%
Illinois	0.18%
Oregon	-0.24%
California	0.28%
New York	-0.97%
Kentucky	1.48%
New Jersey	-1.55%
Missouri	1.71%
Georgia	-1.71%
Utah	1.73%
Colorado	-1.76%
Ohio	1.82%
South Carolina	1.90%
Tennessee	1.96%

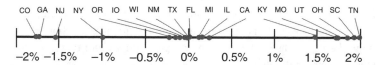

Figure 4.26 The 19 battleground states in 2004 under the whole-number proportional approach

whole-number proportional approach include states such as Texas, Illinois, California, New York, Kentucky, New Jersey, Georgia, Utah, South Carolina, and Tennessee. None of these 10 states was a battleground state in the actual 2004 presidential election. Five of these newcomers are among the nation's 10 largest states (i.e., states with 14 or more electoral votes). Kentucky, Georgia, Utah, South Carolina, and Tennessee are newcomers because of the accident of the numerical breakpoints.

Second, the biggest states are more likely to be battleground states under the whole-number proportional approach (subject to a caveat below concerning the difference between vote percentages and popular votes). The reason is that the share of the popular vote corresponding to one electoral vote is smaller for large states. Eight of the 10 states with 14 or more electoral votes are among the 19 battleground states under the whole-number proportional approach (table 4.24). Moreover, Pennsylvania and North Carolina would be included on the list of battleground states if the percentage window considered by a particular campaign were widened to 3%. In contrast, six of the nation's 10 largest states (California, Texas, New York, Illinois, New Jersey, and North Carolina) are decidedly non-competitive under the current statewide winner-take-all system.

Third, five states (Florida, New Mexico, Wisconsin, Iowa, and Oregon) are battleground states under both the existing statewide winner-take-all-system and the whole-number proportional approach. These states are on the list either because the major parties received close to 50% of the vote in those states in 2000 or because these states happen to have had an odd number of electoral votes in 2000 (and hence have a breakpoint at 50.00%). On the other hand, states with an even number of electoral votes that were battlegrounds under the existing statewide winner-take-all system, such as New Hampshire, would not be battlegrounds under the whole-number proportional approach because there is no breakpoint at 50.00%.

It is, of course, difficult to predict exactly how a new system, such as the whole-number proportional approach, would actually work in practice if all the states were to adopt it for a future presidential election. For one thing, the above discussion is based on *percentages* and therefore somewhat overstates the degree of competitiveness of the larger states under the whole-number proportional approach. Almost all of the 19 or so battleground states under the whole-number proportional approach offer a campaign the possibility of winning or losing only one electoral vote. Changing the statewide percentage of the popular vote in a large state is more costly (in terms of campaigning time, advertising, and organizational efforts) than generating the same percentage change in a small state. Thus, in practice, the largest of the 19 battleground states in table 4.24 might receive less attention because they would offer far less "bang for the buck" to the campaign managers who are responsible for prudently allocating limited resources. If we were to exclude the 10 largest states (i.e., the states with 14 or more electoral votes), the actual list of battleground states under the whole-number proportional approach might consist of the following 11 states (as shown in figure 4.27):

- New Mexico,
- Iowa,
- Wisconsin,
- Oregon,
- Kentucky,
- Missouri,
- Georgia,
- Utah,
- Colorado,
- South Carolina, and
- Tennessee.

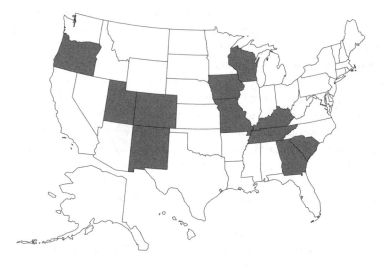

Figure 4.27 The 11 battleground states with greatest "bang for the buck" under the whole-number proportional approach

4.1.14 AMENDMENT 36 IN COLORADO IN 2004

The whole-number proportional approach was on the ballot in November 2, 2004, as a proposed amendment to the Colorado state constitution. It received 35% of the vote. There are three main reasons why the voters defeated Amendment 36 in 2004.

First, Amendment 36 was written so that it would take effect immediately and apply to the November 2004 presidential election. That is, the initiative would have applied to the very election in which the voters were deciding the initiative's fate. Many voters said that they would have approved the change for a subsequent election but that they were troubled by changing the rules of the game in the midst of a presidential campaign.

Second, Amendment 36's retroactivity provision interacted with the changing fortunes of the presidential candidates during the campaign. During the summer of 2004, Bush was expected to carry Colorado easily. Given that expectation, the political effect of Amendment 36 would have been to give four of Colorado's nine electoral votes in 2004 to the candidate who was expected to lose the state (Kerry). Part of the historical context of the 2004 presidential campaign was that Bush received only 271 votes in the Electoral College in 2000 (i.e., one more electoral vote than is necessary to win). In addition, it was widely (and correctly) predicted that the national vote in the Electoral College was likely to be very close in 2004. Therefore, Amendment 36 was perceived to have a strong possibility of affecting the outcome of the 2004 presidential election nationally. Indeed, Bush ultimately received only 16 more electoral votes than he needed in order to win in 2004. Thus, from the beginning, there was little Republican support for Amendment 36 because it was perceived to be a partisan issue. Bill Owens, Colorado's Republican Governor, made a decision to spend over a million dollars in opposition to Amendment 36. Then, as election day approached, some polls showed Kerry almost tied with Bush in Colorado. At that point, Democrats started believing that the measure could cost Kerry four electoral votes, and the proposition's remaining support evaporated.

Third, if Amendment 36 had been adopted, Colorado would have been the only state in the country dividing its electoral votes proportionally. Everyone agreed that the practical political effect of Amendment 36 would be to convert Colorado from a "winner-take-nine" state into a "winner-take-one" state. Many voters in Colorado felt that Colorado's influence would be greatly reduced if it were the only state in the nation to select its presidential electors proportionally. In his campaign against Amendment 36, Governor Owens argued that it did not make sense for just one state to adopt the whole-number proportional approach. The Governor's argument was, in essence, the same argument that Thomas Jefferson had made in his January 12, 1800, letter to James Monroe concerning the district system that had worked to Jefferson's disadvantage by dividing Virginia's electoral votes in the 1796 presidential election (quoted immediately below in the next section).

4.1.15 PRACTICAL POLITICAL IMPEDIMENT CONCERNING THE WHOLE-NUMBER PROPORTIONAL APPROACH

Whatever the merits of the whole-number proportional approach, there is a prohibitive practical impediment associated with the adoption of this approach on a piecemeal basis by individual states, namely the political disadvantage suffered by states that divide their electoral vote in a political environment in which other states do not divide their votes.

Thomas Jefferson summed up this objection in his January 12, 1800, letter to James Monroe arguing that Virginia should switch from its existing district system to the statewide winner-take-all system. As Jefferson wrote:

> "All agree that an election by districts would be best, if it could be general; but while 10. states chuse either by their legislatures or by a general ticket, **it is folly & worse than folly** for the other 6. not to do it."[5] (Emphasis added; spelling and punctuation as per original)

The now-prevailing statewide winner-take-all system became entrenched in the political landscape by the 1830s precisely because virtually all parties came to realize that any fragmentation of a state's electoral votes diminishes a state's political influence in comparison to states employing a statewide winner-take-all approach. Once even one state adopts the statewide winner-take-all approach, it is disadvantageous for any other state not to do so as well.

Suppose, for the purpose of argument, that 50 of the 51 jurisdictions entitled to appoint presidential electors decided to allocate their electoral votes using the whole-number proportional approach. Recall (from table 4.24) that there would be about 19 battleground states under the whole-number proportional approach where one electoral vote would be in play. If even one state with 19 or more electoral votes were to retain the statewide winner-take-all system, then that single state would immediately become the only state that would matter in presidential politics. Indeed, even a single state with 10 or 15 electoral votes would, as a practical matter, become the most important state in an environment in which

---

[5] The entire letter and citations appear in the text and footnotes of section 2.2.3 of this book.

all the other jurisdictions used the whole-number proportional approach. The same argument would apply *a fortiori* if 49, 48, 47, or 46 jurisdictions were to adopt the whole-number proportional approach.

Moreover, if states were to ever start adopting the whole-number proportional approach on a piecemeal basis, each additional state adopting the approach would increase the influence of the remaining states and thereby would decrease the remaining state's incentive to adopt it. Thus, a state-by-state process of adopting the whole-number proportional approach would quickly bring itself to a halt, leaving the states that adopted it without any influence in presidential elections.

Of course, the above impediment associated with piecemeal adoption by the states of the whole-number proportional approach would not apply if it were adopted on a uniform national basis in the form of a federal constitutional amendment. A federal constitutional amendment would, if ratified, take effect simultaneously in all 50 states and the District of Columbia.

4.2 CONGRESSIONAL-DISTRICT APPROACH

The congressional-district approach would retain the existing statewide winner-take-all approach for both of the state's senatorial electors; however, it would use a district-level winner-take-all rule for the state's remaining presidential electors.

Of the three approaches described in chapter 3 and the two approaches described in this chapter, the congressional-district approach is the only approach that has ever been used in the United States. In recent times, the district approach has been used in Maine since 1969 and in Nebraska since 1992. Maine has only two congressional districts, and Nebraska has only three. In the nine presidential elections in which the congressional-district approach has been used in Maine and in the four elections in which it has been used in Nebraska, the presidential candidate carrying the state has also carried all of the state's congressional districts. Thus, the congressional-district approach has had no practical effect in terms of affecting the ultimate disposition of electoral votes in either Maine or Nebraska.

In this section, we will analyze two questions. The first is whether the congressional-district approach, if adopted nationwide, would more accurately reflect the nationwide popular vote than the existing statewide winner-take-all system. The second is whether the approach, if adopted nationwide, would improve the competitiveness of presidential elections on a nationwide basis.

As will be seen in the analysis below, if the congressional-district approach were adopted nationwide,

- it would not accurately reflect the nationwide popular vote; and
- it would not make every state or district competitive, but, instead, would simply create a small group of battleground congressional districts and battleground states (with most districts and most states remaining non-competitive in presidential elections).

We again start our analysis with a close recent election (the 2000 election) because almost any electoral system will yield the desired outcome in a landslide.

In the 2000 presidential election:

- George W. Bush carried 228 of the 435 congressional districts, whereas Al Gore carried 207 districts.
- Bush carried 30 states (having 60 senatorial electors), whereas Gore carried 20 states (having 40 senatorial electors).
- Gore carried the District of Columbia, which has three electoral votes.

If the congressional-district approach were applied to the results of the 2000 presidential election, then Bush would have received 288 electoral votes (53.3% of the total number of electoral votes), and Gore would have received 250 electoral votes (46.5% of the total). That is, the congressional-district approach would have given Bush a 6.8% lead in electoral votes over Gore in 2000.

Gore received 50,992,335 popular votes (50.2% of the two-party popular vote), whereas Bush received 50,455,156 (49.7% of the two-party popular vote). Under the existing statewide winner-take-all system, Bush received 271 electoral votes in 2000 (50.4% of the total number of electoral votes)—a 0.8% lead in electoral votes over Gore.

In summary, the congressional-district approach would have been even less accurate than the existing statewide winner-take-all system in terms of mirroring the nationwide popular vote.

There are three reasons why the congressional-district approach would not accurately reflect the nationwide popular vote in presidential elections.

First, congressional districts are generally skewed in favor of the Republican Party because the Democratic vote is relatively more heavily concentrated in those geographic areas where Democrats are in the majority than is the case for the areas where Republicans are in the majority. This is one reason why Bush carried 228 of the 435 congressional districts, whereas Gore carried only 207 districts in 2000 despite the fact that Gore received 537,179 more popular votes nationwide than Bush.

The Republican geographical bias in congressional districts became more pronounced after the 2000 census. The congressional district boundaries that were in place at the time of the 2000 presidential election were, of course, the ones that were adopted in the early 1990s using data from the 1990 federal census. If the results of the 2000 presidential election are viewed from the perspective of the up-to-date congressional districts based on data from the 2000 federal census (i.e., those first used in the 2002 congressional elections), George W. Bush would have carried 241 (55%) of the 435 congressional districts.[6]

In the 2004 presidential election, George W. Bush carried 255 (59%) of the 435 congressional districts, whereas John Kerry carried 180.[7] Bush also carried 31 (61%) of the 51 jurisdictions entitled to appoint presidential electors. If the congressional-district approach had been in place nationwide for the 2004 presidential election, Bush would have won 317 (59%) of the 538 electoral votes in an election in which he received 51.5% of the two-party popular vote.

Second, the congressional-district approach retains the existing statewide winner-take-all approach for 100[8] of the 538 presidential electors (i.e., the two presidential electors to which each state is entitled regardless of its population). That is, the congressional-district approach overlays a "statewide winner-takes-two" system on top of a "district-wide winner-takes-one" system.

[6] Barone, Michael; Cohen, Michael; and Ujifusa, Grant. 2003. *The 2004 Almanac of American Politics*. Washington, DC: National Journal Group.

[7] America's choice in 2004: Votes by congressional district. *Cook Political Report*. 2005.

[8] This total would be 102 if one were to count the District of Columbia (which has three presidential electors) as a state. The District of Columbia, like the seven states with three electoral votes, employs the winner-take-all rule. The District does not have any representation in Congress.

The third, and most fundamental, reason why the congressional-district approach does not accurately reflect the nationwide popular vote is simply that it is a *district* system. At the end of the day, the congressional-district approach would merely replace one kind of district (the existing state boundaries) with another (the congressional district boundaries) for 435 of the 538 presidential electors. Whenever a single political office is filled by an electoral process in which the winner-take-all rule is applied to geographic areas that are smaller than the entire jurisdiction encompassed by the office, there will be significant differences in the political value of individual votes. The inequality arises because some geographic areas will be battlegrounds, whereas others will not. Inevitably, candidates will compete vigorously for votes in the closely divided areas, while ignoring the voters in non-competitive areas. In addition, there is always the possibility, in any district system, of electing a candidate who did not receive the most popular votes in the jurisdiction as a whole.

Turning now to competitiveness, table 4.25 lists the 55 congressional districts in which the difference between George W. Bush and Al Gore was 4% or less in the 2000 presidential election.[9] Column 2 shows Bush's percentage of the popular vote for President in the district, and column 3 shows Gore's percentage. Column 4 shows the difference.

Overall, table 4.25 shows that

- in 6.7% of the congressional districts (29 of 435), the difference in the presidential vote was 2% or less;
- in 10.8% of the congressional districts (47 of 435), the difference in the presidential vote was 3% or less; and
- in 12.6% of the congressional districts (55 of 435), the difference in the presidential vote was 4% or less.

In short, the vast majority of congressional districts are non-competitive in terms of a presidential election.[10]

One reason why the congressional-district approach is so much less competitive than the existing statewide winner-take-all approach is that congressional districts are gerrymandered in many states. Gerrymandering is most commonly done to give a partisan advantage to

---

[9] *The Cook Political Report.* April 10, 2001.

[10] Of course, the vast majority of congressional districts are also non-competitive in congressional elections.

Table 4.25 THE 55 CLOSEST CONGRESSIONAL DISTRICTS IN THE 2000 PRESIDENTIAL ELECTION

DISTRICT	BUSH	GORE	DIFFERENCE
California–22	49%	45%	4%
Florida–7	51%	47%	4%
Ohio–13	50%	46%	4%
Wisconsin–4	50%	46%	4%
Arizona–5	49%	46%	3%
California–11	50%	47%	3%
California–41	50%	47%	3%
New Hampshire–1	49%	46%	3%
Pennsylvania–4	50%	47%	3%
Pennsylvania–10	50%	47%	3%
Texas–10	46%	43%	3%
California–44	49%	47%	2%
Florida–8	50%	48%	2%
Iowa–4	50%	48%	2%
Minnesota–1	48%	46%	2%
Minnesota–6	48%	46%	2%
Oregon–5	48%	46%	2%
Arkansas–2	49%	48%	1%
Florida–2	49%	48%	1%
Iowa–3	49%	48%	1%
Pennsylvania–21	49%	48%	1%
Tennessee–8	50%	49%	1%
Washington–3	48%	47%	1%
Michigan–10	49%	49%	0%
California–22	49%	45%	4%
Michigan–11	49%	49%	0%
New York–24	48%	48%	0%
Texas–27	49%	49%	0%
Virginia–4	49%	49%	0%
California–23	47%	48%	-1%
New Hampshire–2	47%	48%	-1%
Wisconsin–7	47%	48%	-1%
California–20	48%	50%	-2%
California–28	47%	49%	-2%
New Mexico–1	47%	49%	-2%
Pennsylvania–15	47%	49%	-2%
Texas–25	48%	50%	-2%
Virginia–11	47%	49%	-2%
Washington–2	46%	48%	-2%
Washington–8	47%	49%	-2%

Table 4.25 THE 55 CLOSEST CONGRESSIONAL DISTRICTS IN THE 2000 PRESIDENTIAL ELECTION (cont.)

DISTRICT	BUSH	GORE	DIFFERENCE
Wisconsin–1	47%	49%	-2%
Arkansas–1	47%	50%	-3%
Arkansas–4	47%	50%	-3%
Florida–16	47%	50%	-3%
Michigan–8	47%	50%	-3%
North Carolina–4	48%	51%	-3%
Ohio–1	47%	50%	-3%
Ohio–3	47%	50%	-3%
Pennsylvania–7	47%	50%	-3%
Pennsylvania–8	47%	50%	-3%
Texas–24	48%	51%	-3%
Wisconsin–3	46%	49%	-3%
Florida–5	46%	50%	-4%
Ohio–19	46%	50%	-4%
Pennsylvania–20	47%	51%	-4%
West Virginia–3	47%	51%	-4%

one political party. It is sometimes done to protect congressional incumbents of both parties.

If the presidential election were based on congressional districts, then the incentive for politically motivated districting would be even greater than it is today.

Many current efforts to change the process of congressional districting require districts to be compact in shape and to adhere closely to existing city and county boundaries. Generally, geometrically compact districts that adhere closely to local government boundaries tend to yield non-competitive areas. In most cases, the only way to achieve competitiveness (in the context of the single-member districts) is to intentionally create irregularly shaped districts that make competitiveness the top priority (after population equality). Thus, to the extent that redistricting procedures are changed to favor compact districts adhering to local government boundaries, one can expect to see fewer (not more) competitive districts.

Table 4.26 shows that the congressional districts that are close in the presidential race are heavily concentrated in the 10 largest states. Specifically, 58% of the close congressional districts (32 of the 55) lie in eight of the 10 largest states. Thus, the congressional-district approach would not only focus presidential campaigns on a tiny fraction of the nation's congressional-districts, but it would also concentrate the presidential race on the 10 largest states to a degree that exceeds their share of the nation's population and that exceeds their prominence under the current winner-take-all system. Four of the eight large states in the table are currently competitive statewide in presidential elections (i.e., Pennsylvania, Florida, Ohio, and Michigan), whereas four are not (i.e., California, Texas, New York, and North Carolina).

Table 4.26 CONGRESSIONAL DISTRICTS IN THE 10 LARGEST STATES THAT ARE CLOSE IN THE PRESIDENTIAL ELECTION

STATE	NUMBER OF CONGRESSIONAL DISTRICTS THAT ARE CLOSE IN THE PRESIDENTIAL RACE
California	7
Pennsylvania	7
Florida	5
Ohio	4
Texas	4
Michigan	3
New York	1
North Carolina	1

Votes do not have equal weight under the congressional-district approach. In fact, there are four different inequalities inherent in the congressional-district approach, namely

- inequalities resulting from the fact that each state has two statewide (senatorial) presidential electors regardless of its population;
- inequalities stemming from the decennial apportionment of the membership of the House of Representatives among the states;
- inequalities caused by differences in voter turnout caused by the level of civic participation in the state or the state's rate of population growth; and
- inequalities caused by differences in voter turnout in particular congressional districts.

First, a vote cast in a large state for the two statewide (senatorial) presidential electors has less weight than a vote cast in a small state for its two statewide electors. For example, in the 2000 presidential election, Wyoming had two statewide presidential electors (with a 1990 population of 453,588), whereas California had two statewide presidential electors (with a 1990 population of 29,760,021). As shown in table 4.27 for the presidential elections of 1992, 1996, and 2000, each statewide presidential elector corresponded to 226,794 people in Wyoming but to 14,880,011 people in California. The last column of this table shows the ratio of California's population per electoral vote compared to that of Wyoming— a 65.6-to-1 variation.

Table 4.27 DIFFERENCE IN WEIGHT OF A VOTE CAST FOR THE TWO STATEWIDE PRESIDENTIAL ELECTORS UNDER THE CONGRESSIONAL-DISTRICT APPROACH

STATE	POPULATION	POPULATION CORRESPONDING TO EACH STATEWIDE PRESIDENTIAL ELECTOR	RATIO TO LOWEST
California	29,760,021	14,880,011	65.6
Wyoming	453,588	226,794	1.00

Second, a vote cast in certain states has less weight than a vote cast in certain other states because of inequalities in the apportionment of the membership of the House of Representatives among the several states. For example, in the 1990 census, Wyoming had a population of 453,588, and Montana had 799,065; however both states received one House seat. As shown in table 4.28, in the presidential elections of 1992, 1996, and 2000, each statewide presidential elector corresponded to 226,794 people in Wyoming but to 399,533 in Montana. The last column of this table shows the ratio of Montana's population per electoral vote to that of the lowest in the table (Wyoming)—a 1.76-to-1 variation.

Table 4.28 DIFFERENCE IN WEIGHT OF A VOTE CAST BECAUSE OF CONGRESSIONAL APPORTIONMENT UNDER THE CONGRESSIONAL-DISTRICT APPROACH

STATE	POPULATION	POPULATION CORRESPONDING TO EACH STATEWIDE PRESIDENTIAL ELECTOR	RATIO TO LOWEST
Montana	799,065	399,533	1.76
Wyoming	453,588	226,794	1.00

Numerous other such substantial variations could be cited between various pairs of states, including variations between states with differing numbers of electoral votes.

Third, among states with equal numbers of electoral votes, a vote cast in a state with a lower voter turnout has a greater weight than a vote cast in a state where more votes are cast. Voter turnout may be high in a particular state because of a high level of civic participation (e.g., Utah) or because the state is fast-growing (e.g., Nevada). See table 3.5.

Fourth, a vote cast in a congressional district where fewer total votes are cast has a greater weight than a vote cast in a congressional district where more total votes are cast. There are many congressional districts (typically those with lopsided majorities in favor of one party) where voter turnout is noticeably lower than that of other districts within the state.

Summarizing the above points, if the congressional-district approach were adopted nationwide,
- it would not more accurately reflect the nationwide popular vote than the existing statewide winner-take-all approach, and
- it would not produce greater competition.

4.2.1 PRACTICAL POLITICAL IMPEDIMENT CONCERNING THE CONGRESSIONAL-DISTRICT APPROACH

Whatever the merits of the congressional-district approach, there is a prohibitive practical impediment associated with the adoption of this approach on a piecemeal basis by individual states.

In his January 12, 1800, letter to James Monroe, Thomas Jefferson argued that Virginia should switch from its then-existing district system to the statewide winner-take-all system because of the political disadvantage suffered by states that divided their electoral votes by districts in a political environment in which other states use the winner-take-all approach:

> "All agree that an election by districts would be best, if it could be general; but while 10. states chuse either by their legislatures or by a general ticket, **it is folly & worse than folly** for the other 6. not to do it."[11] (Emphasis added; spelling and punctuation as per original)

---

[11] The entire letter and citations appear in the text and footnotes of section 2.2.3 of this book.

Indeed, the now-prevailing statewide winner-take-all system became entrenched in the political landscape in the 1830s precisely because dividing a state's electoral votes diminishes the state's political influence relative to states employing the statewide winner-take-all approach.

The Florida legislature considered adopting the congressional-district approach in the early 1990s. The proposal failed there largely because of concern that it would reduce the state's political importance in presidential elections. As it happened, George W. Bush carried 13 of Florida's 23 congressional districts in the 2000 presidential election, whereas Gore carried 10. If the congressional-district approach had been used in Florida in the 2000 presidential election (with the electoral system remaining unchanged in all other states), Gore would have been elected President because Bush would not have received all of Florida's 25 electoral votes.

The "folly" of individual states adopting the congressional-district approach on a *piecemeal* basis is shown by the listing of the 55 closest congressional districts in table 4.25. Suppose that 50 of the 51 jurisdictions entitled to appoint presidential electors were to allocate electoral votes by district but that California (with 55 electoral votes in the 2004 presidential election) did not. California would immediately become the only state that would matter in presidential politics. The same thing would happen if two or three medium-sized states were to retain the statewide winner-take-all system while the remaining states decided to employ the congressional-district approach. The congressional-district approach only makes sense if 100% of the states adopt it.

Moreover, if states started adopting the congressional-district approach on a piecemeal basis, each additional state adopting the approach would increase the influence of the remaining states and thereby would increase the disincentive for the remaining states to adopt it. Thus, a state-by-state process adopting the congressional-district approach would bring itself to a halt.

Of course, the above impediment associated with piecemeal adoption of the congressional-district approach would not apply if the system were adopted simultaneously on a nationwide basis as a federal constitutional amendment (such as Senator Mundt's proposed amendment described in section 3.2).

5 | Background on Interstate Compacts

An interstate compact is a contractual agreement between two or more states.

This chapter covers the

- constitutional basis for interstate compacts (section 5.1),
- legal standing of compacts (section 5.2),
- history of compacts (section 5.3),
- subjects covered by compacts (section 5.4),
- parties to compacts (section 5.5),
- formulation of compacts (section 5.6),
- methods by which a state enacts a compact (section 5.7),
- contingent nature of compacts (section 5.8),
- congressional consent and involvement in compacts (section 5.9),
- effect of congressional consent (section 5.10),
- compacts that are contingent on enactment of federal legislation at the time Congress grants its consent to the compact (section 5.11),
- compacts that do not require congressional consent (section 5.12),
- enforcement of compacts (section 5.13),
- amendments to compacts (section 5.14),
- duration, termination, and withdrawals from compacts (section 5.15),
- administration of compacts (section 5.16),
- style of compacts (section 5.17),
- comparison of treaties and interstate compacts (section 5.18),
- comparison of uniform state laws and interstate compacts (section 5.19),

187

- comparison of federal multi-state commissions and inter-state compacts (section 5.20),
- future of interstate compacts (section 5.21), and
- proposals for compacts on elections (section 5.22).

5.1 CONSTITUTIONAL BASIS FOR INTERSTATE COMPACTS

Interstate compacts predate the U.S. Constitution. The Articles of Confederation[1] provided:

> "No two or more States shall enter into any treaty, confeder-ation or alliance whatever between them, without the con-sent of the United States in Congress assembled, specifying accurately the purposes for which the same is to be entered into, and how long it shall continue."[2]

The Continental Congress consented to four interstate compacts under the Articles of Confederation. An interstate compact regulating fishing and navigation on the Chesapeake Bay and the Potomac River received congressional consent under the Articles of Confederation in 1785 and remained in force until 1958.

Article I, section 10, clause[3] of the U.S. Constitution provides:

> "No state shall, without the consent of Congress, ... enter into any agreement or compact with another state...."[4]

The terms "compact" and "agreement" are generally used inter-changeably. As the U.S. Supreme Court wrote in the 1893 case of *Virginia v. Tennessee*:

> "Compacts or agreements ... we do not perceive any difference in the meaning...."[5]

The Supreme Court also wrote:

> "The terms 'agreement' or 'compact,' taken by themselves, are sufficiently comprehensive to embrace all forms of

---

[1] The Articles of Confederation were proposed by the Continental Congress in 1777 and ratified by the states by 1781.

[2] Articles of Confederation. Article VI, clause 2.

[3] The U.S. Constitution was proposed by the Constitutional Convention in 1787 and ratified by the requisite number of states by 1789.

[4] See appendix C for full wording of the compacts clause.

[5] *Virginia v. Tennessee*. 148 U.S. 503 at 520. 1893.

stipulation, written or verbal, and relating to all kinds of subjects...."[6]

The terms "compact" and "agreement" encompass arrangements that are enacted by statutory law as well as those entered into by a state's executive officers and commissions.

5.2 LEGAL STANDING OF INTERSTATE COMPACTS

An interstate compact is, first and foremost, a contract. As the Supreme Court wrote in the 1959 case of *Petty v. Tennessee-Missouri Bridge Commission*:

> "[a] compact is, after all, a contract."[7]

As contracts, compacts enjoy strong protection from the U.S. Constitution. Article I, section 10, clause 1 of the Constitution provides:

> "No State shall ... pass any ... Law impairing the Obligation of Contracts...."[8]

The Council of State Governments summarizes the nature of interstate compacts as follows:

> "Compacts are agreements between two or more states that bind them to the compacts' provisions, just as a contract binds two or more parties in a business deal. As such, compacts are subject to the substantive principles of contract law and are protected by the constitutional prohibition against laws that impair the obligations of contracts (U.S. Constitution, Article I, Section 10).

> "That means that compacting states are bound to observe the terms of their agreements, even if those terms are inconsistent with other state laws. In short, compacts between states are somewhat like treaties between nations. Compacts have the force and effect of statutory law (whether enacted by statute or not) and they take precedence over conflicting state laws, regardless of when those laws are enacted.

---

[6] *Id.* at 517–518.

[7] *Petty v. Tennessee-Missouri Bridge Commission.* 359 U.S. 275 at 285. 1959.

[8] See appendix C for the full wording of the impairments clause.

> "However, unlike treaties, compacts are not dependent solely upon the good will of the parties. Once enacted, compacts may not be unilaterally renounced by a member state, except as provided by the compacts themselves. Moreover, Congress and the courts can compel compliance with the terms of interstate compacts. That's why compacts are considered the most effective means of ensuring interstate cooperation."[9]

Once a state enters into an interstate compact, the state—like an individual, corporation, or any other legal entity—is bound by the compact's terms. The contractual obligations undertaken by a state in an interstate compact bind all state officials. In addition, an interstate compact binds the state legislature because a legislature may not enact any law impairing a contract. Thus, after a state enters into an interstate compact, the state is bound by all the terms of the compact until the state withdraws from the compact in accordance with the compact's terms for withdrawal, until the compact is terminated in accordance with the compact's terms for termination, or until the compact ends in accordance with the compact's stated duration.

States generally enter into interstate compacts in order to obtain some benefit that can only be obtained by cooperative and coordinated action with one or more sister states. In most cases, it would make no sense for a state to agree to the terms of a compact unless certain desired other states simultaneously agreed to abide by the terms of the compact. For example, a state generally would not want to agree to limitations on its use of water in a river basin unless the other states in the basin agreed to limit their water use. When two states are involved in a boundary dispute, neither state would generally want to acknowledge a compromise boundary until the other state accepted the compromise.

When a state enters into an interstate compact (other than a purely advisory compact), it is typically agreeing to a constraint, to one degree or another, on its ability to exercise some power that it otherwise might independently exercise.

5.3 HISTORY OF INTERSTATE COMPACTS

There were four interstate compacts approved under the Articles of Confederation. Three of them were settlements of boundary disputes.

[9] Council of State Governments. 2003. *Interstate Compacts and Agencies 2003.* Lexington, KY: The Council of State Governments. Page 6.

The first regulatory compact was an agreement between Maryland and Virginia concerning fishing and navigation on the Chesapeake Bay and the Potomac River. This compact received congressional consent under the Articles of Confederation in 1785 and remained in force until it was replaced by the Potomac River Compact (which received congressional consent in 1958).

In their seminal 1925 article entitled "The Compact Clause of the Constitution," Felix Frankfurter (subsequently a Justice of the U.S. Supreme Court) and James Landis reported that the vast majority (25 of the 32) of interstate compacts prior to 1921 were for the purpose of resolving boundary disputes.[10]

Prior to 1921, pre-existing agencies of the compacting states administered all interstate compacts.

The modern era of interstate compacts began in 1921. The inadequacies of the port of New York became obvious during World War I. After the war, the states of New York and New Jersey decided that efficient operation and development of the port required closer cooperation and coordination between the two states. The result was the 1921 Port of New York Authority Compact. The 1921 compact broke new ground by establishing a bi-state governmental entity—the Port Authority. Under the compact, the Port Authority is administered by its own governing body—a commission appointed by the governors of the two states.

The compact's intended purposes are summarized in the compact's preamble:

> "Whereas, In the year eighteen hundred and thirty-four the states of New York and New Jersey did enter into an agreement fixing and determining the rights and obligations of the two states in and about the waters between the two states, especially in and about the bay of New York and the Hudson river; and

> "Whereas, Since that time the commerce of the port of New York has greatly developed and increased and the territory in and around the port has become commercially one center or district; and

---

[10] Frankfurter, Felix and Landis, James. 1925. The compact clause of the constitution—A study in interstate adjustments. 34 *Yale Law Journal* 692–693 and 730–732. May 1925.

"Whereas, It is confidently believed that a better co-ordination of the terminal, transportation and other facilities of commerce in, about and through the port of New York, will result in great economies, benefiting the nation, as well as the states of New York and New Jersey; and

"Whereas, The future development of such terminal, transportation and other facilities of commerce will require the expenditure of large sums of money and the cordial co-operation of the states of New York and New Jersey in the encouragement of the investment of capital, and in the formulation and execution of the necessary physical plans; and

"Whereas, Such result can best be accomplished through the co-operation of the two states by and through a joint or common agency."

After 1921, the number of compacts and the variety of topics covered by compacts increased dramatically. Nowadays, about one half of all interstate compacts establish a commission to administer the subject matter of the compact.[11] Compact commissions are generally composed of a specified number of representatives from each party state. Many modern-day compacts receive annual funding from each member state for the operation of the compact commission and its staff.

5.4 SUBJECT MATTER OF INTERSTATE COMPACTS

There are no constitutional restrictions on the subject matter of interstate compacts other than the implicit limitation that the compact's subject matter must be among the powers that the states are permitted to exercise. Thus, interstate compacts have been employed for a wide variety of purposes, including those listed below.

An *advisory compact* establishes a commission that is authorized only to conduct studies and to develop recommendations to solve interstate problems.

Examples of *agricultural compacts* include the Compact on Agricultural Grain Marketing and the Northeast Interstate Dairy Compact.

Two states may enter into a *boundary compact*. A freely negotiated settlement of a boundary dispute is often a desirable alternative to a trial

---

[11] Council of State Governments. 2003. *Interstate Compacts and Agencies 2003.* Lexington, KY: The Council of State Governments.

in the U.S. Supreme Court to establish the official boundaries between two states. The South Dakota–Nebraska Boundary Compact (which received congressional consent in 1990) settled a dispute arising from the fact that the Missouri River had changed its course with the passage of time.

Many *civil defense compacts* were adopted during the Cold War period when the Soviet Union was viewed as a potential aggressor nation. The Emergency Management Assistance Compact (found in appendix N), to which Congress consented in 1996, is a broad compact that effectively replaces the earlier Civil Defense Compact.

Crime-control and *corrections compacts* are traceable to 1910 when Congress gave its consent in advance to four states—Illinois, Indiana, Michigan, and Wisconsin—to enter into an agreement with respect to the exercise of jurisdiction "over offenses arising out of the violation of the laws" of these states on the waters of Lake Michigan.[12] The Interstate Agreement on Detainers is one of the best-known compacts concerning crime. This agreement facilitates speedy and proper disposition of detainers based on indictments, information, or complaints from the jurisdictions that are parties to the compact. The parties to this compact include 48 states, the District of Columbia, Puerto Rico, the Virgin Islands, and the federal government.

In 2000, Congress gave its consent to Kansas and Missouri to enter into the nation's first *cultural compact*. The compact established a metropolitan cultural district governed by a commission.

The first *education compact* pooled the resources of southern states by means of the Southern Regional Education Compact. The aim of the compact was to reduce each state's need to maintain expensive post-graduate and professional schools. There are two additional compacts of this nature: the New England Higher Education Compact and the Western Regional Education Compact. The New Hampshire–Vermont Interstate School Compact has been used to establish two interstate school districts, each involving a New Hampshire town and one or more Vermont towns.

Energy Compacts include the Interstate Compact to Conserve Oil and Gas, the Southern States Energy Compact (originally the Southern Interstate Nuclear Compact), the Midwest Energy Compact, and the Western Interstate Energy Compact (originally the Western Interstate Nuclear Compact).

---

[12] 36 Stat. 882.

Facilities compacts provide for the joint construction and operation of physical facilities—commonly bridges and tunnels. A compact entered into by Maine and New Hampshire dealt with the construction and maintenance of a single bridge over the Piscataqua River.[13] On the other hand, the Port Authority of New York and New Jersey operates extensive facilities, including the Holland and Lincoln Tunnels, the George Washington Bridge, three airports (Kennedy, LaGuardia, and Newark Liberty), the PATH rail system, ferries, industrial development projects, and marine facilities. The Port Authority's police force alone numbers over 1,600.

The four *fisheries compacts* are the Atlantic States Marine Fisheries Compact of 1942, the Pacific States Marine Fisheries Compact of 1947, the Gulf States Marine Fisheries Compact of 1949, and the Connecticut River Basin Atlantic Salmon Compact of 1983.

Flood-control compacts relate to the construction of projects to prevent flooding. A 1957 compact between Massachusetts and New Hampshire established the Merrimack Valley Flood Control Commission, which determines the annual amount of compensation that Massachusetts must pay New Hampshire for loss of tax revenue resulting from the construction of flood-control projects.

The Interstate Compact on Mental Health and New England Compact on Radiological Health Protection are examples of *health compacts.*

Congress encouraged the formation of *low-level radioactive waste compacts* to construct regional waste storage facilities as an alternative to the development of individual storage sites in each state. In particular, the federal Low Level Radioactive Waste Policy Act of 1980[14] (as amended in 1985) encourages the use of interstate compacts to establish and operate regional facilities for management of low-level radioactive waste. A total of 44 states have entered into 10 such compacts. One example is the Southwestern Low-Level Radioactive Waste Disposal Compact in which California agreed to serve, for 35 years, as the host state for the storage of radioactive waste for the states of Arizona, North Dakota, South Dakota, and California (and such other states to which the compact commission might later decide to grant membership).

Because of the sensitive subject matter, radioactive-waste compacts generally attract considerable public attention and generate fierce debate

---

[13] 50 Stat. 536.
[14] 94 Stat. 3347.

in state legislatures. Voters have often become directly involved in radioactive waste compacts by means of the citizen-initiative process, the protest-referendum process, and the legislative referral process.[15]

Marketing and development compacts address a variety of subjects and include the Agricultural Grain Marketing Compact, the Midwest Nuclear Compact promoting the use of nuclear energy, and the Mississippi River Parkway Compact.

The objective of each *metropolitan problems compact* is generally conveyed by in its title. For example, the Washington Metropolitan Area Transit Regulation Compact was entered into by the District of Columbia, Maryland, and Virginia and was granted congressional consent in 1960.[16]

The only *military compact* is the National Guard Mutual Assistance Compact. It provides for the sharing of military personnel and equipment among its member states.

There are 12 *motor vehicle compacts*, including ones that relate to driver's licenses, nonresident violators, equipment safety, and uniform vehicle registration prorogation.

Natural resources compacts are designed to settle disputes and to promote the conservation and development of resources. For example, in 1963, Maryland and Virginia established the Potomac River Fisheries Commission to settle a dispute that had originated during the colonial period. Ever since a royal charter made the river a part of Maryland, Maryland oyster fishermen have resented Virginia oyster fishermen intruding in Maryland's waters. The more recent Connecticut River Basin Atlantic Salmon Restoration Compact involves the return of salmon to the river.[17]

The Columbia River Gorge Compact and the 1900 Palisades Interstate Park Compact are two of the five *parks and recreation compacts*.

Economic interest groups often encourage the establishment of *regulatory compacts*. Such groups typically lobby Congress not to exercise its preemption powers in a particular area by arguing that coordinated action by the states, by means of an interstate compact, is sufficient to solve a problem.

---

[15] See sections 5.7 and 5.13 for discussion of the political controversies, spanning a 20-year period, concerning Nebraska's participation in the Central Interstate Low-Level Radioactive Waste Compact.

[16] 74 Stat. 1031.

[17] 97 Stat. 1983.

The Interstate Sanitation Compact, entered into by New Jersey and New York in 1935 and by Connecticut in 1941, created a commission with the power to abate and prevent pollution in tidal waters of the New York City metropolitan area. Subsequently, the compact was amended to allow the commission to monitor, but not to regulate, air quality. The commission (renamed the Interstate Environmental Commission) shares concurrent regulatory authority with the environmental protection departments of the member states.

The Atlantic States Marine Fisheries Compact does not grant its commission regulatory enforcement powers; however, the commission obtained indirect regulatory authority by a congressional act. In 1986, the Atlantic Striped Bass Conservation Act was amended to offer each concerned state the choice of complying with the management plan developed by the commission or being subject to a fishing moratorium on striped bass imposed by the U.S. Fish and Wildlife Service in the state's coastal waters.[18]

One of the greatest problems in southwestern states—the shortage of water—led to the filing of numerous lawsuits between states in the U.S. Supreme Court. *River basin compacts* provide an alternative to litigation. The first such compact was the Colorado River Compact apportioning waters of the river among various western states. More recently, various mid-Atlantic states have entered into river basin compacts.

A *federal-interstate compact* is an interstate compact to which the federal government is one of the parties.

A *service compact* seeks to eliminate social problems by committing each member state to provide services to legal residents of other member states. The Interstate Compact on the Placement of Children in Interstate Adoption, for example, facilitates the adoption of children by qualified foster parents in other compact states if there are too few families willing to adopt children in the home state. This compact has 50 members—49 states and the Virgin Islands.

In 1934, Congress enacted the Crime Control Consent Act authorizing states to enter into crime-control compacts.[19] The Interstate Compact for Supervision of Parolees and Probationers is based on this statute and is the first interstate compact to have been joined by all states. Puerto Rico

---

[18] 100 Stat. 989, 16 U.S.C. §1857.

[19] *Crime Control Consent Act of 1934*. 48 Stat. 909. 4 U.S.C. §112.

and the Virgin Island also are members. The importance of this compact is illustrated by the fact that more than 300,000 persons are on parole or probation in states other than those in which they committed their crimes.

The Interstate Compact on Juveniles and the Interstate Corrections Compact authorize the return of delinquents and convicts, respectively, to their states of domicile to serve their sentences. Supporters of these compacts believe that rehabilitation of delinquents and convicts will be promoted if they are incarcerated in close proximity to their families.

The levying of state income and sales taxes and the growth of interstate commerce has encouraged states to enter into *tax compacts*. The Great Lakes Interstate Sales Compact was the first multi-state compact to focus on enforcement of state sales and use taxes. New Jersey and New York belong to an agreement providing for a mutual exchange of information relative to purchases by residents of the other state from in-state vendors. The states have also entered into numerous administrative agreements concerning taxation.

Twenty-three states and the District of Columbia are parties to the Multistate Tax Compact. Twenty-one additional states are associate members of the compact by virtue of their participation in, and their providing funding for, various programs established by the compact's commission. The impetus for the Multistate Tax Compact was the 1966 decision of the U.S. Supreme Court in *Northwestern States Portland Cement Company v. Minnesota*. The Court ruled that a state may tax the net income of a foreign corporation (i.e., one chartered in a sister state) if the tax is nondiscriminatory and is apportioned equitably on the basis of the corporation's activities with a nexus to the taxing state.[20]

Felix Frankfurter and James Landis anticipated the possibility of *federal-interstate compacts* in 1925 and wrote:

> "[T]he combined legislative powers of Congress and of the several states permit a wide range of permutations and combinations for governmental action. Until very recently these potentialities have been left largely unexplored.... Creativeness is called for to devise a great variety of legal alternatives to cope with the diverse forms of interstate interests."[21]

---

[20] *Northwestern States Portland Cement Company v. Minnesota.* 358 U.S. 450. 1966.

Frankfurter and Landis's call for creativity led to the first *federal-interstate compact* in 1961. After a prolonged drought in the 1950s made the careful management of Delaware River waters essential, four states and the federal government entered into the Delaware River Basin Compact. Congress enacted the compact into federal law with a provision that the United States be a member of the compact. That law created a commission with a national co-chairman and a state co-chairman. The commission also has additional members from the national and member state governments.

Additionally, the federal government, Maryland, New York, and Pennsylvania entered into the Susquehanna River Basin Compact, which became effective in 1971. This is another example of a federal-interstate compact. It is modeled on the Delaware River Basin Compact.

Federal-interstate compacts have also been employed to promote economic development in large regions of the nation. The Appalachian Regional Compact was the first such compact. It was enacted by Congress and thirteen states in 1965. This compact has a commission with a state co-chairman appointed by the governors involved and a federal co-chairman appointed by the President with the Senate's advice and consent.[22]

A unique federal-interstate agreement resulted from a 1980 congressional statute granting consent to an agreement entered into by the Bonneville Power Administration, a federal entity, with Idaho, Montana, Oregon, and Washington.[23] The term "interstate compact" does not appear in the act, and the agreement was not negotiated by the member states. Instead, the proposed compact was drafted by the Pacific Northwest Electric Power and Conservation Planning Council, which sent the proposal to the states. If the states had not enacted the proposed compact, a federal council would have been appointed by the U.S. Secretary of the Interior to perform the functions of the proposed federal-interstate council, namely preparing of a conservation and electric power plan and implementing a program to protect fish and wildlife. A second unique

---

[21] Frankfurter, Felix and Landis, James. 1925. The compact clause of the constitution—A study in interstate adjustments. 34 *Yale Law Journal* 692–693 and 730–732. May 1925.

[22] *Appalachian Regional Development Act of 1966*, 79 Stat. 5, 40 U.S.C. app. §1.

[23] *Pacific Northwest Electric Power and Conservation Planning Act of 1980*. 94 Stat. 2697. 16 U.S.C. §839b.

feature of this legislation was the provision for membership by a federal agency, rather than the federal government.[24]

In 1990, Congress created a similar temporary body—the Northern Forest Lands Council. The Northern Forest Lands Council Act[25] authorized each of the governors of Maine, New Hampshire, New York, and Vermont to appoint four council members charged with developing plans to maintain the "traditional patterns of land ownership and use" of the northern forest. The council was disbanded in 1994.

The National Criminal Prevention and Privacy Compact Act, enacted by Congress in 1998, established what may be termed a federal-interstate compact that

> "organizes an electronic information sharing system among the Federal Government and the States to exchange criminal history records for non-criminal justice purposes authorized by Federal or State law, such as background checks for governmental licensing and employment."[26]

Federal and state law enforcement officers were not involved in the negotiations leading to this compact. The compact is activated when entered into by two or more states. Article VI of the compact established a Compact Council with authority to promulgate rules and procedures pertaining to use of the Interstate Identification Index System for non-criminal justice purposes. The council is composed of fifteen members appointed by the Attorney General of the United States, including nine members selected from among the law enforcement officers of member states, two at-large members nominated by the Chairman of the Compact Council, two other at-large members, a member of the FBI's advisory policy board, and an FBI employee appointed by the FBI director. The Director of the FBI designates the federal "Compact Officer."

Indian tribe gaming compacts are a new type of compact. The origin of such compacts is the U.S. Supreme Court's 1987 decision in the case of *Cabazon Band of Mission Indians v. California*, which held that

---

[24] Olsen, Darryll and Butcher, Walter R. The Regional Power Act: A model for the nation? *Washington State Policy Notes 35.* Winter 1984. Pages 1–6.

[25] *Northern Forest Lands Council Act of 1990,* 104 Stat. 3359, 16 U.S.C. §2101.

[26] *National Crime Prevention and Privacy Compact Act of 1998.* 112 Stat. 1874. 42 U.S.C. §14611.

a state may not unduly restrict gaming on Indian lands.[27] This decision led to a sharp increase in gaming on Indian lands. Congress became concerned that tribal governments and their members were not actually profiting from the gaming and that organized crime might acquire a stake in such activity. The Indian Gaming Regulatory Act of 1988[28] therefore authorized tribe–state gaming compacts. The 1988 act established three classes of Indian gaming. Class I gaming—primarily social gaming for small prizes—is regulated totally by Indian tribes. Class II gaming—bingo and bingo-type games and non-banking card games—is regulated by tribes, but is subject to limited oversight by the National Indian Gaming Commission. Class III contains all other types of gaming. Class III gaming is prohibited in the absence of a tribal-state compact approved by the U.S. Secretary of the Interior. The compact device permits states to exercise their reserved powers without the need for direct congressional action.

Appendix M contains a listing of 196 active interstate compacts compiled by the National Center for Interstate Compacts (NCIC) of the Council of State Governments (CSG). The Center has also identified 62 defunct or inactive interstate compacts.[29]

5.5 PARTIES TO INTERSTATE COMPACTS

Although most early interstate compacts usually involved only two states, modern-day interstate compacts frequently involve numerous parties.

The parties to an interstate compact are often determined by geography (e.g., the Colorado River Compact and the Great Lakes Basin Compact). Membership in many compacts is defined by the activities in which the states engage. For example, the Interstate Oil Compact encompasses the 22 oil-producing states. The Multistate Lottery Agreement operates a quasi-national lotto game in geographically scattered states. In some cases, compacts are open to all states, and their actual membership is simply determined by whichever states decide to enact the compact. Examples include the Interstate Compact for Adult Offender Supervision (enacted by 38 states) and the Agreement on Detainers (enacted by 47 states).

---

[27] *Cabazon Band of Mission Indians v. California.* 480 U.S. 202. 1987.

[28] *Indian Gaming Regulatory Act of 1988.* 108 Stat. 2467. 25 U.S.C. §2701.

[29] Council of State Governments. 2003. *Interstate Compacts and Agencies 2003.* Lexington, KY: The Council of State Governments.

Today, there are interstate compacts that include as few as two states and compacts that involve all 50 states. Certain interstate compacts include the District of Columbia, the Commonwealth of Puerto Rico, the Virgin Islands, American Samoa, and provinces of Canada. The Interstate Compact for Education, for example, encompasses 48 states, the District of Columbia, American Samoa, Puerto Rico, and the Virgin Islands. In 1949, the Northeastern Interstate Forest Fire Compact became the first interstate compact to include a Canadian province. The Great Lakes Basin Compact (appendix K) includes Ontario and Quebec.

The federal government may be a party to an interstate compact. For example, the membership of the Agreement on Detainers (appendix L) includes 47 states, the District of Columbia, and the federal government as parties.

The Interstate Compact on the Placement of Children and the Interstate Compact on Juveniles are examples of compacts adhered to by all 50 states and the District of Columbia.

States belong to an average of 25.4 interstate compacts.[30] The numbers of compacts entered into range from a low of 16 for Hawaii and Wisconsin to a high of 32 for Colorado and Maryland.

5.6 FORMULATION OF INTERSTATE COMPACTS

Prior to 1930, gubernatorially appointed commissioners negotiated and drafted all interstate compacts. This method is especially appropriate when the contemplated compact requires lengthy negotiations among the prospective parties and frequent consultation with the governors and legislative leaders of the states involved.

Since the 1930s, some interstate compacts (e.g., the Interstate Compact on Parolees and Probationers) have been drafted by non-governmental organizations. Over the years, the National Conference of State Legislatures (NCSL) and the Council of State Governments (CSG) have proposed numerous interstate compacts to the states.[31] Compacts have occasionally been initiated by private citizens. As Marian E. Ridgeway describes in *Interstate Compacts: A Question of Federalism:*

---

[30] Bowman, Ann O'M. 2004. Trends and issues in interstate cooperation. In *The Book of the States 2004 Edition.* Chicago, IL: The Council of State Governments. Page 36.

[31] Hardy, Paul T. 1982. *Interstate Compacts: The Ties That Bind.* Athens, GA: Institute of Government, University of Georgia.

> "The Compact on Education is largely the product of the zeal
> and energy of former governor Terry Sanford of North
> Carolina, acting on a suggestion of James B. Conant in his
> [1964 book] *Shaping Education Policy.*"[32]

Interstate compacts may also originate in state legislatures. A legislature may unilaterally enact a statute that serves as a prospective compact and invitation to other states to join by enacting identical statutes.

In recent years, various industry groups have promoted interstate regulatory compacts in attempts to discourage Congress from exercising its preemption powers over the subject matter involved. These groups argue that a compact obviates the need for federal regulation and that cooperative action by the states can adequately address the problem at hand.

Representatives of the federal government occasionally participate in the negotiation of interstate compacts. Such federal participation is usually at the invitation of the states themselves. Federal participation is, however, sometimes necessary, given the nature of the compact. For example, federal representatives participated from the beginning in the negotiation of the Potomac River Compact. Both the federal government and the District of Columbia are represented on the commission established by the compact.

In the case of the Colorado River Compact, Congress passed legislation[33] in 1921 calling on the seven western states in the Colorado River basin (Arizona, California, Colorado, Nevada, New Mexico, Utah and Wyoming) to enter negotiations to resolve their long-standing water dispute and to provide for the use of the water for agriculture and power generation. Under the terms of the federal legislation, the negotiations were headed by Secretary of Commerce Herbert Hoover. These negotiations led to the Colorado River Compact of 1922.[34,35]

There are no constitutional or statutory restrictions on the length of time for the negotiation of interstate compacts.

---

[32] Ridgeway, Marian E. 1971. *Interstate Compacts: A Question of Federalism.* Carbondale, IL: Southern Illinois University Press. Page 41.

[33] 42 Stat. 171.

[34] Barton, Weldon V. 1967. *Interstate Compacts in the Political Process.* Chapel Hill, NC: University of North Carolina Press.

[35] Zimmerman, Joseph F. 2002. *Interstate Cooperation: Compacts and Administrative Agreements.* Westport, CT: Praeger.

5.7 METHODS BY WHICH A STATE ENACTS AN INTERSTATE COMPACT

A state may enter an interstate compact in several ways. In certain circumstances, the Governor, the head of an administrative department, or a commission may have sufficient legal authority to enter into a compact on a particular subject on behalf of the state. For example, the Multi-State Lottery Agreement was adopted in many states merely by the action of state lottery commissions. The focus of this book is, however, on compacts that require explicit legislative action in order to come into effect.

Enactment of an interstate compact is generally accomplished in the same way that ordinary state laws are enacted. Enactment of a state statute typically requires a majority vote of the state legislature and submission of the legislative bill to the state's Governor for approval or disapproval. If the Governor approves a bill that has been passed by the legislature, then the bill becomes law. All Governors have the power to veto legislation passed by their state legislatures. If a Governor vetoes a bill, the bill may nonetheless become law if the legislature overrides the veto in the manner provided by the state's constitution. Overriding a gubernatorial veto typically requires a super-majority (e.g., a two-thirds vote of all houses of the state legislature). See *The Book of the States* for general information about vetoes in particular states.[36] The veto by the Governor of Vermont of the bill enacting the New England Water Pollution Compact is an example of a gubernatorial veto of a legislative bill enacting an interstate compact.

If a state allows the citizen-initiative process, an interstate compact may be enacted in that fashion. Each state constitution specifies the legislature's role, if any, in the initiative process. For example, in some states, the legislature has the option (sometimes the obligation) of voting on an initiative petition before the proposition is submitted to the voters. See *The Initiative: Citizen Law-Making*[37] for additional information on the citizen-initiative process. The citizen-initiative process may, in general, be used to repeal a state law. Thus, a state law enacting an interstate compact can be subjected to review and possible repeal by the voters. For example, an initiative petition was used in Nebraska in 1988 to force

---

[36] Council of State Governments. 2005. *The Book of the States*. Lexington, KY: The Council of State Governments. 2005 Edition. Volume 37. Pages 161–162.

[37] Zimmerman, Joseph F. 1999. *The Initiative: Citizen Law-Making*. Westport, CT: Praeger. See pages 24-25 for citations to the constitutional and statutory provisions governing the initiative processes in various states.

204 | Chapter 5

a statewide vote on the question of Nebraska's continued participation in the Central Interstate Low-Level Radioactive Waste Compact. The compact (which had been passed several years earlier by the Nebraska legislature) provided for the building of a nuclear waste site in Nebraska. In the statewide vote on Proposition 402 in 1988, Nebraska voters rejected the opportunity to repeal the state's participation in the compact. The compact nonetheless remained controversial, and, in 1999, the Nebraska legislature enacted a law withdrawing the state from the compact.[38]

The protest-referendum process, if available in a given state, provides another way to subject a law enacted by the legislature (including a law enacting an interstate compact) to review by the voters. The protest-referendum process usually must be invoked within a short and limited time after the law was originally passed by the legislature. See *The Referendum: The People Decide Public Policy*[39] for additional information on the protest-referendum process.

In some cases, the state legislature has referred enactment of an interstate compact to the state's voters. For example, the Maine legislature referred the question of enactment of the Texas Low-Level Radioactive Waste Disposal Compact to its voters in 1993. The question on the ballot was:

> "Do you approve of the interstate compact to be made with Texas, Maine and Vermont for the disposal of the State's low-level radioactive waste at a proposed facility in the State of Texas?"

The proposition received 170,411 "yes" votes and 63,672 "no" votes.

The statutory language required to enact an interstate compact at the state level is not complex. For example, the legislation by which the state of Ohio entered into the Great Lakes Basin Compact in 1963 consists of two parts. The first part consists of the following 43-word enacting clause:

> "The 'great lakes basin compact' is hereby ratified, enacted into law, and entered into by this state as a party thereto with

---

[38] See section 5.13 for additional discussion of the political controversies, spanning a 20-year period, concerning Nebraska's participation in the Central Interstate Low-Level Radioactive Waste Compact.

[39] Zimmerman, Joseph F. 1997. *The Referendum: The People Decide Public Policy.* Westport, CT: Praeger.

> any other state or province which, pursuant to Article II of
> said compact, has legally joined in the compact as follows: ..."

The second part consists of the text of the compact (placed inside quotation marks). Appendix K contains the entire text of the Ohio legislation.

Statutory language for enacting an interstate compact at the state level may, or may not, be self-executing. The above Ohio legislation is an example of self-executing legislation—that is, no further action is required by any official or body in Ohio with respect to the process of adopting the compact in Ohio. On the other hand, the statutory language enacting an interstate compact may require that the compact be subsequently executed by the state's Governor, Attorney General, or other official—perhaps at the discretion of the official involved, perhaps after some specified condition is satisfied, or perhaps merely after a certain number of other states have joined the compact. The Interstate Compact for the Supervision of Parolees and Probationers is an example of a non-self-executing compact. That particular compact was enacted in 1936 by the New York Legislature. Because of the opposition of Governor Herbert H. Lehman, the compact remained unexecuted for eight years.

An interstate compact may sometimes be adopted on a temporary basis by executive or administrative action. For example, the Compact for Education stipulates that it may be adopted

> "either by enactment thereof or by adherence thereto by the
> Governor; provided that in the absence of enactment, adherence by the Governor shall be sufficient to make his state a
> party only until December 31, 1967."

The governor authorized participation by Kansas in the Interstate Compact for Supervision of Parolees and Probationers for a period of time prior to enactment of the compact by the legislature.

There are no constitutional or statutory restrictions on the length of time that potential parties to an interstate compact may take in deciding whether to join the compact.[40] Indeed, history is replete with examples of long delays prior to the enactment of interstate compacts. In 1955, the Great Lakes Basin Compact (appendix K) was enacted by the state legislatures in Illinois, Indiana, Michigan, Minnesota, and Wisconsin. It was

---

[40] Of course, a particular compact could explicitly contain a time limitation for its adoption by its prospective members.

enacted in 1956 by the Pennsylvania General Assembly. However, the New York Legislature did not enact the compact until 1960, and the Ohio General Assembly did not enact the compact until 1963. It took twelve years to gain approval from the California and Nevada legislatures for the California-Nevada Water Apportionment Interstate Compact. It took five years to secure the necessary enactments of the Atlantic States Marine Fisheries Compact (which became effective in 1942).

5.8 CONTINGENT NATURE OF COMPACTS

As a general rule, a state enters into an interstate compact in order to obtain some benefit that can only be obtained by mutually agreed coordinated action with its sister state(s). In most cases, it would make no sense for a state to agree to the terms of a compact unless certain desired other states agreed to the compact. Thus, an interstate compact generally does not come into effect until it is approved by a specified number or a specified combination of prospective parties.

A bi-state compact does come into effect until it is adopted by both of the states involved.

A compact involving three or more parties typically contains a specific provision specifying the conditions under which the compact will come into effect. If a compact is silent as to the number of parties necessary to bring it into effect, then, in accordance with standard contract law, it comes into effect only when adopted by all of its named parties.

The Gulf States Marine Fisheries Compact contemplated participation of five states but required only two states to enact the compact in order to bring it into effect.

> "This compact shall become operative immediately as to those states ratifying it whenever any two or more of the States of Florida, Alabama, Mississippi, Louisiana and Texas have ratified it."

The Tri-State Lotto Compact is an example of a multi-state compact that did not come into effect until it was enacted by all of its prospective parties (Maine, New Hampshire, and Vermont).

The Multistate Tax Compact is open to all states and provides:

> "This compact shall enter into force when enacted into law by any seven states. Thereafter, this compact shall become

effective as to any other state upon its enactment thereof."

The Great Lakes Basin Compact was intended to include eight states but came into effect when four states enacted it.

"This compact shall enter into force and become effective and binding when it has been enacted by the legislatures of any four of the states of Illinois, Indiana, Michigan, Minnesota, New York, Ohio, Pennsylvania, and Wisconsin and thereafter shall enter into force and become effective and binding as to any other of said states when enacted by the legislature thereof."

The Great Lakes Basin Compact is noteworthy because it permitted two Canadian provinces to join the Great Lakes Basin Compact. The Canadian provinces did not, however, count toward the threshold of four states necessary to bring the compact into effect.

"The province of Ontario and the province of Quebec, or either of them, may become states party to this compact by taking such action as their laws and the laws of the government of Canada may prescribe for adherence thereto. For the purpose of this compact the word 'state' shall be construed to include a province of Canada."

The Midwest Interstate Passenger Rail Compact came into effect when it was enacted by three states out of a pool of 12 named prospective members. The membership of this compact may be expanded by action of the commission established by the compact.

"The states of Illinois, Indiana, Iowa, Kansas, Michigan, Minnesota, Missouri, Nebraska, North Dakota, Ohio, South Dakota and Wisconsin are eligible to join this compact. Upon approval of the Commission, according to its bylaws, other states may also be declared eligible to join the compact. As to any eligible party state, this compact shall become effective when its legislature shall have enacted the same into law; provided that it shall not become initially effective until enacted into law by any three (3) party states incorporating the provisions of this compact into the laws of such states.

Amendments to the compact shall become effective upon their enactment by the legislatures of all compacting states."[41]

The Central Interstate Low-Level Radioactive Waste Compact named 10 states as eligible for membership. It specified that it would become effective when enacted by any three of the 10 prospective parties. The compact enabled the compact's commission to admit additional states by a unanimous vote.

Sometimes the requirements for bringing a compact into effect are of paramount importance. The original version of the Colorado River Compact was negotiated in 1922 by gubernatorially appointed commissioners from the seven western states involved (Arizona, California, Colorado, Nevada, New Mexico, Utah, and Wyoming). The negotiations were headed by Herbert Hoover, and the compact was signed, amid considerable fanfare, on November 24, 1922, in Santa Fe, New Mexico. The 1922 version provided:

"This compact shall become binding and obligatory when it shall have been approved by the legislatures of each of the signatory states."[42]

The Arizona legislature, however, did not enact a statute approving the 1922 compact. Congress then initiated a revised version of the compact—the Boulder Canyon Project Act of 1928. The 1928 version specified that the compact would come into effect when enacted by six of the seven western states involved, provided that California was one of the six.[43] Arizona, the seventh prospective member, did not approve the 1928 version of compact until 1944.

5.9 CONGRESSIONAL CONSENT AND INVOLVEMENT IN INTERSTATE COMPACTS

Congress may become involved with an interstate compact in one of several different ways:
- consenting to a compact,
- consenting to a compact on behalf of the District of Columbia,

---

[41] Midwest Interstate Passenger Rail Compact. Section 1 of Article X.

[42] See http://ssl.csg.org/compactlaws/coloradoriver.html

[43] 45 Stat.1057.

- making the federal government a party to a compact,
- granting implied consent to a compact,
- consenting in advance to a broad category of compacts, and
- consenting in advance to a particular compact.

The statutory language necessary for congressional consent to an interstate compact is straight-forward.

A joint resolution is generally used if Congress is simply granting its consent. For example, House Joint Resolution 193 (Public Law 104-321)[44] of the 104th Congress entitled "Joint Resolution Granting the consent of Congress to the Emergency Management Assistance Compact" was used to grant consent to the Emergency Management Assistance Compact in 1996. The joint resolution consists of three major parts. In the first part, Congress grants its consent.

"Resolved by the Senate and House of Representatives of the United States in Congress assembled,

"SECTION 1: CONGRESSIONAL CONSENT.
"The Congress consents to the Emergency Management Assistance Compact entered into by Delaware, Florida, Georgia, Louisiana, Maryland, Mississippi, Missouri, Oklahoma, South Carolina, South Dakota, Tennessee, Virginia and West Virginia. The compact reads substantially as follows ... "

The second part of this joint resolution consists of the entire wording of the Emergency Management Assistance Compact (which is inserted in the joint resolution inside quotation marks).

The third part of a joint resolution consenting to a compact generally contains several sections that qualify the grant of consent.

"SECTION 2. RIGHT TO ALTER, AMEND, OR REPEAL.
"The right to alter, amend, or repeal this joint resolution is hereby expressly reserved. The consent granted by this joint resolution shall

(1) not be construed as impairing or in any manner affecting any right or jurisdiction of the United States in and over the subject of the compact;

---

[44] Appendix N contains Public Law 104-321 of 1996 entitled "Joint Resolution Granting the consent of Congress to the Emergency Management Assistance Compact."

(2) not be construed as consent to the National Guard Mutual Assistance Compact;

(3) be construed as understanding that the first paragraph of Article II of the compact provides that emergencies will require procedures to provide immediate access to existing resources to make a prompt and effective response;

(4) not be construed as providing authority in Article IIIA.7 that does not otherwise exist for the suspension of statutes or ordinances;

(5) be construed as understanding that Article IIIC does not impose any affirmative obligation to exchange information, plans, and resource records on the United States or any party which has not entered into the compact; and

(6) be construed as understanding that Article XIII does not affect the authority of the President over the National Guard provided by article I of the Constitution and title 10 of the United States Code.

"SECTION 3. CONSTRUCTION AND SEVERABILITY.
"It is intended that the provisions of this compact shall be reasonably and liberally construed to effectuate the purposes thereof. If any part or application of this compact, or legislation enabling the compact, is held invalid, the remainder of the compact or its application to other situations or persons shall not be affected.

"SECTION 4. INCONSISTENCY OF LANGUAGE.
"The validity of this compact shall not be affected by any insubstantial difference in its form or language as adopted by the States."

When the District of Columbia is a party to a compact, Congress consents to the compact on behalf of the District. When the federal government is a party to a compact, Congress enters into the compact on behalf of the United States. Thus, when Congress acted on the Interstate Agreement on Detainers, it simultaneously consented to the compact on behalf of the District of Columbia, made the federal government a party to the compact, and enacted some additional permanent statutory language (sections 5 and 6). Appendix L contains Public Law 91-538 of 1970 entitled "An Act to enact the Interstate Agreement on Detainers into law." This law begins:

> "*Be it enacted by the Senate and House of Representatives of the United States of America in Congress assembled,*
>
> "[Sec. 1.] That this Act may be cited as the 'Interstate Agreement on Detainers Act.'
>
> "Sec. 2. The Interstate Agreement on Detainers is hereby enacted into law and entered into by the United States on its own behalf and on behalf of the District of Columbia with all jurisdictions legally joining in substantially the following form: ..."

At this point, Public Law 91-538 incorporates the entire Interstate Agreement on Detainers (inside quotation marks).

Public Law 91-538 then concludes with several additional sections:

> "Sec. 3. The term 'Governor' as used in the agreement on detainers shall mean with respect to the United States, the Attorney General, and with respect to the District of Columbia, the Commissioner of the District of Columbia.
>
> "Sec. 4. The term 'appropriate court' as used in the agreement on detainers shall mean with respect to the United States, the courts of the United States, and with respect to the District of Columbia, the courts of the District of Columbia, in which indictments, informations, or complaints, for which disposition is sought, are pending.
>
> "Sec. 5. All courts, departments, agencies, officers, and employees of the United States and of the District of Columbia are hereby directed to enforce the agreement on detainers and to cooperate with one another and with all party States in enforcing the agreement and effectuating its purpose.

"Sec. 6. For the United States, the Attorney General, and for the District of Columbia, the Commissioner of the District of Columbia, shall establish such regulations, prescribe such forms, issue such instructions, and perform such other acts as he deems necessary for carrying out the provisions of this Act.

"Sec. 7. The right to alter, amend, or repeal this Act is expressly reserved.

"Sec. 8. This Act shall take effect on the ninetieth day after the date of its enactment."

Congressional consent to an interstate compact need not be explicit. For example, there is nothing in Public Law 91-538 (quoted above) that specifically mentions that Congress is consenting to the Interstate Agreement on Detainers. The reason is that congressional consent is *implied* by its consent to the compact on behalf of the District of Columbia and by its action making the federal government a party to the compact. As the U.S. Supreme Court observed in the 1893 case of *Virginia v. Tennessee:*

> **"The constitution does not state when the consent of congress shall be given, whether it shall precede or may follow the compact made, or whether it shall be express or may be implied.** In many cases the consent will usually precede the compact or agreement.... But where the agreement relates to a matter which could not well be considered until its nature is fully developed, it is not perceived why the consent may not be subsequently given. [Justice] Story says that **the consent may be implied, and is always to be implied when congress adopts the particular act by sanctioning its objects and aiding in enforcing them;** and observes that where a state is admitted into the Union, notoriously upon a compact made between it and the state of which it previously composed a part, there the act of congress admitting such state into the Union is an implied consent to the terms of the compact. Knowledge by congress of the boundaries of a state and of its political subdivisions may reasonably be presumed, as much of its legislation is affected by them, such as relate to the territorial jurisdiction of the

courts of the United States, the extent of their collection districts, and of districts in which process, civil and criminal, of their courts may be served and enforced."[45] [Emphasis added]

Congressional consent is given in the same way that Congress enacts an ordinary statute. That is, such legislation requires a majority vote of both houses of Congress and approval of the President. As part of the legislative process, the President may veto such legislation. Congress has the power to override a presidential veto by a two-thirds vote in both houses. For example, in 1941, Franklin D. Roosevelt vetoed the bill granting consent to the Republican River Compact (perhaps preferring a Democratic river); however, two years later he signed a bill consenting to a modified version of the compact. Congress's failure to grant its consent for the Connecticut River and Merrimack River Flood Control Compacts in the 1930s has been attributed to the threat of a presidential veto.

There is no constitutional limitation on the amount of time that Congress may take in considering a compact. Maryland, New York, and Pennsylvania enacted the Susquehanna River Basin Compact in 1967 and 1968, but Congress did not grant its consent until 1970. The Washington Metropolitan Area Transit Regulation Compact was approved by Maryland, Virginia, and the District of Columbia in 1958; however, the compact did not receive the consent of Congress until 1960.

Congress is free to grant its unrestricted consent in advance for all compacts pertaining to a particular subject. For example, Congress consented in advance to interstate crime control compacts in the Crime Control Consent Act of 1934.

> *"Be it enacted by the Senate and House of Representatives of the United States of America in congress assembled,*
>
> "[Sec. 1.] That the consent of Congress is hereby given to any two or more States to enter into agreements or compacts for cooperative effort and mutual assistance in the prevention of crime and in the enforcement of their respective criminal laws and policies, and to establish such agencies, joint or otherwise, as they deem desirable for making effective such agreement and compacts.

---

[45] *Virginia v. Tennessee.* 148 U.S. 503 at 521. 1893.

"Sec. 2. The right to alter, amend, or repeal this Act is hereby expressly reserved."

In the Weeks Act of 1911, Congress granted unrestricted consent in advance to interstate compacts formed

"for the purpose of conserving the forests and water supply...."[46]

In the Tobacco Control Act of 1936, Congress authorized tobacco-producing states to enter into interstate compacts

"to enable growers to receive a fair price for such tobacco."[47]

Another example of congressional consent in advance involved the development and operation of airports.[48]

In 1939, President Franklin D. Roosevelt vetoed a bill that would have granted consent in advance to states to enter into compacts relating to fishing in the Atlantic Ocean because he considered the advance authorization to be overly vague.

On rare occasions, Congress has combined consent and advance permission in the same statute. For example, in 1921, it granted its consent to a Minnesota–South Dakota compact relating to criminal jurisdiction over boundary waters and simultaneously granted its consent in advance for a similar compact among Iowa, Minnesota, Nebraska, North Dakota, South Dakota, and Wisconsin.[49]

In 1951, Congress authorized states to enter into interstate civil defense compacts that, upon enactment, were required to be filed with the U.S. House of Representatives and Senate. These compacts were all deemed to have the consent of Congress unless disapproved by a concurrent resolution within 60 days of filing.[50]

Generally, a congressional grant of consent to an interstate compact is for an indefinite period of time. However, Congress originally subjected the Interstate Oil and Gas Compact of 1935 and the Atlantic States Marine Fisheries Compact to sunset provisions. Later, Congress removed the time restrictions on its consent.[51] The 10 compacts (involving a total

---

[46] 36 Stat. 961.

[47] 49 Stat. 1239.

[48] 73 Stat. 333.

[49] 41 Stat. 1447.

[50] 64 Stat. 1249.

[51] 86 Stat. 383 and 64 Stat. 467.

of 44 states) authorized by the Low Level Radioactive Waste Policy Act of 1980 were each approved for a period of five years.[52]

Of course, Congress is not obligated to renew its consent. The controversial Northeast Interstate Dairy Compact established a commission with authority to fix the price of fluid or drinking milk above the minimum prices set by the New England federal milk-marketing order. This compact was enacted by each state legislature in New England. Congress granted its consent to this particular compact for a limited period of time. In the meantime, the compact attracted considerable opposition from consumer groups and mid-western and western dairy states. Consumer advocates opposed the compact because it would increase the retail price of milk, thereby adversely impacting low-income citizens. Representatives of mid-western and western dairy states argued that their farmers suffered from low milk prices because of the compact. Wisconsin dairy farmers, in particular, argued that the compact prevented them from selling their products in New England. The compact became inactive in 2001 when Congress failed to grant an extension of its consent.

Congress may impose conditions in granting its consent. For example, Congress granted its consent to the Wabash Valley Compact in 1959[53] and the Washington Metropolitan Area Transit Regulation Compact in 1960[54] with the proviso that each compact authority was to publish specified data and information. Congress always reserves its authority over navigable waters. It almost always reserves its right to "alter, amend, or repeal" its consent. The Boulder Canyon Project Act of 1928[55] granted congressional consent to the Colorado River Compact subject to several stipulated conditions, including approval of the modified compact by California and five of the other six states involved (it being understood, at the time, that Arizona was unlikely to join immediately).

In the 1962 case of *Tobin v. United States*, the United States Court of Appeals for the District of Columbia Circuit upheld the authority of Congress to attach conditions to a compact.[56] The U.S. Supreme Court declined to review the decision.

---

[52] 94 Stat. 3347.

[53] 73 Stat. 694.

[54] 74 Stat. 1031.

[55] 45 Stat.1057.

[56] *Tobin v. United States.* 306 F.2d 270 at 272–74. 1962.

The Constitution does not detail the specific form or manner by which congressional consent is to be granted. In 1823, the U.S. Supreme Court in *Green v. Biddle* noted this fact in a case involving a congressional statute that granted consent to the admission of Kentucky to the Union and simultaneously referred to the Virginia–Kentucky Interstate Compact of 1789.[57] Kentucky unsuccessfully challenged the compact on the ground that Congress had not explicitly consented to the compact.

The Central Interstate Low-Level Radioactive Waste Compact enabled the commission established by the compact to accept additional states as members by a unanimous vote. The compact (which was submitted to Congress for its consent) contained a provision granting advance congressional consent to any additional new states:

> "The consent given to this compact by the Congress shall extend to any future admittance of new party states under subsections B and C of Article VII of the compact."

5.10 EFFECT OF CONGRESSIONAL CONSENT

The question arises as to whether an interstate compact is converted into federal law when Congress grants its consent. This question is important because it may determine which court has the power to interpret the compact and whether the compact is interpreted under the state or federal law.

The Supreme Court's answer to this question has changed over the years. In 1938, the Court held in the case of *Hinderlider v. La Plata River and Cherry Creek Ditch Company* that congressional consent does not make a compact the equivalent of a United States statute or treaty.[58] The Court modified its *Hinderlider* ruling in *Delaware River Joint Toll Bridge Commission v. Colburn*. The Court expanded the authority of a compact that had been granted consent by Congress and involved

> "a federal 'title, right, privilege, or immunity' which when explicitly identified and claimed in a state court may be reviewed here on certiorari...."[59]

---

[57] *Green v. Biddle*. 21 U.S. 1. 1823.

[58] *Hinderlider v. La Plata River and Cherry Creek Ditch Company*. 304 U.S. 92. 1938.

[59] *Delaware River Joint Toll Bridge Commission v. Colburn*. 320 U.S. 419. 1940.

In 1874, the Supreme Court held in *Murdock v. City of Memphis* that federal courts are required to apply the interpretation of state law by the highest state court in the state.[60]

In 1981, however, the Court overturned *Murdock* in *Cuyler v. Adams*. The Court held that congressional consent converts an interstate compact into federal law provided that the compact's subject matter was

"an appropriate subject for congressional legislation."[61]

By overturning *Murdock*, the Court was free to reject the interpretation provided by the Pennsylvania Supreme Court and to interpret the statute on its own.[62,63]

The question repeatedly arises as to whether the grant of congressional consent to an interstate compact invalidates other federal statutes containing inconsistent provisions. Courts could interpret congressional consent as repealing, relative to the interstate compact, conflicting federal statutes. The question also arises as to the effect of a new federal statute whose provisions conflict with an interstate compact previously approved by Congress. Apparently, the consent would be repealed relative to the conflicting provisions with the exception of any vested rights protected by the Fifth Amendment to the Constitution.

5.11 COMPACTS CONTINGENT ON ENACTMENT OF FEDERAL LEGISLATION

An interstate compact may contain terms specifying that it is contingent on the enactment of federal legislation at the time Congress grants its consent to the compact.

For example, the Belle Fourche River Compact between South Dakota and Wyoming stipulated that it would not become effective unless congressional consent were accompanied by congressional legislation satisfactorily addressing three enumerated points that the compact's parties desired. The compact provided:

---

[60] *Murdock v. City of Memphis.* 87 U.S. 590. 1874.

[61] *Cuyler v. Adams.* 449 U.S. 433. 1981.

[62] Hardy, Paul T. 1982. *Interstate Compacts: The Ties That Bind.* Athens, GA: Institute of Government, University of Georgia.

[63] Zimmerman, Joseph F. 2002. *Interstate Cooperation: Compacts and Administrative Agreements.* Westport, CT: Praeger.

"This compact shall become operative when approved by the legislature of each of the states, and when consented to by the congress of the United States by legislation providing, among other things, that:

"(i) Any beneficial uses hereafter made by the United States, or those acting by or under its authority, within a state, of the waters allocated by this compact, shall be within the allocations hereinabove made for use in that state and shall be taken into account in determining the extent of use within that state;

"(ii) The United States, or those acting by or under its authority, in the exercise of rights or powers arising from whatever jurisdiction the United States has in, over and to the waters of the Belle Fourche River and all its tributaries, shall recognize, to the extent consistent with the best utilization of the waters for multiple purposes, that beneficial use of the waters within the basin is of paramount importance to development of the basin, and no exercise of such power or right thereby that would interfere with the full beneficial use of the waters shall be made except upon a determination, giving due consideration to the objectives of this compact and after consultation with all interested federal agencies and the state officials charged with the administration of this compact, that such exercise is in the interest of the best utilization of such waters for multiple purposes;

"(iii) The United States, or those acting by or under its authority, will recognize any established use, for domestic and irrigation purposes, of the apportioned waters which may be impaired by the exercise of federal jurisdiction in, over, and to such waters; provided, that such use is being exercised beneficially, is valid under the laws of the appropriate state and in conformity with this compact at the time of the impairment thereof, and was validly initiated under state law prior to the initiation or authorization of the federal program or project which causes such impairment."

Congress agreed to the states' request in its legislation granting consent to the Belle Fourche River Compact.

Similarly, the Republican River Compact contained a description of congressional legislation desired by the compact's parties. Again, Congress agreed to the states' request at the time of granting its consent to the compact.

5.12 COMPACTS NOT REQUIRING CONGRESSIONAL CONSENT

Two reasons are generally given as to why the U.S. Constitution requires congressional consent for interstate compacts.

First, congressional consent provides a means of protecting the federal government from efforts by the states to encroach upon its delegated powers and federal supremacy.

Second, congressional consent provides a means of safeguarding the interests of states that are not parties to the compact. For example, absent congressional supervision, upstream states in a river basin might enter into a compact to use water to the extreme disadvantage of downstream states that do not belong to the compact.

At first glance, the Constitution seems to be unambiguous as to the necessity for congressional consent to interstate compacts. Article I, section 10, clause 3 provides:

> "No state shall, without the consent of Congress, … enter into any agreement or compact with another state.…"

The Supreme Court has interpreted this clause to allow states to enter into compacts without Congressional consent. In deciding the 1978 case of *U.S. Steel Corporation v. Multistate Tax Commission*,[64] the Court wrote:

> "Read literally, the Compact Clause would require the States to obtain congressional approval before entering into any agreement among themselves, irrespective of form, subject, duration, or interest to the United States. The difficulties with such an interpretation were identified by Mr. Justice Field in his opinion for the Court in *Virginia v. Tennessee*, supra.[65] His conclusion that the Clause could not be read literally was approved in subsequent dicta, … but this Court did not have

---

[64] *U.S. Steel Corporation v. Multistate Tax Commission*. 434 U.S. 452. 1978.

[65] *Virginia v. Tennessee*. 148 U.S. 503. 1893.

occasion expressly to apply it in a holding until our recent [1976] decision in *New Hampshire v. Maine*[66] ...."[67]

Litigation started in the early 19th century over whether congressional consent to interstate compacts is necessary in all circumstances.

In the 1833 case of *Barron v. Baltimore*, Chief Justice John Marshall wrote:

> "If these compacts are with foreign nations, they interfere with the treaty-making power, which is conferred entirely on the general government; if with each other, for political purposes, they can scarcely fail to interfere with the general purpose and intent of the constitution."[68]

In 1845, the New Hampshire Supreme Court in *Dover v. Portsmouth Bridge* dismissed the contention that an 1819 New Hampshire statute and an 1821 Maine statute that authorized construction of a bridge over navigable waters (the Piscataqua River) without congressional consent violated the U.S. Constitution.[69] The court held that there is no constitutional provision precluding each of the two states from granting authority for the erection of a bridge to the middle of the river.

In 1854, the U.S. Supreme Court held in *Florida v. Georgia* that a boundary compact enacted by the two states would be invalid unless Congress were to grant its consent.[70]

The seminal case on the issue of the necessity for congressional consent to interstate compacts is the 1893 case of *Virginia v. Tennessee*.[71] The two states involved never obtained congressional consent for a boundary agreement that they had reached earlier in the 19th century. The U.S. Supreme Court framed the issue in the case as follows:

> "Is the agreement, made without the consent of congress, between Virginia and Tennessee, to appoint commissioners to run and mark the boundary line between them, within the prohibition of this clause? The terms 'agreement' or

---

[66] *New Hampshire v. Maine.* 426 U.S. 363. 1976.

[67] *U.S. Steel Corporation v. Multistate Tax Commission.* 434 U.S. 452. at 459. 1978.

[68] *Barron v. Baltimore.* 32 U.S. 243. 1833.

[69] *Dover v. Portsmouth Bridge.* 17 N.H. 200. 1845.

[70] *Florida v. Georgia.* 55 U.S. 478. 1854.

[71] *Virginia v. Tennessee.* 148 U.S. 503. 1893.

'compact,' taken by themselves, are sufficiently comprehensive to embrace all forms of stipulation, written or verbal, and relating to all kinds of subjects; to those to which the United States can have no possible objection or have any interest in interfering with, as well as to those which may tend to increase and build up the political influence of the contracting states, so as to encroach upon or impair the supremacy of the United States, or interfere with their rightful management of particular subjects placed under their entire control."[72]

The Court observed:

"There are many matters upon which different states may agree that can in no respect concern the United States. If, for instance, Virginia should come into possession and ownership of a small parcel of land in New York, which the latter state might desire to acquire as a site for a public building, it would hardly be deemed essential for the latter state to obtain the consent of congress before it could make a valid agreement with Virginia for the purchase of the land."[73] [Emphasis added]

The Court continued:

"If Massachusetts, in forwarding its exhibits to the World's Fair at Chicago, should desire to transport them a part of the distance over the Erie canal, it would hardly be deemed essential for that state to obtain the consent of congress before it could contract with New York for the transportation of the exhibits through that state in that way."[74]

Further, the Court stated:

"If the bordering line of two states should cross some malarious and disease-producing district, there could be no possible reason, on any conceivable public grounds, to obtain the consent of congress for the bordering states to agree to unite

---

[72] *Id.* at 517–518.
[73] *Id.* at 518.
[74] *Id.*

in draining the district, and thus removing the cause of disease. So, in case of threatened invasion of cholera, plague, or other causes of sickness and death, it would be the height of absurdity to hold that the threatened states could not unite in providing means to prevent and repel the invasion of the pestilence without obtaining the consent of congress, which might not be at the time in session."[75]

Having established that the requirement for congressional consent is not universal, the Court then recast the issue in the case:

"If, then, the terms 'compact' or 'agreement' in the constitution do not apply to every possible compact or agreement between one state and another, for the validity of which the consent of congress must be obtained, to what compacts or agreements does the constitution apply?"[76]

The Court then answered the question as follows:

"We can only reply by looking at the object of the constitutional provision, and construing the terms 'agreement' and 'compact' by reference to it. It is a familiar rule in the construction of terms to apply to them the meaning naturally attaching to them from their context. 'Noscitur a sociis' is a rule of construction applicable to all written instruments. Where any particular word is obscure or of doubtful meaning, taken by itself, its obscurity or doubt may be removed by reference to associated words; and the meaning of a term may be enlarged or restrained by reference to the object of the whole clause in which it is used.

"Looking at the clause in which the terms 'compact' or 'agreement' appear, it is evident that **the prohibition is directed to the formation of any combination tending to the increase of political power in the states, which may encroach upon or interfere with the just supremacy of the United States.**"[77] [Emphasis added]

---

[75] *Id.*

[76] *Id.*

[77] *Id.* at 519.

The Court continued:

"[Justice] Story, in his Commentaries, (section 1403,) referring to a previous part of the same section of the constitution in which the clause in question appears, observes that its language

'may be more plausibly interpreted from the terms used, 'treaty, alliance, or confederation,' and upon the ground that the sense of each is best known by its association *('noscitur a sociis')* to apply to treaties of a political character; such as treaties of alliance for purposes of peace and war, and treaties of confederation, in which the parties are leagued for mutual government, political co-operation, and the exercise of political sovereignty, and treaties of cession of sovereignty, or conferring internal political jurisdiction, or external political dependence, or general commercial privileges;'

"and that

'the latter clause, 'compacts and agreement,' might then very properly apply to such as regarded what might be deemed mere private rights of sovereignty; such as questions of boundary, interests in land situate in the territory of each other, and other internal regulations for the mutual comfort and convenience of states bordering on each other.'

"And he [Story] adds:

'In such cases the consent of congress may be properly required, in order to check any infringement of the rights of the national government; and, at the same time, a total prohibition to enter into any compact or agreement might be attended with permanent inconvenience or public mischief.' "[78]

The Court continued:

"Compacts or agreements—and we do not perceive any difference in the meaning, except that the word 'compact' is

---

[78] *Id.* at 520–521.

generally used with reference to more formal and serious engagements than is usually implied in the term 'agreement'— cover all stipulations affecting the conduct or claims of the parties. The mere selection of parties to run and designate the boundary line between two states, or to designate what line should be run, of itself imports no agreement to accept the line run by them, and such action of itself does not come within the prohibition. Nor does a legislative declaration, following such line, that is correct, and shall thereafter be deemed the true and established line, import by itself a contract or agreement with the adjoining state. It is a legislative declaration which the state and individuals affected by the recognized boundary line may invoke against the state as an admission, but not as a compact or agreement. The legislative declaration will take the form of an agreement or compact when it recites some consideration for it from the other party affected by it; for example, as made upon a similar declaration of the border or contracting state. The mutual declarations may then be reasonably treated as made upon mutual considerations. The compact or agreement will then be within the prohibition of the constitution, or without it, according as the establishment of the boundary line **may lead or not to the increase of the political power or influence of the states affected, and thus encroach or not upon the full and free exercise of federal authority.**"[79] [Emphasis added]

The Court continued:

"If the boundary established is so run as to cut off an important and valuable portion of a state, the political power of the state enlarged would be affected by the settlement of the boundary; and to an agreement for the running of such a boundary, or rather for its adoption afterwards, the consent of congress may well be required. But the running of a boundary may have no effect upon the political influence of either state; it may simply serve to mark and define that which actually existed before, but was undefined and unmarked. In that

---

[79] *Id.*

case the agreement for the running of the line, or its actual survey, would in no respect displace the relation of either of the states to the general government. There was, therefore, no compact or agreement between the states in this case which required, for its validity, the consent of congress, within the meaning of the constitution, until they had passed upon the report of the commissioners, ratified their action, and mutually declared the boundary established by them to be the true and real boundary between the states. Such ratification was mutually made by each state in consideration of the ratification of the other.

"The constitution does not state when the consent of congress shall be given, whether it shall precede or may follow the compact made, or whether it shall be express or may be implied. In many cases the consent will usually precede the compact or agreement, as where it is to lay a duty of tonnage, to keep troops or ships of war in time of peace, or to engage in war. But where the agreement relates to a matter which could not well be considered until its nature is fully developed, it is not perceived why the consent may not be subsequently given. [Justice] Story says that the consent may be implied, and is always to be implied when congress adopts the particular act by sanctioning its objects and aiding in enforcing them; and observes that where a state is admitted into the Union, notoriously upon a compact made between it and the state of which it previously composed a part, there the act of congress admitting such state into the Union is an implied consent to the terms of the compact. Knowledge by congress of the boundaries of a state and of its political subdivisions may reasonably be presumed, as much of its legislation is affected by them, such as relate to the territorial jurisdiction of the courts of the United States, the extent of their collection districts, and of districts in which process, civil and criminal, of their courts may be served and enforced.

"In the present case the consent of congress could not have preceded the execution of the compact, for until the line was run it could not be known where it would lie, and whether or not it would receive the approval of the states. The preliminary agreement was not to accept a line run, whatever it might be, but to receive from the commissioners designated a report as to the line which might be run and established by them. After its consideration each state was free to take such action as it might judge expedient upon their report. The approval by congress of the compact entered into between the states upon their ratification of the action of their commissioners is fairly implied from its subsequent legislation and proceedings. The line established was treated by that body as the true boundary between the states in the assignment of territory north of it as a portion of districts set apart for judicial and revenue purposes in Virginia, and as included in territory in which federal elections were to be held, and for which appointments were to be made by federal authority in that state, and in the assignment of territory south of it as a portion of districts set apart for judicial and revenue purposes in Tennessee, and as included in territory in which federal elections were to be held, and for which federal appointments were to be made for that state. Such use of the territory on different sides of the boundary designated in a single instance would not, perhaps, be considered as absolute proof of the assent or approval of congress to the boundary line; but the exercise of jurisdiction by congress over the country as a part of Tennessee on one side, and as a part of Virginia on the other, for a long succession of years, without question or dispute from any quarter, furnishes as conclusive proof of assent to it by that body as can usually be obtained from its most formal proceedings."[80]

In summary, despite the absence of congressional consent, the U.S. Supreme Court upheld the interstate compact between Virginia and Tennessee because the compact did not

- increase "the political power of influence" of the party states, or

---

[80] *Id.*

- encroach "upon the full and free exercise of federal authority."

In deciding *Virginia v. Tennessee*, the Court also noted that Congress had relied, over the years, upon the compact's terms for judicial and revenue purposes, thereby implying the grant of consent.

Relying on *Virginia v. Tennessee*, the legislatures of New York and New Jersey did not submit the Palisades Interstate Park Agreement of 1900 to Congress for its consent.

In the same vein, the legislatures of New Jersey and New York initially had no intention of submitting the 1921 Port of New York Authority Compact to Congress, despite the compact's many novel and unique features. The compact simply specified that it would become effective

> "when signed and sealed by the Commissioners of each State as hereinbefore provided and the Attorney General of the State of New York and the Attorney General of New Jersey...."[81]

After the newly created Authority's bankers and bond counsels advised the Authority that potential investors might be hesitant to purchase bonds of such an unusual governmental entity in the absence of congressional consent, the two states sought, and quickly obtained, congressional consent for the compact.[82]

Note that, as a matter of convention, many compacts do not explicitly mention congressional consent, even when it is the intent of the compacting parties to seek it.

In the 1976 case of *New Hampshire v. Maine*, the U.S. Supreme Court reaffirmed the 1893 case of *Virginia v. Tennessee* and decided that an interstate agreement locating an ancient boundary did not require congressional consent.[83]

The 1978 case of *U.S. Steel Corporation v. Multistate Tax Commission*[84] is the most important recent case on the issue of whether

---

[81] *New York Laws of 1921.* Chapter 154.

[82] Zimmerman, Joseph F. 1996. *Interstate Relations: The Neglected Dimension of Federalism.* Westport, CT: Praeger.

[83] *New Hampshire v. Maine.* 426 U.S. 363. 1976.

[84] *U.S. Steel Corporation v. Multistate Tax Commission.* 434 U.S. 454. 1978. Justice Powell wrote the opinion of the Court, joined by Chief Justice Burger and Justices Brennan, Stewart, Marshall, Rehnquist, and Stevens.

congressional consent is necessary for interstate compacts. In that case, the U.S. Supreme Court reaffirmed its 1893 holding in *Virginia v. Tennessee.*[85] The Multistate Tax Compact addresses issues relating to multistate taxpayers and uniformity among state tax systems. Like many compacts, the compact itself is silent as to congressional consent, saying only:

"This compact shall enter into force when enacted into law by any seven states."[86]

The Multistate Tax Compact was submitted to Congress for its consent. However, the compact languished there because of fierce political opposition from various business interests that were concerned about multi-million-dollar tax audits. The compacting states decided to proceed with the implementation of the compact without congressional consent. Predictably, the opponents of the compact, led by U.S. Steel, challenged the constitutionality of their action.

In upholding the constitutionality of the Multistate Tax Compact, despite the lack of congressional consent, the Supreme Court noted that the compact did not

"authorize the member states to exercise any powers they could not exercise in its absence...."[87]

The Court again applied the interpretation of the Compact Clause from its 1893 holding in *Virginia v. Tennessee,* writing that:

"the test is whether the Compact enhances state power *quaod* the National Government."[88]

The dissent of Justice Byron White (joined by Justice Harry Blackmun) in *U.S. Steel Corporation v. Multistate Tax Commission* is noteworthy because it suggests that the Court's majority opinion may have implicitly recognized a second test, namely whether a compact possibly encroaches on non-party states.

"A proper understanding of what would encroach upon federal authority, however, must also incorporate encroach-

---

[85] *Virginia v. Tennessee.* 148 U.S. 503. 1893.

[86] Multistate Tax Compact. Section 1 of Article X.

[87] *U.S. Steel Corporation v. Multistate Tax Commission.* 434 U.S. 454 at 473. 1978. Justice Powell wrote the opinion of the Court, joined by Chief Justice Burger and Justices Brennan, Stewart, Marshall, Rehnquist and Stevens.

[88] *Id.* at 473. 1978.

ments on the authority and power of non-Compact States."[89]

Accordingly, it might be necessary to analyze the impact of a disputed compact on the power of the federal government and on the power of non-member states in order to determine whether Congressional consent is required for a particular compact.

As the Supreme Court noted in *U.S. Steel Corporation v. Multistate Tax Commission:*

> "most multilateral compacts have been submitted for Congressional approval."[90]

Recognizing the historical precedent of submitting compacts to Congress for approval, we have been unable to locate a single case where a court invalidated a compact for lack of consent on the grounds that it impermissibly encroached on federal supremacy.[91]

In analyzing the diverse range of issues on which courts have allowed states to enter into interstate compacts, it is hard to predict circumstances under which a court will invalidate an interstate compact that has not received Congressional approval, except in the rare cases where the compact clearly encroaches on federal supremacy.[92] As Michael S. Greve wrote in 2003:

> "After *U.S. Steel* one can hardly imagine a state compact that would run afoul of the Compact Clause without first, or at

---

[89] *Id.* at 494.

[90] *Id.* at 471.

[91] See *Star Scientific, Inc. v. Beales*, 278 F.3d 339 (4th Cir. 2002) involving the Master Settlement Agreement that resolved the lawsuit between states and major companies in the tobacco industry and established an administrative body to determine compliance with the agreement; *McComb v. Wambaugh*, 934 F.2d 474 (3rd Cir. 1991) involving the Interstate Compact on Placement of Children focusing on adoption and foster care of children; *New York v. Trans World Airlines*, Inc., 728 F.Supp. 162 (S.D.N.Y. 1990) involving a compact among several states to regulate airline advertising; *Breest v. Moran*, 571 F.Supp. 343 (D.R.I. 1983) involving the New England Interstate Corrections Compact allowing for the transfer of prisoners among detention facilities in the New England states.

[92] Even where encroachment arguably occurs, Congressional consent might not be required. For example, encroachment on federal powers arguably occurred in both the Multistate Tax Compact involved in *U.S. Steel Corporation v. Multistate Tax Commission* (434 U.S. 454, 1978) which sought to short-circuit a federal statutory solution to the allocation of interstate taxes and the compact involved in *Star Scientific, Inc. v. Beales*, 278 F.3d 339 (4th Cir. 2002) that resolved the lawsuit between states and major tobacco companies concerning the regulation of national cigarette advertising. Yet, both were held to be valid despite not receiving Congressional consent.

least also, running afoul of other independent constitutional obstacles."[93]

Moreover, in the 1991 case of *McComb v. Wambaugh,* the U.S. Court of Appeals for the Third Circuit held that no encroachment occurs where the subject of the compact concerns

"areas of jurisdiction historically retained by the states."[94]

In *The Law and Use of Interstate Compacts,* Frederick L. Zimmermann[95] and Mitchell Wendell point out:

> "Consent bills for interstate compacts dealing with issues in the realm of state activity, law, and administration, with inter-state jurisdictional problems and with the settlement of inter-state equities, normally serve only to clutter congressional cal-endars and complicate and obstruct interstate cooperation."[96]

A number of compacts involving the concerned states' constitution-ally reserved powers have been submitted to Congress for its consent. On one occasion, one house of Congress declined to grant consent on the grounds that congressional consent was unnecessary. The House of Representatives approved a bill granting consent to the Southern Regional Education Compact; however, the Senate did not concur because it concluded that the subject matter of the compact—educa-tion—was entirely a state prerogative.[97]

5.13 ENFORCEMENT OF INTERSTATE COMPACTS

The granting of consent suggests that Congress may enforce compact provisions; however, in practice, enforcement of interstate compacts is usually left to courts.

Party states have, on numerous occasions, filed suits in the U.S. Supreme Court requesting its interpretation of the provisions of interstate compacts. For example, the Court granted a request by Kansas in 2001 to

---

[93] Compacts, Cartels, and Congressional Consent. 68 Mo. L. Rev. 285 at 308. 2003.

[94] 934 F.2d at 479 (3rd Cir. 1991).

[95] Not to be confused with Joseph F. Zimmerman, co-author of this book.

[96] Zimmermann, Frederick. Lloyd and Wendell, Mitchell. 1976. *The Law and Use of Interstate Compacts.* Lexington, KY: Council of State Governments.

[97] Barton, Weldon V. 1967. *Interstate Compacts in the Political Process.* Chapel Hill, NC: University of North Carolina Press. Pages 132–133.

file a bill of complaint in equity against Colorado in an attempt to resolve disputes pertaining to the Arkansas River Compact. In *Kansas v. Colorado*, the Court rejected Colorado's argument that the 11th Amendment barred a damages award for Colorado's violation of the compact because the damages were losses suffered by individual farmers in Kansas and not by the State of Kansas.[98]

An individual or a state may challenge the validity of a compact in state or federal court. Similarly, an individual or a state may bring suit to have provisions of a compact enforced. In general, the 11th Amendment forbids a federal court from considering a suit in law or equity against a state brought by a citizen of a sister state or a foreign nation. Notwithstanding the 11th Amendment, a citizen can challenge a compact or its execution in a state or federal court in a proceeding to prevent a public officer from enforcing a compact. If brought in a state court, the suit can potentially be removed to a United States District Court under provisions of the Removal of Causes Act of 1920 on the ground the state court

"... might conceivably be interested in the outcome of the case...."[99]

Nebraska's participation in the Central Interstate Low-Level Radioactive Waste Compact created controversy over a 20-year period starting in the 1980s. As discussed in section 5.7, an initiative petition was used in Nebraska in 1988 in an unsuccessful attempt to repeal the law authorizing Nebraska's participation in the compact. Then, in 1999, the legislature decided to withdraw from the compact. Nebraska's change of heart proved costly. The Central Interstate Low-Level Radioactive Waste Commission filed a federal lawsuit resulting from Nebraska's withdrawal from the compact and its alleged refusal to meet its contractual obligations to store the radioactive waste. Waste generators and the compact commission's contractor filed a suit in the U.S. District Court for the District of Nebraska, alleging that the state of Nebraska had deliberately delayed review of their license application for eight years and that it had always intended to deny it. The court ruled in 1999 that Nebraska had waived its 11th Amendment immunity when it joined the

---

[98] *Kansas v. Colorado.* 533 U.S. 1. 2001.

[99] 41 Stat. 554.

compact.[100] In 2001, the U.S. Court of Appeals for the Eighth Circuit affirmed the lower court's decision.[101] In 2004, Nebraska agreed to settle the lawsuit for $141,000,000.[102]

5.14 AMENDMENTS TO INTERSTATE COMPACTS

Party states may amend an interstate compact. Proposed amendments to an interstate compact typically follow the same process employed in the enactment of the original compact by each party (e.g., approval of a bill by the legislature and Governor). For example, the Tri-States Lotto Compact provides:

> "Amendments and supplements to this compact may be adopted by concurrent legislation of the party states."

In addition, the consent of Congress is necessary for an amendment of an interstate compact if the original compact received such consent.

As a matter of practical politics, an objection by a member of Congress who represents an area affected by a compact will often be able to halt congressional consideration of consent. This fact is illustrated by the experience of the New Jersey Legislature and the New York Legislature, which each enacted an amendment to the Port Authority of New York and New Jersey Compact (signed by the two Governors) allowing the Port Authority to initiate industrial development projects. In 1967, Representative Elizabeth Holtzman of New York placed a hold on the consent bill on the grounds that the Port Authority had failed to solve the port's transportation problems. Holtzman argued that the Port Authority should construct a railroad freight tunnel under the Hudson River to obviate the need of trains to travel 125 miles to the north to a rail bridge over the river. She removed the hold upon reaching an agreement with the Authority. The Port Authority agreed that it would finance an independent study of the economic feasibility of constructing such a tunnel. The study ultimately reached the conclusion that a rail freight tunnel would not be economically viable.

The Constitution (section 10 of Article I) authorizes Congress to revise state statutes levying import and export duties; however, it does

---

[100] *Entergy, Arkansas, Incorporated v. Nebraska*, 68 F.Supp.2d 1093 at 1100 (D.Neb.1999).
[101] *Entergy, Arkansas, Incorporated v. Nebraska*, 241 F.3d 979 at 991–992 (8th Cir. 2001).
[102] *Lincoln Journal Star.* July 15, 2005.

not grant similar authority to revise interstate compacts. Congress withdrew its consent to a Kentucky–Pennsylvania Interstate Compact that stipulated that the Ohio River should be kept free of obstructions. In 1855, the U.S. Supreme Court ruled in *Pennsylvania v. Wheeling and Belmont Bridge Company* that the compact was constitutional under the Constitution's Supremacy Clause (Article VI) and that a compact approved by Congress did not restrict Congress's power to regulate an interstate compact.[103] In the 1917 case of *Louisville Bridge Company v. United States*, the Court ruled that Congress may amend a compact even in the absence of a specific provision reserving to Congress the authority to alter, amend, or repeal the compact.[104] A federal statute terminating a compact is not subject to the due process guarantee of the 5th Amendment to the Constitution on the ground that this protection extends only to persons.

5.15 DURATION, TERMINATION, AND WITHDRAWALS

The duration of an interstate compact, the method of terminating a compact, and the method by which a party may withdraw from a compact are generally specified by the compact itself.

5.15.1 DURATION OF AN INTERSTATE COMPACT

The U.S. Constitution does not address the question of the permissible duration of interstate compacts. The 1785 Maryland–Virginia compact regulating fishing and navigation on the Chesapeake Bay and the Potomac was ratified under the Articles of Confederation and remained in effect until 1958 (when it was replaced by the Potomac River Compact).

Some compacts contain a sunset provision specifying the compact's duration. For example, California agreed to serve, for 35 years, as the host state for the storage of radioactive waste for the states of Arizona, North Dakota, South Dakota, and California in the Southwestern Low-Level Radioactive Waste Disposal Compact.

5.15.2 TERMINATION OF AN INTERSTATE COMPACT

Many compacts contain a termination provision. For example, the Colorado River Compact stipulates that termination may be authorized only by a unanimous vote of all party states.

---

[103] *Pennsylvania v. Wheeling and Belmont Bridge Company.* 50 U.S. 647. 1855.

[104] *Louisville Bridge Company v. United States.* 242 U.S. 409. 1917.

The Central Interstate Low-Level Radioactive Waste Compact permits states to withdraw, but that the compact shall not be terminated until all parties leave the compact.

> "G. The withdrawal of a party state from this compact under subsection D of Article VII of the compact or the revocation of a state's membership in this compact under subsection E of Article VII of the compact shall not affect the applicability of this compact to the remaining party states.

> "H. This compact shall be terminated when all party states have withdrawn pursuant to subsection D of Article VII of the compact."

5.15.3 WITHDRAWAL FROM AN INTERSTATE COMPACT

Most compacts (other than those settling boundary disputes) have a provision permitting a party state to withdraw. If a state originally joined a compact by enacting a statute, withdrawal is usually accomplished by enacting a new statute withdrawing from the compact.

Examples of withdrawals include the action of the Maryland General Assembly withdrawing from the Interstate Bus Motor Fuel Tax Compact in 1967 and its action withdrawing from the National Guard Mutual Assistance Compact in 1981. In 1995, the Virginia General Assembly enacted a statute withdrawing from the Atlantic States Marine Fisheries Compact, complaining that Virginia's fishing quotas were too low.

States may withdraw from a compact and then rejoin it. For example, Florida withdrew from the Atlantic States Marine Fisheries Compact and then subsequently rejoined the compact.

Although some compacts allow instantaneous withdrawal, most require a party to provide a specified amount of advance notice before its withdrawal becomes effective. For example, the Interstate Mining Compact authorizes a party state to withdraw its membership one year after the Governor of the withdrawing state notifies the Governors of all the other compacting states.

The Delaware River Basin Compact requires advance notice of at least 20 years for withdrawal, with such notice being allowed only during a five-year window every 100 years.

Section 8.6 contains a considerably more detailed discussion of withdrawals from interstate compacts.

5.16 ADMINISTRATION OF INTERSTATE COMPACTS

About one half of all modern-day interstate compacts establish a commission to administer the subject matter of the compact. The remaining compacts are generally administered by departments and agencies of the party states.

For example, the Driver License Compact (to which 45 states adhere) requires a party state to report each conviction of a driver from another party state for a motor vehicle violation to the licensing authority of the driver's home state. The compact requires the home state to treat the reported violation as if it had occurred in the home state. The compact also requires the licensing authority of each member state to determine whether an applicant for a driver license has held or currently holds a driver's license issued by another party state.

Similarly, the Nonresident Violator Compact (enacted by 44 states) ensures that nonresident drivers answer summonses or appearance tickets for moving violations. This compact (like the Driver License Compact) requires each member state to report each conviction of a driver from another party state for a motor vehicle violation to the licensing authority of the driver's home state. This compact is designed to ensure that nonresident motorists are treated in the same manner as resident motorists and that their due process rights are protected. A driver who fails to respond to an appearance ticket or summons will have his or her license suspended by the issuing state.

5.17 STYLE OF INTERSTATE COMPACTS

As a matter convention, modern interstate compacts are typically organized into articles, with unnumbered sections. After each member state enacts the compact, the various articles of the compact are given numbers and letters in the state's compiled code in accordance with the state's style. Similarly, after Congress consents to a compact, the various articles of the compact may be assigned different letters and numbers. Thus, compacts (and congressional legislation consenting to compacts) typically make reference to enactment of "substantially" the same agreement by other member states.

5.18 COMPARISON OF TREATIES AND COMPACTS

Although interstate compacts bear many similarities to international treaties among nations, they differ in three important respects.

First, Congress may enact a statute that conflicts with an international treaty, whereas a state legislature lacks the authority to enact a statute conflicting with any provision of an interstate compact.

Second, a compact is a contract that is enforceable by courts. In contrast, the procedure for enforcement of an international treaty is specified within the treaty itself. In practice, many treaties contain no specific provision for enforcement and merely rely on the goodwill of the parties.

Third, under the Constitution, the President is granted the sole authority to negotiate a treaty with another nation. In contrast, no provision in the Constitution stipulates the manner of negotiation of interstate compacts. Moreover, Congress has never enacted any general statute specifying procedures to be followed by a state that is contemplating entry into an interstate compact.

There is no international law provision authorizing citizens of a signatory to a treaty to be involved in its termination. In 1838, the U.S. Supreme Court applied this principle of international law to interstate compacts. The Court ruled, in the case of *Georgetown v. Alexander Canal Company*, that citizens whose rights would be affected adversely by a compact are not parties to a compact and that they consequently can have no direct involvement in a compact's termination.[105]

5.19 COMPARISON OF UNIFORM STATE LAWS AND INTERSTATE COMPACTS

The term "uniform state law" usually refers to a law drafted and recommended by the National Conference of Commissioners on Uniform State Laws (NCCUSL), although the term is occasionally used to refer to laws originating elsewhere. The Conference, formed in 1892 upon the recommendation of the American Bar Association, is a non-governmental body. The Conference primarily works on private civil law and is most widely known for its work on the Uniform Commercial Code. Since 1892, the Conference has produced more than 200 recommended laws in areas such as commercial law, family or domestic relations law, estates, probate and trusts, real estate, implementation of full faith and credit, interstate enforcement of judgments, and alternative dispute resolution. There are numerous uniform acts that have been adopted by large

---

[105] *Georgetown v. Alexander Canal Company.* 37 U.S. 91 at 95–96. 1838.

numbers of states, including the Uniform Anatomical Gift Act, the Uniform Fraudulent Transfer Act, the Uniform Interstate Family Support Act, the Uniform Enforcement of Foreign Judgments Act, and the Uniform Transfers to Minors Act.

There is some resemblance between an interstate compact and a uniform state law. Both, for example, entail enactment of identical statutes by a group of states. An interstate compact encompassing all 50 states and the District of Columbia and a uniform state law enacted by the same 51 jurisdictions each has the effect of establishing national policy. There are, however, a number of important differences.

First, the goal of a uniform state law is, almost always, enactment of the identical statute by all states. Many interstate compacts are inherently limited to particular geographic areas (e.g., the Port of New York Authority Compact, the Arkansas River Compact, and the Great Lakes Basin Compact) or to states that are engaged in particular activities (e.g., the Interstate Oil Compact and the Multistate Lottery Agreement).

Second, the effective date of a uniform state law is typically not contingent on identical legislation being passed in any other state. A uniform state law generally takes effect in each state as soon as each state enacts it. That is, a uniform state law stands alone and is not coordinated with the identical laws that other states may, or may not, pass. If it happens that all 50 states enact a particular uniform state law, then the goal of establishing a uniform policy for the entire country is achieved. If a substantial fraction of the states enact a uniform state law, then the goal of uniformity is partially achieved. If only one state enacts a uniform state law, that particular statute serves as the law of that state on the subject matter involved. In contrast, the effective date of a compact is almost always contingent on the enactment by some specified number or some specified combination of states. The reason for this is that states are apt to enter into interstate compacts in order to obtain some benefit that can be obtained only by cooperative and coordinated action with one or more sister states.

Third, although the goal of the National Conference of Commissioners on Uniform State Laws is that identical laws be adopted in all states, it is very common for individual states to amend the Conference's recommended statute in response to local pressures. If the changes are not major, the Conference's goal of uniformity may nonetheless be substantially (albeit not perfectly) achieved. In contrast, adoption of a compact requires a meeting of minds. Because an interstate compact is a contract, each party that desires to adhere to an interstate compact must enact identical wording (except for insubstantial differences such as numbering and punctuation). Variations in substance are not allowed.

Fourth, and most importantly, a uniform state law does not establish a contractual relationship among the states involved. When a state enacts a uniform state law, it undertakes no obligations to other states. The enacting state merely seeks the benefits associated with uniform treatment of the subject matter at hand. Each state's legislature may repeal or amend a uniform state law at any time, at its own pleasure and convenience. There is no procedure for withdrawal (or advance notice for withdrawal) in a uniform state law. A uniform state law does not create any new legal entity, and therefore there is no legal entity from which to withdraw. In contrast, an interstate compact establishes a contractual relationship among its party states. Once a state enters into a compact, it is legally bound to the compact's terms, including the compact's specified restrictions and procedures for withdrawal and the compact's specified procedure for termination of the compact as a whole.

5.20 COMPARISON OF FEDERAL MULTI-STATE COMMISSIONS AND INTERSTATE COMPACTS

Federal multi-state commissions bear some resemblance to the commissions that are established by some interstate compacts. There are, however, a number of important differences between federally created multi-state commissions and interstate compacts.

In 1879, Congress first recognized the need for a governmental body in a multi-state region by establishing the Mississippi River Commission. The enabling statute directed the Commission to deepen channels; improve navigation safety; prevent destructive floods; and promote commerce, the postal system, and trade. The Commission's original members were three officers of the U.S. Army Corps of Engineers, one member of the U.S. Coast and Geodetic Survey, and three citizen members, including two civil engineers. Commission members are nominated by the President, subject to the Senate's advice and consent.

In a similar vein, the Water Resources Planning Act of 1965

authorizes the President, at the request of the concerned governors, to establish other river basin commissions. Such commissions have been created for the Ohio River and Upper Mississippi River basin.

The most well-known multi-state commission—the Tennessee Valley Authority—was created by Congress in 1933. The TVA operates in an area encompassing parts of seven states. Its purposes are to promote agricultural and industrial development, control floods, and improve navigation on the Tennessee River. The President appoints, with the Senate's advice and consent, three TVA commissioners for nine-year terms. The creation of the TVA is credited to populist Senator George Norris of Nebraska, who conducted a crusade for many years against the high rates charged by electric utility companies. Aside from the benefits to the states in the Tennessee Valley, Norris and his supporters argued that the cost of TVA-generated electricity would serve as a yardstick for evaluating the rates charged by private power companies elsewhere in the country.

Although the TVA possesses broad powers to develop the river basin, the authority has largely concentrated its efforts on dams and channels, fertilizer research, and production of electricity. The TVA is generally credited with achieving considerable success in its flood control, land and forest conservation, and river-management activities. At the same time, the TVA has engendered considerable controversy over the years in a number of areas.

There are several differences between federal multi-state commissions and the commissions that are established by interstate compacts.

First, federal multi-state commissions are entirely creatures of the federal government. The states play no official role in enacting the enabling legislation establishing such bodies. In contrast, each state makes its own decision as to whether to enact an interstate compact.

Second, although state officials often provide advice on appointments to federal multi-state commissions, the appointing authority for members of a federal multi-state commissions is entirely federal (i.e., the President). In contrast, the members of a commission established by an interstate compact are typically appointed by the states (e.g., by the Governors).

5.21 FUTURE OF INTERSTATE COMPACTS

In recent years, Congress has, with increasing frequency, exercised its preemption powers to remove regulatory authority totally or partially from the states. This tendency is responsible for the decrease in the number of new regulatory compacts since the mid 1960s.[106] For example, the Mid-Atlantic States Air Pollution Control Compact was entered into by Connecticut, New Jersey, and New York; however, Congress did not consent to the compact and instead enacted the Air Quality Act of 1967,[107] preempting state regulatory authority over air pollution abatement.

There are countervailing tendencies. Economic interest groups frequently lobby for the establishment of regulatory compacts among states, arguing that coordinated action by the states is sufficient to solve a particular problem.

It is reasonable to predict that increasing urban sprawl may someday lead to an interstate compact that establishes an interstate city encompassing an urban area spread over two or more states. Although no such interstate city has been created to date, the New Hampshire–Vermont Interstate School Compact has been used to establish two interstate school districts, each including a New Hampshire town and one or more Vermont towns. In the same vein, Kansas and Missouri have entered into a compact establishing a metropolitan cultural district governed by a commission. The commission's membership is determined by the number of counties that decide to join the district. Eligible counties include one with a population exceeding 300,000 that is adjacent to the state line, one that contains a part of a city with a population exceeding 400,000, and one that is contiguous to one of these.[108]

5.22 PROPOSALS FOR INTERSTATE COMPACTS ON ELECTIONS

There have been suggestions, over the years, for using interstate compacts in the field of elections.

The 1970 U.S. Supreme Court case of *Oregon v. Mitchell* was concerned with congressional legislation to bring about uniformity among state durational residency requirements for voters in presidential elections. In his opinion (partially concurring and partially dissenting), Justice Potter Stewart pointed out that if Congress had not acted, the states could have adopted an interstate compact to accomplish the same

---

[106] Zimmerman, Joseph F. 2005. *Congressional Preemption: Regulatory Federalism* Albany, NY: State University of New York Press.

[107] 81 Stat. 485.

[108] 114 Stat. 909.

objective. Justice Stewart pointed out that a compact involving all the states would, in effect, establish a nationwide policy on residency for election purposes.[109]

In the 1990s, Senator Charles Schumer of New York proposed a bi-state interstate compact in which New York and Texas would pool their electoral votes in presidential elections. Both states were (and still are) non-competitive in presidential politics. Schumer observed that the two states have almost the same number of electoral votes (currently 34 for Texas and 31 for New York) and regularly produce majorities of approximately the same magnitude in favor of each state's respective dominant political party. The Democrats typically carry New York by about 60%, and the Republicans typically carry Texas by about 60%. The purpose of the proposed compact was to create a large super-state (slightly larger than California) that would attract the attention of the presidential candidates during presidential campaigns.

---

[109] *Oregon v. Mitchell.* 400 U.S. 112 at 286–287. 1970.

6 | The Agreement Among the States to Elect the President by National Popular Vote

This chapter

- summarizes the motivation for the authors' proposal to employ an interstate compact to change the system for electing the President and Vice President of the United States (section 6.1),
- presents the text of the authors' proposal, namely the "Agreement Among the States to Elect the President by National Popular Vote" (section 6.2),
- explains the authors' proposed compact (section 6.3),
- mentions federal legislation that might be enacted by Congress in connection with the proposed interstate compact (section 6.4), and
- discusses previous proposals for multi-state electoral legislation (section 6.5).

6.1 MOTIVATION FOR THE PROPOSED INTERSTATE COMPACT

Chapter 1 of this book made the following points:

- Under the winner-take-all rule that is in nearly universal use in the United States, all of a state's electoral votes are controlled by a statewide plurality of the popular votes. Under this rule, a person's vote is nearly worthless unless the voter happens to live in a closely divided battleground state.
- Because only about 18 states are competitive in presidential elections, voters in two-thirds of the states are ignored in presidential elections.
- The existing winner-take-all system divides the nation's 122,000,000 popular votes into 51 separate pools, thereby

regularly manufacturing artificial electoral crises even when the nationwide popular vote is not particularly close. In the past six decades, there have been six presidential elections in which a shift of a small number of votes in one or two states would have elected (and in 2000, did elect) a presidential candidate who lost the popular vote nationwide.

- In about one election in 14, the existing system elects a candidate to the Presidency who did not win the nationwide popular vote.
- The statewide winner-take-all system is the reason why presidential voting does not matter in two thirds of the states, artificial crises are regularly manufactured, and second-place candidates are sometimes elected to the Presidency.

Chapter 2 established the following facts:

- The statewide winner-take-all system is established by state law—not the U.S. Constitution or federal law.
- The U.S. Constitution gives each state the exclusive power to choose the manner of choosing its presidential electors. Unlike the states' power to choose the manner of electing U.S. Representatives and Senators, the states' power to choose the manner of allocating its electoral votes is not subject to Congressional oversight.
- The Founding Fathers did not design or advocate the current system of electing the President. Instead, the current system evolved over a period of decades as a result of political considerations. The statewide winner-take-all rule was used by only three states in the nation's first presidential election (1789). Because each state realized that it diminished its voice by dividing its electoral votes, the statewide winner-take-all rule for the popular election of presidential electors became the norm in the first five decades after the Constitution's ratification.
- Because the power to allocate electoral votes is exclusively a state power and the statewide winner-take-all rule is contained only in state statutes, a federal constitutional

amendment is not necessary to change the existing state laws specifying use of the statewide winner-take-all system. The states have the constitutional power to change the current system.

Chapter 3 analyzed the three most prominent approaches to presidential election reform that have been proposed in the form of a federal constitutional amendment, namely the fractional proportional allocation of electoral votes, allocation of electoral votes by congressional district, and direct nationwide popular election. Each of these three approaches is analyzed in terms of three criteria:

- **Accuracy:** Would it ensure the election to the Presidency of the candidate with the most popular votes nationwide?
- **Competitiveness:** Would it improve upon the current situation in which voters in two-thirds of the states are ignored because they live in presidentially non-competitive states?
- **Equality:** Would every vote be equal?

Chapter 4 analyzed the two most prominent approaches to presidential election reform that can be unilaterally enacted without a federal constitutional amendment and without action by Congress, namely the whole-number proportional approach and the congressional-district approach.

Chapters 3 and 4 reached the conclusion that nationwide popular election of the President is the only approach that satisfies the criteria of accuracy, competitiveness, and equality.

Chapter 5 provided background on interstate compacts and made the following points:

- Interstate compacts are specifically authorized by the U.S. Constitution as a means by which the states may act in concert to address a problem.
- There are several hundred interstate compacts in existence, covering a wide variety of topics.
- An interstate compact is enacted in the same manner as a state law—that is, by a legislative bill receiving gubernatorial approval (or sufficient legislative support to override a gubernatorial veto) or by the citizen-initiative process (in states having this process).

- Interstate compacts typically address problems that cannot be solved unilaterally, but that can be solved by coordinated action. Accordingly, a compact almost always takes effect on a contingent basis—that is, the compact does not take effect until it is enacted by a specified number or combination of states that are sufficient to achieve the compact's goals.
- There are no constitutional restrictions on the subject matter of interstate compacts (other than the implicit limitation that the compact's subject matter must be among the powers that the states are permitted to exercise).
- An interstate compact has the force and effect of statutory law in the states belonging to the compact. The provisions of an interstate compact bind all state officials with the same force as all other state laws. The provisions of a compact are enforceable in court in the same way that any other state law is enforceable—that is, a court may compel a state official to execute the provisions of a compact (by mandamus), and a court may enjoin a state official from violating a compact's provisions (by injunction).
- An interstate compact is a binding contractual arrangement among states involved. The U.S. Constitution prohibits states from impairing the obligations of any contract, including interstate compacts. Thus, each state belonging to an interstate compact is assured that its sister states will perform their obligations under the compact.
- Because a compact is a contract, the provisions of an interstate compact take precedence over any conflicting law of any state belonging to the compact. As long as a state remains a party to a compact, it may not enact a law in conflict with its obligations under the compact. That is, the provisions of an interstate compact take precedence over a conflicting law—even if the conflicting law is enacted after the state enters into the compact.
- A state may withdraw from an interstate compact in accordance with the provisions for withdrawal contained in the compact.

The authors' proposal, namely an interstate compact entitled the "Agreement Among the States to Elect the President by National Popular Vote," would not become effective in any state until it is enacted by states collectively possessing a majority of the electoral votes (that is, 270 of the 538 electoral votes).

The proposed compact does not change a state's internal procedures for operating a presidential election. After the 50 states and the District of Columbia certify their popular vote counts for President in the usual way, a grand total of popular votes would be calculated by adding up the popular vote count from all 51 jurisdictions.

The Electoral College would remain intact under the proposed compact. The compact would simply change the Electoral College from an institution that reflects the voters' state-by-state choices (or, in the case of Maine and Nebraska, district-wide choices) into a body that reflects the voters' nationwide choice. Specifically, the proposed compact would require that each member state award its electoral votes to the presidential candidate who received the largest number of popular votes in all 50 states and the District of Columbia. Because the compact would become effective only when it encompasses states collectively possessing a majority of the electoral votes, the presidential candidate receiving the most popular votes in all 50 states and the District of Columbia would be guaranteed enough electoral votes in the Electoral College to be elected to the Presidency.

Note that every state's popular vote is included in the nationwide total regardless of whether it is a member of the compact. Membership in the compact is not required for the popular votes of a state to count.

Note also that the political complexion of the particular states belonging to the compact does not affect the outcome—that is, the presidential candidate receiving the most popular votes in all 50 states and the District of Columbia is assured sufficient electoral votes to be elected to the Presidency.

6.2 TEXT OF THE PROPOSED COMPACT

This section presents the entire text (888 words) of the proposed "Agreement Among the States to Elect the President by National Popular Vote."

ARTICLE I—MEMBERSHIP

I-1 Any State of the United States and the District of Columbia may become a member of this agreement by enacting this agreement.

ARTICLE II—RIGHT OF THE PEOPLE IN MEMBER STATES TO VOTE FOR PRESIDENT AND VICE PRESIDENT

II-1 Each member state shall conduct a statewide popular election for President and Vice President of the United States.

ARTICLE III—MANNER OF APPOINTING PRESIDENTIAL ELECTORS IN MEMBER STATES

III-1 Prior to the time set by law for the meeting and voting by the presidential electors, the chief election official of each member state shall determine the number of votes for each presidential slate in each State of the United States and in the District of Columbia in which votes have been cast in a statewide popular election and shall add such votes together to produce a "national popular vote total" for each presidential slate.

III-2 The chief election official of each member state shall designate the presidential slate with the largest national popular vote total as the "national popular vote winner."

III-3 The presidential elector certifying official of each member state shall certify the appointment in that official's own state of the elector slate nominated in that state in association with the national popular vote winner.

III-4 At least six days before the day fixed by law for the meeting and voting by the presidential electors, each member state shall make a final determination of the number of popular votes cast in the state for each presidential slate and shall communicate an official statement of such determination within 24 hours to the chief election official of each other member state.

III-5 The chief election official of each member state shall treat as conclusive an official statement containing the number of popular votes in a state for each presidential slate made by the day established by federal law for making a state's final determination conclusive as to the counting of electoral votes by Congress.

III-6 In event of a tie for the national popular vote winner, the presidential elector certifying official of each member state shall certify the appointment of the elector slate nominated in association with the presidential slate receiving the largest number of popular votes within that official's own state.

III-7 If, for any reason, the number of presidential electors nominated in a member state in association with the national popular vote winner is less than or greater than that state's number of electoral votes, the presidential candidate on the presidential slate that has been designated as the national popular vote winner shall have the power to nominate the presidential electors for that state and that state's presidential elector certifying official shall certify the appointment of such nominees.

III-8 The chief election official of each member state shall immediately release to the public all vote counts or statements of votes as they are determined or obtained.

III-9   This article shall govern the appointment of presidential electors in each member state in any year in which this agreement is, on July 20, in effect in states cumulatively possessing a majority of the electoral votes.

ARTICLE IV—OTHER PROVISIONS

IV-1   This agreement shall take effect when states cumulatively possessing a majority of the electoral votes have enacted this agreement in substantially the same form and the enactments by such states have taken effect in each state.

IV-2   Any member state may withdraw from this agreement, except that a withdrawal occurring six months or less before the end of a President's term shall not become effective until a President or Vice President shall have been qualified to serve the next term.

IV-3   The chief executive of each member state shall promptly notify the chief executive of all other states of when this agreement has been enacted and has taken effect in that official's state, when the state has withdrawn from this agreement, and when this agreement takes effect generally.

IV-4   This agreement shall terminate if the electoral college is abolished.

IV-5   If any provision of this agreement is held invalid, the remaining provisions shall not be affected.

ARTICLE V—DEFINITIONS

V-1   For purposes of this agreement,
      "chief executive" shall mean the Governor of a State of the United States or the Mayor of the District of Columbia;

V-2   "elector slate" shall mean a slate of candidates who have been nominated in a state for the position of presidential elector in association with a presidential slate;

V-3   "chief election official" shall mean the state official or body that is authorized to certify the total number of popular votes for each presidential slate;

V-4   "presidential elector" shall mean an elector for President and Vice President of the United States;

V-5   "presidential elector certifying official" shall mean the state official or body that is authorized to certify the appointment of the state's presidential electors;

V-6   "presidential slate" shall mean a slate of two persons, the first of whom has been nominated as a candidate for President of the United States and the second of whom has been nominated as a candidate for Vice President of the United States, or any legal successors to such persons, regardless of whether both names appear on the ballot presented to the voter in a particular state;

V-7   "state" shall mean a State of the United States and the District of Columbia; and

V-8   "statewide popular election" shall mean a general election in which votes are cast for presidential slates by individual voters and counted on a statewide basis.

6.3 EXPLANATION OF THE PROPOSED COMPACT

6.3.1 Explanation of Article I—Membership

Article I of the compact identifies the compact's prospective parties, namely the 51 jurisdictions that are currently entitled to appoint presidential electors under the U.S. Constitution. These 51 jurisdictions include the 50 states and the District of Columbia (which acquired the right to appoint presidential electors under terms of the 23rd Amendment). Elsewhere in the compact, the uncapitalized word "state" (defined in article V of the compact) refers to any of these 51 jurisdictions. The term "member state" refers to a jurisdiction where the compact has been enacted into law and is in effect.

6.3.2 Explanation of Article II—Right of the People in Member States to Vote for President and Vice President

Article II of the compact mandates a popular election for President and Vice President in each member state.

> "Each member state shall conduct a statewide popular election for President and Vice President of the United States."

The term "statewide popular election" is defined in article V of the compact as

> "a general election at which votes are cast for presidential slates by individual voters and counted on a statewide basis."

From the perspective of the operation of the compact, this clause establishes an essential precondition for a nationwide popular vote for President and Vice President, namely that there will be popular votes to count. As discussed in detail in section 2.2, the people of the United States have no federal constitutional right to vote for President and Vice President. The people have acquired the privilege to vote for President and Vice President as a consequence of legislative action by their respective states. Moreover, except in Colorado, the people have no state constitutional right to vote for President and Vice President, and the existing privilege may be withdrawn at any time merely by passage of a state law. Indeed, state legislatures chose the presidential electors in a majority of the states participating in the nation's first presidential election (1789). Moreover, state legislatures have changed the rules for voting for President for purely political reasons. For example, just prior to the 1800 presidential election, the Federalist-controlled legislatures of Massachusetts and New Hampshire—fearing Jeffersonian victories in the popular votes in their states—repealed existing state statutes allowing the people to vote for presidential electors and vested that power in themselves. Article II of the compact precludes the state legislature of a member state from doing this.

Because an interstate compact is a contractual obligation among the member states, the provisions of a compact take precedence over any conflicting law of any member state. This principle applies regardless of when the conflicting law may have been enacted.[1] Thus, once a state enters into an interstate compact and the compact takes effect, the state is bound by the terms of the compact as long as the state remains in the compact. Because a compact is a contract, a state must remain in an interstate compact until the state withdraws from the compact in accordance with the compact's terms for withdrawal. Thus, in reading each provision of a compact, the reader may find it useful to imagine that every section of the compact is preceded by the words

> "Notwithstanding any other provision of law in the member state, whether enacted before or after the effective date of this compact, … ."

Thus, as long as a state remains in the compact, article II of the compact establishes the right of the people in each member state to vote for President and Vice President.

Article II of the compact also requires continued use by member states of another feature of presidential voting that is an essential precondition for a nationwide popular vote for President and Vice President (and that is currently in universal use by the states). Specifically, article II of the compact requires that member states continue to use the short presidential ballot (section 2.2.6) in which the voter is presented with a choice among "presidential slates" containing a specifically named presidential nominee and a vice-presidential nominee.[2] The term "presidential

---

[1] Council of State Governments. 2003. *Interstate Compacts and Agencies 2003.* Lexington, KY: The Council of State Governments. Page 6.

[2] This clause does not prevent a presidential candidate from running with more than one vice-presidential nominee. In 2004, for example, Ralph Nader appeared on the ballot in New York as the presidential nominee of the Independence Party with Jan D. Pierce as his vice-presidential nominee. He simultaneously appeared on the New York ballot as the presidential nominee of the Peace and Justice Party with Peter Miguel Camejo as his

slate" is defined in article V of the compact as

> "a slate of two persons, the first of whom has been nominat-
> ed as a candidate for President of the United States and the
> second of whom has been nominated as a candidate for Vice
> President of the United States, or any legal successors to
> such persons .... "

The continued use of the short presidential ballot is an essential precondition for a nationwide popular vote because it permits the aggregation, from state to state, of the popular votes that have been cast for various presidential slates. If, for example, the voters in a particular state
cast separate votes for individual presidential electors (say, in the manner
shown in the 1964 Vermont ballot shown in figure 2.1 and discussed in
section 2.2.6 or the 1960 Alabama ballot shown in figure 2.13 and discussed in section 2.11), the winning presidential electors from that state
would each inevitably have a different vote count. Thus, there would not
be any single number available to add into the nationwide tally being
accumulated by the presidential slates running in the remainder of the
country.

6.3.3 Explanation of Article III—Manner of Appointing Presidential Electors in Member States

Article III of the compact prescribes the manner by which each state
would appoint its presidential electors under the compact. Article III
establishes the mechanics for a nationwide popular election. The first
three clauses of article III are the main clauses for implementing nationwide popular election of the President and Vice President.

The first clause of article III of the compact provides:

> "Prior to the time set by law for the meeting and voting by the
> presidential electors, the chief election official of each mem-
> ber state shall determine the number of votes for each presi-
> dential slate in each State of the United States and in the
> District of Columbia in which votes have been cast in a
> statewide popular election and shall add such votes together

vice-presidential nominee. There were, necessarily, two different lists of 31 nominees for
presidential elector associated with each of the two Nader "presidential slates" in New
York in 2004. Existing New York law treated and counted Nader's Independence Party
votes separately from Nader's Peace and Justice Party votes. That is, there were two different Nader "presidential slates" in New York in 2004.

to produce a 'national popular vote total' for each presidential slate."

The phrase "the time set by law for the meeting and voting by the presidential electors" refers to the federal law (title 3, chapter 1, section 7 of the United States Code) providing:

"The electors of President and Vice President of each State shall meet and give their votes on the first Monday after the second Wednesday in December next following their appointment at such place in each State as the legislature of such State shall direct."

In 2004, the federally designated day for the meeting of the Electoral College was Monday, December 13.

The term "chief election official" used throughout the compact is defined in article V of the compact as

"the state official or board that is authorized to certify the total number of popular votes cast for each presidential slate."

In most states, the "chief election official" is the Secretary of State or the state canvassing board.

The first clause of article III of the compact requires that the chief election official obtain statements showing the number of popular votes cast for each presidential slate in each state. Then, this clause requires that the popular votes for each presidential slate from all the states be added together to yield a "national popular vote total" for each presidential slate.

Because the purpose of the compact is to achieve a nationwide popular vote for President and Vice President, the popular vote counts from all 50 states and the District of Columbia are included in the "national popular vote total" regardless of whether the jurisdiction is a member of the compact. That is, the compact counts the popular votes from member states on an equal footing with those from non-member states.

Popular votes can, however, only be counted from non-member states if there are popular votes available to count. As already mentioned, Article II of the compact guarantees that each member state will produce a popular vote count because it requires member states to allow their voters to vote for President and Vice President in a "statewide popular election." Even though all states currently permit their voters to vote for presidential electors in a "statewide popular election," non-member states are, of course, not bound by the compact. In the unlikely event that a non-member state were to take the presidential vote away from its own people (as Massachusetts and New Hampshire did, for partisan political reasons, prior to the 1800 presidential election), there would be no popular vote count available from such a state.

Similarly, in the unlikely event that a non-member state were to remove the names of the presidential nominees and vice-presidential nominees from the ballot and present the voters only with names of unpledged candidates for presidential elector (such as the 1960 Alabama ballot shown in figure 2.13 and discussed in section 2.11), there would be no way to associate the vote counts of the various unpledged presidential electors with the nationwide tally being accumulated by any regular "presidential slate" running in the rest of the country.

The compact addresses the above two unlikely possibilities by specifying that the popular votes that are to be aggregated to produce the "national popular vote total" are those that are

> " … cast for each presidential slate in each State of the United States and in the District of Columbia **in which votes have been cast in a statewide popular election**.…" [Emphasis added]

The purpose of the second clause of article III of the compact is to identify the winner of the presidential election:

> "The chief election official of each member state shall designate the presidential slate with the largest national popular vote total as the 'national popular vote winner.' "

The third clause of article III of the compact guarantees that the "national popular vote winner" will end up with a majority of the electoral votes in the Electoral College.

> "The presidential elector certifying official of each member state shall certify the appointment in that official's own state of the elector slate nominated in that state in association with the national popular vote winner."

The third clause of article III of the compact refers to the "presidential elector certifying official" rather than the "chief election official" because these two officials are not the same in every state. For example, in some states, the "presidential elector certifying official" is an official or entity that is not otherwise involved in the administration of elections (e.g., the Governor or the Superior Court). The term "presidential elector certifying official" is defined in article V of the compact.

For purposes of illustration, suppose that the compact was in effect in 2004, and that Colorado was a member of the compact in 2004, and that the Republican presidential slate received the most popular votes in all 50 States and the District of Columbia (as was the case in the 2004 presidential election). In that event, the Colorado Secretary of State would declare the nine presidential electors who had been nominated by the Colorado Republican Party to be elected as Colorado's members of the Electoral College.

Because the purpose of the compact is to implement a nationwide popular election of the President and Vice President, it is the *national* vote total—not each state's separate statewide vote count—that would determine the national winner. Under the compact, the Electoral College would reflect the *nationwide* will of the voters—not the voters' separate statewide wills. Thus, the presidential electors nominated by the Republican Party in *all* states belonging to the compact would have won election as members of the Electoral College in their states. If Colorado voters had favored the Kerry-Edwards slate in 2004, the presidential electors nominated by the Republican Party in Colorado, for example, still would have won election as members of the Electoral College in Colorado in 2004 because the specific purpose of the compact is to award enough electoral votes to win the Presidency to the presidential candidate with the most votes nationwide.

Because the compact becomes effective only when it encompasses states collectively possessing a majority of the electoral votes (i.e., 270 or more of the 538 electoral votes), the presidential slate receiving the most popular votes in all 50 States and the District of Columbia is guaranteed at least 270 electoral votes when the Electoral College meets in mid-December. Given the fact that the Bush-Cheney presidential slate received about 3,500,000 more popular votes in the 50 States and the District of Columbia in 2004 than the Kerry-Edwards slate, the compact would have guaranteed the Bush-Cheney slate a majority of the electoral votes in the Electoral College. Under the compact, the Bush-Cheney slate would have received a majority of the electoral votes even if 59,393 Bush voters in Ohio had switched to Kerry in 2004 thereby giving Kerry a plurality of the popular votes in Ohio. In contrast, under the present system, if Kerry had carried Ohio, Kerry would have received all of Ohio's 20 electoral votes and Kerry would have been elected to the Presidency with 272 electoral votes (to Bush's 266).

The first three clauses of article III of the compact are the main clauses for implementing nationwide popular election of the President and Vice President. The remaining clauses of article III of the compact deal with administrative matters and technical issues.

The fourth clause of article III of the compact requires the timely issuance by each of the compact's member states of an "official statement" of the state's "final determination" of its presidential vote.

> "At least six days before the day fixed by law for the meeting and voting by the presidential electors, each member state shall make a final determination of the number of popular votes cast in the state for each presidential slate and shall communicate an official statement of such determination within 24 hours to the chief election official of each other member state."

The particular deadline in this clause corresponds to the deadline contained in the "safe harbor" provision of federal law (section 5 of title 3, chapter 1 of the United States Code). The phrase "final determination" in this clause corresponds to the term used in the "safe harbor" provision. Section 5 provides:

> "If any State shall have provided, by laws enacted prior to the day fixed for the appointment of the electors, for its final determination of any controversy or contest concerning the appointment of all or any of the electors of such State, by judicial or other methods or procedures, and such determination shall have been made at least six days before the time fixed for the meeting of the electors, such determination made pursuant to such law so existing on said day, and made at least six days prior to said time of meeting of the electors, shall be conclusive, and shall govern in the counting of the electoral votes as provided in the Constitution, and as hereinafter regulated, so far as the ascertainment of the electors appointed by such State is concerned."

The federally established "safe harbor" date for the 2004 presidential election was Monday December 6, 2004.

The fourth clause of article III of the compact, in effect, mandates each member state to comply with the "safe harbor" deadline. As a practical matter, this clause is merely a backstop because the vast majority of states already have specific state statutory deadlines for certifying the results of presidential elections, and these existing statutory deadlines come earlier than the federal "safe harbor" date (appendix T). This clause is a backstop for the additional reason that the U.S. Supreme Court in *Bush v. Gore* effectively treated the "safe harbor" date as a deadline for a state's "final determination" of its presidential election results.[3]

The word "communicated" in the fourth clause of article III of the compact is intended to permit transmission of the "official statement" by secure electronic means that may become available in the future (rather than, say, physical delivery of the official statement by an overnight courier service).

The fifth clause of article III of the compact provides:

> "The chief election official of each member state shall treat as conclusive an official statement containing the number of popular votes in a state for each presidential slate made by the day established by federal law for making a state's final determination conclusive as to the counting of electoral votes by Congress."

When the joint session of Congress counts the electoral votes on January 6th as provided in title 3, chapter 1, section 15 of the United States Code, each state's own "final determination" of its vote is considered "conclusive" as to the counting of electoral votes by Congress if it was finalized by the date established in the "safe harbor" provision of federal law (title 3, chapter 1, section 5). This section makes each state's (and, in particular, each *non-member* state's) final determination of its popular vote similarly "conclusive" when the chief election officials of the compact's member states add up the national popular vote under the terms of the compact.

The sixth clause of article III of the compact deals with the highly unlikely event of a tie in the national popular vote count:

---

[3] *Bush v. Gore.* 531 U.S. 98. 2000.

"In event of a tie for the national popular vote winner, the presidential elector certifying official of each member state shall certify the appointment of the elector slate nominated in association with the presidential slate receiving the largest number of popular votes within that official's own state."

The purpose of the seventh clause of article III of the compact is to ensure that the presidential slate receiving the most popular votes nationwide gets what it is entitled to—namely 100% of the electoral votes of each member state.

"If, for any reason, the number of presidential electors nominated in a member state in association with the national popular vote winner is less than or greater than that state's number of electoral votes, the presidential candidate on the presidential slate that has been designated as the national popular vote winner shall have the power to nominate the presidential electors for that state and that state's presidential elector certifying official shall certify the appointment of such nominees."

The seventh clause of article III of the compact addresses six potential situations that might prevent the national popular vote winner from receiving all of the electoral votes from a member state. These situations arise because of gaps and ambiguities in the widely varying language of state election laws concerning presidential elections.

First, the winning presidential slate might not be on the ballot in a particular member state. Presidential candidates (particularly third-party candidates) frequently fail to get on the ballot in a particular state because they did not comply with the state's ballot-access requirements (or perhaps did not even attempt to be on the ballot in a particular state). If a presidential candidate were to win the popular vote nationally without having qualified to be the ballot in a particular state belonging to the compact, there would no official slate of presidential electors "nominated in association with" the "national popular vote winner" in that particular member state. The remedy for this situation (and each of the other situations described below) is to employ the concept behind the current law for choosing presidential electors in Pennsylvania. Under current Pennsylvania law, each presidential nominee directly nominates the presidential electors who will run in association with the nominee's presidential slate in Pennsylvania.⁴ Thus, under the seventh clause of article III of the compact, the unrepresented presidential candidate would have the power to nominate the presidential electors for the state involved. The state's presidential elector certifying official would then certify the appointment of the candidate's choices for presidential elector. Note that the nomination of the presidential electors would, in this situation, come after the November voting (i.e., after the presidential slate involved had won the nationwide popular vote and had been declared to be the "national popular vote winner").

Second, no presidential electors may be "nominated in association with" the winning presidential slate in a particular member state because of some unforeseen situation that might arise under the language of state election codes. The Republican National Committee scheduled the 2004 Republican National Convention somewhat later than usual. In particular, the convention was scheduled to be held after Alabama's statutory deadline for each political party to file the name of its presidential and vice-presidential nominees with state officials. The scheduling of the convention created the possibility that there would be no Republican presidential slate on the Alabama ballot in 2004. The problem was satisfactorily resolved when the Alabama legislature agreed to pass special legislation in early 2004 to change the state law.

Third, a full slate of presidential electors may not be nominated in association with the winning presidential slate in a particular member state. For example, in 2004, Congressman Sherrod Brown was nominated as a Democratic presidential elector in Ohio. Brown was ineligible to be a presidential elector because the U.S. Constitution provides:

> "No Senator or Representative, or Person holding an Office of Trust or Profit under the United States, shall be appointed an Elector."⁵

---

⁴ The method of direct appointment of presidential electors by the presidential nominee is regularly used in Pennsylvania. Section 2878 of the Pennsylvania election code provides: "The nominee of each political party for the office of President of the United States shall, within thirty days after his nomination by the National convention of such party, nominate as many persons to be the candidates of his party for the office of presidential elector as the State is then entitled to."

⁵ U.S. Constitution. Article II, section 1, clause 2.

Although Brown submitted his resignation and the Ohio Democratic Party nominated a replacement, some contended that Ohio's procedure for filling a vacancy among the list of nominees for presidential elector did not permit naming a replacement in this case because there had been no legal nomination for Brown's position in the first place and hence no vacancy to fill. This contention remained unresolved because Kerry did not carry Ohio in 2004.

Fourth, the possibility exists that more presidential electors might be nominated in association with a presidential candidate than the state is entitled to send to the Electoral College. Fusion voting (section 2.10) creates the possibility that two or more competing slates of presidential electors could be nominated in association with the same presidential slate.

At the present time, fusion voting is routinely and widely used in only one state—New York. Because fusion voting is so routinely used in New York, the procedures for handling fusion voting in connection with presidential elector slates are well established. In 2004, for example, voters in New York had the opportunity to vote for the Bush-Cheney presidential slate on either the Republican Party line or the Conservative Party line (as shown by the voting machine face in figure 2.11). The political parties sharing a presidential nominee in New York nominate a common slate of presidential electors. Thus, the Republican and Conservative parties nominated the same slate of 31 presidential electors for the 2004 presidential election. The popular votes cast for Bush-Cheney on the Republican and Conservative lines were added together and treated as votes for all 31 Republican-Conservative candidates for the position of presidential elector. The popular votes cast for Kerry-Edwards on the Democratic Party line and the Working Families Party line were similarly aggregated and attributed to the common Kerry-Edwards slate of presidential electors. In 2004, the Kerry-Edwards presidential slate received the most popular votes in New York and therefore became entitled to all of New York's 31 electoral votes. The common Kerry-Edwards slate of 31 presidential electors was therefore declared to be elected to the Electoral College in New York. New York's 2004 Certificate of Ascertainment (appendix H) shows this aggregation.

Fusion voting is, however, permissible at the present time under the laws of a dozen and a half other states under various circumstances. Moreover, fusion voting proposals are currently under active consideration in several other states.[6] The laws of states where fusion is not routinely used would almost certainly lead to situations in which two competing elector slates are nominated under the banner of the same presidential slate.

Fifth, there is another way in which more presidential electors might be nominated in association with a particular presidential candidate than the state is entitled to send to the Electoral College. In states permitting presidential write-ins (section 2.8), it is possible for different slates of presidential electors to be written in by the voters in association with the same write-in presidential slate. Thus, a situation akin to fusion might arise in those states in connection with presidential write-ins.

Sixth, in some states permitting presidential write-ins, it is possible that an insufficient number of presidential electors may be nominated in association with a particular presidential slate. For example, the Minnesota election code does not specifically require that a full slate of presidential electors be identified at the time of the advance filing of write-in slates (section 2.8). In fact, it requires advance filing of the name of only one presidential elector even though Minnesota has 10 electoral votes.[7] Moreover, voters in Minnesota may cast write-in votes for President without advance filing.

The eighth clause of article III of the compact enables the public, the press, and political parties to closely monitor the implementation of the compact within each member state:

> "The chief election official of each member state shall immediately release to the public all vote counts or statements of votes as they are determined or obtained."

The unmodified term "statements" is intended to refer to both "official statements" of a state's "final determination" of its presidential vote (the fourth clause of article III of the compact) and any intermediate statements that the chief election official may obtain or consider at any time during the process of determining a state's presidential vote. The unmodified term "statement" is also intended to encompass the variety of types of documentation that may arise under the various practices and

---

[6] There was a statewide ballot proposition in 2002 in Alaska on fusion voting. The proposition was defeated.

[7] Minnesota election law. Section 204B.09, subdivision 3.

procedures of the states for officially recording and reporting their presidential votes. The Certificate of Ascertainment issued by the state in accordance with federal law,[8] for example, would be considered to be a "statement."

Because time is severely limited prior to the constitutionally mandated meeting of the Electoral College in mid-December, the term "immediately" is intended to eliminate any delays that might otherwise apply to the release of information by a public official under general public-disclosure laws.

The ninth clause of article III of the compact provides:

> "This article shall govern the appointment of presidential electors in each member state in any year in which this agreement is, on July 20, in effect in states cumulatively possessing a majority of the electoral votes."

This "governing" clause operates in conjunction with the first clause of article IV of the compact relating to the date when the compact as a whole first comes into effect:

> "This agreement shall take effect when states cumulatively possessing a majority of the electoral votes have enacted this agreement in substantially the same form and the enactments by such states have taken effect in each state."

The ninth clause of article III—the "governing" clause—employs the date of July 20 of a presidential election year because the six-month period starting on this date contains the following six important events relating to presidential elections:

- the national nominating conventions,[9]
- the fall general election campaign period,
- election day on the Tuesday after the first Monday in November,
- the meeting of the Electoral College on the first Monday after the second Wednesday in December,

---

[8] Title 3, chapter 1, section 6 of the United States Code deals with issuance of Certificates of Ascertainment by the states (and is discussed in section 2.4). See appendix A for the provisions of the U.S. Constitution and appendix B for provisions of federal law relating to presidential elections.

[9] All recent national nominating conventions of the major parties have met after July 20.

- the counting of the electoral votes by Congress on January 6, and
- the scheduled inauguration of the President and Vice President for the new term on January 20.

The ninth clause of article III of the compact addresses the question of whether article III governs the conduct of the presidential election in a particular year whereas the first clause of article V specifies when the compact as a whole initially comes into effect. The importance of this distinction is that it is theoretically possible that the compact could come into effect by virtue of enactment by states possessing a majority of the votes in the Electoral College (i.e., 270 or more of the 538 electoral votes), but that, at some future time, the compacting states might no longer possess a majority of the electoral votes. The situation could arise in any of four ways.

First, a future federal census might reduce the number of electoral votes possessed by the compacting states so that they no longer account for a majority of the electoral votes. This could occur if the compacting states happened to lose population relative to the remainder of the country. In that event, the compact provides that the compact as a whole would remain in effect (because the compact would have come into initial effect under the first clause of article IV of the compact); however, article III (the operative article in the compact) would then not "govern" the next presidential election. If additional state(s) subsequently enacted the compact—thereby raising the number of electoral votes possessed by the compacting states above 270 by July 20 of a subsequent presidential election year—article III of the compact would then again govern presidential elections.[10]

As a second example, if one or more states withdrew from the compact and thereby reduced the number of electoral votes possessed by the remaining compacting states below 270 by July 20 of a presidential election year, the compact as a whole would remain in effect, but article III (the operative article in the compact) would not govern the next presidential election.

As a third example, if a new state were admitted to the Union and if the total number of seats in the U.S. House of Representatives (and hence the total number of electoral votes) were permanently or temporarily

---

[10] As a practical matter, the scenario can only arise if the number of electoral votes possessed by states belonging to the compact hovers close to 270.

adjusted upwards, it is conceivable that the compacting states might no longer possess a majority of the new number of electoral votes. If the newly admitted state and/or some combination of other pre-existing state(s) subsequently enacted the compact—thereby raising the number of electoral votes possessed by the compacting states above a majority of the new number of electoral votes—article III of the compact would again govern.

As a fourth example, if the number of U.S. Representatives (set by federal statute) were changed so that the number of electoral votes possessed by the compacting states no longer accounted for a majority of the new number of electoral votes, article III of the compact would not govern the next presidential election. Proposals to change the number of members of the House are periodically floated for a variety of reasons. For example, Representative Tom Davis (R–Virginia) recently proposed increasing the number of Representatives from 435 to 437 on a temporary basis in connection with his bill to give the District of Columbia voting representation in Congress.[11]

As long as the compacting states possess a majority of the electoral votes on July 20 of a presidential election year, article III of the compact would govern the presidential election. In practice, the question as to whether the compact would govern a particular presidential election would be known long before July 20 of the presidential election year. Changes resulting from the census are no surprise because the census does not affect congressional reapportionment until two years after the census.[12] A new state enters the Union only after a time-consuming congressional process. Moreover, no territories are likely to be admitted as a new state in the near future. Enactment of a state law withdrawing from an interstate compact is a time-consuming, multi-step legislative process

---

[11] H.R. 2043—The D.C. Fairness in Representation Act. Introduced May 3, 2005. Based on the 2000 census, Utah is the state that would become entitled, under the existing formula for distributing U.S. Representatives among the states, to the second temporary additional congressional seat. As a matter of practical politics, the two additional seats would be expected to divide equally among the Democrats and Republicans. If the Davis bill were to pass in, say, 2006, there would be 540 electoral votes in the 2008 presidential election. The Davis bill provides that the number of seats in the House would revert to 435 after the 2010 census.

[12] For example, the 2000 federal census did not affect the 2000 presidential election. The results of the 2000 census affected the 2002 congressional election and the 2004 presidential election.

involving the introduction of a bill, action on the bill in a committee in each house of the state legislature, debate and voting on the bill on the floor of each house, and presentation of the bill to the state's Governor for approval or disapproval.[13] In addition, new state laws generally do not take immediate effect but, instead, take effect at a particular future time.[14] Moreover, a withdrawal from the proposed compact cannot take effect during the six-month period between July 20 of a presidential election year and the subsequent January 20 inauguration date (as discussed below). Finally, enactment of any federal statutory change in the number of U.S. Representatives is a time-consuming, multi-step legislative process.

6.3.4 Explanation of Article IV—Additional Provisions

The first clause of article IV of the compact (quoted above) specifies the time when the compact initially would take effect. A state is not counted for purposes of this clause until the compact is "in effect" in the state in accordance with the terms of the state's constitution schedule specifying when state laws take effect.

The same version of a compact must, of course, be enacted by each member state. The phrase "substantially the same form" is found in many interstate compacts and is intended to permit minor variations (e.g., differences in punctuation and numbering or inconsequential typographical errors) that sometimes occur when the same law is enacted by various states.

The second clause of article IV of the compact permits a state to withdraw from the compact but provides for a "blackout" period (of approximately six months) restricting withdrawals:

> "Any member state may withdraw from this agreement, except that a withdrawal occurring six months or less before the end of a President's term shall not become effective until a President or Vice President shall have been qualified to serve the next term."

---

[13] Similarly, the citizen-initiative process is a time-consuming, multi-step process that typically involves an initial filing and review by a designated state official (e.g., the Attorney General), circulation of the petition, and voting in a statewide election (usually a November general election).

[14] State constitutions generally specify when new state laws take effect. A super-majority vote is typically required to give immediate effect to a legislative bill. The details vary from state to state.

The purpose for the delay in the effective date of a withdrawal is to ensure that a withdrawal will not be undertaken—perhaps for partisan political purposes—in the midst of a presidential campaign or in the period between the popular voting in early November and the meeting of the Electoral College in mid-December. This restriction on withdrawals is warranted in light of the subject matter of the proposed interstate compact.[15] The blackout period starts on July 20 of a presidential election year and would normally end on January 20 of the following year (the scheduled inauguration date). Thus, if a statute repealing the compact in a particular state were enacted and came into effect in the midst of the presidential election process, that state's withdrawal from the compact would not take effect until completion of the entire current presidential election cycle. The language used in the compact tracks the wording of the 20th Amendment. The date for the end of the present President's term is fixed by the 20th Amendment as January 20th; however, the 20th Amendment recognizes the possibility that a new President might, under certain circumstances, not have been "qualified" by that date. The blackout period in the compact ends when the entire presidential election cycle is completed under terms of the 20th Amendment.

The third clause of article IV of the compact concerns the process by which each state notifies all the other states of the status of the compact. Notices are required on three occasions—namely when the compact has taken effect in a particular state, when the compact has taken effect generally (that is, when it has been enacted and taken effect in states cumulatively possessing a majority of the electoral votes), and when a state's withdrawal has taken effect.

The fourth clause of article IV provides that the compact would automatically terminate if the Electoral College were to be abolished.

The fifth clause of article IV is a severability clause.

6.3.5 Explanation of Article V—Definitions

Article V of the compact contains definitions.

There are separate definitions for the "chief election official" and the "presidential elector certifying official" because these terms may, in some states, refer to a different official or body.

---

[15] Delays in the effective date of withdrawals are commonplace in interstate compacts (and, indeed, in contracts in general). See section 5.15.3 for additional discussion on withdrawals from interstate compacts in general and section 8.6 for additional discussion on withdrawals from the proposed compact in particular.

The definition of "presidential slate" in Article V of the compact is important because voters cast votes for a team consisting of a presidential and vice-presidential candidate and because the votes for each distinct team are aggregated separately in the national count under the terms of the compact. "Presidential slate" is defined as

> "a slate of two persons, the first of whom has been nominated as a candidate for President of the United States and the second of whom has been nominated as a candidate for Vice President of the United States, or any legal successors to such persons, regardless of whether both names appear on the ballot presented to the voter in a particular state."

The above definition permits the substitution of nominees on a given presidential slate if, for example, a nominee were to die during the presidential election cycle,[16] resign from a slate,[17] or become disqualified.[18]

Because North Dakota's ballot lists only the name of the presidential candidate (figure 2.3), the definition of "presidential slate" in the proposed compact contains a savings clause for North Dakota.

Note that this definition comports with present practice in that it treats a slate as a unit containing two particular candidates in a specified order. As discussed in section 2.10 and shown in figure 2.11, Ralph Nader appeared on the ballot in New York in 2004 as the presidential nominee of both the Independence Party and the Peace and Justice Party. Nader ran with Jan D. Pierce for Vice President on the Independence Party line in New York in 2004, but with Peter Miguel Camejo for Vice President on the Peace and Justice Party line. Thus, there were two different "Nader" presidential slates in New York in 2004. Each "Nader" slate had a different slate of presidential electors in New York in 2004. The votes for these two distinct "presidential slates" were counted separately (as shown on the sixth page of New York's Certificate of Ascertainment in appendix H). There was no fusion of votes between the Independence Party and the Peace and Justice Party in this situation because there were

---

[16] Horace Greeley, the (losing) Democratic presidential nominee in 1872, died between the time of the November voting and the counting of the electoral votes.

[17] Senator Thomas F. Eagleton of Missouri resigned from the 1972 Democratic presidential slate.

[18] A presidential candidate must be a natural-born citizen.

two distinct presidential slates and two distinct slates of presidential electors.

The definition of "statewide popular election" in article V is important. At the present time, all states conduct a "statewide popular election" for President and Vice President. However, if a state were to withdraw from its voters the power to vote for President (as Massachusetts and New Hampshire did in the 1800 presidential election, as described in section 2.2.3), there would be no popular votes available to count from that state. If there is no popular vote to count from a particular state, the "national popular vote total" would necessarily not include that state.

6.4 POSSIBLE FEDERAL LEGISLATION

The enactment of the proposed "Agreement Among the States to Elect the President by National Popular Vote" would provide an excellent opportunity for Congress to review existing federal laws concerning presidential elections.

The proposed "Agreement Among the States to Elect the President by National Popular Vote" is intended to be entirely self-executing. To this end, the compact identifies officials in each member state to perform the necessary tasks of obtaining the popular vote counts from all the states, adding up the votes from all the states to yield the "national popular vote total," and designating the "national popular vote winner." These tasks could be simplified by the establishment of an administrative clearinghouse for these functions. Such a clearinghouse might be established by federal law. Alternatively, the officials of the compacting states might themselves establish such a clearinghouse.

Numerous problems have been identified concerning the existing schedule of events involving the November general election, the "safe harbor" date, the timing of the meeting of the Electoral College in mid-December, the counting of the votes by Congress in early January, and the presidential inauguration scheduled for January 20.

Leonard M. Shambon, an assistant to the co-chairman of the Ford-Carter Commission on Election Reform in 2001 and a member of the advisory board to the Carter-Baker Commission in 2005, described some of the problems associated with the current schedule in a 2004 article entitled "Electoral-College Reform Requires Change of Timing."[19] Many of

---

[19] Shambon, Leonard M. 2004. Electoral-College Reform Requires Change of Timing. *Roll Call.* June 15, 2004.

problems identified in the Shambon article are incorporated in H.R. 1579, introduced by Representative David Price (D–North Carolina) on April 12, 2005.[20] They are discussed further by Suzanne Nelson in an article entitled "Three-Month Period Imperils Presidency."[21]

In addition, Norman Ornstein, a resident scholar at the American Enterprise Institute, described additional potential problems concerning presidential elections in a 2004 article entitled "Want a Scary Scenario for Presidential Chaos? Here Are a Few."[22]

Additional issues have been raised by John C. Fortier, a resident fellow of the American Enterprise Institute and Norman Ornstein in a 2004 article entitled "If Terrorists Attack Our Presidential Elections"[23] and by Jerry H. Goldfeder, an elections law attorney in New York and Adjunct Professor at Fordham University School of Law, in an article entitled "Could Terrorists Derail a Presidential Election?"[24]

6.5 PREVIOUS PROPOSALS FOR MULTI-STATE ELECTORAL LEGISLATION

Several previous proposals contained elements of the proposed "Agreement Among the States to Elect the President by National Popular Vote."[25]

In *Oregon v. Mitchell*, U.S. Supreme Court Justice Potter Stewart pointed out in 1970 that an interstate compact could be employed by the states for electoral purposes. This case concerned congressional legislation establishing uniformity among the states for durational residency requirements for voters in presidential elections. In his opinion (partially concurring and partially dissenting), Justice Potter Stewart observed that if Congress had not enacted federal legislation concerning residency

---

[20] H.R. 1579—To amend title 3, United States Code, to extend the date provided for the meeting of electors of the President and Vice President in the States and the date provided for the joint session of Congress held for the counting of electoral votes, and for other purposes. Introduced April 12, 2005.

[21] Nelson, Suzanne. Three-Month Period Imperils Presidency. *Roll Call.* November 2, 2004.

[22] Ornstein, Norman. 2004. Want a Scary Scenario for Presidential Chaos? Here Are a Few. *Roll Call.* October 21, 2004

[23] Fortier, John C. and Ornstein, Norman. 2004. If Terrorists Attack Our Presidential Elections. 3 *Election Law Journal* 4. Pages 597–612.

[24] Goldfeder, Jerry H. 2005. Could Terrorists Derail a Presidential Election. 32 *Fordham Urban Law Journal* 3. May 2005. Pages 523–566.

[25] None of the proposals discussed in this section was known to the authors of this book at the time when the authors developed their proposed interstate compact in 2004.

requirements, the states could have adopted an interstate compact to accomplish the same objective.[26]

In the 1990s, Senator Charles Schumer (D–New York) proposed a bi-state compact in which New York and Texas would pool their electoral votes in presidential elections. Both states were then (and still are) noncompetitive in presidential politics and receive little attention in presidential campaigns except for fund raising. Schumer observed that the two states have almost the same number of electoral votes (at the time, 33 for New York and 32 for Texas)[27] and the two states regularly produce majorities of approximately the same magnitude in favor of the state's dominant political party. The Democrats typically carry New York by about 60%, and the Republicans typically carry Texas by about 60%. The purpose of the proposed compact was to create a presidentially competitive super-state (slightly larger than California) that would attract the attention of the presidential candidates during presidential campaigns.

After the 2000 election in which George W. Bush was elected to the Presidency without receiving a majority of the popular votes, Robert W. Bennett, Northwestern University Law Professor and former Dean of the Northwestern University School of Law, published a highly creative and innovative idea concerning the Electoral College. At a January 2001 conference and in an April 2001 publication, Bennett observed that that a federal constitutional amendment was not necessary to achieve the goal of nationwide popular election of the President because the states could use their power under Article II of the U.S. Constitution to allocate their electoral votes based on the nationwide popular vote.[28] Bennett expanded his thoughts in subsequent publications suggesting several variations on his basic idea.[29,30] In December 2001, Akhil Reed Amar and Vikram David

[26] *Oregon v. Mitchell.* 400 U.S. 112 at 286–287. 1970.

[27] In the 2004 presidential election, New York had 31 electoral votes, and Texas had 34.

[28] Bennett, Robert W. 2001. Popular election of the president without a constitutional amendment. 4 *Green Bag.* Spring 2001. Posted on April 19, 2001. The January 11–12, 2001, presentation was contained in *Conference Report, Election 2000: The Role of the Courts, The Role of the Media; The Roll of the Dice* (Northwestern University).

[29] Bennett, Robert W. 2002. Popular election of the president without a constitutional amendment. In Jacobson, Arthur J. and Rosenfeld, Michel (editors). *The Longest Night: Polemics and Perspectives on Election 2000.* Berkeley, CA: University of California Press. Pages 391–396.

[30] Bennett, Robert W. 2002. Popular election of the president II: State coordination in popular election of the president without a constitutional amendment. *Green Bag.* Winter 2002.

Amar, citing Bennett, continued the discussion about the fact that the states could allocate their electoral votes to the nationwide winner of the popular vote.[31,32]

In one variation on these proposals, a single state would enact a law that would award its electoral votes to the nationwide winner without regard to whether any other state enacted similar legislation. In another variation, the state laws would be made contingent on the enactment of identical laws by other states. It was further argued the resulting arrangement would not constitute an interstate compact and therefore would not require congressional consent.[33]

These earlier proposals differ from the authors' proposed "Agreement Among the States to Elect the President by National Popular Vote" in several respects.

First, the earlier proposals were not framed as an interstate compact. Interstate compacts are specifically authorized by the U.S. Constitution as a means by which the states may act in concert to address a problem. An arrangement that takes effect only when a specified combination of states agree to participate, that no state would enact without the offer and assurance of complementary action by other states, and that ultimately involves the states acting in concert would probably be regarded by the courts as a contract and hence an "agreement or compact" as that phrase is used in the U.S. Constitution.[34]

Compacts have the specific advantage of making the states' contemplated joint actions into a legally enforceable contractual obligation on all the participating states. This assurance is particularly salient concerning the provision preventing a state from unilaterally withdrawing from the agreed arrangement for partisan political reasons in the midst of a

---

[31] Amar, Akhil Reed and Amar, Vikram David. 2001. How to achieve direct national election of the president without amending the constitution: Part three of a three-part series on the 2000 election and the electoral college. *Findlaw's Writ*. December 28, 2001. http://writ.news.findlaw.com/amar/20011228.html

[32] Amar, Akhil Reed and Amar, Vikram David Amar. 2001. Rethinking the electoral college debate: The Framers, federalism, and one person, one vote. 114 *Harvard Law Review* 2526 at 2549, n. 112.

[33] The question of whether such an arrangement requires congressional consent is separate from the question of whether the arrangement is an interstate compact. As discussed in section 5.12, many interstate compacts do not require congressional consent.

[34] Article I, section 10, clause 3 of the U.S. Constitution states, "No state shall, without the consent of Congress, ... enter into any agreement or compact with another state...."

presidential election campaign or, even more egregiously, after the election results become known in early November but before the Electoral College meets in mid-December. Enforceability is most relevant in the event that the winner of the nationwide popular vote did not carry states having a majority of the electoral votes (as occurred in 1824, 1876, 1892, and 2000). A state whose legislature and Governor are controlled by a political party whose presidential candidate did not win the nationwide popular vote could, in the absence of an enforceable restriction on withdrawal, abandon its obligations at the precise moment when they would matter. Once a state enters into an interstate compact, it may not unilaterally nullify the compact because the Impairments Clause of the U.S. Constitution provides:

> "No State shall ... pass any ... Law impairing the Obligation of Contracts...."[35]

Instead, a party to a contract must withdraw from the agreement in accordance with the agreement's provisions for withdrawal. Most interstate compacts contain provisions that delay the effective date of a state's withdrawal by a certain amount of time that is appropriate given the nature of the compact. As described in sections 6.2.3 and discussed in section 8.6, the proposed "Agreement Among the States to Elect the President by National Popular Vote" has a "blackout" period (of approximately six months) starting on July 20 of a presidential election year and continuing until a President or Vice President shall have been qualified to serve the next term (normally on January 20 of the following year).

Second, earlier proposals did not contain a provision making the effective date of the system contingent on the enactment of substantially identical laws in states that collectively possess a majority of the electoral votes (i.e., 270 of the 538 electoral votes). No single state would be likely to alone enact a law awarding its electoral votes to the nationwide winner. For one thing, such an action would give the voters of all the other states a voice in the selection of the state's own presidential electors, while not giving the state a voice in the selection of presidential electors in other states and would not alone guarantee achievement of the goal of nationwide popular election of the President. Moreover, enactment of such a law in a single state would encourage the presidential can-

---

[35] See appendix C for the full wording of the Impairments Clause.

didates to ignore that state. The effect of such a law in a single state would be to negate the voice of the enacting state in the presidential election, except in the unlikely event that the electoral votes of the other states are so nearly equally divided that the lone enacting state could weigh in on the side of the winner of the nationwide popular vote.

Moreover, the earlier proposals do not work in a even-handed and non-partisan way when the arrangement contains states possessing fewer than a majority of the electoral votes. Suppose, for example, that a group of states that consistently voted Democratic in presidential elections were to participate in an arrangement to award their electoral votes to the nationwide popular vote winner without the electoral-majority threshold. Then, if the Republican presidential candidate won the most popular votes nationwide (but did not carry states with a majority of the electoral votes), the participating (Democratic) states would award their electoral votes to the Republican candidate—thereby helping to achieve the desired result of electing the presidential candidate with the most popular votes nationwide. On the other hand, if the Democratic presidential candidate won the most popular votes nationwide (but did not carry states with a majority of the electoral votes), the similarly situated Democratic presidential candidate would not receive a symmetric benefit. Instead, the Republican candidate would be elected because the Democratic candidate could not receive any additional electoral votes from the group of states involved because the Democratic candidate would already be getting all of the electoral votes from that group of states. In short, a Republican presidential nominee would be the only beneficiary if only Democratic states participated in such an arrangement, and vice versa. In fact, an arrangement without a electoral majority threshold would operate in an even-handed and non-partisan way only in the unlikely that the participating states were equally divided (in terms of electoral votes) among reliably Republican and reliably Democratic states. In contrast, if the states participating in the arrangement possess a majority of the electoral votes, the system operates in an even-handed and non-partisan way without regard to the political complexion of the states that happen to be members of the compact.

If the earlier proposals were altered so that the participating states awarded all of their electoral votes to the popular vote winner calculated only within the group of participating states, then a candidate with a bare majority of the popular votes in that group of states would negate the popular votes of the losing candidate in that group of states—thereby again permitting the Presidency to be won by a candidate who did not receive a nationwide majority of the popular vote.

Third, the statutory language and the operational details were not specified in the earlier proposals.

The authors submit that the proposed "Agreement Among the States to Elect the President by National Popular Vote" does not have the above-mentioned problems of the earlier proposals.

7 | Strategy for Enacting the Proposed Interstate Compact

Public opinion has supported nationwide popular election of the President for over six decades. For example, the Gallup poll in 1944 asked:

"It has been suggested that the electoral vote system be discontinued and Presidents of the United States be elected by total popular vote alone. Do you favor or oppose this proposal?"[1]

In 1977 and 1980, the Gallup poll asked:

"Would you approve or disapprove of an amendment to the Constitution which would do away with the electoral college and base the election of a President on the total vote cast throughout the nation?"[2]

Table 7.1 shows the results for these public opinion polls in 1944, 1977, and 1980.

Table 7.1 PUBLIC SUPPORT FOR NATIONWIDE POPULAR ELECTION OF THE PRESIDENT

	APPROVE	DISAPPROVE	NO OPINION
June 22–27, 1944	65%	23%	13%
January 14–17, 1977	73%	15%	12%
November 7–10, 1980	67%	19%	15%

The Gallup News Service has also reported:

"The greatest level of support, 81%, was recorded after the 1968 election when Richard Nixon defeated Hubert Humphrey in another extremely close election."[3]

---

[1] Gallup News Service. 2000. Americans Have Historically Favored Changing Way Presidents Are Elected. November 10, 2000. Page 1.

[2] *Id.* at 2.

[3] *Id.* at 2.

Public opinion plays only an indirect and muted role in the top-down process of amending the federal constitution. Proposed amendments generally require a two-thirds vote by both houses of Congress, followed by favorable votes in three quarters of the state legislatures.[4]

The authors of this book envision a bottom-up strategy for securing enactment of the proposed "Agreement Among the States to Elect the President by National Popular Vote" (presented in chapter 6). The contemplated process would start where support for this proposal is strongest—the voters. The three-part process would include the following:

(1) **Citizen-Initiative Process:** The citizen-initiative process could be used to place the proposed compact on the ballot in various states in 2006 and 2008. Each ballot measure would enable a state's voters to vote directly on a state law enacting the proposed interstate compact in that state (section 7.1).

(2) **State Legislative Action:** The proposed compact would be introduced into state legislatures throughout the country in 2006 and 2007. There is a possibility that one or more state legislatures might adopt the proposed compact prior to the November 2006 elections. (section 7.2).

(3) **Action by Congress:** After enactment of the compact by numerous states, Congress might take one or more of the following actions in 2008 or 2009 (section 7.3):

(a) consenting to the proposed compact on behalf of the District of Columbia,

(b) streamlining existing federal law regarding the certification by the states of the results of the presidential elections, and

(c) granting consent (expressed or implied) to the proposed compact.

---

[4] For a detailed discussion of various alternative modes of amending the federal constitution, see Orfield, Lester Bernhardt. 1942. *The Amending of the Federal Constitution.* Ann Arbor, MI: The University of Michigan Press.

7.1 DIRECTLY INVOLVING THE PEOPLE

The people in 22 states have reserved to themselves the power to enact state statutes through the citizen-initiative process. In addition, the people in 19 states have reserved to themselves the power to adopt state constitutional amendments through the citizen-initiative process. These 19 states include two states (Florida and Mississippi) that are not among the previously mentioned 22 states with the statutory initiative process. Also, the District of Columbia has a citizen-initiative process for statutes. Table 7.2 shows the 25 jurisdictions that permit either statutory or constitutional initiatives and the number of electoral votes in each. As can be seen, these 25 jurisdictions collectively possess 260 electoral votes (i.e., just short of the 270 electoral votes necessary to elect a President

Table 7.2 THE 25 JURISDICTIONS WITH THE CITIZEN-INITIATIVE PROCESS

STATE	STATUTORY	CONSTITUTIONAL	ELECTORAL VOTES
Alaska	Yes	No	3
Arizona	Yes	Yes	10
Arkansas	Yes	Yes	6
California	Yes	Yes	55
Colorado	Yes	Yes	9
District of Columbia	Yes	No	3
Florida	No	Yes	27
Idaho	Yes	Very limited	4
Illinois	Advisory only	Very limited	21
Maine	Yes	No	4
Massachusetts	Yes	Yes	12
Michigan	Yes	Yes	17
Mississippi	No	Yes	6
Missouri	Yes	Yes	11
Montana	Yes	Yes	3
Nebraska	Yes	Yes	5
Nevada	Yes	Yes	5
North Dakota	Yes	Yes	3
Ohio	Yes	Yes	20
Oklahoma	Yes	Yes	7
Oregon	Yes	Yes	7
South Dakota	Yes	Yes	3
Utah	Yes	No	5
Washington	Yes	No	11
Wyoming	Yes	No	3
Total			**260**

in the Electoral College). See *The Initiative: Citizen Law-Making*[5] for citations to the constitutional and statutory provisions governing the initiative processes in various states.

The effort to secure adoption of the proposed compact could involve with the use of the citizen-initiative process.

The citizen initiative process is, however, problematic in many of the 25 jurisdictions listed in table 7.2. For example, in Illinois, the statutory initiative is advisory only. Moreover, the constitutional initiative in Illinois is limited to matters relating to legislative procedure. As a result, it would not be possible to use the citizen-initiative process for the purpose of enacting the proposed interstate compact in Illinois.

Because there is no statutory initiative in Florida or Mississippi, the constitutional initiative process would have to be invoked in those states in order to adopt the proposed interstate compact. The initiative process for constitutional amendments in Florida is extraordinarily time-consuming and uncertain. The procedure generally includes a preliminary review of the proposition by the Florida Supreme Court (a step that is not governed by any fixed schedule and that can take a year or longer). The initiative process for constitutional amendments in Mississippi is unusually difficult to use.

The first step in invoking the citizen-initiative process in a typical state is to file the proposed legislation with a state official (usually the Attorney General). Ohio, Maine, Massachusetts, and Missouri have extraordinarily early deadlines for starting the citizen-initiative process in order to place a question before the voters.

In Nevada, the citizen-initiative process spans two general elections.

Although the District of Columbia has the citizen-initiative process for statutes, Congress has been the body that has historically granted consent to interstate compacts on behalf of the District. It is not clear, under existing home rule legislation, whether a statutory initiative in the District would be the appropriate legal vehicle for enacting an interstate compact.

In some states, there are significant legal limitations (including both statute law and case law) concerning the circulation of petitions on private property. In some states (such as Alaska and Arizona), weather conditions shorten the time window during which it is practical to circulate

---

[5] Zimmerman, Joseph F. 1999. *The Initiative: Citizen Law-Making.* Westport, CT: Praeger. Pages 24–25.

initiative petitions. Signature gathering is difficult in Michigan because of a combination of the weather and relatively tight legal limitations on petition circulation on private property. In some states, election administrators and the courts are not favorably disposed to the citizen-initiative process, and it is common for ballot measures to be disqualified in pre-election or post-election challenges. Finally, in some states, state constitutional provisions and existing judicial interpretations do not make it clear whether the citizen initiative process is co-extensive with the powers of the state legislature.

On the other hand, in numerous states (including many western states), the citizen-initiative process is an accepted part of the overall political process.

7.2 STATE LEGISLATIVE ACTION

Even if there were no practical or legal obstacles to the effective use of the citizen initiative process, the 25 jurisdictions listed in table 7.2 do not possess a majority of the electoral votes. Thus, at least some state legislatures must enact the proposed interstate compact in order to bring it into effect. In practice, the authors of this book believe that the vast majority of the 270 electoral votes would, as a practical matter, come from state legislatures.

Almost all state legislatures will convene shortly after the November 2006 elections. Most will convene in January and February of 2007. The legislatures of Louisiana and Florida will convene in the spring of 2007. A few legislatures will convene as early as December 2006.

A state legislature enacts an interstate compact in the same way that it enacts an ordinary statute. Enactment of a statute typically requires a majority vote of the legislature and gubernatorial approval. All governors have the power to veto legislation passed by their state legislatures. If a governor vetoes a bill, the legislation may nonetheless become law if the legislature overrides the veto in the manner provided by the state's constitution. Overriding a gubernatorial veto typically requires a super-majority (e.g., two-thirds vote of all houses of the state legislature). See *The Book of the States* for general information about vetoes in particular states.[6]

---

[6] Council of State Governments. 2005. *The Book of the States*. Lexington, KY: The Council of State Governments. 2005 Edition. Volume 37. Pages 161–162.

7.3 CONGRESSIONAL ACTION

The ideal time to seek congressional action on the proposed interstate compact would be after the compact has been adopted by states possessing a majority of the electoral votes. At that time, the group of states supporting the compact might include states that had enacted the compact by means of the citizen-initiative process as well as states where the legislature enacted the compact. The interstate compact might go before Congress in 2008 or 2009.

Congressional action on the proposed compact might include one or both of the following:

- granting the consent of Congress to the proposed interstate compact on behalf of the District of Columbia, and
- amending existing federal laws regarding the timing of the certification of the results of presidential election.

Congress has the option of explicitly consenting to the compact (section 5.10). However, as the U.S. Supreme Court wrote in the 1893 case of *Virginia v. Tennessee,*

> "… consent may be implied, and is always to be implied when congress adopts the particular act by sanctioning its objects and aiding in enforcing them.…"[7]

Thus, enactment of a legislative bill covering either of the above two items would constitute implied consent by Congress to the proposed compact (section 5.9).

The federal legislation concerning the compact could be adopted by a majority vote of both houses of Congress and approval by the President. The President could veto such legislation. If the President vetoes the bill, the Congress could override the veto by a two-thirds vote of both houses.

In the unlikely event that all of the above steps are completed by July 20, 2008, the compact would govern the 2008 presidential election, and the President would, for the first time in American history, be elected by all of the people in an election in which every vote is equal.

If, on the other hand, the compact is not effective by July 20, 2008, the debate on the issue of nationwide popular election of the President would inevitably become a part of the 2008 campaign. Candidates for Senator, Representative, and President would be asked for their position on the

---

[7] *Virginia v. Tennessee.* 148 U.S. 503 at 521. 1893.

issue. Newspapers and television stations would editorialize on the question of how the President should be elected. The travel, advertising, and "on the ground" activity of the presidential candidates would be scrutinized in terms of whether the candidates are, in fact, ignoring voters in two-thirds of the states. In addition, the citizen-initiative process could be used in the November 2008 elections to further demonstrate voter support for nationwide popular election of the President (and to increase the number of states that have enacted the proposed compact). The authors of this book believe that a robust debate on the issue in 2008 will inevitably lead to a nationwide decision to embrace nationwide popular election of the President in time for the 2012 presidential election.

8 | Legal Issues Concerning the Proposed Interstate Compact

The proposed interstate compact entitled the "Agreement Among the States to Elect the President by National Popular Vote" (presented in chapter 6) would change the laws by which presidential electors are appointed in the states belonging to the compact. This chapter addresses the following legal questions in connection with the proposed compact:

- Is the subject matter of the proposed compact appropriate for an interstate compact (section 8.1)?
- May the citizen-initiative process be used to enact interstate compacts in general (section 8.2)?
- May the citizen-initiative process be used to enact a state law concerning the manner of choosing presidential electors (section 8.3)?
- Does the proposed compact encroach on the powers or rights of non-member states (section 8.4)?
- Does the proposed compact impermissibly delegate a state's sovereign power (section 8.5)?
- Is the six-month blackout period for withdrawals from the proposed compact enforceable (section 8.6)?

8.1 IS THE SUBJECT MATTER OF THE PROPOSED COMPACT APPROPRIATE FOR AN INTERSTATE COMPACT?

The U.S. Constitution authorizes states to enter into interstate compacts:

> "No state shall, without the consent of Congress, ... enter into any agreement or compact with another state or with a foreign power."[1]

---

[1] U.S. Constitution. Article I, section 10, clause 3.

The U.S. Constitution places no restriction on the subject matter of an interstate compact other than the implicit limitation that a compact's subject matter must be among the powers that the states are permitted to exercise.

The subject matter of existing interstate compacts varies widely and has included such topics as agriculture, boundaries, bridges, building construction and safety, child welfare, civil defense, conservation, corrections, crime control, cultural issues, education, emergency management, energy, facilities, flood control, gambling and lotteries, health, insurance, interstate school districts, low-level radioactive wastes, metropolitan problems, motor vehicles, national guard, natural resources, navigation, parks and recreation, pest control, planning and development, ports, property, public safety, river basins, taxation, transportation, and water (section 5.4).

Beginning in the 1920s, the states have used interstate compacts in increasingly creative ways. The judiciary has been repeatedly asked to consider the validity of various novel compacts; however, we are aware of no case in which the courts have invalidated an interstate compact.[2]

The subject matter of the proposed "Agreement Among the States to Elect the President by National Popular Vote" concerns the manner of appointment of a state's presidential electors. The U.S. Constitution gives each state the power to select the manner of appointing its presidential electors.[3] As the Supreme Court stated in *McPherson v. Blacker* in 1892:

> "In short, **the appointment and mode of appointment of electors belong exclusively to the states** under the constitution of the United States.... Congress is empowered to determine the time of choosing the electors and the day on which they are to give their votes, which is required to be the same day throughout the United States; but otherwise **the power and jurisdiction of the state is exclusive,** with the exception of the provisions as to the number of electors and the ineligibility of certain persons, so framed that

---

[2] There are cases where a higher court invalidated a ruling by a lower court invalidating an interstate compact. See, for example, *West Virginia ex rel. Dyer v. Sims.* 341 U.S. 22. 1950.

[3] U.S. Constitution. Article II, section 1, clause 2.

congressional and federal influence might be excluded."⁴
[Emphasis added]

Thus, the subject matter of the proposed interstate compact is a state power and an appropriate subject for an interstate compact.

Although there is currently no interstate compact concerned with presidential elections, Justice Potter Stewart noted the possibility of compacts involving elections in his concurring and dissenting opinion in *Oregon v. Mitchell* in 1970. In that case, the U.S. Supreme Court examined the constitutionality of the Voting Rights Act Amendments of 1970 that removed state-imposed durational residency requirements on voters casting ballots in presidential elections. Justice Stewart concurred with the majority that Congress had the power to make durational residency requirements uniform in presidential elections, and observed:

> "Congress could rationally conclude that the imposition of durational residency requirements unreasonably burdens and sanctions the privilege of taking up residence in another State. The objective of § 202 is clearly a legitimate one. Federal action is required if the privilege to change residence is not to be undercut by parochial local sanctions. No State could undertake to guarantee this privilege to its citizens. At most a single State could take steps to resolve that its own laws would not unreasonably discriminate against the newly arrived resident. Even this resolve might not remain firm in the face of discriminations perceived as unfair against those of its own citizens who moved to other States. Thus, the problem could not be wholly solved by a single State, or even by several States, since every State of new residence and every State of prior residence would have a necessary role to play. **In the absence of a unanimous interstate compact, the problem could only be solved by Congress.**"⁵ [Emphasis added]

In summary, the states are constitutionally permitted to use an interstate compact to specify the manner in which they choose their presidential electors.

---

⁴ *McPherson v. Blacker.* 146 U.S. 1 at 35. 1892.
⁵ *Oregon v. Mitchell.* 400 U.S. 112 at 286–287. 1970.

8.2 MAY THE CITIZEN-INITIATIVE PROCESS BE USED TO ENACT AN INTERSTATE COMPACT?

A state may enact an interstate compact in the same manner as it enacts a state law.

The legislative process at the state level generally entails adoption of a proposed legislative bill by a majority vote of each house of the state legislature. All state governors currently have the power to veto bills passed by their legislatures, so bills are presented to the governor for approval or disapproval.[6] If a governor vetoes a bill, the legislation may nonetheless become law if the legislature overrides the veto in the manner specified by the state's constitution. Overriding a gubernatorial veto typically requires a super-majority (typically a two-thirds vote) of both houses of the legislature.[7]

In 22 states, an alternative method, called the *citizen-initiative process*, may be used to enact a state law. In those states (listed in table 7.2), the voters have reserved to themselves the power to enact statutes through the citizen-initiative process.[8] The initiative process is invoked by filing a petition signed by a constitutionally specified number of voters. The voters then decide whether to enact the proposed law in a statewide vote.[9]

In many of these same states, the voters have also reserved to themselves the power to suspend temporarily a law enacted by the legislature and subsequently to vote on whether to retain the law in a statewide referendum—a process called the *protest-referendum*.[10]

The Michigan Constitution (article II, section 9) provides a good description of both the citizen-initiative process and the protest-referendum process:

---

[6] Council of State Governments. 2005. *The Book of the States.* Lexington, KY: The Council of State Governments. 2005 Edition. Volume 37. Pages 161–162.

[7] For simplicity, we refer to the two houses of a state legislature, even though Nebraska has a unicameral state legislature.

[8] Zimmerman, Joseph F. 1999. *The Initiative: Citizen Law-Making.* Westport, CT: Praeger.

[9] In addition, the voters in 19 states may use the citizen-initiative process to propose and enact amendments to the state constitution. These 19 states include two states (Florida and Mississippi) that are not among the group of 22 states with the statutory initiative process. Also, the District of Columbia has a citizen-initiative process for statutes. Thus, there are 25 jurisdictions with the process. See table 7.2 for details.

[10] Zimmerman, Joseph F. 1997. *The Referendum: The People Decide Public Policy.* Westport, CT: Praeger.

"The people reserve to themselves the power to propose laws and to enact and reject laws, called the initiative, and the power to approve or reject laws enacted by the legislature, called the referendum. The power of initiative extends only to laws which the legislature may enact under this constitution. The power of referendum does not extend to acts making appropriations for state institutions or to meet deficiencies in state funds and must be invoked in the manner prescribed by law within 90 days following the final adjournment of the legislative session at which the law was enacted. To invoke the initiative or referendum, petitions signed by a number of registered electors, not less than eight percent for initiative and five percent for referendum of the total vote cast for all candidates for governor at the last preceding general election at which a governor was elected shall be required.

"No law as to which the power of referendum properly has been invoked shall be effective thereafter unless approved by a majority of the electors voting thereon at the next general election.

"Any law proposed by initiative petition shall be either enacted or rejected by the legislature without change or amendment within 40 session days from the time such petition is received by the legislature. If any law proposed by such petition shall be enacted by the legislature it shall be subject to referendum, as hereinafter provided.

"If the law so proposed is not enacted by the legislature within the 40 days, the state officer authorized by law shall submit such proposed law to the people for approval or rejection at the next general election. The legislature may reject any measure so proposed by initiative petition and propose a different measure upon the same subject by a yea and nay vote upon separate roll calls, and in such event both measures shall be submitted by such state officer to the electors for approval or rejection at the next general election.

"Any law submitted to the people by either initiative or referendum petition and approved by a majority of the votes cast thereon at any election shall take effect 10 days after the date of the official declaration of the vote. No law initiated or adopted by the people shall be subject to the veto power of the governor, and no law adopted by the people at the polls under the initiative provisions of this section shall be amended or repealed, except by a vote of the electors unless otherwise provided in the initiative measure or by three-fourths of the members elected to and serving in each house of the legislature. Laws approved by the people under the referendum provision of this section may be amended by the legislature at any subsequent session thereof. If two or more measures approved by the electors at the same election conflict, that receiving the highest affirmative vote shall prevail."[11]

The Arizona Constitution provides:

"The legislative authority of the state shall be vested in the legislature, consisting of a senate and a house of representatives, but the people reserve the power to propose laws and amendments to the constitution and to enact or reject such laws and amendments at the polls, independently of the legislature; and they also reserve, for use at their own option, the power to approve or reject at the polls any act, or item, section, or part of any act, of the legislature."[12]

The Ohio Constitution provides:

"The legislative power of the state shall be vested in a General Assembly consisting of a Senate and House of Representatives, but the people reserve to themselves the power to propose to the General Assembly laws and amendments to the Constitution, and to adopt or reject the same at the polls on a referendum vote as hereinafter provided."[13]

The origin of the citizen-initiative process is generally attributed to various Swiss cantons in the early 19th century.[14] In 1898, the state

---

[11] Michigan Constitution. Article II, section 9.

[12] Arizona Constitution. Article I, section 1.

[13] Ohio Constitution. Article II, section 1.

constitution of South Dakota was amended to permit the citizen-initiative process. Oregon adopted the process in 1902. In 1904, Oregon voters became the first in the United States to use the citizen-initiative process to enact legislation when they enacted a direct primary statute and a local-option liquor statute.[15]

The initiative process spread rapidly to additional states as part of the Progressive movement in the early decades of the 20th century. Maine adopted the initiative and referendum in 1908. In California, the voters adopted the initiative process in the belief that it would reduce the dominance of the state legislature by the railroads and other corporations and that it would reduce the power of political machines. By 1918, 19 states had adopted the initiative. All were west of the Mississippi River, except for Maine, Massachusetts, and Ohio. The initiative process was included in Alaska's original constitution at the time of that state's admission to the Union in 1959.[16]

The question arises as to whether an interstate compact may be enacted by means of the citizen-initiative process.

The scope of the statutory initiative process and the scope of protest-referendum process varies considerably from state to state. Thus, an examination of the provisions of each state constitution is necessary to answer this question.

There is no provision of any state constitution that specifically singles out interstate compacts as being ineligible for enactment by the voters by means of the citizen-initiative process. Likewise, there is no provision of any state constitution that specifically states that interstate compacts are ineligible for temporary suspension and subsequent repeal by the voters by means of the protest-referendum process.

Having said that, there are significant limitations as to subject matter of the citizen-initiative and protest-referendum processes in about half of the states having these processes.[17] The limitations are so severe in Illinois that it would not be possible to enact an interstate compact using

---

[14] Zimmerman, Joseph F. 1999. *The Initiative: Citizen Law-Making.* Westport, CT: Praeger.

[15] *Id.*

[16] *Id.*

[17] Alaska, California, Illinois, Massachusetts, Michigan, Mississippi, Missouri, Montana, Nebraska, Nevada, North Dakota, Ohio, South Dakota, and Wyoming.

the citizen-initiative process in that state.[18] In general, the restraints on the protest-referendum process are more severe than those applying to the initiative process.[19] The constitutional limitations typically relate to appropriations, the judiciary, measures involving the support of governmental operations, and emergency measures.[20]

In short, unless an interstate compact deals with a subject that is outside a state's constitutional power, there is no state with the citizen-initiative process (other than Illinois) where an interstate compact could not, in principle, be adopted by the citizen-initiative process.

There are, in fact, precedents for the use of the citizen-initiative process and protest-referendum processes in connection with interstate compacts.

In 1988, an initiative petition forced a statewide vote on the question of repealing the law providing for Nebraska's participation in the Central Interstate Low-Level Radioactive Waste Compact (enacted several years earlier by the legislature).[21] In the statewide vote on Proposition 402, voters rejected the initiative proposition to repeal the compact.

In South Dakota in 1984, there was a statewide vote on an initiated law to require the approval of the voters of the state on the state's participation in any nuclear-waste-disposal compact. The measure passed 182,952 to 112,161.

In addition, legislatures have occasionally referred enactment of an interstate compact to the state's voters.[22] For example, the Maine legislature referred the question of enactment of the Texas Low-Level Radioactive Waste Disposal Compact to its voters in 1993. The question on the ballot was:

"Do you approve of the interstate compact to be made with Texas, Maine and Vermont for the disposal of the State's low-

---

[18] In Illinois, the statutory initiative process is advisory only, and the constitutional initiative process is limited to matters relating to legislative procedure.

[19] Zimmerman, Joseph F. 1997. *The Referendum: The People Decide Public Policy.* Westport, CT: Praeger.

[20] Zimmerman, Joseph F. 1999. *The Initiative: Citizen Law-Making.* Westport, CT: Praeger.

[21] The protest-referendum process is typically available only for a relatively short period after a state legislature enacts a particular law. After expiration of that period, the citizen-initiative process may be used to repeal an existing law.

[22] State legislatures generally have the power to refer questions to the state's voters.

level radioactive waste at a proposed facility in the State of Texas?"

The proposition received 170,411 "yes" votes and 63,672 "no" votes.

8.3 MAY THE CITIZEN-INITIATIVE PROCESS BE USED TO ENACT THE PROPOSED COMPACT?

The proposed "Agreement Among the States to Elect the President by National Popular Vote" could be brought into effect solely by the collective action of state legislatures. Nonetheless, in order to demonstrate public support for the concept of nationwide popular election of the President, the authors of this book suggest (in chapter 7) that the citizen-initiative process might be used to enact the proposed compact in an initial group of states.

Article II, section 1, clause 2 of the U.S. Constitution (which we will frequently refer to as "Article II" in the remainder of this section) provides:

> "Each State shall appoint, in such Manner as the **Legislature** thereof may direct, a Number of Electors, equal to the whole Number of Senators and Representatives to which the State may be entitled in the Congress...." [Emphasis added]

The use of the word "legislature" in Article II raises the question of whether the citizen-initiative process may be used to enact legislation specifying the manner of choosing presidential electors.

An answer to this question requires an examination of the way that the word "legislature" is used in the U.S. Constitution.

The word "legislature" appears in 15 places in the U.S. Constitution—13 of which relate to the powers of state legislatures.[23] As will become clear later in this section, the word "legislature" is used with two distinct meanings in the U.S. Constitution, namely

- **the state's two legislative chambers**—that is, the state house of representatives and the state senate agreeing on a

---

[23] Two of the 15 occurrences of the word "legislature" in the U.S. Constitution are unrelated to the powers of state legislatures and will therefore not be discussed further in this chapter. The first such provision is the requirement in Article I, section 2, clause 1 that voters for U.S. Representatives have "the Qualifications requisite for Electors of the most numerous Branch of the State Legislature." The second is the requirement in Article VI, clause 2 that "Members of the several State Legislatures" take an oath or affirmation to support the U.S. Constitution.

common action—either by sitting together in a joint convention or adopting a concurrent resolution while sitting separately;[24] or

- **the state's law-making process**—that is, the process of enacting a state law.

These 13 occurrences of the word "legislature" appear in the following 11 provisions of the U.S. Constitution:

- electing United States Senators in the state legislature (prior to ratification in 1913 of the 17th Amendment providing for popular election of Senators);
- filling a U.S. Senate vacancy (prior to the 17th Amendment);
- ratifying a proposed federal constitutional amendment;
- making an application to Congress for a federal constitutional convention;
- choosing the manner of electing U.S. Representatives and U.S. Senators;
- choosing the manner of appointing presidential electors;
- choosing the manner of conducting a popular election to fill a U.S. Senate vacancy (under the 17th Amendment);
- empowering the state's Governor to fill a U.S. Senate vacancy temporarily until the voters fill the vacancy in a popular election (under the 17th Amendment);
- consenting to the purchase of enclaves by the federal government for "forts, magazines, arsenals, dock-yards, and other needful buildings;"
- consenting to the formation of new states from territory of existing state(s); and
- requesting federal assistance to quell domestic violence.

Table 8.1 displays these 11 provisions of the U.S. Constitution referring to the powers of the state "legislature."

8.3.1 Electing U.S. Senators

Under the original Constitution, each state legislature elected the state's two U.S. Senators. Two methods were commonly used by the states. In some states, the two houses of the state legislature met in a joint con-

---

[24] For simplicity, we frequently refer to the "two houses" of a state legislature, even though Nebraska has a unicameral state legislature.

TABLE 8.1 PROVISIONS OF THE U.S. CONSTITUTION REFERRING TO POWERS OF THE STATE "LEGISLATURE"

	POWER	PROVISION OF THE U.S. CONSTITUTION
1	**Electing U.S. Senators** (prior to the 17th Amendment)	"The Senate of the United States shall be composed of two Senators from each State, **chosen by the Legislature thereof,** for six Years; and each Senator shall have one Vote."[25] [Emphasis added]
2	**Filling a U.S. Senate vacancy** (prior to the 17th Amendment)	"... if Vacancies happen by Resignation, or otherwise, during the Recess of the **Legislature** of any State, the Executive thereof may make temporary Appointments until the next Meeting of the **Legislature, which shall then fill such Vacancies.**"[26] [Emphasis added]
3	**Ratifying a proposed federal constitutional amendment**	"The Congress, whenever two thirds of both Houses shall deem it necessary, shall propose Amendments to this Constitution, or, on the Application of the Legislatures of two thirds of the several States, shall call a Convention for proposing Amendments, which, in either Case, shall be valid to all Intents and Purposes, as Part of this Constitution, **when ratified by the Legislatures** of three fourths of the several States, or by Conventions in three fourths thereof, as the one or the other Mode of Ratification may be proposed by the Congress ... "[27] [Emphasis added]
4	**Making an application to Congress for a federal constitutional convention**	"The Congress, whenever two thirds of both Houses shall deem it necessary, shall propose Amendments to this Constitution, or, **on the Application of the Legislatures** of two thirds of the several States, shall call a Convention for proposing Amendments, which, in either Case, shall be valid to all Intents and Purposes, as Part of this Constitution, when ratified by the Legislatures of three fourths of the several States, or by Conventions in three fourths thereof, as the one or the other Mode of Ratification may be proposed by the Congress ... "[28] [Emphasis added]

[25] U.S. Constitution. Article I, section 3, clause 1. Superseded by the 17th Amendment.
[26] U.S. Constitution. Article I, section 3, clause 2. Superseded by the 17th Amendment.
[27] U.S. Constitution. Article V.
[28] U.S. Constitution. Article V.
[29] U.S. Constitution. Article I, section 4, clause 1.

TABLE 8.1 PROVISIONS OF THE U.S. CONSTITUTION REFERRING TO POWERS OF THE STATE "LEGISLATURE" (cont.)

	POWER	PROVISION OF THE U.S. CONSTITUTION
5	**Choosing the manner of electing U.S. Representatives and Senators**	"The Times, Places and Manner of holding Elections for Senators and Representatives, shall be **prescribed in each State by the Legislature** thereof; but the Congress may at any time by Law make or alter such Regulations, except as to the Places of chusing Senators."[29] [Emphasis added]
6	**Choosing the manner of appointing presidential electors**	"Each State shall appoint, in such Manner **as the Legislature thereof may direct,** a Number of Electors, equal to the whole Number of Senators and Representatives to which the State may be entitled in the Congress ...."[30] [Emphasis added]
7	**Choosing the manner of conducting a popular election to fill a U.S. Senate vacancy** (under the 17th Amendment)	"When vacancies happen in the representation of any State in the Senate, the executive authority of such State shall issue writs of election to fill such vacancies: Provided, That the legislature of any State may empower the executive thereof to make temporary appointments until the people fill the vacancies by election **as the legislature may direct.**"[31] [Emphasis added]
8	**Empowering the Governor to fill a U.S. Senate vacancy temporarily until a popular election is held** (under the 17th Amendment)	"When vacancies happen in the representation of any State in the Senate, the executive authority of such State shall issue writs of election to fill such vacancies: Provided, That **the legislature of any State may empower** the executive thereof to make temporary appointments until the people fill the vacancies by election as the legislature may direct."[32] [Emphasis added]
9	**Consenting to the purchase of enclaves by the federal government**	"To exercise exclusive Legislation in all Cases whatsoever, over such District (not exceeding ten Miles square) as may, by Cession of particular States, and the Acceptance of Congress, become the Seat of the Government of the United States, and to exercise like Authority over all Places purchased by the **Consent of the Legislature** of the State in which the Same shall be, for the Erection of Forts, Magazines, Arsenals, dockYards, and other needful Buildings."[33] [Emphasis added]

[29] U.S. Constitution. Article I, section 4, clause 1.
[30] U.S. Constitution. Article II, section 1, clause 2.
[31] U.S. Constitution. 17th Amendment, section 2.
[32] U.S. Constitution. 17th Amendment, section 2.
[33] U.S. Constitution. Article I, section 9, clause 17.

TABLE 8.1 PROVISIONS OF THE U.S. CONSTITUTION REFERRING TO POWERS OF THE STATE "LEGISLATURE" (cont.)

	POWER	PROVISION OF THE U.S. CONSTITUTION
10	**Consenting to the formation of new states from territory of existing state(s)**	"New States may be admitted by the Congress into this Union; but no new State shall be formed or erected within the Jurisdiction of any other State; nor any State be formed by the Junction of two or more States, or Parts of States, without the **Consent of the Legislatures** of the States concerned as well as of the Congress."[34] [Emphasis added]
11	**Requesting federal military assistance to quell domestic violence**	"The United States shall guarantee to every State in this Union a Republican Form of Government, and shall protect each of them against Invasion; and on **Application of the Legislature,** or of the Executive (when the **Legislature** cannot be convened) against domestic Violence."[35] [Emphasis added]

vention in which each state representative and each state senator cast one vote in the election for the state's U.S. Senator. In other states, the state house of representatives and the state senate voted separately on a concurrent resolution expressing their choice for the state's U.S. Senator.[36] Regardless of which method was used, the state's Governor was *not* part of the constitutional process of electing U.S. Senators. Neither the decision of a joint convention of the two houses nor the concurrent resolution agreed to by both houses of the legislature was presented to the Governor for approval or disapproval. In other words, the word "legislature" in the U.S. Constitution, in connection with the election of U.S. Senators (the first entry in table 8.1), refers to the state's two legislative chambers—not to the state's usual process for making laws.

---

[34] U.S. Constitution. Article IV, section 3, clause 1.

[35] U.S. Constitution. Article IV, section 4.

[35] Separate voting for U.S. Senators by the two houses of the state legislature, of course, created the possibility of a deadlock between the two houses. Thus, it became common for U.S. Senate seats to remain vacant for prolonged periods. Article I, section 4, clause 1 of the U.S. Constitution provides that "The Times, Places and Manner of holding Elections for Senators and Representatives, shall be prescribed in each State by the Legislature thereof; but the Congress may at any time by Law make or alter such Regulations, except as to the Places of chusing Senators." In 1866, Congress exercised its power under this constitutional provision to change the "manner" by which state legislatures conducted their Senate elections and to specify the "time" of such elections. Congress required the two houses of each state legislature to meet in a joint convention on a specified day and to meet every day thereafter until a Senator was selected (14 Stat. 243).

8.3.2 Filling a U.S. Senate Vacancy

Similarly, under the original Constitution, a vacancy in the U.S. Senate was filled by action of the state's two legislative chambers (either voting in a joint convention or acting separately by concurrent resolution). That is, the word "legislature" in the U.S. Constitution, in connection with the filling of U.S. Senate vacancies (the second entry in table 8.1), refers to the state's two legislative chambers.

8.3.3 Ratifying a Proposed Federal Constitutional Amendment

The meaning of the word "legislature" in connection with the ratification of amendments to the federal Constitution (the third entry in table 8.1) was decided by the U.S. Supreme Court in *Hawke v. Smith* in 1920.[37] Article V of the U.S. Constitution provides that proposed amendments

> "... shall be valid to all Intents and Purposes, as Part of this Constitution, when ratified by the **Legislatures** of three fourths of the several States...." [Emphasis added]

Before deciding the specific issue in the Hawke case in 1920, the U.S. Supreme Court reviewed the Court's decision in 1798 in *Hollingsworth et al. v. Virginia.*[38] The *Hollingsworth* case explored the two distinct meanings of the word "Congress" in the U.S. Constitution (the analog of the issue concerning the two meanings of the word "legislature").

The U.S. Constitution frequently uses the word "Congress" to refer to the national government's law-making process—that is, the process by which the legislative bills are passed by the two houses of Congress and presented to the President for approval or disapproval. The word "Congress" appears with this meaning in numerous places in the Constitution, including

> "The **Congress** shall have Power To lay and collect Taxes, Duties, Imposts and Excises, to pay the Debts and provide for the common Defence and general Welfare of the United States...."[39] [Emphasis added]

---

[37] *Hawke v. Smith.* 253 U.S. 221. 1920.

[38] *Hollingsworth et al. v. Virginia.* 3 Dall. 378. 1798.

[39] U.S. Constitution. Article I, section 8, clause 1.

The word "Congress" also appears in Article V:

"The **Congress,** whenever two thirds of both Houses shall deem it necessary, shall propose Amendments to this Constitution...." [Emphasis added]

The *Hollingsworth* case addressed the question of whether the word "Congress" in the U.S. Constitution meant

- **the national government's legislative chambers**—that is, the U.S. House of Representatives and U.S. Senate sitting separately and agreeing to a concurrent resolution, or
- **the national government's law-making process.**

In 1798, the U.S. Supreme Court ruled that when the Congress proposes an amendment to the U.S. Constitution, the resolution of ratification need not be submitted to the President for approval or disapproval. Referring to the 1798 *Hollingsworth* case, the Court noted in the 1920 *Hawke* case:

"At an early day this court settled that the submission of a constitutional amendment did not require the action of the President. The question arose over the adoption of the Eleventh Amendment. *Hollingsworth et al. v. Virginia*, 3 Dall. 378. In that case it was contended that the amendment had not been proposed in the manner provided in the Constitution as an inspection of the original roll showed that it had never been submitted to the President for his approval in accordance with article 1, section 7, of the Constitution. The Attorney General answered that **the case of amendments is a substantive act, unconnected with the ordinary business of legislation,** and not within the policy or terms of the Constitution investing the President with a qualified negative [veto] on the acts and resolutions of Congress. In a footnote to this argument of the Attorney General, Justice Chase said:

'There can, surely, be no necessity to answer that argument. **The negative of the President applies only to the ordinary cases of legislation. He has nothing to do with the proposition, or adoption, of amendments to the Constitution.**'

"The court by a unanimous judgment held that the amendment was constitutionally adopted."[40] [Emphasis added]

In other words, the 1798 *Hollingsworth* case concluded that a federal constitutional amendment was *not* the "ordinary business of legislation."

The U.S. Supreme Court then addressed the specific issue in the 1920 *Hawke* case, namely the constitutionality of a 1918 amendment to the Ohio Constitution. This state constitutional amendment extended the protest-referendum process to resolutions of ratification by the Ohio legislature of proposed federal constitutional amendments. Specifically, the 1918 amendment to the Ohio Constitution provided:

"The people also reserve to themselves the legislative power of the referendum on the action of the General Assembly ratifying any proposed amendment to the Constitution of the United States."

The *Hawke* case arose as a result of the Ohio Legislature's ratification of the 18th Amendment prohibiting the manufacture, sale, and transportation of intoxicating liquors for beverage purposes. On January 7, 1919, the Ohio Legislature passed a concurrent resolution[41] ratifying the Amendment.[42] Ohio's ratification was crucial because the U.S. Secretary of State was in possession of resolutions of ratification from 35 other states, and 36 ratifications were sufficient, at the time, to make a pending amendment part of the U.S. Constitution. A protest-referendum petition was quickly circulated in Ohio. Supporters of the 18th Amendment challenged the petition's validity in state court. The Ohio Supreme Court decided that the legislature's ratification of the 18th Amendment should be temporarily suspended and submitted to the state's voters for approval or disapproval in a statewide referendum. The U.S. Supreme Court, however, decided otherwise.

"The argument to support the power of the state to require the approval by the people of the state of the ratification of

---

[40] *Hawke v. Smith.* 253 U.S. 221 at 229–230. 1920.

[41] A concurrent resolution is a type of resolution that is passed by both houses of the legislature but not submitted to the Governor for approval or disapproval.

[42] The resolution of ratification for the 18th Amendment was adopted by the Ohio Legislature in accordance with the long-standing practice in Ohio (and other states) of not submitting the legislature's resolution to the state's Governor for approval or disapproval.

---

amendments to the federal Constitution through the medium of a referendum rests upon the proposition that the federal Constitution requires ratification by the legislative action of the states through the medium provided at the time of the proposed approval of an amendment. This argument is fallacious in this—**ratification by a state of a constitutional amendment is not an act of legislation** within the proper sense of the word. **It is but the expression of the assent of the state to a proposed amendment.**"[43] [Emphasis added]

In short, in connection with ratification of amendments to the U.S. Constitution (the third entry in table 8.1), the word "legislature" in the U.S. Constitution refers to the state's two legislative chambers. Ratification is

- "unconnected with the ordinary business of legislation,"[44] and
- "not an act of legislation."[45]

Appendix U contains the full text of the Supreme Court's 1920 decision in *Hawke v. Smith.*

8.3.4 Making an Application to Congress for a Federal Constitutional Convention

The word "legislature" appears in the U.S. Constitution in connection with one of the two ways by which amendments to the Constitution may be proposed to the states. Article V provides:

"The Congress, whenever two thirds of both Houses shall deem it necessary, shall propose Amendments to this Constitution, or, on the **Application of the Legislatures** of two thirds of the several States, shall call a Convention for proposing Amendments...." [Emphasis added]

State legislatures sometimes call on Congress to convene a federal Constitutional Convention. For example, prior to congressional passage of the 17th Amendment, 26 states had petitioned Congress for a federal Constitutional Convention to consider the specific question of the

---

[43] *Hawke v. Smith.* 253 U.S. 221 at 229–230. 1920.

[44] *Id.* at 230.

[45] *Id.*

popular election of U.S. Senators. In addition, two additional states had, during the period immediately prior to congressional action on the 17th Amendment, issued requests for a federal Constitutional Convention without mentioning the topic to be considered by the Convention. Similarly, by the time Congress acted on the 21st Amendment, almost two-thirds of the states had petitioned Congress for a federal Constitutional Convention to repeal the 18th Amendment.

According to Orfield's *The Amending of the Federal Constitution*, when state legislatures apply to Congress for a federal Constitutional Convention, the long-standing practice of the states has been that the action of the legislature is not presented to the state's Governor for approval or disapproval.[46] Instead, the two houses of the state legislature pass a concurrent resolution. Thus, in connection with applications to Congress for a federal Constitutional Convention (the fourth entry in table 8.1), historical practice indicates that the word "legislature" in the U.S. Constitution refers to the state's two legislative chambers.

8.3.5 Choosing the Manner of Electing U.S. Representatives and Senators

As demonstrated in the previous four sections, judicial precedent and long-standing practice by the states indicate that the word "legislature" in the U.S. Constitution refers, in connection with the first, second, third, and fourth entries in table 8.1, to the state's two legislative chambers— not to the state's Governor or the state's citizen-initiative or protest-referendum processes.

In many other parts of the U.S. Constitution, however, the word "legislature" has a different meaning—namely, the state's law-making process. In these parts of the Constitution, "legislature" includes the state's Governor—an official who is manifestly not part of the state legislature. Moreover, in these parts of the U.S. Constitution, "legislature" may also include the state's voters—who, like the Governor, are plainly not members of the two chambers of the state legislature.

An example of this second meaning of the word "legislature" is found in Article I, section 4, clause 1 of the U.S. Constitution concerning the manner of holding elections for U.S. Representatives and Senators (the fifth entry in table 8.1).

---

[46] Orfield, Lester Bernhardt. 1942. *The Amending of the Federal Constitution*. Ann Arbor: The University of Michigan Press.

"The Times, Places and **Manner** of holding Elections for Senators and Representatives, shall be prescribed in each State by the **Legislature** thereof; but the Congress may at any time by Law make or alter such Regulations, except as to the Places of chusing Senators." [Emphasis added]

The U.S. Supreme Court addressed the meaning of "legislature" in Article I, section 4, clause 1 in *Smiley v. Holm* in 1932.[47] The issue in *Smiley* was whether the Minnesota Governor could veto a law passed by the legislature redrawing the state's congressional districts after the 1930 census. In other words, the question in *Smiley* was whether the word "legislature" refers to the state's two legislative chambers or the state's law-making process which, in Minnesota in 1932, included the Governor.

The question of whether the word "legislature" includes a state's Governor depends, in large part, on the answer to the following question:

"When a state exercises authority pursuant to powers granted to it by the U.S. Constitution in connection with deciding on the manner of electing its U.S. Representatives,

(1) does it derive the power to act solely from the U.S. Constitution, or

(2) does it enact the legislation in accordance with the procedures specified in the state's constitution?"

The 1932 *Smiley* case involving the meaning of the word "legislature" in the U.S. Constitution came to the U.S. Supreme Court over a decade after various cases arising from the adoption of the initiative and referendum processes in the early years of the 20th century. These earlier cases included the 1920 *Hawke* case (discussed above) and the 1916 case of *State of Ohio ex rel. Davis v. Hildebrant* (discussed below). *Smiley* thus provided the Court with the opportunity to put all of these related cases into perspective. The U.S. Supreme Court wrote in *Smiley* in 1932:

"[W]henever the term 'legislature' is used in the Constitution, it is necessary to consider the nature of the particular action in view."[48] [Emphasis added]

---

[47] *Smiley v. Holm.* 285 U.S. 355. 1932.

[48] *Id.* at 366.

Applying this test, the Court found that the term "legislature" in Article I, section 4, clause 1 referred to "making laws"[49] and therefore included the Governor.

> "[I]t follows, in the absence of an indication of a contrary intent, that **the exercise of the authority must be in accordance with the method which the State has prescribed for legislative enactments. We find no suggestion in the Federal constitutional provision of an attempt to endow the legislature of the State with power to enact laws in any manner other than that in which the constitution of the State has provided that laws shall be enacted.**"[50] [Emphasis added]

Thus, the word "legislature" in the U.S. Constitution, in connection with the state's deciding on the "manner of holding Elections" for U.S. Representatives" (the fifth entry in table 8.1), refers to the state's process of making laws—not just to the two chambers of the state legislature.

Appendix V contains the full text of the Supreme Court's 1932 decision in *Smiley v. Holm.*

In 1916, the U.S. Supreme Court addressed the specific question of whether the word "legislature" in Article I, section 4, clause 1 of the U.S. Constitution included the voters acting through the processes of direct democracy. The Supreme Court described the origins of *State of Ohio ex rel. Davis v. Hildebrant* as follows:

> "By an amendment to the Constitution of Ohio, adopted September 3d, 1912, the **legislative power was expressly declared to be vested** not only in the senate and house of representatives of the state, constituting the general assembly, but **in the people,** in whom a right was reserved by way of referendum to approve or disapprove by popular vote any law enacted by the general assembly." [51] [Emphasis added]

The Supreme Court continued:

> "In May, 1915, the general assembly of Ohio passed an act redistricting the state for the purpose of congressional

---

[49] *Id.* at 365.

[50] *Id.* at 368.

[51] *State of Ohio ex rel. Davis v. Hildebrant.* 241 U.S. 565 at 566. 1916.

elections, by which act twenty-two congressional districts were created, in some respects differing from the previously established districts, and this act, after approval by the governor, was filed in the office of the secretary of state. The requisite number of electors under the referendum provision having petitioned for a submission of the law to a popular vote, such vote was taken and the law was disapproved.

"Thereupon, in the supreme court of the state, the suit before us was begun against state election officers for the purpose of procuring a mandamus, directing them to disregard the vote of the people on the referendum, disapproving the law, and to proceed to discharge their duties as such officers in the next congressional election, upon the assumption that the action by way of referendum was void, and that the law which was disapproved was subsisting and valid."[52]

Summarizing the issue, the Supreme Court wrote:

"The right to this relief was based upon the charge that the referendum vote was not and could not be a part of the legislative authority of the state, and therefore could have no influence on the subject of the law creating congressional districts for the purpose of representation in Congress. Indeed, it was in substance charged that both from the point of view of the state Constitution and laws and from that of the Constitution of the United States, especially [clause] 4 of article 1, providing that

'the times, places and manner of holding elections for Senators and Representatives, shall be prescribed in each state by the legislature thereof; but the Congress may at any time by law, make or alter such regulations, except as to the places of choosing Senators;'

and also from that of the provisions of the controlling act of Congress of August 8, 1911 (chap. 5, 37 Stat. at L. 13, Comp. Stat. 1913, 15), apportioning representation among the states, the attempt to make the referendum a component part of the

---

[52] *Id.* at 566–567.

legislative authority empowered to deal with the election of members of Congress was absolutely void. **The court below adversely disposed of these contentions, and held that the provisions as to referendum were a part of the legislative power of the state, made so by the Constitution, and that nothing in the act of Congress of 1911, or in the constitutional provision, operated to the contrary,** and that therefore the disapproved law had no existence and was not entitled to be enforced by mandamus."[53] [Emphasis added]

The U.S. Supreme Court then upheld the Ohio Supreme Court and rejected the argument that the word "legislature" in Article I, section 4, clause 1 of the U.S. Constitution excluded the referendum process. The popular vote rejecting Ohio's redistricting statute was allowed to stand.

Additionally, the Court noted:

"Congress recognize[d] the referendum as part of the legislative authority of a state."[54]

Appendix P contains the full text of the Supreme Court's 1916 decision in *State of Ohio ex rel. Davis v. Hildebrant.*

In 1920, the U.S. Supreme Court distinguished its decision in *Hawke* from its decision in *State of Ohio ex rel. Davis v. Hildebrant* by saying in *Hawke:*

"But it is said this view runs counter to the decision of this court in *Davis v. Hildebrant* (241 U.S. 565) 36 S. Ct. 708. But that case is inapposite. It dealt with article 1 section 4, of the Constitution, which provides that the times, places, and manners of holding elections for Senators and Representatives in each state shall be determined by the respective Legislatures thereof, but that Congress may at any time make or alter such regulations, except as to the place for choosing Senators. As shown in the opinion in that case, Congress had itself recognized the referendum as part of the legislative authority of the state for the purpose stated. It was held, affirming the

---

[53] *Id.* at 568.

[54] *Id.* at 569.

judgment of the Supreme Court of Ohio, that the referendum provision of the state Constitution, when applied to a law redistricting the state with a view to representation in Congress, was not unconstitutional. **Article 1, section 4, plainly gives authority to the state to legislate within the limitations therein named. Such legislative action is entirely different from the requirement of the Constitution as to the expression of assent or dissent to a proposed amendment to the Constitution. In such expression no legislative action is authorized or required.**"[55] [Emphasis added]

Relying on *Smiley v. Holm*[56] and *State of Ohio ex rel. Davis v. Hildebrant*,[57] the Colorado Supreme Court wrote in *Colorado, ex rel. Salazar v. Davidson* in 2003:

"[T]he United States Supreme Court has interpreted the word 'legislature' in Article I to broadly encompass any means permitted by state law [including] citizen referenda and initiatives, mandatory gubernatorial approval, and any other procedures defined by the state." [58,59]

Chief Justice Rehnquist, joined by Justices Thomas and Scalia, affirmed this view in a dissenting opinion when the U.S. Supreme Court denied review of the *Colorado, ex rel. Salazar v. Davidson* decision. Rehnquist stated that the Court had

"explained that the focus of our inquiry was **not on the 'body' but the function performed** [and that] the function referred to by Article I, §4, was **the lawmaking process,** which is defined by state law."[60] [Emphasis added]

[55] *Hawke v. Smith.* 253 U.S. 221 at 230–231. 1920.

[56] *Smiley v. Holm.* 285 U.S. 355. 1932.

[57] *State of Ohio ex rel. Davis v. Hildebrant.* 241 U.S. 565. 1916.

[58] *Colorado, ex rel. Salazar v. Davidson.* 79 P.3d 1221, 1232 (Colorado 2003).

[59] In *Cook v. Gralike*, 531 U.S. 510, 526 n.20 (2001), the Court declined to consider whether the Elections Clause of Art. 1, §4, which is a grant of power to "each State by the Legislature thereof," could be invoked to protect to a statute adopted by referendum. The Court reaffirmed, however, the notion in *Smiley* that "[w]herever the term 'legislature' is used in the Constitution, it is necessary to consider the nature of the particular action in view." *Id.*

[60] *Colorado General Assembly v. Salazar*, 124 S. Ct. 2228 at 2230. 2004.

The distinction between "the lawmaking process" and the two chambers of the state legislature is not new. In fact, this distinction has been made since the earliest days of the U.S. Constitution. When the U.S. Constitution took effect in 1788, two states had the gubernatorial veto.[61,62]

The provisions of the Massachusetts Constitution at the time when the U.S. Constitution took effect were substantially the same as the procedures for gubernatorial approval, veto, and legislative override found in most state constitutions today (and substantially the same as the procedures for presidential veto in the U.S. constitution).

"No bill or resolve of the senate or house of representatives shall become a law, and have force as such, until it shall have been laid before the governor for his revisal; and if he, upon such revision, approve thereof, he shall signify his approbation by signing the same. But if he have any objection to the passing of such bill or resolve, he shall return the same, together with his objections thereto, in writing, to the senate or house of representatives, in whichsoever the same shall have originated, who shall enter the objections sent down by the governor, at large, on their records, and proceed to reconsider the said bill or resolve; but if, after such reconsideration, two-thirds of the said senate or house of representatives shall, notwithstanding the said objections, agree to pass the same, it shall, together with the objections, be sent to the other branch of the legislature, where it shall also be reconsidered, and if approved by two-thirds of the members present, shall have the force of law; but in all such cases, the vote of both houses shall be determined by yeas and nays; and the names of the persons voting for or against the said bill or resolve shall be entered upon the public records of the commonwealth."[63]

---

[61] Kole, Edward A. 1999. *The First 13 Constitutions of the First American States.* Haverford, PA: Infinity Publishing.

[62] Kole, Edward A. *The True Intent of the First American Constitutions of 1776–1791.* Haverford, PA: Infinity Publishing.

[63] Massachusetts Constitution of 1780. Chapter I, Section I, Article II.

On November 20, 1788, both chambers of the Massachusetts legislature approved legislation specifying the manner for electing U.S. representatives. This legislation was forwarded to Governor John Hancock, and he approved it.[64]

The New York Constitution of 1777 was in effect when the U.S. Constitution took effect. The New York Constitution (like many state constitutions of the colonial era and immediate post-independence era) had a Governor's Council.[65] In particular, the New York Constitution required that all bills passed by the legislature be submitted to a Council of Revision composed of the Governor, the Chancellor, and judges of the state supreme court. A two-thirds vote of both houses of the legislature was necessary to override a veto by the Council. On January 23, 1789, the New York legislature approved legislation specifying the manner for electing U.S. representatives. The bill was presented to the Council; the Council approved the bill; and the bill became law.

Article I, section 4, clause 1 of the U.S. Constitution covers the manner of electing U.S. Senators as well as the manner of electing U.S. Representatives.

> "The Times, Places and **Manner** of holding Elections for **Senators** and Representatives, shall be prescribed in each State by the **Legislature** thereof...." [Emphasis added]

The two meanings of the word "legislature" in the U.S. Constitution are dramatically illustrated by the actions of the first New York legislature that met under the U.S. Constitution. As mentioned in section 8.3.1, the state's Governor was not part of the constitutional process of electing U.S. Senators under the original Constitution. The two chambers of the state legislature elected the state's U.S. Senators. The Governor of New York was, however, part of the law-making process that decided the *manner* of electing U.S. Senators. For example, in 1789, both houses of the New York legislature passed a bill providing for the manner of electing U.S. Senators. This bill was presented to the Council composed of the Governor, the Chancellor, and the judges of the state supreme court. The

---

[64] Smith, Hayward H. 2001. *Symposium, Law of Presidential Elections: Issues in the Wake of Florida 2000.* History of the Article II Independent State legislature Doctrine. 29 *Florida State University Law Review* 731-785 at 760. Issue 2.

[65] Currently, Massachusetts has a Governor's Council and New Hampshire has an Executive Council.

Council vetoed the bill.[66] That bill did not become law. In short, when a state chose the "manner" of electing its U.S. Senators, the word "legislature" in the U.S. Constitution meant "the lawmaking process" (which included the Governor and Council); however, when the state elected its U.S. Senators, the same word "legislature" meant only the two legislative chambers (which did not include the Governor or the Council).

Congressional districting is arguably the most important aspect of the "manner" of electing U.S. Representatives. In recent years, the voters have used the processes of direct democracy not only to review congressional districting plans enacted by the state legislature (as they did in Ohio in the 1916 case of *State of Ohio ex rel. Davis v. Hildebrant*), but also to entirely exclude the state legislature from the process of congressional districting. For example, Arizona voters recently approved an initiative establishing a non-partisan commission to draw the state's congressional districts. The voters' decision to exclude the state legislature power from the redistricting process was taken by the voters unilaterally through the citizen-initiative process—without the involvement, much less the consent, of the state legislature. The power of congressional redistricting in Arizona now resides in the non-partisan commission. Similar initiative measures were on the ballot in the November 2005 elections in California and Ohio (but were defeated). Initiative petitions were in circulation in 2005 in Florida and Massachusetts for similar measures.

In summary, present-day practice, practice at the time of ratification of the U.S. Constitution, and court decisions consistently support the interpretation that the word "legislature" in article I, section 4, clause 1 of the U.S. Constitution (the fifth entry in table 8.1) does not refer to the two chambers of the state legislature but, instead, refers to the "lawmaking process" that includes

- the state's Governor, an official who is manifestly not a member of the two chambers of the state legislature, and
- in states having the citizen-initiative process and protest-referendum process, the state's voters, who, like the Governor, are manifestly not members of the two chambers of the state legislature.

---

[66] DenBoer, Gordon; Brown, Lucy Trumbull; and Hagermann, Charles D. (editors). 1986. *The Documentary History of the First Federal Elections 1788–1790*. Madison, WI: University of Wisconsin Press. Volume III.

8.3.6 Choosing the Manner of Appointing Presidential Electors

The word "legislature" appears in Article II of the U.S. Constitution (the sixth entry in table 8.1).

> "Each State shall appoint, in such Manner **as the Legislature thereof may direct,** a Number of Electors, equal to the whole Number of Senators and Representatives to which the State may be entitled in the Congress...."[67] [Emphasis added]

In *U.S. Term Limits v. Thornton,* the U.S. Supreme Court in 1995 noted the parallelism between the use of the word "legislature" in Article I, section 4, clause 1 (relating to the "manner" of electing U.S. Representatives) and the word "legislature" in Article II. The Court wrote,

> "... the provisions governing elections reveal the Framers' understanding that powers over the election of federal officers had to be delegated to, rather than reserved by, the States. It is surely no coincidence that **the context of federal elections provides one of the few areas in which the Constitution expressly requires action by the States,** namely that
>
> > '[t]he Times, Places and **Manner** of holding Elections for Senators and Representatives, shall be prescribed in each State by the **legislature** thereof.' [Art I., §4, cl. 4.]
>
> **"This duty parallels the duty under Article II** that
>
> > 'Each State shall appoint, in such **Manner** as the **Legislature** thereof may direct, a Number of Electors.' Art II., §1, cl. 2.
>
> "These Clauses are express delegations of power to the States to act with respect to federal elections."[68] [Emphasis added]

The parallelism noted by the Court supports the power of the people to act legislatively through the citizen-initiative process concerning the manner of electing presidential electors.

---

[67] U.S. Constitution. Article II, section 1, clause 2.

[68] *U.S. Term Limits v. Thornton.* 514 U.S. 779 at 805. 1995.

The question of whether the word "legislature" includes the state's initiative and referendum processes depends, in large part, on the answer to the following question:

> "When a state exercises authority pursuant to powers granted to it by the U.S. Constitution in connection with deciding on the manner of choosing its presidential electors,
>
> > (1) does it derive the power to act solely from the U.S. Constitution, or
> >
> > (2) does it enact the legislation in accordance with the procedures specified in the state's constitution?"

The leading U.S. Supreme Court case interpreting Article II, section 1, clause 2 of the U.S. Constitution is the 1892 case of *McPherson v. Blacker*.[69] In *Blacker*, the U.S. Supreme Court rejected a challenge to Michigan legislation providing for selection of presidential electors by district, as opposed to the statewide winner-take-all method that Michigan had been using prior to 1892 and that had become the national norm. In that case, the Court analyzed the meaning of the word "legislature" as used in Article II and noted that the interpretation of this word was governed by fundamental law of the state. The U.S. Supreme Court wrote:

> "The state does not act by its people in their collective capacity, but through such political agencies as are duly constituted and established. The legislative power is the supreme authority, **except as limited by the constitution of the state,** and the sovereignty of the people is exercised through their representatives in the legislature, **unless by the fundamental law power is elsewhere reposed.** The constitution of the United States frequently refers to the state as a political community, and also in terms to the people of the several states and the citizens of each state. What is forbidden or required to be done by a state is forbidden or required of the legislative power under state constitutions as they exist."[70] [Emphasis added]

---

[69] *McPherson v. Blacker.* 146 U.S. 1. 1892.

[70] *Id.* at 27.

The possibility that a state's legislative power might be "reposed" in a place other than the state legislature is noteworthy, given that the case was decided when the idea of the citizen-initiative process was an active topic of public debate (just before South Dakota became the first state to adopt the citizen-initiative process in 1898).

Given that the citizen-initiative process is generally considered to be a co-equal grant of authority to that given to the state's legislature, the treatment of the initiative process as a legislative power is consistent with the fundamental law of states that have the initiative process.

There are two cases that have specifically involved the question of whether the word "legislature" in Article II of the U.S. Constitution includes the initiative and referendum processes.[71]

The first case arose as a result of a 1919 law entitled "An act granting to women the right to vote for presidential electors." This law was passed by the two houses of the Maine legislature and presented to the state's Governor. The Governor signed the law. Under the protest-referendum provisions of the Maine Constitution, if a petition protesting a just-enacted law is filed with the signatures of at least 10,000 voters, the new law is temporarily suspended and referred to the voters for their approval or disapproval in a statewide referendum. A petition was circulated and duly filed with the Governor's office concerning this statute. Before proceeding with the referendum, the Governor raised the question of whether the referendum provision of the Maine Constitution applied to legislation involving the manner of appointing the state's presidential electors. Specifically, he propounded the following question to the Justices of the Maine Supreme Judicial Court:

> "Is the effect of the act of the Legislature of Maine of 1919, entitled 'An act granting to women the right to vote for presidential electors,' approved by the Governor on March 28, 1919, suspended by valid written petitions of not less than

---

[71] Court cases specifically interpreting the word "legislature" in Article II in relation to the initiative or referendum process are necessarily rare for several reasons. First, the initiative and referendum processes are only slightly more than 100 years old. Second, the initiative or referendum processes are available in fewer than one half of the states. Third, only a handful of the laws that a state enacts in a typical year involve the conduct of elections. Fourth, few new state laws involve the manner of conducting congressional and senatorial elections, and even fewer relate to presidential elections. Fifth, the vast majority of new state laws each year are enacted without the use of either the initiative or referendum processes.

10,000 electors, addressed to the Governor and filed in the office of the secretary of state within 90 days after the recess of the Legislature, requesting that it be referred to the people, and should the act be referred to the people as provided in article 4 of the Constitution of Maine, as amended by Amendment 31, adopted September 14, 1908?"

On August 28, 1919, the Maine Supreme Judicial Court unanimously answered this question in the affirmative. Relying extensively on the 1892 decision of the U.S. Supreme Court in *McPherson v. Blacker*,[72] the Maine Supreme Judicial Court wrote:

"The language of section 1, subd. 2, is clear and unambiguous. It admits of no doubt as to where the constitutional power of appointment is vested, namely, in the several states.

'Each state shall appoint in such manner as the Legislature thereof may direct'

are the significant words of the section, and their plain meaning is that **each state is thereby clothed with the absolute power to appoint electors in such manner as it may see fit, without any interference or control on the part of the federal government,** except, of course, in case of attempted discrimination as to race, color, or previous condition of servitude under the fifteenth amendment. The clause,

'in such manner as the Legislature thereof may direct,'

means, simply that **the state shall give expression to its will, as it must, of necessity, through its law-making body, the Legislature.** The will of the state in this respect must be voiced in legislative acts or resolves, which shall prescribe in detail the manner of choosing electors, the qualifications of voters therefor, and the proceedings on the part of the electors when chosen.

---

[72] *McPherson v. Blacker.* 146 U.S. 1. 1892. The *Blacker* case is also discussed in section 2.2.5 and later in this section. The complete opinion of the U.S. Supreme Court in the *Blacker* case is found in appendix O.

"**But these acts and resolves must be passed and become effective in accordance with and in subjection to the Constitution of the state, like all other acts** and resolves having the force of law. **The Legislature was not given in this respect any superiority over or independence from the organic law of the state in force at the time when a given law is passed.** Nor was it designated by the federal Constitution as a mere agency or representative of the people to perform a certain act, as it was under article 5 in ratifying a federal amendment, a point more fully discussed in the answer to the question concerning the federal prohibitory amendment. 107 Atl. 673. **It is simply the ordinary instrumentality of the state, the legislative branch of the government, the law-making power, to put into words the will of the state in connection with the choice of presidential electors. The distinction between the function and power of the Legislature in the case under consideration and its function and power as a particular body designated by the federal Constitution to ratify or reject a federal amendment is sharp and clear and must be borne in mind.**

"It follows, therefore, that under the provisions of the federal Constitution the state by its legislative direction may establish such a method of choosing its presidential electors as it may see fit, and may change that method from time to time as it may deem advisable; but **the legislative acts both of establishment and of change must always be subject to the provisions of the Constitution of the state in force at the time such acts are passed** and can be valid and effective only when enacted in compliance therewith."[73] [Emphasis added]

The Court continued:

"It is clear that this act, extending this privilege to women, constitutes a change in the method of electing presidential electors....

---

[73] *In re Opinion of the Justices.* 107 A. 705. 1919.

"... this state during the century of its existence prior to 1919, had by appropriate legislative act or resolve directed that only male citizens were qualified to vote for presidential electors. By the act of 1919 it has attempted to change that direction, by extending the privilege of suffrage, so far as presidential electors are concerned, to women. Had this act been passed prior to the adoption of the initiative and referendum amendment in 1908, it would have become effective, so far as legal enactment is concerned, without being referred to the people; but now under Amendment 31 such reference must be had, if the necessary steps therefor are taken."

"... **This is the public statute of a law-making body, and is as fully within the control of the referendum amendment as is any other of the 239 public acts passed at the last session of the Legislature,** excepting, of course, emergency acts. **It is shielded from the jurisdiction of that referendum neither by the state nor by the federal Constitution.** In short, the state, through its Legislature, has taken merely the first step toward effecting a change in the appointment of presidential electors; but, because of the petitions filed, it must await the second step which is the vote of the people. The legislative attempt in this case cannot be fully effective until

'thirty days after the Governor shall have announced by public proclamation that the same has been ratified by a majority of the electors voting thereon at a general or special election.'"[74] [Emphasis added]

Appendix Q contains the entire text of the Court's opinion in *In re Opinion of the Justices.*

---

[74] *Id.*

[75] There was a flurry of activity concerning women's suffrage at the time. The Maine legislature adopted its contested law on women's suffrage in presidential elections on March 28, 1919. Congress proposed the women's suffrage amendment to the U.S. Constitution on June 4, 1919 and sent it to the states for ratification. The Maine Supreme Judicial Court announced its decision on August 28, 1919. The Maine Legislature ratified the proposed federal constitutional amendment on November 5, 1919. Tennessee's ratification on August 18, 1920, brought the 19th Amendment to the U.S. Constitution into effect.

When the voters of Maine voted on the suspended law, it was passed by a vote of 88,080 to 30,462.[75]

The second case involving an interpretation of the word "legislature" in Article II of the U.S. Constitution came just prior to the November 2, 2004, presidential election. *Napolitano v. Davidson* involved a federal court challenge to an initiative petition proposing an amendment to the Colorado Constitution to adopt the whole-number proportional approach for choosing the state's presidential electors (section 4.1.14). In that case, a Colorado voter asked that the Colorado Secretary of State be enjoined from holding the election on the proposed amendment. The plaintiff alleged that Amendment 36 violated Article II of the U.S. Constitution in that the voters were attempting to unconstitutionally preempt the role of the "legislature" in connection with the manner of appointing presidential electors.

The Colorado Attorney General defended the Secretary of State. Two representatives of those who had signed initiative petitions to place Amendment 36 on the ballot (the "proponents") were granted the right to intervene in the litigation. Additionally, one Democratic and one Republican candidate for presidential elector in the November 2004 election attempted to intervene.[76]

The Colorado Attorney General unqualifiedly defended the substantive provisions of Amendment 36. In response to the claim that the voters' exercise of the initiative power to allocate presidential electors infringed upon Article II, the Attorney General stated that, when the people of Colorado use the initiative process, they act as the "legislature." Specifically, the State of Colorado took the position that its voters were fully empowered to act, pursuant to Article II, to allocate presidential electors.

> "Article II, §1 authorizes each state to act in a lawmaking capacity to select the manner in which it appoints its presidential electors.... For example, the lawmaking authority conferred by Article II, §1 encompasses the people's power of referendum when such power is provided by the state constitution. *Cf. Hildebrant*, 241 U.S. at 569.[77] It follows that **the**

---

[76] The Elector-Intervenors were permitted to brief each of their legal arguments. After addressing the substance of their arguments, however, Judge Babcock ruled from the bench that their attempted intervention was not authorized, as they lacked standing to participate in the litigation.

[77] Appendix P contains the opinion of the U.S. Supreme Court in the case of *State of Ohio ex rel. Davis v. Hildebrant* cited by the Colorado Attorney General.

lawmaking authority conferred by Article II, §1 also encompasses the people's power of initiative where the people are empowered by the state constitution to legislate via initiative....

"The Proposal (to proportionally allocate presidential electors based on the state's popular vote) is an initiative by the people of Colorado as authorized by the Colorado Constitution. As such, it **is an exercise of legislative power** for the purpose of appointing presidential electors. **The Proposal, therefore, is authorized by Article II, §1.**"[78] [Emphasis added]

By the time the matter was fully briefed for the court, early voting had commenced in Colorado. Most absentee ballots had been sent to voters. A little more than one week remained until election day. On October 26, 2004, Judge Lewis Babcock heard the motions for preliminary injunction, filed by the plaintiff and the elector-intervenors, as well as the motions to dismiss filed by the Colorado Attorney General and the petition's proponents. Judge Babcock denied the former and granted the latter, clearing the way for a vote by the people on Amendment 36 on November 2, 2004.

From the bench, Judge Babcock noted that the matter was not ripe for adjudication, as an actual controversy could be said to exist only if the election were held and a majority of voters approved the proposed change in the method of allocating Colorado's presidential electors. Until that time, any opinion would only be advisory in nature.

Judge Babcock also noted that the issues involved in this case should be resolved in the first instance by the Colorado state courts and, therefore, that it was proper for the federal courts to abstain from intervening in this matter. Indeed, the Colorado challenge to the initiative petition on Amendment 36 was unusual in that it started in federal court. Most challenges to initiative and referendum petitions start in state courts.

In his oral ruling, Judge Babcock noted that the elector-intervenors had argued that Amendment 36 was "patently unconstitutional." The judge expressly stated that this was not the case, but he added that

---

[78] The Secretary of State's Combined Motion to Dismiss and Response to Motion for Preliminary Injunction at 21–22, filed in *Napolitano v. Davidson*, Civil Action No. 04-B-2114, D.Colo. (2004).

because he did not have to reach the merits of the case, his ruling should not be taken as a judicial imprimatur concerning the constitutionality of Amendment 36.

In order to obtain a preliminary injunction, one generally must establish (among other things) that there is a substantial likelihood of prevailing on the merits when the matter goes to trial. This standard generally applies when one seeks to enjoin an election or any part of the election process.[79] The federal district court, in evaluating the motions for preliminary injunction, did not find that either the plaintiff or the elector-intervenors had a substantial likelihood of success on the merits with regard to their argument that Amendment 36 violated Article II.

On November 2, 2004, Amendment 36 was rejected by the voters (section 4.1.14), so none of the legal issues raised by the pre-election lawsuit was subsequently addressed in court. Nonetheless, the voters' right to use the initiative process to change the manner of appointing presidential electors in Colorado was not disturbed by the judiciary.

Long-standing historical practice by the states is consistent with the 1920 decision by the Maine Supreme Judicial Court and the outcome of the 2004 litigation in Colorado concerning the meaning of the word "legislature" in Article II of the U.S. Constitution.

When the U.S. Constitution took effect in 1788, the gubernatorial veto existed in Massachusetts and New York.[80,81]

On November 20, 1788, both chambers of the Massachusetts legislature approved legislation specifying the manner for appointing the state's presidential electors. This legislation was presented to Governor John Hancock—an official who was manifestly not part of the two chambers of the state legislature. Governor Hancock approved the legislation.[82]

In New York, a comprehensive bill was introduced in the Senate on December 13, 1788, for electing presidential electors, U.S. Representatives, and U.S. Senators. The Federalists controlled the state

---

[79] *Libertarian Party v. Buckley.* 938 F.Supp. 687, 690 (D. Colo. 1997). See also *Chandler v. Miller.* 520 U.S. 305, 311. 1997.

[80] Kole, Edward A. 1999. *The First 13 Constitutions of the First American States.* Haverford, PA: Infinity Publishing.

[81] Kole, Edward A. *The True Intent of the First American Constitutions of 1776–1791.* Haverford, PA: Infinity Publishing.

[82] Smith, Hayward H. 2001. Symposium, Law of Presidential Elections: Issues in the Wake of Florida 2000, History of the Article II Independent State legislature Doctrine, 29 *Florida State University Law Review* 731 at 760.

Senate, and the Anti-Federalists controlled the Assembly. The two houses could not agree on the method by which the legislature would elect
presidential electors or U.S. Senators because each house wanted to
enhance its own power in the process. The three issues were therefore
considered separately.

As previously mentioned (section 8.3.5), the legislature passed legislation on January 27, 1789, providing the "manner" of electing U.S.
Representatives (including the districts to be used). That bill was submitted to the Council of Revision composed of the Governor, the
Chancellor, and the judges of the state supreme court. The Council
approved the bill; the bill became law; and the elections of U.S.
Representatives were held on March 3, 1789, in accordance with that law.

In addition (section 8.3.5), the legislature passed a bill in 1789 providing for the manner of electing U.S. Senators. This bill was presented to
the Council, but the Council vetoed the bill, and the bill did not become
law.

The legislature also debated a bill entitled "An act for regulating the
manner of appointing electors who are to elect the President, and Vice-
President of the United States of America."[83] That is, the legislation specifying the manner of appointing presidential electors was in the same
form as the vetoed bill specifying the manner of electing U.S.
Representatives and U.S. Senators. That is, the legislature debated the bill
concerning the manner of appointing presidential electors as an ordinary
legislative bill—not as a concurrent resolution to be voted upon only by
the two houses.

As it happened the two chambers of the New York legislature did not
reach an agreement on the manner of appointing presidential electors in
time for the first presidential election. Consequently, New York did not
cast any electoral votes in the 1789 presidential election. Later, a bill was
passed by both chambers of the legislature and submitted to the Council
in time for the 1792 presidential election. It took effect.

Thus, actual practice in the two states that had the gubernatorial veto
at the time when the U.S. Constitution first took effect indicates that, in
connection with the state's decision on the manner of appointing

---

[83] DenBoer, Gordon; Brown, Lucy Trumbull; and Hagermann, Charles D. (editors). 1986.
The Documentary History of the First Federal Elections 1788–1790. Madison, WI:
University of Wisconsin Press. Volume III. Pages 217–435.

presidential electors, the word "legislature" in Article II meant the state's lawmaking process—not just the two chambers of the state legislature.

Present-day practice by the states is consistent with practice from the time when the U.S. Constitution first took effect. Table 8.2 shows the section of each state's current law specifying the manner of appointing

Table 8.2 PRESENT-DAY PRACTICE BY THE STATES CONCERNING THE MEANING OF THE WORD "LEGISLATURE" IN CONNECTION WITH STATE LAWS SPECIFYING THE MANNER OF APPOINTING PRESIDENTIAL ELECTORS

STATE	SECTION	WAS THE LEGISLATURE'S BILL PRESENTED TO THE STATE'S GOVERNOR?
Alabama	Ala.Code § 17-19-4	Yes
	Ala.Code § 17-19-5	Yes
	Ala. Code § 17-19-6	Yes
Alaska	AK ST § 15.15.450	Yes
Arizona	A.R.S. § 16-650	Yes
Arkansas	Ar. Code §7-8-304	Yes
California	Cal.Elec.Code § 15505	Yes
Colorado	C.R.S. § 1-11-106	Yes
	Section. 20 of Schedule to	No—Provision of 1876
	Colorado Constitution	Colorado Constitution
Connecticut	C.G.S. § 9-315	Yes
Delaware	15 Del. C. § 5703	Yes
	15 Del. C. § 5711	Yes
District of Columbia	D.C. Code, Sect. 1-1001.10	Yes
Florida	F.S.A. § 9.103.011	Yes
Georgia	Ga. Code Ann., § 21-2-499	Yes
Hawaii	H.R.S. § 2-14-24	Yes
Idaho	ID ST § 34-1215	Yes
Illinois	10 ILCS 5/21-2	Yes
	10 ILCS 5/21-3	Yes
Indiana	IC 3-12-5-7	Yes
Iowa	I.C.A. § 50.45	Yes
Kansas	KS ST § 25-702	Yes
Kentucky	KRS § 118.425	Yes
Louisiana	LSA-R.S. 18:1261	Yes
Maine	21-A M.R.S. § 723	Yes
	21-A M.R.S. § 802	Yes
Maryland	MD Code § 11-601	Yes
Massachusetts	M.G.L.A. 54 § 118	Yes
Michigan	M.C.L.A. 168.42	Yes
Minnesota	M.S.A. § 208.05	Yes
Mississippi	Miss. Code Ann. § 23-15-605	Yes
Missouri	V.A.M.S. 128.070	Yes

Table 8.2 PRESENT-DAY PRACTICE BY THE STATES CONCERNING THE MEANING OF THE WORD "LEGISLATURE" IN CONNECTION WITH STATE LAWS SPECIFYING THE MANNER OF APPOINTING PRESIDENTIAL ELECTORS (cont.)

STATE	SECTION	WAS THE LEGISLATURE'S BILL PRESENTED TO THE STATE'S GOVERNOR?
Montana	Mt. St. §13-25-103	Yes
	Mt. St. §13-1-103	Yes
Nebraska	NE ST § 32-710	Yes
	NE ST § 32-1040	Yes
Nevada	N.R.S. 293.395	Yes
New Hampshire	N.H. Rev. Stat. § 659:81	Yes
New Jersey	§19:3-26	Yes
New Mexico	N. M. S. A. 1978, § 1-15-14	Yes
New York	§ 12-102	Yes
North Carolina	N.C.G.S.A. § 163-210	Yes
North Dakota	ND ST 16.1-14-01	Yes
Ohio	R.C. § 3505.33	Yes
Oklahoma	26 Okl.St.Ann. § 7-136	Yes
	26 Okl.St.Ann. § 10-103	Yes
Oregon	O.R.S. § 254.065	Yes
Pennsylvania	25 P.S. § 3166	Yes
Rhode Island	§ 17-4-10	Yes
South Carolina	Code 1976 § 7-19-70	Yes
South Dakota	SDCL. § 12-20-35	Yes
Tennessee	T. C. A. § 2-8-110	Yes
Texas	§ 192.005	Yes
Utah	Utah Code 20A-4-304	Yes
	Utah Code 20A-13-302	Yes
Vermont	VT ST T. 17 § 2731	Yes
	VT ST T. 17 § 2592	Yes
Virginia	§ 24.2-675	Yes
	§ 24.2-673	Yes
Washington	Rev. Code Wash. (ARCW) § 29A.56.320[84]	Yes
West Virginia	Article VII, Section 3 of West Virginia constitution[85]	No
Wisconsin	W.S.A. 5.01	Yes
Wyoming	WY ST § 22-17-117	Yes
	WY ST § 22-19-103	Yes

[84] Article III, section 4 of the Washington State Constitution specifies that, in all elections, the candidate "having the highest number of votes shall be declared duly elected."

[85] Article VII, section 3 (ratified November 4, 1902) specifies that, in all elections, the candidate with "the highest number of votes for either of said offices, shall be declared duly elected thereto."

presidential electors.[86] In every state, the law was not enacted merely by action of the two chambers of the state legislature but, instead, was presented to the state's Governor for approval or disapproval.

None of the state laws in table 8.2 was enacted by means of the citizen-initiative process; however, there have been numerous initiatives and referenda over the years on provisions of state election laws involving the manner of electing presidential electors.

On February 23, 1917, Maine voted on a "Proposed Constitutional Amendment Granting Suffrage to Women upon Equal Terms with Men." The proposition received 20,604 "yes" vote and 38,838 "no" votes.

In 1919, the Maine Supreme Judicial Court upheld a statewide referendum on a state statute entitled "An act granting to women the right to vote for presidential electors."[87]

In the late 1950s and early 1960s, there was considerable controversy in Michigan (and other states) concerning the coattail effect of votes cast for President on races for lower offices. In particular, Republican county and township officeholders in Michigan sought to eliminate the voter's option to vote for all nominees of one party by casting a single so-called *straight-party* vote. When the Republicans ended 14 years of Democratic control of the Governor's office in 1962, the new Republican Governor and the Republican legislature enacted a statute requiring that voters cast a separate vote for President and a separate vote for each other office on the ballot (the so-called *Massachusetts ballot*).[88] A protest-referendum petition was circulated and filed, thereby suspending the statute. The voters rejected the statute in the November 1964 elections. Thus, presidential electors remained tethered in Michigan to the party's candidates for other offices (if the voter so desired).

Similarly, in 1972, an initiative petition was filed in Maine proposing to change the form of the ballot from party columns to individual offices (the Massachusetts ballot). This proposition passed by a vote of 110,867 to 64,506.

In 1976, an Oklahoma court wrote the following in *McClendon v. Slater* about state legislation concerning the manner of appointing presidential electors:

---

[86] That is, the statewide winner-take-all rule in 48 states and the District of Columbia and the congressional district system in Maine and Nebraska.

[87] *In re Opinion of the Justices.* 107 Atl. 705. 1919.

[88] Michigan Public Act 240 of 1964.

"It is fundamental that each state and its Legislature, under a Republican form of government possess all power to protect and promote the peace, welfare and safety of its citizens. The only restraints placed thereon are those withdrawn by the United States Constitution and the state's fundamental law. Art. V, ss 1 and 2 express that these reservations **or withdrawals in the people under the Constitution of the State of Oklahoma are two in nature and as explicitly set out in Art. V, s 2 to be the 'initiative' and the 'referendum' processes.** For our purpose, **no other withdrawal or restraint is placed upon the broad fundamental powers of this state's Legislature** by Art. V of the State Constitution."[89] [Emphasis added]

More recently, voters have considered initiatives for instant run-off voting for presidential electors and other offices in Alaska in 2002, requirements for voter identification in Arizona in 2004, and voting by convicted felons in Massachusetts in 2000.

In *Commonwealth ex rel. Dummit v. O'Connell*, the Kentucky Court of Appeals wrote the following in 1944 in connection with a state law permitting soldiers to vote by absentee ballot for U.S. Representatives, U.S. Senators, and presidential electors:

"[T]he legislative process must be completed in the manner prescribed by the State Constitution in order to result in a valid enactment, even though that enactment be one which the Legislature is authorized by the Federal Constitution to make."[90]

It is important to note that the decision of the U.S. Supreme Court in *Bush v. Gore* in 2000 did nothing to change the meaning of the word "legislature" in the U.S. Constitution in Article II. In that case, the Court settled the dispute over Florida's 2000 presidential vote by halting the manual recount of ballots that the Florida Supreme Court had ordered.

Referring to the 1892 case of *McPherson v. Blacker*, the U.S. Supreme Court wrote in *Bush v. Gore*:[91]

---

[89] *McClendon v. Slater.* 554 P.2d 774, 776 (Ok. 1976).

[90] *Commonwealth ex rel. Dummit v. O'Connell.* 181 S.W.2d 691, 694 (Ky. Ct. App. 1944).

[91] *McPherson v. Blacker.* 146 U.S. 1 at 27. 1892.

"The individual citizen has no federal constitutional right to vote for electors for the President of the United States unless and until the state legislature chooses a statewide election as the means to implement its power to appoint members of the Electoral College. U.S. Const., Art. II, §1. **This is the source for the statement in *McPherson v. Blacker*, 146 U.S. 1, 35 (1892), that the State legislature's power to select the manner for appointing electors is plenary;** it may, if it so chooses, select the electors itself, which indeed was the manner used by State legislatures in several States for many years after the Framing of our Constitution. *Id.*, at 28-33. History has now favored the voter, and in each of the several States the citizens themselves vote for Presidential electors. When the state legislature vests the right to vote for President in its people, the right to vote as the legislature has prescribed is fundamental; and one source of its fundamental nature lies in the equal weight accorded to each vote and the equal dignity owed to each voter. The State, of course, after granting the franchise in the special context of Article II, can take back the power to appoint electors. See *id.*, at 35."[92] [Emphasis added]

The U.S. Supreme Court did not change the prevailing definition of the word "legislature" in *Bush v. Gore* but, instead, identified the source (i.e., *McPherson v. Blacker*) of the undisputed statement that the "legislature" is indeed supreme in matters of choosing the manner of appointing a state's presidential electors. The issues in *Bush v. Gore* did not concern the way that Florida's election code was originally enacted (e.g., whether the election code was presented to the Governor for approval or disapproval or whether the voters had perhaps enacted the election code through the citizen-initiative process). Indeed, the Florida election code at issue in *Bush v. Gore* was not enacted by the legislature alone but, instead, was enacted as part by the ordinary lawmaking process involving presentation of the bill to the Governor for approval or disapproval (as shown in table 8.2).

Rather, *Bush v. Gore* was concerned with the breadth of authority of the Florida Supreme Court to establish a recount process *not found in*

---

[92] *Bush v. Gore.* 531 U.S. 98 at 104. 2000.

Florida's pre-existing legislation after the voters had cast their votes on November 7, 2000. The U.S. Supreme Court specifically identified two issues to be decided in *Bush v. Gore*, namely

(1) "whether the Florida Supreme Court established new standards for resolving Presidential election contests, thereby violating Art. II, §1, cl. 2, of the United States Constitution and failing to comply with 3 U.S.C. §5, ..."[93] and

(2) "whether the use of standardless manual recounts violates the Equal Protection and Due Process Clauses."[94]

In reaching its decision in *Bush v. Gore*, the Court referred to the "safe harbor" provision (3 U.S.C. §5).

> "If any State shall have provided, **by laws enacted prior to the day fixed for the appointment of the electors,** for its final determination of any controversy or contest concerning the appointment of all or any of the electors of such State, by judicial or other methods or procedures, and such determination shall have been made at least six days before the time fixed for the meeting of the electors, such determination made pursuant to such law so existing on said day, and made at least six days prior to said time of meeting of the electors, shall be conclusive, and shall govern in the counting of the electoral votes as provided in the Constitution, and as hereinafter regulated, so far as the ascertainment of the electors appointed by such State is concerned."[95] [Emphasis added]

The Court ruled (on December 12, 2000) that insufficient time remained to conduct a constitutional recount before the meeting of the Electoral College scheduled for December 18, 2000. Because there was insufficient time for a constitutional recount, Bush's 537-vote plurality that had already been certified under terms of the Florida election code was allowed to stand.[96]

---

[93] *Bush v. Gore.* 531 U.S. 98 at 103. 2000. See Appendix B for the complete wording of the so-called "safe harbor" provision—Title 3, Chapter 1, section 5 of the United States Code.

[94] *Bush v. Gore.* 531 U.S. 98 at 103. 2000.

[95] Title 3, chapter 1, section 5 of the United States Code.

[96] *Bush v. Gore.* 531 U.S. 98 at 110. 2000.

In *Bush v. Gore*, the Supreme Court did not address the issue of whether the Florida voters could substitute themselves for the legislature, through the citizen-initiative process or the protest-referendum process, concerning the manner of choosing presidential electors in Florida. In fact, the 1892 case *(McPherson v. Blacker)* cited by the Court in *Bush v. Gore* specifically mentioned the possibility that a state's legislative power might be "reposed" in a place other than the state legislature.

> **"The legislative power is the supreme authority, except as limited by the constitution of the state,** and the sovereignty of the people is exercised through their representatives in the legislature, **unless by the fundamental law power is elsewhere reposed."**[97] [Emphasis added]

The citizen-initiative process—representing the authority of the citizens of a state to make their own laws—is consistent with the two exceptions contained in *McPherson v. Blacker*, namely that the legislature's power is supreme "except as limited by the constitution of the state" and except when "power is elsewhere reposed" "by the [state's] fundamental law." Initiatives are limitations on the power of the legislature because they enable the voters to displace the legislature by enacting laws of their own design. The initiative process is established by the state's fundamental law (i.e., constitution). Indeed, initiatives are the obvious alternative place where the state's legislative power might be "elsewhere reposed."

The citizen-initiative process has consistently been viewed as a limitation on the state legislature. For example, in 1964, *Lucas v. Forty-Fourth General Assembly*[98] approved the use of the initiative to "obtain relief against alleged malapportionment" of state legislative seats. In 1975, *Chapman v. Meier*[99] concerned the adoption of an initiative substituting the voters' will for the legislature's unwillingness to act. As a reservation of legislative power by the voters, the initiative process is necessarily an element of the fundamental law. In *Eastlake v. Forest City Enterprises, Inc.*, the U.S. Supreme Court wrote in 1976:

> "Under our constitutional assumptions, all power derives from the people, who can delegate it to representative instru-

---

[97] *McPherson v. Blacker.* 146 U.S. 1 at 25. 1892.

[98] *Lucas v. Forty-Fourth General Assembly.* 377 U.S. 713 at 732–733. 1964.

[99] *Chapman v. Meier.* 420 U.S. 1 at 21. 1975.

ments which they create. See e.g., *The Federalist*, No. 39 (J. Madison). **In establishing legislative bodies, the people can reserve to themselves power to deal directly with matters which might otherwise be assigned to the legislature.**"[100,101] [Emphasis added]

In commenting on *Bush v. Gore* in *Breaking the Deadlock*, Judge Richard Posner wrote:

> "[I]t is important that the approach be understood, and not rejected out of hand as meaning, for example, that the governor of a state cannot veto a proposed law on the appointment of the state's Presidential electors or that the state's supreme court cannot invalidate an election law as unconstitutional. **Article II does not regulate the process by which state legislation is enacted and validated,** any more than it precludes interpretation. **But once the law governing appointment of the state's presidential electors is duly enacted,** upheld, and interpreted, (so far as interpretation is necessary to fill gaps and dispel ambiguities), the legislature has spoken and **the other branches of the state government must back off....**"[102] [Emphasis added]

Bush v. Gore was not about "the process by which state legislation is enacted" but, instead, was about the extent to which the Florida Supreme should "back off."

In summary, present-day practice by the states, actual practice by the states at the time that the U.S. Constitution took effect, legal commentary, and court decisions are consistent in supporting the view that the word "legislature" in Article II, section 1, clause 2 of the U.S. Constitution (the sixth entry in table 8.1) means the state's lawmaking process—a process that includes the state's Governor and the state's voters in states having citizen-initiative and protest-referendum procedures.

---

[100] *Eastlake v. Forest City Enterprises, Inc.* 426 U.S. 668 at 672. 1976.

[101] *Cf. James v. Valtierra,* 401 U.S. 137, 141 (1971) "[p]rovisions for referendums demonstrate devotion to democracy."

[102] Posner, Richard A. 2001. *Breaking the Deadlock: The 2000 Election, the Constitution, and the Courts.* Princeton, NJ: Princeton University Press. Page 111.

As Kirby stated in 1962,

"it is safe to assume that state legislatures are limited by constitutional provisions for veto, referendum, and initiative in prescribing the manner of choosing presidential electors."[103]

8.3.7 Choosing the Manner of Conducting a Popular Election to Fill a U.S. Senate Vacancy

The 17th Amendment (providing for popular election of U.S. Senators) was ratified in 1913—in the midst of the period (1898–1918) when 19 states were adopting the initiative and referendum processes.[104,105] The 17th Amendment provides:

"When vacancies happen in the representation of any State in the Senate, the executive authority of such State shall issue writs of election to fill such vacancies: Provided, That the legislature of any State may empower the executive thereof to make temporary appointments until the people fill the vacancies by election **as the legislature may direct.**" [Emphasis added]

The phrase "as the legislature may direct" in the 17th Amendment parallels the wording of Article II of the U.S. Constitution concerning presidential electors, namely

"Each State shall appoint, in such Manner **as the Legislature thereof may direct,** a Number of Electors, equal to the whole Number of Senators and Representatives to which the State may be entitled in the Congress...."[106] [Emphasis added]

Moreover, the phrase "as the legislature may direct" in the 17th Amendment and Article II parallels the wording of Article I, section 4,

---

[103] Kirby, J. 1962. Limitations on the powers of the state legislatures over presidential elections. 27 *Law and Contemporary Problems* 495 at 504.

[104] Zimmerman, Joseph F. 1999. *The Initiative: Citizen Law-Making.* Westport, CT: Praeger.

[105] Zimmerman, Joseph F. 1997. *The Referendum: The People Decide Public Policy.* Westport, CT: Praeger.

[106] U.S. Constitution. Article II, section 1, clause 2.

clause 1 of the U.S. Constitution concerning the "manner" of holding elections for U.S. Representatives and Senators, namely

> "The Times, Places and Manner of holding Elections for Senators and Representatives, shall be **prescribed in each State by the Legislature thereof;** but the Congress may at any time by Law make or alter such Regulations, except as to the Places of chusing Senators." [Emphasis added]

The practice of the states in enacting laws to implement the 17th Amendment is shown in table 8.3. This table shows the section of each state's law that specifies the manner of holding the popular election to fill a vacancy in the U.S. Senate under the 17th Amendment and the section that specifies whether the Governor is empowered to make temporary appointments to the U.S. Senate prior to the vacancy-filling election. As can be seen, in no state was the enactment of implementing legislation for the 17th Amendment accomplished merely by action of the two chambers of the legislature. Instead, the actual practice of all states has been to treat the word "legislature" in the 17th Amendment to mean the "lawmaking process." The "lawmaking process" concerning the 17th Amendment has involved legislative bills that have been presented to the state's Governor for approval or disapproval and the use of the citizen-initiative process (in the cases of Arkansas in 1938 and Alaska in 2004).

Arkansas's implementation of the 17th Amendment is noteworthy for two reasons. First, its current implementation was proposed by a citizen-initiative petition that was adopted by the voters in the November 8, 1938, general election. Second, Arkansas's implementation was in the form of an amendment to the state constitution as distinguished from a statutory enactment.[107] In other words, neither the "legislature" nor "legislation" was involved in implementing the 17th Amendment in Arkansas.

The November 2004 elections provided two additional examples of the interpretation given to the word "legislature" by the states in connection with the 17th Amendment.

When U.S. Senator John Kerry was running for President in 2004, the Democratic-controlled legislature in Massachusetts passed a bill changing the procedure for filling U.S. Senate vacancies in Massachusetts. Under the pre-existing Massachusetts law, the Governor had the power to

---

[107] Section 1 Amendment 29 adopted November 8, 1938.

Table 8.3 PRACTICE BY THE STATES CONCERNING THE MEANING OF THE WORD "LEGISLATURE" IN CONNECTION WITH STATE LAWS SPECIFYING THE IMPLEMENTATION OF THE 17TH AMENDMENT

STATE	SECTION	WAS THE LEGISLATURE'S BILL PRE-SENTED TO THE STATE'S GOVERNOR?
Alabama	Ala.Code § 36-9-7	Yes
	Ala.Code § 36-9-8	Yes
Alaska	AK ST § 15.40.140	No–Citizen-initiative process
	AK ST § 15.40.145	
Arizona	A.R.S. § 16-222	Yes
Arkansas	Const. Am. 29, § 1	No–Citizen-initiative process
California	Cal.Elec.Code § 10720	Yes
Colorado	C.R.S.A. § 1-12-201	Yes
Connecticut	C.G.S.A. § 9-211	Yes
Delaware	DE ST TI 15 § 7321	Yes
Florida	F.S.A. § 100.161	Yes
Georgia	Ga. Code Ann., § 21-2-542	Yes
Hawaii	HI ST § 17-1	Yes
Idaho	ID ST § 59-910	Yes
Illinois	10 ILCS 5/25-8	Yes
Indiana	IC 3-13-3-1	Yes
Iowa	I.C.A. § 69.8	Yes
Kansas	KS ST § 25-318	Yes
Kentucky	KRS § 63.200	Yes
Louisiana	LSA-R.S. 18:1278	Yes
Maine	21-A M.R.S.A. § 391	Yes
Maryland	MD Code, Election Law, § 8-602	Yes
Massachusetts	M.G.L.A. 54 § 140	Yes
Michigan	M.C.L.A. 168.105	Yes
Minnesota	M.S.A. § 204D.28	Yes
Mississippi	Miss. Code Ann. § 23-15-855	Yes
Missouri	V.A.M.S. 105.040	Yes
Montana	Mt. St. 13-25-202	Yes
Nebraska	NE ST § 32-565	Yes
Nevada	N.R.S. 304.030	Yes
New Hampshire	N.H. Rev. Stat. § 661:5	Yes
New Jersey	§19:3-26	Yes
New Mexico	N. M. S. A. 1978, § 1-15-14	Yes
New York	Mckinney's Consolidated Laws of New York, Chapter 47, Article 3	Yes
North Carolina	N.C.G.S.A. § 163-12	Yes
North Dakota	ND ST 16.1-13-08	Yes
Ohio	R.C. § 3521.02	Yes
Oklahoma	26 Okl. St.Ann. § 12-101	Yes

ation of the vacancy). Thus, a special Senate election would have beenation of the vacancy). Thus, a special Senate election would have beenation of the vacancy). Thus, a special Senate election would have beenation of the vacancy). Thus, a special Senate election would have beenation of the vacancy). Thus, a special Senate election would have beenation of the vacancy). Thus, a special Senate election would have beenation of the vacancy). Thus, a special Senate election would have beenation of the vacancy). Thus, a special Senate election would have been

Table 8.3 PRACTICE BY THE STATES CONCERNING THE MEANING OF THE WORD "LEGISLATURE" IN CONNECTION WITH STATE LAWS SPECIFYING THE IMPLEMENTATION OF THE 17TH AMENDMENT (cont.)

STATE	SECTION	WAS THE LEGISLATURE'S BILL PRESENTED TO THE STATE'S GOVERNOR?
Oregon	O.R.S. § 188.120	Yes
Pennsylvania	25 P.S. § 2776	Yes
Rhode Island	§ 17-4-9	Yes
South Carolina	Code 1976 § 7-19-20	Yes
South Dakota	SDCL. § 12-11-4	Yes
	SDCL. § 12-11-5	Yes
Tennessee	T. C. A. § 2-16-101	Yes
Texas	§ 204.001	Yes
	§ 204.002	Yes
	§ 204.003	Yes
	§ 204.004	Yes
Utah	§ 20A-1-502	Yes
Vermont	VT ST T. 17 § 2621	Yes
	VT ST T. 17 § 2622	Yes
Virginia	§ 24.2-207	Yes
Washington	RCW 29A.28.030	Yes
	RCW 29A.28.041	Yes
West Virginia	W. Va. Code, § 3-10-3	Yes
Wisconsin	W.S.A. 17.18	Yes
	W.S.A. 8.50	Yes
Wyoming	WY ST § 22-18-111	Yes

appoint a temporary replacement who would serve until the next general election. In other words, if Democrat Kerry had won the Presidency in November 2004, then the Republican Governor of Massachusetts would have been able to appoint a Republican to serve in the then-closely-divided U.S. Senate until November 2006 (almost two full years). Under the bill that the legislature passed, the Senate seat would remain vacant until a special election could be held (between 145 and 160 days after the creation of the vacancy). Thus, a special Senate election would have been held in Massachusetts in the spring of 2005 if Kerry had been elected President. The legislative bill was presented to Governor Mitt Romney for his approval or disapproval. That is, the constitutional phrase "as the Legislature thereof may direct" was interpreted to mean the law-making process. Predictably, the Republican Governor vetoed the bill passed by the Democratic legislature. As it happened, the legislature overrode the Governor's veto, and the bill became law.

The election of U.S. Senator Frank Murkowski as Governor of Alaska in 2002 created a vacancy in the U.S. Senate. Murkowski appointed his daughter Lisa to serve the last two years of his Senate term, thereby focusing public attention on the operation of the 17th Amendment in Alaska. An initiative petition was circulated and filed to require that, in the future, a vacancy in the U.S. Senate would remain vacant until a special election could be called. The Alaska Constitution enables the legislature to keep an initiative proposition off the ballot if the legislature responds to the petition by enacting a "substantially" similar law. The legislature's bill resembled the proposal in the petition in that it required a special election to fill a Senate vacancy; however, the legislature's bill differed from the petition in that it authorized the Governor to appoint a temporary Senator prior to the popular election. This legislature's bill was presented to the Governor for his approval or disapproval, and he signed it. The petition's sponsors protested that the legislature's alternative approach was not substantially the same as the initiative proposition because it gave the Governor's appointee the advantage of incumbency in the special election.

On August 20, 2004, the Alaska Supreme Court decided that the legislature's alternative was not substantially the same as the proposition in the initiative petition.[108] At the same time, the Court refused to consider a pre-election challenge to the use of the citizen-initiative process to change the manner of filling a vacancy in the U.S. Senate on the grounds that the U.S. Constitution required the "legislature" to make the decision. The Alaska Supreme Court allowed the voters to vote on the proposition in the petition in the November 2004 election. The voters then enacted the proposition in the petition (Ballot Measure 4) in the November 2004 election by a margin of 165,017 to 131,821.[109]

That is, the phrase "as the Legislature thereof may direct" in the 17th Amendment (the seventh entry in table 8.1) has been interpreted as the state's entire law-making process—not action by the two chambers of state's legislature.

---

[108] *State of Alaska et al. v. Trust the People Initiative Committee.* Supreme Court Order No. S-11288.

[109] In the same election, the voters elected Lisa Murkowski to a full six-year term in the Senate by a margin of 149,446 to 139,878.

8.3.8 Empowering the Governor to Temporarily Fill a U.S. Senate Vacancy Until a Popular Election Is Held

The word "legislature" also appears in the 17th Amendment in connection with temporary appointments to the U.S. Senate.

> "When vacancies happen in the representation of any State in the Senate, the executive authority of such State shall issue writs of election to fill such vacancies: Provided, That **the legislature of any State may empower the executive thereof to make temporary appointments until the people fill the vacancies by election** as the legislature may direct." [Emphasis added]

As shown in table 8.3, the word "legislature" in the 17th Amendment (the eighth entry in table 8.1) has meant the state's entire law-making process—not action by the two chambers of state's legislature.

8.3.9 Consenting to the Federal Purchase of Enclaves

The U.S. Constitution empowers Congress to exercise exclusive

> "... Authority over all Places purchased by the **Consent of the Legislature** of the State in which the Same shall be, for the Erection of Forts, Magazines, Arsenals, dock-Yards, and other needful Buildings."[110] [Emphasis added]

Prior to ratification of the U.S. Constitution, the states had been paying for the operation and maintenance of 13 lighthouses. Moreover, in 1789, several additional lighthouses were under construction. When the first Congress met in 1789, it offered to fund the operation and maintenance of all the lighthouses; however, Congress insisted that the sites become federal enclaves. Accordingly, Congress passed the Lighthouse Act on August 7, 1789, offering permanent funding for lighthouses on the condition that the state "legislatures" consented to the creation of the federal enclaves by August 15, 1790.[111] The Constitution required consent from the state "legislatures" and thus set the stage for a contemporary

---

[110] U.S. Constitution. Article I, section 9, clause 17.

[111] Grace, Adam S. 2005. *Federal-State "Negotiations" over Federal Enclaves in the Early Republic: Finding Solutions to Constitutional Problems at the Birth of the Lighthouse System.* Berkeley, CA: Berkeley Electronic Press. Working Paper 509. http://law.bepress.com/expresso/eps/509. Pages 1–11.

interpretation of the word "legislature" in the Enclaves Clause of the U.S. Constitution. The question was whether the word "legislature" referred to the two chambers of the state legislature or "the lawmaking process."

At the time when the U.S. Constitution took effect, the gubernatorial veto existed in Massachusetts and New York.[112] Both chambers of the legislatures of Massachusetts and New York approved legislation consenting to the cession of their lighthouses. These legislative bills were then presented, respectively, to the Governor of Massachusetts (an official who was manifestly not part of the state legislature) and the New York Council of Revision (a body composed of the Governor and other officials who were manifestly not part of the state legislature). The Massachusetts legislation became law on June 10, 1790,[113] and the New York legislation became law on February 3, 1790.[114] Cession legislation was similarly enacted in New York in connection with the construction of a new lighthouse at Montauk in 1792—with the legislative bill again being presented to the Governor and the Council.[115]

Thus, practice by the states in connection with the ninth entry in table 8.1 has interpreted the word "legislature" to mean the state's lawmaking process in connection with the consent by a state to the acquisition of enclaves by the federal government (the ninth entry in Table 8.1).

8.3.10 Consenting to the Formation of New States from Territory of Existing States

The U.S. Constitution provides:

> "... No new State shall be formed or erected within the Jurisdiction of any other State; nor any State be formed by the Junction of two or more States, or Parts of States, without the **Consent of the Legislatures** of the States concerned as well as of the Congress."[116] [Emphasis added]

As of the time of the writing of this edition, the authors believe that this usage of the word "legislature" refers to the state's law-making

---

[112] Kole, Edward A. 1999. *The First 13 Constitutions of the First American States.* Haverford, PA: Infinity Publishing.

[113] Ch. 4, 1790 Massachusetts Laws 77.

[114] New York, Ch. 3, February 3, 1790.

[115] New York, Ch. 4, December 18, 1792.

[116] U.S. Constitution. Article IV, section 3, clause 1.

process in connection with the consent of a state to the formation of a new state from its territory (the 10th entry in table 8.1).

8.3.11 Requesting Federal Military Assistance to Quell Domestic Violence

The U.S. Constitution provides:

> "The United States shall guarantee to every State in this Union a Republican Form of Government, and shall protect each of them against Invasion; and on **Application of the Legislature,** or of the Executive (when the Legislature cannot be convened) against domestic Violence."[117] [Emphasis added]

This provision of the U.S. Constitution (the Guarantee Clause) specifically creates a contrast between the state's "executive" and the "legislature."

The Guarantee Clause has been only rarely invoked. On April 4, 1842, Rhode Island Governor Samuel Ward King requested that President John Tyler provide federal military aid to quell a potential insurrection, known as the Dorr Rebellion, in which an alternative government for Rhode Island was attempting to gain recognition and legitimacy. The Governor's request was not accompanied by any action by the state legislature. President Tyler took no action in response to the Governor's request.[118]

Then, in 1844, the Freeholders' legislature of Rhode Island passed a resolution requested that President John Tyler provide federal military aid to quell the Dorrites. Again, President Tyler took no action in response to the Legislature's resolution.[119]

The Guarantee Clause of the U.S. Constitution distinguishes the state's "legislature" from the state's Governor. These two requests concerning the Dorr Rebellion in Rhode Island suggest that the word "legislature" Article IV, section 4 of the U.S. Constitution (the 11th entry in table 8.1) was interpreted, in Rhode Island in the 1840s, to mean the two chambers of the state legislature.

---

[117] U.S. Constitution. Article IV, section 4.

[118] Wiecek, William M. 1972. *The Guarantee Clause of the U.S. Constitution.* Ithaca, NY: Cornell University Press. Page 105.

[119] Gettleman, Marvin E. 1973. *The Dorr Rebellion: A Study in American Radicalism 1833–1849.* New York, NY: Random House. Page 105.

8.3.12 Pre-Election Challenges Versus Post-Election Litigation

The use of the citizen-initiative process to enact the proposed interstate compact can be challenged either before or after the statewide vote on the statute proposed by a petition.

Both state and federal courts have been reluctant, as a general principle, to intervene in the citizen-initiative process prior to enactment of a proposition by the voters. In "Pre-Election Judicial Review of Initiatives and Referendums," James Gordon and David Magleby wrote:

> "Most courts will not entertain a challenge to a measure's substantive validity before the election. A minority of courts, however, are willing to conduct such review. Arguably, pre-election review of a measure's substantive validity involves issuing an advisory opinion, violates ripeness requirements and the policy of avoiding unnecessary constitutional questions, and is an unwarranted judicial intrusion into a legislative process." [120]

The numerous practical difficulties with pre-election judicial challenges to ballot propositions partly explain judicial reluctance to such challenges. As Justice William O. Douglas wrote in his concurring opinion in *Ely v. Klahr* in 1971:

> "We are plagued with election cases coming here on the eve of election, with the remaining time so short we do not have the days needed for oral argument and for reflection on the serious problems that are usually presented." [121]

The practical difficulties associated with pre-election challenges have been compounded in recent years by the increasing use of absentee voting and early voting (where walk-in polling places are operated at designated locations, such as government buildings, for several weeks prior to election day).

The general reluctance of courts to prevent a vote on ballot measures proposed by the citizen-initiative process is illustrated by the efforts in the early 1990s to enact state constitutional amendments imposing term

---

[120] Gordon, James D. and Magleby, David B. 1989. Pre-Election Judicial Review of Initiatives and Referendums. 64 *Notre Dame Law Review* 298–320 at 303.

[121] *Ely v. Klahr.* 403 U.S. 103 at 120–121. 1971.

limits on members of the U.S. House of Representatives and U.S. Senate. Many questioned whether the proposed state constitutional amendments were consistent with the specific federal constitutional provisions establishing qualifications for these federal offices. Despite pre-election legal challenges to the initiative petitions in some states, in no instance did the courts prevent a vote by the people on the grounds that congressional term limits violated the U.S. Constitution. It was only after these propositions had been enacted by the voters in a number of states that the courts examined the constitutional validity of the ballot propositions. In 1995, the U.S. Supreme Court held that term limits on members of the U.S. House of Representatives and U.S. Senate could not be imposed at the state level.[122]

More recently, the California Supreme Court refused, on July 26, 2005, to remove an initiated proposition from the ballot in California's November 8, 2005, statewide election. The court order stated:

> "The stay issued by the Court of Appeal as part of its July 22, 2005, decision, restraining the Secretary of State from taking any steps, pending the finality of the Court of Appeal's decision, to place Proposition 80 in the ballot pamphlet or on the ballot of the special election to be held on November 8, 2005, is vacated. As the Court of Appeal recognized, California authorities establish that
>
> > 'it is usually more appropriate to review constitutional and other challenges to ballot propositions or initiative measures after an election rather than to disrupt the electoral process by preventing the exercise of the people's franchise, in the absence of some clear showing of invalidity.' (*Brosnahan v. Eu* (1982) 31 Cal.3d 1, 4.)
>
> "Because, unlike the Court of Appeal, at this point we cannot say that it is clear that article XII, section 5, of the California Constitution precludes the enactment of Proposition 80 as an initiative measure, we conclude that the validity of Proposition 80 need not and should not be determined prior to the November 8, 2005 election. Accordingly, the Secretary

---

[122] *U.S. Term Limits v. Thornton.* 514 U.S. 779. 1995.

of State and other public officials are directed to proceed with all the required steps to place Proposition 80 in the ballot pamphlet and on the ballot of the special election to be held on November 8, 2005. After that election, we shall determine whether to retain jurisdiction in this matter and resolve the issues raised in the petition."[123]

8.3.13 Curability of the Potential Invalidity of Popular Voting

Were a court decision to invalidate a popular vote in favor of the proposed interstate compact on state constitutional grounds applicable to one particular state or on federal constitutional grounds applicable to all states, the fact would remain that the people would have spoken in favor of nationwide popular election of the President in those states where the people had voted on the invalidated ballot measures. The favorable public vote would remain as a political fact. In that event, practical political considerations suggest that legislators in any affected state would probably be willing to correct the technical defect concerning the method of enactment of the compact in their state by re-enacting the compact in the legislature. The proposed compact is not inherently adverse to the interests of state legislators, and there is no reason that state legislators are, as a group, any less likely to favor the concept of nationwide popular election of the President than the public at large. It should, therefore, be possible to re-enact the proposed compact in the legislatures of many or all states where the voters spoke in favor of the compact. Regardless of the extent to which the citizen-initiative process may be used to spotlight the issue of the nationwide popular election of the President, state legislatures must necessarily provide most of the support needed to bring the proposed compact into effect.

8.4 DOES THE PROPOSED COMPACT ENCROACH ON THE POWERS OF NON-MEMBER STATES?

An interstate compact may potentially affect non-member states. For example, upstream states in a river basin might enter into a compact to use water to the extreme disadvantage of downstream states that do not belong to the compact.

---

[123] *Independent Energy Producers Association et al., Petitioners, v. Bruce McPherson, as Secretary of State, etc., Respondent; Robert Finkelstein et al., Real Parties in Interest.* Case number S135819. July 26, 2005.

Justice White's dissent in *U.S. Steel Corp. v. Multistate Tax Commission* in 1978 raises the possibility that a court would consider the question of whether a particular interstate compact adversely encroaches on the powers of non-member states.

> "A proper understanding of what would encroach upon federal authority, however, must also incorporate encroachments on the authority and power of non-Compact States."[124]

The U.S. Supreme Court has twice considered, but rejected, arguments that an interstate compact was unconstitutional because it impaired the sovereign rights of non-member states or enhanced the political power of the member states at the expense of other states. For example, in *U.S. Steel Corp. v. Multistate Tax Commission*, the Supreme Court wrote in 1978:

> "Appellants' final Compact Clause argument charges that the Compact impairs the sovereign rights of nonmember States. Appellants declare, without explanation, that if the use of the unitary business and combination methods continues to spread among the Western States, unfairness in taxation— presumably the risks of multiple taxation—will be avoidable only through the efforts of some coordinating body. Appellants cite the belief of the Commission's Executive Director that the Commission represents the only available vehicle for effective coordination, and conclude that **the Compact exerts undue pressure to join upon nonmember States in violation of their "sovereign right" to refuse.**

> "We find no support for this conclusion. It has not been shown that any unfair taxation of multistate business resulting from the disparate use of combination and other methods will redound to the benefit of any particular group of States or to the harm of others. Even if the existence of such a situation were demonstrated, it could not be ascribed to the existence of the Compact. **Each member State is free to adopt**

---

[124] *U.S. Steel Corp. v. Multistate Tax Commission.* 434 U.S. at 494. 1978.

the auditing procedures it thinks best, just as it could if the Compact did not exist. Risks of unfairness and double taxation, then, are independent of the Compact.

"Moreover, **it is not explained how any economic pressure that does exist is an affront to the sovereignty of nonmember States.** Any time a State adopts a fiscal or administrative policy that affects the programs of a sister State, pressure to modify those programs may result. Unless that pressure transgresses the bounds of the Commerce Clause or the Privileges and Immunities Clause of Art. IV, 2, see, e.g., *Austin v. New Hampshire*, 420 U.S. 656 (1975), it is not clear how our federal structure is implicated. Appellants do not argue that an individual State's decision to apportion nonbusiness income—or to define business income broadly, as the regulations of the Commission actually do—touches upon constitutional strictures. This being so, we are not persuaded that the same decision becomes a threat to the sovereignty of other States if a member State makes this decision upon the Commission's recommendation."[125] [Emphasis added]

In *Northeast Bancorp, Inc. v. Board of Governors of the Federal Reserve System*, the U.S. Supreme Court wrote in 1985 that it

"do[es] not see how the statutes in question ... enhance the *political* power of the New England states at the expense of other States...."[126]

Justice White's criterion has never been embraced to invalidate any compact. In any event, it is unlikely that the courts would apply his criterion to the proposed "Agreement Among the States to Elect the President by National Popular Vote" because both member and non-member states would be treated equally in that the popular votes of all 50 states and the District of Columbia would be added together to obtain a nationwide popular vote total for each presidential slate.

---

[125] *Id.* at 477–478.

[126] *Northeast Bancorp, Inc. v. Board of Governors of the Federal Reserve System.* 472 U.S. 159 at 176. 1985.

8.5 DOES THE PROPOSED COMPACT IMPERMISSIBLY DELEGATE A STATE'S SOVEREIGN POWER?

No court has invalidated an interstate compact on the grounds that the compact impermissibly has delegated a state's sovereign power. Indeed, the purpose of almost every interstate compact[127] is, as Marian Ridgeway put it in *Interstate Compacts: A Question of Federalism,*

> "[to] shift a part of a state's authority to another state or states."[128]

Nonetheless, the question arises as to whether the proposed "Agreement Among the States to Elect the President by National Popular Vote" would be an impermissible delegation of a state's sovereign power. In particular, the following question might be raised:

> May a state delegate, under the auspices of an interstate compact, the choice of its presidential electors to the collective choice of the voters of a group of states?

This inquiry requires an examination of whether the appointment of a state's presidential electors is one of its sovereign powers and, if so, whether that power can be shared with voters throughout the United States.

8.5.1 A State's "Sovereign Powers" May Be Delegated by an Interstate Compact

The sovereign authority of a state is not easily defined. The federal courts have not defined sovereignty, although they have attempted to describe it on various occasions. In *Hinderlider v. La Plata River and Cherry Creek Ditch Co.* in 1938, the U.S. Supreme Court traced the history of compacts during the colonial period and immediately thereafter and viewed compacts as a corollary to the ability of independent nations to enter into treaties with one another.

> "The compact—the legislative means [for resolving conflicting claims]—adapts to our Union of sovereign States the age-old treaty making power of sovereign nations."[129]

[127] Except for purely advisory compacts.

[128] Ridgeway, Marian E. 1971. *Interstate Compacts: A Question of Federalism.* Carbondale, IL: Southern Illinois University Press. Page 300.

[129] *Hinderlider v. La Plata River & Cherry Creek Ditch Co.* 304 U.S. 92 at 104. 1938.

In the 1992 case of *Texas Learning Technology Group v. Commissioner of Internal Revenue*, the Fifth Circuit wrote:

> "The power to tax, the power of eminent domain, and the police power are the generally acknowledged sovereign powers."[130]

The appropriation power is another example of a power that is viewed as fundamental to a state.

The filling of public positions that are central to the operation of state government (including legislative, executive, or judicial positions and the position of delegate to a state constitutional convention) is regarded as a sovereign state power.[131,132]

The historical practice of the states, the long history of approvals of interstate compacts by Congress, and court decisions all support the view that a state's sovereign powers may be granted to a group of states acting through an interstate compact. For example, New York and New Jersey delegated certain sovereign powers to the Port Authority of New York and New Jersey, including the power of eminent domain and the power to exempt property from taxation. New York and New Jersey granted the power to tax to the commission created by the 1953 New York–New Jersey Waterfront Compact. Such delegation was upheld in 1944 in *Commissioner of Internal Revenue v. Shamberg's Estate.*[133]

The Ohio River Valley Water Sanitation Compact provided:

> "The signatory states agree to appropriate for the salaries, office and other administrative expenses, their proper proportion of the annual budget as determined by the Commission and approved by the governors of the signatory states...."

---

[130] *Texas Learning Technology Group v. Commissioner of Internal Revenue.* 958 F.2d 122 at 124 (5th Cir. 1992).

[131] See, e.g., *Kingston Associates Inc. v. LaGuardia,* 281 N.Y.S. 390, 398 (S.Ct. 1935) (the exercise of public offices within the legislative, executive, or judicial branches of government); *People v. Brady,* 135 N.E. 87, 89 (Ill. 1922) (same); *People v. Hardin,* 356 N.E.2d 4 (Ill. 1976) (the power to appoint officials to commissions or agencies within the three branches of state government); *State v. Schorr,* 65 A.2d 810, 813 (Del. 1948) (same); and *Forty-Second Legislative Assembly v. Lennon,* 481 P.2d 330, 330 (Mont. 1971) (the role of a delegate to a state constitutional convention).

[132] Engdahl. 1965. Characterization of Interstate Arrangements: When Is a Compact Not a Compact? 64 *Michigan Law Review* 63 at 64–66.

[133] *Commissioner of Internal Revenue v. Shamberg's Estate* 144 F.2d 998 at 1005–1006. (2nd Cir. 1944).

In *West Virginia ex rel. Dyer v. Sims* (discussed at greater length in section 8.6.2), the U.S. Supreme Court upheld the delegation of West Virginia's appropriation power and wrote in 1950:

> "The issue before us is whether the West Virginia Legislature had authority, under her Constitution, to enter into a compact which involves delegation of power to an interstate agency and an agreement to appropriate funds for the administrative expenses of the agency.

> "That a legislature may delegate to an administrative body the power to make rules and decide particular cases is one of the axioms of modern government. The West Virginia court does not challenge the general proposition but objects to the delegation here involved because it is to a body outside the State and because its Legislature may not be free, at any time, to withdraw the power delegated.... **What is involved is the conventional grant of legislative power. We find nothing in that to indicate that West Virginia may not solve a problem such as the control of river pollution by compact and by the delegation, if such it be, necessary to effectuate such solution by compact**.... Here, the State has bound itself to control pollution by the more effective means of an agreement with other States. The Compact involves a reasonable and carefully limited delegation of power to an interstate agency."[134] [Emphasis added]

In the 1970 U.S. Supreme Court case of *Oregon v. Mitchell*, Justice Potter Stewart (concurring in part and dissenting in part) pointed out that if Congress had not acted to bring about uniformity among state durational residency requirements for voters casting ballots in presidential elections, then the states could have adopted an interstate compact to do so.[135] The right to vote for a presidential elector is not beyond the reach of an interstate compact.

In short, there is nothing about the nature of an interstate compact that fundamentally prevents the delegation of a state's sovereign power to a group of compacting states.

---

[134] *West Virginia ex rel. Dyer v. Sims.* 341 U.S. 22 at 30–31. 1950.

[135] *Oregon v. Mitchell.* 400 U.S. 112 at 286–287.

As Ridgeway wrote:

"If the state chooses to inaugurate some new pattern of local government [by means of an interstate compact] that is not in conflict with the state's constitution, it can do so, as long as the people lose none of their **ultimate power to control the state itself.**"[136] [Emphasis added]

This statement reflects various court decisions that emphasize the ability of a sovereign entity to operate independently of any other.[137]

8.5.2 The Proposed Compact Does Not Delegate a Sovereign State Power

There is no authority from any court regarding whether presidential electors exercise a sovereign power of their state. Given the temporary nature of the function of presidential electors, it is doubtful that a court would rule that presidential electors exercise inherent governmental authority. In contrast to members of the legislative, executive, or judicial branches of state government or members of a state constitutional convention, the function that presidential electors perform is not one that addresses the sovereign governance of the state. Instead, presidential electors decide the identity of the chief executive of the federal government. That is, the selection of electors is not in any way a manifestation of the way in which the state itself is governed.

If the power to determine a state's electors is deemed not to be a sovereign power of the state, then the ability to delegate it is unquestioned. No court has invalidated an interstate compact for delegating a power that is not central to the organic ability of a state to operate independently as a political and legal entity, no matter how broad the delegation. In *Hinderlider v. La Plata River and Cherry Creek Ditch Co.*, the U.S. Supreme Court ruled that a compact to administer an interstate stream was

"binding upon the citizens of each State and all water claimants, even where the State had granted the water rights before it entered into the compact."[138]

---

[136] Ridgeway, Marian E. 1971. *Interstate Compacts: A Question of Federalism.* Carbondale, IL: Southern Illinois University Press.

[137] See, for example, the 1793 case of *Chisholm v. Georgia* for a discussion of the historic origins of state sovereignty.

[138] *Hinderlider v. La Plata River and Cherry Creek Ditch Company.* 304 U.S. 92 at 106. 1938.

Given the states' exclusive role under the Constitution to determine the manner of appointing its presidential electors,[139] if the determination of a state's electors is a sovereign power and its delegation would shift political power to the group of compacting states, the proposed compact will not be deemed to compromise federal supremacy.[140] The fact of the delegation would not, in and of itself, violate the U.S. Constitution.

8.6 IS THE SIX-MONTH BLACKOUT PERIOD FOR WITHDRAWALS FROM THE COMPACT ENFORCEABLE?

This section begins by discussing the importance of the withdrawal provisions of the proposed "Agreement Among the States to Elect the President by National Popular Vote" and then considers the

- withdrawal provisions of typical interstate compacts (section 8.6.1),
- legal enforceability of withdrawal provisions of the proposed compact (section 8.6.2), and
- additional state and federal limitations on withdrawals from the proposed compact (section 8.3.3).

The proposed "Agreement Among the States to Elect the President by National Popular Vote" permits any member state to withdraw, subject to the limitation that a withdrawal cannot take effect during a six-month period between July 20 of a presidential election year and January 20 of the following year. This blackout period contains the following six events relating to presidential elections:

(1) national nominating conventions,[141]

(2) the fall campaign period,

(3) election day in early November,

(4) the meeting of the Electoral College in mid-December,

(5) the counting of the electoral votes by Congress on January 6, and

(6) the inauguration of the President and Vice President for the new term on January 20.

The blackout period in the proposed compact is aimed at preventing a withdrawal, for partisan political reasons, in the midst of the

---

[139] *McPherson v. Blacker.* 146 U.S. 1. 1892.

[140] See *Northeast Bancorp, Inc. v. Board of Governors of the Federal Reserve System.* 472 U.S. 159 at 176. 1985.

[141] All recent national nominating conventions of the major parties have occurred after July 20 of the presidential election year.

presidential election process and, in particular, during the especially sensitive 35-day period between election day in early November and the meeting of the Electoral College in mid-December.

Withdrawal from the proposed compact requires passage of legislation to repeal the compact. Because most state legislatures are not in session in November and December, it would be necessary to call the legislature into special session for this purpose. Governors generally have the power to call their state legislatures into special session. In some cases, legislative leaders have an independent power to convene a special session. All Governors have the power to veto legislative bills.[142] Thus, unless the legislative leadership possesses the power to convene a special session and has a veto-proof majority, the Governor's support would, as a practical matter, be required for any politically motivated effort to repeal the compact. An additional obstacle to a politically motivated repeal of the compact arises from the fact that most state constitutions specify that new state laws do not take immediate effect—that is, the effective date for new legislation is automatically delayed by a designated amount of time. Immediate effect would be required for a politically motivated withdrawal from the compact because such an effort would necessarily occur during the 35-day window between election day in early November and the meeting of the Electoral College in mid-December. Most constitutions require a super-majority (typically two-thirds) in both houses of the legislature to give immediate effect to new legislation. In addition, many state constitutions impose significant state-specific constitutional limitations applicable to the repeal or amendment of legislation enacted by the citizen-initiative process (section 8.6.3).

Having said all that, at any given time, a certain small number of states would inevitably have the lopsided political control that could, in theory, permit the proposed compact to be repealed during the 35-day period between election day in early November and the meeting of the Electoral College in mid-December. Even then, such a repeal would be politically relevant only if

- the number of electoral votes cast in favor of the nation-wide popular vote winner by the compacting states remain-

---

[142] In North Carolina, a gubernatorial veto can be overridden by a majority vote of both houses. In other states, a super-majority vote of both houses is necessary to override a veto.

ing after the withdrawal, when added to the electoral votes cast in favor of the nationwide winner by all non-compacting states, were less than 270; and

- the winner of the nationwide popular vote is different from the winner of the electoral vote (computed using the statewide winner-take-all rule).

If all of the above conditions were to converge, then it would be possible—absent the compact's six-month blackout period—for a state to escape its obligation to award its electoral votes to the nationwide popular vote winner at the very moment when it would matter. Such a result would be unfair to voters, candidates, political parties, and the states that entered the compact in reliance on each member state fulfilling its obligations under the compact.

The question therefore arises as to the enforceability of the blackout period for withdrawals contained in the proposed compact.

8.6.1 Withdrawal Provisions of Typical Interstate Compacts

An interstate compact is, first of all, a contract. Consequently, the general principles of contract law apply to interstate compacts. Unless a contract provides otherwise, a contract may be amended or terminated only by unanimous consent of its signatories. In particular, unless a contract provides otherwise, a party cannot unilaterally renounce a contract.

With the exception of compacts that are presumed to be permanent (for example, those settling boundary disputes), almost all interstate compacts permit a party state to withdraw. Moreover, almost all compacts specify the procedures that a party state must follow in order to withdraw.

A small number of interstate compacts permit any party state to withdrawal instantaneously. For example, the Boating Offense Compact provides:

"Any party state may withdraw from this compact by enacting a statute repealing the same."

The Interstate Compact on Licensure of Participants in Horse Racing with Parimutuel Wagering permits instantaneous withdrawal as soon as the Governor of the withdrawing state performs the task of notifying the other compacting states.

"Any party state may withdraw from this compact by enacting a statute repealing this compact, but no such withdrawal shall become effective until the head of the executive branch of the withdrawing state has given notice in writing of such withdrawal to the head of the executive branch of all other party states."

In contrast, the vast majority of interstate compacts impose both a notification requirement for withdrawal and a delay before a withdrawal becomes effective. The length of the delay is typically calibrated based on the nature of the compact. Compacts frequently specify that a withdrawal does not interrupt, in midstream, any process that began while the withdrawing state was part of the compact and that a withdrawal does not cancel obligations that a withdrawing state incurred while it was part of the compact.

For example, the compact on the Interstate Taxation of Motor Fuels Consumed by Interstate Buses permits withdrawal after one year's notice.

"This compact shall enter into force when enacted into law by any 2 states. Thereafter it shall enter into force and become binding upon any state subsequently joining when such state has enacted the compact into law. Withdrawal from the compact shall be by act of the legislature of a party state, but shall not take effect until one year after the governor of the withdrawing state has notified the governor of each other party state, in writing, of the withdrawal."

The Interstate Mining Compact contains similar provisions.

The delay is generally based on the subject matter of the compact. The delay is typically lengthy when the compact's remaining parties may need time to make alternative arrangements or to adjust economically to a withdrawal. For example, the Rhode Island–Massachusetts Interstate Low-Level Radioactive Waste Management Compact requires that a withdrawing state give notice five years in advance.

"Any party state may withdraw from this compact by repealing its authorizing legislation, and such rights of access to regional facilities enjoyed by generators in that party state shall thereby terminate. However, no such withdrawal shall

> take effect until five years after the governor of the with-
> drawing state has given notice in writing of such withdrawal
> to the Commission and to the governor of each party state."

Some compacts impose a longer withdrawal period for a member having a special obligations under the compact. For example, the Southwestern Low-Level Radioactive Waste Disposal Compact imposes a five-year delay for withdrawal on the state that receives and stores the radioactive waste (California in this case), but only a two-year delay on the non-host states (Arizona, North Dakota, and South Dakota). A host state withdrawal would require that all of the non-host states scramble to find an alternative place to store their radioactive waste, whereas a withdrawal by a non-host state would merely necessitate economic readjustment at the facility operated by the host state.

> "A party state, other than the host state, may withdraw from
> the compact by repealing the enactment of this compact, but
> this withdrawal shall not become effective until two years
> after the effective date of the repealing legislation....
>
> "If the host state withdraws from the compact, the withdraw-
> al shall not become effective until five years after the effec-
> tive date of the repealing legislation."

The Texas Low-Level Radioactive Waste Disposal Compact similarly imposes a longer time delay for withdrawal by hosts than non-hosts.

The Delaware River Basin Compact requires advance notice of at least 20 years for withdrawal, with such notice being allowed only during a five-year window every 100 years.

> "The duration of this compact shall be for an initial period of
> 100 years from its effective date, and it shall be continued for
> additional periods of 100 years if not later than 20 years nor
> sooner than 25 years prior to the termination of the initial
> period or any succeeding period none of the signatory States,
> by authority of an act of its Legislature, notifies the commis-
> sion of intention to terminate the compact at the end of the
> then current 100-year period."

Some compacts provide that a state's withdrawal will not affect any legal action or process that was undertaken while the withdrawing party was still part of the compact. For example, the Agreement on Detainers provides:

"This agreement shall enter into full force and effect as to a party state when such state has enacted the same into law. A state party to this agreement may withdraw herefrom by enacting a statute repealing the same. However, the withdrawal of any state shall not affect the status of any proceedings already initiated by inmates or by state officers at the time such withdrawal takes effect, nor shall it affect their rights in respect thereof."

The Interstate Compact on the Placement of Children (one of the compacts to which all 50 states and the District of Columbia belong) provides:

"This compact shall be open to joinder by any state, territory or possession of the United States, the District of Columbia, the Commonwealth of Puerto Rico, and, with the consent of Congress, the Government of Canada or any province thereof. It shall become effective with respect to any such jurisdiction when such jurisdiction has enacted the same into law. Withdrawal from this compact shall be by the enactment of a statute repealing the same, but shall not take effect until two years after the effective date of such statute and until written notice of the withdrawal has been given by the withdrawing state to the Governor of each other party jurisdiction. Withdrawal of a party state shall not affect the rights, duties and obligations under this compact of any sending agency therein with respect to a placement made prior to the effective date of withdrawal."

The Interstate Compact on Juveniles (another compact to which all 50 states and the District of Columbia adhere) provides:

"That this compact shall continue in force and remain binding upon each executing state until renounced by it. Renunciation of this compact shall be by the same authority which executed it, by sending six months' notice in writing of its intention to withdraw from the compact to the other states party hereto. The duties and obligations of a renouncing state under Article VII hereof shall continue as to parolees and probationers residing therein at the time of withdrawal until retaken or finally discharged. Supplementary agreements entered into under Article X hereof shall be subject to renunciation as provided by such supplementary agreements, and shall not be subject to the six months' renunciation notice of the present Article."

The Multistate Tax Compact provides:

"Any party state may withdraw from this compact by enacting a statute repealing the same. No withdrawal shall affect any liability already incurred by or chargeable to a party state prior to the time of such withdrawal.

"No proceeding commenced before an arbitration board prior to the withdrawal of a state and to which the withdrawing state or any subdivision thereof is a party shall be discontinued or terminated by the withdrawal, nor shall the board thereby lose jurisdiction over any of the parties to the proceeding necessary to make a binding determination therein."

The Interstate Agreement Creating a Multistate Lottery (MUSL) delays return of the departing lottery's share of the prize reserve fund until the expiration of the period for winners to claim their lotto prizes.

"That MUSL shall continue in existence until this agreement is revoked by all of the party lotteries. The withdrawal of one or more party lotteries shall not terminate this agreement among the remaining lotteries....

"A party lottery wishing to withdraw from this agreement shall give the board a six months notice of its intention to withdraw....

"In the event that a party lottery terminates, voluntarily or involuntarily, or MUSL is terminated by agreement of the parties, the prize reserve fund share of the party lottery or lotteries shall not be returned to the party lottery or lotteries until the later of one year from and after the date of termination or final resolution of any pending unresolved liabilities arising from transactions processed during the tenure of the departing lottery or lotteries. The voluntary or involuntary termination of a party lottery or lotteries does not cancel any obligation to MUSL which the party lottery or lotteries incurred before the withdrawal date."

Many compacts specifically provide that a state's withdrawal will not affect any obligations that the withdrawing state incurred while it was part of the compact. For example, the Multistate Tax Compact provides:

"No withdrawal shall affect any liability already incurred by or chargeable to a party state prior to the time of such withdrawal."

The Rhode Island–Massachusetts Interstate Low-Level Radioactive Waste Management Compact and Central Interstate Low-Level Radioactive Waste Compact have a similar provision.

Occasionally, a compact permits a member state to withdraw selectively from its obligations under the compact—that is, to withdraw from the compact with respect to some states, but to remain in the compact with respect to other states. For example, the Interpleader Compact provides:

"This compact shall continue in force and remain binding on a party state until such state shall withdraw therefrom. To be valid and effective, any withdrawal must be preceded by a formal notice in writing of one year from the appropriate authority of that state. Such notice shall be communicated to the same officer or agency in each party state with which the notice of adoption was deposited pursuant to Article VI. In the event that a state wishes to withdraw with respect to one or more states, but wishes to remain a party to this compact with other states party thereto, its notice of withdrawal shall be communicated only to those states with respect to which withdrawal is contemplated."

Although withdrawals from interstate compacts are relatively rare, they do occur. For example, Florida withdrew from the Atlantic States Marine Fisheries Compact in 1995. Maryland withdrew from the Interstate Bus Motor Fuel Tax Compact in 1967 and from the National Guard Mutual Assistance Compact in 1981.

8.6.2 Enforceability of Compact Provisions

The Impairments Clause of the U.S. Constitution restricts the action of all state legislatures concerning contracts:

> "No State shall ... pass any ... Law impairing the Obligation of Contracts...."[143]

The courts have long held that a state belonging to an interstate compact may not unilaterally renounce the agreement. The U.S. Supreme Court addressed this issue in a 1950 case involving the Ohio River Valley Water Sanitation Compact. The parties to this compact included eight states and the federal government. The compact established a commission consisting of representatives from each of the governmental units. It provided that each party state would pay a specified share of the operating expenses of the compact's commission.

> "The signatory states agree to appropriate for the salaries, office and other administrative expenses, their proper proportion of the annual budget as determined by the Commission and approved by the governors of the signatory states, one half of such amount to be prorated among the several states in proportion of their population within the district at the last preceding federal census, the other half to be prorated in proportion to their land area within the district."

There was considerable political division in West Virginia over the desirability of the compact. The legislature ratified the compact and, in 1949, appropriated $12,250 as West Virginia's initial contribution to the expenses of the compact's commission. The state Auditor, however, refused to make the payment from the state treasury. He argued that the legislature's approval of the compact violated the state constitution in two respects. First, the Auditor argued that the compact was unconstitutional because it delegated the state's police power to an interstate agency involving other states and the federal government. Second, the Auditor argued that the compact was invalid because it bound the West Virginia Legislature to make appropriations for the state's share of the commission's operating expenses in violation of a general provision of

---

[143] U.S. Constitution. Article I, section 10, clause 3. See appendix C for the full wording of the Impairments Clause.

the state constitution concerning the incurring of "debts." The West Virginia State Water Commission supported the compact and went to court requesting a mandamus order to compel the Auditor to make the payment from the state treasury. The Supreme Court of Appeals of West Virginia invalidated the legislature's ratification of the compact on the grounds that the compact violated the state constitution.

In 1950, the U.S. Supreme Court reversed the state ruling and prevented West Virginia from avoiding its obligations under the compact. The Court wrote in *West Virginia ex rel. Dyer v. Sims:*

> "But a compact is after all a legal document.... **It requires no elaborate argument to reject the suggestion that an agreement** solemnly entered into between States by those who alone have political authority to speak for a State **can be unilaterally nullified,** or given final meaning by an organ of one of the contracting States. **A State cannot be its own ultimate judge in a controversy with a sister State.**"[144] [Emphasis added]

The U.S. Supreme Court continued:

> "That a legislature may delegate to an administrative body the power to make rules and decide particular cases is one of the axioms of modern government. The West Virginia court does not challenge the general proposition but objects to the delegation here involved **because it is to a body outside the State and because its Legislature may not be free, at any time, to withdraw the power delegated.**... What is involved is the conventional grant of legislative power. We find nothing in that to indicate that West Virginia may not solve a problem such as the control of river pollution by compact and by the delegation, if such it be, necessary to effectuate such solution by compact.... Here, the State has bound itself to control pollution by the more effective means of an agreement with other States. **The Compact involves a reasonable and carefully limited delegation of power to an interstate agency.**"[145] [Emphasis added]

---

[144] *West Virginia ex rel. Dyer v. Sims.* 341 U.S. 22 at 28. 1950.
[145] *Id.* at 30–31.

Justice Robert Jackson's concurring opinion set forth an additional justification for Court's decision. Justice Jackson suggested that the Supreme Court did not need to interpret the West Virginia state constitution in order to conclude that the compact bound West Virginia. Instead, he stated that West Virginia was estopped from changing its position after each of the other governmental entities relied upon, and changed their position because of, the compact.

> **"West Virginia assumed a contractual obligation** with equals by permission of another government that is sovereign in its field (the federal government). After Congress and **sister states had been induced to alter their positions and bind themselves to terms of a covenant,** West Virginia should be estopped from repudiating her act. For this reason, I consider that whatever interpretation she put on the generalities of her Constitution, **she is bound by the Compact.**"[146]
> [Emphasis added]

The pre-ratification expectations of states joining a compact are especially important whenever there is a post-ratification dispute among compacting parties concerning voting rights within the compact. In one case, Nebraska (which was obligated to store radioactive waste under the terms of a compact) sought additional voting power on the compact's commission after the compact had gone into effect. A majority (but not all) of the compact's other members consented to Nebraska's request. Nebraska's request was, however, judicially voided in 1995 in *State of Nebraska v. Central Interstate Low-Level Radioactive Waste Commission*

> "because changes in 'voting power' substantially alter the original expectations of the majority of states which comprise the compact."[147]

Amplifying the principle of *West Virginia ex rel. Dyer v. Sims*, the courts have noted that a single state cannot obstruct the workings of a compact. In *Hess v. Port Authority Trans-Hudson Corp.*, the U.S. Supreme Court held in 1994 that a compact is

---

[146] *Id.* at 36.

[147] *State of Nebraska v. Central Interstate Low-Level Radioactive Waste Commission.* 902 F.Supp. 1046, 1049 (D.Neb. 1995).

"... not subject to the unilateral control of any one of the States...."[148]

Similarly, in *Lake Country Estates, Inc. v. Tahoe Regional Planning Agency*, the U.S. Supreme Court in 1979 held that a member state may not unilaterally veto the actions of a compact's commission. Instead, the remedy of an aggrieved state consists of withdrawing from the compact in accordance with the compact's terms for withdrawal.[149]

In *Kansas City Area Transportation Authority v. Missouri*, the Eighth Circuit in 1981 held that a member state may not legislatively burden the other member states unless they concur.[150]

Moreover, a compacting state, motivated by politics, may be prevented from undermining the workings of that compact. In the 1993 case of *Alcorn v. Wolfe*, the removal of an appointee to a compact commission, initiated by a Governor to inject his political influence into the operations of the commission, was invalidated because it

"clearly frustrate[d] one of the most important objectives of the compact."[151]

In *State of Nebraska v. Central Interstate Low-Level Radioactive Waste Commission*, Nebraska was estopped in 1993 from seeking equitable relief to prevent a compact, of which it was a member, from pursuing its central mission.[152] In *New York v. United States*, the U.S. Supreme Court held that the estoppel doctrine was applicable only to the states that have adopted the interstate compact.[153]

In short, a state may be estopped from withdrawing from a compact in any manner not permitted by the terms of the compact.

The six-month blackout period for withdrawing from the proposed "Agreement Among the States to Elect the President by National Popular Vote" is reasonable and appropriate in order to ensure that a politically

[148] *Hess v. Port Authority Trans-Hudson Corp.* 513 U.S. 30 at 42. 1994.

[149] *Lake Country Estates, Inc. v. Tahoe Regional Planning Agency.* 440 U.S. 391 at 399 and 402. 1979.

[150] *Kansas City Area Transportation Authority v. Missouri.* 640 F.2d 173 at 174 (8th Cir.). 1979.

[151] *Alcorn v. Wolfe.* 827 F.Supp. 47, 53 (D.D.C. 1993).

[152] *State of Nebraska v. Central Interstate Low-Level Radioactive Waste Commission.* 834 F.Supp. 1205 at 1215 (D.Neb. 1993).

[153] *New York v. United States.* 505 U.S. 144 at 183. 1992.

motivated member state does not change its position after the candidates, the political parties, the voters, and the other compacting states have proceeded through the presidential campaign and presidential election cycle in reliance on each compacting state fulfilling its obligations under the compact.

8.6.3 Additional State and Federal Constraints on Withdrawal

There are two additional potential constraints on a withdrawal from the "Agreement Among the States to Elect the President by National Popular Vote" that are applicable to the 35-day period between election day in November and the meeting of the Electoral College in mid-December.

The first constraint is applicable if the compact were to be enacted in a particular state using the citizen-initiative process. In 11 states, there are state constitutional limitations concerning the repeal or amendment of a statute originally enacted by the voters by means of the citizen-initiative process.[154] In seven of these states, the constraint on the legislature runs for a specific period of time. In four of the 11 states, the constraint is permanent—that is, the voters must be consulted in a subsequent ref-

Table 8.4 STATE CONSTITUTIONAL LIMITATIONS ON THE REPEAL OR AMENDMENT OF STATUTES ORIGINALLY ENACTED BY THE VOTERS THROUGH THE CITIZEN-INITIATIVE PROCESS

STATE	LIMITATION
Alaska	No repeal within two years; amendment by majority vote anytime
Arizona	Three-quarters vote to amend; amending legislation must "further the purpose" of the measure
Arkansas	Two-thirds vote to amend or repeal
California	No amendment or repeal of an initiative statute by the legislature unless the initiative specifically permits it
Michigan	Three-quarters vote to amend or repeal
Nebraska	Two-thirds vote to amend or repeal
Nevada	No amendment or repeal within three years of enactment
North Dakota	Two-thirds vote to amend or repeal within seven years of effective date
Oregon	Two-thirds vote to amend or repeal within two years of enactment
Washington	Two-thirds vote to amend or repeal within two years of enactment
Wyoming	No repeal within two years of effective date; amendment by majority vote any time

---

[154] National Conference on State Legislatures.

erendum about any proposed repeal or amendment. Table 8.4 briefly describes these constitutional limitations. Appendix R contains the complete constitutional provisions.

In addition to the above constitutional limitations, public opinion acts as an inhibition against legislative repeal of, or substantive amendments to, a statute that the voters originally enacted by means of the citizen-initiative process. This political inhibition is particularly forceful in western states that have the citizen-initiative process.

Second, there is a federal law that would likely be interpreted to constrain repeal of the proposed compact withdrawal during the 35-day period between "the day fixed for the appointment of the electors" (that is, election day in early November) and the meeting of the Electoral College in mid-December. The federal "safe harbor" provision (quoted in full in section 8.3.6) gives preference to presidential election returns that are in accord with

> "laws enacted prior to the day fixed for the appointment of the electors....″[155]

In the 1960 presidential election, for example, John F. Kennedy won the nationwide popular vote by 114,673 votes. However, his electoral-vote majority depended on the fact that he had carried Illinois by 4,430 popular votes and South Carolina by 4,732 votes. Some members of the South Carolina legislature suggested that the legislature ignore the popular vote count in the state, change the rules for awarding the state's electoral votes after election day, and appoint all the state's presidential electors themselves. One reason that nothing came of this suggestion was that the "safe harbor" provision requires that an ascertainment of a state's votes based on the laws that existed prior to election day be treated as "conclusive" in the national count of the electoral votes. Nothing came of similar post-election suggestions that the Florida Legislature appoint all of the state's presidential electors in 2000.

---

[155] See section 8.3.6 for the complete wording of this provision (title 3, chapter 1, section 6 of the United States Code).

9 | Administrative Issues Concerning the Proposed Interstate Compact

The proposed "Agreement Among the States to Elect the President by National Popular Vote" (presented in chapter 6) raises several issues concerning the administration of elections, including the following:

- Does the proposed compact impose any significant additional financial cost or administrative burden on state election officials (section 9.1)?
- How would recounts be handled (section 9.2)?

9.1 DOES THE PROPOSED COMPACT IMPOSE ANY SIGNIFICANT FINANCIAL COST OR ADMINISTRATIVE BURDEN ON STATE ELECTION OFFICIALS?

Under the proposed interstate compact, a presidential election would be conducted by each state in the same way that it is now conducted. The proposed compact makes no changes in a state's laws or procedures for preparing ballots; administering polling places; counting votes at the precinct level; or aggregating the vote counts from the precincts to determine the total number of popular votes cast for each presidential slate in the state.

Under the statewide winner-take-all system currently used by 48 states and the District of Columbia, the state's chief election official (or state canvassing board) certifies the election of the entire list of presidential electors that is affiliated with the presidential slate that received the most votes in the state. For example, if the Republican presidential slate carries the state, the state's chief election official certifies the election of the entire slate of Republican presidential electors for the state. These presidential electors collectively represent the will of their state's voters.

The system currently used in Maine and Nebraska is different. The state's chief election official certifies the election of a presidential elector affiliated with the presidential slate that carried each separate congressional district in the state. Each district-level presidential elector represents the will of the voters in the district involved. In addition, the chief election official certifies two presidential electors affiliated with the presidential slate that carried the state. These two senatorial presidential electors collectively represent the will of the voters in their state. For example, if the Democratic presidential slate carries the state and the 1st congressional district, the state's chief election official certifies the election of three Democratic presidential electors (two senatorial electors and one district elector from the 1st district). If the Republican presidential slate carries the 2nd congressional district, the state's chief election official certifies the election of one Republican presidential elector for that district. In this example, two senatorial presidential electors collectively represent the will of their state's voters; the Democratic elector from the 1st district represents the will of that district's voters; and the Republican elector from the 2nd district represents the will of that district's voters.

The only change introduced by the proposed compact occurs *after* a state has finished tallying the statewide total number of popular votes cast for each presidential slate. At that point, there is one additional step under the proposed compact. The votes cast for each presidential slate in all 50 states and the District of Columbia would be added together to produce a national grand total for each presidential slate (section 6.3.3). This is, of course, the same adding-up process that the media, the political parties, and various watchdog groups already do on election night and in the days following each presidential election. Under the proposed compact, the presidential slate with the largest national grand total from all 50 states and the District of Columbia would be designated as the "national popular vote winner." The chief election official of each state belonging to the compact would then certify the election of the entire slate of presidential electors that is affiliated with the presidential slate that has been designated as the "national popular vote winner." For example, if the Democratic presidential slate is the "national popular vote winner," the state's chief election official in every state belonging to the compact would certify the election of the slate of Democratic presidential electors.

The effect of the proposed compact would be that all the presidential electors of all states belonging to the compact would be affiliated with the presidential slate that received the largest total number of popular votes in all 50 states and the District of Columbia. These presidential electors from the states belonging to the compact will collectively represent the nationwide will of the voters. Under the proposed compact, the presidential electors will meet in mid-December and cast their electoral votes. Because the proposed compact only goes into effect when it has been enacted by states possessing a majority of the electoral votes, the presidential slate receiving the most popular votes from all 50 states and the District of Columbia will receive a majority of the electoral votes in the Electoral College.

As can be seen, there is no significant additional administrative burden or financial cost associated with the proposed interstate compact.

9.2 HOW WOULD RECOUNTS BE HANDLED?

Before discussing the mechanics of recounts, let us recognize that there would be less opportunity for a close election under nationwide popular election of the President than under the prevailing statewide winner-take-all system. A close outcome is considerably less likely in an election with a single pool of votes than in an election in which there are 51 separate pools and hence 51 separate opportunities for a close outcome. Moreover, a close outcome is considerably less likely in larger pool than in a smaller one. Thus, a close outcome is less likely in a single pool of 122,000,000 popular votes than in 51 separate pools each averaging 2,392,159 votes (1/51 of 122,000,000).

The 2000 presidential election is remembered as being close because George W. Bush's total of 2,912,790 popular votes in Florida was a mere 537 more than Gore's statewide total of 2,912,353. Under the statewide winner-take-all rule used in Florida (and almost all other states), the 537-vote lead entitled Bush to all 25 of Florida's electoral votes. There was, however, nothing particularly close about the 2000 presidential election on a nationwide basis. Al Gore had a nationwide lead of 537,179 popular votes. Gore's nationwide lead was larger than, for example, Nixon's lead of 510,314 in 1968 and Kennedy's lead of 118,574 in 1960.[1] The closeness of the 2000 presidential election was an artificial crisis manufactured by Florida's use of the statewide winner-take-all system. No one would even have considered a recount in 2000 if the nationwide

---

[1] Congressional Quarterly. 2002. *Presidential Elections 1789–2002*. Washington, DC: CQ Press. Pages 146 and 148.

popular vote had controlled the outcome. No one would have cared whether Bush did, or did not, carry Florida by 537 popular votes.

Similarly, the 2004 election was also not close in terms of the nationwide popular vote. President George W. Bush had a nationwide lead of about 3,500,000 popular votes. However, people had to wait until the morning of Wednesday November 3, 2004, to find out the outcome of the popular vote in Ohio. A switch of 59,388 popular votes in Ohio would have given Kerry all of Ohio's 20 electoral votes and the Presidency. Again, the illusion of closeness resulted from the statewide winner-take-all system used in Ohio—not because the election was genuinely close on a nationwide basis.

In fact, no presidential election since the 19th century has been won by fewer than 100,000 votes on a nationwide basis. The closest presidential election since 1900 was the 1960 election in which John F. Kennedy led Richard M. Nixon by 118,574 popular votes nationwide. A margin of 118,574 popular votes is not particularly close on a nationwide basis. Such a margin would have been unlikely to be questioned. No margin of that size is likely to be overturned by any recount. The 1960 election is remembered as being close because a switch of 4,430 votes in Illinois and a switch 4,782 votes in South Carolina would have given Nixon a majority of the electoral votes. If Nixon had carried both of those states, Kennedy still would have been ahead nationwide by almost 110,000 popular votes, but Nixon would have won the Presidency. The 1960 election then would have become yet another election in which the winner of the nationwide popular vote did not win the Presidency. In any case, the perceived closeness of the 1960 election was an illusion manufactured by the statewide winner-take-all system used in Illinois and South Carolina—not because the nationwide margin of 118,574 was ever likely to be overturned by any recount.

Table 9.1 shows the popular vote count for the Democratic and Republican presidential candidates in each presidential election since 1900 (except that Theodore Roosevelt's vote is shown for the 1912 presidential election because he polled more votes as nominee of the Progressive Party than did the Republican nominee, William Howard Taft). Column 4 shows the difference between the first- and second-place candidates. None of these elections was particularly close in terms of the nationwide popular vote. This is true even though the number of votes cast nationwide in the early years of the 20th century was only about 10% of the present-day turnout of 122,000,000 votes.

Table 9.1 **WINNING MARGINS IN PRESIDENTIAL ELECTIONS BETWEEN 1900 AND 2004**

ELECTION	DEMOCRAT	REPUBLICAN	DIFFERENCE
1900	6,357,698	7,219,193	861,495
1904	5,083,501	7,625,599	2,542,098
1908	6,406,874	7,676,598	1,269,724
1912	6,294,326	4,120,207	2,174,119
1916	9,126,063	8,547,039	579,024
1920	9,134,074	16,151,916	7,017,842
1924	8,386,532	15,724,310	7,337,778
1928	15,004,336	21,432,823	6,428,487
1932	22,818,740	15,760,426	7,058,314
1936	27,750,866	16,679,683	11,071,183
1940	27,343,218	22,334,940	5,008,278
1944	25,612,610	22,021,053	3,591,557
1948	24,105,810	21,970,064	2,135,746
1952	27,314,992	33,777,945	6,462,953
1956	26,022,752	35,590,472	9,567,720
1960	34,226,731	34,108,157	118,574
1964	43,129,566	27,178,188	15,951,378
1968	31,275,166	31,785,480	510,314
1972	29,170,383	47,169,911	17,999,528
1976	40,830,763	39,147,793	1,682,970
1980	35,483,883	43,904,153	8,420,270
1984	37,577,185	54,455,075	16,877,890
1988	41,809,074	48,886,097	7,077,023
1992	44,909,326	39,103,882	5,805,444
1996	47,402,357	39,198,755	8,203,602
2000	50,992,335	50,455,156	537,179
2004	59,028,111	62,040,610	3,012,499

Even the highly controversial 1876 presidential election was not close in terms of the nationwide popular vote. Democrat Samuel J. Tilden received 4,288,191 popular votes—254,694 more than the 4,033,497 popular votes received by Rutherford B. Hayes. Tilden's percentage lead of 3.05% was greater than George W. Bush's 2004 lead of 2.8%. The 1876 election is remembered as having been close because Hayes had extremely narrow popular-vote leads in several states, namely

- 889 votes in South Carolina,
- 922 votes in Florida,
- 1,050 votes in Oregon,

- 1,075 votes in Nevada, and
- 2,798 votes in California.[2,3,4,5]

Again, the closeness of the 1876 presidential election was an artificial crisis created by the statewide winner-take-all system.

Having said that, even with a single pool of 122,000,000 votes, it is conceivable that the nationwide popular vote could some day be extremely close (say, a few hundred or a few thousand votes out of 122,000,000). In that event, the vote count and the inevitable recount would be handled in the same way as it is currently handled—that is, under the generally serviceable laws that govern all elections. An extremely close election will almost inevitably engender controversy. The guiding principle in such circumstances should be that all votes should be counted fairly and expeditiously. Of course, if the nationwide popular vote count were extremely close on a nationwide basis, it would be very likely that the vote count would, simultaneously, be close in a number of states.

In terms of logistics, the personnel and procedures for a nationwide recount are already in place because every state is always prepared to conduct a statewide recount after any election. Indeed, there are statewide recounts for certain statewide offices and ballot propositions in virtually every election cycle. As Senator David Durenberger (R-Minnesota) said in the Senate in 1979:

> "There is no reason to doubt the ability of the States and localities to manage a recount, and nothing to suggest that a candidate would frivolously incur the expense of requesting one. And even if this were not the case, the potential danger in selecting a President rejected by a majority of the voters far outweighs the potential inconvenience in administering a recount."[6]

[2] Congressional Quarterly. 2002. *Presidential Elections 1789–2002.* Washington, DC: CQ Press. Page 125.

[3] Morris, Roy B. 2003. *Fraud of the Century: Rutherford B. Hayes, Samuel Tilden, and the Stolen Election of 1876.* Waterville, ME: Thorndike Press.

[4] Robinson, Lloyd. 1996. *The Stolen Election: Hayes versus Tilden—1876.* New York, NY: Tom Doherty Associates Books.

[5] Rehnquist, William H. 2004. *Centennial Crisis: The Disputed Election of 1876.* New York, NY: Alfred A. Knopf.

[6] *Congressional Record.* July 10, 1979. Pages 17706–17707.

Senator Birch Bayh (D-Indiana) summed up the concerns about extremely close elections and recounts in a Senate speech by saying:

> "Fraud is an ever present possibility in the electoral college system, even if it rarely has become a proven reality. With the electoral college, relatively few irregular votes can reap a healthy reward in the form of a bloc of electoral votes, because of the unit rule or winner take all rule. Under the present system, fraudulent popular votes are much more likely to have a great impact by swinging enough blocs of electoral votes to reverse the election. A like number of fraudulent popular votes under direct election would likely have little effect on the national vote totals.

> "I have said repeatedly in previous debates that there is no way in which anyone would want to excuse fraud. We have to do everything we can to find it, to punish those who participate in it; but **one of the things we can do to limit fraud is to limit the benefits to be gained by fraud.**

> **"Under a direct popular vote system, one fraudulent vote wins one vote in the return. In the electoral college system, one fraudulent vote could mean 45 electoral votes, 28 electoral votes.**

> "So the incentive to participate in 'a little bit of fraud,' if I may use that phrase advisedly, can have the impact of turning a whole electoral block, a whole State operating under the unit rule. Therefore, so the incentive to participate in fraud is significantly greater than it would be under the direct popular vote system."[7] [Emphasis added]

---

[7] *Congressional Record.* March 14, 1979. Page 5000.

10 | Epilogue

The epilogue to this book will be written by the people, the state legislatures, and the Congress as they consider the proposed "Agreement Among the States to Elect the President by National Popular Vote" described in this book.

APPENDIX A
U. S. Constitutional Provisions on Presidential Elections

ARTICLE II, SECTION 1, CLAUSE 1
The executive Power shall be vested in a President of the United States of America. He shall hold his Office during the Term of four Years, and, together with the Vice President, chosen for the same Term, be elected, as follows

ARTICLE II, SECTION 1, CLAUSE 2
Each State shall appoint, in such Manner as the Legislature thereof may direct, a Number of Electors, equal to the whole Number of Senators and Representatives to which the State may be entitled in the Congress: but no Senator or Representative, or Person holding an Office of Trust or Profit under the United States, shall be appointed an Elector.

ARTICLE II, SECTION 1, CLAUSE 3
The Electors shall meet in their respective States, and vote by Ballot for two Persons, of whom one at least shall not be an Inhabitant of the same State with themselves. And they shall make a List of all the Persons voted for, and of the Number of Votes for each; which List they shall sign and certify, and transmit sealed to the Seat of the Government of the United States, directed to the President of the Senate. The President of the Senate shall, in the Presence of the Senate and House of Representatives, open all the Certificates, and the Votes shall then be counted. The Person having the greatest Number of Votes shall be the President, if such Number be a Majority of the whole Number of Electors appointed; and if there be more than one who have such Majority, and have an equal Number of Votes, then the House of Representatives shall immediately chuse by Ballot one of them for President; and if no Person have a Majority, then from the five highest on the List the said House shall in like

Manner chuse the President. But in chusing the President, the Votes shall be taken by States, the Representation from each State having one Vote; A quorum for this Purpose shall consist of a Member or Members from two thirds of the States, and a Majority of all the States shall be necessary to a Choice. In every Case, after the Choice of the President, the Person having the greatest Number of Votes of the Electors shall be the Vice President. But if there should remain two or more who have equal Votes, the Senate shall chuse from them by Ballot the Vice President.

ARTICLE II, SECTION 1, CLAUSE 4

The Congress may determine the Time of chusing the Electors, and the Day on which they shall give their Votes; which Day shall be the same throughout the United States.

12th AMENDMENT

The Electors shall meet in their respective states, and vote by ballot for President and Vice-President, one of whom, at least, shall not be an inhabitant of the same state with themselves; they shall name in their ballots the person voted for as President, and in distinct ballots the person voted for as Vice-President, and they shall make distinct lists of all persons voted for as President, and of all persons voted for as Vice-President, and of the number of votes for each, which lists they shall sign and certify, and transmit sealed to the seat of the government of the United States, directed to the President of the Senate;—The President of the Senate shall, in the presence of the Senate and House of Representatives, open all the certificates and the votes shall then be counted;—The person having the greatest number of votes for President, shall be the President, if such number be a majority of the whole number of Electors appointed; and if no person have such majority, then from the persons having the highest numbers not exceeding three on the list of those voted for as President, the House of Representatives shall choose immediately, by ballot, the President. But in choosing the President, the votes shall be taken by states, the representation from each state having one vote; a quorum for this purpose shall consist of a member or members from two-thirds of the states, and a majority of all the states shall be necessary to a choice. And if the House of Representatives shall not choose a President whenever the right of choice shall devolve upon them, before the fourth day of March next following, then the Vice-President shall act as President, as in the case of the death or other constitutional disability of the President. The person having the greatest number of votes as Vice-President, shall be the Vice-President, if such number be a majority of the whole number of Electors appointed, and if no person have a majority, then from the two highest numbers on the list, the Senate shall choose the Vice-President; a quorum for the purpose shall consist of two-thirds of the whole number of Senators, and a majority of the whole number shall be necessary to a choice. But no person constitutionally ineligible to the office of President shall be eligible to that of Vice-President of the United States.

14th AMENDMENT-SECTIONS 2 AND 3

Section 2. Representatives shall be apportioned among the several States according to their respective numbers, counting the whole number of persons in each State, excluding Indians not taxed. But when the right to vote at any election for the choice of electors for President and Vice President of the United States, Representatives in Congress, the Executive and Judicial officers of a State, or the members of the Legislature thereof, is denied to any of the male inhabitants of such State, being twenty-one years of age, and citizens of the United States, or in any way abridged, except for participation in rebellion, or other crime, the basis of representation therein shall be reduced in the proportion which the number of such male citizens shall bear to the whole number of male citizens twenty-one years of age in such State.

Section 3. No person shall be a Senator or Representative in Congress, or elector of President and Vice President, or hold any office, civil or military, under the United States, or under any State, who, having previously taken an oath, as a member of Congress, or as an officer of the United States, or as a member of any State legislature, or as an executive or judicial officer of any State, to support the Constitution of the United States, shall have engaged in insurrection or rebellion against the same, or given aid or comfort to the enemies thereof. But Congress may by a vote of two-thirds of each House, remove such disability.

15th AMENDMENT-SECTION 1

Section 1. The right of citizens of the United States to vote shall not be denied or abridged by the United States or by any State on account of race, color, or previous condition of servitude.

19th AMENDMENT

The right of citizens of the United States to vote shall not be denied or abridged by the United States or by any State on account of sex.

Congress shall have power to enforce this article by appropriate legislation.

20th AMENDMENT – SECTIONS 1-5

Section 1. The terms of the President and Vice President shall end at noon on the 20th day of January, and the terms of Senators and Representatives at noon on the 3d day of January, of the years in which such terms would have ended if this article had not been ratified; and the terms of their successors shall then begin.

Section 2. The Congress shall assemble at least once in every year, and such meeting shall begin at noon on the 3d day of January, unless they shall by law appoint a different day.

Section 3. If, at the time fixed for the beginning of the term of the President, the President elect shall have died, the Vice President elect shall become President. If a President shall not have been chosen before the time fixed for the beginning of his term, or if the President elect shall have failed to qualify, then the Vice President elect shall act as President until a President shall have qualified; and the Congress may by law provide for the case wherein neither a President elect nor a Vice President elect shall have qualified, declaring who shall then act as President, or the manner in which one who is to act shall be selected, and such person shall act accordingly until a President or Vice President shall have qualified.

Section 4. The Congress may by law provide for the case of the death of any of the persons from whom the House of Representatives may choose a President whenever the right of choice shall have devolved upon them, and for the case of the death of any of the persons from whom the Senate may choose a Vice President whenever the right of choice shall have devolved upon them.

Section. 5. Sections 1 and 2 shall take effect on the 15th day of October following the ratification of this article.

22nd AMENDMENT – SECTION 1

Section 1. No person shall be elected to the office of the President more than twice, and no person who has held the office of President, or acted as President, for more than two years of a term to which some other person was elected President shall be elected to the office of the President more than once. But this Article shall not apply to any person holding the office of President when this Article was proposed by the Congress, and shall not prevent any person who may be holding the office of President, or acting as President, during the term within which this Article becomes operative from holding the office of President or acting as President during the remainder of such term.

23rd AMENDMENT

Section 1. The District constituting the seat of government of the United States shall appoint in such manner as the Congress may direct:

A number of electors of President and Vice President equal to the whole number of Senators and Representatives in Congress to which the District would be entitled if it were a state, but in no event more than the least populous state; they shall be in addition to those appointed by the states, but they shall be considered, for the purposes of the election of President and Vice President, to be electors appointed by a state; and they shall meet in the District and perform such duties as provided by the twelfth article of amendment.

Section 2. The Congress shall have power to enforce this article by appropriate legislation.

24th AMENDMENT

Section 1. The right of citizens of the United States to vote in any primary or other election for President or Vice President, for electors for President or Vice President, or for Senator or Representative in Congress, shall not be denied or abridged by the United States or any state by reason of failure to pay any poll tax or other tax.

Section 2. The Congress shall have power to enforce this article by appropriate legislation.

25th AMENDMENT

Section 1. In case of the removal of the President from office or of his death or resignation, the Vice President shall become President.

Section 2. Whenever there is a vacancy in the office of the Vice President, the President shall nominate a Vice President who shall take office upon confirmation by a majority vote of both Houses of Congress.

Section 3. Whenever the President transmits to the President pro tempore of the Senate and the Speaker of the House of Representatives his written declaration that he is unable to discharge the powers and duties of his office, and until he transmits to them a written declaration to the contrary, such powers and duties shall be discharged by the Vice President as Acting President.

Section 4. Whenever the Vice President and a majority of either the principal officers of the executive departments or of such other body as Congress may by law provide, transmit to the President pro tempore of the Senate and the Speaker of the House of Representatives their written declaration that the President is unable to discharge the powers and duties of his office, the Vice President shall immediately assume the powers and duties of the office as Acting President.

Thereafter, when the President transmits to the President pro tempore of the Senate and the Speaker of the House of Representatives his written declaration that no inability exists, he shall resume the powers and duties of his office unless the Vice President and a majority of either the principal officers of the executive department or of such other body as Congress may by law provide, transmit within four days to the President pro tempore of the Senate and the Speaker of the House of Representatives their written declaration that the President is unable to discharge the powers and duties of his office. Thereupon Congress shall decide the issue, assembling within forty-eight hours for that purpose if not in session. If the Congress, within twenty-one days after receipt of the latter written declaration, or, if Congress is not in session, within twenty-one days after Congress is required to assemble, determines by two-thirds vote of both Houses that the President is unable to discharge the powers and duties of his office, the Vice President shall continue to discharge the same as Acting President; otherwise, the President shall resume the powers and duties of his office.

26th AMENDMENT

Section 1. The right of citizens of the United States, who are eighteen years of age or older, to vote shall not be denied or abridged by the United States or by any State on account of age.

Section 2. The Congress shall have the power to enforce this article by appropriate legislation.

APPENDIX B
Federal Law on Presidential Elections

UNITED STATES CODE
TITLE 3, CHAPTER 1. PRESIDENTIAL ELECTIONS AND VACANCIES

Time of appointing electors

§1. The electors of President and Vice President shall be appointed, in each State, on the Tuesday next after the first Monday in November, in every fourth year succeeding every election of a President and Vice President.

Failure to make choice on prescribed day

§2. Whenever any State has held an election for the purpose of choosing electors, and has failed to make a choice on the day prescribed by law, the electors may be appointed on a subsequent day in such a manner as the legislature of such State may direct.

Number of electors

§3. The number of electors shall be equal to the number of Senators and Representatives to which the several States are by law entitled at the time when the President and Vice President to be chosen come into office; except, that where no apportionment of Representatives has been made after any enumeration, at the time of choosing electors, the number of electors shall be according to the then existing apportionment of Senators and Representatives.

Vacancies in electoral college

§4. Each State may, by law, provide for the filling of any vacancies which may occur in its college of electors when such college meets to give its electoral vote.

Determination of controversy as to appointment of electors

§5. If any State shall have provided, by laws enacted prior to the day fixed for the appointment of the electors, for its final determination of any controversy or contest concerning the appointment of all or any of the electors of such State, by judicial or other methods or procedures, and such determination shall have been made at least six days before the time fixed for the meeting of the electors, such determination made pursuant to such law so existing on said day, and made at least six days prior to said time of meeting of the electors, shall be conclusive, and shall govern in the counting of the electoral votes as provided in the Constitution, and as hereinafter regulated, so far as the ascertainment of the electors appointed by such State is concerned.

Credentials of electors; transmission to archivist of the united states and to congress; public inspection

§6. It shall be the duty of the executive of each State, as soon as practicable after the conclusion of the appointment of the electors in such State by the final ascertainment, under and in pursuance of the laws of such State providing for such ascertainment, to communicate by registered mail under the seal of the State to the Archivist of the United States a certificate of such ascertainment of the electors appointed, setting forth the names of such electors and the canvass or other ascertainment under the laws of such State of the number of votes given or cast for each person for whose appointment any and all votes have been given or cast; and it shall also thereupon be the duty of the executive of each State to deliver to the electors of such State, on or before the day on which they are required by section 7 of this title to meet, six duplicate-originals of the same certificate under the seal of the State; and if there shall have been any final determination in a State in the manner provided for by law of a controversy or contest concerning the appointment of all or any of the electors of such State, it shall be the duty of the executive of such State, as soon as practicable after such determination, to communicate under the seal of the State to the Archivist of the United States a certificate of such determination in form and manner as the same shall have been made; and the certificate or certificates so received by the Archivist of the United States shall be preserved by him for one year and shall be a part of the public records of his office and shall be open to public inspection; and the Archivist of the United States at the first meeting of Congress thereafter shall transmit to the two Houses of Congress copies in full of each and every such certificate so received at the National Archives and Records Administration.

Meeting and vote of electors

§7. The electors of President and Vice President of each State shall meet and give their votes on the first Monday after the second Wednesday in December next following their appointment at such place in each State as the legislature of such State shall direct.

Manner of voting

§8. The electors shall vote for President and Vice President, respectively, in the manner directed by the Constitution.

Certificates of votes for president and vice president

§9. The electors shall make and sign six certificates of all the votes given by them, each of which certificates shall contain two distinct lists, one of the votes for President and the other of the votes for Vice President, and shall annex to each of the certificates one of the lists of the electors which shall have been furnished to them by direction of the executive of the State.

Sealing and endorsing certificates

§10. The electors shall seal up the certificates so made by them, and certify upon each that the lists of all the votes of such State given for President, and of all the votes given for Vice President, are contained therein.

Disposition of certificates

§11. The electors shall dispose of the certificates so made by them and the lists attached thereto in the following manner:

First. They shall forthwith forward by registered mail one of the same to the President of the Senate at the seat of government.

Second. Two of the same shall be delivered to the secretary of state of the State, one of which shall be held subject to the order of the President of the Senate, the other to be preserved by him for one year and shall be a part of the public records of his office and shall be open to public inspection.

Third. On the day thereafter they shall forward by registered mail two of such certificates and lists to the Archivist of the United States at the seat of government, one of which shall be held subject to the order of the President of the Senate. The other shall be preserved by the Archivist of the United States for one year and shall be a part of the public records of his office and shall be open to public inspection.

Fourth. They shall forthwith cause the other of the certificates and lists to be delivered to the judge of the district in which the electors shall have assembled.

Failure of certificates of electors to reach president of the senate or archivist of the united states; demand on state for certificate

§12. When no certificate of vote and list mentioned in sections 9 and 11 and of this title from any State shall have been received by the President of the Senate or by the Archivist of the United States by the fourth Wednesday in December, after the meeting of the electors shall have been held, the President of the Senate or, if he be absent from the seat of government, the Archivist of the United States shall request, by the most expeditious method available, the secretary of state of the State to send up the certificate and list lodged with him by the electors of such State; and it shall be his duty upon receipt of such request immediately to transmit same by registered mail to the President of the Senate at the seat of government.

Same; demand on district judge for certificate

§13. When no certificates of votes from any State shall have been received at the seat of government on the fourth Wednesday in December, after the meeting of the electors shall have been held, the President of the Senate or, if he be absent from the seat of government, the Archivist of the United States shall send a special messenger to the district judge in whose custody one certificate of votes from that State has been lodged, and such judge shall forthwith transmit that list by the hand of such messenger to the seat of government.

Forfeiture for messenger's neglect of duty

§14. Every person who, having been appointed, pursuant to section 13 of this title, to deliver the certificates of the votes of the electors to the President of the Senate, and having accepted such appointment, shall neglect to perform the services required from him, shall forfeit the sum of $1,000.

Counting electoral votes in congress

§15. Congress shall be in session on the sixth day of January succeeding every meeting of the electors. The Senate and House of Representatives shall meet in the Hall of the House of Representatives at the hour of 1 o'clock in the afternoon on that day, and the President of the Senate shall be their presiding officer. Two tellers shall be previously appointed on the part of the Senate and two on the part of the House of Representatives, to whom shall be handed, as they are opened by the President of the Senate, all the certificates and papers purporting to be certificates of the electoral votes, which certificates and papers shall be opened, presented, and acted upon in the alphabetical order of the States, beginning with the letter A; and said tellers, having then read the same in the presence and hearing of the two Houses, shall make a list of the votes as they shall appear from the said certificates; and the votes having been ascertained and counted according to the rules in this subchapter provided, the result of the same shall be delivered to the President of the Senate, who shall thereupon announce the state of the vote, which announcement shall be deemed a sufficient declaration of the persons, if any, elected President and Vice President of the United States, and, together with a list of the votes, be entered on the Journals of the two Houses. Upon such reading of any such certificate or paper, the President of the Senate shall call for objections, if any. Every objection shall be made in writing, and shall state clearly and concisely, and without argument, the ground thereof, and shall be signed by at least one Senator and one Member of the House of Representatives before the same shall be received. When all objections so made to any vote or paper from a State shall have been received and read, the Senate shall thereupon withdraw, and such objections shall be submitted to the Senate for its decision; and the Speaker of the House of Representatives shall, in like manner, submit such objections to the House of Representatives for its decision; and no electoral vote or votes from any State which shall have been regularly given by electors whose appointment has been lawfully certified to according to section 6 of this title from which but one return has been received shall be rejected, but the two Houses concurrently may reject the vote or votes when they agree that such vote or votes have not been so regularly given by electors whose appointment has been so certified. If more than one return or paper purporting to be a return from a State shall have been received by the President of the Senate, those votes, and those only, shall be counted which shall have been regularly given by the electors who are shown by the determination mentioned in section 5 of this title to have been appointed, if the determination in said section provided for shall have been made, or by such successors or substitutes, in case of a vacancy in the board of electors so ascertained, as have been appointed to fill such vacancy in the mode provided by the laws of the

State; but in case there shall arise the question which of two or more of such State authorities determining what electors have been appointed, as mentioned in section 5 of this title, is the lawful tribunal of such State, the votes regularly given of those electors, and those only, of such State shall be counted whose title as electors the two Houses, acting separately, shall concurrently decide is supported by the decision of such State so authorized by its law; and in such case of more than one return or paper purporting to be a return from a State, if there shall have been no such determination of the question in the State aforesaid, then those votes, and those only, shall be counted which the two Houses shall concurrently decide were cast by lawful electors appointed in accordance with the laws of the State, unless the two Houses, acting separately, shall concurrently decide such votes not to be the lawful votes of the legally appointed electors of such State. But if the two Houses shall disagree in respect of the counting of such votes, then, and in that case, the votes of the electors whose appointment shall have been certified by the executive of the State, under the seal thereof, shall be counted. When the two Houses have voted, they shall immediately again meet, and the presiding officer shall then announce the decision of the questions submitted. No votes or papers from any other State shall be acted upon until the objections previously made to the votes or papers from any State shall have been finally disposed of.

Same; seats for officers and members of two houses in joint meeting

§16. At such joint meeting of the two Houses seats shall be provided as follows: For the President of the Senate, the Speaker's chair; for the Speaker, immediately upon his left; the Senators, in the body of the Hall upon the right of the presiding officer; for the Representatives, in the body of the Hall not provided for the Senators; for the tellers, Secretary of the Senate, and Clerk of the House of Representatives, at the Clerk's desk; for the other officers of the two Houses, in front of the Clerk's desk and upon each side of the Speaker's platform. Such joint meeting shall not be dissolved until the count of electoral votes shall be completed and the result declared; and no recess shall be taken unless a question shall have arisen in regard to counting any such votes, or otherwise under this subchapter, in which case it shall be competent for either House, acting separately, in the manner hereinbefore provided, to direct a recess of such

House not beyond the next calendar day, Sunday excepted, at the hour of 10 o'clock in the forenoon. But if the counting of the electoral votes and the declaration of the result shall not have been completed before the fifth calendar day next after such first meeting of the two Houses, no further or other recess shall be taken by either House.

Same; limit of debate in each house

§17. When the two Houses separate to decide upon an objection that may have been made to the counting of any electoral vote or votes from any State, or other question arising in the matter, each Senator and Representative may speak to such objection or question five minutes, and not more than once; but after such debate shall have lasted two hours it shall be the duty of the presiding officer of each House to put the main question without further debate.

Same; parliamentary procedure at joint meeting

§18. While the two Houses shall be in meeting as provided in this chapter, the President of the Senate shall have power to preserve order; and no debate shall be allowed and no question shall be put by the presiding officer except to either House on a motion to withdraw.

Vacancy in offices of both president and vice president; officers eligible to act

§19. (a)

   (1) If, by reason of death, resignation, removal from office, inability, or failure to qualify, there is neither a President nor Vice President to discharge the powers and duties of the office of President, then the Speaker of the House of Representatives shall, upon his resignation as Speaker and as Representative in Congress, act as President.

   (2) The same rule shall apply in the case of the death, resignation, removal from office, or inability of an individual acting as President under this subsection.

(b) If, at the time when under subsection (a) of this section a Speaker is to begin the discharge of the powers and duties of the office of President, there is no Speaker, or the Speaker fails to qualify as Acting President, then the President pro tempore of the Senate shall, upon his resignation as President pro tempore and as Senator, act as President.

(c) An individual acting as President under subsection (a) or subsection (b) of this section shall continue to act until the expiration of the then current Presidential term, except that
  (1) if his discharge of the powers and duties of the office is founded in whole or in part on the failure of both the President-elect and the Vice-President-elect to qualify, then he shall act only until a President or Vice President qualifies; and
  (2) if his discharge of the powers and duties of the office is founded in whole or in part on the inability of the President or Vice President, then he shall act only until the removal of the disability of one of such individuals.

(d)
  (1) If, by reason of death, resignation, removal from office, inability, or failure to qualify, there is no President pro tempore to act as President under subsection (b) of this section, then the officer of the United States who is highest on the following list, and who is not under disability to discharge the powers and duties of the office of President shall act as President: Secretary of State, Secretary of the Treasury, Secretary of Defense, Attorney General, Secretary of the Interior, Secretary of Agriculture, Secretary of Commerce, Secretary of Labor, Secretary of Health and Human Services, Secretary of Housing and Urban Development, Secretary of Transportation, Secretary of Energy, Secretary of Education, Secretary of Veterans Affairs.
  (2) An individual acting as President under this subsection shall continue so to do until the expiration of the then current Presidential term, but not after a qualified and prior-entitled individual is able to act, except that the removal of the disability of an individual higher on the list contained in paragraph (1) of this subsection or the ability to qualify on the part of an individual higher on such list shall not terminate his service.
  (3) The taking of the oath of office by an individual specified in the list in paragraph (1) of this subsection shall be held to constitute his resignation from the office by virtue of

the holding of which he qualifies to act as President.

(e) Subsections (a), (b), and (d) of this section shall apply only to such officers as are eligible to the office of President under the Constitution. Subsection (d) of this section shall apply only to officers appointed, by and with the advice and consent of the Senate, prior to the time of the death, resignation, removal from office, inability, or failure to qualify, of the President pro tempore, and only to officers not under impeachment by the House of Representatives at the time the powers and duties of the office of President devolve upon them.

(f) During the period that any individual acts as President under this section, his compensation shall be at the rate then provided by law in the case of the President.

Resignation or refusal of office

§20. The only evidence of a refusal to accept, or of a resignation of the office of President or Vice President, shall be an instrument in writing, declaring the same, and subscribed by the person refusing to accept or resigning, as the case may be, and delivered into the office of the Secretary of State.

Definitions

§21. As used in this chapter the term –

(a) "State" includes the District of Columbia.

(b) "executives of each State" includes the Board of Commissioners * of the District of Columbia.

APPENDIX C
U. S. Constitution on
Interstate Compacts and Contracts

ARTICLE I, SECTION 10, CLAUSE 3

No State shall, without the Consent of Congress, lay any Duty of Tonnage, keep Troops, or Ships of War in time of Peace, enter into any Agreement or Compact with another State, or with a foreign Power, or engage in War, unless actually invaded, or in such imminent Danger as will not admit of delay.

ARTICLE I, SECTION 10, CLAUSE 1

No State shall enter into any Treaty, Alliance, or Confederation; grant Letters of Marque and Reprisal; coin Money; emit Bills of Credit; make any Thing but gold and silver Coin a Tender in Payment of Debts; pass any Bill of Attainder, ex post facto Law, or Law impairing the Obligation of Contracts, or grant any Title of Nobility.

APPENDIX D
Minnesota Laws on Presidential Elections

208.02. ELECTION OF PRESIDENTIAL ELECTORS

Presidential electors shall be chosen at the state general election held in the year preceding the expiration of the term of the president of the United States.

208.03. NOMINATION OF PRESIDENTIAL ELECTORS

Presidential electors for the major political parties of this state shall be nominated by delegate conventions called and held under the supervision of the respective state central committees of the parties of this state. On or before primary election day the chair of the major political party shall certify to the secretary of state the names of the persons nominated as Presidential electors and the names of the party candidates for president and vice-president.

208.04. PREPARATION OF BALLOTS

Subdivision 1. When Presidential electors are to be voted for, a vote cast for the party candidates for president and vice-president shall be deemed a vote for that party's electors as filed with the secretary of state. The secretary of state shall certify the names of all duly nominated Presidential and vice-Presidential candidates to the county auditors of the counties of the state. Each county auditor, subject to the rules of the secretary of state, shall cause the names of the candidates of each major political party and the candidates nominated by petition to be printed in capital letters, set in type of the same size and style as for candidates on the state white ballot, before the party designation. To the left of, and on the same line with the names of the candidates for president and vice-president, near the margin, shall be placed a square or box, in which the voters may indicate their choice by marking an "X."

The form for the Presidential ballot and the relative position of the several candidates shall be determined by the rules applicable to other state officers. The state ballot, with the required heading, shall be printed on the same piece of paper and shall be below the Presidential ballot with a blank space between one inch in width.

Subdivision 2. The rules for preparation, state contribution to the cost of printing, and delivery of Presidential ballots are the same as the rules for white ballots under section 204D.11, subdivision 1.

208.05. STATE CANVASSING BOARD

The state canvassing board at its meeting on the second Tuesday after each state general election shall open and canvass the returns made to the secretary of state for Presidential electors, prepare a statement of the number of votes cast for the persons receiving votes for these offices, and declare the person or persons receiving the highest number of votes for each office duly elected. When it appears that more than the number of persons to be elected as Presidential electors have the highest and an equal number of votes, the secretary of state, in the presence of the board shall decide by lot which of the persons shall be declared elected. The governor shall transmit to each person declared elected a certificate of election, signed by the governor, sealed with the state seal, and counter-signed by the secretary of state.

208.06. ELECTORS TO MEET AT CAPITOL; FILLING OF VACANCIES

The Presidential electors, before 12:00 M. on the day before that fixed by congress for the electors to vote for president and vice-president of the United States, shall notify the governor that they are at the state capitol and ready at the proper time to fulfill their duties as electors. The governor shall deliver to the electors present a certificate of the names of all the electors. If any elector named therein fails to appear before 9:00 a.m. on the day, and at the place, fixed for voting for president and vice-president of the United States, the electors present shall, in the presence of the governor, immediately elect by ballot a person to fill the vacancy. If more than the number of persons required have the highest and an equal number of votes, the governor, in the presence of the electors attending, shall decide by lot which of those persons shall be elected.

208.07. CERTIFICATE OF ELECTORS

Immediately after the vacancies have been filled, the original electors present shall certify to the governor the names of the persons elected to complete their number, and the governor shall at once cause written notice to be given to each person elected to fill a vacancy. The persons so chosen shall be Presidential electors and shall meet and act with the other electors.

208.08. ELECTORS TO MEET AT STATE CAPITOL

The original and substituted Presidential electors, at 12:00 M., shall meet in the executive chamber at the state capitol and shall perform all the duties imposed upon them as electors by the constitution and laws of the United States and this state.

204B.07. NOMINATING PETITIONS

Subdivision 1. Form of petition. A nominating petition may consist of one or more separate pages each of which shall state:

(a) The office sought;

(b) The candidate's name and residence address, including street and number if any; and

(c) candidate's political party or political principle expressed in not more than three words. No candidate who files for a partisan office by nominating petition shall use the term "nonpartisan" as a statement of political principle or the name of the candidate's political party. No part of the name of a major political party may be used to designate the political party or principle of a candidate who files for a partisan office by nominating petition, except that the word "independent" may be used to designate the party or principle. A candidate who files by nominating petition to fill a vacancy in nomination for a nonpartisan office pursuant to section 204B.13, shall not state any political principle or the name of any political party on the petition.

Subdivision 2. Petitions for presidential electors. This subdivision does not apply to candidates for Presidential elector nominated by major political parties. Major party candidates for Presidential elector are certified under section 208.03. Other Presidential electors are nominated by petition pursuant to this section. On petitions nominating Presidential electors, the names of the candidates for president and vice-president shall be added to the political party or political principle stated on the petition. One petition may be filed to nominate a slate of Presidential electors equal in number to the number of electors to which the state is entitled.

Subdivision 3. Number of candidates nominated. No nominating petition shall contain the name of more than one candidate except a petition jointly nominating individuals for governor and lieutenant governor or nominating a slate of Presidential electors.

Subdivision 4. Oath and address of signer. Following the information required by subdivisions 1 and 2 and before the space for signing, each separate page that is part of the petition shall include an oath in the following form:

> "I solemnly swear (or affirm) that I know the contents and purpose of this petition, that I do not intend to vote at the primary election for the office for which this nominating petition is made, and that I signed this petition of my own free will."

Notarization or certification of the signatures on a nominating petition is not required. Immediately after the signature, the signer shall write on the petition the signer's residence address including street and number, if any, and mailing address if different from residence address.

Subdivision 5. Sample forms. An official with whom petitions are filed shall make sample forms for nominating petitions available upon request.

Subdivision 6. Penalty. An individual who, in signing a nominating petition, makes a false oath is guilty of perjury.

204B.09. TIME AND PLACE OF FILING AFFIDAVITS AND PETITIONS

Subdivision 1. Candidates in state and county general elections.

(a) Except as otherwise provided by this subdivision, affidavits of candidacy and nominating petitions for county, state, and federal offices filled at the state general election shall be filed not more than 70 days nor less than 56 days before the state primary. The affidavit may be prepared and signed at any time between 60 days before the filing period opens and the last day of the filing period.

(b) Notwithstanding other law to the contrary, the affidavit of candidacy must be signed in the presence of a notarial officer or an individual authorized to administer oaths under section 358.10.

(c) This provision does not apply to candidates for Presidential elector nominated by major political parties. Major party candidates for Presidential elector are certified under section 208.03. Other candidates for Presidential electors may file petitions on or before the state primary day pursuant to section 204B.07. Nominating petitions to fill vacancies in nominations shall be filed as provided in section 204B.13. No affidavit or petition shall be accepted later than 5:00 p.m. on the last day for filing.

(d) Affidavits and petitions for offices to be voted on in only one county shall be filed with the county auditor of that county. Affidavits and petitions for offices to be voted on in more than one county shall be filed with the secretary of state.

Subdivision 1a. Absent candidates. A candidate for special district, county, state, or federal office who will be absent from the state during the filing period may submit a properly executed affidavit of candidacy, the appropriate filing fee, and any necessary petitions in person to the filing officer. The candidate shall state in writing the reason for being unable to submit the affidavit during the filing period. The affidavit, filing fee, and petitions must be submitted to the filing officer during the seven days immediately preceding the candidate's absence from the state. Nominating petitions may be signed during the 14 days immediately preceding the date when the affidavit of candidacy is filed.

Subdivision 2. Other elections. Affidavits of candidacy and nominating petitions for city, town or other elective offices shall be filed during the time and with the official specified in chapter 205 or other applicable law or charter, except as provided for a special district candidate under subdivision 1a. Affidavits of candidacy and applications filed on behalf of eligible voters for school board office shall be filed during the time and with the official specified in chapter 205A or other applicable law.

Subdivision 3. Write-in candidates.

(a) A candidate for state or federal office who wants write-in votes for the candidate to be counted must file a written request with the filing office for the office sought no later than the fifth day before the general election. The filing officer shall provide copies of the form to make the request.

(b) A candidate for president of the United States who files a request under this subdivision must include the name of a candidate for vice-president of the United States. The request must also include the name of at least one candidate for Presidential elector. The total number of names of candidates for Presidential elector on the request may not exceed the total number of electoral votes to be cast by Minnesota in the presidential election.

(c) A candidate for governor who files a request under this subdivision must include the name of a candidate for lieutenant governor.

APPENDIX E
Minnesota 2004 Certificate of Ascertainment

STATE of MINNESOTA

EXECUTIVE DEPARTMENT

TIM PAWLENTY
GOVERNOR

CERTIFICATE OF ASCERTAINMENT
OF APPOINTMENT OF ELECTORS
FOR PRESIDENT AND VICE PRESIDENT
OF THE UNITED STATES
FOR THE STATE OF MINNESOTA

To: John W. Carlin
Archivist of the United States
National Archives and Records Administration
c/o Office of the Federal Register (NF)
8601 Adelphi Road
College Park, MD 20740-6001

I, Tim Pawlenty, Governor of the State of Minnesota, do hereby certify the following:

In accordance with Article 2, Section 1 of the Constitution of the United States, the Legislature of the State of Minnesota directed that the electors for President and Vice President of the United States be elected at the General Election conducted on November 2, 2004.

At the General Election held in this State on November 2, 2004, the following persons received the greatest number of votes cast for the office of Electors for President and Vice President of the United States, and are duly elected to fill such office:

State of Minnesota
Certificate of Ascertainment, 2004, Page 2 of 8

Minnesota Democratic-Farmer-Labor Party
Electors pledged to John F. Kerry for President of the United States
and John Edwards for Vice President of the United States.
These candidates for presidential elector each received 1,445,014
votes:

> Sonja Berg, of St. Cloud
> Vi Grooms-Alban, of Cohasset
> Matthew Little, of Maplewood
> Michael Meuers, of Bemidji
> Tim O'Brien, of Edina
> Lil Ortendahl, of Osakis
> Everett Pettiford, of Minneapolis
> Jean Schiebel, of Brooklyn Center
> Frank Simon, of Chaska
> Chandler Harrison Stevens, of Austin

I further certify that the returns of the votes cast for Presidential Electors at the General Election were canvassed and certified by the State Canvassing Board on the 16th day of November, 2004 in accordance with the laws of the State of Minnesota, and that the number of votes cast for each candidate for Presidential Elector at the General Election is as follows:

Green Party of Minnesota
Electors pledged to David Cobb for President of the United States
and Pat LaMarche for Vice President of the United States.
These candidates for presidential elector each received 4,408 votes:

> Scott Bol
> Kellie Burriss
> Michael Cavlan
> Amber Garlan
> Jenny Heiser
> Molly Nutting
> Douglas Root
> Mark Wahl
> Annie Young
> Dean Zimmermann

State of Minnesota
Certificate of Ascertainment 2004, Page 3 of 8

Republican Party of Minnesota
Electors pledged to George W. Bush for President of the United States
and Dick Cheney for Vice President of the United States.
Each elector received 1,346,695 votes:

George Cable
Jeff Carnes
Ronald Eibensteiner
Angie Erhard
Eileen Fiore
Walter Klaus
Michelle Rifenberg
Julie Rosendahl
Lyall Schwarzkopf
Armin Tesch

Socialist Equality Party
Electors pledged to Bill Van Auken for President of the United States
and Jim Lawrence for Vice President of the United States.
These candidates for presidential elector each received 539 votes:

Nathan Andrew
Dan W. Blais
William J. Campbell-Bezat
Christopher M. Isett
Cory R. Johnson
Cynthia B. Moore
Thomas G. Moore
Stephen M. Paulson
Emanuele Saccarelli
James Strouf

State of Minnesota
Certificate of Ascertainment 2004, Page 4 of 8

Socialist Workers Party
Electors pledged to Roger Calero for President of the United States
and Arrin Hawkins for Vice President of the United States.
These candidates for presidential elector each received 416 votes:

> Dennis Drake
> Rebecca L. Ellis
> Catherine S. Fowlkes
> Allan J. Grady
> Bryce J. Grady
> Louise M. Halverson
> Bernadette Kuhn
> Thomas O'Brien
> Michael Pennock
> Sandra M. Sherman

Christian Freedom Party
Electors pledged to Thomas J. Harens for President of the United States
and Jennifer A. Ryan for Vice President of the United States.
These candidates for presidential elector each received 2,387 votes:

> Gail Froncek
> Brian Harens
> Kaja R. King
> Wayne Kruekeberg
> Sally Paulsen
> Janine Quaile
> Susan Smith
> Nadine Snyder
> Susan M. Style
> John Vinje

State of Minnesota
Certificate of Ascertainment 2004, Page 5 of 8

Better Life Party
Electors pledged to Ralph Nader for President of the United States
and Peter Miguel Camejo for Vice President of the United States.
These candidates for presidential elector each received 18,683 votes:

Cassandra Lynn Carlson
Enrique Pedro Gentzsch
Rhoda Jean Gilman
Kari Elizabeth Kyle
Linda Shannon Mann
Corey Scott Mattson
Lois Minna Piper
Preston George Piper
Matthew Alan Ryg
Suzanne Shelley Skorich

Constitution Party
Electors pledged to Michael Peroutka for President of the United States
and Chuck Baldwin for Vice President of the United States.
These candidates for presidential elector each received 3,074 votes:

Arthur Becker
Patricia Becker
Kent Berdahl
Bill Dodge
Rev. Dr. Tom Jestus Sr.
Lars Johnson
Don Koehler
Marilyn Nibbe
John Robillard
Wayne Zimmerscheid

State of Minnesota
Certificate of Ascertainment 2004, Page 6 of 8

Libertarian Party
Electors pledged to Michael Badnarik for President of the United States
and Richard Campagna for Vice President of the United States.
These candidates for presidential elector each received 4,639 votes:

Stephen Baker
Kathy Helwig
Beatrice Kurk
Jeremy Mackinney
Mary O'Connor
Corey Stern
Shelby Thorsted
David Wiester
Colin Wilkinson
Jill Wilkinson

Elector Pledged to Declared Write-In Candidates
Debra Joyce Renderos for President of the United States
and Oscar Renderos Castillo for Vice President of the United States.
This candidate for presidential elector received 2 votes:

Henry Ford

Elector Pledged to Declared Write-In Candidates
Martin Wishnatsky for President of the United States
and Andrew Vanyo for Vice President of the United States.
This candidate for presidential elector received 2 votes:

Chris Welle

State of Minnesota
Certificate of Ascertainment 2004, Page 7 of 8

Elector Pledged to Declared Write-In Candidates
Walt Brown for President of the United States
and Mary Alice Herbert for Vice President of the United States.
This candidate for presidential elector received 2 votes:

    Kari B. Garcia-Fisher

Electors Pledged to Declared Write-In Candidates
John Joseph Kennedy for President of the United States
and Daniel Robert Rezac for Vice President of the United States.
These candidates for presidential elector each received 4 votes:

    Donna Finnala
    Leonard Finnala
    Anita Hameister
    Jeff Hovde
    Darlene Jaskulke
    Jesse James Morris
    Joshua J. Morris
    Teresa A. Morris
    Julie Wellen

Electors Pledged to Declared Write-In Candidates
Joy Elaina Graham-Pendergast for President of the United States
and Ronald M. LeFeber for Vice President of the United States.
These candidates for presidential elector each received 1 vote:

    Daniel J. Coellinger
    Chris Haness
    B. Johnson

State of Minnesota
Certificate of Ascertainment 2004, Page 8 of 8

IN WITNESS WHEREOF,
I have set my hand and the Great Seal
of the State of Minnesota at the Capitol
in Saint Paul this 8th day of December,
2004, being the 228th year of
Independence, and the 146th year of
Statehood.

TIM PAWLENTY
Governor

ATTEST:

MARY KIFFMEYER
Secretary of State

APPENDIX F
Maine 2004 Certificate
of Ascertainment

STATE OF MAINE

Certificate of Ascertainment of Electors

I, John Elias Baldacci, Governor of the State of Maine, do hereby certify that Jill Duson of Portland; Samuel Shapiro of Waterville; Lu Bauer of Standish and David Garrity of Portland have been duly chosen and appointed

ELECTORS OF PRESIDENT AND VICE PRESIDENT
OF THE UNITED STATES

for the State of Maine, at an election for that purpose which was held on the Tuesday following the first Monday in November, in the year two thousand and four, in accordance with the provisions of the laws of the State of Maine and in conformity with the Constitution and laws of the United States, for the purpose of giving their votes for President and Vice President of the United States for the respective terms commencing on the twentieth day of January, in the year two thousand and five; and

I further certify, that, the votes given at said election for Electors of President and Vice President of the United States as appears by the returns from the several cities, towns and plantations in the State, which were duly received and examined by me in accordance with the laws, were as follows:

The LIBERTARIAN PARTY Electors supporting the candidacy of Michael Badnarik for President and Richard Campagna for Vice President received the following votes:

First Congressional District
Mark Cenci, Portland   1,047

Second Congressional District
Dana Snowman, Alton   918

At-Large
Richard W. Eaton, Westbrook   1,965

At-Large
Geoffrey H. Keller, Dayton   1,965

The REPUBLICAN PARTY Electors supporting the candidacy of George W. Bush for President and Dick Cheney for Vice President received the following votes:

First Congressional District
Kenneth M. Cole, III, Falmouth   165,824

Second Congressional District
Katherine L. Watson, Pittsfield   164,377

At-Large
Peter E. Cianchette, South Portland   330,201

At-Large
James D. Tobin, Bangor   330,201

The GREEN INDEPENDENT PARTY Electors supporting the candidacy of David Cobb for President and Patricia LaMarche for Vice President received the following votes:

First Congressional District
Larry Dean Lofton-McGee, Augusta   1,468

Second Congressional District
Heather E. Garrold, Brooks   1,468

At-Large
Charlene Decker, Machias   2,936

At-Large
Ruth Z. Gabey, West Gardiner   2,936

The DEMOCRATIC PARTY Electors supporting the candidacy of John F. Kerry for President and John Edwards for Vice President received the following votes:

First Congressional District
Jill Duson, Portland   211,703

Second Congressional District
Samuel Shapiro, Waterville   185,139

At-Large
Lu Bauer, Standish   396,842

At-Large
David Garrity, Portland   396,842

The BETTER LIFE PARTY Electors supporting the candidacy of Ralph Nader for President and Peter Miguel Camejo for Vice President received the following votes:

First Congressional District
Rosemary L. Whittaker, South Portland   4,004

Second Congressional District
Christopher M. Droznick, Auburn   4,065

At-Large
Nancy Oden, Jonesboro   8,069

At-Large
J. Noble Snowdeal, Jonesboro   8,069

The CONSTITUTION PARTY Electors supporting the candidacy of Michael Anthony Peroutka for President and Chuck Baldwin for Vice President received the following votes:

First Congressional District
Stanley Jones, Hallowell   346

Second Congressional District
Harvey R. Lord, Paris   389

At-Large
Mary-Ann Greiner, St. George   735

At-Large
Patricia Truman, Hallowell   735

In Testimony Whereof, I have caused the Great Seal of the State of Maine to be hereunto affixed, given under my hand, this twenty-third day of November in the year two thousand and four.

John Elias Baldacci, Governor

Dan A. Gwadosky, Secretary of State

APPENDIX G
Nebraska 2004 Certificate
of Ascertainment

STATE OF NEBRASKA
ELECTORAL COLLEGE
CERTIFICATE OF ASCERTAINMENT

We, Mike Johanns, Governor of the State of Nebraska, and John A. Gale, Secretary of State of the State of Nebraska, do hereby certify the following is a certified list of the five Presidential Electors in and for the State of Nebraska, including the names of the Presidential and Vice Presidential candidates and the votes received by each as duly canvassed by the State Canvassing Board on November 29, 2004.

Republican Party   **George W. Bush, President/Dick Cheney, Vice President**
                        Statewide Total Votes Received: 512,814

Electors: Ms. Kay Orr 1610 Brent Blvd. Lincoln, NE 68506 (At Large)
             Mr. Ken Stinson 14349 Hamilton St. Omaha, NE 68154 (At Large)

             First Congressional District Total Votes Received: 169,888
             The Honorable Curt Bromm 1448 N Pine St. Wahoo, NE 68066 (1st District)

             Second Congressional District Total Votes Received: 153,041
             Mr. Michael John Hogan 16212 Wakely St. Omaha, NE 68118 (2nd District)

             Third Congressional District Total Votes Received: 189,885
             Mr. Bill Barrett P.O. Box 366 Lexington, NE 68850 (3rd District)

Democratic Party   **John F. Kerry, President/John Edwards, Vice President**
                        Statewide Total Votes Received: 254,328

Electors: Ms. Carol Yoakum 1145 Rose St., #117 Lincoln, NE 68502-2268 (At Large)
             Mr. Frank Johannsen HC 86, Box 149 Bayard, NE 69334 (At Large)

             First Congressional District Total Votes Received: 96,314
             The Honorable Diana Schimek 2321 Camelot Ct. Lincoln, NE 68512 (1st District)

             Second Congressional District Total Votes Received: 97,858
             Ms. Sandi Skorniak 6324 Blondo St. Omaha, NE 68104 (2nd District)

             Third Congressional District Total Votes Received: 60,156
             Deb Hardin Quirk P.O. Box 1142 Hastings, NE 68902 (3rd District)

Libertarian Party   **Michael Badnarik, President/Richard V. Campagna, Vice President**
                         Statewide Total Votes Received: 2,041

Electors: Mr. Paul Tripp 12216 Poppleton Plz., #238 Omaha, NE 68144 (At Large)
             Ms. Nydra Smart 310 Fawn Ct. Bellevue, NE 68005-2006 (At Large)

             First Congressional District Total Votes Received: 656
             Mr. Gerald F. Kosch 775 N 11th St, #4 David City, NE 68632 (1st District)

             Second Congressional District Total Votes Received: 813
             Mr. Jack Graziano 1513 N 112th Ct., #5413 Omaha, NE 68154

             Third Congressional District Total Votes Received: 572
             Mr. Jerry Hickman Rt. 2 Box 91 Loup City, NE 68853-9632

<u>Nebraska Party</u>   **Michael Anthony Peroutka, President/Chuck Baldwin, Vice President**
Statewide Total Votes Received: 1,314

Electors: Mr. Duane Dufek Box 555 Creighton, NE 68729 (At Large)
Mr. Gene Dobias 510 Washington Ave. Creighton, NE 68729 (At Large)

First Congressional District Total Votes Received: 405
Mr. Peter Rosberg 83626 557 Ave. Norfolk NE 68701 (1st District)

Second Congressional District Total Votes Received: 305
Mr. Tim Larson 15709 O Cir. Omaha, NE 68135 (2nd District)

Third Congressional District Total Votes Received: 604
Mr. Joseph Rosberg 54288 874 Rd. Wausa, NE 68786

<u>Green Party</u>   **David Cobb, President/Patricia LaMarche, Vice President**
Statewide Total Votes Received: 978

Electors: Mr. Tim Jensen 307 W. Charleston, #1232 Lincoln, NE 68528 (At Large)
Ms. Elaine Santore 609 N 17th St. Lincoln, NE 68508 (At Large)

First Congressional District Total Votes Received: 453
Ms. Ginny Crisco 1601 F St. Lincoln, NE 68508 (1st District)

Second Congressional District Total Votes Received: 261
Mr. Charles Ostdiek 3808 Harney St., #4 Omaha, NE 68131(2nd District)

Third Congressional District Total Votes Received: 264
Mr. Josh Skufca 3058 S. 41 Omaha, NE 68105 (3rd District)

<u>By Petition</u>   **Roger Calero, President/Arrin Hawkins, Vice President**
Statewide Total Votes Received: 82

Electors: Mr. Nelson F. Gonzalez 4731 S 24th St., Apt. 209 Omaha, NE 68107 (At Large)
Mr. David Z. Rosenfeld 4841 S 24th St. Omaha, NE 68107 (At Large)

First Congressional District Total Votes Received: 30
Ms. Lisa J. Krueger 5951 Oakridge Dr. Lincoln, NE 68516 (1st District)

Second Congressional District Total Votes Received: 23
Ms. Lisa M. Rottach 4841 S 24th St. Omaha, NE 68107 (2nd District)

Third Congressional District Total Votes Received: 29
Mr. Wayne Honsermeier 1206 Nebraska Hwy 2 Phillips, NE 68865 (3rd District)

<u>By Petition</u>   **Ralph Nader, President, Peter Miguel Camejo, Vice President**
Statewide Total Votes Received: 5,698

Electors: Ms. Diana McIntyre-Wright 5621 Dogwood Dr. Lincoln, NE 68516 (At Large)
Ms. Irma Sarata 2000 SW 47th St. Lincoln, NE 68522 (At Large)

First Congressional District Total Votes Received: 2,025
Ms. Amber McIntyre 5621 Dogwood Dr. Lincoln, NE 68516 (1st District)

Second Congressional District Total Votes Received: 1,731
Ms. Susan Robinson 9815 Pasadena Ave. Omaha, NE 68124 (2nd District)

Third Congressional District Total Votes Received: 1,942
Mr. Lee R. Heerten HC 81 PO Box 121 Springview, NE 68778

We hereby certify the names of the Republican Party Electors associated with the Bush-Cheney ticket have been duly appointed and notified by certified mail by the Governor and will appear at the State Capitol, Lincoln, Nebraska on the 13th day of December 2004, for the purpose of casting Nebraska's five Electoral College votes.

We hereunto affix our signatures this 13th day of December, 2004, at Lincoln, Nebraska.

Mike Johanns
Governor

John A. Gale
Secretary of State

APPENDIX H
New York 2004 Certificate
of Ascertainment

STATE OF NEW YORK

BY

George E. Pataki

GOVERNOR

I, **GEORGE E. PATAKI**, Governor of the State of New York, do hereby certify, that the statement containing the Canvass and Certificate of Determination by the State Board of Canvassers of the State of New York, as to **ELECTORS of PRESIDENT and VICE-PRESIDENT** hereto annexed, and certified by the Chairperson of the State Board of Elections of said State, under her seal of office, contains a true and correct list setting forth the names of Electors of President and Vice-President, elected in said State, at the General Election held in said State on the Tuesday after the First Monday in November (November second), in the year two thousand four, pursuant to the Constitution and Laws of the United States and of the State of New York, to wit:

Joseph Ashton	Bertha Lewis
Bill De Blasio	Alan Lubin
Molly Clifford	Thomas Manton
Lorraine Cortes-Vazquez	Dennis Mehiel
Inez Dickens	June O'Neill
Danny Donahue	David Paterson
Herman D. Farrell	Jose Rivera
Virginia Fields	Rich Schaffer
Emily Giske	Chung Seto
Bea Gonzalez	Sheldon Silver
Alan Hevesi	Eliot Spitzer
Frank Hoare	Antoine Thompson
Virginia Kee	Paul Tokasz
Peggy Kerry	Bill Wood
Denise King	Robert Zimmerman
Len Lenihan	

And further that the Statement of Canvass and Certificate of Determination certified by the Chairperson of the State Board of Elections of said State, as aforesaid, correctly sets forth the Canvass of Determination under the Laws of said State of New York, of the number of votes given or cast for each person for whose elections any and all votes have been given or cast at said election as aforesaid.

In Testimony Whereof, The Great Seal of the State is hereunto affixed.

Witness my hand at the City of Albany, the tenth day of December, in the year two thousand four.

Attested by

Secretary of State

We, the State Board of Elections, constituting the State Board of Canvassers, having canvassed the whole number of votes given for the office of ELECTOR of PRESIDENT and VICE-PRESIDENT at the general election held in said State, on the Second day of November, 2004, according to the certified statement of canvass received by the State Board of Elections, in the manner directed by law, do hereby determine, declare and certify that

Joseph Ashton	Bertha Lewis
Bill De Blasio	Alan Lubin
Molly Clifford	Thomas Manton
Lorraine Cortes-Vazquez	Dennis Mehiel
Inez Dickens	June O'Neill
Danny Donahue	David Paterson
Herman D. Farrell	Jose Rivera
Virginia Fields	Rich Schaffer
Emily Giske	Chung Seto
Bea Gonzalez	Sheldon Silver
Alan Hevesi	Eliot Spitzer
Frank Hoare	Antoine Thompson
Virginia Kee	Paul Tokasz
Peggy Kerry	Bill Wood
Denise King	Robert Zimmerman
Len Lenihan	

were, by the greatest number of votes given at said election duly elected ELECTOR of PRESIDENT and VICE-PRESIDENT of the United States.

GIVEN under our hands in Sloatsburg, New York, the 6th day of December in the year two thousand four.

Carol Berman	Commissioner
Neil W. Kelleher	Commissioner
Evelyn J. Aquila	Commissioner
Helena Moses Donohue	Commissioner

STATE OF NEW YORK   :
                                          : ss:
STATE BOARD OF ELECTIONS :

I certify that I have compared the foregoing with the original certificate filed in this office, and that the same is a correct transcript therefrom and of the whole of such original.

GIVEN under my hand and official seal of office of the State Board of Elections, in Sloatsburg, New York, this 6th day of December in the year two thousand four.

Carol Berman
Carol Berman   Chairperson

STATE OF NEW YORK, ss:

Statement of the whole number of votes cast for all the candidates for the office of ELECTOR OF PRESIDENT and VICE-PRESIDENT at a General Election held in said State on the Second day of November, 2004.

The whole number of votes given for the office of ELECTOR OF PRESIDENT and VICE-PRESIDENT was **7,448,266** of which

		REPUBLICAN	CONSERVATIVE	TOTAL
George E. Pataki	received	2,806,993	155,574	2,962,567
Alexander F. Treadwell	received	2,806,993	155,574	2,962,567
Joseph Bruno	received	2,806,993	155,574	2,962,567
Charles Nesbitt	received	2,806,993	155,574	2,962,567
Mary Donohue	received	2,806,993	155,574	2,962,567
Rudolph Giuliani	received	2,806,993	155,574	2,962,567
Charles Gargano	received	2,806,993	155,574	2,962,567
Joseph Mondello	received	2,806,993	155,574	2,962,567
J. Patrick Barrett	received	2,806,993	155,574	2,962,567
John F. Nolan	received	2,806,993	155,574	2,962,567
Robert Davis	received	2,806,993	155,574	2,962,567
Peter J. Savago	received	2,806,993	155,574	2,962,567
Maggie Brooks	received	2,806,993	155,574	2,962,567
Catherine Blaney	received	2,806,993	155,574	2,962,567
Howard Mills	received	2,806,993	155,574	2,962,567
John Cahill	received	2,806,993	155,574	2,962,567
Rita DiMartino	received	2,806,993	155,574	2,962,567
Libby Pataki	received	2,806,993	155,574	2,962,567
Stephen Minarik	received	2,806,993	155,574	2,962,567
Raymond Meier	received	2,806,993	155,574	2,962,567
Thomas M. Reynolds	received	2,806,993	155,574	2,962,567
Adam Stoll	received	2,806,993	155,574	2,962,567
Herman Badillo	received	2,806,993	155,574	2,962,567
Jane Forbes Clark	received	2,806,993	155,574	2,962,567
James Garner	received	2,806,993	155,574	2,962,567
Shawn Marie Levine	received	2,806,993	155,574	2,962,567
Viola J. Hunter	received	2,806,993	155,574	2,962,567
Laura Schreiner	received	2,806,993	155,574	2,962,567
Carmen Gomez Goldberg	received	2,806,993	155,574	2,962,567
Bernadette Castro	received	2,806,993	155,574	2,962,567
Cathy Jimino	received	2,806,993	155,574	2,962,567

		DEMOCRATIC	WORKING FAM.	TOTAL
Joseph Ashton	received	4,180,755	133,525	4,314,280
Bill De Blasio	received	4,180,755	133,525	4,314,280
Molly Clifford	received	4,180,755	133,525	4,314,280
Lorraine Cortes-Vazquez	received	4,180,755	133,525	4,314,280
Inez Dickens	received	4,180,755	133,525	4,314,280
Danny Donahue	received	4,180,755	133,525	4,314,280
Herman D. Farrell	received	4,180,755	133,525	4,314,280
Virginia Fields	received	4,180,755	133,525	4,314,280
Emily Giske	received	4,180,755	133,525	4,314,280
Bea Gonzalez	received	4,180,755	133,525	4,314,280
Alan Hevesi	received	4,180,755	133,525	4,314,280
Frank Hoare	received	4,180,755	133,525	4,314,280
Virginia Kee	received	4,180,755	133,525	4,314,280
Peggy Kerry	received	4,180,755	133,525	4,314,280
Denise King	received	4,180,755	133,525	4,314,280
Len Lenihan	received	4,180,755	133,525	4,314,280
Bertha Lewis	received	4,180,755	133,525	4,314,280
Alan Lubin	received	4,180,755	133,525	4,314,280
Thomas Manton	received	4,180,755	133,525	4,314,280
Dennis Mehiel	received	4,180,755	133,525	4,314,280
June O'Neill	received	4,180,755	133,525	4,314,280
David Paterson	received	4,180,755	133,525	4,314,280
Jose Rivera	received	4,180,755	133,525	4,314,280
Rich Schaffer	received	4,180,755	133,525	4,314,280
Chung Seto	received	4,180,755	133,525	4,314,280
Sheldon Silver	received	4,180,755	133,525	4,314,280
Eliot Spitzer	received	4,180,755	133,525	4,314,280
Antoine Thompson	received	4,180,755	133,525	4,314,280
Paul Tokasz	received	4,180,755	133,525	4,314,280
Bill Wood	received	4,180,755	133,525	4,314,280
Robert Zimmerman	received	4,180,755	133,525	4,314,280

		INDEPENDENCE	TOTAL
Fran Siems	received	84,247	84,247
Barbara Smith	received	84,247	84,247
Theresa Smith	received	84,247	84,247
Joseph Baruth	received	84,247	84,247
Howard Edelbaum	received	84,247	84,247
Bryan Puertas	received	84,247	84,247
Barbara Pershay	received	84,247	84,247
Elizabeth Allen	received	84,247	84,247
Paul Gouldin	received	84,247	84,247
Joan Fleischman	received	84,247	84,247
Ken Gallashaw	received	84,247	84,247
Robert Conroy	received	84,247	84,247
Bobby Soto	received	84,247	84,247
Lenora Fulani	received	84,247	84,247
Harry Kresky	received	84,247	84,247
Amy Jo Butler	received	84,247	84,247
Rebecca Seward	received	84,247	84,247
Lili Vega	received	84,247	84,247
Jeff Graham	received	84,247	84,247
Patricia Anken	received	84,247	84,247
Judith Resen	received	84,247	84,247
Paul Caputo	received	84,247	84,247
Jessie Field	received	84,247	84,247
Sarah Lyons	received	84,247	84,247
Judith A. Orsini	received	84,247	84,247
Lee Kolesnikoff	received	84,247	84,247
Ben Curtis	received	84,247	84,247
Lorraine Stevens	received	84,247	84,247
Frank Mackay	received	84,247	84,247
Eileen Trace	received	84,247	84,247
Richard Schulman	received	84,247	84,247

		PEACE & JUSTICE	TOTAL
Sally J. Cass	received	15,626	15,626
Mitchel Cohen	received	15,626	15,626
Millicent Y. Collins	received	15,626	15,626
Edward T. Dodge	received	15,626	15,626
Mark A. Dunlea	received	15,626	15,626
J. David Edelstein	received	15,626	15,626
James Farney	received	15,626	15,626
Leslie Farney	received	15,626	15,626
Anthony Gronowicz	received	15,626	15,626
Howie Hawkins	received	15,626	15,626
Gerald F. Kann	received	15,626	15,626
Alan B. Kendrick-Bowser	received	15,626	15,626
James C. Lane	received	15,626	15,626
Peter LaVenia	received	15,626	15,626
Daniella Liebling	received	15,626	15,626
Joseph Lombardo	received	15,626	15,626
Ronald J. MacKinnon	received	15,626	15,626
Jessica L. Maxwell	received	15,626	15,626
Robin L. Miller	received	15,626	15,626
Steven Penn	received	15,626	15,626
Stephen H. Reynolds	received	15,626	15,626
Rebecca Rotzler	received	15,626	15,626
Leigh C. Safford	received	15,626	15,626
Eric Salzman	received	15,626	15,626
Lorna Salzman	received	15,626	15,626
Rachel Treichler	received	15,626	15,626
Jason West	received	15,626	15,626
Betty K. Wood	received	15,626	15,626
Paul H. Zulkowitz	received	15,626	15,626

		SOCIALIST WORKERS	TOTAL
Michael J. Fitzsimmons	received	2,405	2,405
Olga L. Rodriguez	received	2,405	2,405

		LIBERTARIAN	TOTAL
Richard A. Cooper	received	11,607	11,607
Dawn Davis	received	11,607	11,607
Donald H. Davis	received	11,607	11,607
Robert S. Flanzer	received	11,607	11,607
Christopher B. Garvey	received	11,607	11,607
David A. Harnett	received	11,607	11,607
James E. Harris	received	11,607	11,607
Loretta K. Hetzner	received	11,607	11,607
Werner Hetzner	received	11,607	11,607
David J. Hopwood	received	11,607	11,607
Nicolas Leobold	received	11,607	11,607
Jim Lesczynski	received	11,607	11,607
Adam Martin	received	11,607	11,607
Bruce A. Martin	received	11,607	11,607
Crystal Martin	received	11,607	11,607
William P. McMillen	received	11,607	11,607
Ronald G. Moore	received	11,607	11,607
John C. Mounteer	received	11,607	11,607
Christian Padgett	received	11,607	11,607
Audrey M. Pappaeliou	received	11,607	11,607
Gary S. Popkin	received	11,607	11,607
Louise Popkin	received	11,607	11,607
Eleanor Rosenblatt	received	11,607	11,607
Catherine Ruks	received	11,607	11,607
Thomas Ruks	received	11,607	11,607
Norma Segal	received	11,607	11,607
Donald Silberger	received	11,607	11,607
Sam Sloan	received	11,607	11,607
Thomas Robert Stevens	received	11,607	11,607
Michael L. Trombetta	received	11,607	11,607
Alexander E. Ulmann, III	received	11,607	11,607

GIVEN under our hands in Sloatsburg, New York, the 6th day of December in the year two thousand four.

Carol Berman   Commissioner
Neil W. Kelleher   Commissioner
Evelyn J. Aquila   Commissioner
Helena Moses Donohue Commissioner

STATE OF NEW YORK   :
                   : ss:
STATE BOARD OF ELECTIONS :

    I certify that I have compared the foregoing with the original certificate filed in this office, and that the same is a correct transcript therefrom and of the whole of such original.

GIVEN under my hand and official seal of office of the State Board of Elections, in the City of Albany, this 6th day of December, 2004.

Peter S. Kosinski   Deputy Executive Director

APPENDIX I
Mississippi 2004 Certificate of Ascertainment

CERTIFICATE OF ASCERTAINMENT

TO: THE HONORABLE JOHN W. CARLIN
ARCHIVIST OF THE UNITED STATES
NATIONAL ARCHIVES AND RECORDS ADMINISTRATION

I, HALEY BARBOUR, Governor of the State of Mississippi, in accordance with Chapter 1, Section 6 of Title 3, United States Code, do hereby certify as follows:

At the General Election held on Tuesday, November 2, 2004, the qualified electors of the state at large elected and appointed six (6) Presidential and Vice Presidential Electors for the State of Mississippi; and

There was no controversy or contest concerning the election of all or of any of such Electors; and

Pursuant to the applicable laws of this state, final ascertainment has now been made of the results of the November 2, 2004, General Election, and the following named persons have been elected and appointed to serve as, and to discharge the duties of, Presidential and Vice Presidential Electors for the State of Mississippi:

ELECTORS FOR GEORGE W. BUSH FOR PRESIDENT AND DICK CHENEY FOR VICE PRESIDENT (REPUBLICAN PARTY)

Mr. James H. "Jimmy" Creekmore	684,981
Mr. Victor Mavar	684,981
Mr. W.D. "Billy" Mounger	684,981
Mr. Wayne Parker	684,981
Mr. John F. Phillips	684,981
Dr. Kelly S. Segars	684,981.

I do further certify that the number of votes cast at the November 2, 2004, General Election for the other candidates for election as Presidential and Vice Presidential Electors has been finally ascertained to be:

ELECTORS FOR JOHN F. KERRY FOR PRESIDENT AND JOHN EDWARDS FOR VICE PRESIDENT (DEMOCRATIC PARTY)

Mr. Gary Bailey	458,094
Ms. Janice Carr	458,094
Mr. Robert Hooks	458,094
Ms. Tamara Longmire	458,094
Mrs. Tyna Stewart	458,094
Mr. Al Tate	458,094

ELECTORS FOR MICHAEL BADNARIK FOR PRESIDENT AND RICHARD V. CAMPAGNA FOR VICE PRESIDENT (LIBERTARIAN PARTY)

Mr. Mark G. Bushman	1,793
Mr. Victor G. Dostrow	1,793
Ms. Lana Renee Ethridge	1,793
Mr. Lewis W. Napper	1,793
Mr. Harold M. Taylor	1,793
Ms. Leighanne A. Taylor	1,793

417

ELECTORS FOR DAVID COBB FOR PRESIDENT AND PATRICIA LAMARCHE FOR VICE PRESIDENT (GREEN PARTY)

Mr. Sherman Lee Dillon	1,073
Mr. Ray Gebhart	1,073
Ms. Jan Hillegas	1,073
Mr. Greg Johnson	1,073
Mr. Claude Evan Peacock	1,073
Ms. Gwendolyn M. Wages	1,073

ELECTORS FOR JAMES HARRIS FOR PRESIDENT AND MARGARET TROWE FOR VICE PRESIDENT (INDEPENDENT)

Ms. Barbara Bell	1,268
Mr. Roy Bell	1,268
Ms. Joann Hogan	1,268
Ms. Penny Hogan	1,268
Mr. R.C. Howard	1,268
Ms. Linda Miles	1,268

ELECTORS FOR RALPH NADER FOR PRESIDENT AND PETER MIGUEL CAMEJO FOR VICE PRESIDENT (REFORM PARTY)

Mr. Rodney (Billy) Fulgham	3,177
Ms. Carroll Grantham	3,177
Mr. John A. Hailey	3,177
Ms. Lamonica L. Magee	3,177
Mr. Billy Minshew	3,177
Mr. Christopher Minshew	3,177

ELECTORS FOR MICHAEL A. PEROUTKA FOR PRESIDENT AND CHUCK BALDWIN FOR VICE PRESIDENT (CONSTITUTION PARTY)

Mr. John C. Bethea	1,759
Mr. Jim Bourland	1,759
Mr. Tim Delrie	1,759
Mr. Thomas R. Floyd	1,759
Mr. Leslie Riley	1,759
Mr. Steve C. Thornton	1,759.

IN WITNESS WHEREOF, I have hereunto set my hand and caused the Great Seal of the State of Mississippi to be affixed.

DONE at the Capitol, in the City of Jackson, this the 22nd day of March, in the year of our Lord, Two thousand and five, and of the Independence of the United States of America, the two hundred and twenty ninth.

GOVERNOR

BY THE GOVERNOR

SECRETARY OF STATE

APPENDIX J
Dates Appearing on Certificates of Ascertainment for 2000 and 2004 Presidential Elections

TABLE J.1 KEY DATES IN 2000 AND 2004 PRESIDENTIAL ELECTION PROCESS

	DATE FOR 2000	DATE FOR 2004
Election day	November 7, 2000	November 2, 2004
Safe harbor day	December 12, 2000	December 7, 2004
Electoral college meeting day	December 18, 2000	December 13, 2004

TABLE J.2 DATES APPEARING ON 2000 AND 2004 CERTIFICATES OF ASCERTAINMENT

JURISDICTION	DATE FOR 2000	DATE FOR 2004
Alabama	December 8, 2000	November 29, 2004
Alaska	December 5, 2000	December 7, 2004
Arizona	December 4, 2000	November 22, 2004
Arkansas	November 30, 2000	November 23, 2004
California	December 14, 2000	December 13, 2004
Colorado	December 4, 2000	December 13, 2004
Connecticut	November 29, 2000	November 24, 2004
Delaware	December 4, 2000	November 30, 2004
District of Columbia	December 6, 2000	December 7, 2004
Florida	November 26, 2000	November 18, 2004
Georgia	December 1, 2000	November 23, 2004
Hawaii	November 27, 2000	November 22, 2004
Idaho	November 22, 2000	November 17, 2004
Illinois	November, 27, 2000	December 3, 2004
Indiana	December 5, 2000	December 7, 2004
Iowa	December 14, 2000	December 13, 2004
Kansas	December 6, 2000	December 8, 2004
Kentucky	December 4, 2000	December 1, 2004
Louisiana	November 21, 2000	November 16, 2004
Maine	November 27, 2000	November 23, 2004
Maryland	December 18, 2000	December 13, 2004
Massachusetts	December 6, 2000	December 13, 2004

420 | *Appendix J*

TABLE J.2 DATES APPEARING ON 2000 AND 2004 CERTIFICATES OF ASCERTAINMENT *(cont.)*

JURISDICTION	DATE FOR 2000	DATE FOR 2004
Michigan	November 30, 2000	November 30, 2004
Minnesota	December 5, 2000	November 30, 2004
Mississippi	December 7, 2000	December 13, 2004
Missouri	December 11, 2000	December 13, 2004
Montana	December 6, 2000	December 8, 2004
Nebraska	December 18, 2000	December 13, 2004
Nevada	December 4, 2000	December 7, 2004
New Hampshire	December 6, 2000	December 1, 2004
New Jersey	December 8, 2000	December 13, 2004
New Mexico	December 5, 2000	December 3, 2004
New York	December 12, 2000	December 6, 2004
North Carolina	December 8, 2000	December 1, 2004
North Dakota	November 27, 2000	December 3, 2004
Ohio	December 11, 2000	December 6, 2004
Oklahoma	December 8, 2000	December 13, 2004
Oregon	No date	No date
Pennsylvania	December 14, 2000	December 10, 2004
Rhode Island	November 22, 2000	November 23, 2004
South Carolina	November 28, 2000	December 3, 2004
South Dakota	November 28, 2000	December 13, 2004
Tennessee	November 28, 2000	December 7, 2004
Texas	November 27, 2000	November 18, 2004
Utah	December 1, 2000	December 13, 2004
Vermont	December 9, 2000	December 3, 2004
Virginia	November 29, 2000	December 13, 2004
Washington	December 7, 2000	December 9, 2004
West Virginia	December 11, 2000	December 13, 2004
Wisconsin	December 11, 2000	December 6, 2004
Wyoming	November 22, 2000	December 2, 2004

APPENDIX K
Ohio Adoption of the
Great Lakes Basin Compact

SECTION 6161.01 (EFFECTIVE ON OCTOBER 9, 1963)

The "great lakes basin compact" is hereby ratified, enacted into law, and entered into by this state as a party thereto with any other state or province which, pursuant to Article II of said compact, has legally joined in the compact as follows:

GREAT LAKES BASIN COMPACT

The party states solemnly agree:

ARTICLE I

The purposes of this compact are, through means of joint or co-operative action:

(A) To promote the orderly, integrated, and comprehensive development, use, and conservation of the water sources of the great lakes basin (hereinafter called the basin);

(B) To plan for the welfare and development of the water resources of the basin as a whole, as well as for those portions of the basin which may have problems of special concern;

(C) To make it possible for the states of the basin and their people to derive the maximum benefit from utilization of public works, in the form of navigational aids or otherwise, which may exist or which may be constructed from time to time;

(D) To advise in securing and maintaining a proper balance among industrial, commercial, agricultural, water supply, residential, recreational, and other legitimate uses of the water resources of the basin;

(E) To establish and maintain an intergovernmental agency to the end that the purposes of this compact may be accomplished more effectively.

ARTICLE II

(A) This compact shall enter into force and become effective and binding when it has been enacted by the legislatures of any four of the states of Illinois, Indiana, Michigan, Minnesota, New York, Ohio, Pennsylvania, and Wisconsin and thereafter shall enter into force and become effective and binding as to any other of said states when enacted by the legislature thereof.

(B) The province of Ontario and the province of Quebec, or either of them, may become states party to this compact by taking such action as their laws and the laws of the government of Canada may prescribe for adherence thereto. For the purpose of this compact the word "state" shall be construed in include a province of Canada.

ARTICLE III

The great lakes commission created by Article IV of this compact shall exercise its powers and perform its functions in respect to the basin which, for the purposes of this compact, shall consist of so much of the following as may be within the party states:

(A) Lakes Erie, Huron, Michigan, Ontario, St. Clair, Superior, and the St. Lawrence River, together with any and all natural or man-made water interconnections between or among them;

(B) All rivers, ponds, lakes, streams, and other watercourses which, in their natural state or in their prevailing condition, are tributary to Lakes Erie, Huron, Michigan, Ontario, St. Clair, and Superior, or any of them, or which comprise part of any watershed draining into any of said lakes.

ARTICLE IV

(A) There is hereby created an agency of the party states to be known as the great lakes commission (hereinafter called the commission). In that name the commission may sue and be sued, acquire, hold and convey real and personal property, and any interest therein. The commission shall have a seal with the words "the great lakes commission" and such other design as it may prescribe engraved thereon by which it shall authenticate its proceedings. Transactions involving real or personal property shall conform to the laws of the state in which the property is located, and the commission may by bylaws provide for the execution and acknowledgement of all instruments in its behalf.

(B) The commission shall be composed of not less than three commissioners nor more than five commissioners from each party state designated or appointed in accordance with the law of the state which they represent and serving and subject to removal in accordance with such law.

(C) Each state delegation shall be entitled to three votes in the commission. The presence of commissioners from a majority of the party states shall constitute a quorum for the transaction of business at any meeting of the commission. Actions of the commission shall be by a majority of the votes cast except that any recommendations made pursuant to Article VI of this compact shall require an affirmative vote of not less than a majority of the votes cast from each of a majority of the states present and voting.

(D) The commissioners of any two or more party states may meet separately to consider problems of particular interest to their states but no action taken at any such meeting shall be deemed an action of the commission unless and until the commission shall specifically approve the same.

(E) In the absence of any commissioner, his vote may be cast by another representative or commissioner of his state provided that said commissioner or other representative casting said vote shall have a written proxy in proper form as may be required by the commission.

(F) The commission shall elect annually from among its members a chairman and vice-chairman. The commission shall appoint an executive director who shall also act as secretary-treasurer, and who shall be bonded in such amount as the commission may require. The executive director shall serve at the pleasure of the commission and at such compensation and under such terms and conditions as may be fixed by it. The executive director shall be custodian of the records of the commission with authority to affix the commission's official seal and to attest and certify such records or copies thereof.

(G) The executive director, subject to the approval of the commission in such cases as its bylaws may provide, shall appoint and remove or discharge such personnel as may be necessary for the performance of the commission's functions. Subject to the aforesaid approval, the executive director may fix their compensation, define their duties, and require bonds of such of them as the commission may designate.

(H) The executive director, on behalf of, as trustee for, and with the approval of the commission, may borrow, accept, or contract for the services of personnel from any state or government or any subdivision or agency thereof, from any intergovernmental agency, or from any institution, person, firm, or corporation; and may accept for any of the commission's purposes and functions under this compact any and all donations, gifts, and grants of money, equipment, supplies, materials, and services from any state or government or any subdivision or agency thereof or intergovernmental agency or from any institution, person, firm, or corporation and may receive and utilize the same.

(I) The commission may establish and maintain one or more offices for the transacting of its business and for such purposes the executive director, on behalf of, as trustee for, and with the approval of the commission, may acquire, hold, and dispose of real and personal property necessary to the performance of its functions.

(J) No tax levied or imposed by any party state or any political subdivision thereof shall be deemed to apply to property, transactions, or income of the commission.

(K) The commission may adopt, amend, and rescind bylaws, rules, and regulations for the conduct of its business.

(L) The organization meeting of the commission shall be held within six months from the effective date of this compact.

(M) The commission and its executive director shall make available to the party states any information within its possession and shall always provide free access to its records by duly authorized representatives of such party states.

(N) The commission shall keep a written record of its meetings and proceedings and shall annually make a report thereof to be submitted to the duly designated official of each party state.

(O) The commission shall make and transmit annually to the legislature and governor of each party state a report covering the activities of the commission for the preceding year and embodying such recommendations as may have been adopted by the commission. The commission may issue such additional reports as it may deem desirable.

ARTICLE V

(A) The members of the commission shall serve without compensation, but the expenses of each commissioner shall be met by the state which he represents in accordance with the law of that state. All other expenses incurred by the commission in the course of exercising the powers conferred upon it by this compact, unless met in some other manner specifically provided by this compact, shall be paid by the commission out of its own funds.

(B) The commission shall submit to the executive head or designated officer of each party state a budget of its estimated expenditures for such period as may be required by the laws of the state for presentation to the legislature thereof.

(C) Each of the commission's budgets of estimated expenditures shall contain specific recommendations of the amount or amounts to be appropriated by each of the party states. Detailed commission budgets shall be recommended by a majority of the votes cast, and the costs shall be allocated equitably among the party states in accordance with their respective interests.

(D) The commission shall not pledge the credit of any party state. The commission may meet any of it obligations in whole or in part with funds available to it under Article IV (H) of this compact, provided that the commission takes specific action setting aside such funds prior to the incurring of any obligations to be met in whole or in part in this manner. Except where the commission makes use of funds available to it under Article IV (H) hereof, the commission shall not incur any obligations prior to the allotment of funds by the party states adequate to meet the same.

(E) The commission shall keep accurate accounts of all receipts and disbursements. The receipts and disbursements of the commission shall be subject to the audit and accounting procedures established under the bylaws. However, all receipts and disbursements of funds handled by the commission shall be audited yearly by a qualified public accountant and the report of the audit shall be included in and become a part of the annual report of the commission.

(F) The accounts of the commission shall be open at any reasonable time for inspection by such agency, representative, or representatives of the party states as may be duly constituted for that purpose and by others who may be authorized by the commission.

ARTICLE VI

The commission shall have power to:

(A) Collect, correlate, interpret, and report on data relating to the water resources and the use thereof in the basin or any portion thereof;

(B) Recommend methods for the orderly, efficient, and balanced development, use, and conservation of the water resources of the basin or any portion thereof to the party states and to any other governments or agencies having interests in or jurisdiction over the basin or any portion thereof;

(C) Consider the need for and desirability of public works and improvements relating to the water resources in the basin or any portion thereof;

(D) Consider means of improving navigation and port facilities in the basin or any portion thereof;

(E) Consider means of improving and maintaining the fisheries of the basin or any portion thereof;

(F) Recommend policies relating to water resources including the institution and alteration of flood plain and other zoning laws, ordinances, and regulations;

(G) Recommend uniform or other laws, ordinances, or regulations relating to the development, use, and conservation of the basin's water resources to the party states or any of them and to other governments, political subdivisions, agencies, or intergovernmental bodies having interests in or jurisdiction sufficient to affect conditions in the basin or any portion thereof;

(H) Consider and recommend amendments or agreements supplementary to this compact to the party states or any of them, and assist in the formulation and drafting of such amendments or supplementary agreements;

(I) Prepare and publish reports, bulletins, and publications appropriate to this work and fix reasonable sale prices therefor;

(J) With respect to the water resources of the basin or any portion thereof, recommend agreements between the governments of the United States and Canada;

(K) Recommend mutual arrangements expressed by concurrent or reciprocal legislation on the part of congress and the parliament of Canada including but not limited to such agreements and mutual arrangement as are provided for by Article XIII of the Treaty of 1909 Relating to Boundary Waters and Questions Arising Between the United States and Canada. (Treaty Series, No. 548);

(L) Co-operate with the governments of the United States and of Canada, the party states and any public or private agencies or bodies having interests in or jurisdiction sufficient to affect the basin or any portion thereof;

(M) At the request of the United States, or in the event that a province shall be a party state, at the request of the government of Canada, assist in the negotiation and formulation of any treaty or other mutual arrangement or agreement between the United States and Canada with reference to the basin or any portion thereof;

(N) Make any recommendation and do all things necessary and proper to carry out the powers conferred upon the commission by this compact, provided that no action of the commission shall have the force of law in, or be binding upon, any party state.

ARTICLE VII

Each party state agrees to consider the action the commission recommends in respect to:

(A) Stabilization of lake levels;

(B) Measures for combating pollution, beach erosion, floods, and shore inundation;

(C) Uniformity in navigation regulations within the constitutional powers of the states;

(D) Proposed navigation aids and improvements;

(E) Uniformity or effective co-ordinating action in fishing laws and regulations and co-operative action to eradicate destructive and parasitical forces endangering the fisheries, wild life, and other water resources;

(F) Suitable hydroelectric power developments;

(G) Co-operative programs for control of soil and bank erosion for the general improvement of the basin;

(H) Diversion of waters from and into the basin;

(I) Other measures the commission may recommend to the states pursuant to Article VI of this compact.

ARTICLE VIII

This compact shall continue in force and remain binding upon each party state until renounced by act of the legislature of such state, in such form and manner as it may choose and as may be valid and effective to repeal a statute of said state, provided that such renunciation shall not become effective until six months after notice of such action shall have been officially communicated in writing to the executive head of the other party states.

ARTICLE IX

It is intended that the provisions of this compact shall be reasonably and liberally construed to effectuate the purposes thereof. The provisions of this compact shall be severable and if any phrase, clause, sentence, or provision of this compact is declared to be contrary to the constitution of any party state or of the United States, or in the case of a province, to the British North America Act of 1867 as amended, or the applicability thereof to any state, agency, person, or circumstance is held invalid, the constitutionality of the remainder of this compact and the applicability thereof to any state, agency, person, or circumstance shall not be affected thereby, provided further that if this compact shall be held contrary to the constitution of the United States, or in the case of a province, to the British North America Act of 1867 as amended, or of any party state, the compact shall remain in full force and effect as to the remaining states and in full force and effect as to the state affected as to all severable matters.

APPENDIX L
Congressional Consent to the Interstate Agreement on Detainers

PUBLIC LAW 91-538 OF 1970

AN ACT
To enact the Interstate Agreement on Detainers into law

Be it enacted by the Senate and House of Representatives of the United States of America in congress assembled, That this Act may be cited as the "Interstate Agreement on Detainers Act".

Sec. 2. The Interstate Agreement on Detainers is hereby enacted into law and entered into by the United States on its own behalf and on behalf of the District of Columbia with all jurisdictions legally joining in substantially the following form:

"The contracting States solemnly agree that:

"Article I
"The party States find that charges outstanding against a prisoner, detainers based on untried indictments, informations, or complaints and difficulties in securing speedy trial of persons already incarcerated in other jurisdictions, produce uncertainties which obstruct programs of prisoner treatment and rehabilitation. Accordingly, it is the policy of the party States and the purpose of this agreement to encourage the expeditious and orderly disposition of such charges and determination of the proper status of any and all detainers based on untried indictments, informations, or complaints. The party States also find that proceedings with reference to such charges and detainers, when emanating from another jurisdiction, cannot properly be had in the absence of coop-

429

erative procedures. It is the further purpose of this agreement to provide such cooperative procedures.

"Article II

"As used in this agreement:

"(a) 'State' shall mean a State of the United States; the United States of America; a territory or possession of the United States; the District of Columbia; the Commonwealth of Puerto Rico.

"(b) 'Sending State' shall mean a State in which a prisoner is incarcerated at the time that he initiates a request for final disposition pursuant to article III hereof or at the time that a request for custody or availability is initiated pursuant to article IV hereof.

"(c) 'Receiving State' shall mean the State in which trial is to be had on an indictment, information, or complaint pursuant to article III or article IV hereof.

"Article III

"(a) Whenever a person has entered upon a term of imprisonment in a penal or correctional institution of a party State, and whenever during the continuance of the term of imprisonment there is pending in any other party State any untried indictment, information, or complaint on the basis of which a detainer has been lodged against the prisoner, he shall be brought to trial within one hundred and eighty days after he shall have caused to be delivered to the prosecuting officer and the appropriate court of the prosecuting officer's jurisdiction written notice of the place of his imprisonment and his request for a final disposition to be made of the indictment, information, or complaint: Provided, That, for good cause shown in open court, the prisoner or his counsel being present, the court having jurisdiction of the matter may grant any necessary or reasonable continuance. The request of the prisoner shall be accompanied by a certificate of the appropriate official having custody of the prisoner, stating the term of commitment under which the prisoner is being held, the time already served, the time remaining to be served on the sentence, the amount of good time earned, the time of parole eligibility of the prisoner, and any decision of the State parole agency relating to the prisoner.

"(b) The written notice and request for final disposition referred to in paragraph (a) hereof shall be given or sent by the prisoner to the warden, commissioner of corrections, or other official having custody of him, who shall promptly forward it together with the certificate to the appropriate prosecuting official and court by registered or certified mail, return receipt requested.

"(c) The warden, commissioner of corrections, or other official having custody of the prisoner shall promptly inform him of the source and contents of any detainer lodged against him and shall also inform him of his right to make a request for final disposition of the indictment, information, or complaint on which the detainer is based.

"(d) Any request for final disposition made by a prisoner pursuant to paragraph (a) hereof shall operate as a request for final disposition of all untried indictments, informations, or complaints on the basis of which detainers have been lodged against the prisoner from the State to whose prosecuting official the request for final disposition is specifically directed. The warden, commissioner of corrections, or other official having custody of the prisoner shall forthwith notify all appropriate prosecuting officers and courts in the several jurisdictions within the State to which the prisoner's request for final disposition is being sent of the proceeding being initiated by the prisoner. Any notification sent pursuant to this paragraph shall be accompanied by copies of the prisoner's written notice, request, and the certificate. If trial is not had on any indictment, information, or complaint contemplated hereby prior to the return of the prisoner to the original place of imprisonment, such indictment, information, or complaint shall not be of any further force or effect, and the court shall enter an order dismissing the same with prejudice.

"(e) Any request for final disposition made by a prisoner pursuant to paragraph (a) hereof shall also be deemed to be a waiver of extradition with respect to any charge or proceeding contemplated thereby or included therein by reason of paragraph (d) hereof, and a waiver of extradition to the receiving State to serve any sentence there imposed upon him after completion of his term of imprisonment in the sending State. The request for final disposition shall also constitute a consent by the prisoner to the production of his body in any court where his presence may be required in order to effectuate the purposes of this agreement and a further consent voluntarily to be returned to the original place of imprisonment in accordance with the provisions of this agreement. Nothing in this paragraph shall prevent the imposition of a concurrent sentence if otherwise permitted by law.

"(f) Escape from custody by the prisoner subsequent to his execution of the request for final disposition referred to in paragraph (a) hereof shall void the request.

"Article IV

"(a) The appropriate officer of the jurisdiction in which an untried indictment, information, or complaint is pending shall be entitled to have a prisoner against whom he has lodged a detainer and who is serving a term of imprisonment in any party State made available in accordance with article V(a) hereof upon presentation of a written request for temporary custody or availability to the appropriate authorities of the State in which the prisoner is incarcerated: Provided, That the court having jurisdiction of such indictment, information, or complaint shall have duly approved recorded, and transmitted the request: And provided further, That there shall be a period of thirty days after receipt by the appropriate authorities before the request be honored, within which period the Governor of the sending State may disapprove the request for temporary custody or availability, either upon his own motion or upon motion of the prisoner.

"(b) Upon request of the officer's written request as provided in paragraph (a) hereof, the appropriate authorities having the prisoner in custody shall furnish the officer with a certificate stating the term of commitment under which the prisoner is being held, the time already served, the time remaining to be served on the sentence, the amount of good time earned, the time of parole eligibility of the prisoner, and any decisions of the State parole agency relating to the prisoner. Said authorities simultaneously shall furnish all other officers and appropriate courts in the receiving State who has lodged detainers against the prisoner with similar certificates and with notices informing them of the request for custody or availability and of the reasons therefor.

"(c) In respect of any proceeding made possible by this article, trial shall be commenced within one hundred and twenty days of the arrival of the prisoner in the receiving State but for good cause shown in open court, the prisoner or his counsel being present, the court having jurisdiction of the matter may grant any necessary or reasonable continuance.

"(d) Nothing contained in this article. shall be construed to deprive any prisoner of any right which he may have to contest the legality of his delivery as provided in paragraph (a) hereof, but such delivery may not be opposed or denied on the ground that the executive authority of the sending State has not affirmatively consented to or ordered such delivery.

"(e) If trial is not had on any indictment, information, or complaint contemplated hereby prior to the prisoner's being returned to the original place of imprisonment pursuant to article V(e) hereof, such indictment, information, or complaint shall not be of any further fore or effect, and the court shall enter an order dismissing the same with prejudice.

"Article V

"(a) In response to a request made under article III or article IV hereof, the appropriate authority in it sending State shall offer to deliver temporary custody of such prisoner to the appropriate authority in the State Where such indictment, information, or complaint is pending against such person in order that speedy and efficient prosecution may be had. If the request for final disposition is made by the prisoner, the offer of temporary custody shall accompany the written notice provided for in article III of this agreement. In the case of a

Federal prisoner, the appropriate authority in the receiving
State shall be entitled to temporary custody as provided by
this agreement or to the prisoner's presence in Federal custody at the place of trial, whichever custodial arrangement
may be approved by the custodian.

"(b) The officer or other representative of a State accepting
an offer of temporary custody shall present the following
upon demand:

"(1) Proper identification and evidence of his authority to act
for the State into whose temporary custody this prisoner is to
be given.

"(2) A duly certified copy of the indictment, information, or
complaint on the basis of which the detainer has been lodged
and on the basis of which the request for temporary custody
of the prisoner has been made.

"(c) If the appropriate authority shall refuse or fail to accept
temporary custody of said person, or in the event that an
action on the indictment, information, or complaint on the
basis of which the detainer has been lodged is not brought to
trial within the period provided in article III or article IV hereof, the appropriate court of the jurisdiction where the indictment, information, or complaint has been pending shall enter
an order dismissing the same with prejudice, and any detainer based thereon shall cease to be of any force or effect.

"(d) The temporary custody referred to in this agreement
shall be only for the purpose of permitting prosecution on the
charge or charges contained in one or more untried indictments, informations or complaints which form the basis of
the detainer or detainers or for prosecution on any other
charge or charges arising out of the same transaction. Except
for his attendance at court and while being transported to or
from any place at which his presence may be required, the
prisoner shall be held in a suitable jail or other facility regularly used for persons awaiting prosecution.

"(e) At the earliest practicable time consonant with the purposes of this agreement, the prisoner shall be returned to the
sending State.

"(f) During the continuance of temporary custody or while the prisoner is otherwise being made available for trial as required by this agreement, time being served on the sentence shall continue to rim but good time shall be earned by the prisoner only if, and to the extent that, the law and practice of the jurisdiction which imposed the sentence may allow.

"(g) For all purposes other than that for which temporary custody as provided in this agreement is exercised, the prisoner shall be deemed to remain in the custody of and subject to the jurisdiction of the sending State and any escape from temporary custody may be dealt with in the same manner as an escape from the original place of imprisonment or in any other manner permitted by law.

"(h) From the time that a party State receives custody of a prisoner pursuant to this agreement until such prisoner is returned to the territory and custody of the sending State, the State in which the one or more untried indictments informations, or complaints are pending or in which trial is being had shall be responsible for the prisoner and shall also pay all costs of transporting, caring for, keeping, and returning the prisoner. The provisions of this paragraph shall govern unless the States concerned shall have entered into a supplementary agreement providing for a different allocation of costs and responsibilities as between or among themselves. Nothing herein contained shall be construed to alter or affect any internal relationship among the departments, agencies, and officers of and in the government of a party State, or between a party State and its subdivisions, as to the payment of costs, or responsibilities therefor.

"Article VI

"(a) In determining the duration and expiration dates of the time periods provided in articles III and IV of this agreement, the running of said time periods shall be tolled whenever and for as long as the prisoner is unable to stand trial, as determined by the court having jurisdiction of the matter.

"(b) No provision of this agreement, and no remedy made

available by this agreement shall apply to any person who is adjudged to be mentally ill.

"Article VII

"Each State party to this agreement shall designate an officer who, acting jointly with like officers of other party States shall promulgate rules and regulations to carry out more effectively the terms and provisions of this agreement, and who shall provide, within and without the State, information necessary to the effective operation of this agreement.

"Article VIII

"This agreement shall enter into full force and effect as to a party State when such State has enacted the same into law. A State party to this agreement may withdraw herefrom by enacting a statute repealing the same. However, the withdrawal of any State shall not affect the status of any proceedings already initiated by inmates or by State officers at the time such withdrawal takes effect, nor shall it affect their rights in respect thereof.

"Article IX

"This agreement shall be liberally construed so as to effectuate its purposes. The provisions of this agreement shall be severable and if any phrase, clause, sentence, or provision of this agreement is declared to be contrary to the constitution of any party State or of the United States or the applicability' thereof to any government, agency, person, or circumstance is held invalid the validity of the remainder of this agreement and the applicability thereof to any government, agency, person or circumstance shall not be affected thereby. If this agreement shall be held contrary to the constitution of any State party hereto, the agreement shall remain in full force and effect as to the remaining States and in full force and effect as to the State affected as to all severable matters."

Sec. 3. The term "Governor" as used in the agreement on detainers shall mean with respect to the United States, the Attorney General, and with respect to the District of Columbia, the Commissioner of the District of Columbia.

Sec. 4. The term "appropriate court" as used in the agreement on detainers shall mean with respect to the United States, the courts of the United States, and with respect to the District of Columbia, the courts of the District of Columbia, in which indictments, informations, or complaints, for which disposition is sought, are pending.

Sec. 5. All courts, departments, agencies officers, and employees of the United States and of the District of Columbia are hereby directed to enforce the agreement on detainers and to cooperate with one another and with all party States in enforcing the agreement and effectuating its purpose.

Sec. 6. For the United States, the Attorney General, and for the District of Columbia, the Commissioner of the District of Columbia, shall establish such regulations, prescribe such forms, issue such instructions, and perform such other acts as he deems necessary for carrying out the provisions of this Act.

Sec. 7. The right to alter, amend, or repeal this Act is expressly reserved.

Sec. 8. This Act shall take effect on the ninetieth day after the date of its enactment.

APPENDIX M:
List of Interstate Compacts

The National Center for Interstate Compacts of the Council of State Governments has compiled the following list of 196 interstate compacts believed to be currently in force.

The National Center for Interstate Compacts (NCIC) is designed to be an information clearinghouse, a provider of training and technical assistance, and a primary facilitator in assisting states in their review, revision, and creation of new interstate compacts to solve multi-state problems or, provide alternatives to federal preemption. As such, the NCIC combines policy research and best practices, and functions as a membership association, serving the needs of compact administrators, compact commissions, and state agencies where interstate compacts are in effect.

For additional information on the National Center for Interstate Compacts (NCIC), contact John Mountjoy, Director of the National Center for Interstate Compacts at 859-244-8256 or jmountjoy@csg.org. The web address of NCIC is http://www.csg.org/CSG/Programs/National+Center+for+Interstate+Compacts/default.htm. The web address of the Council of state governments is http://www.csg.org.

LIST OF INTERSTATE COMPACTS
- Apalachicola-Chattahoochee-Flint River Basin Compact,
- Alabama-Coosa-Tallapossa River Basin Compact,
- Animas-La Plata Project Compact,
- Appalachian States Low-Level Radioactive Waste Compact,
- Arkansas-Mississippi Great River Bridge Construction Compact Arkansas,
- Arkansas River Basin Compact of 1970,
- Arkansas River Compact of 1949,

- Arkansas River Compact of 1965 (Arkansas River Basin Compact, Kansas, Oklahoma),
- Atlantic States Marine Fisheries Compact Delaware,
- Bay State–Ocean State Compact,
- Bear River Compact,
- Belle Fourche River Compact,
- Chesapeake Bay Commission Agreement (Bi/Tri-State Agreement on the Chesapeake Bay) – Chesapeake Bay Commission,
- Bi-State Criminal Justice Center Compact Arkansas,
- Bi-State Development Agency Compact Missouri (Bi-State Metropolitan District),
- Boating Offense Compact,
- Breaks Interstate Park Compact,
- Buffalo and Fort Erie Bridge Compact New York,
- Bus Taxation Proration and Reciprocity Agreement,
- California-Nevada Compact for Jurisdiction on Interstate Waters,
- Canadian River Compact – Canadian River Compact Commission,
- Central Interstate Low-Level Radioactive Waste Compact – Central Interstate Low-Level Radioactive Waste Commission,
- Central Midwest Low-Level Radioactive Waste Compact,
- Chesapeake Regional Olympic Games Authority,
- Chickasaw Trail Economic Development Compact,
- Colorado River Compact,
- Colorado River Crime Enforcement Compact (Interstate Compact for Jurisdiction on the Colorado River),
- Columbia River Compact (Oregon-Washington Columbia River Fish Compact),
- (Columbia River Gorge Compact) – Columbia River Gorge Commission,
- Compact for Pension Portability for Educators,
- (Connecticut–New York) Railroad Passenger Transportation Compact,
- Connecticut River Atlantic Salmon Compact – Connecticut River Atlantic Salmon Compact Commission,
- Connecticut River Valley Flood Control Compact,
- Costilla Creek Compact Colorado,
- Cumberland Gap National Park Compact Virginia,

- Cumbres and Toltec Scenic Railroad Compact,
- Delaware River and Bay Authority Compact (Delaware–New Jersey Compact),
- Delaware River Basin Compact – Delaware River Basin Commission,
- Delaware River Joint Toll Bridge Compact,
- Delaware River and Port Authority Compact – Delaware River Port Authority,
- Delaware Valley Urban Area Compact – Delaware Valley Regional Planning Commission,
- Delmarva Advisory Council Agreement Virginia,
- Desert Pacific Economic Region Compact
- Drivers' License Compact–American Association of Motor Vehicle Administrators,
- Emergency Management Assistance Compact,
- Great Lakes Basin Compact Indiana – Great Lakes Basin Commission,
- Great Lakes Forest Fire Compact – Great Lakes Forest Fire Compact Board,
- Gulf States Marine Fisheries Compact,
- Historic Chattahoochee Compact,
- International Registration Plan,
- International Fuel Tax Agreement (Motor Carriers),
- Interpleader Compact,
- Interstate Adoption Assistance Compact,
- (Interstate) Agreement on Qualification of Educational Personnel,
- (Interstate) Civil Defense (and Disaster Compact),
- (Interstate) Compact for (on) Adoption and Medical Assistance,
- Interstate Compact for Adult Offender Supervision,
- (Interstate) Compact for Education (Compact) – Education Commission of the States,
- (Interstate) Compact(s) on Parole and Probation (the Supervision of Parolees and Probationers) (for the Supervision of) (Interstate Compact for Supervision of Parolees and Probationers),
- (Interstate) Civil Defense (and Disaster) Compact,
- Interstate Compact on Energy (Midwest Energy Compact),
- Interstate Compact on Industrialized/Modular Buildings,

- Interstate Compact on Juveniles – Association of Juvenile Compact Administrators,
- Interstate Compact on Licensure of Participants in Live Racing with Parimutuel Wagering,
- Interstate (Compact on) Pest Control Compact – Interstate Pest Control Governing Board,
- (Interstate) Compact on (The) Placement of Children,
- Interstate (Compact to Conserve) Oil and Gas Compact Illinois – Interstate Oil and Gas Compact Commission,
- Interstate Corrections Compact,
- Interstate Dealer Licensing Compact,
- Interstate Earthquake Emergency Compact,
- Interstate Forest Fire Suppression Compact,
- Interstate Furlough Compact Utah,
- Interstate High Speed Intercity Rail Passenger Network Compact/Interstate High Speed Rail Compact,
- Interstate Insurance Receivership Compact,
- Interstate Jobs Protection Compact,
- Interstate Library Compact,
- Interstate Mining Compact – Interstate Mining Compact Commission,
- (Interstate) Mutual Aid (Agreements) Compact,
- Interstate Rail Passenger Network Compact,
- Interstate Solid Waste Compact,
- (Interstate) (Uniform) Agreement on Detainers (Interstate Compact on),
- Interstate Water Supply Compact (Vermont-New Hampshire),
- (Interstate) Wildlife Violator Compact,
- Jennings Randolph Lake Project Compact,
- Kansas City Area Transportation District and Authority Compact,
- Kansas-Missouri Flood Prevention and Control Compact Missouri,
- (Kansas/Nebraska) Big Blue River Compact,
- Klamath River Compact,
- La Plata River Compact,
- Low-Level Radioactive Waste Disposal,

- Live Horseracing Compact (the Interstate Compact on Licensure of Participants in Horse Racing with Pari-Mutuel Wagering),
- Maine-New Hampshire School District Compact,
- Mentally Disordered Offender Compact,
- Middle Atlantic (Interstate) Forest Fire Protection Compact,
- Midwestern Higher Education Compact – Midwestern Higher Education Commission,
- Midwest Interstate Passenger Rail Compact,
- Midwest Interstate Low-Level Radioactive Waste Compact,
- Minnesota-Wisconsin Boundary (Area) Compact,
- Mississippi River Interstate Pollution Phase Out Compact,
- Missouri And Kansas Metropolitan Culture District Compact,
- Missouri River Toll Bridge Compact,
- Motor Vehicle Safety Equipment Compact,
- Multistate Highway Transportation Agreement,
- Multistate Lottery Agreement
- Multistate Tax Compact–the Multistate Tax Commission,
- Mutual Interstate Aid Agreements and Compacts,
- Mutual/Military Aid Compact,
- National Crime Prevention and Privacy Compact,
- National Guard Mutual Assistance Compact,
- National Guard Mutual Assistance Counter-Drug Activities Compact,
- New England Compact on Radiological Health Protection,
- New England Compact on Involuntary Detention for Tuberculosis Control,
- New England (Interstate) Corrections Compact,
- New England Higher Education Compact – New England Board of Higher Education,
- New England Interstate Water Pollution Control Compact – New England Interstate Water Pollution Control Commission,
- New England States Emergency Military Aid Compact,
- New England (State) Police Compact Massachusetts,
- New England Truckers Compact,
- New England Truck Permit Agreement for Oversize, Non-Divisible, Interstate Loads,

- New Hampshire–Massachusetts Interstate Sewage and Waste Disposal Facilities Compact,
- New Hampshire-Vermont Interstate School Compact (Hanover-Norwich District),
- New Hampshire-Vermont Interstate Sewage And Waste Disposal Facilities Compact,
- New Jersey–Pennsylvania Turnpike Bridge Compact,
- New York–New Jersey Port Authority Compact – The Port Authority of New York & New Jersey,
- New York-Vermont Interstate School Compact,
- Nonresident Violator Compact – American Association of Motor Vehicle Administrators,
- Northern New England Low-Level Radioactive Waste Compact,
- Northeast Interstate Dairy Compact,
- Northeast Interstate Low-Level Radioactive Waste Management Compact,
- Northeast Mississippi – Northwest Alabama Railroad Authority Compact,
- Northeastern (Interstate) Forest Fire Protection Compact – Northeastern Forest Fire Protection Commission,
- Northeast Interstate Dairy Compact – Northeast Interstate Dairy Compact Committee,
- Northeast Interstate Low-Level Radioactive Waste Management Compact,
- Northwest (Interstate) Compact on Low-Level Radioactive Waste Management,
- Nurse Licensure Compact,
- Ogdensburg Bridge and Port Authority,
- Ohio River Valley Water Sanitation Compact – Ohio River Valley Sanitation Commission,
- Out-of-State Parollee Supervision,
- Pacific Marine Fisheries Compact – Pacific States Marine Fisheries Commission,
- Pacific Ocean Resources Compact,
- Pacific States Agreement on Radioactive Materials Transportation,
- Palisades Interstate Park Compact New Jersey – Palisades Interstate Park Commission,

- Pecos River Compact Texas – Pecos River Compact Commission,
- Portsmouth-Kittery Bridge Compact,
- Potomac Highlands Airport Authority,
- Potomac River Bridges Towing Compact,
- Potomac River Compact of 1958,
- Potomac Valley Compact (Conservancy District) (Potomac River Basin Interstate Compact of 1940),
- Pymatuning Lake Compact,
- Quad Cities Interstate Metropolitan Authority Compact,
- Red River Compact – Red River Compact Commission,
- Republican River Compact,
- Rio Grande Interstate Compact – Rio Grande Compact Commission,
- Rocky Mountain Low-Level Radioactive Waste Compact,
- Sabine River Compact,
- Snake River Compact,
- South Central (Interstate) Forest Fire Protection Compact,
- South Platte River Compact,
- Southern Dairy Compact,
- Southern Growth Policies (Agreements) (Board) (Compact) – Southern Growth Policies Board,
- Southern (Interstate) (Energy) (Nuclear) Compact (Southern States Energy Compact),
- Southeastern (Interstate) Forest Fire Protection Compact,
- Southeast Interstate Low-Level Radioactive Waste (Management) Compact – Southeast Interstate Low-Level Radioactive
- Waste Commission,
- (Southern) Rapid Rail Transit Compact (Mississippi-Louisiana-Alabama-Georgia Rapid Rail Transit Compact),
- Southern Regional Education Compact – Southern Regional Education Board,
- Southwestern Low-Level Radioactive Waste Disposal Compact,
- Susquehanna River Basin Compact – Susquehanna River Basin Commission,
- Tahoe Regional Planning Compact,
- Tangipahoa River Waterway Compact,

- Taxation of Motor Fuels Consumed by Interstate Buses,
- Tennessee-Tombigbee Waterway Development Compact
  Compact – Tennessee Tombigbee Waterway Development
  Authority,
- Tennessee Interstate Furlough Compact,
- (Texas) Low-Level Radioactive Waste Disposal Compact,
- (The) Interstate Compact on Agricultural Grain Marketing,
- (The) (Interstate) Compact on Mental Health,
- Thames River Flood Control Compact,
- Tri-State Agreement on the Chesapeake Bay,
- Tri-State Delta Economic Compact,
- Tri-State Lotto Compact,
- Tri-State Sanitation Compact (Interstate Environmental
  Commission, Tri-State Compact),
- Tuberculosis Control Compact,
- Unclaimed (Abandoned or Uniform) Property Compact (Act)
  (Uniform Disposition of Unclaimed Property Act),
- Upper Colorado River Basin Compact,
- Upper Niobrara River Compact,
- Vehicle Equipment Safety Compact – American Association of
  Motor Vehicle Administrators,
- Wabash Valley Compact,
- Washington Metropolitan Area Transit Authority – Washington
  Metropolitan Area Transit Authority,
- Washington Metropolitan Area Transit District,
- Waterfront Commission Compact,
- Western (Interstate) Corrections Compact,
- Western Interstate Nuclear (Energy) (Cooperation) Compact,
- Western Regional (Higher) Education Compact – Western
  Interstate Commission for Higher Education,
- Wheeling Creek Watershed Protection and Flood Prevention
  Compact,
- Woodrow Wilson Bridge and Tunnel Compact, and
- Yellowstone River Compact.

*The above information is reprinted here with the kind permission
of the National Center for Interstate Compacts.*

APPENDIX N:
Congressional Consent to the Emergency Management Assistance Compact

PUBLIC LAW 104-321 OF 1996

JOINT RESOLUTION
Granting the consent of Congress to
the Emergency Management Assistance Compact

Resolved by the Senate and House of Representatives of the United States of America in Congress assembled,

SECTION 1. CONGRESSIONAL CONSENT.

The Congress consents to the Emergency Management Assistance Compact entered into by Delaware, Florida, Georgia, Louisiana, Maryland, Mississippi, Missouri, Oklahoma, South Carolina, South Dakota, Tennessee, Virginia, and West Virginia. The compact reads substantially as follows:

"Emergency Management Assistance Compact

"ARTICLE I.
"PURPOSE AND AUTHORITIES.
"This compact is made and entered into by and between the participating member states which enact this compact, hereinafter called party states. For the purposes of this compact, the term 'states' is taken to mean the several states, the Commonwealth of Puerto Rico, the District of Columbia, and all U.S. territorial possessions.
"The purpose of this compact is to provide for mutual assis-

tance between the states entering into this compact in managing any emergency disaster that is duly declared by the Governor of the affected state, whether arising from natural disaster, technological hazard, man-made disaster, civil emergency aspects of resources shortages, community disorders, insurgency, or enemy attack.

"This compact shall also provide for mutual cooperation in emergency-related exercises, testing, or other training activities using equipment and personnel simulating performance of any aspect of the giving and receiving of aid by party states or subdivisions of party states during emergencies, such actions occurring outside actual declared emergency periods. Mutual assistance in this compact may include the use of the states' National Guard forces, either in accordance with the National Guard Mutual Assistance Compact or by mutual agreement between states.

"ARTICLE II.
"GENERAL IMPLEMENTATION.
"Each party state entering into this compact recognizes that many emergencies transcend political jurisdictional boundaries and that intergovernmental coordination is essential in managing these and other emergencies under this compact. Each state further recognizes that there will be emergencies which require immediate access and present procedures to apply outside resources to make a prompt and effective response to such an emergency. This is because few, if any, individual states have all the resources they may need in all types of emergencies or the capability of delivering resources to areas where emergencies exist.

"The prompt, full, and effective utilization of resources of the participating states, including any resources on hand or available from the federal government or any other source, that are essential to the safety, care, and welfare of the people in the event of any emergency or disaster declared by a party state, shall be the underlying principle on which all articles of this compact shall be understood.

"On behalf of the Governor of each state participating in the compact, the legally designated state official who is assigned responsibility for emergency management will be responsible for formulation of the appropriate interstate mutual aid plans and procedures necessary to implement this compact.

"ARTICLE III.

"PARTY STATE RESPONSIBILITIES.

"A. It shall be the responsibility of each party state to formulate procedural plans and programs for interstate cooperation in the performance of the responsibilities listed in this article. In formulating such plans, and in carrying them out, the party states, insofar as practical, shall:

"1. Review individual state hazards analyses and, to the extent reasonably possible, determine all those potential emergencies the party states might jointly suffer, whether due to natural disaster, technological hazard, man-made disaster, emergency aspects of resources shortages, civil disorders, insurgency, or enemy attack;

"2. Review party states' individual emergency plans and develop a plan which will determine the mechanism for the interstate management and provision of assistance concerning any potential emergency;

"3. Develop interstate procedures to fill any identified gaps and to resolve any identified inconsistencies or overlaps in existing or developed plans;

"4. Assist in warning communities adjacent to or crossing the state boundaries;

"5. Protect and assure uninterrupted delivery of services, medicines, water, food, energy and fuel, search and rescue, and critical lifeline equipment, services, and resources, both human and material;

"6. Inventory and set procedures for the interstate loan and delivery of human and material resources, together with procedures for reimbursement or forgiveness; and

"7. Provide, to the extent authorized by law, for temporary suspension of any statutes or ordinances that restrict the implementation of the above responsibilities.

"B. The authorized representative of a party state may

request assistance to another party state by contacting the authorized representative of that state. The provisions of this compact shall only apply to requests for assistance made by and to authorized representatives. Requests may be verbal or in writing. If verbal, the request shall be confirmed in writing within thirty days of the verbal request. Requests shall provide the following information:

"1. A description of the emergency service function for which assistance is needed, including, but not limited to, fire services, law enforcement, emergency medical, transportation, communications, public works and engineering, building, inspection, planning and information assistance, mass care, resource support, health and medical services, and search and rescue;

"2. The amount and type of personnel, equipment, materials and supplies needed, and a reasonable estimate of the length of time they will be needed; and

"3. The specific place and time for staging of the assisting party's response and a point of contact at that location.

"C. There shall be frequent consultation between state officials who have assigned emergency management responsibilities and other appropriate representatives of the party states with affected jurisdictions and the United States Government, with free exchange of information, plans, and resource records relating to emergency capabilities.

"ARTICLE IV.
"LIMITATIONS.
"Any party state requested to render mutual aid or conduct exercises and training for mutual aid shall take such action as is necessary to provide and make available the resources covered by this compact in accordance with the terms hereof; provided that it is understood that the state rendering aid may withhold resources to the extent necessary to provide reasonable protection for such state.

"Each party state shall afford to the emergency forces of any party state, while operating within its state limits under the terms and conditions of this compact, the same powers, except that of arrest unless specifically authorized by the receiving state, duties, rights, and privileges as are afforded forces of the state in which they are performing emergency services. Emergency forces will continue under the command and control of their regular leaders, but the organizational units will come under the operational control of the emergency services authorities of the state receiving assistance. These conditions may be activated, as needed, only subsequent to a declaration of a state emergency or disaster by the governor of the party state that is to receive assistance or upon commencement of exercises or training for mutual aid and shall continue so long as the exercises or training for mutual aid are in progress, the state of emergency or disaster remains in effect, or loaned resources remain in the receiving state, whichever is longer.

"ARTICLE V.
"LICENSES AND PERMITS.
"Whenever any person holds a license, certificate, or other permit issued by any state party to the compact evidencing the meeting of qualifications for professional, mechanical, or other skills, and when such assistance is requested by the receiving party state, such person shall be deemed licensed, certified, or permitted by the state requesting assistance to render aid involving such skill to meet a declared emergency or disaster, subject to such limitations and conditions as the Governor of the requesting state may prescribe by executive order or otherwise.

"ARTICLE VI.
"LIABILITY.
"Officers or employees of a party state rendering aid in another state pursuant to this compact shall be considered agents of the requesting state for tort liability and immunity purposes. No party state or its officers or employees rendering aid in another state pursuant to this compact shall be liable on account of any act or omission in good faith on the part of such forces while so engaged or on account of the mainte-

nance or use of any equipment or supplies in connection therewith. Good faith in this article shall not include willful misconduct, gross negligence, or recklessness.

"ARTICLE VII.
"SUPPLEMENTARY AGREEMENTS.
"Inasmuch as it is probable that the pattern and detail of the machinery for mutual aid among two or more states may differ from that among the states that are party hereto, this compact contains elements of a broad base common to all states, and nothing herein shall preclude any state entering into supplementary agreements with another state or affect any other agreements already in force between states. Supplementary agreements may comprehend, but shall not be limited to, provisions for evacuation and reception of injured and other persons and the exchange of medical, fire, police, public utility, reconnaissance, welfare, transportation and communications personnel, and equipment and supplies.

"ARTICLE VIII.
"COMPENSATION.
"Each party state shall provide for the payment of compensation and death benefits to injured members of the emergency forces of that state and representatives of deceased members of such forces in case such members sustain injuries or are killed while rendering aid pursuant to this compact, in the same manner and on the same terms as if the injury or death were sustained within their own state.

"ARTICLE IX.
"REIMBURSEMENT.
"Any party state rendering aid in another state pursuant to this compact shall be reimbursed by the party state receiving such aid for any loss or damage to or expense incurred in the operation of any equipment and the provision of any service in answering a request for aid and for the costs incurred in connection with such requests; provided, that any aiding party state may assume in whole or in part such loss, damage,

expense, or other cost, or may loan such equipment or donate such services to the receiving party state without charge or cost; and provided further, that any two or more party states may enter into supplementary agreements establishing a different allocation of costs among those states. Article VIII expenses shall not be reimbursable under this article.

"ARTICLE X.

"EVACUATION.

"Plans for the orderly evacuation and interstate reception of portions of the civilian population as the result of any emergency or disaster of sufficient proportions to so warrant, shall be worked out and maintained between the party states and the emergency management/services directors of the various jurisdictions where any type of incident requiring evacuations might occur. Such plans shall be put into effect by request of the state from which evacuees come and shall include the manner of transporting such evacuees, the number of evacuees to be received in different areas, the manner in which food, clothing, housing, and medical care will be provided, the registration of the evacuees, the providing of facilities for the notification of relatives or friends, and the forwarding of such evacuees to other areas or the bringing in of additional materials, supplies, and all other relevant factors. Such plans shall provide that the party state receiving evacuees and the party state from which the evacuees come shall mutually agree as to reimbursement of out-of-pocket expenses incurred in receiving and caring for such evacuees, for expenditures for transportation, food, clothing, medicines, and medical care, and like items. Such expenditures shall be reimbursed as agreed by the party state from which the evacuees come. After the termination of the emergency or disaster, the party state from which the evacuees come shall assume the responsibility for the ultimate support of repatriation of such evacuees.

"ARTICLE XI.

"IMPLEMENTATION.

"A. This compact shall become effective immediately upon its Effective date. enactment into law by any two states. Thereafter, this compact shall become effective as to any other state upon enactment by such state.

"B. Any party state may withdraw from this compact by enacting a statute repealing the same, but no such withdrawal shall take effect until thirty days after the Governor of the withdrawing state has given notice in writing of such withdrawal to the Governors of all other party states. Such action shall not relieve the withdrawing state from obligations assumed hereunder prior to the effective date of withdrawal.

"C. Duly authenticated copies of this compact and of such supplementary agreements as may be entered into shall, at the time of their approval, be deposited with each of the party states and with the Federal Emergency Management Agency and other appropriate agencies of the United States Government.

"ARTICLE XII.

"VALIDITY.

"This compact shall be construed to effectuate the purposes stated in Article I. If any provision of this compact is declared unconstitutional, or the applicability thereof to any person or circumstances is held invalid, the constitutionality of the remainder of this compact and the applicability thereof to other persons and circumstances shall not be affected.

"ARTICLE XIII.

"ADDITIONAL PROVISIONS.

"Nothing in this compact shall authorize or permit the use of military force by the National Guard of a state at any place outside that state in any emergency for which the President is authorized by law to call into federal service the militia, or for any purpose for which the use of the Army or the Air Force would in the absence of express statutory authorization be prohibited under § 1385 of Title 18 of the United States Code.".

SEC. 2. RIGHT TO ALTER, AMEND, OR REPEAL.

The right to alter, amend, or repeal this joint resolution is hereby expressly reserved. The consent granted by this joint resolution shall-

    (1) not be construed as impairing or in any manner affecting any right or jurisdiction of the United States in and over the subject of the compact;

    (2) not be construed as consent to the National Guard Mutual Assistance Compact;

    (3) be construed as understanding that the first paragraph of Article II of the compact provides that emergencies will require procedures to provide immediate access to existing resources to make a prompt and effective response;

    (4) not be construed as providing authority in Article III A. 7. that does not otherwise exist for the suspension of statutes or ordinances;

    (5) be construed as understanding that Article III C. does not impose any affirmative obligation to exchange information, plans, and resource records on the United States or any party which has not entered into the compact; and

    (6) be construed as understanding that Article XIII does not affect the authority of the President over the National Guard provided by article I of the Constitution and title 10 of the United States Code.

SEC. 3. CONSTRUCTION AND SEVERABILITY.

It is intended that the provisions of this compact shall be reasonably and liberally construed to effectuate the purposes thereof. If any part or application of this compact, or legislation enabling the compact, is held invalid, the remainder of the compact or its application to other situations or persons shall not be affected.

SEC. 4. INCONSISTENCY OF LANGUAGE.

The validity of this compact shall not be affected by any insubstantial difference in its form or language as adopted by the States.

APPENDIX O:
U. S. Supreme Court Decision in
McPherson v. Blacker (1892)

U.S. SUPREME COURT
146 U.S. 1
McPherson et al. v. Blacker, Secretary of State
No. 1,170
October 17, 1892

Statement by Mr. Chief Justice FULLER:

William McPherson, Jr., Jay A. Hubbell, J. Henry Carstens, Charles E. Hiscock, Otto Ihling, Philip T. Colgrove, Conrad G. Swensburg, Henry A. Haigh, James H. White, Fred. Slocum, Justus S. Stearns, John Millen, Julius T. Hannah, and J. H. Comstock filed their petition and affidavits in the supreme court of the state of Michigan on May 2, 1892, as nominees for presidential electors, against Robert R. Blacker, secretary of state of Michigan, praying that the court declare the act of the legislature, approved May 1, 1891, (Act No. 50, Pub. Acts Mich. 1891,) entitled "An act to provide for the election of electors of president and vice president of the United States, and to repeal all other acts and parts of acts in conflict herewith," void and of no effect, and that a writ of mandamus be directed to be issued to the said secretary of state, commanding him to cause to be delivered to the sheriff of each county in the state, between the 1st of July and the 1st of September, 1892, "a notice in writing that at the next general election in this state, to be held on Tuesday, the 8th day of November, 1892, there will be chosen (among other officers to be named in said notice) as many electors of president and vice president of the United States as this state may be entitled to elect senators and representatives in the congress."

The statute of Michigan (1 How. Ann. St. Mich. 147, c. 9, p. 133) provided: "The secretary of the state shall, between the 1st day of July and

457

the 1st day of September preceding a general election, direct and cause to be delivered to the sheriff of each county in this state a notice in writing that, at the next general election, there will be chosen as many of the following officers as are to be elected at such general election, viz.: A governor, lieutenant governor, secretary of state, state treasurer, auditor general, attorney general, superintendent of public instruction, commissioner of state land office, members of the state board of education, electors of president and vice president of the United States, and a representative in congress for the district to which each of such counties shall belong."

A rule to show cause having been issued, the respondent, as secretary of state, answered the petition, and denied that he had refused to give the notice thus required, but he said "that it has always been the custom in the office of the secretary of state, in giving notices under said section 147, to state in the notice the number of electors that should be printed on the ticket in each voting precinct in each county in this state, and following such custom with reference to such notice, it is the intention of this respondent in giving notice under section 147 to state in said notice that there will be elected one presidential elector at large and one district presidential elector and two alternate presidential electors, one for the elector at large and one for the district presidential elector, in each voting precinct, so that the election may be held under and in accordance with the provisions of Act No. 50 of the Public Acts of the state of Michigan of 1891."

By an amended answer the respondent claimed the same benefit as if he had demurred.

Relators relied in their petition upon various grounds as invalidating Act No. 50 of the Public Acts of Michigan of 1891, and, among them, that the act was void because in conflict with clause 2 of section 1 of article 2 of the constitution of the United States, and with the fourteenth amendment to that instrument, and also in some of its provisions in conflict with the act of congress of February 3, 1887, entitled "An act to fix the day for the meeting of the electors of president and vice president, and to provide for and regulate the counting of the votes for president and vice president, and the decision of questions arising thereon." The supreme court of Michigan unanimously held that none of the objections urged against the validity of the act were tenable; that it did not conflict with clause 2, 1, art. 2, of the constitution, or with the fourteenth amendment thereof; and that the law was only inoperative so far as in conflict with the law of congress in a matter in reference to which congress had the right to legislate. The opinion of the court will be found reported, in advance of the official series, in 52 N. W. Rep. 469.

Judgment was given, June 17, 1892, denying the writ of mandamus, whereupon a writ of error was allowed to this court.

The October term, 1892, commenced on Monday, October 10th, and on Tuesday, October 11th, the first day upon which the application could be made, a motion to advance the case was submitted by counsel, granted at once in view of the exigency disclosed upon the face of the papers, and the cause heard that day. The attention of the court having been called to other provisions of the election laws of Michigan than those supposed to be immediately involved, (Act No. 190, Pub. Acts Mich. 1891, pp. 258, 263,) the chief justice, on Monday, October 17th, announced the conclusions of the court, and directed the entry of judgment affirming the judgment of the supreme court of Michigan, and ordering the mandate to issue at once, it being stated that this was done because immediate action under the state statutes was apparently required and might be affected by delay, but it was added that the court would thereafter file an opinion stating fully the grounds of the decision.

Act No. 50 of the Public Acts of 1891 of Michigan is as follows:

> "An act to provide for the election of electors of president and vice president of the United States, and to repeal all other acts and parts of acts in conflict herewith.
>
> "*Section 1.* The people of the state of Michigan enact that, at the general election next preceding the choice of president and vice president of the United States, there shall be elected as many electors of president and vice president as this state may be entitled to elect of senators and representatives in congress in the following manner, that is to say: There shall be elected by the electors of the districts hereinafter defined one elector of president and vice president of the United States in each district, who shall be known and designated on the ballot, respectively, as 'eastern district elector of president and vice president of the United States at large,' and 'western district elector of president and vice president of the United States at large.' There shall also be elected, in like manner, two alternate electors of president and vice presi-

dent, who shall be known and designated on the ballot as 'eastern district alternate elector of president and vice president of the United States at large,' and 'western district alternate elector of president and vice president of the United States at large;' for which purpose the first, second, sixth, seventh, eighth, and tenth congressional districts shall compose one district, to be known as the 'Eastern Electoral District,' and the third, fourth, fifth, ninth, eleventh, and twelfth congressional districts shall compose the other district, to be known as the 'Western Electoral District.' There shall also be elected, by the electors in each congressional district into which the state is or shall be divided, one electors of president and vice president, and one alternate elector of president and vice president, the ballots for which shall designate the number of the congressional district and the persons to be voted for therein, as 'district elector' and 'alternate district elector' of president and vice president of the United States, respectively.

"*Sec. 2.* The counting, canvassing, and certifying of the votes cast for said electors at large and their alternates, and said district electors and their alternates, shall be done as near as may be in the same manner as is now provided by law for the election of electors or president and vice president of the United States.

"*Sec. 3.* The secretary of state shall prepare three lists of the names of the electors and the alternate electors, procure thereto the signature of the governor, affix the seal of the state to the same, and deliver such certificates thus signed and sealed to one of the electors, on or before the first Wednesday of December next following said general election. In case of death, disability, refusal to act, or neglect to attend, by the hour of twelve o'clock at noon of said day, of either of said electors at large, the duties of the office shall be performed by the alternate electors at large, that is to say: The eastern district alternate elector at large shall supply the place of the eastern district elector at large, and the western district alternate elector at large shall supply the place of the western district elector at large. In like case, the alternate congressional district elector shall supply the place of the congressional district elector. In case two or more persons have an equal and the highest number of votes for any office created by this act as canvassed by the board of state canvassers, the legislature in joint convention shall choose one of said persons to fill such office, and it shall be the duty of the governor to convene the legislature in special session for such purpose immediately upon such determination by said board of state canvassers.

"*Sec. 4.* The said electors of president and vice president shall convene in the senate chamber at the capital of the state at the hour of twelve o'clock at noon, on the first Wednesday of December immediately following their election, and shall proceed to perform the duties of such electors as required by the constitution and the laws of the United States. The alternate electors shall also be in attendance, but shall take no part in the proceedings, except as herein provided.

"*Sec. 5.* Each of said electors and alternate electors shall receive the sum of five dollars for each day's attendance at the meetings of the electors as above provided, and five cents per mile for the actual and necessary distance traveled each way in going to and returning from said place of meeting, the same to be paid by the state treasurer upon the allowance of the board of state auditors.

"*Sec. 6.* All acts and parts of acts in conflict with the provisions of this act are hereby repealed." Pub. Acts Mich. 1891, pp. 50, 51.

Section 211 of Howell's Annotated Statutes of Michigan (volume 1, c. 9, p. 145) reads:

"For the purpose of canvassing and ascertaining the votes given for electors of president and vice president of the United States, the board of state canvassers shall meet on the Wednesday next after the third Monday of November, or on such other day before that time as the secretary of state shall appoint; and the powers, duties, and proceedings of said board, and of the secretary of state, in sending for, examining, ascertaining, determining, certifying, and recording the votes and results of the election of such electors, shall be in all respects, as near as may be, as hereinbefore provided in relation to sending for, examining, ascertaining, determining, certifying, and recording the votes and results of the election of state officers."

Section 240 of Howell's Statutes, in force prior to May 1, 1891, provided: "At the general election next preceding the choice of president and vice president of the United States, there shall be elected by general ticket as many electors of president and vice president as this state may be entitled to elect of senators and representatives in congress."

The following are sections of article 8 of the constitution of Michigan:

"Sec. 4. The secretary of state, state treasurer, and commissioner of the state land office shall constitute a board of state auditors, to examine and adjust all claims against the state, not otherwise provided for by general law. They shall constitute a board of state canvassers, to determine the result of all elections for governor, lieutenant governor, and state officers, and of such other officers as shall by law be referred to them. *"Sec. 5.* In case two or more persons have an equal and the highest number of votes for any office, as canvassed by the board of state canvassers, the legislature in joint convention shall choose one of said persons to fill such office. When the determination of the board of state canvassers is contested, the legislature in joint convention shall decide which person is elected." 1 How. Ann. St. Mich. p. 57.

Reference was also made in argument to the act of congress of February 3, 1887, to fix the day for the meeting of the electors of president and vice president, and to provide for and regulate and counting of the votes. 24 St. p. 373.

Henry M. Duffield, W. H. H. Miller, and Fred A. Baker, for plaintiff in error.

Otto Kirchner, A. A. Ellis, and John W. Champlin, for defendant in error.

Mr. Chief Justice FULLER, after stating the facts in the foregoing language, delivered the opinion of the court. The supreme court of Michigan held, in effect, that if the act in question were invalid, the proper remedy had been sought. In other words, if the court had been of opinion that the act was void, the writ of mandamus would have been awarded.

And having ruled all objections to the validity of the act urged as arising under the state constitution and laws adversely to the plaintiffs in error, the court was compelled to, and did, consider and dispose of the contention that the act was invalid because repugnant to the constitution and laws of the United States.

We are not authorized to revise the conclusions of the state court on these matters of local law, and, those conclusions being accepted, it follows that the decision of the federal questions is to be regarded as necessary to the determination of the cause. *De Saussure v. Gaillard*, 127 U.S. 216, 8 Sup. Ct. Rep. 1053.

Inasmuch as, under section 709 of the Revised Statutes of the United States, we have jurisdiction by writ of error to re-examine and reverse or affirm the final judgment in any suit in the highest court of a state in which a decision could be had, where the validity of a statute of the state is drawn in question on the ground that it is repugnant to the constitution and laws of the United States, and the decision is in favor of its validity, we perceive no reason for holding that this writ was improvidently brought.

It is argued that the subject-matter of the controversy is not of judicial cognizance, because it is said that all questions connected with the election of a presidential elector are political in their nature; that the court has no power finally to dispose of them; and that its decision would be subject to review by political officers and agencies, as the state board of canvassers, the legislature in joint convention, and the governor, or, finally, the congress.

But the judicial power of the United States extends to all cases in law or equity arising under the constitution and laws of the United States, and this is a case so arising, since the validity of the state law was drawn in question as repugnant to such constitution and laws, and its validity was sustained. *Boyd v. State*, 143 U.S. 135, 12 Sup. Ct. Rep. 375. And it matters not that the judgment to be reviewed may be rendered in a proceeding for mandamus. *Hartman v. Greenhow*, 102 U.S. 672.

As we concur with the state court, its judgment has been affirmed; if we had not, its judgment would have been reversed. In either event, the questions submitted are finally and definitely disposed of by the judgment which we pronounce, and that judgment is carried into effect by the transmission of our mandate to the state court.

The question of the validity of this act, as presented to us by this record, is a judicial question, and we cannot decline the exercise of our jurisdiction upon the inadmissible suggestion that action might be taken by political agencies in disregard of the judgment of the highest tribunal of the state, as revised by our own.

On behalf of plaintiffs in error it is contended that the act is void because in conflict with (1) clause 2, 1, art. 2, of the constitution of the United States; (2) the fourteenth and fifteenth amendments to the constitution; and (3) the act of congress, of February 3, 1887.

The second clause of section 1 of article 2 of the constitution is in these words: "Each state shall appoint, in such manner as the legislature thereof may direct, a number of electors, equal to the whole number of senators and representatives to which the state may be entitled in the congress; but no senator or representative, or person holding an office of trust or profit under the United States, shall be appointed an elector."

The manner of the appointment of electors directed by the act of Michigan is the election of an elector and an alternate elector in each of the twelve congressional districts into which the state of Michigan is divided, and of an elector and an alternate elector at large in each of two districts defined by the act. It is insisted that it was not competent for the legislature to direct this manner of appointment, because the state is to appoint as a body politic and corporate, and so must act as a unit, and cannot delegate the authority to subdivisions created for the purpose; and it is argued that the appointment of electors by districts is not an appointment by the state, because all its citizens otherwise qualified are not permitted to vote for all the presidential electors.

"A state, in the ordinary sense of the constitution," said Chief Justice Chase, (*Texas v. White*, 7 Wall. 700, 731,) "is a political community of free citizens, occupying a territory of defined boundaries, and organized under a government sanctioned and limited by a written constitution, and established by the consent of the governed." The state does not act by its people in their collective capacity, but through such political agencies as are duly constituted and established. The legislative power is the supreme authority, except as limited by the constitution of the state, and the sovereignty of the people is exercised through their representatives in the legislature, unless by the fundamental law power is elsewhere reposed. The constitution of the United States frequently refers to the state as a political community, and also in terms to the people of the several states and the citizens of each state. What is forbidden or required to be done by a state is forbidden or required of the legislative power under state constitutions as they exist. The clause under consideration does not read that the people or the citizens shall appoint, but that "each state shall;" and if the words, "in such manner as the legislature thereof may direct," had been omitted, it would seem that the legislative power of appointment could not have been successfully questioned in the absence of any provision in the state constitution in that regard. Hence the insertion of those words, while operating as a limitation upon the state in respect of any attempt to circumscribe the legislative power, cannot be held to operate as a limitation on that power itself.

If the legislature possesses plenary authority to direct the manner of appointment, and might itself exercise the appointing power by joint ballot or concurrence of the two houses, or according to such mode as designated, it is difficult to perceive why, if the legislature prescribes as a method of appointment choice by vote, it must necessarily be by general ticket, and not by districts. In other words, the act of appointment is none the less the act of the state in its entirety because arrived at by districts, for the act is the act of political agencies duly authorized to speak for the state, and the combined result is the expression of the voice of the state, a result reached by direction of the legislature, to whom the whole subject is committed.

By the first paragraph of section 2, art. 1, it is provided: "The house of representatives shall be composed of members chosen every second year by the people of the several states, and the electors in each state shall have the qualifications requisite for electors of the most numerous branch of the state legislature;" and by the third paragraph, "when vacancies happen in the representation from any state, the executive authority thereof shall issue writs of election to fill such vacancies." Section 4 reads: "The times, places, and manner of holding elections for senators and representatives shall be prescribed in each state by the legislature thereof; but the congress may at any time by law make or alter such regulations, except as to the places of choosing senators."

Although it is thus declared that the people of the several states shall choose the members of congress, (language which induced the state of New York to insert a salvo as to the power to divide into districts, in its resolutions of ratification,) the state legislatures, prior to 1842, in prescribing the times, places, and manner of holding elections for representatives, had usually apportioned the state into districts, and assigned to each a representative; and by act of congress of June 25, 1842 , (carried forward as section 23 of the Revised Statutes,) it was provided that, where a state was entitled to more than one representative, the election should be by districts. It has never been doubted that representatives in congress thus chosen represented the entire people of the state acting in their sovereign capacity.

By original clause 3, 1, art. 2, and by the twelfth amendment, which superseded that clause in case of a failure in the election of president by the people the house of representatives is to choose the president; and "the vote shall be taken by states, the representation from each state having one vote." The state acts as a unit, and its vote is given as a unit, but that vote is arrived at through the votes of its representatives in congress elected by districts.

The state also acts individually through its electoral college, although, by reason of the power of its legislature over the manner of appointment, the vote of its electors may be divided.

The constitution does not provide that the appointment of electors shall be by popular vote, nor that the electors shall be voted for upon a general ticket, nor that the majority of those who exercise the elective franchise can alone choose the electors. It recognizes that the people act through their representatives in the legislature, and leaves it to the legislature exclusively to define the method of effecting the object.

The framers of the constitution employed words in their natural sense; and, where they are plain and clear, resort to collateral aids to interpretation is unnecessary, and cannot be indulged in to narrow or enlarge the text; but where there is ambiguity or doubt, or where two views may well be entertained, contemporaneous and subsequent practical construction is entitled to the greatest weight. Certainly, plaintiffs in error cannot reasonably assert that the clause of the constitution under consideration so plainly sustains their position as to entitle them to object that contemporaneous history and practical construction are not to be allowed their legitimate force, and, conceding that their argument inspires a doubt sufficient to justify resort to the aids of interpretation thus afforded, we are of opinion that such doubt is thereby resolved against them, the contemporaneous practical exposition of the constitution being too strong and obstinate to be shaken or controlled. *Stuart v. Laird,* 1 Cranch, 299, 309.

It has been said that the word "appoint" is not the most appropriate word to describe the result of a popular election. Perhaps not; but it is sufficiently comprehensive to cover that mode, and was manifestly used as conveying the broadest power of determination. It was used in article 5 of the articles of confederation, which provided that "delegates shall be annually appointed in such manner as the legislature of each state shall direct;" and in the resolution of congress of February 21, 1787, which declared it expedient that "a convention of delegates who shall have been appointed by the several states" should be held. The appointment of delegates was, in fact, made by the legislatures directly, but that involved no denial of authority to direct some other mode. The constitutional convention, by resolution of September 17, 1787, expressed the opinion that the congress should fix a day "on which electors should be appointed by the states which shall have ratified the same," etc., and that, "after such publication, the electors should be appointed, and the senators and representatives elected."

The journal of the convention discloses that propositions that the president should be elected by "the citizens of the United States," or by the "people," or "by electors to be chosen by the people of the several states," instead of by the congress, were voted down, (Jour. Conv. 286, 288; 1 Elliot, Deb. 208, 262,) as was the proposition that the president should be "chosen by electors appointed for that purpose by the legislatures of the states," though at one time adopted, (Jour. Conv. 190; 1 Elliot, Deb. 208, 211, 217;) and a motion to postpone the consideration of the choice "by the national legislature," in order to take up a resolution providing for electors to be elected by the qualified voters in districts, was negatived in committee of the whole, (Jour. Conv. 92; 1 Elliot, Deb. 156.) Gerry proposed that the choice should be made by the state executives; Hamilton, that the election be by electors chosen by electors chosen by the people; James Wilson and Gouverneur Morris were strongly in favor of popular vote; Ellsworth and Luther Martin preferred the choice by electors elected by the legislatures; and Roger Sherman, appointment by congress. The final result seems to have reconciled contrariety of views by leaving it to the state legislatures to appoint directly by joint ballot or concurrent separate action, or through popular election by districts or by general ticket, or as otherwise might be directed.

Therefore, on reference to contemporaneous and subsequent action under the clause, we should expect to find, as we do, that various modes of choosing the electors were pursued, as, by the legislature itself on joint ballot; by the legislature through a concurrent vote of the two houses; by vote of the people for a general ticket; by vote of the people in districts; by choice partly by the people voting in districts and partly by the people voting in districts and partly by the candidates voted for by the people in districts; and in other ways, as, notably, by North Carolina in 1792, and Tennessee in 1796 and 1800. No question was raised as to the power of the state to appoint in any mode its legislature saw fit to adopt, and none that a single method, applicable without exception, must be pursued in the absence of an amendment to the constitution. The district system was largely considered the most equitable, and Madison wrote that it was that system which was contemplated by the framers of the constitution, although it was soon seen that its adoption by some states might place them at a disadvantage by a division of their strength, and that a uniform rule was preferable.

At the first presidential election, the appointment of electors was made by the legislatures of Connecticut, Delaware, Georgia, New Jersey, and South Carolina. Pennsylvania, by act of October 4, 1788, (Acts Pa. 1787-88, p. 513,) provided for the election of electors on a general ticket. Virginia, by act of November 17, 1788, was divided into 12 separate districts, and an elector elected in each district, while for the election of congressmen the state was divided into 10 other districts. Laws Va. Oct. Sess. 1788, pp. 1, 2. In Massachusetts, the general court, by resolve of November 17, 1788, divided the state into districts for the election of representatives in congress, and provided for their election, December 18, 1788, and that at the same time the qualified inhabitants of each district should give their votes for two persons as candidates for an elector of president and vice president of the United States, and, from the two persons in each district having the greatest number of votes, the two houses of the general court by joint ballot should elect one as elector, and in the same way should elect two electors at large. Mass. Resolves 1788, p. 53. In Maryland, under elected on general ticket, five being residents elected on general ticket, five being residents of the Western Shore, and three of the Eastern Shore. Laws Md. 1788, c. 10. In New Hampshire an act was passed November 12, 1788, (Laws N. H. 1789, p. 169,) providing for the election of five electors by majority popular vote, and in case of no choice that the legislature should appoint out of so many of the candidates as equaled double the number of electors elected. There being no choice, the appointment was made by the legislature. The senate would not agree to a joint ballot, and the house was compelled, that the vote of the state might not be lost, to concur in the electors chosen by the senate. The state of New York lost its vote through a similar contest. The assembly was willing to elect by joint ballot of the two branches or to divide the electors with the senate, but the senate would assent to nothing short of a complete negative upon the action of the assembly, and the time for election passed without an appointment. North Carolina and Rhode Island had not then ratified the constitution.

Fifteen states participated in the second presidential election, in nine of which electors were chosen by the legislatures. Maryland, Laws Md. 1790, c. 16; Laws 1791, c. 62,) New Hampshire, (Laws N. H. 1792, pp. 398, 401,) and Pennsylvania, (Laws Pa. 1792, p. 240,) elected their electors on a general ticket, and Virginia by districts, (Laws Va. 1792, p. 87.) In Massachusetts the general court, by resolution of June 30, 1792, divided the state into four districts, in each of two of which five electors were elected, and in each of the other two three electors. Mass. Resolves, June, 1792, p. 25. Under the apportionment of April 13, 1792, North Carolina was entitled to ten members of the house of representatives. The legislature was not in session, and did not meet until November 15th, while under the act of congress of March 1, 1792, (1 St. p. 239,) the electors were to assemble on December 5th. The legislature passed an act dividing the state into four districts, and directing the members of the legislature residing in each district to meet on the 25th of November, and choose three electors. 2 Ired. N. C. Laws, 1715-1800, c. 15 of 1792. At the same session an act was passed dividing the state into districts for the election of electors in 1796, and every four years thereafter. Id. c. 16.

Sixteen states took part in the third presidential election, Tennessee having been admitted June 1, 1796. In nine states the electors were appointed by the legislatures, and in Pennsylvania and New Hampshire by popular vote for a general ticket. Virginia, North Carolina, and Maryland elected by districts. The Maryland law of December 24, 1795, was entitled "An act to alter the mode of electing electors," and provided for dividing the state into ten districts, each of which districts should "elect and appoint one person, being a resident of the said district, as an elector." Laws Md. 1795, c. 73. Massachusetts adhered to the district system, electing one elector in each congressional district by a majority vote. It was provided that, if no one had a majority, the legislature should make the appointment on joint ballot, and the legislature also appointed two electors at large in the same manner. Mass. Resolves, June, 1796, p. 12. In Tennessee an act was passed August 8, 1796, which provided for the election of three electors, "one in the district of Washington, one in the district of Hamilton, and one in the district of Mero," and, "that the said electors may be elected with as little trouble to the citizens as possible," certain persons of the counties of Washington, Sullivan, Green, and Hawkins were named in the act and appointed electors to elect an elector for the district of Washington; certain other persons of the counties of Knox, Jefferson, Sevier, and Blount were by name appointed to elect an elector for the district of Hamilton; and certain others of the counties of Davidson, Sumner, and Tennessee to elect an elector for the district of Mero. Laws Tenn. 1794, 1803, p. 209; Acts 2d Sess. 1st Gen. Assem. Tenn. c. 4. Electors were chosen by the persons thus designated.

In the fourth presidential election, Virginia, under the advice of Mr. Jefferson, adopted the general ticket, at least "until some uniform mode of choosing a president and vice president of the United States shall be prescribed by an amendment to the constitution." Laws Va. 1799-1800, p. 3. Massachusetts passed a resolution providing that the electors of that state should be appointed by joint ballot of the senate and house. Mass. Resolves, June, 1800, p. 13. Pennsylvania appointed by the legislature, and, upon a contest between the senate and house, the latter was forced to yield to the senate in agreeing to an arrangement which resulted in dividing the vote of the electors. 26 Niles" Reg. 17. Six states, however, chose electors by popular vote, Rhode Island supplying the place of Pennsylvania, which had theretofore followed that course. Tennessee, by act October 26, 1799, designated persons by name to choose its three electors, as under the act of 1796. Laws Tenn, 1794-1803, p. 211; Acts 2d Sess. 2d Gen. Assem, Tenn. c. 46.

Without pursuing the subject further, it is sufficient to observe that, while most of the states adopted the general ticket system, the district method obtained in Kentucky until 1824; in Tennessee and Maryland until 1832; in Indiana in 1824 and 1828; in Illinois in 1820 and 1824; and in Maine in 1820, 1824, and 1828. Massachusetts used the general ticket system in 1804, (Mass. Resolves, June, 1804, p. 19;) chose electors by joint ballot of the legislature in 1808 and in 1816, (Mass. Resolves 1808, pp. 205, 207, 209; Mass. Resolves 1816, p. 233;) used the district system again in 1812 and 1820, (Mass. Resolves 1812, p. 94; Mass. Resolves 1820, p. 245;) and returned to the general ticket system in 1824, (Mass. Resolves 1824, p. 40.) In New York the electors were elected in 1828 by districts, the district electors choosing the electors at large. Rev. St. N. Y. 1827, tit. 6, p. 24. The appointment of electors by the legislature, instead of by popular vote, was made use of by North Carolina, Vermont, and New Jersey in 1812.

In 1824 the electors were chosen by popular vote, by districts, and by general ticket, in all the states excepting Delaware, Georgia, Louisiana, New York, South Carolina, and Vermont, where they were still chosen by the legislature. After 1832 electors were chosen by general ticket in all the states excepting South Carolina, where the legislature chose them up to and including 1860. Journals 1860, Senate, pp. 12, 13; House, 11, 15, 17. And this was the mode adopted by Florida in 1868, (Laws 1868, p. 166,) and by Colorado in 1876, as prescribed by section 19 of the schedule to the constitution of the state, which was admitted into the Union, August 1, 1876, (Gen. Laws Colo. 1877, pp. 79, 990.)[1]

Mr. Justice Story, in considering the subject in his Commentaries on the Constitution, and writing nearly 50 years after the adoption of that instrument, after stating that "in some states the legislatures have direct-

---

[1] See Stanwood, Presidential Elections, (3d Ed.) and Appleton, Presidential Counts, passim; 2 Lalor, Enc. Pol. Science, 68; 4 Hild. Hist. U. S. (Rev. Ed.) 39, 382, 689; 5 Hild. Hist. U. S. 389, 531; 1 Schouler, Hist. U. S. 72, 334; 2 Schouler, Hist. U. S. 184; 3 Schouler, Hist. U. S. 313, 439; 2 Adams, Hist. U. S. 201; 4 Adams, Hist. U. S. 285; 6 Adams, Hist. U. S. 409, 413; 9 Adams, Hist. U. S. 139; 1 McMaster, Hist. Peopel U. S. 525; 2 McMaster, Hist. People U. S. 85, 509; 3 McMaster, Hist. People U. S. 188, 189, 194, 317; 2 Scharf, Hist. Md. 547; 2 Bradf. Mass. 335; Life of Plumer, 104; 3 Niles' Reg. 160; 5 Niles' Reg. 372; 9 Niles' Reg. 319, 349; 10 Niles' Reg. 45, 177, 409; 11 Niles' Reg.

ly chosen the electors by themselves; in others, they have been chosen by the people by a general ticket throughout the whole state; and in others, by the people by electoral districts, fixed by the legislature, a certain number of electors being apportioned to each district,"-adds: "No question has ever arisen as to the constitutionality of either mode, except that by a direct choice by the legislature. But this, though often doubted by able and ingenious minds, (3 Elliot, Deb. 100, 101,) has been firmly established in practice ever since the adoption of the constitution, and does not now seem to admit of controversy, even if a suitable tribunal existed to adjudicate upon it." And he remarks that "it has been thought desirable by many statesmen to have the constitution amended so as to provide for a uniform mode of choice by the people." Story, Const. (1st Ed.) 1466.

Such an amendment was urged at the time of the adoption of the twelfth amendment, the suggestion being that all electors should be chosen by popular vote, the states to be divided for that purpose into districts. It was brought up again in congress in December, 1813, but the resolution for submitting the amendment failed to be carried. The amendment was renewed in the house of representatives in December, 1816, and a provision for the division of the states into single districts for the choice of electors received a majority vote, but not two thirds. Like amendments were offered in the senate by Messrs. Sanford of New York, Dickerson of New Jersey, and Macon of North Carolina. December 11, 1823, Senator Benton introduced an amendment providing that each legislature should divide its state into electoral districts, and that the voters of each district "should vote, in their own proper persons," for president and vice president, but it was not acted upon. December 16 and December 24, 1823, amendments were introduced in the senate by Messrs. Dickerson, of New Jersey, and Van Buren, of New York, requiring the choice of electors to be by districts; but these and others failed of adoption, although there was favorable action in that direction by the senate in 1818, 1819, and 1822. December 22, 1823, an amendment was introduced in the house by Mr. McDuffie, of South Carolina, providing that electors should be chosen by districts assigned by the legislatures, but

---

[2] 1 Benton, Thirty Years' View, 37; 5 Benton, Cong. Deb. 110, 677; 7 Benton, Cong. Deb. 472-474, 600; 3 Niles' Reg. 240, 334; 11 Niles' Reg. 258, 274, 293, 349; Annals Cong. (1812-13,) 847.

action was not taken[2]. The subject was again brought forward in 1835, 1844, and subsequently, but need not be further dwelt upon, except that it may be added that, on the 28th of May, 1874, a report was made by Senator Morton, chairman of the senate committee on privileges and elections, recommending an amendment dividing the states into electoral districts, and that the majority of the popular vote of each district should give the candidate one presidential vote, but this also failed to obtain action. In this report it was said: "The appointment of these electors is thus placed absolutely and wholly with the legislatures of the several states. They may be chosen by the legislature, or the legislature may provide that they shall be elected by the people of the state at large, or in districts, as are members of congress, which was the case formerly in many states; and it is not doubt competent for the legislature to authorize the governor, or the supreme court of the state, or any other agent of its will, to appoint these electors. This power is conferred upon the legislatures of the states by the constitution of the United States, and cannot be taken from them or modified by their state constitutions any more than can their power to elect senators of the United States. Whatever provisions may be made by statute, or by the state constitution, to choose electors by the people, there is no doubt of the right of the legislature to resume the power at any time, for it can neither be taken away nor abdicated." Senate Rep. 1st Sess. 43d Cong. No. 395.

From this review, in which we have been assisted by the laborious research of counsel, and which might have been greatly expanded, it is seen that from the formation of the government until now the practical construction of the clause has conceded plenary power to the state legislatures in the matter of the appointment of electors.

Even in the heated controversy of 1876-77 the electoral vote of Colorado cast by electors chosen by the legislature passed unchallenged, and our attention has not been drawn to any previous attempt to submit to the courts the determination of the constitutionality of state action.

In short, the appointment and mode of appointment of electors belong exclusively to the states under the constitution of the United States. They are, as remarked by Mr. Justice Gray *in Re Green*, 134 U.S. 377, 379, 10 S. Sup. Ct. Rep. 586, "no more officers or agents of the United States than are the members of the state legislatures when acting as electors of federal senators, or the people of the states when acting as the electors of representatives in congress." Congress is empowered to determine the time of choosing the electors and the day on which they are to give their votes, which is required to be the same day throughout the United States; but otherwise the power and jurisdiction of the state is exclusive, with the exception of the provisions as to the number of electors and the ineligibility of certain persons, so framed that congressional and federal influence might be excluded.

The question before us is not one of policy. but of power; and, while public opinion had gradually brought all the states as matter of fact to the pursuit of a uniform system of popular election by general ticket, that fact does not tend to weaken the force of contemporaneous and long-continued previous practice when and as different views of expediency prevailed. The prescription of the written law cannot be overthrown because the states have laterally exercised, in a particular way, a power which they might have exercised in some other way. The construction to which we have referred has prevailed too long and been too uniform to justify us in interpreting the language of the constitution as conveying any other meaning than that heretofore ascribed, and it must be treated as decisive.

It is argued that the district mode of choosing electors, while not obnoxious to constitutional objection, if the operation of the electoral system had conformed to its original object and purpose, had become so in view of the practical working of that system. Doubtless it was supposed that the electors would exercise a reasonable independence and fair judgment in the selection of the chief executive, but experience soon demonstrated that, whether chosen by the legislatures or by popular suffrage on general ticket or in districts, they were so chosen simply to register the will of the appointing power in respect of a particular candidate. In relation, then, to the independence of the electors, the original expectation may be said to have been frustrated. Miller, Const. Law, 149; Rawle, Const. 55; Story, Const. 1473; Federalist, No. 68. But we can perceive no reason for holding that the power confided to the states by the constitution has ceased to exist because the operation of the system has not fully realized the hopes of those by whom it was created. Still less can we recognize the doctrine that because the constitution has been found in the march of time sufficiently comprehensive to be applicable to conditions not within the minds of its framers, and not arising in their time, it may therefore be wrenched from the subjects expressly embraced within it, and amended by judicial decision without action by the designated organs in the mode by which alone amendments can be made. Nor are we able to discover any conflict between this act and the fourteenth and fifteenth amendments to the constitution. The fourteenth amendment provides:

> *"Section 1.* All persons born or naturalized in the United States, and subject to the jurisdiction thereof, are citizens of the United States and of the state wherein they reside. No state shall make or enforce any law which shall abridge the privileges or immunities of citizens of the United States; nor shall any state deprive any person of life, liberty, or property without due process of law, nor deny to any person within its jurisdiction the equal protection of the laws.
>
> *"Sec. 2.* Representatives shall be apportioned among the several states according to their respective numbers, counting the whole number of persons in each state, excluding Indians not taxed. But when the right to vote at any election for the choice of electors for president and vice president of the United States, representatives in congress, the executive and judicial officers of a state, or the members of the legislature thereof, is denied to any of the male inhabitants of such state, being twenty-one years of age, and citizens of the United States, or in any way abridged, except for participation in rebellion or other crime, the basis of representation therein shall be reduced in the proportion which the number of such male citizens shall bear to the whole number of male citizens twenty-one years of age in such state."

The first section of the fifteenth amendment reads: "The right of citizens of the United States to vote shall not be denied or abridged by the United States or by any state on account of race, color, or previous condition of servitude."

In the Slaughterhouse Cases, 16 Wall. 36, this court held that the first clause of the fourteenth amendment was primarily intended to confer citizenship on the negro race; and, secondly, to give definitions of citizenship of the United States, and citizenship of the states; and it recognized the distinction between citizenship of a state and citizenship of the United States by those definitions; that the privileges and immunities of citizens of the states embrace generally those fundamental civil rights for the security and establishment of which organized society was instituted, and which remain, with certain exceptions mentioned in the federal constitution, under the care of the state governments; while the privileges and immunities of citizens of the United States are those which arise out of the nature and essential character of the national government, the provisions of its constitution, or its laws and treaties made in pursuance thereof; and that it is the latter which are placed under the protection of congress by the second clause of the fourteenth amendment.

We decided in *Minor v. Happersett*, 21 Wall. 162, that the right of suffrage was not necessarily one of the privileges or immunities of citizenship before the adoption of the fourteenth amendment, and that that amendment does not add to these privileges and immunities, but simply furnishes an additional guaranty for the protection of such as the citizen already has; that, at the time of the adoption of that amendment, suffrage was not coextensive with the citizenship of the state, nor was it at the time of the adoption of the constitution; and that neither the constitution nor the fourteenth amendment made all citizens voters.

The fifteenth amendment exempted citizens of the United States from discrimination in the exercise of the elective franchise on account of race, color, or previous condition of servitude. The right to vote in the states comes from the states, but the right of exemption from the prohibited discrimination comes from the United States. The first has not been granted or secured by the constitution of the United States, but the last has been. *U. S. v. Cruikshank*, 92 U.S. 542; *U. S. v. Reese*, Id. 214.

If, because it happened, at the time of the adoption of the fourteenth amendment, that those who exercised the elective franchise in the state of Michigan were entitled to vote for all the presidential electors, this right was rendered permanent by that amendment, then the second clause of article 2 has been so amended that the states can no longer appoint in such manner as the legislatures thereof may direct; and yet no such result is indicated by the language used, nor are the amendments necessarily inconsistent with that clause. The first section of the fourteenth amendment does not refer to the exercise of the elective franchise, though the second provides that if the right to vote is denied or abridged to any male inhabitant of the state having attained majority, and being a citizen of the United States, then the basis of representation to which each state is entitled in the congress shall be proportionately reduced. Whenever presidential electors are appointed by popular election, then the right to vote cannot be denied or abridged without invoking the penalty; and so of the right to vote for representatives in congress, the executive and judicial officers of a state, or the members of the legislature thereof. The right to vote intended to be protected refers to the right to vote as established by the laws and constitution of the state. There is no color for the contention that under the amendments every male inhabitant of the state, being a citizen of the United States, has from the time of his majority a right to vote for presidential electors.

The object of the fourteenth amendment in respect of citizenship was to preserve equality of rights and to prevent discrimination as between citizens, but not to radically change the whole theory of the relations of the state and federal governments to each other, and of both governments to the people. *In re Kemmler,* 136 U.S. 436, 10 Sup. Ct. Rep. 930.

The inhibition that no state shall deprive any person within its jurisdiction of the equal protection of the laws was designed to prevent any person or class of persons from being singled out as a special subject for discriminating and hostile legislation. *Milling Co. v. Pennsylvania,* 125 U.S. 181, 188, Sup. Ct. Rep. 737.

In *Hayes v. Missouri,* 120 U.S. 68, 71, 7 S. Sup. Ct. Rep. 350, Mr. Justice Field, speaking for the court, said: "The fourteenth amendment to the constitution of the United States does not prohibit legislation which is limited either in the objects to which it is directed or by the territory within which it is to operate. It merely requires that all persons subjected to such legislation shall be treated alike, under like circumstances and conditions, both in the privileges and in the liabilities imposed. As we said in *Barbier v. Connolly,* speaking of the fourteenth amendment: 'Class legislation, discriminating against some and favoring others, is prohibited; but legislation which, in carrying out a public purpose, is limited in its application, if within the sphere of its operation it affects alike all persons similarly situated, is not within the amendment' 113 U.S. 27, 32, 5 S. Sup. Ct. Rep. 357."

If presidential electors are appointed by the legislatures, no discrimination is made; if they are elected in districts where each citizen has an equal right to vote, the same as any other citizen has, no discrimination is made. Unless the authority vested in the legislatures by the second clause of section 1 of article 2 has been divested, and the state has lost its power of appointment, except in one manner, the position taken on behalf of relators is untenable, and it is apparent that neither of these amendments can be given such effect.

The third clause of section 1 of article 2 of the constitution is: "The congress may determine the time of choosing the electors, and the day on which they shall give their votes; which day shall be the same throughout the United States."

Under the act of congress of March 1, 1792, (1 St. p. 239, c. 8,) it was provided that the electors should meet and give their votes on the first Wednesday in December at such place in each state as should be directed by the legislature thereof, and by act of congress of January 23, 1845, (5 St. p. 721,) that the electors should be appointed in each state on the Tuesday next after the first Monday in the month of November in the year in which they were to be appointed: provided, that each state might by law provide for the filling of any vacancies in its college of electors when such college meets to give its electoral vote: and provided that when any state shall have held an election for the purpose of choosing electors, and has failed to make a choice on the day prescribed, then the electors may be appointed on a subsequent day, in such manner as the state may by law provide. These provisions were carried forward into sections 131, 133, 134, and 135 of the Revised Statutes, (Rev. St. tit. 3, c. 1, p. 22.)

By the act of congress of February 3, 1887, entitled "An act to fix the day for the meeting of the electors of president and vice president," etc., (24 St. p. 373.) it was provided that the electors of each state should meet and give their votes on the second Monday in January next following their appointment. The state law in question here fixes the first Wednesday of December as the day for the meeting of the electors, as originally designated by congress. In this respect it is in conflict with the act of congress, and must necessarily give way. But this part of the act is not so inseparably connected, in substance, with the other parts as to work the destruction of the whole act. Striking out the day for the meeting, which had already been otherwise determined by the act of congress, the act remains complete in itself, and capable of being carried out in accordance with the legislative intent. The state law yields only to the extent of the collision. *Cooley, Const. Lim.* *178; *Com. v. Kimball,* 24 Pick. 359; *Houston v. Moore,* 5 Wheat. 1, 49. The construction to this effect by the state court is of persuasive force, if not of controlling weight.

We do not think this result affected by the provision in Act No. 50 in relation to a tie vote. Under the constitution of the state of Michigan, in case two or more persons have an equal and the highest number of votes for any office, as canvassed by the board of state canvassers, the legislature in joint convention chooses one of these persons to fill the office. This rule is recognized in this act, which also makes it the duty of the governor in such case to convene the legislature in special session for the purpose of its application, immediately upon the determination by the board of state canvassers.

We entirely agree with the supreme court of Michigan that it cannot be held, as matter of law, that the legislature would not have provided for being convened in special session but for the provision relating to the time of the meeting of the electors contained in the act, and are of opinion that that date may be rejected, and the act be held to remain otherwise complete and valid.

And as the state is fully empowered to fill any vacancy which may occur in its electoral college, when it meets to give its electoral vote, we find nothing in the mode provided for anticipating such an exigency which operates to invalidate the law. We repeat that the main question arising for consideration is one of power, and not of policy, and we are unable to arrive at any other conclusion than that the act of the legislature of Michigan of May 1, 1891, is not void as in contravention of the constitution of the United States, for want of power in its enactment.

The judgment of the supreme court of Michigan must be affirmed.

APPENDIX P:
U. S. Supreme Court Decision in *State of Ohio Ex Rel. Davis v. Hildebrandt* (1916)

U.S. Supreme Court

241 U.S. 565

STATE OF OHIO ON RELATION OF DAVID DAVIS, Plff. in Err.,

v.

CHARLES Q. HILDEBRANT,

Secretary of State of Ohio, State Supervisor and Inspector of Elections, and State Supervisor of Elections, et al.

No. 987

Submitted May 22, 1916

Decided June 12, 1916

Messrs. Sherman T. McPherson and J. Warren Keifer for plaintiff in error.

Mr. Edward C. Turner, Attorney General of Ohio, and Messrs. Edmond H. Moore and Timothy S. Hogan for defendants in error.

Mr. Chief Justice White delivered the opinion of the court:

By an amendment to the Constitution of Ohio, adopted September 3d, 1912, the legislative power was expressly declared to be vested not only in the senate and house of representatives of the state, constituting the general assembly, but in the people, in whom a right was reserved by way of referendum to approve or disapprove by popular vote any law enacted by the general assembly. And by other constitutional provisions the machinery to carry out the referendum was created. Briefly they were this: Within a certain time after the enactment of a law by the senate and house of representatives, and its approval by the governor, upon petition of 6 per centum of the voters, the question of whether the law should become operative was to be submitted to a vote of the people, and, if approved, the law should be operative; and, if not approved, it should have no effect whatever.

In May, 1915, the general assembly of Ohio passed an act redistricting the state for the purpose of congressional elections, by which act twenty-two congressional districts were created, in some respects differing from the previously established districts, and this act, after approval by the governor, was filed in the office of the secretary of state. The requisite number of electors under the referendum provision having petitioned for a submission of the law to a popular vote, such vote was taken and the law was disapproved. Thereupon, in the supreme court of the state, the suit before us was begun against state election officers for the purpose of procuring a mandamus, directing them to disregard the vote of the people on the referendum, disapproving the law, and to proceed to discharge their duties as such officers in the next congressional election, upon the assumption that the action by way of referendum was void, and that the law which was disapproved was subsisting and valid. The right to this relief was based upon the charge that the referendum vote was not and could not be a part of the legislative authority of the state, and therefore could have no influence on the subject of the law creating congressional districts for the purpose of representation in Congress. Indeed, it was in substance charged that both from the point of view of the state Constitution and laws and from that of the Constitution of the United States, especially 4 of article 1, providing that 'the times, places and manner of holding elections for Senators and Representatives, shall be prescribed in each state by the legislature thereof; but the Congress may at any time by law, make or alter such regulations, except as to the places of choosing Senators;' and also from that of the provisions of the controlling act of Congress of August 8, 1911 (chap. 5, 37 Stat. at L. 13, Comp. Stat. 1913, 15), apportioning representation among the states, the attempt to make the referendum a component part of the legislative authority empowered to deal with the election of members of Congress was absolutely void. The court below adversely disposed of these contentions, and held that the provisions as to referendum were a part of the legislative power of the state, made so by the Constitution, and that nothing in the act of Congress of 1911, or in the constitutional provision, oper-

ated to the contrary, and that therefore the disapproved law had no existence and was not entitled to be enforced by mandamus.

Without going into the many irrelevant points which are pressed in
the argument, and the various inapposite authorities cited, although we
have considered them all, we think it is apparent that the whole case and
every real question in it will be disposed of by looking at it from three
points of view,-the state power, the power of Congress, and the operation
of the provision of the Constitution of the United States, referred to.

1. As to the state power, we pass from its consideration, since it is
   obvious that the decision below is conclusive on that subject, and
   makes it clear that, so far as the state had the power to do it, the
   referendum constituted a part of the state Constitution and laws,
   and was contained within the legislative power; and therefore the
   claim that the law which was disapproved and was no law under
   the Constitution and laws of the state was yet valid and operative
   is conclusively established to be wanting in merit.

2. So far as the subject may be influenced by the power of Congress,
   that is, to the extent that the will of Congress has been expressed
   on the subject, we think the case is equally without merit. We say
   this because we think it is clear that Congress, in 1911, in enacting
   the controlling law concerning the duties of the states, through
   their legislative authority, to deal with the subject of the creation of
   congressional districts, expressly modified the phraseology of the
   previous acts relating to that subject by inserting a clause plainly
   intended to provide that where, by the state Constitution and laws,
   the referendum was treated as part of the legislative power, the
   power as thus constituted should be held and treated to be the state
   legislative power for the purpose of creating congressional districts
   by law. This is the case since, under the act of Congress dealing
   with apportionment, which preceded the act of 1911, by 4 if was
   commanded that the existing districts in a state should continue in
   force 'until the legislature of such state, in the manner herein prescribed, shall redistrict such state' (act of February 7, 1891, chap.
   116, 26 Stat. at L. 735); while in the act of 1911 there was substituted a provision that the redistricting should be made by a state 'in

484 | Appendix P

the manner provided by the laws thereof.' And the legislative history of this last act leaves no room for doubt that the prior words were stricken out and the new words inserted for the express purpose, in so far as Congress had power to do it, of excluding the possibility of making the contention as to referendum which is now urged. Cong. Rec. vol. 47, pp. 3436, 3437, 3507

3. To the extent that the contention urges that to include the referendum within state legislative power for the purpose of apportionment is repugnant to 4 of article 1 of the Constitution and hence void, even if sanctioned by Congress, because beyond the constitutional authority of that body, and hence that it is the duty of the judicial power so to declare, we again think the contention is plainly without substance, for the following reasons: It must rest upon the assumption that to include the referendum in the scope of the legislative power is to introduce a virus which destroys that power, which in effect annihilates representative government, and causes a state where such condition exists to be not republican in form, in violation of the guaranty of the Constitution. Const. 4, art. 4. But the proposition and the argument disregard the settled rule that the question of whether that guaranty of the Constitution has been disregarded presents no justiciable controversy, but involves the exercise by Congress of the authority vested in it by the Constitution. *Pacific States Teleph. & Teleg. Co. v. Oregon,* 223 U.S. 118 , 56 L. ed. 377, 32 Sup. Ct. Rep. 224. In so far as the proposition challenges the power of Congress, as manifested by the clause in the act of 1911, treating the referendum as a part of the legislative power for the purpose of apportionment, where so ordained by the state Constitutions and laws, the argument but asserts, on the one hand, that Congress had no power to do that which, from the point of view of 4 of article 1, previously considered, the Constitution expressly gave the right to do. In so far as the proposition may be considered as asserting, on the other hand, that any attempt by Congress to recognize the referendum as a part of the legislative authority of a state is obnoxious to a republican form of government as provided by 4 of article 4, the contention necessarily but reasserts the proposition on that subject previously adversely disposed of. And that this is the inevitable

result of the contention is plainly manifest, since at best the proposition comes to the assertion that because Congress, upon whom the Constitution has conferred the exclusive authority to uphold the guaranty of a republican form of government, has done something which it is deemed is repugnant to that guaranty, therefore there was automatically created judicial authority to go beyond the limits of judicial power, and, in doing so, to usurp congressional power, on the ground that Congress had mistakenly dealt with a subject which was within its exclusive control, free from judicial interference.

It is apparent from these reasons that there must either be a dismissal for want of jurisdiction, because there is no power to re- examine the state questions foreclosed by the decision below, and because of the want of merit in the Federal questions relied upon, or a judgment of affirmance, it being absolutely indifferent, as to the result, which of the two be applied. In view, however, of the subject-matter of the controversy and the Federal characteristics which inhere in it, we are of opinion, applying the rule laid down in *Swafford v. Templeton*, 185 U.S. 487 , 46 L. ed. 1005, 22 Sup. Ct. Rep. 783, the decree proper to be rendered is one of affirmance, and such a decree is therefore ordered.

Affirmed.

APPENDIX Q:
Maine Supreme Court Opinion for
In re Opinion of the Justices (1919)

Maine Supreme Court
107 A. 705
In re Opinion of the Justices
August 28, 1919

Answer to question propounded to the Justices of the Supreme Judicial Court by the Governor.

To the Honorable Carl E. Milliken, Governor of Maine:

The undersigned Justices of the Supreme Judicial Court, having considered the question propounded by you under date of July 9, 1919, concerning the necessity of submitting by referendum to the qualified voters of the state a certain act of the Legislature of Maine, entitled "An act granting to women the right to vote for presidential electors," respectfully submit the following answer:

The request contains certain recitals of fact, the substance of which is that the above statute was passed by the concurrent action of both branches of the Legislature and was duly approved by the Governor; that the Legislature adjourned without day on April 4, 1919, and within 90 days thereafter petitions, apparently bearing the requisite number of signatures, were filed with the secretary of state, requesting that this act be referred to the people under Amendment 31 of article 4 of the Constitution of Maine, known as the initiative and referendum amendment.

QUESTION.

"Is the effect of the act of the Legislature of Maine of 1919, entitled 'An act granting to women the right to vote for presidential electors,' approved by the Governor on March 28, 1919, suspended by valid written petitions of not less than 10,000 electors, addressed to the Governor and filed in the office of the secretary of state within 90 days after the recess of the Legislature, requesting that it be referred to the people, and should the act be referred to the people as provided in article 4 of the Constitution of Maine, as amended by Amendment 31, adopted September 14, 1908?"

ANSWER.

This question we answer in the affirmative. In our opinion this legislative act comes within the provisions of the initiative and referendum amendment, and should be referred to the people for adoption or rejection by them.

To solve this problem it is necessary to pursue the same general course as in deciding the question concerning the prohibitory amendment to the federal Constitution, by an examination, first, of the provisions and requirements of the Constitution of the United States relating to this subject-matter, and, second, of the provisions and requirements of the Constitution of Maine.

The first question that naturally arises is this: Where, under the federal Constitution, is lodged the power of determining in what manner presidential electors shall be chosen and of prescribing the qualifications of the voters therefor?

It was competent for the people of the United States, in creating the compact known as the federal Constitution, to lodge this power wherever they saw fit. It was a matter wholly within their discretion. It is a well-known historical fact that there was a long and spirited debate in the constitutional convention over this very question; that is, the method to be adopted in electing the chief magistrate of the nation. Many plans were submitted, such as election by Congress, by the people at large, by the chief executives of the several states, and by electors appointed by the Legislatures. 1 Elliot, Deb. 208, 211, 217, 262.

Finally the following provisions, which were presented by Gouveneur Morris for the special committee, were adopted by the convention after much discussion, and were incorporated in article 11 of the perfected instrument, where they stand unchanged today, viz.:

"Each state shall appoint, in such manner as the Legislature thereof may direct, a number of electors equal to the whole number of Senators and Representatives to which the state may be entitled in the Congress," etc. Article 2, § 1, subd. 2.

"The Congress may determine the time of choosing the electors, and the day on which they shall give their votes, which day shall be the same throughout the United States." Article 2, § 1, subd. 4.

These two subdivisions comprise all the provisions of the federal Constitution applicable to the point in issue here. Under section 1, subd. 4, Congress is given the power to determine the date of holding presidential elections and of the meeting of the electors, but that marks the limit of its constitutional power. *In re Green,* 134 U. S. 377, 10 Sup. Ct. 586, 33 L. Ed. 951. All other powers in connection with this subject are expressly reserved to the states. *McPherson v. Blacker,* 146 U. S. 1, 13 Sup. Ct. 3, 36 L. Ed. 869; *Pope v. Williams,* 193 U. S. 621, 24 Sup. Ct. 573, 48 L. Ed. 817 .

In the case last cited the Supreme Court of the United States say:

"The privilege to vote in a state is within the jurisdiction of the state itself, to be exercised as the state may direct, and upon such terms as to it may seem proper, provided, of course, no discrimination is made between individuals in violation of the federal Constitution."

The word "appoint" as employed in subdivision 2 has been interpreted to be sufficiently comprehensive to include the result of a popular election and to convey the broadest powers of determination. *McPherson v. Blacker,* 146 U. S. 1, 27, 13 Sup. Ct. 3, 36 L. Ed. 869.

The language of section 1, subd. 2, is clear and unambiguous. It admits of no doubt as to where the constitutional power of appointment is vested, namely, in the several states. "Each state shall appoint in such manner as the Legislature thereof may direct" are the significant words of the section, and their plain meaning is that each state is thereby clothed with the absolute power to appoint electors in such manner as it may see fit, without any interference or control on the part of the federal government, except, of course, in case of attempted discrimination as to race, color, or previous condition of servitude under the fifteenth amendment. The clause, "in such manner as the Legislature thereof may direct," means, simply that the state shall give expression to its will, as it must, of necessity, through its law-making body, the Legislature. The will of the state in this respect must be voiced in legislative acts or resolves, which shall prescribe in detail the manner of choosing electors, the qualifications of voters therefor, and the proceedings on the part of the electors when chosen.

But these acts and resolves must be passed and become effective in accordance with and in subjection to the Constitution of the state, like all other acts and resolves having the force of law. The Legislature was not given in this respect any superiority over or independence from the organic law of the state in force at the time when a given law is passed. Nor was it designated by the federal Constitution as a mere agency or representative of the people to perform a certain act, as it was under article 5 in ratifying a federal amendment, a point more fully discussed in the answer to the question concerning the federal prohibitory amendment. 107 Atl. 673. It is simply the ordinary instrumentality of the state, the legislative branch of the government, the law-making power, to put into words the will of the state in connection with the choice of presidential electors. The distinction between the function and power of the Legislature in the case under consideration and its function and power as a particular body designated by the federal Constitution to ratify or reject a federal amendment is sharp and clear and must be borne in mind.

It follows, therefore, that under the provisions of the federal Constitution the state by its legislative direction may establish such a method of choosing its presidential electors as it may see fit, and may change that method from time to time as it may deem advisable; but the legislative acts both of establishment and of change must always be subject to the provisions of the Constitution of the state in force at the time such acts are passed and can be valid and effective only when enacted in compliance therewith.

In the exercise of the power thus conferred by the federal Constitution, various methods of electing presidential electors were adopted in the early days by the several states, as set forth in detail in *McPherson v. Blacker,* 146 U. S. at pages 29 to 35, 13 Sup. Ct. 3, 36 L. Ed. 869.

In our own state the same holds true to a certain extent. Prior to 1847 the legislative direction expressed itself in the form of a joint resolution, passed every fourth year, at the session immediately preceding a presidential election. These resolves had the force of law, and with the exception of those of 1820 and 1824 they were uniformly presented to and were approved by the Governor.

Prior to 1840 the district prevailed in whole or in part. Res. 1820, c. 19; 1824, c. 76; 1828, c. 23; 1832, c. 65; 1836, c. 9. In 1840 (Res c. 55) 10 electors at large were provided for, and since that time the electors have been chosen at large upon a single ballot. This method was followed in 1844. Res. 1844, c. 295.

Under the resolves of 1820, 1824, and 1828, the qualifications of voters for representatives and senators to the Legislature were made the qualifications of voters for presidential electors. By the resolves of 1832 and 1836, the qualifications of voters for representatives alone were made the test, and by the resolve of 1840 this was changed to qualifications of voters for senators alone.

The Legislature of 1847 directed for the first time by a general act, instead of by a quadrennial resolve, the manner in which the voters should proceed in the election of presidential electors (Pub. L. 1847, c. 26), and, following the resolves of 1840 and 1844, prescribed the qualified voters therefor to be "the people of this state qualified to vote for senators in its Legislature." This qualification established by the act of 1847 has been preserved in all the subsequent revisions. R. S. 1857, c. 4, § 79; R. S. 1871, c. 4, § 78; R. S. 1883, c. 4, § 86; R. S. 1903, c. 6, § 123; R. S. 1916, c. 7, § 57. And such was the law of this state when the act in question (chapter 120 of the Public Laws of 1919) was passed. The qualification of voters for senators, as well as for representatives, is fixed by the Constitution of Maine as "every male citizen of the United States of the age of twenty-one years and upwards," etc. Article 2, § 1. Therefore, prior to the act of 1919, only male citizens could vote for presidential electors. It is clear that this act, extending this privilege to women, constitutes a change in the method of electing presidential electors, and is a virtual amendment of R. S. 1916, c. 7, § 57, not in express terms, but by necessary implication.

In other words, this state during the century of its existence prior to 1919, had by appropriate legislative act or resolve directed that only male citizens were qualified to vote for presidential electors. By the act of 1919 it has attempted to change that direction, by extending the privilege of suffrage, so far as presidential electors are concerned, to women. Had this act been passed prior to the adoption of the initiative and referendum amendment in 1908, it would have become effective, so far as legal enactment is concerned, without being referred to the people; but now under Amendment 31 such reference must be had, if the necessary steps therefor are taken.

The language of that amendment is as follows:

> "No act or joint resolution of the Legislature, except such orders or resolutions as pertain solely to facilitating the performance of the business of the Legislature, of either branch, or of any committee or officer thereof, or appropriate money therefor or for the payment of salaries fixed by law, shall take effect until ninety days after the recess of the Legislature passing it, unless in case of emergency," etc.

None of the exceptions applies here. Section 17 provides that upon written petition of not less than 10,000 electors, filed in the office of the Secretary of State within 90 days after the recess of the Legislature, requesting that-

> "one or more acts, bills, resolves or resolutions, or part or parts thereof passed by the Legislature, not then in effect by reason of the provisions of the preceding section be referred to the people, such acts, bills, resolves or resolutions shall not take effect until thirty days after the Governor shall have announced by public proclamation that the same have been ratified by a majority of the electors voting thereon at a general or special election."

It is evident that the act in question falls within the terms and scope of this amendment. This is an ordinary legislative act, a bill in the form prescribed by Amendment 31. It is entitled "An act granting," etc. The enacting clause is, "Be it enacted by the people of the state of Maine." It was presented to the Governor for his approval, and was signed by him, as required by section 2 of part third of article 4 of the Constitution of Maine, viz.:

> "Every bill or resolution having the force of law, to which the concurrence of both houses may be necessary, ... which shall have passed both houses, shall be presented to the Governor,

and if he approves, he shall sign it," etc.

It has been published as chapter 120 of Public Laws of 1919.

This is not a mere joint resolution, addressed to the Governor, asking for the removal of a public official, as in *Moulton v. Scully*, 111 Me. 428, 89 Atl. 944, nor is it a joint resolution ratifying an amendment to the federal Constitution, as in the other question propounded to us herewith, in neither of which cases did the referendum attach, because neither resolution had the force of law. This is the public statute of a law-making body, and is as fully within the control of the referendum amendment as is any other of the 239 public acts passed at the last session of the Legislature, excepting, of course, emergency acts. It is shielded from the jurisdiction of that referendum neither by the state nor by the federal Constitution. In short, the state, through its Legislature, has taken merely the first step toward effecting a change in the appointment of presidential electors; but, because of the petitions filed, it must await the second step which is the vote of the people. The legislative attempt in this case cannot be fully effective until "thirty days after the Governor shall have announced by public proclamation that the same has been ratified by a majority of the electors voting thereon at a general or special election."

It follows that, for the reasons already stated, this question is answered in the affirmative.

Very respectfully,

LESLIE C. CORNISH

ALBERT M. SPEAR

GEORGE M. HANSON

WARREN C. PHILBROOK

CHARLES J. DUNN

JOHN A. MORRILL

SCOTT WILSON

LUERE B. DEASY

APPENDIX R:
State Constitutional Provisions Relating to Repealing or Amending Voter Initiatives

ALASKA CONSTITUTION-ARTICLE XI

SECTION 6. ENACTMENT. If a majority of the votes cast on the proposition favor its adoption, the initiated measure is enacted. If a majority of the votes cast on the proposition favor the rejection of an act referred, it is rejected. The lieutenant governor shall certify the election returns. An initiated law becomes effective ninety days after certification, is not subject to veto, and may not be repealed by the legislature within two years of its effective date. It may be amended at any time. An act rejected by referendum is void thirty days after certification. Additional procedures for the initiative and referendum may be prescribed by law.

ARIZONA CONSTITUTION-ARTICLE 4, PART 1(6)

(A) Veto of initiative or referendum. The veto power of the governor shall not extend to an initiative measure approved by a majority of the votes cast thereon or to a referendum measure decided by a majority of the votes cast thereon.

(B) Legislature's power to repeal initiative or referendum. The legislature shall not have the power to repeal an initiative measure approved by a majority of the votes cast thereon or to repeal a referendum measure decided by a majority of the votes cast thereon.

(C) Legislature's power to amend initiative or referendum. The legislature shall not have the power to amend an initiative measure approved by a majority of the votes cast thereon, or to amend a referendum measure decided by a majority of the votes cast thereon, unless the amending legislation furthers the purposes of such measure and at least three-fourths of the members of each house of the legislature, by a roll call of ayes and nays, vote to amend such measure.

ARKANSAS CONSTITUTION-AMENDMENT

No Veto: The veto power of the Governor or Mayor shall not extend to measures initiated by or referred to the people.

Amendment and Repeal: No measure approved by a vote of the people shall be amended or repealed by the General Assembly or by any City Council, except upon a yea and nay vote on roll call of two-thirds of all the members elected to each house of the General Assembly, or of the City Council, as the case may be.

CALIFORNIA CONSTITUTION-ARTICLE 2, SECTION 10(C)

The Legislature may amend or repeal referendum statutes. It may amend or repeal an initiative statute by another statute that becomes effective only when approved by the electors unless the initiative statute permits amendment or repeal without their approval.

MASSACHUSETTS CONSTITUTION-AMENDMENT ARTICLE 4

Section 3. Amendment of Proposed Amendments. – A proposal for an amendment to the constitution introduced by initiative petition shall be voted upon in the form in which it was introduced, unless such amendment is amended by vote of three-fourths of the members voting thereon in joint session, which vote shall be taken by call of the yeas and nays if called for by any member.

MICHIGAN CONSTITUTION-ARTICLE 2, SECTION 9

Initiative; duty of legislature, referendum. Any law proposed by initiative petition shall be either enacted or rejected by the legislature without change or amendment within 40 session days from the time such petition is received by the legislature. If any law proposed by such petition shall be enacted by the legislature it shall be subject to referendum, as hereinafter provided.

Legislative rejection of initiated measure; different measure; submission to people. If the law so proposed is not enacted by the legislature within the 40 days, the state officer authorized by law shall submit such proposed law to the people for approval or rejection at the next general election. The legislature may reject any measure so proposed by initiative petition and propose a different measure upon the same subject by a yea and nay vote upon separate roll calls, and in such event both measures shall be submitted by such state officer to the electors for approval or rejection at the next general election.

Initiative or referendum law; effective date, veto, amendment and repeal. Any law submitted to the people by either initiative or referendum petition and approved by a majority of the votes cast thereon at any election shall take effect 10 days after the date of the official declaration of the vote. No law initiated or adopted by the people shall be subject to the veto power of the governor, and no law adopted by the people at the polls under the initiative provisions of this section shall be amended or repealed, except by a vote of the electors unless otherwise provided in the initiative measure or by three-fourths of the members elected to and serving in each house of the legislature. Laws approved by the people under the referendum provision of this section may be amended by the legislature at any subsequent session thereof. If two or more measures approved by the electors at the same election conflict, that receiving the highest affirmative vote shall prevail.

NEBRASKA CONSTITUTION-ARTICLE III, SECTION 2

. . . The Legislature shall not amend, repeal, modify, or impair a law enacted by the people by initiative, contemporaneously with the adoption of this initiative measure or at any time thereafter, except upon a vote of at least two -thirds of all the members of the Legislature.

NEVADA CONSTITUTION-ARTICLE 19, SECTION 2

3. . . . An initiative measure so approved by the voters shall not be amended, annulled, repealed, set aside or suspended by the legislature within 3 years from the date it takes effect....

NORTH DAKOTA CONSTITUTION-ARTICLE 3, SECTION 8

. . . A measure approved by the electors may not be repealed or amended by the legislative assembly for seven years from its effective date, except by a two-thirds vote of the members elected to each house...

WASHINGTON CONSTITUTION, ARTICLE 2, SECTION 41

. . . No act, law or bill approved by a majority of the electors voting thereon shall be amended or repealed by the legislature within a period of two years following such enactment: Provided, That any such act, law or bill may be amended within two years after such enactment at any regular or special session of the legislature by a vote of two-thirds of all the members elected to each house with full compliance with section 12, Article III, of the Washington Constitution, and no amendatory law adopted in accordance with this provision shall be subject to referendum. But such enactment may be amended or repealed at any general regular or special election by direct vote of the people thereon. These provisions supersede the provisions of subsection (c) of section 1 of this article as amended by the seventh amendment to the Constitution of this state.

WYOMING CONSTITUTION-ARTICLE 3, SECTION 52

(f) If votes in an amount in excess of fifty percent (50%) of those voting in the general election are cast in favor of adoption of an initiated measure, the measure is enacted. If votes in an amount in excess of fifty percent (50%) of those voted in the general election are cast in favor of rejection of an act referred, it is rejected. The secretary of state shall certify the election returns. An initiated law becomes effective ninety (90) days after certification, is not subject to veto, and may not be repealed by the legislature within two (2) years of its effective date. It may be amended at any time. An act rejected by referendum is void thirty (30) days after certification. Additional procedures for the initiative and referendum may be prescribed by law.

APPENDIX S:
Supporters in Congress of Nationwide Popular Election of the President in Roll Calls and Sponsors of Constitutional Amendments

S.1 ALABAMA

SPONSOR OF A CONSTITUTIONAL AMENDMENT	VOTED FOR SJR 28 IN 1979 ROLL CALL	VOTED FOR HJR 681 IN 1969 ROLL CALL
Rep. John H. Buchanan (R) • HJR 228 - 95th Congress • HJR 288 - 96th Congress		Rep. John H. Buchanan (R)
		Rep. William Dickinson (R)
Rep. William Edwards (R) • HJR 138 - 95th Congress • HJR 189 - 96th Congress • HJR 195 - 97th Congress		Rep. William Edwards (R)
	Sen. Donald Stewart (D)	

S.2 ALASKA

SPONSOR OF A CONSTITUTIONAL AMENDMENT	VOTED FOR SJR 28 IN 1979 ROLL CALL	VOTED FOR HJR 681 IN 1969 ROLL CALL
Sen. Maurice Gravel (D) • SJR 1 - 94th Congress • SJR 1 - 95th Congress • SJR 1 - 96th Congress • SJR 28 - 96th Congress	Sen. Maurice Gravel (D)	

S.3 ARIZONA

SPONSOR OF A CONSTITUTIONAL AMENDMENT	VOTED FOR SJR 28 IN 1979 ROLL CALL	VOTED FOR HJR 681 IN 1969 ROLL CALL
		Rep. John Rhodes (R)
		Rep. Sam Steiger (R)
Rep. Morris K. Udall (D) • HJR 168 - 95th Congress		Rep. Morris K. Udall (D)
Sen. Dennis DeConcini (D) • SJR 1 - 95th Congress • SJR 1 - 96th Congress • SJR 28 - 96th Congress • SJR 3 - 97th Congress • SJR 17 - 98th Congress • SJR 297 - 102nd Congress	Sen. Dennis DeConcini (D)	

S.3 ARKANSAS

SPONSOR OF A CONSTITUTIONAL AMENDMENT	VOTED FOR SJR 28 IN 1979 ROLL CALL	VOTED FOR HJR 681 IN 1969 ROLL CALL
Rep. William Vollie Alexander Jr. (D) • HJR 137 - 93rd Congress		Rep. William Vollie Alexander Jr. (D)
		Rep. John Hammerschmidt (R)
		Rep. Wilbur Mills (D)
Sen. David H. Pryor (D) • SJR 1 - 96th Congress • SJR 28 - 96th Congress • SJR 3 - 97th Congress • SJR 17 - 98th Congress • SJR 163 - 101st Congress • SJR 297 - 102nd Congress	Sen. David H. Pryor (D)	Rep. David H. Pryor (D)

S.5 CALIFORNIA

SPONSOR OF A CONSTITUTIONAL AMENDMENT	VOTED FOR SJR 28 IN 1979 ROLL CALL	VOTED FOR HJR 681 IN 1969 ROLL CALL
		Rep. Glenn Anderson (D)
Rep. Jim Bates (D) • HJR 137 - 101st Congress		
Rep. Anthony Beilenson (D) • HJR 9 - 102nd Congress		
Rep. Alphonza Bell (R) • HJR 237 - 93rd Congress		Rep. Alphonza Bell (R)
Sen. Barbara Boxer (D) • HJR 5 - 100th Congress		
Rep. George Brown (D) • HJR 228 - 95th Congress • HJR 254 - 96th Congress		Rep. George Brown (D)
Rep. Clair Burgener (R) • HJR 228 - 95th Congress		
		Rep. Phillip Burton (D)
Rep. Tom Campbell (R) • HJR 180 - 104th Congress • HJR 43 - 105th Congress		
		Rep. Donald Clausen (R)
		Rep. Delwin Clawson (R)
Rep. Anthony Coelho (D) • HJR 254 - 96th Congress		
		Rep. Jeffery Cohelan (D)
		Rep. James Corman (D)
Sen. Alan Cranston (D) • SJR 1 - 94th Congress • SJR 1 - 95th Congress • SJR 1 - 96th Congress • SJR 28 - 96th Congress • SJR 3 - 97th Congress • SJR 297 - 102nd Congress	Sen. Alan Cranston (D)	
Rep. George Danielson (D) • HJR 207 - 93rd Congress • HJR 149 - 95th Congress • HJR 7 - 96th Congress		
Rep. Ronald Dellums (D) • HJR 117 - 104th Congress		

S.5 CALIFORNIA *(cont.)*

SPONSOR OF A CONSTITUTIONAL AMENDMENT	VOTED FOR SJR 28 IN 1979 ROLL CALL	VOTED FOR HJR 681 IN 1969 ROLL CALL
Rep. Calvin Dooley (D) • HJR 28 - 103rd Congress		
		Rep. William Edwards (D)
Rep. Vic Fazio (D) • HJR 254 - 96th Congress		
Sen. Diane Feinstein (D) • SJR 11 - 109th Congress		
Rep. Bob Filner (D) • HJR 103 - 108th Congress		
		Rep. Charles Gubser (R)
		Rep. Richard Hanna (D)
Rep. Mark W. Hannaford (D) • HJR 229 - 95th Congress		
Rep. Augustus Hawkins (D) • HJR 384 - 95th Congress		Rep. Augustus Hawkins (D)
Rep. Andrew Hinshaw (R) • HJR 207 - 93rd Congress		
Rep. Chester Holifield (D) • HJR 207 - 93rd Congress		Rep. Chester Holifield (D)
		Rep. Craig Hosmer (R)
		Rep. Harold Johnson (D)
Rep. William M. Ketchum (R) • HJR 168 - 95th Congress • HJR 230 - 95th Congress • HJR 384 - 95th Congress		
Rep. Jay Kim (R) • HJR 28 - 103rd Congress		
Rep. John H. Krebs (D) • HJR 228 - 95th Congress		
Rep. Robert L. Leggett (D) • HJR 207 - 93rd Congress • HJR 231 - 95th Congress		Rep. Robert L. Leggett (D)
Rep. James F. Lloyd (D) • HJR 168 - 95th Congress		

S.5 CALIFORNIA *(cont.)*

SPONSOR OF A CONSTITUTIONAL AMENDMENT	VOTED FOR SJR 28 IN 1979 ROLL CALL	VOTED FOR HJR 681 IN 1969 ROLL CALL
Rep. Zoe Lofgren (D) • HJR 112 - 108th Congress • HJR 50 - 109th Congres		
		Rep. William Mailliard (R)
Rep. Matthew Martinez (D) • HJR 137 - 101st Congress		
		Rep. Robert Mathias (R)
Rep. Alfred McCandless (R) • HJR 28 - 103rd Congress		
		Rep. Paul McCloskey (R)
		Rep. John McFall (D)
		Rep. George Miller (D)
Rep. John Moss (D) • HJR 70 - 95th Congress • HJR 168 - 95th Congress		Rep. John Moss (D)
Rep. Jerry M. Patterson (D) • HJR 231 - 95th Congress • HJR 397 - 95th Congress • HJR 254 - 96th Congress		
Rep. Nancy Pelosi (D) • HJR 137 - 101st Congress		
		Rep. Jerry Pettis (R)
Rep. Shirley N. Pettis (R) • HJR 228 - 95th Congress		
		Rep. Thomas Rees (D)
Rep. Edward R. Roybal (D) • HJR 228 - 95th Congress		
Rep. Bernice Sisk (D) • HJR 207 - 93rd Congress		
		Rep. Allen Smith (R)
Rep. Fortney Stark (D) • HJR 228 - 95th Congress • HJR 299 - 96th Congress • HJR 36 - 109th Congress • HJR 50 - 109th Congress		

S.5 CALIFORNIA *(cont.)*

SPONSOR OF A CONSTITUTIONAL AMENDMENT	VOTED FOR SJR 28 IN 1979 ROLL CALL	VOTED FOR HJR 681 IN 1969 ROLL CALL
		Rep. Burt Talcott (R)
Rep. Walter R. Tucker III (D) • HJR 65 - 103rd Congress		
Sen. John Tunney (D) • SJR 1 - 94th Congress		Rep. John Tunney (D)
Rep. Lionel Van Deerlin (D) • HJR 254 - 96th Congress		Rep. Lionel Van Deerlin (D)
		Rep. Jerome Waldie (D)
		Rep. Charles Wiggins (R)
Rep. Charles H. Wilson (D) • HJR 231 - 95th Congress		Rep. Charles H. Wilson (D)
		Rep. Robert Wilson (R)
Rep. Lynn Woolsey (D) • HJR 50 - 109th Congress		

S.6 COLORADO

SPONSOR OF A CONSTITUTIONAL AMENDMENT	VOTED FOR SJR 28 IN 1979 ROLL CALL	VOTED FOR HJR 681 IN 1969 ROLL CALL
	Sen. William Armstrong (R)	
		Rep. Wayne Aspinall (D)
		Rep. Donald Brotzman (R)
Sen. Ben Campbell (R) • HJR 9 - 102nd Congress		
Rep. Frank Evans (D) • HJR 137 - 93rd Congress		Rep. Frank Evans (D)
Sen. Gary W. Hart (D) • SJR 1 - 94th Congress • SJR 1 - 95th Congress	Sen. Gary W. Hart (D)	
Sen. Floyd Haskell (D) • SJR 1 - 95th Congress • SJR 1 - 99th Congress		
		Rep. Byron Rogers (D)

S.7 CONNECTICUT

SPONSOR OF A CONSTITUTIONAL AMENDMENT	VOTED FOR SJR 28 IN 1979 ROLL CALL	VOTED FOR HJR 681 IN 1969 ROLL CALL
		Rep. Emilio Daddario (D)
Rep. Robert Giaimo (D) • HJR 137 - 93rd Congress		Rep. Robert Giaimo (D)
Rep. Stewart McKinney (R) • HJR 197 - 95th Congress		
		Rep. Thomas Meskill (R)
		Rep. John Monagan (D)
Rep. Bill Ratchford (D) • HJR 254 - 96th Congress		
Sen. Abaraham A. Ribicoff (D) • SJR 1 - 94th Congress • SJR 1 - 95th Congress • SJR 1 - 96th Congress • SJR 28 - 96th Congress	Sen. Abaraham A. Ribicoff (D)	
Rep. Ronald A. Sarasin (R) • HJR 300 - 93rd Congress • HJR 230 - 95th Congress		
		Rep. William St. Onge (D)
		Rep. Lowell Palmer Weicker (R)

S.8 DELAWARE

SPONSOR OF A CONSTITUTIONAL AMENDMENT	VOTED FOR SJR 28 IN 1979 ROLL CALL	VOTED FOR HJR 681 IN 1969 ROLL CALL
		Rep. William Victor Roth (R)
Sen. Thomas Carper (D) • HJR 137 - 101st Congress		

S.9 FLORIDA

SPONSOR OF A CONSTITUTIONAL AMENDMENT	VOTED FOR SJR 28 IN 1979 ROLL CALL	VOTED FOR HJR 681 IN 1969 ROLL CALL
Rep. Jim Bacchus (D) • HJR 506 - 102nd Congress • HJR 28 - 103rd Congress		
Rep. Charles E. Bennett (D) • HJR 13 - 93rd Congress • HJR 3 - 94th Congress • HJR 33 - 95th Congress • HJR 24 - 96th Congress • HJR 20 - 97th Congress • HJR 11 - 98th Congress • HJR 19 - 99th Congress • HJR 12 - 100th Congress • HJR 11 - 101st Congress • HJR 9 - 102nd Congress		Rep. Charles E. Bennett (D)
		Rep. Herbert Burke (R)
		Rep. William Cramer (R)
Rep. Dante Fascell (D) • HJR 207 - 93rd Congress		Rep. Dante Fascell (D)
		Rep. Louis Frey (R)
Rep. Don Fuqua (D) • HJR 31 - 93rd Congress		
Rep. Sam Gibbons (D) • HJR 228 - 95th Congress • HJR 261 - 96th Congress		Rep. Sam Gibbons (D)
Rep. Alcee Hastings (D) • HJR 28 - 103rd Congress • HJR 17 - 109th Congress		
Rep. Claude Pepper (D) • HJR 207 - 93rd Congress • HJR 228 - 95th Congress • HJR 288 - 96th Congress		Rep. Claude Pepper (D)
		Rep. Paul Rogers (D)

S.10 GEORGIA

SPONSOR OF A CONSTITUTIONAL AMENDMENT	VOTED FOR SJR 28 IN 1979 ROLL CALL	VOTED FOR HJR 681 IN 1969 ROLL CALL
		Rep. John Davis (D)
		Rep. Phillip Landrum (D)
Rep. John Lewis (D) • HJR 137 - 101st Congress • HJR 9 - 102nd Congress		
		Rep. Robert G. Stephens, Jr. (D)
		Rep. Standish Thompson (R)

S.11 HAWAII

SPONSOR OF A CONSTITUTIONAL AMENDMENT	VOTED FOR SJR 28 IN 1979 ROLL CALL	VOTED FOR HJR 681 IN 1969 ROLL CALL
Rep. Cecil Heftel (D) • HJR 168 - 95th Congress		
Sen. Daniel K. Inouye (D) • SJR 1 - 94th Congress • SJR 1 - 95th Congress • SJR 1 - 96th Congress • SJR 28 - 96th Congress • SJR 3 - 97th Congress • SJR 362 - 100th Congress	Sen. Daniel K. Inouye (D)	
Sen. Spark Matsunaga (D) • SJR 1 - 95th Congress • SJR 1 - 96th Congress • SJR 28 - 96th Congress • SJR 3 - 97th Congress • SJR 17 - 98th Congress	Sen. Spark M. Matsunaga (D)	Rep. Spark M. Matsunaga (D)
		Rep. Patsy Mink (D)

S.12 IDAHO

SPONSOR OF A CONSTITUTIONAL AMENDMENT	VOTED FOR SJR 28 IN 1979 ROLL CALL	VOTED FOR HJR 681 IN 1969 ROLL CALL
Sen. Frank F. Church (D) • SJR 1 - 94th Congress • SJR 1 - 95th Congress	Sen. Frank F. Church (D)	
		Rep. Orval Hansen (R)
Rep. George Hansen (R) • HJR 207 - 93rd Congress		

S.13 ILLINOIS

SPONSOR OF A CONSTITUTIONAL AMENDMENT	VOTED FOR SJR 28 IN 1979 ROLL CALL	VOTED FOR HJR 681 IN 1969 ROLL CALL
Rep. John Anderson (R) • HJR 228 - 95th Congress • HJR 288 - 96th Congress		Rep. John Anderson (R)
Rep. Frank Annunzio (D) • HJR 137 - 93rd Congress		Rep. Frank Annunzio (D)
		Rep. Leslie Arends (R)
Rep. Rod Blagojevich (D) • HJR 23 - 106th Congress		
Rep. Harold Collier (R) • HJR 137 - 93rd Congress • HJR 462 - 93rd Congress		Rep. Harold Collier (R)
		Rep. George Collins (D)[1]
Rep. Cardiss Collins (D) • HJR 229 - 95th Congress • HJR 137 - 101st Congress • HJR 28 - 103rd Congress • HJR 117 - 104th Congress		
Rep. Philip Crane (R) • HJR 28 - 105th Congress		
Sen. Richard Durbin (D) • HJR 60 - 103rd Congress • SJR 56 -106th Congress		
		Rep. John Erlenborn (R)

---

[1] The roll call does not make clear whether this Representative Collins or the one from Texas voted for HJR 681 in 1969.

S.13 ILLINOIS *(cont.)*

SPONSOR OF A CONSTITUTIONAL AMENDMENT	VOTED FOR SJR 28 IN 1979 ROLL CALL	VOTED FOR HJR 681 IN 1969 ROLL CALL
Rep. Lane Evans (D) • HJR 506 - 102nd Congress • HJR 28 - 103rd Congress • HJR 23 - 106th Congress • HJR 17 - 109th Congress		
		Rep. Paul Findley (R)
		Rep. Kenneth Gray (D)
Rep. Robert Hanrahan (R) • HJR 207 - 93rd Congress		
Rep. Jesse Jackson Jr. (D) • HJR 109 - 108th Congress • HJR 36 - 109th Congress		
		Rep. John Kluczynski (D)
Rep. Ray LaHood (R) • HJR 28 - 105th Congress • HJR 23 - 106th Congress		
Rep. William O. Lipinski (D) • HJR 9 - 102nd Congress • HJR 28 - 105th Congress		
Rep. Robert McClory (R) • HJR 118 - 95th Congress • HJR 197 - 95th Congress • HJR 240 - 96th Congress		Rep. Robert McClory (R)
		Rep. Robert Michel (R)
		Rep. Abner Mikva (D)
		Rep. William Murphy (D)
Rep. Charles Price (D) • HJR 228 - 95th Congress • HJR 261 - 96th Congress		Rep. Charles Price (D)
		Rep. Roman Pucinski (D)
		Rep. Thomas Railsback (R)
		Rep. Charlotte Reid (R)
		Rep. Daniel Rostenkowski (D)

S.13 ILLINOIS *(cont.)*

SPONSOR OF A CONSTITUTIONAL AMENDMENT	VOTED FOR SJR 28 IN 1979 ROLL CALL	VOTED FOR HJR 681 IN 1969 ROLL CALL
Rep. Martin A. Russo (D) • HJR 288 - 96th Congress • HJR 384 - 96th Congress		
Rep. Janice Schakowsky (D) • HJR 109 - 108th Congress		
		Rep. George Shipley (D)
		Rep. William Springer (R)
Sen. Aldai Stevenson III (D) • SJR 1 - 94th Congress • SJR 1 - 95th Congress • SJR 1 - 96th Congress • SJR 28 - 96th Congress	Sen. Aldai Stevenson III (D)	
		Rep. Sidney Yates (D)

S.14 INDIANA

SPONSOR OF A CONSTITUTIONAL AMENDMENT	VOTED FOR SJR 28 IN 1979 ROLL CALL	VOTED FOR HJR 681 IN 1969 ROLL CALL
		Rep. Edwin Adair (R)
Sen. Birch E. Bayh (D) • SJR 1 - 94th Congress • SJR 1 - 95th Congress • SJR 123 - 95th Congress • SJR 1 - 96th Congress • SJR 28 - 96th Congress	Sen. Birch E. Bayh (D)	
Rep. Adam Benjamin Jr. (D) • HJR 384 - 95th Congress		
		Rep. John Brademas (D)
Rep. William Bray (R) • HJR 137 - 93rd Congress		Rep. William Bray (R)
Rep. Floyd Fithian (D) • HJR 521 - 94th Congress • HJR 350 - 95th Congress • HJR 208 - 96th Congress • HJR 254 - 96th Congress		
Rep. Lee Hamilton (D) • HJR 137 - 93rd Congress • HJR 207 - 95th Congress • HJR 137 - 101st Congress • HJR 9 - 102nd Congress • HJR 28 - 103rd Congress • HJR 28 - 105th Congress		Rep. Lee Hamilton (D)
Rep. Andrew Jacobs Jr. (D) • HJR 28 - 103rd Congress • HJR 33 - 103rd Congress • HJR 117 - 104th Congress • HJR 180 - 104th Congress		Rep. Andrew Jacobs Jr. (D)
		Rep. Ray Madden (D)
		Rep. John Myers (R)
Rep. Tim Roemer (D) • HJR 506 - 102nd Congress		
		Rep. Richard Roudebush (R)
Rep. John Roush (D) • HJR 106 - 93rd Congress		
		Rep. Roger Zion (R)

S.15 IOWA

SPONSOR OF A CONSTITUTIONAL AMENDMENT	VOTED FOR SJR 28 IN 1979 ROLL CALL	VOTED FOR HJR 681 IN 1969 ROLL CALL
Rep. Berkley W. Bedell (D) • HJR 229 - 95th Congress • HJR 230 - 95th Congress • HJR 254 - 96th Congress		
Rep. Michael T. Blouin (D) • HJR 1100 - 94th Congress • HJR 676 - 95th Congress		
Sen. Richard Clark (D) • SJR 1 - 94th Congress • SJR 1 - 95th Congress		
	Sen. John Culver (D)	Rep. John Culver (D)
Rep. James Leach (R) • HJR 585 - 96th Congress • HJR 516 - 102nd Congress • HJR 113 - 106th Congress		
		Rep. Frederick Schwengel (R)

S.16 KANSAS

SPONSOR OF A CONSTITUTIONAL AMENDMENT	VOTED FOR SJR 28 IN 1979 ROLL CALL	VOTED FOR HJR 681 IN 1969 ROLL CALL
Sen. Robert J. Dole (R) • SJR 1 - 94th Congress • SJR 1 - 95th Congress • SJR 1 - 96th Congress • SJR 28 - 96th Congress • SJR 3 - 97th Congress • SJR 17 - 98th Congress	Sen. Robert J. Dole (R)	
Rep. Dan Glickman (D) • HJR 673 - 100th Congress • HJR 137 - 101st Congress • HJR 516 - 102nd Congress • HJR 28 - 103rd Congress		
Sen. James Pearson (R) • SJR 1 - 94th Congress		
Rep. William Roy (D) • HJR 207 - 93rd Congress		
		Rep. Garner Shriver (R)
		Rep. Joe Skubitz (R)
Rep. James Slattery (D) • HJR 137 - 101st Congress		
Rep. Edward Winn (R) • HJR 231 - 95th Congress		Rep. Edward Winn (R)

S.17 KENTUCKY

SPONSOR OF A CONSTITUTIONAL AMENDMENT	VOTED FOR SJR 28 IN 1979 ROLL CALL	VOTED FOR HJR 681 IN 1969 ROLL CALL
Rep. Scotty Baesler (D) • HJR 28 - 103rd Congress		
Rep. John Breckinridge (D) • HJR 384 - 95th Congress		
		Rep. Tim Carter (R)
		Rep. William Cowger (R)
Sen. Wendell H. Ford (D) • SJR 1 - 94th Congress • SJR 1 - 95th Congress • SJR 1 - 96th Congress • SJR 28 - 96th Congress • SJR 3 - 97th Congress • SJR - 17 - 98th Congress	Sen. Wendell H. Ford (D)	
Sen. Walter Huddleston (D) • SJR 1 - 94th Congress • SJR 1 - 95th Congress • SJR 1 - 96th Congress • SJR 28 - 96th Congress • SJR 3 - 97th Congress • SJR 17 - 98th Congress	Sen. Walter Huddleston (D)	
		Rep. William Natcher (D)
Rep. Carl D. Perkins (D) • HJR 228 - 95th Congress		Rep. Carl D. Perkins (D)
		Rep. Marion Snyder (R)
		Rep. Frank Stubblefield (D)
		Rep. John Watts (D)

S.18 LOUISIANA

SPONSOR OF A CONSTITUTIONAL AMENDMENT	VOTED FOR SJR 28 IN 1979 ROLL CALL	VOTED FOR HJR 681 IN 1969 ROLL CALL
		Rep. Thomas Hale Boggs (D)
Sen. John Breaux (D) • HJR 229 - 95th Congress		
		Rep. Edwin Edwards (D)
Rep. Thomas J. Huckaby (D) • HJR 516 - 102nd Congress • HJR 526 - 102nd Congress		
Sen. John B. Johnston Jr. (D) • SJR 1 - 96th Congress • SJR 28 - 96th Congress	Sen. John B. Johnston Jr. (D)	
Rep. Richard A. Tonry (D) • HJR 228 - 95th Congress		

S.19 MAINE

SPONSOR OF A CONSTITUTIONAL AMENDMENT	VOTED FOR SJR 28 IN 1979 ROLL CALL	VOTED FOR HJR 681 IN 1969 ROLL CALL
Rep. Thomas Andrews (D) • HJR 28 - 103rd Congress		
Rep. David Emery (R) • HJR 228 - 95th Congress		
Sen. William Hathaway (D) • SJR 1 - 94th Congress)		Rep.. William Hathaway (D
		Rep. Peter Kyros (D)

S.20 MARYLAND

SPONSOR OF A CONSTITUTIONAL AMENDMENT	VOTED FOR SJR 28 IN 1979 ROLL CALL	VOTED FOR HJR 681 IN 1969 ROLL CALL
		Rep. John Glenn Beall (R)
Rep. Elijah E. Cummings (D) • HJR 109 - 108th Congress		
		Rep. George Fallon (D)
		Rep. Samuel Friedel (D)
		Rep. Edward Garmatz (D)
		Rep. Gilbert Gude (R)
		Rep. Lawrence Hogan (R)
		Rep. Clarence Long (D)
Sen. Charles McCurdy Mathias Jr. (R) • SJR 1 - 94th Congress • SJR 1 - 95th Congress • SJR 1 - 96th Congress • SJR 28 - 96th Congress • SJR 8 - 97th Congress • SJR 17 - 98th Congress	Sen. Charles McCurdy Mathias Jr. (R)	
Rep. Kweisi Mfume (D) • HJR 117 - 104th Congress		
Rep. Parren Mitchell (D) • HJR 229 - 95th Congress • HJR 261 - 96th Congress		
		Rep. Rogers Morton (R)
Rep. Gladys Spellman (D) • HJR 384 - 95th Congress		
Rep. Albert Wynn (D) • HJR 103 - 108th Congress		

S.21 MASSACHUSETTS

SPONSOR OF A CONSTITUTIONAL AMENDMENT	VOTED FOR SJR 28 IN 1979 ROLL CALL	VOTED FOR HJR 681 IN 1969 ROLL CALL
Rep. Chester Atkins (D) • HJR 137 - 101st Congress		
Rep. Edward Boland (D) • HJR 137 - 93rd Congress		Rep. Edward Boland (D)
Sen. Edward W. Brooke (R) • SJR 1 - 94th Congress • SJR 1 - 95th Congress		
		Rep. James Burke (D)
Rep. Silvio Conte (R) • HJR 300 - 93rd Congress • HJR 38 - 94th Congress • HJR 45 - 95th Congress • HJR 230 - 95th Congress • HJR 231 - 95th Congress • HJR 373 - 95th Congress • HJR 150 - 96th Congress		Rep. Silvio Conte (R)
Rep. William D. Delahunt (D) • HJR 5 - 107th Congress • HJR 103 - 108th Congress • HJR 8 - 109th Congress		
Rep. Brian Donnelly (D) • HJR 288 - 96th Congress		
		Rep. Harold Donohue (D)
Rep. Barney Frank (D) • HJR 137 - 101st Congress • HJR 9 - 102nd Congress • HJR 28 - 103rd Congress • HJR 117 - 104th Congress • HJR 28 - 105th Congress • HJR 17 - 109th Congress • HJR 36 - 109th Congress		
		Rep. Margaret Heckler (R)
		Rep. Hastings Keith (R)
Sen. Ted Kennedy (D) • SJR 1 - 94th Congress • SJR 1 - 95th Congress • SJR 1 - 96th Congress • SJR 28 - 96th Congress	Sen. Ted Kennedy (D)	

S.21 MASSACHUSETTS *(cont.)*

SPONSOR OF A CONSTITUTIONAL AMENDMENT	VOTED FOR SJR 28 IN 1979 ROLL CALL	VOTED FOR HJR 681 IN 1969 ROLL CALL
Rep. Torbert MacDonald (D) • HJR 336 - 94th Congress		Rep. Torbert MacDonald (D)
Rep. Edward Markey (D) • HJR 373 - 95th Congress		
		Rep. Frank Morse (R)
		Rep. David Obey (D)
		Rep. Thomas O'Neill (D)
		Rep. Philip Philbin (D)
Rep. Gerry Studds (D) • HJR 208 - 93rd Congress • HJR 384 - 95th Congress • HJR 261 - 96th Congress • HJR 591 - 96th Congress • HJR 70 - 97th Congress • HJR 124 - 98th Congress • HJR 137 - 101st Congress • HJR 117 - 104th Congress		
Sen. Paul Tsongas (D) • SJR 1 - 96th Congress • SJR 28 - 96th Congress	Sen. Paul Tsongas (D)	

S.22 MICHIGAN

SPONSOR OF A CONSTITUTIONAL AMENDMENT	VOTED FOR SJR 28 IN 1979 ROLL CALL	VOTED FOR HJR 681 IN 1969 ROLL CALL
Rep. James A. Barcia (D) • HJR 117 - 104th Congress		
Rep. James J. Blanchard (D) • HJR 168 - 95th Congress		
Rep. David Bonior (D) • HJR 230 - 95th Congress • HJR 145 - 102nd Congress • HJR 28 - 103rd Congress		
Rep. William Broomfield (R) • HJR 137 - 93rd Congress • HJR 288 - 94th Congress		Rep. William Broomfield (R)
		Rep. Garry Brown (R)
Rep. Milton R. Carr (D) • HJR 397 - 95th Congress • HJR 261 - 96th Congress		
Rep. Elford Cederberg (R) • HJR 168 - 95th Congress		Rep. Elford Cederberg (R)
Rep. Charles Chamberlain (R) • HJR 202 - 93rd Congress		Rep. Charles Chamberlain (R)
Rep. John Conyers Jr. (D) • HJR 137 - 93rd Congress • HJR 109 - 108th Congress		Rep. John Conyers Jr. (D)
Rep. George Crockett (D) • HJR 137 - 101st Congress		
Rep. John David Dingell Jr. (D) • HJR 137 - 93rd Congress		Rep. John David Dingell Jr. (D)
Rep. Marvin Esch (R) • HJR 137 - 93rd Congress		Rep. Marvin Esch (R)
		Rep. Gerald Ford (R)
Rep. W. D. Ford (D) • HJR 137 - 93rd Congress • HJR 229 - 95th Congress • HJR 288 - 96th Congress		Rep. W. D. Ford (D)
Sen. Robert Griffin (R) • SJR 1 - 94th Congress		

S.22 MICHIGAN *(cont.)*

SPONSOR OF A CONSTITUTIONAL AMENDMENT	VOTED FOR SJR 28 IN 1979 ROLL CALL	VOTED FOR HJR 681 IN 1969 ROLL CALL
Sen. Philip Hart (D) • SJR 1 - 94th Congress		
Sen. Rupert Hartke (D) • SJR 1 - 94th Congress		
Rep. James Harvey (R) • HJR 207 - 93rd Congress		Rep. James Harvey (R)
Rep. Dale E. Kildee (D) • HJR 229 - 95th Congress • HJR 254 - 96th Congress • HJR 261 - 96th Congress		
Sen. Carl Levin (D) • SJR 1 - 96th Congress • SJR 28 - 96th Congress • SJR 3 - 97th Congress • SJR 17 - 98th Congress • SJR 362 - 100th Congress • SJR 163 - 101st Congress	Sen. Carl Levin (D)	
		Rep. Jack McDonald (R)
Rep. Lucien Nedzi (D) • HJR 168 - 95th Congress • HJR 231 - 95th Congress • HJR 384 - 95th Congress		Rep. Lucien Nedzi (D)
Rep. James O'Hara (D) • HJR 137 - 93rd Congress • HJR 139 - 93rd Congress • HJR 207 - 93rd Congress • HJR 208 - 93rd Congress		Rep. James O'Hara (D)
Rep. Carl D. Pursell (R) • HJR 168 - 95th Congress • HJR 230 - 95th Congress		
Sen. Donald Riegle (D) • SJR 1 - 95th Congress • SJR 1 - 96th Congress • SJR 28 - 96th Congress	Sen. Donald Riegle (D)	Rep. Donald Riegle (D)
		Rep. Philip Ruppe (R)
Rep. Harold Sawyer (R) • HJR 384 - 95th Congress		

S.22 MICHIGAN *(cont.)*

SPONSOR OF A CONSTITUTIONAL AMENDMENT	VOTED FOR SJR 28 IN 1979 ROLL CALL	VOTED FOR HJR 681 IN 1969 ROLL CALL
Rep. Bart Stupak (D) • HJR 28 - 103rd Congress		
		Rep. Guy Vander Jagt (R)
Rep. Howard Wolpe (D) • HJR 288 - 96th Congress		

S.23 MINNESOTA

SPONSOR OF A CONSTITUTIONAL AMENDMENT	VOTED FOR SJR 28 IN 1979 ROLL CALL	VOTED FOR HJR 681 IN 1969 ROLL CALL
Sen. Wendell Anderson (D) • SJR 1 - 95th Congress		
		Rep. John Blatnik (D)
Sen. Dave Durenberger (R) • SJR 1 - 96th Congress • SJR 28 - 96th Congress • SJR 3 - 97th Congress	Sen. Dave Durenberger (R)	
Rep. Donald Fraser (D) • HJR 207 - 93rd Congress • HJR 384 - 95th Congress		Rep. Donald Fraser (D)
Rep. William Frenzel (R) • HJR 300 - 93rd Congress • HJR 253 - 95th Congress		
Sen. Hubert Humphrey (D) • SJR 1 - 94th Congress • SJR 1 - 95th Congress		
Rep. Joseph Karth (D) • HJR 204 - 94th Congress		Rep. Joseph Karth (D)
		Rep. Odin Langen (R)
Rep. Bill Luther (D) • HJR 117 - 104th Congress • HJR 28 - 105th Congress		
		Rep. Clark MacGregor (R)
Rep. Betty McCollum (D) • HJR 103 - 108th Congress		
Rep. David Minge (D) • HJR 28 - 103rd Congress • HJR 23 - 106th Congress		

522 | *Appendix S*

S.23 MINNESOTA

SPONSOR OF A CONSTITUTIONAL AMENDMENT	VOTED FOR SJR 28 IN 1979 ROLL CALL	VOTED FOR HJR 681 IN 1969 ROLL CALL
Sen. Walter Mondale (D) • SJR 1 - 94th Congress		
		Rep. Ancher Nelsen (R)
Rep. Richard M. Nolan (D) • HJR 229 - 95th Congress • HJR 308 - 96th Congress		
Rep. Collin Peterson (D) • HJR 28 - 103rd Congress		
Rep. Albert H. Quie (R) • HJR 151 - 94th Congress • HJR 434 - 95th Congress		Rep. Albert H. Quie (R)
Rep. Bruce F. Vento (D) • HJR 288 - 96th Congress • HJR 137 - 101st Congress		
		Rep. John Zwach (R)

S.24 MISSISSIPPI

SPONSOR OF A CONSTITUTIONAL AMENDMENT	VOTED FOR SJR 28 IN 1979 ROLL CALL	VOTED FOR HJR 681 IN 1969 ROLL CALL
Rep. Gene Taylor (D) • HJR 506 - 102nd Congress		

S.25 MISSOURI

SPONSOR OF A CONSTITUTIONAL AMENDMENT	VOTED FOR SJR 28 IN 1979 ROLL CALL	VOTED FOR HJR 681 IN 1969 ROLL CALL
Rep. Richard Bolling (D) • HJR 207 - 93rd Congress		
Rep. William D. Burlison (D) • HJR 137 - 93rd Congress • HJR 786 - 94th Congress • HJR 39 - 95th Congress • HJR 228 - 95th Congress • HJR 229 - 95th Congress • HJR 281 - 95th Congress • HJR 384 - 95th Congress • HJR 397 - 95th Congress • HJR 254 - 96th Congress • HJR 261 - 96th Congress • HJR 288 - 96th Congress • HJR 299 - 96th Congress • HJR 308 - 96th Congress • HJR 332 - 96th Congress		Rep. William D. Burlison (D)
Sen. John C. Danforth (R) • SJR 1 - 95th Congress • SJR 1 - 96th Congress • SJR 28 - 96th Congress	Sen. John C. Danforth (R)	
Rep. Pat Danner (D) • HJR 117 - 104th Congress • HJR 28 - 105th Congress		
Rep. Richard Gephardt (D) • HJR 228 - 95th Congress		
		Rep. William Raleigh Hull (D)
		Rep. William Hungate (D)
		Rep. Richard Ichord (D)
		Rep. William Randall (D)
Sen. William Symington (D) • SJR 1 - 94th Congress		
Rep. James Symington (D) • HJR 300 - 93rd Congress		Rep. James Symington (D)

S.25 MISSOURI *(cont.)*

SPONSOR OF A CONSTITUTIONAL AMENDMENT	VOTED FOR SJR 28 IN 1979 ROLL CALL	VOTED FOR HJR 681 IN 1969 ROLL CALL
Rep. Alan Wheat (D) • HJR 137 - 101st Congress • HJR 145 - 102nd Congress • HJR 65 - 103rd Congress		
Rep. Robert Young (D) • HJR 261 - 96th Congress		

S.26 MONTANA

SPONSOR OF A CONSTITUTIONAL AMENDMENT	VOTED FOR SJR 28 IN 1979 ROLL CALL	VOTED FOR HJR 681 IN 1969 ROLL CALL
Sen. Max Baucus (D) • HJR 197 - 95th Congress • HJR 229 - 95th Congress • HJR 230 - 95th Congress • SJR 3 - 97th Congress • SJR 17 - 98th Congress	Sen. Max Baucus (D)	
Sen. Michael Mansfield (D) • SJR 1 - 94th Congress		
		Rep. Arnold Olsen (D)

S.27 NEBRASKA

SPONSOR OF A CONSTITUTIONAL AMENDMENT	VOTED FOR SJR 28 IN 1979 ROLL CALL	VOTED FOR HJR 681 IN 1969 ROLL CALL
Rep. John J. Cavanaugh (D) • HJR 228 - 95th Congress • HJR 332 - 96th Congress		
		Rep. Glenn Cunningham (R)
		Rep. Robert Denney (R)
Sen. J. James Exon (D) • SJR 3 - 97th Congress • SJR 362 - 100th Congress • SJR 163 - 101st Congress • SJR 302 - 102nd Congress • SJR 173 - 103rd Congress	Sen. J. James Exon (D)	
		Rep. David Martin (R)
Sen. Edward Zorinsky (D) • SJR 1 - 95th Congress • SJR 1 - 96th Congress • SJR 28 - 96th Congress	Sen. Edward Zorinsky (D)	

S.28 NEVADA

SPONSOR OF A CONSTITUTIONAL AMENDMENT	VOTED FOR SJR 28 IN 1979 ROLL CALL	VOTED FOR HJR 681 IN 1969 ROLL CALL
Sen. Harry M. Reid (D) • SJR 297 - 102nd Congress		

S.29 NEW HAMPSHIRE

SPONSOR OF A CONSTITUTIONAL AMENDMENT	VOTED FOR SJR 28 IN 1979 ROLL CALL	VOTED FOR HJR 681 IN 1969 ROLL CALL
Sen. Thomas J. McIntyre (D) • SJR 1 - 94th Congress • SJR 1 - 95th Congress		
		Rep. Louis Wyman (R)

S.30 NEW JERSEY

SPONSOR OF A CONSTITUTIONAL AMENDMENT	VOTED FOR SJR 28 IN 1979 ROLL CALL	VOTED FOR HJR 681 IN 1969 ROLL CALL
		Rep. William Cahill (R)
Rep. Dominick Daniels (D) • HJR 137 - 93rd Congress		Rep. Dominick Daniels (D)
		Rep. Florence Dwyer (R)
Rep. Edwin Forsythe (R) • HJR 207 - 93rd Congress		
		Rep. Peter Frelinghuysen (R)
		Rep. Cornelius Gallagher (D)
		Rep. Henry Helstoski (D)
Rep. James J. Howard (D) • HJR 228 - 95th Congress • HJR 288 - 96th Congress • HJR 130 - 97th Congress		Rep. James J. Howard (D)
Rep. William J. Hughes (D) • HJR 114 - 95th Congress		
		Rep. John Hunt (R)
Rep. Joseph G. Minish (D) • HJR 231 - 95th Congress		Rep. Joseph G. Minish (D)
Rep. Edward Patten (D) • HJR 820 - 93rd Congress		Rep. Edward Patten (D)
Rep. Matthew Rinaldo (R) • HJR 300 - 93rd Congress		
Rep. Peter Rodino (D) • HJR 144 - 95th Congress		Rep. Peter Rodino (D)
		Rep. Charles Sandman (R)
		Rep. Frank Thompson (D)
Rep. William Widnall (R) • HJR 208 - 93rd Congress		Rep. William Widnall (R)
Sen. Harrison Williams (D) • SJR 1 - 94th Congress • SJR 1 - 95th Congress • SJR 1 - 96th Congress • SJR 28 - 96th Congress	Sen. Harrison Williams (D)	

S.31 NEW MEXICO

SPONSOR OF A CONSTITUTIONAL AMENDMENT	VOTED FOR SJR 28 IN 1979 ROLL CALL	VOTED FOR HJR 681 IN 1969 ROLL CALL
		Rep. Manuel Lujan (R)
Sen. Joseph Montoya (D) • SJR 1 - 94th Congress		

S.32 NEW YORK

SPONSOR OF A CONSTITUTIONAL AMENDMENT	VOTED FOR SJR 28 IN 1979 ROLL CALL	VOTED FOR HJR 681 IN 1969 ROLL CALL
Rep. Joseph P. Addabbo (D) • HJR 207 - 93rd Congress • HJR 168 - 95th Congress		Rep. Joseph P. Addabbo (D)
Rep. Herman Badillo (D) • HJR 207 - 93rd Congress		
		Rep. Mario Biaggi (D)
Rep. Jonathan Bingham (D) • HJR 352 - 95th Congress • HJR 384 - 95th Congress		Rep. Jonathan Bingham (D)
Rep. Frank James Brasco (D) • HJR 137 - 93rd Congress		Rep. Frank James Brasco (D)
		Rep. Daniel Button (R)
		Rep. Hugh Carey (D)
		Rep. Emanuel Celler (D)
Rep. Shirley A. Chisholm (D) • HJR 137 - 93rd Congress • HJR 300 - 93rd Congress • HJR 254 - 96th Congress		Rep. Shirley A. Chisholm (D)
		Rep. Barber Conable (R)
		Rep. James Delaney (D)
Rep. Thomas J. Downey (D) • HJR 229 - 95th Congress • HJR 288 - 96th Congress		
		Rep. Thaddeus Dulski (D)
Rep. Eliot L. Engel (D) • HJR 17 - 109th Congress		
		Rep. Leonard Farbstein (D)

S.32 NEW YORK *(cont.)*

SPONSOR OF A CONSTITUTIONAL AMENDMENT	VOTED FOR SJR 28 IN 1979 ROLL CALL	VOTED FOR HJR 681 IN 1969 ROLL CALL
Rep. Hamilton Fish Jr. (R) • HJR 137 - 93rd Congress • HJR 50 - 94th Congress		Rep. Hamilton Fish Jr. (R)
		Rep. Jacob Gilbert (D)
Rep. James Russell Grover Jr. (R) • HJR 137 - 93rd Congress		Rep. James Russell Grover Jr. (R)
		Rep. Seymour Halpern (R)
Rep. James Hanley (D) • HJR 228 - 95th Congress • HJR 261 - 96th Congress		Rep. James Hanley (D)
Rep. James Hastings (R) • HJR 207 - 93rd Congress		Rep. James Hastings (R)
		Rep. Frank Horton (R)
Sen. Jacob Javits (R) • SJR 1 - 94th Congress • SJR 1 - 95th Congress • SJR 1 - 96th Congress • SJR 28 - 96th Congress	Sen. Jacob Javits (R)	
		Rep. Carleton King (R)
		Rep. Edward Koch (D)
		Rep. Allard Lowenstein (D)
		Rep. Richard McCarthy (D)
		Rep. Robert McEwen (R)
		Rep. Martin McKneally (R)
Rep. Michael McNulty (D) • HJR 28 - 103rd Congress • HJR 60 - 103rd Congress • HJR 28 - 105th Congress • HJR 23 - 106th Congress • HJR 103 - 108th Congress • HJR 17 - 109th Congress		
Rep. Donald Mitchell (R) • HJR 750 - 94th Congress • HJR 168 - 95th Congress • HJR 228 - 95th Congress • HJR 288 - 96th Congress		

S.32 NEW YORK *(cont.)*

SPONSOR OF A CONSTITUTIONAL AMENDMENT	VOTED FOR SJR 28 IN 1979 ROLL CALL	VOTED FOR HJR 681 IN 1969 ROLL CALL
Rep. Susan Molinari (R) • HJR 28 - 103rd Congress		
		Rep. John Murphy (D)
Rep. Jerrold Nadler (D) • HJR 109 - 108th Congress		
Rep. Richard L. Ottinger (D) • HJR 231 - 95th Congress • HJR 384 - 95th Congress • HJR 288 - 96th Congress		Rep. Richard L. Ottinger (D)
Rep. Major Owens (D) • HJR 117 - 104th Congress • HJR 109 - 108th Congress		
		Rep. Otis Pike (D)
		Rep. Alexander Pirnie (R)
Rep. Bertram Podell (D) • HJR 207 - 93rd Congress		Rep. Bertram Podell (D)
Rep. Charles B. Rangel (D) • HJR 300 - 95th Congress		
		Rep. Ogden Reid (D)
Rep. Frederick Richmond (D) • HJR 229 - 95th Congress • HJR 254 - 96th Congress		
		Rep. Howard Robison (R)
		Rep. John Rooney (D)
Rep. Benjamin Rosenthal (D) • HJR 207 - 93rd Congress		Rep. Benjamin Rosenthal (D)
		Rep. William Ryan (D)
		Rep. James Scheuer (D)
Rep. Jose E. Serrano (D) • HJR 103 - 108th Congress • HJR 50 - 109th Congress		
		Rep. Henry Smith (R)
		Rep. Samuel Stratton (D)
Rep. Anthony Weiner (D) • HJR 103 - 108th Congress		

S.32 NEW YORK *(cont.)*

SPONSOR OF A CONSTITUTIONAL AMENDMENT	VOTED FOR SJR 28 IN 1979 ROLL CALL	VOTED FOR HJR 681 IN 1969 ROLL CALL
Rep. Theodore S. Weiss (D) • HJR 228 - 95th Congress		
Rep. Lester L. Wolff (D) • HJR 208 - 93rd Congress • HJR 228 - 95th Congress		Rep. Lester L. Wolff (D)
		Rep. John Wydler (R)

S.33 NORTH CAROLINA

SPONSOR OF A CONSTITUTIONAL AMENDMENT	VOTED FOR SJR 28 IN 1979 ROLL CALL	VOTED FOR HJR 681 IN 1969 ROLL CALL
		Rep. James Broyhill (R)
		Rep. Lawrence Fountain (D)
		Rep. Nick Galifianakis (D)
		Rep. David Henderson (D)
		Rep. Charles Jonas (R)
Rep. Walter Beaman Jones Sr. (D) • HJR 207 - 93rd Congress		Rep. Walter Beaman Jones Sr. (D)
		Rep. Wilmer Mizell (R)
		Rep. Lunsford Preyer (D)
		Rep. Earl Ruth (R)
		Rep. Roy Taylor (D)

S.34 NORTH DAKOTA

SPONSOR OF A CONSTITUTIONAL AMENDMENT	VOTED FOR SJR 28 IN 1979 ROLL CALL	VOTED FOR HJR 681 IN 1969 ROLL CALL
		Rep. Mark Andrews (R)
Sen. Quentin N. Burdick (D) • SJR 1 - 94th Congress • SJR 1 - 96th Congress • SJR 28 - 96th Congress • SJR 17 - 98th Congress	Sen. Quentin N. Burdick (D)	

S.35 OHIO

SPONSOR OF A CONSTITUTIONAL AMENDMENT	VOTED FOR SJR 28 IN 1979 ROLL CALL	VOTED FOR HJR 681 IN 1969 ROLL CALL
Rep. Thomas Ashley (D) • HJR 137 - 93rd Congress		Rep. Thomas Ashley (D)
		Rep. William Ayers (R)
		Rep. Jackson Betts (R)
		Rep. Frank Bow (R)
		Rep. Clarence J. Brown (R)
Rep. Charles J. Carney (D) • HJR 35 - 94th Congress • HJR 40 - 95th Congress • HJR 384 - 95th Congress		
		Rep. Donald Clancy (R)
Rep. Dennis Eckart (D) • HJR 9 - 102nd Congress		
		Rep. Michael Feighan (D)
Sen. John H. Glenn Jr. (D) • SJR 1 - 94th Congress • SJR 1 - 95th Congress • SJR 1 - 96th Congress • SJR 3 - 97th Congress • SJR 17 - 98th Congress	Sen. John H. Glenn Jr. (D)	
		Rep. William Harsha (R)
		Rep. Wayne Hays (D)
Rep. Dennis J. Kucinich (D) • HJR 109 - 108th Congress		
		Rep. Delbert Latta (R)
Rep. Thomas Luken (D) • HJR 228 - 95th Congress		
		Rep. William McCulloch (R)
Sen. Howard M. Metzenbaum (D) • SJR 1 - 95th Congress • SJR 1 - 96th Congress • SJR 3 - 97th Congress • SJR 17 - 98th Congress	Sen. Howard M. Metzenbaum (D)	
		Rep. Clarence Miller (R)
		Rep. William Minshall (R)

S.35 OHIO *(cont.)*

SPONSOR OF A CONSTITUTIONAL AMENDMENT	VOTED FOR SJR 28 IN 1979 ROLL CALL	VOTED FOR HJR 681 IN 1969 ROLL CALL
		Rep. Charles Mosher (R)
Rep. Ronald Mottl (D) • HJR 168 - 95th Congress		
Rep. Donald J. Pease (D) • HJR 168 - 95th Congress • HJR 229 - 95th Congress • HJR 288 - 96th Congress		
Rep. John F. Seiberling (D) • HJR 229 - 95th Congress		
		Rep. John Stanton (R)
Rep. Louis Stokes (D) • HJR 254 - 96th Congress		Rep. Louis Stokes (D)
Sen. Robert Taft Jr. (R) • SJR 1 - 94th Congress		Rep. Robert Taft Jr. (R)
Rep. James A. Traficant Jr. (D) • HJR 511 - 102nd Congress • HJR 117 - 104th Congress		
Rep. Charles Vanik (D) • HJR 139 - 93rd Congress		Rep. Charles Vanik (D)
Rep. Charles Whalen (R) • HJR 300 - 93rd Congress • HJR 345 - 94th Congress • HJR 238 - 95th Congress		Rep. Charles Whalen (R)
		Rep. Chalmers Wylie (R)

S.36 OKLAHOMA

SPONSOR OF A CONSTITUTIONAL AMENDMENT	VOTED FOR SJR 28 IN 1979 ROLL CALL	VOTED FOR HJR 681 IN 1969 ROLL CALL
		Rep. Carl Albert (D)
Sen. Dewey F. Bartlett (R) • SJR 1 - 95th Congress		
		Rep. Page Belcher (R)
Sen. Henry Bellmon (R) • SJR 101 - 93rd Congress • SJR 1 - 94th Congress • SJR 1 - 95th Congress • SJR 1 - 96th Congress • SJR 28 - 96th Congress	Sen. Henry Bellmon (R)	
Sen. David L. Boren (D) • SJR 3 - 97th Congress • SJR 17 - 98th Congress • SJR 297 - 102nd Congress • SJR 302 - 102nd Congress	Sen. David L. Boren (D)	
		Rep. John Camp (R)
		Rep. Edmond Edmondson (D)
		Rep. John Jarman (D)
		Rep. Thomas Steed (D)

S.37 OREGON

SPONSOR OF A CONSTITUTIONAL AMENDMENT	VOTED FOR SJR 28 IN 1979 ROLL CALL	VOTED FOR HJR 681 IN 1969 ROLL CALL
Rep. John Dellenback (R) • HJR 78 - 93rd Congress • HJR 137 - 93rd Congress		Rep. John Dellenback (R)
Rep. Robert B. Duncan (D) • HJR 229 - 95th Congress • HJR 230 - 95th Congress		
		Rep. Edith Green (D)
Sen. Mark O. Hatfield (R) • SJR 1 - 94th Congress • SJR 1 - 95th Congress • SJR 1 - 96th Congress • SJR 28 - 96th Congress • SJR 8 - 97th Congress • SJR 17 - 98th Congress	Sen. Mark O. Hatfield (R)	
Sen. Robert W. Packwood (R) • SJR 1 - 94th Congress • SJR 1 - 95th Congress • SJR 1 - 96th Congress • SJR 28 - 96th Congress	Sen. Robert W. Packwood (R)[2]	
Rep. Albert Ullman (D) • HJR 384 - 95th Congress		Rep. Albert Ullman (D)
		Rep. Wendell Wyatt (R)

---

[2] Senator Packwood was announced in favor of SJR 28, but did not cast a vote in the roll call.

S.38 PENNSYLVANIA

SPONSOR OF A CONSTITUTIONAL AMENDMENT	VOTED FOR SJR 28 IN 1979 ROLL CALL	VOTED FOR HJR 681 IN 1969 ROLL CALL
Rep. Joseph Ammerman (D) • HJR 384 - 95th Congress		
		Rep. William Barrett (D)
Rep. Edward George Biester Jr. (R) • HJR 207 - 93rd Congress		Rep. Edward George Biester Jr. (R)
		Rep. James Byrne (D)
Rep. Frank Clark (D) • HJR 137 - 93rd Congress		Rep. Frank Clark (D)
		Rep. Robert Corbett (R)
		Rep. Robert Coughlin (R)
		Rep. John Dent (D)
Rep. Robert Edgar (D) • HJR 230 - 95th Congress • HJR 384 - 95th Congress		
Rep. Joshua Eilberg (D) • HJR 127 - 95th Congress		Rep. Joshua Eilberg (D)
Rep. Allen E. Ertel (D) • HJR 384 - 95th Congress • HJR 288 - 96th Congress		
		Rep. Edwin Eshleman (R)
Rep. Daniel J. Flood (D) • HJR 137 - 93rd Congress • HJR 288 - 96th Congress		Rep. Daniel J. Flood (D)
		Rep. James Fulton (R)
Rep. Joseph Gaydos (D) • HR 2063 - 95th Congress		Rep. Joseph Gaydos (D)
Rep. William F. Goodling (R) • HJR 150 - 96th Congress		
		Rep. George Goodling (R)
		Rep. William Green (D)
Rep. James Greenwood (R) • HJR 28 - 103rd Congress		
		Rep. Albert Johnson (R)

S.38 PENNSYLVANIA

SPONSOR OF A CONSTITUTIONAL AMENDMENT	VOTED FOR SJR 28 IN 1979 ROLL CALL	VOTED FOR HJR 681 IN 1969 ROLL CALL
Rep. Joseph P. Kolter (D) • HJR 506 - 102nd Congress		
Rep. Peter H. Kostmayer (D) • HJR 506 - 102nd Congress		
Rep. Joseph McDade (R) • HJR 207 - 93rd Congress		Rep. Joseph McDade (R)
Rep. Paul McHale (D) • HJR 28 - 103rd Congress		
		Rep. William Moorhead (D)
		Rep. Thomas Morgan (D)
Rep. Austin Murphy (D) • HJR 228 - 95th Congress • HJR 288 - 96th Congress		
		Rep. Robert Nix (D)
		Rep. Frederick Rooney (D)
		Rep. John Saylor (R)
		Rep. Herman Schneebeli (R)
Sen. Richard Schweiker (R) • SJR 1 - 94th Congress • SJR 1 - 95th Congress		
		Rep. Joseph Vigorito (D)
		Rep. George Watkins (R)
		Rep. Lawrence Williams (R)
Rep. Gus Yatron (D) • HJR 139 - 93rd Congress • HJR 168 - 95th Congress • HJR 231 - 95th Congress • HJR 261 - 96th Congress		Rep. Gus Yatron (D)

S.39 RHODE ISLAND

SPONSOR OF A CONSTITUTIONAL AMENDMENT	VOTED FOR SJR 28 IN 1979 ROLL CALL	VOTED FOR HJR 681 IN 1969 ROLL CALL
Rep. Edward P. Beard (D) • HJR 168 - 95th Congress		
Sen. John H. Chafee (R) • SJR 1 - 95th Congress • SJR 1 - 96th Congress • SJR 28 - 96th Congress • SJR 3 - 97th Congress • SJR 17 - 98th Congress	Sen. John H. Chafee (R)	
Sen. John Pastore (D) • SJR 1 - 94th Congress		
Sen. Claiborne Pell (D) • SJR 1 - 94th Congress • SJR 1 - 95th Congress • SJR 1 - 96th Congress • SJR 28 - 96th Congress • SJR 3 - 97th Congress • SJR 17 - 98th Congress	Sen. Claiborne Pell (D)	
		Rep. Fernand St. Germain (D)
Rep. Robert Tiernan (D) • HJR 208 - 93rd Congress		Rep. Robert Tiernan (D)

S.40 SOUTH CAROLINA

SPONSOR OF A CONSTITUTIONAL AMENDMENT	VOTED FOR SJR 28 IN 1979 ROLL CALL	VOTED FOR HJR 681 IN 1969 ROLL CALL
Rep. John Wilson Jenrette Jr. (D) • HJR 384 - 95th Congress		

S.41 SOUTH DAKOTA

SPONSOR OF A CONSTITUTIONAL AMENDMENT	VOTED FOR SJR 28 IN 1979 ROLL CALL	VOTED FOR HJR 681 IN 1969 ROLL CALL
Sen. James G. Abourezk (D) • SJR 1 - 94th Congress • SJR 1 - 95th Congress		
Sen. Thomas A Daschle (D) • SJR 297 - 102nd Congress		
Sen. Tim Johnson (D) • HJR 145 - 102nd Congress • HJR 28 - 103rd Congress • SJR 56 - 106th Congress		
Sen. George McGovern (D) • SJR 1 - 94th Congress	Sen. George McGovern (D)	

S.42 TENNESSEE

SPONSOR OF A CONSTITUTIONAL AMENDMENT	VOTED FOR SJR 28 IN 1979 ROLL CALL	VOTED FOR HJR 681 IN 1969 ROLL CALL
		Rep. William Anderson (D)
Sen. Howard H. Baker Jr. (R) • SJR 1 - 94th Congress • SJR 1 - 95th Congress • SJR 1 - 96th Congress • SJR 28 - 96th Congress • SJR 3 - 97th Congress	Sen. Howard H. Baker Jr. (R)	
		Rep. Leonard Blanton (D)
Rep. William Boner (D) • HJR 252 - 96th Congress		
Rep. Bob Clement (D) • HJR 28 - 103rd Congress		
		Rep. Richard Fulton (D)
		Rep. John Kyl (R)
	Sen. James Sasser (D)	

S.43 TEXAS

SPONSOR OF A CONSTITUTIONAL AMENDMENT	VOTED FOR SJR 28 IN 1979 ROLL CALL	VOTED FOR HJR 681 IN 1969 ROLL CALL
	Sen. Lloyd Millard Bentsen Jr. (D)	
Rep. Jack Bascom Brooks (D) • HJR 137 - 93rd Congress • HJR 80 - 97th Congress • HJR 5 - 98th Congress • HJR 5 - 99th Congress • HJR 5 - 100th Congress • HJR 2 - 101st Congress		Rep. Jack Bascom Brooks (D)
		Rep. George H.W. Bush (R)
		Rep. Earle Cabell (D)
		Rep. Robert Casey (D)
		Rep. James Collins (R)[3]
Rep. Lloyd Doggett (D) • HJR 36 - 109th Congress		Rep. Henry Gonzalez (D)
Rep. Henry Gonzalez (D) • HJR 167 - 93rd Congress		Rep. Henry Gonzalez (D)
Rep. Gene Green (D) • HJR 28 - 103rd Congress • HJR 117 - 104th Congress • HJR 180 - 104th Congress • HJR 28 - 105th Congress • HJR 132 - 106th Congress • HJR 3 - 107th Congress • HJR 103 - 108th Congress • HJR 8 - 109th Congress		
Rep. Sam Blakeley Hall (D) • HJR 384 - 95th Congress		
		Rep. Abraham Kazen (D)
Rep. Dale Milford (D) • HJR 239 - 93rd Congress • HJR 230 - 95th Congress		
		Rep. Herbert Roberts (D)
Rep. Bill Sarpalius (D) • HJR 28 - 103rd Congress		

[3] The roll call does not make clear whether this Representative Collins or the one from Illinois voted for HJR 681 in 1969.

| Appendix S

S.43 TEXAS *(cont.)*

SPONSOR OF A CONSTITUTIONAL AMENDMENT	VOTED FOR SJR 28 IN 1979 ROLL CALL	VOTED FOR HJR 681 IN 1969 ROLL CALL
		Rep. Olin Teague (D)
		Rep. Richard White (D)
		Rep. James Claude Wright (D)
		Rep. John Young (D)

S.44 UTAH

SPONSOR OF A CONSTITUTIONAL AMENDMENT	VOTED FOR SJR 28 IN 1979 ROLL CALL	VOTED FOR HJR 681 IN 1969 ROLL CALL
Sen. E. J. Garn (R) • SJR 1 - 95th Congress • SJR 1 - 96th Congress • SJR 28 - 96th Congress • SJR 3 - 97th Congress	Sen. E. J. Garn (R)	
Rep. James Hansen (R) • HJR 28 - 103rd Congress		
		Rep. Sherman Lloyd (R)
Sen. Frank Moss (D) • SJR 1 - 94th Congress		
Rep. Bill Orton (D) • HJR 506 - 102nd Congress • HJR 169 - 103rd Congress • HJR 36 - 104th Congress		
Rep. Douglas Owens (D) • HJR 347 - 93rd Congress		
Rep. Karen Shepherd (D) • HJR 28 - 103rd Congress		

S.45 VERMONT

SPONSOR OF A CONSTITUTIONAL AMENDMENT	VOTED FOR SJR 28 IN 1979 ROLL CALL	VOTED FOR HJR 681 IN 1969 ROLL CALL
Sen. Patrick J. Leahy (D) • SJR 1 - 95th Congress • SJR 1 - 96th Congress • SJR 28 - 96th Congress • SJR 3 - 97th Congress	Sen. Patrick J. Leahy (D)	
Rep. Bernard Sanders (I) • HJR 28 - 103rd Congress		
Sen. Robert T. Stafford (R) • SJR 1 - 94th Congress • SJR 1 - 95th Congress • SJR 1 - 96th Congress • SJR 28 - 96th Congress • SJR 17 - 98th Congress	Sen. Robert T. Stafford (R)	Rep. Robert T. Stafford (R)

S.46 VIRGINIA

SPONSOR OF A CONSTITUTIONAL AMENDMENT	VOTED FOR SJR 28 IN 1979 ROLL CALL	VOTED FOR HJR 681 IN 1969 ROLL CALL
Rep. Rick Boucher (D) • HJR 28 - 105th Congress • HJR 23 - 106th Congress		
		Rep. Joel Broyhill (R)
Rep. Leslie Byrne (D) • HJR 28 - 103rd Congress		
Rep. Thomas Downing (D) • HJR 207 - 93rd Congress • HJR 43 - 94th Congress		Rep. Thomas Downing (D)
		Rep. John Marsh (D)
		Rep. Richard Poff (R)
		Rep. William Scott (R)
		Rep. William Wampler (R)
		Rep. George Whitehurst (R)

S.47 WASHINGTON

SPONSOR OF A CONSTITUTIONAL AMENDMENT	VOTED FOR SJR 28 IN 1979 ROLL CALL	VOTED FOR HJR 681 IN 1969 ROLL CALL
		Rep. Brockman Adams (D)
Rep. Brian Baird (D) • HJR 103 - 108th Congress • HJR 8 - 109th Congress		
Rep. Norman Dicks (D) • HJR 384 - 95th Congress		
		Rep. Thomas Foley (D)
		Rep. Julia Hansen (D)
Rep. Floyd Hicks (D) • HJR 300 - 93rd Congress		Rep. Floyd Hicks (D)
Sen. Henry M. Jackson (D) • SJR 1 - 94th Congress • SJR 1 - 95th Congress • SJR 1 - 96th Congress • SJR 28 - 96th Congress • SJR 3 - 97th Congress • SJR 17 - 98th Congress	Sen. Henry M. Jackson (D)	
Sen. Warren G. Magnuson (D) • SJR 1 - 94th Congress • SJR 1 - 95th Congress • SJR 1 - 96th Congress • SJR 28 - 96th Congress	Sen. Warren G. Magnuson (D)	
		Rep. Catherine May (R)
Rep. Mike McCormack (D) • HJR 281 - 95th Congress		
Rep. Jim McDermott (D) • HJR 117 - 104th Congress • HJR 50 - 109th Congress		
Rep. Lloyd Meeds (D) • HJR 66 - 94th Congress • HJR 228 - 95th Congress		Rep. Lloyd Meeds (D)
		Rep. Thomas Pelly (R)
Rep. Joel Pritchard (R) • HJR 384 - 95th Congress		

S.48 WEST VIRGINIA

SPONSOR OF A CONSTITUTIONAL AMENDMENT	VOTED FOR SJR 28 IN 1979 ROLL CALL	VOTED FOR HJR 681 IN 1969 ROLL CALL
	Sen. Robert Byrd (D)	
		Rep. Kenneth Hechler (D)
		Rep. James Kee (D)
Rep. Robert H. Mollohan (D) • HJR 197 - 95th Congress • HJR 308 - 96th Congress		Rep. Robert H. Mollohan (D)
Sen. Jennings Randolph (D) • SJR 1 - 94th Congress • SJR 1 - 95th Congress • SJR 1 - 96th Congress • SJR 28 - 96th Congress • SJR 3 - 97th Congress • SJR 17 - 98th Congress	Sen. Jennings Randolph (D)	
		Rep. John Mark Slack (D)
		Rep. Harley Staggers (D)
Rep. Robert E. Wise Jr. (D) • HJR 137 - 101st Congress • HJR 28 - 103rd Congress • HJR 117 - 104th Congress • HJR 28 - 105th Congress		

S.49 WISCONSIN

SPONSOR OF A CONSTITUTIONAL AMENDMENT	VOTED FOR SJR 28 IN 1979 ROLL CALL	VOTED FOR HJR 681 IN 1969 ROLL CALL
Rep. Alvin J. Baldus (D) • HJR 231 - 95th Congress		
		Rep. John Byrnes (R)
Rep. Robert J. Cornell (D) • HJR 229 - 95th Congress		
		Rep. Glenn Davis (R)
Rep. Robert Kastenmeier (D) • HJR 62 - 94th Congress • HJR 70 - 95th Congress • HJR 57 - 96th Congress		Rep. Robert Kastenmeier (D)
Rep. Gerald D. Kleczka (D) • HJR 145 - 102nd Congress • HJR 60 - 103rd Congress		
Sen. Gaylord Nelson (D) • SJR 1 - 94th Congress	Sen. Gaylord Nelson (D)	
Sen. William Proxmire (D) • SJR 1 - 94th Congress • SJR 1 - 95th Congress • SJR 1 - 96th Congress • SJR 28 - 96th Congress • SJR 3 - 97th Congress • SJR 17 - 98th Congress	Sen. William Proxmire (D)	
		Rep. Henry Reuss (D)
		Rep. Henry Schadeberg (R)
Rep. William Steiger (R) • HJR 207 - 93rd Congress		Rep. William Steiger (R)
		Rep. Vernon Thomson (R)
		Rep. Clement Zablocki (D)

S.50 WYOMING

SPONSOR OF A CONSTITUTIONAL AMENDMENT	VOTED FOR SJR 28 IN 1979 ROLL CALL	VOTED FOR HJR 681 IN 1969 ROLL CALL
		Rep. John Wold (R)

APPENDIX T:
State Statutory Deadlines for Certification of Elections

TABLE T.1 STATE STATUTORY DEADLINES FOR CERTIFICATION OF ELECTIONS FOR THE 50 STATES AND DISTRICT OF COLUMBIA

JURISDICTION	CERTIFIER	CERTIFICATION DEADLINE
Alabama	Governor	Within 22 days after the election
Alaska	Director	No date specified
Arizona	Secretary of State	On the third Monday following a general election
Arkansas	Governor	Within 20 days after the election
California	Secretary of State	On the first Monday in the month following the election
Colorado	Secretary of State	No later than the fifteenth day after any election
Connecticut	Secretary of State/ Superior Court	Last Wednesday in the month in which votes were cast
Delaware	Board of Elections	No date specified
District of Columbia	Superior Court	No date specified
Florida	Canvassing Commission	No date specified
Georgia	Secretary of State	No later than 5:00 p.m. on the four-teenth ay following the date on which such election was conducted
Hawaii	Governor	No later than 4:30 p.m. on the last day in the month of the election or as soon as returns received from all counties
Idaho	Secretary of State	On or before the second Wednesday in December next after such election
Illinois	Governor	Within 31 days after holding the election
Indiana	Secretary of State	Not later than noon on the last Tuesday in November
Iowa	Governor	At the expiration of 10 days after the completed canvass
Kansas	Governor	Before the first Wednesday in December next after such election

TABLE T.1 STATE STATUTORY DEADLINES FOR CERTIFICATION OF ELECTIONS FOR THE 50 STATES AND DISTRICT OF COLUMBIA (cont.)

Kentucky	State Board	State Board shall meet to count when all the returns are in or no later than the third Monday after the election
Louisiana	Governor	On or before the 12th day after the general election
Maine	Governor	Within 20 days after the election.
Maryland	Board of Canvassers	Within 35 days of the election
Massachusetts	Governor	Within 10 days after they have been transmitted to the Secretary of State
Michigan	Secretary of State	On or before the 20th day after the election and no later than the 40th day
Minnesota	Governor	On the second Tuesday after each state general election the state canvassing board shall open and canvass the returns
Mississippi	Secretary of State	Within 30 days after the date of the election
Missouri	Governor	Within two days after the election, the clerks shall, within eight days after they receive the returns, certify and transmit them to the Governor
Montana	Secretary of State	No date specified
Nebraska	Secretary of State	Within 40 days
Nevada	Governor	On the fourth Tuesday of November open canvass the vote, must be completed within 20 days
New Hampshire	Governor	No date specified
New Jersey	Secretary of State	No later than the 28th day after the election
New Mexico	Secretary of State	On the third Tuesday after each election board will meet to canvass and declare the results of the election
New York	State Board of Elections	No date specified
North Carolina	Governor	Board of elections shall meet at 11:00 a.m. on the seventh day after every election or a reasonable time thereafter if the counting of the votes has not been completed
North Dakota	Secretary of State	Within ten days and before 4 p.m. on the tenth day following any general election
Ohio	Board of Elections	No date specified

TABLE T.1 STATE STATUTORY DEADLINES FOR CERTIFICATION OF ELECTIONS FOR THE 50 STATES AND DISTRICT OF COLUMBIA (cont.)

Oklahoma	Secretary of State	Election board shall convene on the day of and remaining session until all returns are delivered
Oregon	Secretary of State	No later than the 30th day after any election
Pennsylvania	Governor	No date specified
Rhode Island	State Board	State board shall commence the canvass at 9:00 p.m. on election day and shall continue and complete the tabulation with all reasonable expedition
South Carolina	State Board	State board shall meet within 10 days after any general election
South Dakota	Governor	Within seven days after the day of election
Tennessee	Secretary of State	No date specified
Texas	Secretary of State	No date specified
Utah	Lieutenant Governor	Fourth Monday of November at noon
Vermont	Canvassing Committee	Canvassing committee shall meet at 10:00 A.M. one week after the day of the election
Virginia	State Board	Fourth Monday in November, if the Board is unable to ascertain results on that day, the meeting shall stand adjourned for not more three days
Washington	Secretary of State	Not later than 30 days after the election
West Virginia	Board of Canvassers	Fifth day after every election
Wisconsin	Elections Board	The first day of December following a general election
Wyoming	Canvassing Board	No later than the second Wednesday following the election

Appendix U:
U. S. Supreme Court Decision in
Hawke v. Smith

U.S. SUPREME COURT
253 U.S. 221
HAWKE V. SMITH, SECRETARY OF STATE OF OHIO. NO. 582.
ARGUED APRIL 23, 1920
DECIDED JUNE 1, 1920

Mr. J. Frank Hanly, of Indianapolis, Ind., for plaintiff in error.

Mr. Lawrence Maxwell, of Cincinnati, Ohio, for defendant in error.

Mr. Justice DAY delivered the opinion of the Court.

Plaintiff in error (plaintiff below) filed a petition for an injunction in the court of common pleas of Franklin county, Ohio, seeking to enjoin the secretary of state of Ohio from spending the public money in preparing and printing forms of ballot for submission of a referendum to the electors of that state on the question of the ratification which the General Assembly had made of the proposed Eighteenth Amendment to the federal Constitution. A demurrer to the petition was sustained in the court of common pleas. Its judgment was affirmed by the Court of Appeals of Franklin County, which judgment was affirmed by the Supreme Court of Ohio, and the case was brought here.

A joint resolution proposing to the states this amendment to the Constitution of the United States was adopted on the 3d day of December, 1917. 40 Stat. 1050. The amendment prohibits the manufacture, sale or transportation of intoxicating liquors within, the importation thereof into, or the exportation thereof from, the United States and all territory subject to the jurisdiction thereof for beverage purposes. The several states were given concurrent power to enforce the amendment by appropriate legislation. The resolution provided that the amendment should be inoperative unless ratified as an amendment of the

Constitution by the Legislatures of the several states, as provide in the Constitution, within seven years from the date of the submission thereof to the states. The Senate and House of Representatives of the state of Ohio adopted a resolution ratifying the proposed amendment by the General Assembly of the state of Ohio, and ordered that certified copies of the joint resolution of ratification be forwarded by the Governor to the Secretary of State at Washington and to the presiding officer of each House of Congress. This resolution was adopted on January 7, 1919; on January 27, 1919, the Governor of Ohio complied with the resolution. On January 29, 1919, the Secretary of State of the United States proclaimed the ratification of the amendment, naming 36 states as having ratified the same, among them the state of Ohio.

The question for our consideration is: Whether the provision of the Ohio Constitution, adopted at the general election, November, 1918, extending the referendum to the ratification by the General Assembly of proposed amendments to the federal Constitution is in conflict with article 5 of the Constitution of the United States. The amendment of 1918 provides:

> "The people also reserve to themselves the legislative power of the referendum on the action of the General Assembly ratifying any proposed amendment to the Constitution of the United States."

Article 5 of the federal Constitution provides:

> "The Congress, whenever two-thirds of both houses shall deem it necessary, shall propose amendments to this Constitution, or, on the application of the Legislatures of two-thirds of the several states, shall call a convention for proposing amendments, which, in either case, shall be valid to all intents and purposes, as part of this Constitution, when ratified by the Legislatures of three-fourths of the several states, or by conventions in three-fourths thereof, as the one or the other mode of ratification may be proposed by the Congress: Provided that no amendment which may be made prior to the year one thousand eight hundred and eight shall in any manner affect the first and fourth clauses in the ninth section of the first article; and that no state, without its consent, shall be

deprived of its equal suffrage in the Senate."

The Constitution of the United States was ordained by the people, and, when duly ratified, it became the Constitution of the people of the United States. *McCulloch v. Maryland*, 4 Wheat. 316, 402. The states surrendered to the general government the powers specifically conferred upon the nation, and the Constitution and the laws of the United States are the supreme law of the land.

The framers of the Constitution realized that it might in the progress of time and the development of new conditions require changes, and they intended to provide an orderly manner in which these could be accomplished; to that end they adopted the fifth article.

This article makes provision for the proposal of amendments either by two-thirds of both houses of Congress, or on application of the Legislatures of two-thirds of the states; thus securing deliberation and consideration before any change can be proposed. The proposed change can only become effective by the ratification of the Legislatures of three-fourths of the states, or by conventions in a like number of states. The method of ratification is left to the choice of Congress. Both methods of ratification, by Legislatures or conventions, call for action by deliberative assemblages representative of the people, which it was assumed would voice the will of the people.

The fifth article is a grant of authority by the people to Congress. The determination of the method of ratification is the exercise of a national power specifically granted by the Constitution; that power is conferred upon Congress, and is limited to two methods, by action of the Legislatures of three-fourths of the states, or conventions in a like number of states. *Dodge v. Woolsey*, 18 How. 331, 348. The framers of the Constitution might have adopted a different method. Ratification might have been left to a vote of the people, or to some authority of government other than that selected. The language of the article is plain, and admits of no doubt in its interpretation. It is not the function of courts or legislative bodies, national or state, to alter the method which the Constitution has fixed.

All of the amendments to the Constitution have been submitted with a requirement for legislative ratification; by this method all of them have been adopted.

The only question really for determination is: What did the framers of the Constitution mean in requiring ratification by "legislatures"? That was not a term of uncertain meaning when incorporated into the Constitution. What it meant when adopted it still means for the purpose of interpretation. A Legislature was then the representative body which made the laws of the people. The term is often used in the Constitution with this evident meaning. Article 1, section 2, prescribes the qualifications of electors of Congressmen as those "requisite for electors of the most numerous branch of the state Legislature." Article 1, section 3, provided that Senators shall be chosen in each state by the Legislature thereof, and this was the method of choosing senators until the adoption of the Seventeenth Amendment, which made provision for the election of Senators by vote of the people, the electors to have the qualifications requisite for electors of the most numerous branch of the state Legislature. That Congress and the states understood that this election by the people was entirely distinct from legislative action is shown by the provision of the amendment giving the Legislature of any state the power to authorize the executive to make temporary appointments until the people shall fill the vacancies by election. It was never suggested, so far as we are aware, that the purpose of making the office of Senator elective by the people could be accomplished by a referendum vote. The necessity of the amendment to accomplish the purpose of popular election is shown in the adoption of the amendment. In article 4 the United States is required to protect every state against domestic violence upon application of the Legislature, or of the executive when the Legislature cannot be convened. Article 6 requires the members of the several Legislatures to be bound by oath, or affirmation, to support the Constitution of the United States. By article 1, section 8, Congress is given exclusive jurisdiction over all places purchased by the consent of the Legislature of the state in which the same shall be. Article 4, section 3, provides that no new states shall be carved out of old states without the consent of the Legislatures of the states concerned.

There can be no question that the framers of the Constitution clearly understood and carefully used the terms in which that instrument referred to the action of the Legislatures of the states. When they intended that direct action by the people should be had they were no less accurate in the use of apt phraseology to carry out such purpose. The members of the House of Representatives were required to be chosen by the people of the several states. Article 1, section 2.

The Constitution of Ohio in its present form, although making provision for a referendum, vests the legislative power primarily in a General Assembly, consisting of a Senate and House of Representatives. Article 2, section 1, provides:

> "The legislative power of the state shall be vested in a General Assembly consisting of a Senate and House of Representatives, but the people reserve to themselves the power to propose to the General Assembly laws and amendments to the Constitution, and to adopt or reject the same at the polls on a referendum vote as hereinafter provided."

The argument to support the power of the state to require the approval by the people of the state of the ratification of amendments to the federal Constitution through the medium of a referendum rests upon the proposition that the federal Constitution requires ratification by the legislative action of the states through the medium provided at the time of the proposed approval of an amendment. This argument is fallacious in this—ratification by a state of a constitutional amendment is not an act of legislation within the proper sense of the word. It is but the expression of the assent of the state to a proposed amendment.

At an early day this court settled that the submission of a constitutional amendment did not require the action of the President. The question arose over the adoption of the Eleventh Amendment. *Hollingsworth et al. v. Virginia*, 3 Dall. 378. In that case is was contended that the amendment had not been proposed in the manner provided in the Constitution as an inspection of the original roll showed that it had never been submitted to the President for his approval in accordance with article 1, section 7, of the Constitution. The Attorney General answered that the case of amendments is a substantive act, unconnected with the ordinary business of legislation, and not within the policy or terms of the Constitution investing the President with a qualified negative on the acts and resolutions of Congress. In a footnote to this argument of the Attorney General, Justice Chase said:

> "There can, surely, be no necessity to answer that argument. The negative of the President applies only to the ordinary cases of legislation. He has nothing to do with the proposi-

tion, or adoption, of amendments to the Constitution."

The court by a unanimous judgment held that the amendment was constitutionally adopted.

It is true that the power to legislate in the enactment of the laws of a state is derived from the people of the state. But the power to ratify a proposed amendment to the federal Constitution has its source in the federal Constitution. The act of ratification by the state derives its authority from the federal Constitution to which the state and its people have alike assented.

This view of the amendment is confirmed in the history of its adoption found in 2 Watson on the Constitution, 1301 et seq. Any other view might lead to endless confusion in the manner of ratification of federal amendments. The choice of means of ratification was wisely withheld from conflicting action in the several states.

But it is said this view runs counter to the decision of this court in *Davis v. Hildebrant*, 241 U.S. 565, 36 S. Ct. 708. But that case is inapposite. It dealt with article 1 section 4, of the Constitution, which provides that the times, places, and manners of holding elections for Senators and Representatives in each state shall be determined by the respective Legislatures thereof, but that Congress may at any time make or alter such regulations, except as to the place for choosing Senators. As shown in the opinion in that case, Congress had itself recognized the referendum as part of the legislative authority of the state for the purpose stated. It was held, affirming the judgment of the Supreme Court of Ohio, that the referendum provision of the state Constitution, when applied to a law redistricting the state with a view to representation in Congress, was not unconstitutional. Article 1, section 4, plainly gives authority to the state to legislate within the limitations therein named. Such legislative action is entirely different from the requirement of the Constitution as to the expression of assent or dissent to a proposed amendment to the Constitution. In such expression no legislative action is authorized or required.

It follows that the court erred in holding that the state had authority to require the submission of the ratification to a referendum under the state Constitution, and its judgment is reversed and the cause remanded for further proceedings not inconsistent with this opinion.

Reversed.

Appendix V:
U. S. Supreme Court Decision in
Smiley v. Holm (1932)

U.S. SUPREME COURT
SMILEY V. HOLM, 285 U.S. 355 (1932)
285 U.S. 355
SMILEY V. HOLM, AS SECRETARY OF STATE OF MINNESOTA
NO. 617.
ARGUED MARCH 16, 17, 1932
DECIDED APRIL 11, 1932

Messrs. George T. Simpson, Alfred W. Bowen, W. Yale Smiley, John A. Weeks, and F. J. Donahue, all of Minneapolis, Minn., for petitioner.

Messrs. Henry N. Benson, Atty. Gen., and William H. Gurnee, Asst. Atty. Gen., both of St. Paul, Minn., for respondent.

Mr. Chief Justice HUGHES delivered the opinion of the Court.

Under the reapportionment following the fifteenth decennial census, as provided by the Act of Congress of June 18, 1929 (c. 28, 22, 46 Stat. 21, 26 (2 USCA 2a)), Minnesota is entitled to nine Representatives in Congress, being one less than the number previously allotted. In April, 1931, the bill known as House File No. 1456 (Laws Minn. 1931, p. 640), dividing the state into nine congressional districts and specifying the counties of which they should be composed, was passed by the House of Representatives and the Senate of the state, and was transmitted to the Governor, who returned it without his approval. Thereupon, without further action upon the measure by the House of Representatives and the Senate, and in compliance with a resolution of the House of Representatives, House File No. 1456 was deposited with the secretary of state of Minnesota. This suit was brought by the petitioner as a "citizen, elector and taxpayer" of the state to obtain a judgment declaring invalid all fillings for nomination for the office of Representative in Congress, which should designate a subdivision of the state as a congressional district, and to enjoin the secretary of state from giving notice of the holding of elections for that office in such subdivisions. The petition alleged that House File No. 1456 was a nullity, in that, after the Governor's veto, it was not repassed by the Legislature as required by law, and also in that the proposed congressional districts were not "compact" and did not "contain an equal number of inhabitants as nearly as practicable" in accordance with the Act of Congress of August 8, 1911.[1]

The respondent, secretary of state, demurred to the petition upon the ground that it did not state facts sufficient to constitute a cause of action. He maintained the validity of House File No. 1456 by virtue of the authority conferred upon the Legislature by article 1, 4, of the Federal Constitution, and he insisted that the act of Congress of August 8, 1911, was no longer in force, and that the asserted inequalities in redistricting presented a political and not a judicial question. The trial court sustained the demurrer, and its order was affirmed by the Supreme Court of the state. 238 N. W. 494. The action was then dismissed upon the merits, and the Supreme Court affirmed the judgment upon its previous opinion. 238 N. W. 792. This Court granted a writ of certiorari. 284 U.S. 616, 52 S. Ct. 266, 76 L. Ed.

---

[1] The Act of August 8, 1911, c. 5, 37 Stat. 13 (2 USCA 2 and note, 3-5), provided for the apportionment of Representatives in Congress among the several states under the thirteenth census. After fixing the total number of Representatives and their apportionment, in sections 1 and 2, the act provided as follows:

"Sec. 3. That in each State entitled under this apportionment to more than one Representative, the Representatives to the Sixty-third and each subsequent Congress shall be elected by districts composed of a contiguous and compact territory, and containing as nearly as practicable an equal number of inhabitants. The said districts shall be equal to the number of Representatives to which such State may be entitled in Congress, no district electing more than one Representative.

"Sec. 4. That in case of an increase in the number of Representatives in any State under this apportionment such additional Representative or Representatives shall be elected by the State at large and the other Representatives by the districts now prescribed by law until such State shall be redistricted in the manner provided by the laws thereof and in accordance with the rules enumerated in section three of this Act; and if there be no charge in the number of Representatives from a State, the Representatives thereof shall be elected from the districts now prescribed by law until such State shall be redistricted as herein prescribed.

"Sec. 5. That candidates for Representative or Representatives to be elected at large in any State shall be nominated in the same manner as candidates for governor, unless otherwise provided by the laws of such State."

Article 1, 4, of the Constitution of the United States, provides:

"The times, places and manner of holding elections for senators and representatives, shall be prescribed in each state by the legislature thereof; but the Congress may at any time by law make or alter such regulations, except as to the places of choosing senators."

Under the Constitution of Minnesota, the "legislature" consists "of the senate and house of representatives." Const. Minn. art. 4, 1. Before any bill passed by the Senate and House of Representatives "becomes a law," it must "be presented to the governor of the state," and if he returns it, within the time stated, without his approval, the bill may become a law provided it is reconsidered and thereupon passed by each house by a two-thirds vote. *Id.* art. 4, 11. The state Constitution also provides that, after each Federal census, "the legislature shall have the power to prescribe the bounds of congressional ... districts." *Id.* art. 4, 23. We do not understand that the Supreme Court of the state has held that, under these provisions, a measure redistricting the state for congressional elections could be put in force by the Legislature without participation by the Governor, as required in the case of legislative bills, if such action were regarded as a performance of the function of the Legislature as a law-making body. No decision to that effect has been cited. It appears that "on seven occasions" prior to the measure now under consideration the Legislature of Minnesota had "made state and federal reapportionments in the form of a bill for an act which was approved by the Governor."[2] While, in the instant case, the Supreme Court regarded that procedure as insufficient to support the petitioner's contention as to practical construction, that question was dismissed from consideration because of the controlling effect which the court ascribed to the federal provision. 238 N. W. page 500. The court expressed the opinion that "the various provisions of our state Constitution cited in the briefs are of little importance in relation to the matter now in controversy"; that "the power of the state Legislature to prescribe congressional districts rests exclusively and solely in the language of article 1, 4, of the United States Constitution." *Id.* 238 N. W. page 497. Construing that provision, the court reached the conclu-

---

[2] See Laws of Minnesota 1858, c. 83; 1872, c. 21; 1881, c. 128; 1891, c. 3; 1901, c. 92; 1913, c. 513; 1929, c. 64.

sion that the Legislature in redistricting the state was not acting strictly in the exercise of the lawmaking power, but merely as an agency, discharging a particular duty in the manner which the Federal Constitution required. Upon this point the court said (*Id.* 238 N. W. page 499):

> "The Legislature in districting the state is not strictly in the discharge of legislative duties as a lawmaking body, acting in its sovereign capacity, but is acting as representative of the people of the state under the power granted by said article 1, 4. It merely gives expression as to district lines in aid of the election of certain federal officials; prescribing one of the essential details serving primarily the federal government and secondly the people of the state. The Legislature is designated as a mere agency to discharge the particular duty. The Governor's veto has no relation to such matters; that power pertains, under the state Constitution, exclusively to state affairs. The word 'legislature' has reference to the well-recognized branch of the state government-created by the state as one of its three branches for a specific purpose-and when the framers of the Federal Constitution employed this term, we believe they made use of it in the ordinary sense with reference to the official body invested with the functions of making laws, the legislative body of the state; and that they did not intend to include the state's chief executive as a part thereof. We would not be justified in construing the term as being used in its enlarged sense as meaning the state or as meaning the lawmaking power of the state."

The question then is whether the provision of the Federal Constitution, thus regarded as determinative, invests the Legislature with a particular authority, and imposes upon it a corresponding duty, the definition of which imports a function different from that of lawgiver, and thus renders inapplicable the conditions which attach to the making of state laws. Much that is urged in argument with regard to the meaning of the term "Legislature" is beside the point. As this Court said in *Hawke v. Smith*, No. 1, 253 U.S. 221, 227, 40 S. Ct. 495, 497, 10 A. L. R. 1504, the term was not one "of uncertain meaning when incorporated into the Constitution. What it meant when adopted it still means for the purpose of interpretation. A Legislature was then the representative body which made the laws of the people." The question here is not with respect to the "body" as thus described but as to the function to be performed. The use in the Federal Constitution of the same term in different relations does not always imply the performance of the same function. The Legislature may act as an electoral body, as in the choice of United States Senators under article 1, 3, prior to the adoption of the Seventeenth Amendment. It may act as a ratifying body, as in the case of proposed amendments to the Constitution under article 5. *Hawke v. Smith*, No. 1, supra; *Hawke v. Smith*, No. 2, 253 U.S. 231, 40 S. Ct. 498; *Leser v. Garnett*, 258 U.S. 130, 137, 42 S. Ct. 217. It may act as a consenting body, as in relation to the acquisition of lands by the United States under article 1, 8, par. 17. Wherever the term "legislature" is used in the Constitution, it is necessary to consider the nature of the particular action in view. The primary question now before the Court is whether the function contemplated by article 1, 4, is that of making laws.

Consideration of the subject-matter and of the terms of the provision requires affirmative answer. The subject-matter is the "times, places and manner of holding elections for senators and representatives." It cannot be doubted that these comprehensive words embrace authority to provide a complete code for congressional elections, not only as to times and places, but in relation to notices, registration, supervision of voting, protection of voters, prevention of fraud and corrupt practices, counting of votes, duties of inspectors and canvassers, and making and publication of election returns; in short, to enact the numerous requirements as to procedure and safeguards which experience shows are necessary in order to enforce the fundamental right involved. And these requirements would be nugatory if they did not have appropriate sanctions in the definition of offenses and punishments. All this is comprised in the subject of "times, places and manner of holding elections," and involves lawmaking in its essential features and most important aspect.

This view is confirmed by the second clause of article 1, 4, which provides that "the Congress may at any time by law make or alter such regulations," with the single exception stated. The phrase "such regulations" plainly refers to regulations of the same general character that the legislature of the State is authorized to prescribe with respect to congressional elections. In exercising this power, the Congress may supplement these state regulations or may substitute its own. It may impose additional penalties for the violation of the state laws or provide independent sanctions. It "has a general supervisory power over the whole subject." *Ex parte Siebold*, 100 U.S. 371, 387; *Ex parte Yarbrough*, 110 U.S. 651, 661, 4 S. Ct. 152; *Ex parte Clarke*, 100 U.S. 399 ; *United States v. Mosley*, 238 U.S. 383, 386, 35 S. Ct. 904; *Newberry v. United States*, 256 U.S. 232, 255, 41 S. Ct. 469. But this broad authority is conferred by the constitutional provision now under consideration, and is exercised by the Congress in making "such regulations"; that is, regulations of the sort which, if there be no overruling action by the Congress, may be provided by the Legislature of the state upon the same subject.

The term defining the method of action, equally with the nature of the subject matter, aptly points to the making of laws. The state Legislature is authorized to "prescribe" the times, places, and manner of holding elections. Respondent urges that the fact that the words "by law" are found in the clause relating to the action of the Congress, and not in the clause giving authority to the state Legislature, supports the contention that the latter was not to act in the exercise of the lawmaking power. We think that the inference is strongly to the contrary. It is the nature of the function that makes the phrase "by law" apposite. That is the same whether it is performed by state or national Legislature, and the use of the phrase places the intent of the whole provision in a strong light. Prescribing regulations to govern the conduct of the citizen, under the first clause, and making and altering such rules by law, under the second clause, involve action of the same inherent character.

As the authority is conferred for the purpose of making laws for the state, it follows, in the absence of an indication of a contrary intent, that the exercise of the authority must be in accordance with the method which the state has prescribed for legislative enactments. We find no suggestion in the federal constitutional provision of an attempt to endow the Legislature of the state with power to enact laws in any manner other than that in which the Constitution of the state has provided that laws shall be enacted. Whether the Governor of the state, through the veto power, shall have a part in the making of state laws, is a matter of state polity. Article 1, 4, of the Federal Constitution, neither requires nor excludes such participation. And provision for it, as a check in the legislative process, cannot be regarded as repugnant to the grant of legislative authority. At the time of the adoption of the Federal Constitution, it appears that only two states had provided for a veto upon the passage of legislative bills; Massachusetts, through the Governor, and New York, through a council of revision.[3] But the restriction which existed in the case of these states was well known. That the state Legislature might be subject to such a limitation, either then or thereafter imposed as the several states might think wise, was no more incongruous with the grant of legislative authority to regulate congressional elections than the fact that the Congress in making its regulations under the same provision would be subject to the veto power of the President, as provided in article 1, 7. The latter consequence was not expressed, but there is no question that it was necessarily implied, as the Congress was to act by law; and there is no intimation, either in the debates in the Federal Convention or in contemporaneous exposition, of a purpose to exclude a similar restriction imposed by state Constitutions upon state Legislatures when exercising the lawmaking power.

The practical construction of article 1, 4, is impressive. General acquiescence cannot justify departure from the law, but long and continuous interpretation in the course of official action under the law may aid in removing doubts as to its meaning. This is especially true in the case of constitutional provisions governing the exercise of political rights, and hence subject to constant and careful scrutiny. Certainly, the terms of the constitutional provision furnish no such clear and definite support for a contrary construction as to justify disregard of the established practice in the states. *McPherson v. Blacker,* 146 U.S. 1, 36, 13 S. Ct. 3; *Missouri Pacific Railway Co. v. Kansas,* 248 U.S. 276, 284, 39 S. Ct. 93, 2 A. L. R. 1589; *Myers v. United States,* 272 U.S. 52, 119, 136 S., 47 S. Ct. 21; The *Pocket Veto Case,* 279 U.S. 655, 688-690, 49 S. Ct. 463, 64 A. L. R. 1434. That

---

[3] The Constitution of Massachusetts of 1780 provided for the Governor's veto of "bills" or "resolves." Part Second, ch. 1, 1, art. 2; 3 Thorpe, *American Charters, Constitutions and Organic Laws,* 1893, 1894. The council of revision in New York, which had the veto power under the first Constitution of 1777 (art. 3), was composed of the Governor, the chancellor, and the judges of the Supreme Court, "or any two of them, together with the Governor." The veto power was given to the Governor alone by the Constitution of 1821. Article 1, 12, 3 Thorpe, op. cit. 2628, 2641, 2642. In South Carolina, the veto power had been given by the Constitution of 1776 to the "president" (article 7), but under the Constitution of 1778 the Governor had no veto power; see article 14, 6 Thorpe, op. cit., 3244, 3252.

practice is eloquent of the conviction of the people of the states, and of
their representatives in state Legislatures and executive office, that in
providing for congressional elections, and for the districts in which they
were to be held, these Legislatures were exercising the lawmaking power
and thus subject, where the state Constitution so provided, to the veto of
theGovernor as a part of the legislative process. The early action in
Massachusetts under this authority was by "resolves," and these, under
the Constitution of 1780, were required to be submitted to the Governor,
and it appears that they were so submitted and approved by him.[4] In New
York, from the outset, provision for congressional districts was made by
statute,[5] and this method was followed until 1931. The argument based on
the disposition, during the early period, to curtail executive authority in
the states, and on the long time which elapsed in a number of states
before the veto power was granted to the Governor, is of slight weight in
the light of the fact that this power was given in four states shortly after
the adoption of the Federal Constitution,[6] that the use of this check has
gradually been extended, and that the uniform practice (prior to the questions raised in relation to the present reapportionment) has been to provide for congressional districts by the enactment of statutes with the participation of the Governor wherever the state Constitution provided for
such participation as part of the process of making laws. See *Moran v.
Bowley*, 347 Ill. 148, 179 N. E. 526, 527; *Koening v. Flynn*, 258 N. Y. 292,
300, 179 N. E. 705; *Carroll v. Becker* (Mo. Sup.) 45 S.W.(2d) 533; *State ex
rel. Schrader v. Polley*, 26 S. D. 5, 7, 127 N. W. 848. The Attorney General
of Minnesota, in his argument in the instant case, states: "It is conceded
that until 1931 whenever the State of Minnesota was divided into districts
for the purpose of congressional elections such action was taken by the
legislature in the form of a bill and presented to and approved by the governor." That the constitutional provision contemplates the exercise of the

---

[4] Const. Mass. 1780; 3 Thorpe, op. cit. 1893, 1894, Mass. Resolves, Oct.Nov., 1788, c. XLIX,
p. 52; May-June, 1792, c. LXIX, p. 23.

[5] New York, Laws of 1789, c. 11; 1797, c. 62; 1802, c. 72. See Koenig v. Flynn, 258 N. Y. 292.

[6] Georgia, Const. 1789, art. 2, 10, 2 Thorpe, op. cit. 788; Pennsylvania, Const. 1790, art. 1,
22, 5 Thorpe, op. cit., 3094; New Hampshire, Const. 1792; Part Second, 44, 4 Thorpe, op.
cit., 2482; Kentucky, Const. 1792, art. 1, 28, 3 Thorpe, op. cit., 1267. In Vermont, the
Constitution of 1793 (chapter 2, 16) gave the Governor and council a power of suspension similar to that for which provision had been made in the Constitution of 1786 (chapter 2, 14) before the admission of Vermont to the Union. See, also, Constitution of 1777
(chapter 2, 14), 6 Thorpe, op. cit., 3744, 3757, 3767.

lawmaking power was definitely recognized by the Congress in the Act of August 8, 1911,[7] which expressly provided in section 4 for the election of Representatives in Congress, as stated, "by the districts now prescribed by law until such State shall be redistricted in the manner provided by the laws thereof, and in accordance with the rules enumerated in section three of this Act." The significance of the clause "in the manner provided by the laws thereof" is manifest from its occasion and purpose. It was to recognize the propriety of the referendum in establishing congressional districts where the state had made it a part of the legislative process. "It is clear," said this Court in *Davis v. Hildebrant*, 241 U.S. 565, 568, 36 S. Ct. 708, 710, "that Congress, in 1911, in enacting the controlling law concerning the duties of the states, through their legislative authority, to deal with the subject of the creation of congressional districts, expressly modified the phraseology of the previous acts relating to that subject by inserting a clause plainly intended to provide that where, by the state Constitution and laws, the referendum was treated as part of the legislative power, the power as thus constituted should be held and treated to be the state legislative power for the purpose of creating congressional districts by law."

The case of *Davis v. Hildebrant*, supra, arose under the amendment of 1912 to the Constitution of Ohio reserving the right "by way of referendum to approve or disapprove by popular vote any law enacted by the general assembly." *Id.*, 241 U. S. page 566, 36 S. Ct. 708, 709. The act passed by the General Assembly of Ohio in 1915, redistricting the state for the purpose of congressional elections, was disapproved under the referendum provision, and the validity of that action was challenged under article 1, 4, of the Federal Constitution. The Supreme Court of the state, denying a mandamus to enforce the disapproved act, "held that the provisions as to referendum were a part of the legislative power of the state, made so by the Constitution, and that nothing in the act of Congress of 1911, or in the constitutional provision, operated to the contrary, and that therefore the disapproved law had no existence." *Id.* 241 U. S. page 567, 36 S. Ct. 708, 709. This Court affirmed the judgment of the state court. It is manifest that the Congress had no power to alter article 1, 4, and that the act of 1911, in its reference to state laws, could but operate as a legislative recognition of the nature of the authority deemed to have been

---

[7] See note 1.

conferred by the constitutional provision. And it was because of the authority of the state to determine what should constitute its legislative process that the validity of the requirement of the state Constitution of Ohio, in its application to congressional elections, was sustained. This was explicitly stated by this Court as the ground of the distinction which was made in *Hawke v. Smith No. 1*, supra, where, referring to the Davis Case, the Court said: "As shown in the opinion in that case, Congress had itself recognized the referendum as part of the legislative authority of the state for the purpose stated. It was held, affirming the judgment of the Supreme Court of Ohio, that the referendum provision of the state Constitution, when applied to a law redistricting the state with a view to representation in Congress, was not unconstitutional. Article 1, section 4, plainly gives authority to the state to legislate within the limitations there-in named. Such legislative action is entirely different from the require-ment of the Constitution as to the expression of assent or dissent to a pro-posed amendment to the Constitution. In such expression no legislative action is authorized or required."

It clearly follows that there is nothing in article 1, 4, which precludes a state from providing that legislative action in districting the state for congressional elections shall be subject to the veto power of the Governor as in other cases of the exercise of the lawmaking power. Accordingly, in this instance, the validity of House File No. 1456 cannot be sustained by virtue of any authority conferred by the Federal Constitution upon the Legislature of Minnesota to create congressional districts independently of the participation of the Governor as required by the state Constitution with respect to the enactment of laws.

The further question has been presented whether the Act of Congress of August 8, 1911,[8] is still in force. The state court held that it was not, that it had been wholly replaced by the Act of June 18, 1929. Sections 1 and 2 of the former act, making specific provision for the apportionment under the thirteenth census, are, of course, superseded; the present question relates to the other sections. These have not been expressly repealed. The act of 1929 repeals "all other laws and parts of laws" that are inconsistent with its provisions (section 21 (46 Stat. 26, 13 USCA 1 note)). The peti-tioner urges that this act contains nothing inconsistent with sections 3, 4,

---

[8] See note 1.

and 58 of the act of 1911, and the only question is whether these sections by their very terms have ceased to be effective. It is pointed out that the provisions of the act of 1911 were carried into the United States Code. U. S. C., tit. 2, 2-5 (2 USCA 2 and note 3-5). Inclusion in the Code does not operate as a re-enactment; it establishes "prima facie the laws of the United States, general and permanent in their nature, in force on the 7th day of December, 1925." Act of June 30, 1926, c. 712, 44 Stat. 777. While sections 3 and 4 of the act of 1911 expressly referred to "this apportionment" (the one made by that Act), the argument is pressed that they contain provisions setting forth a general policy which was intended to apply to the future creation of congressional districts, and the election of Representatives, until Congress should provide otherwise.

There are three classes of states with respect to the number of Representatives under the present apportionment pursuant to the act of 1929, (1) where the number remains the same, (2) where it is increased, and (3) where it is decreased. In states where the number of Representatives remains the same, and the districts are unchanged, no question is presented; there is nothing inconsistent with any of the requirements of the Congress in proceeding with the election of Representatives in such states in the same manner as heretofore. Section 4 of the act of 1911 (2 USCA 4) provided that, in case of an increase in the number of Representatives in any state, "such additional Representative or Representatives shall be elected by the State at large and the other Representatives by the districts now prescribed by law" until such state shall be redistricted. The Constitution itself provides in article 1, 2, that "The house of representatives shall be composed of members chosen every second year by the people of the several states," and we are of the opinion that under this provision, in the absence of the creation of new districts, additional Representatives allotted to a state under the present reapportionment would appropriately be elected by the state at large. Such a course, with the election of the other Representatives in the existing districts until a redistricting act was passed, would present no inconsistency with any policy declared in the act of 1911.

Where, as in the case of Minnesota, the number of Representatives has been decreased, there is a different situation, as existing districts are not at all adapted to the new apportionment. It follows that in such a case, unless and until new districts are created, all Representatives allotted to the state must be elected by the state at large. That would be required, in the absence of a redistricting act, in order to afford the representation to which the state is constitutionally entitled, and the general provisions of the act of 1911 cannot be regarded as intended to have a different import.

This conclusion disposes of all the questions properly before the Court. Questions in relation to the application of the standards defined in section 3 of the act of 1911 to a redistricting statute, if such a statute should hereafter be enacted, are wholly abstract. The judgment is reversed, and the cause is remanded for further proceedings not inconsistent with this opinion.

It is so ordered.

Mr. Justice CARDOZO took no part in the consideration and decision of this case.

Appendix W:
Speech of Senator Birch Bayh (D-Indiana) on March 14, 1979

Mr. President, today we begin debate on a constitutional amendment to abolish the Electoral College and establish direct popular election of the President and Vice President. This proposal has been studied intensively in the Senate for well over a decade, but has only once reached the Senate floor and has never reached a vote. In 1970 it was approved in the House by a vote of 339 to 70, but the Senate was denied its opportunity to vote due to a filibuster, which occurred during the closing days of the session when many of the Senators were running for election and there was the problem of getting them back, so we took it off the calendar and it was never voted on by the Senate.

I am confident that the 96th Congress will pass this joint resolution by the necessary two-thirds vote and the State Legislatures will ratify this amendment, thereby finally providing our political system with a safe and fair means of electing the President and Vice President.

John Roche once described the Electoral College as "merely a jerry-rigged improvisation which has subsequently been endowed with a high theoretical content. The future was left to cope with the problem of what to do with this Rube Goldberg mechanism."

That two-sentence quote from John Roche carries a lot of meaning for anyone who has had a chance to really study the way in which the electoral college actually works.

Despite its eccentricities the electoral college is not a lovable old mechanism to be kept and treasured. Mr. President, the electoral college is not harmless. If, as its defenders like to say, it has worked it has worked oftentimes in strange ways. It carries with it always the risk that it may not work at all. As the Presidential election of 1980 approaches, I hope that the Congress will take heed of the ominous rumblings we have had from this cumbersome counting machine in the past, and begin the amendment process that would provide the country with political protection from a breakdown which could occur anytime in the future. To finally replace the electoral college with direct election is simply to give us insurance before it is needed.

I have read with a great deal of interest certain editorials of very distinguished columnists, the essence of which was, "If it ain't broke, Birch, don't fix it."

That is almost like saying, "If your house is not on fire, don't take out fire insurance. If you don't have heart trouble or if you don't have cancer or if you haven't had an accident on the way to the Senate that broke both legs and put you in the hospital at $150 a day, don't take out health insurance."

What we are trying to do in this effort is not to revolutionize the electoral process or dramatically change the constitutional structure of this country; what we are trying to do is put a little grease on a very squeaky wheel, which has come very close to having consequences which could prove unacceptable to the people of this country.

The electoral college has given problems since it was first created. Speaking in Federalist 67 of the manner of electing a President which had been chosen by the 1787 convention, Alexander Hamilton said:

> "There is hardly any part of the system which could have been attended with greater difficulty in the arrangements of it than this...."

That was Alexander Hamilton speaking, yet we are going to be told here by some of the opponents of this effort that the Founding Fathers had infinite wisdom and all believed they had come forth with a majestic solution to electing the President. Not so, Mr. President.

The manner of electing the President was debated extensively during the summer of 1787. Debate centered mainly between those who believed in a direct popular vote and those who wanted election by the National Legislature. However, John Feerick, chairman of the American Bar Association Committee on Election Reform, an outstanding scholar of the workings and mechanism of the electoral college, reports from the historical records, that on July 25 the following proposals were all debated but none adopted:

> "Among the proposals made, but not adopted were that he be chosen by: Congress and, when running for re-election, by

electors appointed by the state legislatures; the chief executives of the states, with the advice of their councils, or, if not councils, with the advice of electors chosen by their legislatures, with the votes of all states equal; the people; and the people of each state choosing its best citizen and Congress, or electors chosen by it, selecting the President from those citizens."

A committee of 11 finally was appointed to break the deadlock over how votes for President would be apportioned in the National Legislature. The committee discarded the legislative election method, and in the final days of the convention recommended a system of intermediate electors. Their recommendation was accepted.

I will say, Mr. President, that this was after the great compromise which put the union together. The Federal system had already been formulated; the compromise between the large and small States, the large States being represented in the House and the small being represented in the Senate.

The electoral college was not considered to be an indispensable part of that compromise. It was not even considered at that time.

Clearly, the electoral college system was neither the most obvious, the most popular nor the most inspired of the Founding Father's great works in framing the Constitution. What is more, the Founders did not envision political parties, the unit rule, or popular election of electors. These aspects of the present system of electing a President evolved quickly and changed the system dramatically, but not by design of the delegates to the 1787 Convention.

James Madison, one of the original Founding Fathers, wrote some 36 years later, as he looked back on his offspring:

"The difficulty of finding an unexceptionable process for appointing the Executive Organ of a Government such as that of the U.S., was deeply felt by the Convention; and as the final arrangement took place in the latter stages of the session, it was not exempt from a degree of the hurrying influence produced by fatigue and impatience in all such bodies, tho' the degree was much less than usually prevails in them."

For its time, however, the electoral college made some sense.

I think it would be wrong for me to stand here and criticize this as a solution, but this was done 200 years ago by our Founding Fathers. We were living in a different age. The Founding Fathers were dealing with a much different society and the electoral college was a device for that society. The land mass of the country was huge; communication was primitive; and education was limited at best. Lack of information about possible Presidential candidates was in fact a very real consideration. Direct election would have been a difficult proposition, a reality which James Madison, one of its strong proponents, acknowledged reluctantly. Added to this were the problems involving suffrage. Out of a total population of 4,000,000, almost 700,000 were slaves, almost 90 percent of the South. It was not possible to count the slaves along the lines of a 3 to 5 compromise type of solution in a direct popular vote system. This would have let to northern-dominated elections and would have been wholly unacceptable unless the slaves were permitted to vote which was equally unacceptable.

James Madison spoke to this problem on July 19, 1787:

> "There was one difficulty however of a serious nature attending an immediate choice by the people. The right of suffrage was much more diffusive in the Northern than the Southern States; and the latter could have no influence in the election on the score of the Negroes. The substitution of electors obviated this difficulty."

From the beginning the electoral college did not work as intended. Those who feel this has been a perfect mechanism should harken back to 1800. By 1800, the first crisis occurred when Burr and Jefferson tied in the electoral vote for President. Thus, the election was put to the House of Representatives. After 36 ballots and 6 days, Jefferson finally won, but it was clear that an amendment was needed. In 1804 the 12th amendment was ratified, solving only the immediate problem of the 1800 election, but leaving the already outmoded electoral college in place.

As has been often said, the system has backfired three times. In the elections of 1824, 1876 and 1888 the candidate who received the most votes did not win. That is three election out of the 39 which have recorded popular votes, or a failure rate of 8 percent. Each of these elections has shown some peculiar flaw of the electoral college system.

Mr. President, as I pointed out just a moment ago, those who say, "If it ain't broke, don't fix it," are poor readers of history.

A failure rate of 8 percent, and some very near misses that increase the almost failure rate to an unacceptable level, hardly support the notion that "it ain't broke."

I will deal with these near misses of more recent vintage in the memory of most of us in just a moment.

The election of 1824 ended up in the House of Representatives. It taught us a lesson to be carried to this day. What happened then was remembered 144 years later and hovered behind the fears about George Wallace's third party candidacy in 1968. Despite a popular vote plurality of 40,000 votes out of almost 400,000 votes cast-a 10 percent popular vote plurality—Andrew Jackson did not receive sufficient electoral votes to win. During the period between the election and House action, the Nation was subjected to the spectacle of the asking and the suspected granting of every manner of favor as Jackson and Adams vied for the votes of House Members. Charges of a corrupt deal followed Adams through his presidency and as a result of his anger over the election, Andrew Jackson formed our modern Democratic Party.

With direct election, no such deal-making or charges of deal-making ever would be possible. In the unlikely event that the leading candidate does not receive 40 percent of the popular vote, an event which has occurred only once in our history, the people themselves will get to choose the candidate they prefer in a runoff election.

The decision will not be made in a smoke-filled room where the vote of representatives could likely go to the highest bidder.

The election of 1876 was the result of a system steeped in corruption before the election, a nation not yet recovered from the bitterness and division of a Civil War and a system that permitted fraud in a handful of States to decide an election. Even President Rutherford Hayes, in his diary, admits that Samuel Tilden, in fact, won the Presidency. Fraud is an ever present possibility in the electoral college system, even if it rarely has become a proven reality. With the electoral college, relatively few irregular votes can reap a healthy reward in the form of a bloc of electoral votes, because of the unit rule or winner take all rule. Under the present system, fraudulent popular votes are much more likely to have a great impact by swinging enough blocs of electoral votes to reverse the election. A like number of fraudulent popular votes under direct election would likely have little effect on the national vote totals.

I have said repeatedly in previous debates that there is no way in which anyone would want to excuse fraud. We have to do everything we can to find it, to punish those who participate in it; but one of the things we can do to limit fraud is to limit the benefits to be gained by fraud.

Under a direct popular vote system, one fraudulent vote wins one vote in the return. In the electoral college system, one fraudulent vote could mean 45 electoral votes, 28 electoral votes.

So the incentive to participate in "a little bit of fraud," if I may use that phrase advisedly, can have the impact of turning a whole electoral block, a whole State operating under the unit rule. Therefore, so the incentive to participate in fraud is significantly greater than it would be under the direct popular vote system.

In addition, there is one other incentive, it seems to me, which does not exits today, to guard against fraud under the direct popular vote. In a direct popular vote, each vote counts. It does not make any difference whether you are going to win or lose by 1 vote or a million. Each vote adds to the national total. So each precinct committeeman and committee-woman standing at that polling place, representing his or her party, has an incentive to police each of those votes to see that it is a legitimate vote.

On the other hand, in the electoral college system, in which, if you are going to lose by 100,000, you might as well lose by 200,000, because either way you lose all the electors, there is no benefit given to the party that comes close. There is no incentive to either the winner or the loser at the precinct level to get out more votes; because once you have lost a State by one vote, you have lost everything you had to lose—namely, all the electoral votes. In a direct popular election each vote would count on the national scale, committeewoman would know in advance that that was going to be the case. You would have a much more severe policing of the precincts as the voters were counted, and you would have a self-policing mechanism the likes of which is not present in many precincts today.

We may cite New York in 1976 as an example. Cries of voting irregularities arose on election night. At stake were 41 electoral votes—more than enough to elect Ford over Carter in the electoral college. Carter's popular margin was 290,000. The calls for recount were eventually dropped, but if fraud had been present in New York, Carter's plurality of 290,000 would have been enough to determine the outcome of the entire national election. Under direct election, Carter's entire national margin of 1.7 million votes would have had to have been irregular to affect the outcome.

Fraud was also involved in the election of 1888, but there is no question that Grover Cleveland won the popular vote by a 23,000 plurality and lost the electoral vote 219 to 182, simply because the electoral system allowed it to happen. Had Cleveland not been so willing to return to public life; had he, like Jackson, gone home and created a great storm of controversy, we have no way of knowing how the people would have reacted.

What happened in 1888 represents the greatest danger presented to us by the electoral college. Of course, no one can foretell with accuracy what would be the reaction in the United States in the second half of the twentieth century if the duly elected President were not the popular vote winner. But we should be thinking about it. There have been three near misses in the last five elections.

Let us think of that. There have been three near misses in the last five elections. It may be broken; it sure is rumbling and sputtering, if in three of the last five Presidential elections we almost had a miscarriage of what we traditionally would call electoral justice.

When we consider our present day increased suffrage, widespread education, ever-present communications systems, and, perhaps most important, popular dissatisfaction with and distrust in the political process, it is reasonable to predict that there would be a political crisis if a President were elected and tried to govern after receiving fewer votes than the candidate against whom he was running. Surely, there is nothing speculative in the view that the mandate of the President to lead would be severely, perhaps irreparably, weakened.

This morning, about 12:30 or 1 o'clock, I stood at Andrews Air Force base with my son and others of my countrymen, with my heart in my throat, as Air Force I came wheeling to a stop and the Marine Corps Band played "Hail to the Chief." As the President of the United States left the plane, to the cheers of the multitude, I could not help thinking how difficult a burden that man carries. It has become almost impossible to be a good President of the United States because of the complex society in which we live today.

It would increase the difficulty of governing for any President if he knew in the back of his mind, if Congress knew, if the people knew, that the man sitting down there, calling orders in the White House, was not the choice of most of the people, but was defeated by the popular vote in the last election.

Mr. President, that is what concerns me-not that the President who has fewer votes might not be an outstanding President. He or she might be a great American, but how could such a President lead our people effectively if more voters chose his opponent. We are living in a time when the people are looking with great dissatisfaction, distrust, and disenchantment at the political process, and I do not know how the public would respond to the leadership of a President who is not the choice of the people of this country.

Mr. President, I emphasize that the danger that the electoral college will produce a President who is not the choice of the voters is not remote-it is not a speculative danger. On several occasions in this century, a shift of less than 1 percent of the popular vote would have produced an electoral majority for the candidate who received fewer popular votes. I repeat: A change of 1 percent would have produced this electoral majority for the candidate who received fewer popular votes.

To reflect on recent years 1960, 1968, and 1976, most of us remember those years. We should remember the dangers that have been all too close.

To this day we cannot be absolutely certain whether John Kennedy in fact won the popular vote or not in 1960.

If you look at the record, in the States of Alabama and Mississippi, States where unpledged Democratic electors were run and some of them won positions as Presidential electors, many did not vote for President Kennedy when the electoral college met; yet the popular votes for these electors was included in the Kennedy tally by the television networks and by the newspapers and most of those who did the counting.

So we really do not know what the national tally was. We do know it was frighteningly close to a backfire, though we do know if there had been a change of a few thousand votes in the State of Illinois we would have had a much different situation.

Most frightening in this election was an attempt by a Republican elector from Oklahoma to combine with other conservative electors, to disregard the popular vote and vote a Byrd-Goldwater ticket out of the electoral college.

My distinguished colleague, the Senator from Virginia, should be assured that we mean no disrespect for his distinguished father who was highly considered by many people throughout the country and performed a great service in this body. I use this as an example to show what actually has, in fact, happened under the system. Persons not even on the ballot have been urged in the electoral college-and in recent years.

Henry Irwin sent the following telegram in 1960 to his fellow electors:

"I am an Oklahoma Republican elector. The Republican Electors cannot deny election to Kennedy. Sufficient conservative Democratic electors available to deny labor socialist nominee. Would you consider Byrd President, Goldwater Vice President, or wire any acceptable substitute. All replies strict confidence."

That is a fact. That is not some cheap TV-only novel that we have to watch interspersed with commercials.

In 1968, which concerned me, very frankly, much more, we entered an election and built a strategy based on the notion George Wallace could deadlock the electoral college and broker the Presidency there.

Here are the questions and answers by candidate Wallace in a press conference:

"Question. If none of the three candidates get a majority, is the election going to be decided in the Electoral College or in the House of Representatives?

Wallace. I think it would be settled in the electoral college.

"Question. Two of the candidates get together or their electors get together and determine who is to be President?

Wallace. That is right."

In other words, the Constitution requires that, when the votes are cast by the electors in December, if a majority is not received by one candidate then the matter goes to the House of Representatives. But what Governor Wallace was saying plainly, openly, for everyone to see, was that he intended to broker his support to one of the other candidates in the electoral college, and it was perfectly legal under the Constitution. We are not accusing him of being devious-quite the contrary, he was quite open and flagrant-what he was trying to do he nearly accomplished. His purpose was to get electors, and he got 36. If there had been a change of a handful of votes, neither Nixon nor Humphrey would have had a majority of electoral votes, and Wallace would have prevented the matter from going to the House of Representatives. He would first sit down with Mr. Nixon, and then Mr. Humphrey, or vice versa, and cut a deal.

But I am here to say, without any irreverence to either one of these men, practical politics being what it is, one of those would have literally purchased, and I use the term advisedly, purchased the Wallace electors and the decision would have been made then in the Electoral College. There the independent Wallace electors would have joined in the electors of the other candidates and there would have been a majority without the matter having to go to the House of Representatives.

Wallace managed to get his name on the ballot in all 50 States and came within 54,000 votes of accomplishing this goal. We can only speculate how the American people at the height of the controversy over the Vietnam war would have reacted to the kind of deals that might well have taken place between election day and the meeting of the electors.

We might even ask ourselves more significantly how the voters would react today where their faith and confidence in the political processes and the political leaders of our country has gone even lower than it was at the height of the Vietnam War.

In the last election, in 1976, a change of less than 9,500 votes combined, in Ohio and Hawaii would have made Ford the President while Carter had an almost 1.7 million vote plurality. Such a misfiring of the system in our present climate could have grave consequences for our system and for the person charged with carrying out the duties of the Presidency.

One of the things that I have really appreciated about the particular effort that many of us have been involved in over the years is that it is a really bipartisan, multiphilosophy effort. We cannot say everyone who is for direct election belongs to one party or one part of either party. It has been a conglomeration of Senators, House Members, and individual citizens who are concerned about the problem.

One of our distinguished allies from the moment he had the opportunity to serve on the American Bar Association panel back in the late 1960's, was our distinguished colleague, the senior Senator from Oklahoma, Senator Bellmon. He will have his say on this and so I will not relate his experience as he sat there and watched how this system really works and determined that he was not going to support the electoral college system which prior to that time he had thought benefited his relatively sparsely populated State.

The reason I bring this up right now is that I recall after that spectacle of election night, with Carter with almost a 2 million vote plurality, and Ford with a change of less than 10,000 votes having the opportunity to get an electoral college majority. I called Henry Bellmon and I said:

> "Henry, what do you think? Do you think we ought to give it another try?"

He said:

> "Well, I have been intending to call you. If that had backfired and Ford had been elected it would have been good for the Republicans but it would have been bad for the Republic."

That takes a pretty big man to say something like that, but that is the truth.

I would have said the same thing about the 1968 election. As most of you know, I am not one of Richard Nixon's most avid supporters. But if Nixon had a plurality of that popular vote he ought to be elected President, and we should not have some gerry rigged kind of situation to end up with throwing out the popular vote winner.

In a runaway election—like that of 1972—any system will produce an electoral victory for the popular vote winner. But the real test of a system is whether it really will stand the test in close elections and in elections as close as that of 1960 the present system offered only a 50-50 chance that the electoral results would agree with the popular vote. For an election as close as 1968, where some 500,000 popular votes separated the candidates, there was one chance in three that the electoral vote winner would not be the popular vote winner as well. Even in the 1976 election, where Mr. Carter's plurality was1.7 million, our statistical experts who run this through their computers tell us the chance of misfiring was one out of every four. According to the evidence, the danger of an electoral backfire is clear and present.

It is easy for us to forget, when a near miss is past, that we should prepare for the future. Not enough of us remember the flood of magazine and newspaper articles speculating on disaster when the possibility of an electoral college backfire was imminent in 1968.

And I think it is important that we remember that in the days just prior to the 1976 election the cry began again only to subside when all turned out to be safe. I would hope that we would not allow ourselves to wait until the electoral college actually does backfire again before we rouse ourselves to act. Insurance cannot be bought after the house has burned down.

Forgive me for reminiscing just a moment at this hour of the evening, but I cannot help but remark to my very sincere colleague and some who study and write about this outside of this Chamber: We talk about: "Well it never has backfired. It ain't broke. Don't fix it." This is not all that important.

It was that similar kind of cry that some of us faced when we tried to amend the Constitution with the 25th amendment. "Two hundred years of history had never presented us with a sequence of circumstances that would be met by filling a Vice-Presidential vacancy, so you do not really need to act." Or, "Put it aside. Wait for another day. Other things are more important."

As a matter of fact, the ink was hardly dry on the 25th Amendment when we were confronted with a crisis, a dual crisis, where it was necessary to appoint two Vice Presidents.

My judgment is that if it had not been for the 25th Amendment, this Congress and the country would have been subjected to tortuous and divisive impeachment trials the like of which would have done severe damage to this country. But the Congress in its wisdom then did not put it off. It acted and, hopefully, Congress will take out the same kind of insurance policy so far as our electoral process is concerned.

Mr. President, the history of the electoral college is not significant simply because it has carried the threat of misfiring. Its very nature is contrary to the political ideals which we as a nation have come to realize over the years. In a very basic way, the electoral college is inimical to our political life. Unlike any other election in the United States from county commissioner to U.S. Senator, in a Presidential election all votes do not count the same.

What we want to do is to see that we return the election of the President and the Vice President to the same basis which has held up and held up very well in the election of every other official in the country. Under the electoral college, one American's vote is not equal to another's, simply on the basis of where he happens to live. Only with the direct election systems would all votes be equal. The electoral college's strange alchemy of apportioning electoral votes plus its "winner-take-all" rule produces the anomalous result that, for example, a citizen from Iowa's vote is actually worth less that his neighbor's in Illinois, but more than his neighbor's in Nebraska. This effect is contrary to our experience in all other elections and the principles behind our form of government. I am sometimes told that with direct election I am trying to make a major change in our political system. Far from it. With direct election, I think, we would simply be bringing our method of Presidential choice in line with all the rest of our voting process.

We worry a great deal nowadays about the "empty voting booth" in America. We speculate on why so few of us choose to take advantage of our right to vote.

The fact of the matter is I think a lot of people are smart enough to know that in that electoral college their votes do not count in some circumstances, and in others they count for the candidate they actually voted against. The time has come to put this aside so that I, in Indiana, when I vote for Carter, do not have my vote cast for Ford; and when a colleague of mine in Ohio, who voted for Ford, just as surely had that vote counted for Carter.

The time has come to convince people that if they come to the polls, their vote is going to count no matter whether the state goes big for the candidate they want or big against their candidate, or get out and vote, and see that those votes are counted.

Mr. President, in my opinion, the inequities inherent in the electoral college are also inimical to voter participation. The electoral college system provides a disincentive to voter turnout, and this is reflected in the way Presidential campaigns are conducted. It makes no difference to a Presidential candidate how many people show up on election day in any state so long as he receives a plurality of one, for that one extra vote determines the outcome of the State's bloc of electoral votes. The votes constituting the plurality over the winner's vote of one are actually worthless. Conversely, all the votes for the loser are not simply lost; they are in effect recast for the winner along with the State's bloc of electoral votes.

580 | Appendix W

These iniquities are of great consequence to the way campaigns are run and thus on the degree of encouragement by candidates for voter participation. With the electoral college, some States are inherently more influential than others, helping a candidate to decide where he will spend his time and effort. Therefore he will, in all likelihood, ignore much of the plains and mountain states and the South. If he reasonably expects to either win or lose a state, however, he will probably write it off as well. Thus, few Democratic candidates go to Massachusetts or Rhode Island, or Republicans to Wyoming. The Electoral College gives neither the candidate nor the national party any motivation to either work to turn out the votes in those States, or widen the margin of victory if he expects to win, or narrow it if he expects to lose.

There is no advantage in building significant margins of victory. As an example of what I mean, in 1976 Mr. Ford picked up 45 electoral votes in California with a 127,000 plurality; Mr. Carter earned 45 electoral votes in five Southern States with a 1,044,000 plurality. The difference in popular votes made no difference in the electoral votes.

Winning under direct election, however, depends precisely on a party's ability to get out the vote and to build sizable pluralities in every community simply because every vote counts and, therefore, no State nor population can easily be ignored.

Mr. President, there is little doubt that American citizens are ready to abolish the electoral college and establish direct election in its place. For over 10 years, polls have shown that support of direct election is over 75 percent, and that support comes from every region of the country, every political ideology, both parties and independents, all races and religions, all professions and economic strata, consistently across the board. The amendment is endorsed by an array of national organizations including the America Bar Association, the US Chamber of Commerce, AFL-CIO, UAW, League of Women Voters, Common Cause, National Federation of Independent Businesses, the ACLU, National Small Business Association, the ADA, the American Federation of Teachers, and the National Farmer's Union.

You name it, the list is long. This is another example of why we have frustrations in our society, where the people are out ahead of our leaders.

When I ask a question why should we have the direct election for President, most people look back at me and say, "Why shouldn't we?" Most people think it already exists.

All the more reason to fear the consequences when they awaken on election night or the morning after and find out that although candidate A has scored a smashing popular vote victory, because of the nuances of the electoral college system, his opponent, who may have garnered, perhaps, only 40 percent of the popular vote still, because of his concentrated effort in the large metropolitan areas, where we can elect a President of the United States by carrying 10 states, plus the District of Columbia, has turned out to be a loser who becomes the winner. The people of this country will scratch their heads and say, "It can't happen here." Let us act now so that it will not happen here.

In the 95th Congress it was cosponsored by 45 Senators, including 28 Senators from small States. It has broad support in the House where it passed by an 83-percent vote in 1969.

The direct election amendment should have been before this body years ago, but despite 43 days of hearings, including 9 in the last congress, for one reason or another, direct election has consistently been delayed in committee until floor action was virtually impossible. Now we have an opportunity to take advantage of all this study and to come to grips with the issue on the merits. I am sure that my 36 colleagues who have chosen to cosponsor the direct election amendment in the beginning of this 96th Congress join me in urging that in 1979 the time has come to replace the strange mode of Presidential election which was left to us in the last harried hours of the constitutional convention. It is time, Mr. President that we in Congress take the action that a great majority of our constituents long have supported and for which many of our colleagues have labored, and pass the direct election amendment. It is long overdue.

I invite any of my colleagues who remain yet uncertain, and who have heard varying arguments about why it is not in their interest, their State's interest, the country's interest, perhaps even the world's interest, to change the electoral process for President, to look at that strange amalgam of U.S. Senators who have joined in supporting this measure.

It is impossible to find one philosophical strain, one political strain, or one geographical strain. It is hard to convince a CLAIBORNE PELL or a JOHN CHAFEE, or a FRANK CHURCH or a JAKE GARN that the small States are going to be disadvantaged by the change. It is hard to convince JAKE JAVITS, JOHN GLENN, HOWARD METZENBAUM, CARL LEVIN that the large States are going to be disadvantaged. The fact of the matter is the going to be disadvantaged if this process backfires, and the country will be served if we are successful in our efforts.[1]

---

[1] *Congressional Record.* March 14, 1979. Pages 4999–5003.

Elect...
Popular Vot...

Illinois State Senator Jacqueline ...
January 19, 2006. Chief co-sponsors incl...
Don Harmon (D), and Mattie Hunter (D). Co...
James T. Meeks (I) and Iris Y. Martinez (D).

94TH GENERAL ASSEMBLY
State of Illinois
2005 and 2006
SB2724

Introduced 1/19/2006, by Sen. Jacqueline Y. Collins

SYNOPSIS AS INTRODUCED:

New Act

    Creates the Agreement Among the States to Elect the President by
National Popular Vote Act. Ratifies and approves the Agreement Among the
States to Elect the President by National Popular Vote. Provides that the
agencies and officers of this State and its subdivisions shall enforce the
compact and do all things appropriate to effect its purpose and intent
that may be within their respective jurisdictions.

                LRB094 17171 BDD 52459 b

FISCAL NOTE ACT
MAY APPLY

Appendix X:
Sources of Information on the Web

Interstate Compacts

The National Center for Interstate Compacts (NCIC) of the Council for
State Governments (CSG) maintains a web site on interstate compacts at
http://www.csg.org/CSG/Programs/National+Center+for
+Interstate+Compacts/default.htm

The NCIC web site contains links to the texts of the interstate compacts currently in force at
http://www.csg.org/CSG/Programs/National+Center+for
+Interstate+Compacts/statutes.htm

Uniform State Laws

The National Conference of Commissioners on Uniform State Laws
(NCCUSL) maintains a web site on uniform state laws at
http://www.nccusl.org

Electoral College

The National Archives and Records Administration (NARA) maintains a
web site on the Electoral College, including the Certificates of
Ascertainment from 2000 and 2004 presidential elections, at
http://www.archives.gov/federal_register/electoral_
college/index.html

The web site of the Federal Election Commission (FEC) on the
Electoral College is at
http://www.fec.gov/pages/ecmenu2.htm

Fair Vote – Center for Voting and Democracy

www.FairVote.org

A BILL FOR

SB2724   LRB094 17171 BDD 52459 b

1   AN ACT concerning interstate compacts.

2   **Be it enacted by the People of the State of Illinois,**

3   **represented in the General Assembly:**

4   **Section 1.** Short title. This Act may be cited as the

5   Agreement Among the States to Elect the President by National

6   Popular Vote Act.

7   **Section 5.** Ratification and approval of compact. The State

8   of Illinois ratifies and approves the following compact:

9   "Agreement Among the States to Elect the President by National

10   Popular Vote

11   Article I-Membership

12   Any State of the United States and the District of Columbia

13   may become a member of this agreement by enacting this

14   agreement.

15   Article II-Right of the People in Member States to Vote for

16   President and Vice President

17   Each member state shall conduct a statewide popular

18   election for President and Vice President of the United States.

19   Article III-Manner of Appointing Presidential Electors in

20   Member States

21   Prior to the time set by law for the meeting and voting by

22   the presidential electors, the chief election official of each

23   member state shall determine the number of votes for each

24   presidential slate in each State of the United States and in

25   the District of Columbia in which votes have been cast in a

26   statewide popular election and shall add such votes together to

27   produce a "national popular vote total" for each presidential

28   slate.

29   The chief election official of each member state shall

SB2724   - 2 -   LRB094 17171 BDD 52459 b

1   designate the presidential slate with the largest national
2   popular vote total as the "national popular vote winner."

3   The presidential elector certifying official of each
4   member state shall certify the appointment in that official's
5   own state of the elector slate nominated in that state in
6   association with the national popular vote winner.

7   At least six days before the day fixed by law for the
8   meeting and voting by the presidential electors, each member
9   state shall make a final determination of the number of popular
10   votes cast in the state for each presidential slate and shall
11   communicate an official statement of such determination within
12   24 hours to the chief election official of each other member
13   state.

14   The chief election official of each member state shall
15   treat as conclusive an official statement containing the number
16   of popular votes in a state for each presidential slate made by
17   the day established by federal law for making a state's final
18   determination conclusive as to the counting of electoral votes
19   by Congress.

20   In event of a tie for the national popular vote winner, the
21   presidential elector certifying official of each member state
22   shall certify the appointment of the elector slate nominated in
23   association with the presidential slate receiving the largest
24   number of popular votes within that official's own state.

25   If, for any reason, the number of presidential electors
26   nominated in a member state in association with the national
27   popular vote winner is less than or greater than that state'
28   number of electoral votes, the presidential candidate on the
29   presidential slate that has been designated as the national
30   popular vote winner shall have the power to nominate the
31   presidential electors for that state and that state's
32   presidential elector certifying official shall certify the
33   appointment of such nominees.

34   The chief election official of each member state shall
35   immediately release to the public all vote counts or statements
36   of votes as they are determined or obtained.

SB2724 - 3 - LRB094 17171 BDD 52459 b

1   This article shall govern the appointment of presidential
2   electors in each member state in any year in which this
3   agreement is, on July 20, in effect in states cumulatively
4   possessing a majority of the electoral votes.

5   Article IV-Other Provisions

6   This agreement shall take effect when states cumulatively
7   possessing a majority of the electoral votes have enacted this
8   agreement in substantially the same form and the enactments by
9   such states have taken effect in each state.

10   Any member state may withdraw from this agreement, except
11   that a withdrawal occurring six months or less before the end
12   of a President's term shall not become effective until a
13   President or Vice President shall have been qualified to serve
14   the next term.

15   The chief executive of each member state shall promptly
16   notify the chief executive of all other states of when this
17   agreement has been enacted and has taken effect in that
18   official's state, when the state has withdrawn from this
19   agreement, and when this agreement takes effect generally.

20   This agreement shall terminate if the electoral college is
21   abolished.

22   If any provision of this agreement is held invalid, the
23   remaining provisions shall not be affected.

24   Article V-Definitions

25   For purposes of this agreement, "chief executive" shall
26   mean the Governor of a State of the United States or the Mayor
27   of the District of Columbia;

28   "elector slate" shall mean a slate of candidates who have
29   been nominated in a state for the position of presidential
30   elector in association with a presidential slate;

31   "chief election official" shall mean the state official or
32   body that is authorized to certify the total number of popular
33   votes for each presidential slate;

34   "presidential elector" shall mean an elector for President

SB2724   - 4 -   LRB094 17171 BDD 52459 b

1   and Vice President of the United States;

2   "presidential elector certifying official" shall mean the

3   state official or body that is authorized to certify the

4   appointment of the state's presidential electors;

5   "presidential slate" shall mean a slate of two persons, the

6   first of whom has been nominated as a candidate for President

7   of the United States and the second of whom has been nominated

8   as a candidate for Vice President of the United States, or any

9   legal successors to such persons, regardless of whether both

10   names appear on the ballot presented to the voter in a

11   particular state;

12   "state" shall mean a State of the United States and the

13   District of Columbia; and

14   "statewide popular election" shall mean a general election

15   in which votes are cast for presidential slates by individual

16   voters and counted on a statewide basis.".

17   **Section 10.** Enforcement. The agencies and officers of this

18   State and its subdivisions shall enforce this compact and do

19   all things appropriate to effect its purpose and intent that

20   may be within their respective jurisdictions.

Bibliography

Abbott, David W. and Levine, James P. 1991. *Wrong Winner: The Coming Debacle in the Electoral College.* Westport, CT: Praeger.

Amar, Akhil Reed and Amar, Vikram David Amar. 2001. How to achieve direct national election of the president without amending the constitution: Part three of a three-part series on the 2000 election and the electoral college. *Findlaw's Writ.* December 28, 2001.
http://writ.news.findlaw.com/amar/20011228.html.

Amar, Akhil Reed and Amar, Vikram David. 2001. Rethinking the electoral college debate: The Framers, federalism, and one person, one vote. 114 *Harvard Law Review* 2526.

American Bar Association Commission on Electoral College Reform. 1967. *Electing the President: A Report of the Commission on Electoral College Reform.* Chicago, IL: American Bar Association.

American Enterprise Institute for Public Policy Research. 1969. *Proposals for Revision of the Electoral College System: Legislative Analysis.* Washington, DC: AEI.

Barone, Michael; Cohen, Michael; and Ujifusa, Grant. 2003. *The 2004 Almanac of American Politics.* Washington, DC: National Journal Group.

Barton, Weldon V. 1967. *Interstate Compacts in the Political Process.* Chapel Hill, NC: University of North Carolina Press.

Bayh, Birch. 1969. Electing a president: The case for direct election. 6 *Harvard Journal on Legislation* 1.

Bennett, Robert W. 2001. Popular election of the president without a constitutional amendment. 4 *Green Bag.* Spring 2001. Posted on April 19, 2001.

Bennett, Robert W. 2002. Popular election of the president without a constitutional amendment. In Jacobson, Arthur J. and Rosenfeld, Michel (editors). *The Longest Night: Polemics and Perspectives on Election 2000.* Berkeley, CA: University of California Press. Pages 391-396.

Bennett, Robert W. 2002. Popular election of the president II: State coordination in popular election of the president without a constitutional amendment. *Green Bag.* Winter 2002.

Bennett, Robert W. 2006. *Taming the Electoral College.* Stanford, CA: Stanford University Press.

Berns, Walter (editor). 1992. *After the People Vote: A Guide to the Electoral College*. Washington, DC: The AEI Press.

Best, Judith A. 1996. *Choice of the People? Debating the Electoral College*. Lanham, MD: Rowman & Littlefield.

Best, Judith Vairo. 1975. *The Case Against Direct Election of the President: A Defense of the Electoral College*. Ithaca, NY: Cornell University Press.

Bowman, Ann O'M. 2004. Trends and issues in interstate cooperation. In *The Book of the States 2004 Edition*. Chicago, IL: The Council of State Governments.

Brams, Steven J. 1978. *The Presidential Election Game*. New Haven, CT: Yale University Press.

Brown, Everett Sumerville. 1938. *Ratification of the Twenty-First Amendment to the Constitution of the United States*. Ann Arbor, MI: The University of Michigan Press.

Busch, Andrew E. 2001. The development and democratization of the electoral college. In Gregg, Gary L. II (editor). *Securing Democracy: Why We Have an Electoral College*. Wilmington, DE: ISI Books.

Chace, James. 2004. 1912: *Wilson, Roosevelt, Taft & Debs—The Election that Changed the Country*. New York, NY: Simon and Schuster.

Committee for the Study of the American Electorate (2004). "President Bush, Mobilization Drives Propel Turnout to Post-1968 High." November 4, 2004.

Congressional Quarterly. 1979. *Presidential Elections Since 1789*. Second Edition. Washington, DC: CQ Press.

Congressional Quarterly. 2002. *Presidential Elections 1789–2002*. Washington, DC: CQ Press.

Cook, Charlie. 2004. Convention dispatches—As the nation goes, so do swing states. *Charlie Cook's Political Report*. August 31, 2004.

Cook, Charlie. 2005. Off to the races: 435 ways to parse the presidential election results. *Charlie Cook's Political Report*. March 29, 2005.

Council of State Governments. 2003. *Interstate Compacts and Agencies 2003*. Lexington, KY: The Council of State Governments.

Council of State Governments. 2005. *The Book of the States*. Lexington, KY: The Council of State Governments. 2005 Edition. Volume 37.

DenBoer, Gordon; Brown, Lucy Trumbull; and Hagermann, Charles D. (editors). 1984. *The Documentary History of the First Federal Elections 1788–1790*. Madison, WI: University of Wisconsin Press. Volume II.

DenBoer, Gordon; Brown, Lucy Trumbull; and Hagermann, Charles D. (editors). 1986. *The Documentary History of the First Federal Elections 1788–1790*. Madison, WI: University of Wisconsin Press. Volume III.

DenBoer, Gordon; Brown, Lucy Trumbull; Skerpan, Alfred Lindsay; and Hagermann, Charles D. (editors). 1989. *The Documentary History of the First Federal Elections 1788-1790.* Madison, WI: University of Wisconsin Press. Volume IV.

Dover, Edwin D. 2003. *The Disputed Presidential Election of 2000: A History and Reference Guide.* Westport, CT: Greenwood Press.

Dunn, Susan. 2004. Jefferson's Second Revolution: *The Elections Crisis of 1800 and the Triumph of Republicanism.* Boston, MA: Houghton Mifflin.

Edwards, George C., III. 2004. *Why the Electoral College Is Bad for America.* New Haven, CT: Yale University Press.

FairVote. 2005. *The Shrinking Battleground: The 2008 Presidential Election and Beyond.* Takoma Park, MD: The Center for Voting and Democracy. www.fairvote.org/shrinking.

FairVote. 2005. *Who Picks the President?* Takoma Park, MD: The Center for Voting and Democracy. www.fairvote.org/whopicks.

Ferling, John. 2004. *Adams vs. Jefferson: The Tumultuous Election of 1800.* Oxford, UK: Oxford University Press.

Ford, Paul Leicester. 1905. *The Works of Thomas Jefferson.* New York, NY: G.P. Putnam's Sons. 9:90.

Fortier, John C. and Ornstein, Norman. 2004. If Terrorists Attack Our Presidential Elections. 3 *Election Law Journal* 4, 597–612.

Frankfurter, Felix and Landis, James. 1925. The compact clause of the constitution—A study in interstate adjustments. 34 *Yale Law Journal* 692–693 and 730–732. May 1925.

Gallup News Service. 2000. Americans have Historically Favored Changing Way Presidents Are Elected. November 10, 2000.

Gettleman, Marvin E. 1973. *The Dorr Rebellion: A Study in American Radicalism 1833–1849.* New York, NY: Random House.

Goldfeder, Jerry H. 2005. Could Terrorists Derail a Presidential Election. 32 *Fordham Urban Law Journal* 3, 523–566. May 2005.

Gordon, James D. and Magleby, David B. 1989. Pre-Election Judicial Review of Initiatives and Referendums. 64 *Notre Dame Law Review* 298–320.

Grace, Adam S. 2005. *Federal-State "Negotiations" over Federal Enclaves in the Early Republic: Finding Solutions to Constitutional Problems at the Birth of the Lighthouse System.* Berkeley, CA: Berkeley Electronic Press. Working Paper 509. http://law.bepress.com/expresso/eps/509.

Grant, George. 2004. *The Importance of the Electoral College.* San Antonio, TX: Vision Forum Ministries.

Gregg, Gary L. II. (editor). 2001. *Securing Democracy: Why We Have an Electoral College*. Wilmington, DE: ISI Books.

Hardy, Paul T. 1982. *Interstate Compacts: The Ties That Bind*. Athens, GA: Institute of Government, University of Georgia.

Jacobson, Arthur J. and Rosenfeld, Michel (editors). 2002. *The Longest Night: Polemics and Perspectives on Election 2000*. Berkeley, CA: University of California Press.

Jensen, Merrill and Becker, Robert A. (editors). 1976. *The Documentary History of the First Federal Elections 1788–1790*. Madison, WI: University of Wisconsin Press. Volume I.

Kirby, J. 1962. Limitations on the powers of the state legislatures over presidential elections. 27 *Law and Contemporary Problems* 495.

Kole, Edward A. 1999. *The First 13 Constitutions of the First American States*. Haverford, PA: Infinity Publishing.

Kole, Edward A. 1992. *The True Intent of the First American Constitutions of 1776–1791*. Haverford, PA: Infinity Publishing.

Kuroda, Tadahisa. 1994. *The Origins of the Twelfth Amendment: The Electoral College in the Early Republic, 1787–1804*. Westport, CT: Greenwood Press.

Leach, Richard H. and Sugg, Redding S. Jr. 1959. *The Administration of Interstate Compacts*. Louisiana State University Press.

LeVert, Suzanne. 2004. *The Electoral College*. New York, NY: Franklin Watts.

Longley, Lawrence D. and Braun, Alan G. 1972. *The Politics of Electoral College Reform*. New Haven, CT: Yale University Press.

Longley, Lawrence D. and Peirce, Neal R. 1999. *The Electoral College Primer 2000*. New Haven, CT: Yale University Press.

Morris, Roy B. 2003. *Fraud of the Century: Rutherford B. Hayes, Samuel Tilden, and the Stolen Election of 1876*. Waterville, ME: Thorndike Press.

Nelson, Suzanne. Three-Month Period Imperils Presidency. *Roll Call*. November 2, 2004.

New York Daily News. 2000. Bush Set to Fight an Electoral College Loss: They're Not Only Thinking the Unthinkable, They're Planning for It. *New York Daily News*. November 1, 2000.

Nivola, Pietro S. 2005. *Thinking About Political Polarization*. Washington, DC: The Brookings Institution. Policy Brief 139. January 2005.

Orfield, Lester Bernhardt. 1942. *The Amending of the Federal Constitution*. Ann Arbor, MI: The University of Michigan Press.

Ornstein, Norman. 2004. *Roll Call*. October 21, 2004.

Peirce, Neal R. 1968. *The People's President: The Electoral College in American History and Direct-Vote Alternative.* New York, NY: Simon and Schuster.

Peirce, Neal R. and Longley, Lawrence D. 1981. *The People's President: The Electoral College in American History and the Direct-Vote Alternative, Revised Edition.* New Haven, CT: Yale University Press.

Peterson, Svend. 1981. *A Statistical History of the American Presidential Elections: With Supplementary Tables Covering 1968–1980.* Westport, CT: Greenwood Press Reprint.

Posner, Richard A. 2001. *Breaking the Deadlock: The 2000 Election, the Constitution, and the Courts.* Princeton, NJ: Princeton University Press.

Rehnquist, William H. 2004. *Centennial Crisis: The Disputed Election of 1876.* New York, NY: Alfred A. Knopf.

Ridgeway, Marian E. 1971. *Interstate Compacts: A Question of Federalism.* Carbondale, IL: Southern Illinois University Press.

Robinson, Lloyd. 1996. *The Stolen Election: Hayes versus Tilden—1876.* New York, NY: Tom Doherty Associates Books.

Ross, Tara. 2004. *Enlightened Democracy: The Case for the Electoral College.* Los Angeles, CA: World Ahead Publishing Company.

Schumaker, Paul D. and Loomis, Burdett A. (editors). 2002. *Choosing a President.* New York, NY: Chatham House Publishers.

Schlesinger, Arthur M., Jr. and Hewson, Martha S. 2002. Philadelphia, PA: Chelsea House Publishers.

Schlesinger, Arthur M., Jr. and Israel, Fred L. (editors). 2002. *History of American Presidential Elections 1878–2001.* Philadelphia, PA: Chelsea House Publishers. (11 volumes).

Shambon, Leonard M. 2004. Electoral-College Reform Requires Change of Timing. *Roll Call.* June 15, 2004.

Smith, Hayward H. 2001. *Symposium, Law of Presidential Elections: Issues in the Wake of Florida 2000.* History of the Article II Independent State legislature Doctrine. 29 *Florida State University Law Review* 731–785. Issue 2.

Stanwood, Edward. 1912. *A History of the Presidency from 1897 to 1909.* Boston, MA: Houghton Mifflin Company.

Stanwood, Edward. 1916. *A History of the Presidency from 1897 to 1916.* Boston, MA: Houghton Mifflin Company.

Stanwood, Edward. 1924. *A History of the Presidency from 1788 to 1897.* Boston, MA: Houghton Mifflin Company.

Tribe, Laurence H. 2000. *American Constitutional Law.* Third Edition. Volume 1. New York, NY: Foundation Press.

U.S. House of Representatives Committee on the Judiciary. 1969. *Electoral College Reform: Hearings on H.J. Res. 179, H.J. Res. 181, and Similar Proposals to Amend the Constitution Relating to Electoral College Reform.* 91st Congress, 1st Session. February 5, 6, 19, 20, 26, and 27; March 5, 6, 12, and 13, 1969. Washington, DC: U.S. Government Printing Office.

U.S. House of Representatives Committee on the Judiciary. 1999. *Proposals for Electoral College Reform: Hearing on H.J. Res. 28 and H.J. Res. 43.* 105th Congress, 1st Session. September 4, 1997. Washington, DC: U.S. Government Printing Office.

U.S. Senate Committee on the Judiciary. 1967. *Election of the President: Hearings on S.J. Res. 4, 7, 11, 12, 28, 58, 62, 138; and 139, 89th Congress; and S.J. Res. 2, 3, 6, 7, 12, 15, 21, 25, 55, 84, and 86.* 89th Congress, 2nd Session and 90th Congress, 1st Session. February 28–August 23, 1967. Washington, DC: U.S. Government Printing Office.

U.S. Senate Committee on the Judiciary. 1969. *Electing the President: Hearings on S.J. Res. 1, S.J. Res. 2, S.J. Res. 4, S.J. Res. 12, S.J. Res. 18, S.J. Res. 20, S.J. Res. 25, S.J. Res. 30, S.J. Res. 31, S.J. Res. 33, S.J. Res. 71, and S.J. Res. 72 to Amend the Constitution Relating to Electoral College Reform.* 91st Congress, 1st Session. January 23 and 24; March 10, 11, 12, 13, 20 and 21; April 30; and May 1 and 2, 1969. Washington, DC: U.S. Government Printing Office.

U.S. Senate Committee on the Judiciary. 1969. *Direct Popular Election of the President: Report, with Additional Minority, Individual, and Separate Views on H.J. Res. 681, Proposing an Amendment to the Constitution of the United States Relating to the Election of the President and Vice President.* 91st Congress, 1st Session. Washington, DC: U.S. Government Printing Office.

U.S. Senate Committee on the Judiciary. 1975. *Direct Popular Election of the President: Report (to Accompany S.J. Res. 1).* 94th Congress, 1st Session. Washington, DC: U.S. Government Printing Office.

U.S. Senate Committee on the Judiciary. 1977. *The Electoral College and Direct Election: Hearings on the Electoral College and Direct Election of the President and Vice President (S.J. Res. 1, 8, and 18): Supplement.* 95th Congress, 1st Session. July 20, 22 and 28; and August 2, 1977. Washington, DC: U.S. Government Printing Office.

U.S. Senate Committee on the Judiciary. 1979. *Direct Popular Election of the President and Vice President of the United States: Hearings on S.J. Res. 28, Joint Resolution Proposing an Amendment to the Constitution to Provide for the Direct Popular Election of the President and Vice President of the United States.* 96th Congress, 1st Session. March 27 and 30; and April 3, and 9, 1979. Washington, DC: U.S. Government Printing Office.

U.S. Senate Committee on the Judiciary. 1993. *The Electoral College and Direct Election of the President: Hearing on S.J. Res. 297, S.J. Res. 302, and S.J. Res 312, Measures Proposing Amendments to the Constitution Relating to the Direct Election of the President and Vice President of the United States.* 102nd Congress, 2nd Session. July 22, 1992. Washington, DC: U.S. Government Printing Office.

White, Theodore H. 1969. *The Making of the President 1968.* New York, NY: Atheneum Publishers.

Wiecek, William M. 1972. *The Guarantee Clause of the U.S. Constitution.* Ithaca, NY: Cornell University Press.

Wilmerding, Lucius Jr. 1958. *The Electoral College.* Boston, MA: Beacon Press.

Zimmermann, Frederick L. and Wendell, Mitchell. 1976. *The Law and Use of Interstate Compacts.* Lexington, KY: Council of State Governments.

Zimmerman, Joseph F. 1992. *Contemporary American Federalism.* Westport, CT: Praeger.

Zimmerman, Joseph F. 1996. *Interstate Relations: The Neglected Dimension of Federalism.* Westport, CT: Praeger.

Zimmerman, Joseph F. 1997. *The Recall: Tribunal of the People.* Westport, CT: Praeger.

Zimmerman, Joseph F. 1997. *The Referendum: The People Decide Public Policy.* Westport, CT: Praeger.

Zimmerman, Joseph F. 1999. *The Initiative: Citizen Law-Making.* Westport, CT: Praeger.

Zimmerman, Joseph F. 2002. *Interstate Cooperation: Compacts and Administrative Agreements.* Westport, CT: Praeger.

Zimmerman, Joseph F. 2004. *Interstate Economic Relations.* Albany, NY: State University of New York Press.

Zimmerman, Joseph F. 2005. *Congressional Preemption: Regulatory Federalism* Albany, NY: State University of New York Press.

INDEX

W